MW01073191

The New Father

A Dad's Guide to the toddler Years

"I'll teach you about trucks, William, and you teach me about life."

The New Father

A Dad's Guide to the toddler Years

Armin A. Brott

Abbeville Press • Publishers
New York • London • Paris

For Talya and Tirzah,
who remind me every day about what's really important in life;
and my sweetest Evie,
who makes the colors more intense.

EDITOR: Jacqueline Decter
DESIGNER: Celia Fuller
PRODUCTION EDITOR: Owen Dugan
PRODUCTION MANAGER: Elizabeth Gaynor

 Inquiries should be addressed to Abbeville Publishing Group, 22 Cortlandt Street, New York, N.Y. 10007. The text of this book was set in Bodoni Book. Printed and bound in the United States of America.

First edition
10 9 8 7 6 5 4 3 2

Cover photograph by Milton Heiberg.
For cartoon credits, see page 223.

Library of Congress Cataloging-in-Publication Data
Brott, Armin A.
A dad's guide to the toddler years / Armin A. Brott. — 1st ed.
p. cm. — (The new father)
Includes bibliographical references and index.
ISBN 0-7892-0396-0 (pb). — ISBN 0-7892-0480-0 (hc)
1. Toddlers. 2. Toddlers—Care. 3. Father and child. I. Title. II. Series.
HQ774.5.B757 1998
649'.122—dc21 96-32876

Contents

Acknowledgments

Many of the people who helped with the previous books in this series were, remarkably, willing to put up with me again. This book wouldn't have been possible without them.

Andrea Adam helped edit the first draft; Sharon Braz reviewed the section on big-time communication breakdowns between partners; Gene and June Brott, my parents, also read the early versions, baby-sat, and were a constant source of emotional and financial support; Jim Cameron and all the folks at the Center for Human Development freely shared their research and their wisdom about temperament; Phil and Carolyn Cowan, who have studied fathers and families for decades, met with me and helped hone my ideas; Jackie Decter guided the whole thing through from start to finish and made it all coherent; Celia Fuller bought the shirts and did the design; Ken Guilmartin and Edwin Gordon spent a huge amount of time with me discussing the importance of teaching music to children; Amy Handy copyedited the manuscript and, as usual, made a ton of insightful comments; Jim Levine put it all together; Eric Mindich suggested beefing up the financial sections; Jeff Porter, accountant and financial planner extraordinaire, reviewed the sections on financial and tax planning and home buying and made them far more accurate and accessible; Dawn Swanson, the children's librarian at the Berkeley Public Library, helped me select and arrange the children's books; Eric Tyson reviewed, commented on, and added to the sections on estate planning and college savings.

"I was just telling them that there used to be a show called 'Father Knows Best.'"

Introduction

What image comes to mind when you hear the word *toddler*? Probably that of a small child, not nearly as helpless as an infant, walking, falling, walking again. A child brimming with confidence and eager to learn.

Much of the same could be said about the fathers of toddlers as well. You've learned a huge amount over the year or so since your child was born and you're really getting the hang of this parenting thing. But as confident as you are, something still happens every day that reminds you that there's still plenty more to learn.

Over the next two years your child will go from crawling to standing to walking to running, and from one- and two-syllable words to telling you that you don't know anything about anything. Parenting columnist Lawrence Kutner likens toddlerhood to a musical fugue in which "the themes of intellectual, physical, emotional, and social development intertwine." But the focus of this book isn't really on that. Sure, we'll spend some time discussing your child's growth and identifying developmental milestones. If you want an exhaustive study of child development, however, you need look no further than your local library or bookstore.

The New Father: A Dad's Guide to the Toddler Years is primarily about you and *your* musical fugue, about how *fathers* develop and grow over time. And that's something you can't find anywhere else.

In writing this book I talked extensively with dozens of leading experts and studied the research and writings of many more. I also drew from my own experiences as the father of two, as well as from the interviews I've done with hundreds of fathers about their experiences and feelings. It is my hope that giving you access to all this wisdom and experience will leave you far better prepared to meet the challenges of being—and staying—an active, involved father.

The big question, of course, is, Why bother to be involved? Three simple reasons: it's good for your kids, it's good for you, and it's good for your relationship with your partner.

"The evidence is quite robust that kids who have contact with a father have an advantage over kids without that kind of contact," says Norma Radin, who has conducted research on fathers for more than twenty years. And these benefits are evident very early in life. In one study, Radin found that children who were raised by actively involved fathers scored higher on verbal ability tests than children raised in more traditional families by less-involved fathers. In another study, toddlers whose fathers took a special interest in child care were consistently rated two to six months ahead of schedule on tests of development, problem-solving skills, and even social skills. And there's also a strong connection between kids' math skills and the amount of contact they have with their fathers.

Working fathers also benefit greatly from being involved with their kids. Too many men worry that there's no real way to balance their work and family lives, and that taking an active role at home would be committing career suicide. But the truth is that men who put child rearing high up on their list of priorities are on average more successful in their careers at midlife than men who focus only on their work. Fatherhood also seems to "promote men's abilities to understand themselves as adults and to sympathetically care for other adults," says fatherhood researcher John Snarey. Men who take an active role at home are—by the time their children are grown—better managers, community leaders, and mentors. Overall, they're more concerned with the generation coming up than with themselves.

And finally, being an active, involved father has a positive impact on men's relationships with their partners. Division-of-labor issues are right up there with money as the top marital stressor. Not surprisingly, the more support your partner gets from you, the happier she'll be in her marriage and the better she'll perform as a parent. And that will make her a happier woman, which will make you happier as well and will make your relationship last longer.

How This Book Is Organized

Because babies (and their fathers) develop so quickly, the previous book in this series, *The New Father: A Dad's Guide to the First Year,* was organized month by month, a format that enabled us to capture the rapid changes that you and your baby were undergoing. But as your baby ages and as you gain in experience, neither of you is developing quite as quickly and a month-by-month approach would have been too cumbersome. Instead, while we're still going through your baby's and your development in chronological order, we've divided things up into three-month blocks. Each of these quarterly chapters is further divided into the following four sections:

What's Going On with the Baby

In this section we take a brief yet extremely important look at how your toddler is developing physically, intellectually, verbally, and emotionally/socially. In many ways your toddler's growth parallels your own growth as a father. And much of what you'll be experiencing over the next few years will be closely related to your child's development. So knowing the basics of child development will not only help you understand your child, but will give you a better, deeper understanding of yourself.

As you no doubt already know, children develop on very different schedules and the range of "normal" development is quite broad. Dividing the book into three-month sections should take care of most—but probably not all—of the variations, so you might want to keep an extra bookmark in chapters immediately preceding and following the one you're reading. If your baby seems to be two chapters (six months or so) ahead of her age, call Oprah. If she's two chapters behind, however, check with your pediatrician.

What You're Going Through

With no real social support and almost no one to talk to about parenting feelings and concerns, far too many fathers end up thinking not only that they're absolutely alone in what they're experiencing but that they're abnormal as well. Chances are, however, that with very few exceptions what you're going through at any particular moment of your fatherhood is fairly similar to what millions of fathers before you have felt and millions more after you will. Just as babies develop along a more or less predictable path, so do fathers. And in this section of each chapter, we'll examine what fathers typically go through at that particular time, so you'll be able to monitor your own physical and emotional development. We'll talk about the emotional ups and downs, the joys, the frustrations, the anger, the confusion, the incredible pride, and the confidence that fatherhood brings to all of us.

You and Your Baby

Besides being very important, this section is undoubtedly the most fun. It gives you all the tools you'll need to get to know your child better and to create the deepest, closest possible relationship with her—even if all you have is only half an hour a day. We'll deal with activities as diverse as playing games, reading, music, making art, cooking, potty training, computers, discipline, handling your child's fears, and overcoming gender stereotypes.

Family Matters

Although the focus of this book is mostly on you and your toddler, you're still very much part of a family, which includes your partner and any other children you might have. For that reason, we've included a separate section to discuss all the things that can have a major impact on everyone in your house. We'll talk about finances, family planning, nutrition, looking for preschools, finding dentists, dealing with tantrums, how your child's temperament affects the whole family, improving communication with your partner, sex, and much more.

A Note on Terminology

He and She

As the father of two daughters, I find it annoying to read a piece of parenting advice that constantly refers to the child in question as "he." And I'm sure parents of boys feel the same way when the situation is reversed. So in an attempt to annoy everyone equally, I simply alternate between "he" and "she" as often as possible. There are, of course, some sections in the book that apply only to boys or to girls, and in those cases the appropriate pronoun is used. Otherwise, the terms are completely interchangeable, and hopefully there's an equal number of both.

You're Not in This Thing Alone, You Know . . .

Whether the mother of your child is your wife, your lover, your girlfriend, your live-in companion, your ex, or your fiancée, she plays an important role in your child's and your life—you wouldn't be a father without her. To keep from making any kind of statement about the importance (or lack of importance, depending on how you feel) of marriage, I've decided to keep referring to the mother of your child as your "partner," as I did in *The New Father: A Dad's Guide to the First Year.*

What's All This *TNF I* Stuff?

This book, like child and father development, is part of an ongoing process that began with *The Expectant Father: Facts, Tips, and Advice for Dads-to-Be* and continued with *The New Father: A Dad's Guide to the First Year.* And like most ongoing processes, previously mastered skills become the basis for learning new ones. Simply put, this means that while all the information in this book is completely new, some of the topics have been touched on in previous volumes. In each case I give the exact page(s) reference and use an abbreviation to indicate where the idea first came up. If you've got a copy of either or both these books around, you can check these references. If not, don't worry; everything covered here stands on its own. *TNF I* is, not surprisingly, *The New Father: A Dad's Guide to the First Year. TEF* is *The Expectant Father: Facts, Tips, and Advice for Dads-to-Be.*

The All-Important Disclaimer . . .

I'm not a pediatrician, financial planner, accountant, or lawyer, nor do I play one on TV. This means that even though all the medical, financial, and legal advice in this book has been suggested by the experts and proven to work by real people (including me, in most cases), you should still check with an appropriate professional before trying it out on yourself and your family.

12–15 MONTHS

Getting Off on the Right (or Left) Foot

What's Going On with the Baby

Physically

- By the end of this period, your baby will be most comfortable in a fully upright position. He'll be able to walk by himself and will insist on doing so. And when he's not walking, he'll be climbing.
- Your child's favorite activity now is emptying and filling containers of all kinds (although he really is much better at emptying). In a matter of seconds he can empty dresser drawers, kitchen cabinets, refrigerator, and bookshelves. "There seems to be a general pattern in children this age of emptying things that no one else wants emptied," writes child development expert Frank Caplan.
- His fine motor coordination is greatly improved. He can turn the pages of a book one at a time and now releases objects as accurately and gracefully as he picks them up—a skill he's finding invaluable when he throws a ball. He can also draw a straight line (if you do one first).
- He loves to play all sorts of physical games. Chase me/catch me, rolling balls back and forth, and wrestling are big favorites.
- He's trying really, really hard to turn doorknobs. If you're lucky, it'll be a few more months before he successfully puts together grasping and twisting.

Intellectually

- In his ongoing attempt to trash your home, your toddler will be picking up, rotating, dropping, tasting, stacking (then knocking over), and throwing everything he can get his hands on, thus giving him a crash course in shape, texture, taste, density, balance, and aerodynamics.

- He has a clearer understanding of his own limitations and is getting better at using tools—including adults—to get what he wants. He'll use a stick to get something out from under the couch and will demand that you help him achieve his desire to swing on a swing all day.
- He's much better at distinguishing sizes and shapes and has a well-developed sense of how things "should be." He may occasionally put a square peg in a square hole and, if you turn a familiar object (like a book) upside down, he'll turn it right-side up.
- His memory continues to improve, and he can now look for an object he hasn't seen being hidden. He's also developing a sense of time: that things (like naps) follow other things (like meals).
- He's fascinated by hinged objects—especially books—not so much for what's in them but for the sheer feeling of accomplishment he gets when he turns the pages.

Verbally

- According to psychologist Fitzhugh Dodson, there are two phases of language learning: passive language (what you understand) and active language (what you can actually say). Most of the language learning your toddler will do over the course of the next twelve months will be passive.
- By the end of the fifteenth month he'll identify upon request his shoes, clothes, and body parts; familiar people and objects; and one or two pictures from a favorite book.
- Although he has a speaking vocabulary of fewer than ten words, he's already trying to put them together two at a time: "Bye-bye, Daddy" and "No, baby" are among the first "sentences."
- He can also do some pretty good cow, dog, and cat imitations.
- He's becoming aware of the expressive function of language and has developed an uncanny ability to pick out—and endlessly repeat—the one swear word you accidentally slipped into a ten-minute-long conversation.
- His understanding of the symbolic use of words is growing. If he knows the word *pool,* for example, he may use it when he sees a duck pond, a puddle on the street, or even the ocean. However, he may also call every cat, horse, goat, pig, llama, or other hairy, four-legged animal a "dog."

Emotionally/Socially

- He's becoming fiercely independent, demanding to push his stroller instead of riding in it. He'll also insist on feeding himself, but will end up with more on his face, his cheeks, walls, the high-chair tray, or the floor than in his mouth.

- Doing things on his own is not all there is to being independent. Your toddler wants to separate himself physically from you as well—but not for too long. Pretending to be on a scouting expedition, he'll stroll a short distance away, casually looking back over his shoulder to make sure you haven't gone anywhere. But independence is a pretty scary thing to a one-year-old, so a second or two after you disappear from his view, he'll scamper back and cling to you for all he's worth. He'll repeat the process of going away and coming back at least until he's through college.
- As he slowly becomes secure with the idea that you'll always be there for him, your child's shyness around strangers and his fear of separation should decrease.
- As those fears disappear, however, they are replaced by other, even more irrational-seeming ones: the vacuum cleaner and the neighborhood dogs that never bothered him before suddenly terrify him; he now needs a night-light in his room; and he may refuse to take a bath, fearing that he'll get sucked down the drain.
- With all the places he has to go and things he has to do, your baby won't want to waste his precious time eating, and may refuse to do so. He will also regard sleep as a major imposition and will probably refuse to nap.

What You're Going Through

Physical Exhaustion

Being a father can be an exhausting proposition, and I'm not talking about sleep deprivation (which has probably passed for the most part by now anyway). Just trying to keep up with a toddler as she careens happily through her day can be enough to drop even a world-class athlete to his knees.

In our prefatherhood days, most of us never did anything to prepare for all the stooping (to get kids into and out of their car seats), bending (to put away hundreds of toys a day), wrestling, pushing (swings or strollers), chasing (to make sure the baby stays out of trouble), schlepping (all those extra bags of groceries in and out of the car), holding (it's fun, but it's hard to keep up for more than a few blocks), and carrying (sleeping children seem to weigh a lot more than awake ones). Not to mention all that extra laundry and housecleaning. Is it any wonder that just about every father I know has a bad back?

It's crucial to take care of yourself physically as well as psychologically. Not doing so can make it impossible for you to take care of anyone else. Here are a few things you can do:

- Get plenty of exercise—with a special concentration on stretches and strength-building exercises for your back. And don't forget to eat right, too.
- See your doctor regularly.
- Don't suppress your emotions. Getting depressed can make you care less—and do less—about yourself.
- Treat yourself nicely. Take some breaks, get an occasional massage, buy yourself something special once in a while.
- Get some intellectual stimulation. With all the reading you're doing with your baby, don't forget to do some for yourself as well.

What You're Going Through

A Conflict between Separateness and Connectedness

As we will see later in this chapter, your child has been struggling to strike a balance between being dependent on you and independent from you. But your baby isn't the only one in your immediate family who's dealing with separation issues.

As a parent, you are probably struggling with an adult version of separation anxiety: a conflict between wanting to be needed by your child (wanting to keep her a baby), and wanting to push her toward independence.

The great irony here (to me, anyway) is that the attachment that we've tried so hard to achieve with our children is inextricably related to separating from them. In fact, "The task of becoming attached includes beginning to understand separateness," says Ellen Galinsky, head of the Work and Family Institute. It really seems that the stronger your attachment to the child, the more likely you are to be affected by the separation.

There are, of course, two common ways to deal with adult separation anxiety: push the baby to be more independent, or encourage her to be more dependent on you. Adopting either approach by itself will guarantee disaster for your child as well as for your family. As with just about anything else to do with parenting, the trick is to find the balance between the available extremes. And the first step is to become aware of what might be motivating you to take certain steps.

WHY YOU MAY BE PUSHING YOUR CHILD TO BE MORE INDEPENDENT

- Your child may be quieter than you'd like her to be.
- She may not be as curious as you think she should be.
- You may be afraid that your child is too clingy or dependent and that if she doesn't start learning to take care of herself she'll grow up to be a wimp.
- You may be afraid that your child is controlling you, that you're losing your independence, and that she's making too many demands on your time and affection. This is an especially common fear among fathers whose kids are temperamentally "difficult."
- Particularly if you're a stay-at-home dad or if you're especially involved, you may be afraid that besides having lost your career, you've lost your prestige and your masculinity.

Pushing early self-reliance tends to be thought of as a "dad thing," but mothers are far from immune from trying to make their kids more independent. But before you start worrying about these things, remember this:

- If your child seems clingy, there's probably a reason for it. Only when she feels secure in your relationship will she be ready to separate from you.
- Learn to take pride in what she does do, rather than in what you think she should do—she's your child, but she's not you and she won't do exactly what you think she should.
- If you feel that your baby isn't growing up as quickly as you think she should, you may push her to go places or do things she isn't ready for, says psychiatrist Stanley Greenspan. This can lead to your being further disappointed when the baby fails to live up to your too-high expectations, and to her feeling guilty and inadequate because she can't make you happy.

Some potential negative side effects of pushing independence on your child too much or too soon:

- You may suddenly start working longer hours, coming home later, or doing just about anything to stay away from home more.
- You might begin distancing yourself from your partner as well as the baby, feeling that you have to make up for all the time you haven't been getting for yourself since the baby came.

". . . and so the princess and the prince lived happily ever after. The end. Now get some sleep. We want you to be fresh as a daisy for your first day of college tomorrow."

- You may become less affectionate with your child—especially if you have a boy.
- Your child may come to feel unloved and uncared for, as though you're trying to get rid of her.

WHY YOU MAY BE SUBTLY ENCOURAGING YOUR CHILD TO BE MORE DEPENDENT

- You may be saddened that your baby is growing up so quickly. As young as she still is, she's already outgrown certain adorable behaviors and gestures, and you may almost wish that she'd stay this age forever.
- You may be afraid of being rejected or abandoned by your toddler. This feeling tends to arise at times when you really want to sit quietly and snuggle with the baby and she squirms off your lap and runs away.

Although it is usually thought of as more of a "mom thing," there are plenty of fathers who are reluctant to let their kids go. If you're feeling this way, think about this:

- Don't think the baby doesn't need you or love you, in fact she needs you more than ever. She needs your support and love to let her know that growing up (which she's going to do whether you like it or not) is okay.
- Your feeling that your baby's youth has somehow been "lost" runs parallel to her feelings of exploring unknown territory. Taking pride in her independence and all the "big girl" things she can do is an important part of building her self-esteem and independence.
- You may think you want your baby to be a baby forever, but is that what you really want? To be changing this baby's diapers for the next fifty years? I don't think so.

Here are some of the potential negatives of limiting independence:

- You can hover too much, never allowing your child to make the mistakes she needs to make in order to learn.
- You can be too overprotective and not give the child enough room to explore.
- You can limit her contacts with other people, feeling that any free time she has should be spent with you.
- You may refrain from setting limits or disciplining your child for fear of driving her away.
- You may spoil the child or become excessively aggressive in trying to win her love.

RECOGNIZING YOUR LIMITATIONS

Before Clint Eastwood (as Dirty Harry) was inviting people to "Go ahead, make my day," he was advising people that "a man's got to know his limitations."

In family and parenting experts Phil and Carolyn Cowans' research, one of the factors they found that differentiates fathers from nonfathers is that fathers do a better job discriminating between what they can and can't control. This skill—as absolutely basic as it sounds—is something that can actually take years to develop. "We heard men working on it when they discussed their struggles with wanting it all—job advancement, involved relationships with their wives and children, time for themselves—while accepting the fact that no matter how hard they tried, some things had to be put aside for the time being," write the Cowans. "It is our impression that as a group, men who were not parents had fewer competing demands to balance, were less aware of their limitations, and more invested in maintaining at least the illusion of personal control."

You and Your Baby

Play

The first few months of your baby's second year have been full of dramatic changes, and the ways he plays are no exception. Only a few months ago he depended on you to decide what he'd play with, and he could pay attention to only one object (or person) at a time (see *TNF I,* pages 162–67).

But in just the past few weeks, the baby has begun to assume a less passive role in his playtime. One of the first changes you'll notice is that he will start using "gestures or vocalizations to signal a desire to share attention and to establish the topic of the conversation to follow," says researcher Kim Whaley. At just about the same time, your baby will start putting two playthings together—most likely by giving you a toy and trying to get you to play with him. "The ability to coordinate attention marks a pivotal change in the infant's communicative competence," adds Whaley.

Here are some appropriate toys and activities for the next six months or so:

15–18 MONTHS

TOYS THAT:

- The baby can safely chew on (soft plastic or padded blocks, for example).
- Can be washed.
- Stimulate the senses by incorporating lots of different noises, textures, colors—the more the better.
- Encourage manual dexterity by requiring that the baby twist, turn, poke, flick, and/or snap them to get a response.
- Encourage the use of both hands: Duplo (the bigger Lego blocks), toy farms with animals, and the like are great.
- Have wheels that can easily be pulled, pushed, dragged, or shoved. Lawn mowers, buggies, strollers, and "popcorn poppers" are all good. If your child still isn't very steady on her feet, make sure to get toys that won't fall over, roll away, or collapse if leaned on.
- Develop sorting and categorizing skills, such as containers or toy trucks for filling and dumping, measuring spoons, and shape sorters (although it'll be a few months before the baby will be able to get the round block in the round hole very regularly).
- Are real. Old telephones (without cords) and even that extra computer keyboard you've got lying around, for example, are more interesting to many kids than their fake counterparts.

- Bounce. Just about any kind of ball will amuse just about any kind of kid.

ACTIVITIES THAT:

- Promote manual dexterity, such as touching games ("This little piggy went to market . . . ," "Round and round the garden went the teddy bear . . .") and playing ball (this usually means rolling a ball back and forth; the baby will be able to heave a ball in a few months but won't be able to catch one for another year).
- Promote awareness of size, shape, color, spatial concepts (in/out, up/down, and so forth). Emptying, dumping, and refilling everything from buckets to bathtubs and kitchen cabinets build awareness of in and out; toys that nest and stack are great for teaching about size and so are large boxes the baby can crawl into.
- Continue to teach about consequences. Although we talked a lot about this in *TNF I,* it's still a developing skill. Try tying a string to a favorite toy, handing the other end of the string to the baby, and asking her to get the toy. Will she pull the string? Also, have her turn the lights and the television on and off. Does she understand the connection between flipping the switch and what happens next?

18–21 MONTHS

TOYS: All of the above, plus toys that:

- The baby can pound, smack, beat, and smash. Hammer-and-peg boards and sandbox toys are always big hits at this age.
- The baby can ride on. Four-wheelers are better (more stable) than trikes. Skip the batteries (the baby hasn't been walking long enough to need a break) and forget the pedals (it's too early).
- Encourage sorting. The baby's getting much better at putting the right block in the right hole on her shape sorter. She should also be able to stack a series of increasingly larger rings on a cylinder in the right order.

ACTIVITIES: All of the above, plus those that:

- Encourage body-part identification (Where's your nose?).
- Continue to encourage turning, twisting, and so on. My older daughter used to entertain herself for hours by locking and unlocking the doors to the car and the house.
- Continue to promote awareness of size, color, and spatial relationships.
- Promote independence. Let the baby ask you for help before offering any.

See how long it takes her or how many tries she needs to learn new skills. For example, watch as she figures out how to sit down on a baby-sized chair. At first she'll climb on front first. But after a few falls she'll figure out that backing on works better.

- Use real tools. Let your baby sweep, push the vacuum, wipe up the floor, and shave you. An electric razor is no problem, but if you use a razor and shaving cream, you might want to leave the blade off the handle the first few times. The lathering is the most fun anyway. Then shave one side of your face and show her the difference between smooth and scratchy.
- Continue to promote parent-child attachment. Peekaboo and other hiding games are great.
- Promote art awareness. See pages 27–30 for more on this.
- Encourage physical fitness, such as dancing to music, chasing, wrestling, and early attempts at gymnastics. For much more on the importance of physical play, see pages 154–56.

PLAYTHINGS TO AVOID FOR THIS GENERAL AGE GROUP

- Complicated things. Simplicity is the key here. Your baby doesn't need fancy attachments, cellular phones, fax machines, and the like. Busy boxes are generally unappreciated by kids this age.

"What arrow?"

- Antiques. Unless they're exceptionally sturdy, conform to today's more stringent safety standards, and aren't covered in lead paint, leave them in the attic.
- Anything with springs, pinch points, or sharp edges.
- Anything that has a heating element or an electrical cord (battery-operated toys—provided that the battery can't be accessed by the child—are okay).
- Anything with small, detachable parts.
- Balloons (the Consumer Product Safety Commission says balloons are the leading cause of childhood suffocation deaths: 110 kids have died since 1973).
- Audio tapes. They're great fun to unwind, but not nearly as much fun to get back in the cassette. CDs are at least as interesting to play with (they're shinier, for one thing) and are pretty much indestructible.
- Gender-specific toys. There is absolutely no reason why boys can't play with dolls, vacuums, brooms, and kitchen sets, or why girls can't play with cars, walkie-talkies, and balls. In fact, one of my younger daughter's favorite activities is shooting her fifty Hot Wheels cars one at a time down her loop-de-loop track. Don't push any particular toys at your child—just make them available and try to incorporate them into your playtime. If your child sees you using them, he or she will want to do the same.

Computer Readiness

Although your child has been walking for only a few months, it's not too early to begin introducing him to some of the high-tech equipment he's likely to encounter as he grows up. And computers are the place to start.

A lot of parents have some legitimate questions about the sensibility and worthwhileness (and even the danger) of starting kids on computers at a very early age. Here are a few of these concerns:

- Will exposing a child to computers make him antisocial or lead to his spending all his time in front of the screen instead of doing other things? Most early childhood experts believe that initially the novelty of the computer may suck children away from other activities, but this is really no different from what happens with any new toy. Your child needs a wide variety of things to play with and learn from. So as long as you don't try to make the computer replace all your child's other toys, it will be just another toy in his toybox within a few weeks.
- Can little kids really learn anything from computers? Absolutely. Although computers are not nearly as social as reading, they are far more interactive than television and offer many opportunities for creativity (without, for example, all the mess of finger paints). At this age kids can use computers to learn shapes, colors, and opposites. As they get older, computers can

Hardware—and Software—for Little Kids

Using a standard keyboard and mouse requires a level of hand-eye coordination that your child won't have for another year or so. Fortunately, several companies make child-friendly keyboards and input devices (mice, trackballs, joysticks, and so forth) for younger kids. Perhaps the best of the bunch is the Comfy Keyboard; designed to take a serious beating, this sturdy keyboard has no letters, just buttons with pictures of shapes and colors. It comes with special software appropriate for kids as young as twelve months. My younger daughter was introduced to it at about fifteen months and loved it from the start.

assist them in learning upper- and lower-case letters, word recognition, pattern recognition, spelling, reading, arithmetic, reasoning skills, and hand-eye coordination, says computer expert Mario Pagnoni.

At this age, however, the goal of exposing your child isn't really to teach him anything. It's just another way of getting him involved. Kids as young as fifteen months can turn the computer on, put disks in, and take them out.

Computers are not for all children, of course. Before starting a computer-readiness program at your house, the following five criteria should be satisfied:

- You need to have a computer.
- You have to be interested in spending some time with the child—you can't just plunk him down in front of the computer and expect him to enjoy the experience. Kids this age can't operate a conventional mouse anyway.
- He should be at least twelve months old.
- He should have a firm grasp of cause-and-effect relationships (I push the Enter key and something happens on the screen).
- He must be interested. One way to increase the chances he'll be interested is to let him watch you work on your computer; another is to let him bang around on an old keyboard (if you don't have one, you can probably buy a used one at a flea market for about five dollars).

Reading

At about fifteen months your baby has put his passive reading days behind him and is taking on a much more aggressive and participatory attitude toward books.

He'll babble along with you now as you read, and make unsolicited (but often appropriate) animal sounds. And if you pause briefly while reading a

Poetry for Babies?

In a recent national survey, researcher Ann Terry found that children's taste in poetry is just about as lowbrow as my own. Overall, kids seem to like:

- poems they can understand
- narrative poems
- poems with rhyme, rhythm, and a sense of excitement
- poems about animals or familiar experiences
- limericks of all sorts

They don't like:

- poems with a lot of figurative language and imagery
- highly abstract poems that do not make sense to them or do not relate to their own experiences
- haiku

familiar story, he'll often "fill in" a missing word or two—usually the last word in a sentence or rhyme. Over the next few months he'll try to seize control of your reading sessions by pointing to illustrations and insisting that you identify them.

But no matter how great your baby's newfound power, his excitement at his own recently acquired mobility is so consuming that he'll start squirming within minutes after he gets in your lap. Don't be offended or try to limit his movements. If he wants to go, let him. He'll be back soon enough.

To encourage your baby's interest in books and to give him more control over his reading material, consider making a low bookshelf for him, one where the books face cover out, so he can bring you his current favorites. Having a baby-accessible bookshelf will also allow your child the opportunity to pull a few books down and "read" by himself.

Flap books are great for this age, particularly ones with thick pages that the baby can open himself. Before reading a flap book to your baby for the first time, go through it once yourself and test all the flaps; unopened (and hard-to-open) flaps can frustrate even the most eager little fingers. Interactive books and those dealing with real-world themes are also big hits. At this stage babies crave familiarity and will request the same two or three books over and over. For variety—as well as your own sanity—try to slip in a new one every few days.

Whatever you're reading, use a pleasant, conversational manner and be theatrical—adopt a different voice for each character. Your baby won't be interested in plot for a few more months, so don't be afraid to interrupt your reading to "discuss" with your baby what's happening in the story or in the illustrations. Another fun thing to do occasionally is to replace a book character's name with your child's (when reading to my younger daughter, for example, I turned Goldilocks into Talyalocks).

ADDING TO YOUR LIBRARY

Keep reading your child's favorites until either he gets sick of them or they fall apart (but if the latter happens before the former, you might have to go out and buy another copy). Most of the books listed on pages 78–79 and 149 in *TNF I* are still fine for this age. As you introduce new books, though, you might want to consider adding some of these developmentally appropriate titles to your collection:

Airport, Bryon Barton
Are You There, Bear? Ron Maris
Crash! Bang! Boom! (and others), Peter Spier
The Cupboard, John Burningham
Dear Zoo, Rod Campbell
Duck, David Lloyd
Goodnight, Goodnight (and others), Eve Rice
Have You Seen My Duckling? (and many others), Nancy Tafuri
In Our House, Anne Rockwell
Listen to the Rain, Bill Martin, Jr., and John Archambault
Max's Ride, Rosemary Wells
Mommy Buy Me a China Doll, Harve Zemach
My Brown Bear Barney, Dorothy Butler
Toolbox, Anne Rockwell
Two Shoes, New Shoes (and many others), Shirley Hughes
The Very Hungry Caterpillar (and many, many others), Eric Carle

CONCEPTS

100 First Words to Say with Your Baby, Edwina Riddel
In the Morning, Anne Rockwell
I Touch (and many others), Rachel Isadora
Slam Bang, John Burningham

Art

GETTING READY. OR, FRANKLY, MY DEAR, I DON'T . . .

Making art with a toddler can be incredible fun—and incredibly messy. Now that you've been warned, if you don't take the necessary precautions, it's your own fault:

The Basics

- **Drawing implements.** Nontoxic markers are the best bet. They come in a wide variety of sizes, colors, and scents. Crayons aren't practical at this age—they crumble and can get ground into carpets and floors. Pencils need too much adult involvement (either to sharpen them or to make sure the baby doesn't stab herself with the sharp point).
- **Painting implements.** Use long-handled (8-inch minimum), wide (at least 3/8-inch) brushes. Little kids can't—and won't—do much with anything smaller.
- **Paper to draw, paint, or glue on.** Construction (thick) paper is the staple here. It's available at toy, art-supply, and stationery stores. Children's art projects also provide a great opportunity to start a recycling program at home and at work. Instead of tossing out all those old reports, flip them over and let your baby create on the other side.
- **Things to learn from.** At this age, your child is still exploring the world with all her senses. So give her art supplies that stimulate as many senses as possible, such as scented markers and textured papers.
- **Things not to eat.** Make sure everything your baby uses in her art projects is absolutely nontoxic, washable, and too big to be a choking hazard.

- Cover every surface—walls, floors, tabletops, chairs—with paper. If you're still concerned, move the whole show outside onto the sidewalk or into the backyard, where you can just hose everything off.
- Use an easel or tape paper right to the table. It's far too frustrating for the baby to have to hold the paper steady and draw on it at the same time.
- Observe the dress code. Kids this age usually don't like to wear aprons, so have them either work naked (always fun) or wear old clothes that are okay to trash.
- Use *tiny* amounts—a thin film of paint or glue on the inside of a shallow container is fine. You can refill it as often as you need to, and if anything falls, there won't be much to clean up.
- Dilute. Most of the paint you get at craft stores is quite concentrated. Diluting it 25–50 percent with dishwashing liquid will help the paint wash out of the clothes later (and last longer, too). It also serves to deter kids from putting the paint in their mouths.
- Don't give too many choices. Asking "Do you want red or green?" is okay.

Asking "What colors do you want?" is an invitation to a power struggle (unless you're prepared to give in to your child's every demand).

- Pay attention. Your child's attention span ranges from about three seconds to fifteen minutes. If you notice any indications of boredom, such as walking away, crying, or eating the supplies, offer another art-related activity or shut things down for the day.
- Don't interfere. Showing your baby once or twice how to use a brush or a marker is okay. But telling him which colors to use, showing him where to draw, or making *any* kind of correction is inappropriate. The object here is not to teach art or to create the next little Picasso. It is simply to introduce your child—in a no-pressure, no-expectation kind of way—to the creative process and to the idea that art can be fun.
- Monitor your expectations. Even if your child *is* the next Picasso, there's a good chance that she won't create anything remotely recognizable (except perhaps a line, a circle, or a spiral) for another year.
- Stop caring. The more concerned you are about the mess or about your child wasting or destroying the supplies (they love to shred paper, put glue in their hair, and use markers as hammers), the less fun you'll let your baby have. So do what you can to prepare. Then take a deep breath, and relax.

Given your child's age, attention span, interest, and level of hand-eye coordination, the range of age-appropriate art projects is fairly limited. Here, though, are some big hits and the supplies you'll need:

- Drawing. Paper, markers.
- Collages. Objects that will help your baby use all her senses: smelly seeds (fennel, coriander, and so forth); anything that has an interesting shape or texture or that makes an interesting sound when touched; glue; and just about anything you might otherwise be tempted to throw away—egg and juice cartons, cereal boxes, bottle caps, bubble wrap, cotton balls (clean).
- Painting. Paint; paper; potatoes or sponges (for cutting out patterns and making prints); toy cars, sticks, or anything else that can be dipped in paint and make an interesting mark on paper.

DISPLAY

Whatever your child creates, be sure to display it someplace—on the fridge, on a bulletin board, taped to the wall. You do not have to compliment the work very much; just having your child's work up where she can see it herself is enough to make her feel proud of herself.

Family Matters

Separation Anxiety

Try to think about things from your baby's perspective for a second: For most of your life you've controlled everything that happened in the world: who and what came and went, how long they stayed, what they did while they were there. But for the past few months, your grip seems to be slipping. Things seem to be coming and going all by themselves. And the people you thought you could always count on to be there for you have developed a nasty habit of disappearing just when you need them most. Even worse, people you *don't* know—and aren't sure you want to know—keep on trying to pick you up and take you away. The universe is clearly in chaos, and given the way things are going you can't really be sure that the people you're most attached to will ever come back.

All this, according to researchers Barbara and Philip Newman, is what separation anxiety is all about. And from your baby's perspective, the best way to put herself back in the driver's seat is to cry. "That's it," she says. "If I cry, my parents won't leave. I just know it."

DEALING WITH SEPARATION ANXIETY

Some babies get it, others don't. Kids who have had regular contact with lots of friendly, loving people will probably have an easier time adapting to brief separations than those who have spent all their time with one or two people.

They'll be more comfortable with strangers and more confident that their parents and other loved ones will return eventually.

In an unusual but far from uncommon manifestation of separation anxiety, many kids about this age develop some sleep problems; they view going to sleep as yet another assault on their ability to control the world. It can also be confusing and frightening for a child to go to sleep in the dark and wake up in the light or to see you wearing one thing when you put her to bed and something else in the morning. Staying awake can seem like a surefire way to make certain that everything (and everyone) stays right where they're supposed to.

Here are some things you can do to help your child manage her separation anxieties:

- **Be firm but reassuring.** Tell the baby where you're going and that you'll be back soon.
- **Don't say you'll miss her.** She'll only feel guilty that she's making you unhappy. She'll also wonder why you would do something to deliberately make yourself unhappy. And finally, if you're sad or upset at leaving her, that's what your baby will think is the appropriate reaction to separation.
- **Don't sneak away.** If you're leaving, say good-bye like a man. Tiptoeing away will undermine your baby's trust in you.
- **Don't give in to crying.** If you're sure the baby is in good hands, leave—with a smile on your face.
- **Don't force.** Let the baby stay in your arms for a while longer if she needs to and don't make fun of her if she wants to bury her head in your shoulder.
- **Try to use sitters the baby knows.** If you have to use someone new, have him or her arrive fifteen to twenty minutes before you go out so he or she can get acquainted with the baby while you are there. Either way, train sitters in your baby's bedtime ritual.
- **Leave while the baby is awake.** Waking up in the middle of the night to a strange (or even a familiar but unexpected) sitter can be terrifying to a child.
- **Be patient.** Don't trivialize the baby's feelings about your leaving. *You* know you'll be back; the baby isn't so sure. So give her plenty of time to adjust to any new situation.
- **Play.** Object-permanence games (see *TNF I*, page 121) help reinforce the idea that things—and especially people—don't disappear forever.
- **Establish routines.** Doing things on a regular schedule (such as dropping the baby off at day care immediately after breakfast or reading two stories right before bed) can help your child understand that some things in life can be counted on.

- **Develop a strong attachment.** Singing, playing, reading, and talking together all help build a strong, loving bond between you and your baby and help her feel more secure. The more secure she is, the less she'll worry about being abandoned.
- **Ask questions.** You'll have a better chance of finding out what your child is afraid of if you do. The thing that scares most kids the most, for example, is not the dark but being alone. So make sure your child has a favorite toy or other security object at night. And leave a light on so she can see she's not alone.
- **Give the baby plenty of space.** If you hover, she'll get the idea that you're afraid of leaving her by herself and that there's actually something to fear from being alone.
- **Distract.** Encourage independence by suggesting that the baby play with her train set while you wash the dishes.
- **Relax.** Babies will pick up on your mood; if you're nervous they'll figure that they should be too.
- **Let the baby follow you around.** This builds a sense of security and confidence that you're there—just in case she needs you.
- **Know your baby's temperament.** (For a discussion of temperament, see pages 73–79.) If your child has a low frustration tolerance, she won't want you to leave her and may cry all day after being separated. Your slow-to-adapt child won't want you to leave either, but when you do, she'll usually cry only for a few minutes. She may cry again when you return, though, because your coming back is as much of a transition as your leaving was.

INDEPENDENCE VS. DEPENDENCE

From your baby's perspective, separation anxiety can be a real problem. But from your perspective, it's a positive (albeit frequently frustrating) sign, marking the beginning of your baby's struggle between independence and dependence. It's a scary time for the baby, and you can see his ambivalence dozens of times every day as he alternates between clinging and pushing you away.

At this stage, says British child-care expert Penelope Leach, "his own emotions are his worst enemy"—just when it seems that your baby should be needing you less, he actually needs you more. You're the grown-up, so it's up to you to help your baby make some sense of his conflicting emotions, as well as to nurture his independence while supporting his dependence. But beware: it's extremely easy to get trapped in a vicious circle of dependence and independence. Here's how:

IF YOU . . .	HE FEELS . . .	WHICH, IN TURN, MAKES HIM FEEL . . .
Interfere with his independence and his developing ego	frustration, anger, and hate	anxious and afraid
Interfere with his need to be dependent on you and his desire to cling	anxiety and fear	angry, hateful, and frustrated

Safety Update

Now that your child is vertical, he can get into a lot more trouble much more quickly than just a few months ago. That means that in addition to childproofing your home (see *TNF I*, pages 138–41) you're going to need to take some extra safety precautions.

ESPECIALLY IN THE GARAGE, BASEMENT, WORKSHOP, AND OUTSIDE

- Keep all dangerous chemicals, paints, thinners, gas, oil, weed killers, fertilizers, and so forth securely locked up.
- If you have an extra refrigerator or freezer, make sure it is locked (not just shut). It's easier than you think for a toddler to pull open the door, climb in after something particularly attractive, and get stuck inside. If the refrigerator/freezer isn't being used, take the doors off.
- Be particularly careful when backing out of the garage or driveway. Your baby might run after you to say one more good-bye or to get one more kiss and. . . .

ESPECIALLY AROUND SWIMMING POOLS

- Put a fence around it, although not an electrified one. (Don't laugh; I actually heard of a couple who installed an electrified fence around their pool to keep the dog out, but succeeded in electrocuting one of their children.)
- Keep furniture, plants, toys, or anything else that can be used to climb on away from the fence.
- Get a pool cover that is strong enough for an adult to walk on.
- Make sure you have the proper poolside safety equipment (life preserver, poles, and so on).

"Do you know where the fire extinguisher is, Dad?"

- Keep a phone nearby for emergency purposes.
- Never let your child in the pool area without at least one adult present.

GENERAL SAFETY

- Scuff up the soles of any new shoes with sandpaper. Slippery shoes and slippery floors aren't a good combination.
- Be cautious around strange—and even familiar—pets. Animals may not be as responsive to your child's hugs and kisses as you'd like them to be.
- Remember the twelve-inch rule. To keep babies from grabbing things from counters and tabletops, pediatrician William Sears suggests making sure that objects are at least twelve inches from the edge. That way, your curious baby won't be able to reach them.
- Keep all automatic or self-closing doors either locked or secured in the open position. Kids can (and do) get stuck.
- Reminder: Never leave your child alone—or with another child less than eleven years old—in or near water, even if he seems to be sitting up nicely by himself in the bathtub. And while we're on the subject, be sure to dump the water out of any buckets or pans you happen to have standing around. A lot of horrible things can happen in just one second.

15–18 MONTHS

Keeping Communication Open

What's Going On With the Baby

Physically

- As if making up for the lull in motor development of the past few months, your toddler will be a blur of activity, rushing from room to room investigating everything.
- Early in the second quarter of your toddler's second year, her walking will still be somewhat clumsy: getting herself into motion is difficult, her legs will move stiffly, and she'll hold her arms away from her body for balance. Most of the time she'll stop by falling.
- By the end of this quarter starting and stopping will be no problem (although she'll still have a tough time negotiating corners upright).
- Her balance is also improving. If she holds on to something, she can actually stand on one foot.
- She loves to show off her strength, often grunting theatrically as she struggles to pick up or push around the biggest things she can get her hands on.
- She may be able to throw a small ball, but can't catch. And although she'd like to kick a ball, more often than not she ends up stepping on it instead.

  Note: If your child isn't walking unassisted by the end of her eighteenth month, check with your pediatrician.

Intellectually

- Most of your child's development in this period will be physical rather than intellectual.

- She'll continue to use trial and error to solve problems and will expand her use of tools to retrieve out-of-reach items. (If a toy is on a blanket, for example, she may pull the blanket toward her instead of walking over to get the toy.)
- She still struggles with the conflict between autonomy and dependence—refusing your requests to do even the most basic things, but wanting to keep you well within sight as she explores new places.
- She has a very short attention span and may flit from activity to activity. Expecting a lot of rational thought from a child this age is a waste of time, as is giving her long explanations of whys and why nots.
- Toddlers love routines and rituals. Establishing patterns now, such as bath-story-bedtime and park-lunch-nap, will help you minimize some of the problems you're likely to encounter later on.
- She's developing an imagination. She'll crawl on the floor, pretending to be a dog, and she'll "eat" food pictured in a book. The downside to this is that if your child continues imagining things even after she falls asleep (and most do), she may begin to have nightmares. Since kids can't really tell the difference between dreams and reality, nightmares at this age can be particularly frightening.

Verbally

- Your toddler continues to discover the power of language. She tries as often as possible to combine words, and she knows that phrases like "up me," "gimme ba-ba," and "book read" will get her picked up, fed, or read to.
- Her mimicking skills are moving into high gear, and she'll try to repeat any word you can throw at her.
- She loves singing and will join in on familiar songs wherever and whenever she can. Although far from fluent, your baby is beginning to understand the humorous uses of language. My younger daughter had the "moo-moo," "woof-woof," "quack-quack" parts of "Old MacDonald's Farm" down at fifteen months, but insisted that the chorus was "E-I-E-I-EEEEEEEE."
- She may also sing, hum, and bounce to music when she's alone.

Emotionally/Socially

- The first half of the second year may be marked by great frustration and contradictions, feelings that frequently result in tantrums. Unable to express their wants in words, kids this age often become enraged. They also "get angry both when their parents withhold help and when they proffer needed assistance," writes child development expert Frank Caplan. Overall, "they get angry because they are not big or strong enough for the tasks they set for themselves." Some tantrums, especially the ones that involve breath-holding, can be quite spectacular. (See pages 70–71 for more on this.)

- Most of the time, however, your toddler is a pretty happy soul. Her sense of humor is developing nicely, and she's truly amused by her own movement—sliding, dropping things, falling down on purpose.
- She can also understand verbal humor, particularly when it deals with incongruities. For example, after emphatically refusing your lunchtime offer of a banana, a bowl of cereal, or a cheese sandwich, she may laugh hysterically if you suggest a spoonful of dirt.
- She still plays alongside, not *with,* other toddlers. In fact, the only people she really wants to socialize with are her parents. During this period she may begin bringing you favorite books so you can read to her.

What You're Going Through

Thinking About Sex

Sex may mean very different things to you and your partner:

YOU MAY . . .	SHE MAY . . .
♦ See sex as a way of setting the stage for verbal intimacy.	♦ See verbal intimacy as a way of setting the stage for sex.
♦ Want sex as a way of feeling closer to her.	♦ Want sex when she's already feeling close to you.
♦ Need sex to establish an emotional connection with your partner.	♦ Need an emotional connection with you before being interested in sex.

POTENTIAL CONFLICTS

YOU MAY . . .

- Complain about the actual sex more than your partner, says psychologist Aaron Hass: the quantity, the quality, her lack of seductive behavior, her lack of taking the initiative.

- Be feeling excluded from your baby by your partner and may want to have sex as a way of reconnecting with your partner.
- Be embarrassed to admit that you feel too exhausted, unsure, overwhelmed by family responsibilities even to think about sex.
- Find it difficult to contemplate sex—especially oral sex—after remembering all the blood from the birth. You may be feeling that she's somehow been disfigured and get turned off as a result.
- Feel guilty about what pregnancy did to her body.
- Feel guilty about the pain she was in during pregnancy and be afraid of having her go through the same thing again (this is a common fear, even if you're using birth control).
- Feel that your partner prefers the baby to you if she rejects your advances.

SHE MAY . . .

- Complain that you don't talk to her, you aren't affectionate enough, you take her for granted, you don't understand her or her feelings. "Sexual excitement is very much a function of the strength of her loving feelings for her man and her perception of his love for her," says Hass.
- Be withholding sex as a way of getting back at you for not sharing equally in the distribution of household labor or for escaping into work.
- Be "affectioned out" from taking care of the baby all day.
- Be too sleep-deprived to show much sexual interest in you.
- Have less interest in sex, find intercourse painful, or have difficulty reaching orgasm. Twenty percent of women suffer from one or more of these problems longer than a year after the baby, says Dr. Dwenda K. Gjerdingen of the University of Minnesota.
- Not be feeling enough of a connection with you: after focusing predominantly on the baby, she may not know what she and you have in common anymore.
- Think that you find her less attractive than you used to. She also may find *herself* less attractive.
- Be more comfortable interacting with a child because the child expects less of her.

BOTH OF YOU MAY . . .

- Find it hard to admit to the other your basic need for support, comfort, love. The result can often be mutual blaming and resentment.
- Be reluctant to allow yourselves to get aroused. You might be afraid of being interrupted by the baby or you might feel guilty about satisfying your own needs when you should really be doing something to take care of the baby.

(A recent survey by *Parenting* magazine found that parents kiss their children twice as much as they do each other.)

- Have stopped touching each other because you're afraid that a stroke or a touch might be misinterpreted as a sexual overture (see *TNF I*, page 51). A new mother "may think her mate is obsessed with sexual desires," says Hass, "when what he really needs is reassurance that she still loves him and he has not been replaced by the baby." Sounds silly, but it isn't.

SOLUTIONS

- Make sure there are opportunities for verbal as well as sexual intimacy. And while you're at it, get rid of the idea that there's always a connection between the two.
- Eliminate sex (for a while). Spend some time getting used to each other in a nonsexual way.
  - hold hands
  - stroke her hair

The Ultimate Aphrodisiac

According to Aaron Hass, the most frequent complaint from wives about husbands is that they aren't involved enough with the children. And—from her point of view, anyway—if you don't love the kids, you don't love her. "A man, therefore, who does not actively father will inevitably trigger his wife's resentment," says Hass.

The solution? Be an active, involved father.

"There is no more powerful aphrodisiac to a mother than to see her husband lovingly engaged with their children," says Hass. "When your wife sees your involvement with her children, she will want to see you happy. She will, therefore, want to satisfy your sexual desires. She will be more likely to suggest that just the two of you get away for a night or a weekend so that you can have more intimate time together. She will be more open to sexual experimentation. . . . She will be more sexually creative. She will take pains to make sure the children are tucked away early in the evening so that you can have uninterrupted time together. And, of course, when your wife is happier, her own libido is more likely to assert itself."

Whew! If that doesn't make you want to quit your job and take care of your children, nothing will.

- ◊ kiss her when walking through the kitchen
- ◊ give each other massages, back rubs, and so forth
- ◊ make out

- Schedule sex—it doesn't have to be spontaneous like it was (see page 51 for more on this).
- Go on dates.

Dating Your Partner: A Few Requirements

- Don't try to make up for lost time. Packing too many things into a single evening can put a lot of pressure on both of you.
- Make it clear that there are no strings attached. Either of you may be suspicious that the "date" will be used as a way of getting the other in the sack.
- Don't talk about the baby. Let's be realistic: the baby is the one you and your partner are trying to get away from, the one who has consumed so much of your time that the two of you have neglected each other.

You and Your Baby

Dealing with Your Baby's Fears

Even though your baby's world is growing at an incredible clip, it's still a fairly small, well-managed, and—above all—safe little place. But the more she separates from you and the more independent she becomes, the scarier the world gets.

Babies may seem fairly unpredictable to us, but they are essentially creatures of habit who crave familiarity and routine. And just about everything your child will fear in her first three years of life will be the result of a break in her routines or an unfamiliar, unanticipated, or surprising event.

Stranger anxiety (see *TNF I,* pages 149–50) and separation anxiety (pages 30–32) were undoubtedly your baby's first fears. At about fifteen months, fear of the bath and of getting their hair washed top most kids' lists (see the chart on pages 42–45 for a list of some of the most common early-toddlerhood fears, a little about what they might mean, and a few suggestions for handling them). And by the time they're twenty-one months old, they've graduated to being afraid of dogs, the dark (and associated monsters), and loud noises (sirens, vacuums, car backfirings, and so forth)—in that order.

Many of your child's fears, writes child psychologist Selma Fraiberg, are "essentially a fear of his own impulses which are transferred to objects or phenomena outside himself. . . . Normally the fear will subside when the child has learned to control successfully the particular impulse which is disturbing him."

FIGHTING FEARS

Here are some general guidelines for helping your child deal with her fears.

TRY TO DISCOVER THE CAUSE

Starting when she was about eighteen months old, my younger daughter suddenly started crying hysterically every time I put her down on the sidewalk. After a few months, I figured out that she was afraid that the cars would hop the curb and run us down—a perfectly reasonable fear. My wife and I explained to her many, many times that cars live in the street and that they aren't allowed where people walk. That seemed to take the edge off the fear. But a few days later when we were out for a walk a car pulled into a driveway right in front of us, and my daughter went ballistic again. In her view, I'd been lying to her and cars really were after her.

Once you've figured out what's troubling your child, keep the following in mind:

- Acknowledge that your child's fears are real. Let her know that everyone has fears and that being afraid is perfectly normal. You might want to tell your child about some of the fears you had when you were a kid.
- Read. There are plenty of good books about how kids triumph over all sorts of potentially scary situations.
- Don't tell her she really isn't—or shouldn't be—afraid of some thing, place, or person. Instead, comfort her, tell her you'll always be there to help her.
- Never force your child to confront her fears (gently demonstrating that vacuums and baths really won't hurt the baby is okay, but don't push). And never laugh at or tease a fearful child; this will only make things worse.

CONTROL YOUR OWN REACTIONS

Thrust into a situation she's never been in before—especially a scary one—your baby probably won't know how to react. So she'll look to you for some visual or verbal cues as to how *you* think she should respond.

In one recent study, researcher James Sorce and his associates conducted a fascinating experiment designed to see whether parents' facial expressions—happy, fearful, interested, or angry—have any influence on their children's behavior in potentially dangerous situations. Sorce placed the babies and one of their parents on opposite sides of a "visual cliff"—a long, piece of sturdy but transparent Plexiglas that traversed a dangerous-looking (to the babies,

THE FEAR	WHAT IT MIGHT MEAN	WHAT TO DO ABOUT IT
Bath/hair washing	♦ Fear of getting washed down the drain and thrown away (if soap suds go down the drain, the hair can go too, and if the hair goes, why not the whole body?). ♦ Fear of the noise of the water. ♦ Fear of the hot water. ♦ Fear of getting things in the eyes and losing vision—if you can't see the world, you can't control it.	♦ Get a special toy that your baby can play with only in the bathtub. ♦ Take baths with your baby. ♦ Show her that big things (like you and she) can't go down the drain. ♦ Have her get in one toe at a time, then a leg, then the bottom. ♦ Wash her with a washcloth instead of sticking her head under water.
Vacuum cleaner	♦ Fear of being disposed of just like the dust (similar to fear of baths, above). ♦ Fear of loud noises, of being yelled at.	♦ Have the baby explore the vacuum, and perhaps even push it around a little while it's off. ♦ Have one of the baby's toys go for a "ride" on the vacuum. ♦ Hold the baby while vacuuming. ♦ Let the baby turn it on and off, thus giving her control over the noise.
Haircuts	♦ Fear of being disposed of (same "logic" as getting rid of soap suds).	♦ Have the baby check out the barber first, and watch a few strangers get haircuts. ♦ Take the baby (with another adult) to watch you get a haircut. ♦ Find a child-friendly barber who has lots of experience with kids.

THE FEAR	WHAT IT MIGHT MEAN	WHAT TO DO ABOUT IT
Haircuts *(continued)*		♦ Learn to cut hair yourself. ♦ Let your child cut the hair of her dolls, bears, and so on to practice. ♦ Have her sit in your lap during the haircut. ♦ Skip the hair washing—too many fears combined.
Monsters	♦ Fear of the unknown. ♦ Fear of being separated from you. ♦ Fear that there is something so powerful and unpredictable that even *you* (the all-powerful parent) can't control it.	♦ Write a "No Monsters Allowed" sign (or one warning of a monster-eating kid inside the room). ♦ Check under the bed and in closets for monsters. ♦ Watch out for mixed messages. Telling your child monsters don't exist and then putting up signs or looking under the bed can be confusing. Try a compromise approach, such as, "There really aren't any monsters, but if there were, they would read this sign and stay out." ♦ Have a large, sturdy toy "stand guard" over the baby's room. ♦ Give the baby a magic wand or a special magic button to push that makes monsters disappear instantly. ♦ Cut down on prebedtime scary things (including stories, growling, and making faces). ♦ Leave on a night-light.

(continued on page 44)

THE FEAR	WHAT IT MIGHT MEAN	WHAT TO DO ABOUT IT
Sleep or dark	♦ Fear of losing control. ♦ Fear that loved ones and loved things won't be there later.	♦ Establish a comfortable bedtime routine. ♦ Emphasize the big-kid bed. ♦ Tell baby that everyone else she knows is sleeping (name them one at a time). ♦ Tell baby that you—and everyone else—will be there in the morning. ♦ Leave a light on.
Scary stories	♦ Similar to monsters, night, dark.	♦ No scary stories before bed or, if the problem is severe, no scary stories at all, even during the day. ♦ Cuddle while reading. ♦ Edit or cut out the scary parts. ♦ Make sure she knows the story isn't real. ♦ Use a night-light.
Animals	♦ Fear of the unfamiliar (not human). ♦ Fear of being eaten. ♦ Fear of being bitten. ♦ Fear of not being able to control her own impulses or live up to her parents' expectations.	♦ Read lots of books about friendly animals (the *Carl* books, by Alexandra Day, are great for this). ♦ Teach baby the proper way to behave with pets: no fingers in animals' noses, and so on. Take her hand and show her the right way to pet an animal. ♦ Teach baby to recognize inviting and hostile animal gestures.

THE FEAR	WHAT IT MIGHT MEAN	WHAT TO DO ABOUT IT
Animals *(continued)*		♦ Ask pet owners if their animal is friendly before letting your baby anywhere near it. ♦ Hold your baby's hand near unfamiliar pets. ♦ Never force the baby to touch animals if she doesn't want to.
Doctors/ dentists	♦ Fear of strangers. ♦ Fear of new situations, smells, sights. ♦ Fear of pain. ♦ Fear that there's really something wrong (you wouldn't go to the doctor if there weren't, right?).	♦ Talk about the doctor, about how pediatricians love kids and want to make them feel good. ♦ Play through it (see below)—have baby do to her stuffed animals what the doctor will do to her. ♦ Do *not* lie—don't say there won't be shots or that the shots won't hurt. ♦ Schedule appointment for noncranky times. ♦ Switch to a same-sex doctor (don't worry about offending yours, he or she is very familiar with these requests).

anyway) surface. He then induced the babies to crawl across the "cliff" to retrieve a tempting toy from the parent. The results were illuminating: of the seventeen children who saw a fearful expression, *none* crossed the cliff. And only two of the eighteen confronted with an angry expression did. Of the nineteen who saw happy faces, however, fourteen crossed, and so did eleven of the fifteen whose parent's expression was one of "sincere interest."

Your reactions influence your baby in other areas as well. When she's learning to walk, for example, she'll probably fall down twenty times a minute and get right back up without the slightest complaint. But if you gasp and lunge across the room to "save" her, she'll probably start crying, thinking that since you're scared, she should be too. And in just a few years she'll be able to overreact on her own, without your help: when you were a kid you could probably take a pretty good tumble, get right up, and forget all about it. But if you saw blood, you'd start crying.

WATCH WHAT YOU SAY

Like your physical reaction, your verbal reaction can have a great influence on how your baby deals with fear.

- Bring up and discuss potentially scary situations in advance. Say things like, "We're going to . . . but . . ."
- Well-intentioned warnings such as, "Oh, there's nothing to be afraid of," usually backfire. In your baby's mind, if there really wasn't anything to be afraid of, you wouldn't have said anything at all.
- Also, don't say things like, "Be careful, this might be a little scary." Your baby will actually think you want her to be scared.
- Don't go overboard on safety issues. Warnings like the ones you heard from your parents ("Don't talk to strangers," "Don't take candy from strangers," "Don't get into a car with strangers") can give a child a nearly irrational fear of, well, strangers.
- Think about potential mixed messages: now that you've got your baby scared away from the hot stove, do you think she's going to be happy about eating some hot breakfast cereal or, even worse, getting into a bathtub filled with hot water?

PLAY IT OUT

One of the things infants and toddlers are most afraid of is being out of control. Letting them play through scary situations—either ones that just happened or ones they're anticipating—can help them regain that important feeling of being in charge. So, if your child is afraid of doctors, get her a toy doctor's kit, complete with stethoscope and syringe, so she can examine—and give shots to—all her stuffed animals. If she's afraid of *real* animals, try a small but ferocious-looking stuffed one she can tame.

EXPECT THE IRRATIONAL . . . AND TRY NOT TO LAUGH

A friend of mine told me about taking her two-year-old daughter, Arielle, to the barber for her first haircut. They'd talked things over, read some books about haircuts, given the stuffed animals trims, and everything was going fine—until the barber made the first cut. All of a sudden Arielle winced and let out an incredibly loud "Ouch"—a wail she repeated with every snip of the scissors. There wasn't anything wrong, but little Arielle, who knew that cutting her finger hurt, figured that cutting her hair would hurt too.

SECURITY OBJECTS

About half of all kids need, want, use, or demand some kind of security objects: blankets, pacifiers, toys, and so on. Don't discourage this—she'll give it up when she's ready to. Trying to break a security-object habit can make your baby feel even more needy than before, creating a pattern that may result in her using, in later years, such "adult" security devices as alcohol and drugs.

So if you think your child is developing a real fondness for a particular object, go out and buy one or two more identical ones to keep in the closet. The first one might get lost, shredded, or so filthy that it can't be salvaged.

Nutrition Update

BALANCED MEALS? GOOD LUCK!

Getting your baby to eat balanced meals is one of the most frustrating tasks you'll have during his second year of life. For a week it may seem that no matter what kind of delicacies you prepare, he won't eat anything but plain rice and soy sauce. Then, all of a sudden, he'll refuse to eat rice and won't be satisfied with anything but macaroni and cheese. Believe me, this happens all the time.

Part of the problem, of course, is that you and your baby haven't agreed on what, exactly, a balanced meal is—and you won't for quite a few years. Fortunately, you don't have to. In a classic study, Dr. Clara Davis allowed a group of year-old babies to choose freely from a sampling of foods (that carefully omitted high-sugar foods, candy, cookies, and soft drinks). She found that on a

MOST ALLERGENIC FOODS	LEAST ALLERGENIC FOODS
♦ Egg whites	♦ Rice
♦ Wheat and yeast	♦ Oats
♦ Milk and other dairy products	♦ Barley
♦ Citrus fruits	♦ Carrots
♦ Berries	♦ Squash
♦ Tomatoes	♦ Apricots
♦ Chocolate	♦ Peaches
♦ Nuts	♦ Apples
♦ Shellfish	♦ Lamb

"Because I'm *a* sovereign, *and a sovereign is* allowed *not to eat his spinach if he doesn't want to."*

day-to-day basis the babies' diets were indeed out of balance. But over the course of a few months—a far more critical time frame—their diets were actually quite well balanced.

Still, having a kid eat nothing but bananas for two weeks at a stretch (as my younger daughter did) can be a little disconcerting. The only time this kind of eating truly is a problem is if the baby has absolutely no fruits or vegetables for more than a week—a situation that's probably more your fault than the baby's. If this happens, call your pediatrician; he or she may be able to suggest some alternate sources of those crucial nutrients.

Overall, you probably won't be able to do much to change your baby's eating habits. But if you're really worried, here are some suggestions that might help:

- Introduce a wide variety of foods—even if the baby won't touch any of them.
- Serve small portions; large ones can be a little scary.
- Keep a log of what the baby eats over the course of a week—just to see how he's doing.
- Don't give up after only one try.
- Don't make a huge battle out of it.

Diagnosing Food Allergies

Correctly diagnosing food allergies is tricky, even for professionals. Since trace amounts of the most common allergens are present in many foods, pinpointing the single offending ingredient is extremely difficult. Casein (a milk protein), for example, is sometimes found in tuna and even in nondairy ice creams. Chili recipes often include peanuts, and just try to find a packaged product that doesn't contain corn, or at least corn syrup.

If you suspect your toddler is allergic, but her reactions aren't severe, keep a diary of everything she eats and all her symptoms for at least two weeks. This may seem like a real pain, but the diary will help you and your pediatrician identify the source of the problem.

Because the only proven way to treat food allergies is to avoid the offending foods, your pediatrician may, after reviewing the diary, prescribe an elimination diet. These diets typically last two weeks and include only the least allergenic foods possible (see page 47). If the symptoms don't improve after a few weeks, you can assume your child doesn't have a food allergy. But if the symptoms do improve, other foods are introduced, one at a time, a few days apart. If a reaction occurs, the new food is eliminated again and reintroduced after the symptoms have subsided (to make sure the first reaction wasn't just a coincidence). Because most allergies are eventually outgrown, however, many doctors recommend reintroducing previously eliminated foods every three months or so.

Elimination diets may sound simple, but don't start one without your doctor's supervision. Too many parents misdiagnose food allergies and eliminate too many foods. "Most kids are allergic to only one or two foods," says Ann Muñoz-Furlong, who founded the Food Allergy Network. Muñoz-Furlong warns that pulling kids—toddlers in particular—off too many foods can lead to an unbalanced diet or even malnutrition.

A word of caution: if your pediatrician immediately recommends diagnostics such as skin-prick tests, or treatments like immunotherapy, get a second opinion. A lot of these tests are inconvenient, expensive, and, worst of all, ineffective.

To get more information on food allergies, call the Food Allergy Network at (703) 691-3179.

- Don't beg; it will just give your baby an inflated view of her own abilities to control you.
- Don't punish the baby for not eating what you serve.
- Go along with the craziness; let the baby knock himself out.
- Don't use dessert as a bribe (for more on this, see page 132).

Be sure to read the "Food and Your Child's Temperament" section on page 133.

Family Matters

Communication

MORE CH-CH-CH-CHANGES

Nearly all the couples in Jay Belsky's exhaustive studies of new parents experienced a drop in the quality of their communication. Half the time it was permanent. Here are some factors Belsky and several other researchers have identified as contributing to a decline in couples' communication skills:

- "A new child deprives a couple of many of the mechanisms they once used to manage differences," says Belsky. For example, a couple that had disagreements about who did what around the house might solve the problem by getting a housekeeper. But once the baby arrives, strained finances might preclude a cleaning person and the once painless who-does-what disagreements now need to be confronted.
- The lack of spontaneity. Before your baby was born, if you wanted to go to a movie or just sit around and talk, you could just do it. But now, as parents, you don't have that luxury. If you want to go out, you have to get a sitter a day or so in advance, make sure the baby is fed, and be back at a certain time.
- Physical exhaustion. Even if you and your partner stay home together, there's a better than even chance you'll be too tired to stay awake for an entire conversation.
- There's a general decline in intimacy-promoting activities such as sex, getting together with friends, and so forth.
- With so much time and energy focused on the baby, you and your partner may find that your pool of common interests is shrinking fast.
- There's a lot less time and money left to pursue individual interests and activities outside the home. As a result, many new parents find that their communication skills have "rusted." They don't have nearly as many new things to talk about and they've lost (partially, at least) the ability to hear and understand each other.

- If you or your partner has left the workplace, you've lost a rich source of conversational topics; there are now a lot fewer stories to tell about people at the office.

Here are some things you and your partner can do to keep (or get) your communication on track:

- Get a family calendar. This can keep double-booking and scheduling miscommunications to a minimum.
- Set aside at least fifteen minutes a day to talk about things other than the baby. It's harder than you think. See the "(Re)Learning to Talk" section below for more.
- Go out on dates (with your partner, of course). Spending time alone with your partner is absolutely critical to the long-term health of your marriage. Get a sitter if you can, or ask friends or relatives to step in. You might also want to set up an informal baby-sitting cooperative with a few other parents in your neighborhood; they need to get out as much as you and your partner do (see page 40 for more on this).
- Do something special for each other. But be flexible and understanding. If you've made surprise plans and your partner is too exhausted, it doesn't mean she doesn't love you. Try again another night or put the "surprise" on the calendar.
- Schedule sex. It sounds terribly unromantic, but just having the big S on the calendar may actually make it *more* fun. And anyway, if you're still interested, this may be the only way it's going to happen. Weekdays may be out, but if you use your weekends wisely, you should still be able to rechristen every room in your house.
- If your partner is at home with the baby during the day, try to give her some time every day when she can be completely alone and doesn't have to take care of anyone but herself. If you're the primary caretaker, do the same for yourself.
- Don't blame the baby for your troubles. Too many couples interpret their communication problems as a sign that the baby pushed them apart and that they shouldn't have become parents.
- Talk to other people. Talk to other couples with kids to find out what they've been through, what works, and what doesn't. You might also join a new parents' or new fathers' group.

(RE)LEARNING TO TALK

"I get the picture sometimes of two people who may be very much in love and very much together, having private dreams that shape their lives, but not letting each other know the content," says Phil Cowan. Frequent, open, and honest communication is "the key to an effective transition from couple to family," he adds. But because so many couples seem to forget how, let's go over the basics:

- **Open your mouth.** Although many men have been socialized into thinking that we don't have strong feelings or emotional needs, this obviously isn't true. Nevertheless, many men are reluctant to talk to their partners about their needs and feelings, fearing that they'll seem weak in the eyes of their partners and will be letting them down.
- **Close your mouth and open your ears.** One of the most widespread stereotypes about men and women is that women are more open than men about discussing their feelings and emotions. If your partner is a natural talker, great. But plenty of new mothers need some gentle, supportive encouragement. "A great deal of needless suffering goes on because mothers and fathers are ashamed to express feelings they have that seem 'unmotherly' or 'unfatherly,'" writes Phil Cowan. So encourage her to talk, ask her about her deepest feelings about the baby, tell her you love her, reassure her that you'll be there for her.
- **Speak the same language.** Sounds silly, but it's not. Some of the biggest communication breakdowns come because people don't (or can't or won't) agree on the definition of some very basic words. For example, does the word *love* mean the same thing to you and your partner? Do the two of you express your love for each other in the same way? Probably not. Men commonly express love for their partners (and other people) by *doing* things (that may be how the whole "good provider" thing got started). Women, however, are more likely to express their love *verbally*. Unfortunately, most people want to be communicated with in their own language. Consequently, what you *do* may not be loving enough for your partner and what she *says* may not be enough for you. Learning to understand and express love differently is like learning a new language. Granted, it's a little more complicated than high school French, but it can be done.

Here are some ground rules for putting your newly polished communication skills to work:

- Schedule a special time and place for your discussions. Let's face it: if you can't have sex without a schedule, you won't be able to have a serious conversation without one either.
- Tell her what's on your mind. Tackle one issue at a time and stay away from phrases like "you always . . . ," "you never . . . ," or anything else guaranteed to put a quick end to your conversations.

- Ask her to tell you what she heard you say. Just saying, "I understand what you're saying" isn't enough here. It's important to have your partner tell you in her own words what you've just told her.
- Confirm for her that she heard you correctly. Tell her again if she didn't.
- Go back to Step 2, but switch roles: she talks, you listen.
- Learn to compromise. Understanding each other's concerns is a great place to start, but it doesn't do much good if you can't figure out how to bridge the gaps.
- Get professional help if you need it. Set up a monthly or quarterly appointment with a marriage counselor to give you and your partner a safe place to discuss your relationship, differences, problems, worries, and so forth.

FIGHTING CAN BE A GOOD THING . . .

Parenting approaches are the source of just about as many marital spats as money and division of labor. Naturally, you should avoid having huge fights in front of your children. (Kids are scared and confused when their parents yell at each other, and researchers have found that the angrier the parents, the more distressed the children.)

But this doesn't mean that whenever the kids are around, you and your partner always have to see eye to eye (or at least seem to). In fact, just the opposite

"They're playing the blame *game."*

"Repression and denial have always worked for Dad."

is true: "Children of parents who have regular and resolved fights have higher levels of interpersonal poise and self-esteem than those whose parents have chronic unresolved fights or those whose parents appear not to fight at all," writes psychologist Brad Sachs.

Children can also learn plenty from watching their parents disagree—provided they do it civilly. "Occasionally divided ranks will encourage and stimulate a child's capacity to negotiate, bargain, and present her own case against the opinions of others," writes child-rearing columnist Lilian Katz.

So let your child see you and your partner squabble about easily resolvable things and schedule weekly or, if necessary, daily meetings away from the kids to discuss the bigger issues.

Big or small, if you do ever have a disagreement in front of your child, pay close attention to how you make up afterward. "It is probably useful for young children to observe how adults renegotiate their relationship following a squabble or moments of hostility," says Katz. "These observations can reassure the child that when distance and anger come between her and members of the family, the relationship is not over but can be resumed to be enjoyed again."

GO AHEAD, GET ANGRY

Don't go too far out of your way to avoid fighting with your partner. In fact, you may be far better off releasing some steam in her direction (in a reasonable way) than suppressing it. "In trying to avoid conflict, we may create even more," says Sachs. "What we risk by venting our anger out loud is generally far less threatening than what we risk by suppressing it," says Sachs. "Internalized anger causes emotional and physical symptoms like depression, alienation, ulcers, fatigue, backaches, and high blood pressure. Also, we have to remember that if we don't express it directly, it will come out anyway, but sideways, in a way we can't control. The phone message that we forget to deliver to our partner, the medicine we forget to give to the baby, the check we forget to deposit, can all be passive aggressions directed against our spouse when we're afraid of what we're feeling."

18–21 MONTHS

Still Wild (or Mild) after All These Months

What's Going On with the Baby

Physically

- No longer content just to walk forward, your toddler can now walk backward and sideways. He may even be able to run. (Well, sort of. It really looks more like a clumsy speed walk.)
- He can kick a ball without stepping on it and can, at long last, throw overhand.
- As his hand-eye coordination improves, your toddler loves piecing things together. He does simple puzzles (in which each piece fits in a separate hole) and can build a tower five or six blocks high. He'll also put blocks or Duplo or Lego pieces together to make long, straight walls. There's still room for improvement; when hammering, he finds it nearly impossible to keep the head of the hammer straight and, more often than not, it lands sideways.
- All his block building, besides improving his coordination, is teaching him about balance. Will a big block stay on top of a little one?
- He's getting really good at undressing himself. But his dressing skills—if he has any at all—are still pretty much confined to not squirming for a few seconds and allowing you to slip something on him.
- He's experimenting with using forks and spoons, but not the way you'd hoped. He holds his fork in one hand, picks up a piece of food and pushes it onto the tine with the other.
- He still has trouble turning the pages of a book one at a time.

Intellectually

- Despite the major intellectual advances he's made over the past eighteen months, your toddler is still a fairly egotistical little creature, believing that he is the source of all action. Child psychologist Selma Fraiberg beautifully describes his attitude about the world: "The magician is seated in his high chair and looks upon the world with favor. He is at the height of his powers. If he closes his eyes, he causes the world to disappear. If he opens his eyes, he causes the world to come back. . . . If desire arises within him, he utters the magic syllables that cause the desired object to appear. His wishes, his thoughts, his gestures, his noises command the universe."
- Despite his self-centered view of the world, your toddler is beginning to become aware of the ownership of objects. He can (but may not want to) distinguish between "mine" and "yours."
- His sense of object permanence is becoming more sophisticated, and he now anticipates where objects "should" be. If a ball rolls under the couch, for example, he'll run to the back of the couch, knowing the ball will be there soon. And as you pass the gas station down the block from your house and turn onto your street, he'll begin to get excited, knowing he'll be home soon.
- Your toddler has been getting increasingly negative and contrary lately: the first word out of his mouth in any given situation is usually "No," he'll refuse to do almost anything you ask, and he deliberately dawdles when he knows you're in a hurry. For a toddler to do just the opposite of what you want him to do "strikes him as being the very essence of his individuality," writes Selma Fraiberg.
- He still has some difficulty with time concepts: "now," "later," "yesterday," and "tomorrow" mean nothing to him.

Verbally

- Although your toddler knows between ten and forty words (girls are usually more articulate at this stage than boys), "No" is by far the most popular.
- He now makes a serious effort to repeat what you say, using a kind of shorthand. For example, if you say, "No, you can't pour your milk on the floor," he'll probably reply, "Pour milk floor." Language expert James Britton has found that toddlers repeat the words that carry the most information, while omitting the less important words.

- He will frequently ask you to identify unfamiliar (and sometimes quite familiar) objects. And when you're reading to him, he can name a few objects from a favorite book.
- Kids this age are beginning to grasp the concept of pronouns and can make subtle distinctions: "don't hit him" is different from "don't hit her."
- For the first time, you toddler is now capable of engaging in "conversation." Instead of responding physically to your questions (by going somewhere, pointing to something, or doing something), he may use words.

Emotionally/Socially

- He still can't really differentiate between inanimate objects and people, and treats other toddlers accordingly—poking, hitting, biting, and pushing them. This kind of behavior is usually not hostile—your toddler is learning some valuable lessons about actions and reactions.
- Although he is expressing some interest in interacting and socializing with other kids, your toddler still usually plays alone, pausing once in a while to defend his property rights or to snatch something away from a "playmate." Despite his seeming lack of interest, he is learning a massive amount by imitating his friends (they, presumably, are also learning from him).
- If they haven't already, this is about the time when girls discover their vaginas and boys their penises. Boys may even get, albeit rarely, an erection. This is absolutely normal for kids this age, and every attempt should be made *not* to make a big deal of it (see pages 174–75 for more on this).
- Still plenty of tantrums.
- Your toddler may exhibit an early interest in toilet training by occasionally letting you know when he has a wet or soiled diaper.

What You're Going Through

A Fear of Being Rejected by Your Baby

One of these days, you're going to run to comfort your crying child. Oh, you've done it before, but this time it'll be different. This time, instead of running to meet you, your child will see you and scream, "No! I want Mommy!" or "I Hate you," or "You're a bad daddy!"

There's not really anything I or anyone else can say that will make you feel any less rejected or despised when those horrible words pop out of your child's mouth. The first time (and the tenth and the twentieth) my older daughter said something like that to me, I nearly cried.

Remember, though, that your child has no idea that he's hurting you with his words. Feelings are still something new to him, and he may just be experimenting to see how you'll react. Rather than withdraw completely or punish your child (even subtly) for wounding you, here are a few other approaches:

- Acknowledge that your child is upset. Say something like, "You're really mad, aren't you?"
- Reassure him that you love him.
- During a calm moment much later, talk with him a little about how it feels when your feelings are hurt. But don't go on too long about this; the last thing you want to do is put your child in charge of your self-esteem (or to make him feel as though he's in charge of it).
- Try some sarcasm. Saying, "Yep, you're right. I'm the world's worst father and everyone hates me," may shock your child so much that he'll rush to your defense.

Eventually, you'll learn to ignore (or at least pay less attention to) your child's slings and arrows. And you'll find that things have a way of coming full circle. When my younger daughter was about eighteen months old, she went through a stage when she wouldn't let me put her down. In fact, she wouldn't let anyone else—my wife included—pick her up. On one occasion, after carrying her around for about eight hours straight, my legs and shoulders had gone completely numb and I had to take a break. So I told my daughter I was going to take her to mommy for a while, and I did exactly that. The hand-off went fairly well, but the moment I turned to walk away my daughter shrieked, "Daddy! Help me, Daddy! I need you!"

Being a Father Can Make You Smarter . . .

Well, maybe not, but there's no question that becoming a parent can have a major impact on the way you think. According to researchers Newman and Newman, parenting:

- Has the "potential consequence of expanding the realm of consciousness." It can increase your capacity to put the past, present, and future into the proper perspective.
- Makes you think more flexibly. The need to protect and nurture their children requires parents to develop skills in anticipating—and preparing for—the future, including making appropriate contingency plans.

"I know what you're going through. I, too, spent several years as a small child."

- Gets you to put together a consistent philosophy of life and to seek to raise your children according to your central values and goals.
- Makes you a bit more forgiving of people's weaknesses and perhaps look a little harder to find their strengths and potential.
- "Requires and promotes the capacity to hold two or more opposing ideas in the mind at the same time." For example, most new couples say that having children brought them closer together. At the same time, though, they say that labor around the house has been divided along traditional lines, causing fights about the division of labor.

Themes of attachment and separation are another area where adults can have two opposing ideas at the same time, say psychologists Barbara and Philip Newman. Most parents want to remain close to their children. They continue to have a strong bond of affection for their children, and they worry about their children's safety and welfare. At the same time, they take pride in signs of their children's independence and encourage their children to be self-sufficient.

The capacity to hold two or more opposing ideas in the mind at once is widely considered to be one of the characteristics of adult cognition.

You and Your Baby

Play

In the last few months of your baby's second year, three major play-related developments occur, usually in rapid succession:

- He learns to play with others his own age.
- He learns to play alone.
- He learns to tell the difference between what's pretend and what's real.

PLAY WITH PEERS

If your child has been thinking of himself as the center of the solar system, he certainly considered you and your partner to be nearby planets, orbiting around him contentedly. The gravitational pull connecting you to your child was so strong that, in the words of Bruno Bettelheim, "in the long run he can have pleasure only if his delight is validated for him by that of his parents."

But just recently he's realized that there are other objects floating around out there. And some of them seem to be stars—just like him.

Several researchers have analyzed infant-parent interaction with and without a peer present. When both parent and peer were in the room, the children paid more attention to the peer than to the parent, says Whaley. The researchers suggest that toddlers relate to peers better because they share more common play interests than parents are likely to.

PLAYING ALONE

"By twenty-one months, the child is well aware that he or she influences behavior and has now become his or her own source of stimulation rather than relying on adults," says Whaley. Ordinarily, being ignored isn't considered to be a compliment. But if you and your baby are together and he wants to spend some time playing by himself, consider yourself praised: if he wasn't absolutely sure he could count on you to be there in an emergency, he'd never take his eyes off you.

A Few Fun Educational Activities for Kids This Age

- Take a nature walk. Pick up things and discuss them. You'd be amazed at the variety of stuff there is just lying around and at the variety of educational opportunities. (Picking up a leaf, for example, can spark a great discussion about how nutrients get from the root of the tree to the leaves and about the difference between deciduous and evergreen trees). Activities like nature walks also encourage observation skills, and you'll probably find that your child is spotting a lot more interesting things than you are.
- Play matching games. Cut postcards in half and have the baby match the halves. Or, in a more advanced version, match playing cards.
- Cook. Make simple edible recipes together, or just make some Oobleck—a kind of moldable dough that kids love to play with. (Mix 1 pound of cornstarch, 1½ cups of cold water, and some food coloring together until smooth. That's it.) Besides teaching all sorts of great things—measuring, textures, how things change shape and form when heated or cooled—cooking with your child will subtly teach him some valuable lessons about men's and women's roles in society. But best of all, it's a lot of fun. (See pages 159–65 for more on cooking with kids.)
- Build a fort out of chairs and blankets. Learn about structure, balance, privacy, light, and dark.

"See, son? He's not gone. He just turned into 'Splashy the Puddleman.'"

A Few Equipment-Buying Tips

- Make sure anything you buy for use by your child can be easily used. For example, if you have a minibasketball hoop, make sure the child—not just you—can hit a few jumpers. If it's too high, she'll get frustrated and quit.
- Chairs should be wider at bottom than at top to reduce the chance of their tipping over. They should also be low enough so that the baby can get up and sit down without having to ask for help.
- Tables should be high enough to fit comfortably above your child's knees while she's sitting on her chair.

The capacity to be alone is a critical sign of emotional maturity, says English pediatrician and psychoanalyst D. W. Winnicott. And as usual, your role as a father needs to be adjusted in response to your child's growth and development. "Toddler learning now depends in part on the freedom a child is given to explore the environment," says Whaley. "There is now a shift from adult as participant to adult as audience."

Although your child may be playing alone, he'll often accompany himself by singing, humming, laughing, or squealing. "Children as they exercise their bodies feel such an exuberance that they often cannot remain silent but loudly express their joy in what their bodies can do, without knowing that this is its cause," says Bruno Bettelheim. The bottom line is that they've just begun to discover some of the wonderful things their spry young bodies can do, and it feels incredibly good. And anything that makes him feel good enough to squeal is worth doing again.

According to Bettelheim, learning to take pleasure in our own bodies is an important developmental stage. "The pleasure we derive from the experience that our bodies and minds are operating and serving us well," he says, "forms the basis for all feelings of well-being."

PRETEND PLAY

"Pretend play actually fosters cognitive and social development," says Bettelheim. Children who have well-developed pretending skills tend to be well liked by their peers and to be viewed as peer leaders. This is a result of their advanced communication skills, their greater ability to take the point of view of others, and their ability to reason about social situations. "Children who have been

Thinking Music

Ever since you were just a few years old, you've been able to summon up images of objects or people, or imagine words and sentences or entire conversations without actually speaking a word. That's what *thinking* is.

In music, the same basic process is called *audiation*. "To audiate is to hear and comprehend music that is not physically present, just as to think is to hear and give meaning to language, the sound of words not physically present," write Richard Grunow, Edwin Gordon, and Christopher Azzara. Just as you can't develop as a person without thinking, "without audiation, no musical growth can take place," they add.

Sound complicated? It really isn't. Think of all those times you haven't been able to stop humming a particular melody, or the times you've taught someone else a song. That's audiating.

One of the best things you can do to help your child build her audiating skills is to expose her to music without words. Because language development receives so much emphasis in our culture, the words of a song may distract your child from being aware of the music itself. In the case of kids with limited language skills, the words can actually slow down musical development. If a child's "language has not developed well enough to sing the words of the song," writes Gordon, "she may not attempt to sing the song at all."

Please remember that as important as it is to expose your child to music, having the stereo going twenty-four hours a day isn't necessary or helpful. Learning to listen to and appreciate silence is important too. It is during periods of silence that your child has the opportunity to exercise her developing powers of audiation by remembering, thinking about, and experimenting with the music she has already heard.

encouraged in a playful, imaginative approach to the manipulation and exploration of materials and objects through fantasy show more complex language use and more flexible approaches to problem solving," Bettelheim says.

Encourage your child's pretending any way you can: play imitation games, act out stories with your child and his toys, or write your own plays. If your child develops an interest in toys traditionally associated with the opposite sex, don't make a big deal of it. (When my older daughter was nearly two, she decided that she was Oliver Twist. She responded only when addressed as

Oliver, and insisted that my wife and I act the parts of the various villains and heroes from the movie. This little phase lasted well over a year and a half.)

Making Music

"In general, the more you and your child have become actively involved in music . . . the more your child's attention span and appetite for music will increase," writes music educator Edwin Gordon.

Even if you haven't done much more than sing a couple of lullabies or leave the radio on a few hours a day, you'll notice that your baby has become a much more active music listener than he was in his first year (see *TNF I*, pages 176–78). He clearly recognizes familiar songs and tries to sing along. At this stage, he won't be able to get more than a note or two—usually the last one in the song or phrase—the "O" in "E-I-E-I-O," for example. But he's delighted to be able to do even that.

By the time he's about two and a half, he'll add the first few notes and an occasional short phrase in the middle of a song as well (all of "E-I-E-I-O," perhaps, or maybe even "Yes, sir. Yes, sir. Three bags full").

If you haven't done so already, make singing part of your everyday routine. Since your child is taking a more active role in singing, select songs that are short and repetitive, and change your focus from singing *to* the child to singing *with* him. Encourage him to make up his own songs and have him teach you the words or melody.

If you'd like a little help selecting music, several companies produce sets of developmentally appropriate tapes that are aimed at children but that you'll like too. A few are listed in the Resources guide on page 216.

You'll also notice that the way he moves to music is quite different now. Just a few months ago, his arm and leg movements seemed almost random. But now, just before his second birthday, he has adopted his very own, unique rhythmic "gestures"—shaking, wiggling, half-crouching, or bouncing up and down—that are different from those of every other child his age. As before, your child's movements—which now come in groups of three to seven "pulses"—may not seem to have much to do with the music he's hearing. They are, however, definitely in response to the music and are internally very consistent, meaning that you can almost set your watch by the pulses.

The way your child moves to music is an expression of some primal part of his personality. So let him do what he wants—don't tell him how to move, show him new routines, or move his arms or legs for him. That's the surest way to stifle his budding self-expression.

"Do we have something with more of a chararcter driven plot?"

Keep on Reading

DEALING WITH BOREDOM

After reading the same book six times at a single sitting (or several hundred times over the course of a few months), you might find yourself less than completely enthusiastic about reading it again. If (when) this happens, spice things up by making some deliberate mistakes in the text, just to see if your baby is on the ball: switch characters' names, say "in" instead of "out," and so forth.

YOUR ATTENTION, PLEASE

The average almost-two-year-old's attention span is about three minutes, so try to get in at least three or four reading sessions each day. But be prepared: the range varies enormously. When my older daughter was this age, she could easily spend an hour listening, but at the same age my younger daughter wouldn't sit still for more than thirty seconds at a stretch. Please also remember that attention span is *not* an indication of intelligence. Despite her seeming indifference, my younger daughter still ran around the house most of the day demanding to be read to and still managed to memorize at least as many books as her seemingly more attentive peers.

ADDING TO YOUR LIBRARY

If your child is still interested in the same books that interested him a year ago, don't worry. And don't push him to give up old favorites. "When a child has gotten all he can from the book or when the problems that directed him to it have been outgrown," says Bruno Bettelheim, "he'll be ready to move on to something else."

This doesn't mean, though, that you can't introduce new titles. Big hits for this age group include books that introduce numbers, sizes, shapes, colors, opposites, special concepts (up, down, in, out), and that discuss body parts. Here's a short list of some of my developmentally appropriate favorites for this age:

Across the Stream (and many others), Mirra Ginsburg
Can't You Sleep, Little Bear?, Martin Waddell
Caps for Sale, Esphyr Slobodkina
Each Peach Pear Plum, Janet Ahlberg, Allan Ahlberg
Freight Train, Donald Crews
Golden Bear, Ruth Young
A Good Day, A Good Night, Cindy Wheeler
Holes and Peeks (and many others), Ann Jonas
How Do I Put it On?, Shigeo Watanabe
Jesse Bear, What Will You Wear?, Nancy Carlstrom, Bruce Degen
Jump, Frog, Jump, Robert Kalan
Kitten Can . . ., Bruce McMillan
Little Gorilla, Ruth Borenstein
Lunch, Denise Fleming
Mouse Paint, Ellen Walsh
Owl Babies, Martin Waddell
Planting a Rainbow (and many others), Lois Ehlert
Ten, Nine, Eight, Molly Bang
What Do You See?, Bill Martin, Jr.
Where Does the Brown Bear Go?, Nicki Weiss
Wynken, Blynken and Nod, Eugene Field

CONCEPTS

Becca Backward, Becca Frontward: A Book of Concept Pairs, Bruce McMillan
Who Said Red, Mary Serfozo
On Market Street, Arnold Lobel
One Wolly Wombat, Rod Drinca, Kerry Argent
(For more concept books, see pages 109–10 and 152.)

POETRY
A Child's Garden of Verses, Robert Louis Stevenson
Jamberry, Bruce Degen
Rainbow in the Sky, Louis Untermeyer (editor)
(For more poetry books, see pages 110 and 153.)

Family Matters

Tantrums

WHAT CAUSES THEM

In some cases as early as twelve months, but most frequently between fifteen and eighteen months, almost all kids begin having regular tantrums. According to pediatrician T. Berry Brazelton, toddler temper tantrums are perfectly normal and are the result of the child's "inner turmoil."

One of the major sources of turmoil is the frustration that results from the child's inability to use his limited verbal skills to express his specific needs and wants. Generally speaking, the more verbal the child (hence the better able to explain his needs), the less he'll be frustrated and the fewer tantrums he'll have. Many kids, however, are frustrated by their body's inability to respond to their mind's rather sophisticated requests or desires.

Either way, frustrations build up over the course of a day or two until the child finally is no longer able to control herself and explodes. Just to put this into perspective, consider this: nearly 15 percent of twelve-month-olds and 20 percent of twenty-four-month-olds have two or more tantrums *per day.*

Besides frustration, of course, there are a variety of other factors that may account for tantrums:

- Your child is trying to assert herself. She may feel she's lost your attention and will do whatever it takes to get it back.
- She may be frightened at how angry her frustrations make her, and may be trying to attract your attention, hoping you'll help her regain control over her life and emotions.
- Illness, hunger, exhaustion, overstimulation.
- Too much discipline. You may have set too many limits, laid down too many rigid or inconsistent rules.
- Not enough discipline. You may have imposed too few rules or established erratic or inconsistent limits. Tantrums may be, in a sense, a plea for more effective limit setting.

- Temperament. Low-frustration-tolerance, slow-adaptability kids are much more susceptible to tantrums (see pages 73–79 for a discussion of temperament). This susceptibility to tantrums can also result in parent-child personality clashes.
- Family stress. Divorce, separation, or even a major change in work schedule or lifestyle can be tough for kids to deal with.

WHAT TO DO ABOUT THEM

When your child is in the midst of a tantrum, he is no longer a member of the human race. So reasoning, shouting, hitting, and punishment will have little (if any) effect. Here are a few things that may work to minimize the tantrum and its effect on everyone:

- Don't panic. That's just what your child is trying to get you to do. If you get upset and rant, you'll only make things worse.
- Use humor. Say something completely silly. If that doesn't work, get down on the floor and thrash around in your own tantrum. This may snap him out of it by showing him how ridiculous a tantrum looks.
- Walk away. In many circumstances, no audience equals no performance.

Breath Holding/Passing Out

Starting at about eighteen months, babies who have finished in the top 10 percent of Tantrums 101 are invited to get advanced training, this time in how to scare the hell out of their parents by holding their breath and passing out.

The bad news about breath holding is that it is incredibly frightening (how could a child's turning blue and keeling over *not* be?). But the good news is that besides taking ten years off your life, it isn't all that dangerous. What usually happens is that the child starts to cry, takes a huge breath—and holds it. If he holds it long enough, he may lose consciousness, but the moment he does, he'll start breathing immediately and usually recover within seconds.

So why do kids really hold their breath? "When all else seems to fail in battling for control," says temperament researcher Jim Cameron, "holding one's breath becomes the ultimate stronghold—no one can make you breathe."

Breath holding is more common among active, intense, slow-adapting-to-change toddlers (see pages 73–79 for more on this). According to Cameron, "The more energetic they are, the less they want to stop what they're doing or to shift to things you want them to do." In addition, since active kids spend

- Stand firm. If the tantrum is the result of some disciplinary measure, tell your child that the rule still stands and will continue to do so until he calms down.
- Explain. Say things like, "I know you're upset because you really wanted to read that story. . . ."
- Time out. If things are really getting out of hand, put the child by himself someplace and explain (privately) that he won't be able to be with other people until he calms down. Again, the no-audience-equals-no-performance theory applies here.
- Protect your child. Kicking, swinging, and throwing things can hurt not only other people but the child as well. Holding him firmly but calmly often calms an out-of-control kid.
- *After* the tantrum, reassure the child that you're still there for him, that you still love him. But *do not* reward him for stopping.

more time practicing large motor skills (running, crawling, and so on) than other kids, the joy of doing these things is greater. "They can become addicted to the pleasure of imposing their newfound abilities in any possible situation so they don't want to stop," says Cameron. They also may be a little behind in verbal skills, making it harder for them to argue with you.

If your child has started holding, or trying to hold, his breath, some special handling is required:

- Give him extra time to adjust to change. Instead of one ten-minute warning, give notice at ten, five, three, and one minute.
- Don't react intensely to your child's reactions. The bigger your reaction, the more likely your child will make breath-holding a regular part of his anger routine. Also, don't become overly permissive out of fear of triggering another breath-holding episode.
- Talk, talk, talk. Encourage your child to use words. As frightening as these fits are, they won't last forever. The more verbal your child becomes, the faster they'll fade.
- Do not attempt to "shock" your child back to reality by slapping him or throwing water in his face. According to Cameron, this can "leave a kid feeling defeated and helpless, feelings which can lead to other problems later on." Instead, hold your child.

WHAT *NOT* TO DO

- Don't shout. Any big reaction proves that the tantrum was the right approach.
- Don't try to argue with a kid who's in the middle of a tantrum. You'll be wasting your breath.
- No physical punishment. Another waste of time, since most of the time your child isn't in control of the tantrum anyway.
- Don't give in. Doing so offers kids conclusive evidence that tantrums do, indeed, work.

HOW TO PREVENT THEM

There's nothing you can do to prevent tantrums completely. But there are a few preemptive steps you can take that should greatly reduce the frequency and severity of these little outbursts:

- Be a reliable source of help and support.
- Know—and pay close attention to—your child's temperament (see pages 73–79). Don't try to force an irregular child to be regular, or a slow-to-warm child to warm quickly.
- Give your child plenty of opportunities throughout the day to let off steam—physical play, running around, and so forth—as well as some occasional periods without rules (or with as few as possible).
- Encourage your child to talk about the things that make him angry. And be supportive and empathetic when he does.
- Make sure your child gets enough food and sleep. Shortages of either can make kids cranky and more susceptible to having tantrums.
- Think carefully before you say no. Is what you're rejecting really that big a deal? Giving in—perhaps partially, with some conditions or time limits—can give kids more control, thus reducing tantrum possibilities.
- Compromise as much as possible. Offering a *firm* "two more minutes," gives the child a lot more control than insisting on his doing what you want him to do immediately.
- Avoid yes/no questions and open questions ("Which pair of socks do you want to wear?"). Give choices instead: "Do you want the red ones or the blue ones?"
- Compliment good behavior regularly. Tell your child you understand that doing some things is hard and frustrating, but that you appreciate his efforts.

Public Tantrums

Sometimes I'm absolutely convinced that my children subscribe to some kind of special, underground newsletter filled with super-secret techniques they can use to drive adults nuts. And I'm sure one of the most popular features is "Tantrums in the Produce Section, or 25 Surefire Ways to Embarrass Your Parents into Giving You What You Want NOW!"

Besides the techniques described above, there are a few special ways of handling public tantrums:

- Isolation. Take the child to the bathroom, outside, to the car—anywhere you and he can be more or less alone.
- Ignore the audience. You'll be mortified at what your child is doing—and even more mortified at what spectators will think *you're* doing to the child. If your child is particularly theatrical, he's liable to attract quite a crowd. If the peanut gallery gets overly aggressive or hostile, Brazelton suggests that you ask for volunteers to take over for you.

"Rachel! *If you can't even stay focused on spreading* peat *moss, how do you expect to get into* law *school?"*

- Give clear, concise warnings. "Daddy and Mommy are going out later, and Grandpa will be baby-sitting. We'll be there when you wake up." Or, "Five more minutes, then we have to start cleaning up." I've found that setting a timer helps a lot: "When the buzzer goes off, we'll have to . . ."

Temperament

As we discussed in *TNF I*, pages 89–96, your child's temperament will remain fairly constant throughout his life. But now that he's no longer an infant, you should take a look at the kind of emotional and behavioral characteristics you're likely to see in the toddler years.

The nine basic temperament traits we covered in that volume are pretty much the same. However, because your child's emotions are so much more sophisticated than they were a year ago, I've taken the advice of the folks at the Center for Human Development in Oregon and divided the Sensitivity category into two related but separate categories: Emotional Sensitivity and Sensory Awareness. The ten categories they suggest are outlined on pages 74–77.

The Ten Temperament Traits of Toddlers

1. **Approach/Withdrawal:** Your child's initial reactions to new experiences, meeting new people, tasting new foods, being in new situations, and so on.

APPROACHING TODDLERS

- are the opposite of shy
- lack fear in potentially dangerous situations
- may be friendly with strangers
- separate easily from parents; may get lost in crowds or stores
- may be impulsive
- approach new situations with great interest

WITHDRAWING TODDLERS

- are usually shy
- need time to warm up to new experiences
- say they don't like things before trying them
- may be picky—eating only certain foods, playing with only certain toys
- usually have difficulty separating from parents
- show fear in seemingly safe situations
- are cautious
- hesitate before investigating strange sounds
- stand back and watch when first entering a playground

---

2. **Adaptability:** Similar to Approach/Withdrawal, but deals with your child's longer-term reactions to changes in routines or expectations, new places, or new ideas.

FAST-ADAPTING TODDLERS

- are usually compliant
- tend to "go with the flow" when new changes are imposed
- may lack assertiveness
- like change and may get bored when there isn't enough change taking place
- can be compliant with peer pressure

SLOW-ADAPTING TODDLERS

- often refuse to comply with almost anything
- need time to adjust to imposed transitions and ideas
- like to follow their own agendas, and can be bossy and stubborn
- may be quick to anger and slow to get over being angry
- get "locked in" on what they are doing
- may be judgmental
- protest loudly against taking medicine
- may have trouble getting to sleep in unfamiliar places

3. **Intensity:** Your child's overall volume level, both when happy or unhappy.

LOW-INTENSITY TODDLERS

- are "hard to read"—they have emotions, but it is difficult for others to notice
- may seem apathetic
- are sometimes mistakenly viewed as uninvolved, low in motivation or intelligence

HIGH-INTENSITY TODDLERS

- put a lot of energy into their emotional expressions
- shout instead of speaking
- may scream so loudly it hurts your ears
- are emphatic in voice and physical gesturing
- have intense reactions to new toys

---

4. **Mood:** Your child's dominant outlook—optimistic or pessimistic—over the course of a typical day.

POSITIVE-MOOD TODDLERS

- are rarely bothered by anything
- can be described as happy-go-lucky
- may lack seriousness
- may be easily taken advantage of
- tend to trust easily
- expect goodness/success

NEGATIVE-MOOD TODDLERS

- are often in a negative mood, angry, depressed, disappointed, and so on
- unlikely to be conned
- may be skeptical
- extend trust slowly
- expect the worst
- complain when given a bath
- don't like traveling in a car or stroller
- cry often and easily

---

5. **Activity level:** Your child's overall preference for active or inactive play; his overall energy level throughout the day.

LOW-ACTIVITY TODDLERS

- may take a long time to complete tasks
- may avoid activities that require a lot of physical energy
- may dislike active family pastimes
- may nag parents to keep them entertained
- seem to absorb a lot of info by watching quietly

HIGH-ACTIVITY TODDLERS

- are often extremely active—running wildly, talking incessantly
- are usually *not* clinically hyperactive
- may be aggressive during play
- are often fidgety or restless
- may, however, be able to sit quietly in front of video or TV for extended period
- have to be watched carefully to prevent accidents

(continued on page 76)

6. **Regularity:** The day-to-day predictability of your child's basic biological functions: hunger, sleep, and elimination. Each should be rated on its own scale.

HIGHLY REGULAR TODDLERS
- may be easy to train if bowels are predictable
- adjust easily to regular eating and bedtime schedules
- are so regular you can set your clock by them
- struggle with changes in eating and sleeping routines

IRREGULAR TODDLERS
- may be difficult to potty train
- have bedtime struggles due to irregularity in sleep patterns
- may not be hungry at meals, but want food at a different time every day
- have highly irregular sleep/nap patterns

---

7. **Emotional Sensitivity:** The ease or difficulty with which a child responds emotionally to a situation. This trait has two subcategories: one for sensitivity to his own feelings, and one for sensitivity to others' feelings.

EMOTIONALLY INSENSITIVE TODDLERS
- rarely display emotions
- can be "instigators" who like to start a little trouble now and then
- can be budding con artists who enjoy manipulating a situation to their advantage
- can have what seems to be a mean or cruel streak
- often are oblivious to others' feelings
- don't seem bothered by others' insensitive behavior

EMOTIONALLY SENSITIVE TODDLERS
- tend to be fearful
- get upset when teased
- are sensitive to how others are treated
- seem particularly tuned in to others' feelings
- may worry a lot
- may cry easily
- may be "people pleasers"
- get their feelings hurt easily

---

8. **Sensory Awareness:** Your toddler's sensitivity in each of his sensory areas: pain, touch, taste, smell, hearing, and sight. Each channel is rated on a separate scale. *Note:* it's quite possible for a child to be very aware in some areas and quite unaware in others.

LOW-SENSORY-AWARENESS TODDLERS
- may have dull senses
- can miss a lot of things going on around them—they just don't seem to notice
- can have excellent concentration; aren't distracted by sensory input

HIGH-SENSORY-AWARENESS TODDLERS
- may have sharp senses
- may be distracted by sensory input
- can be picky, finicky, or particular
- sometimes complain about things others don't notice, such as temperature changes or itchy clothes

9. **Distractibility:** The ease with which your toddler is distracted by all the things going on around him.

LOW-DISTRACTIBILITY TODDLERS

- tend to stick with tasks until they are completed
- often have terrific memories
- may become caught up in their own world, not noticing things going on around them
- can be excellent naggers who challenge the parents' ability to not give in
- when upset, can be calmed by only one or two people

HIGH-DISTRACTIBILITY TODDLERS

- have short attention spans
- notice things easily
- may have trouble concentrating on complex tasks
- may leave belongings scattered everywhere
- tend to be forgetful
- when learning something new, will stop when hearing people or sounds

---

10. **Persistence:** Similar to Distractibility, but goes beyond the initial reaction and concerns the length of time your child will continue to make an effort—even when the task gets hard.

HIGH-PERSISTENCE TODDLERS

- rarely give up on difficult tasks
- take on challenges well beyond their skill level
- sometimes persist at things that are unimportant
- may tend to do things the hard way because they don't like to ask for help
- may take things too seriously
- may be perfectionists
- may have long attention spans
- may want to stick with a game long, long, long after you're ready to quit

LOW-PERSISTENCE TODDLERS

- are frustrated easily, even by simple tasks
- may throw tantrums in response to frustration
- if interrupted, won't return to original task
- may get angry and give up
- may demand help from parents, grandparents, and other caregivers
- may struggle to master self-care skills such as toilet learning and dressing
- tend to stick with things they are naturally good at, and can look highly persistent when not frustrated
- tend to "let go" easily
- won't play in playground for more than five minutes at a stretch

Again, because your child is far more sophisticated than a year ago, the rating system is too. Here's the rating scale suggested by the Center for Human Development.

TRAIT		RATING	
APPROACH/WITHDRAWAL	Outgoing	1 2 3 4 5	Slow-to-warm
What is your child's first and usual reaction to new people, situations, places?			
ADAPTABILITY	Easy-going	1 2 3 4 5	Strong-willed
Does your child adapt quickly to new ideas, new places, changes in routine or schedule?			
INTENSITY	Mild reactions	1 2 3 4 5	Dramatic reactions
How loud or physically dramatic is your child when expressing strong feelings?			
MOOD	Happy-go-lucky	1 2 3 4 5	Serious, displeased
Is your child primarily an optimist or a pessimist? Lighthearted or serious?			
ACTIVITY LEVEL	Calm and slow-moving	1 2 3 4 5	Wild and quick-moving
Left to his own devices, would your child be on the go or idle?			
REGULARITY			
Hunger	Wants food at same time every day	1 2 3 4 5	Irregular eater
Sleep	Tired on schedule	1 2 3 4 5	No schedule
Toileting	BMs at same time every day	1 2 3 4 5	Try and guess
Does your child normally eat, go to bed, wake up, and have bowel movements at the same time every day?			
EMOTIONAL SENSITIVITY			
Own feelings	Unaware of emotions	1 2 3 4 5	Feels emotions strongly
Others' feelings	Doesn't notice others' feelings	1 2 3 4 5	Highly sensitive to others' feelings
Does your child often get upset over nothing, or does he rarely get upset even when circumstances suggest that he could? Does your child feel sympathy or empathy for others?			

TRAIT		RATING	
SENSORY AWARENESS			
Pain	What nail in my foot?	1 2 3 4 5	EEEOOWWWWHH!!
Touch	No reaction to contact	1 2 3 4 5	Easily irritated or pleased by contact
Taste	Can't make subtle distinctions	1 2 3 4 5	Notices tiny variations
Smell	Doesn't notice odors	1 2 3 4 5	Human bloodhound
Hearing/Sound	Noise is no problem	1 2 3 4 5	Sensitive to sounds
Vision/Lights	Visually sensitive	1 2 3 4 5	Visually insensitive
DISTRACTIBILITY	Not easily diverted	1 2 3 4 5	Easily diverted
Is your child very aware and easily distracted by noises and people? Can you distract him from upset feelings by redirecting his attention?			
PERSISTENCE	Hard to stop	1 2 3 4 5	Stops easily
Does your child stick with things even when frustrated? Can he stop an activity when asked to?			

After you've evaluated your toddler, take a quick look at your own temperament and see how the two of you compare. If you'd like a much more detailed analysis of your child's temperament, contact Temperament Talk (see Resources guide, page 217).

21–24 MONTHS

What Are Daddies Made Of?

What's Going On with the Baby

Physically

- Now that your toddler has fairly good control over her legs, she's decided to use them all the time.
- She runs (but still has some problems slowing down and turning corners), jumps forward with both feet, kicks a ball without stepping on it, rarely falls anymore, stands on her tiptoes, climbs stairs by herself (holding on to a railing), can push herself along in a toy car, and may even be able to pedal a small tricycle.
- And she hasn't forgotten about her arms and hands: she draws nicely controlled straight lines, throws a ball into a basket, makes beautiful mud pies, spends hours opening and closing screw-top containers, can put together more complex puzzles, and still stacks, piles, tears, and pours anything she can get her hands on. She can even unzip her pants (but can't zip them up), and can put her shoes on (but can't lace them).

Intellectually

- Although time still doesn't mean much to her, she's learned about sequences (first we'll put on your shoes, then we'll go for a walk), and can differentiate between "one" and "many" (although she'll probably say "two" for anything above one).
- She's expanding her knowledge of spatial concepts—climbing into boxes, climbing (or being held) as high as possible, pouring things back and forth.

- She now thinks through possible solutions to problems instead of physically acting them out. For example, if an object is out of reach, she won't jump up to get it and probably won't try to knock it down with a stick. Instead, she'll bring a chair over, climb up, and grab what she wants.
- She's learning to tell the difference between animate and inanimate. She spends a lot of time staring at and comparing objects that move by themselves (dogs, people, fish) and those that need some outside intervention (blocks, bikes).
- She still has a tendency to regard everything—animate or not—as her personal property.
- She also deliberately imitates your every activity (sweeping, washing dishes, brushing teeth), but *only while you're there with her.*

Verbally

- She uses longer, more complex sentences and is beginning to use language in situations where she once used emotions: she'll ask for desired objects by name and say "change my diaper" instead of crying.
- She also delights in the power that naming objects gives her, and labels everything she possibly can.
- She likes nursery rhymes and, if you pause for a few seconds, she'll fill in the last word of a couplet ("Hickory, dickory, dock/ The mouse ran up the ____"). And if you're reading a familiar book and make a mistake, she won't let you get away with it.
- She's tightening her grasp on pronouns, correctly using "I," "mine," "his," and "hers." But she may get confused when trying to use two pronouns in the same sentence: "I want to do it yourself," for example.

Emotionally/Socially

- The contrary, negative, temper-tantrum phase is passing, and your toddler is getting more cheerful and more cooperative. She'll come when you call her and may even put away some of her toys (if you ask really, really nicely).
- Nevertheless, she's still easily frustrated, often to tears, by the internal conflict between independence and dependence. She still walks away from you but comes flying back for reassurance that you're still there; she truly wants to please you by doing the "right thing," but she still needs to test your limits by disobeying.
- Perhaps as a result of this conflict, your toddler is also developing a lot of fears of things she may have loved before: night, dogs, bugs, vacuum cleaners.

She may also be getting more fearful of things that she was only slightly afraid of before: loud noises, big trucks, and people (especially doctors).
- She's developing a wider range of emotions: she's now quite affectionate with her friends, family, stuffed animals, and even pictures in books. She loves to "baby" her dolls (and even her parents), covering them with blankets and putting them to "bed." Her whole body lights up when praised and her feelings are genuinely hurt when criticized.

What You're Going Through

Your Changing Identity

There's an old saying in the Talmud that a man has three names: the one his parents gave him at birth, the one that others call him, and the one he calls himself. A person's identity, according to the rabbis, is a rather amorphous thing. What the rabbis don't talk about is that all three of those names are subject to change over time—especially the one you give yourself. The way you view yourself today may have nothing to do with how you'll see yourself tomorrow.

This point is nicely illustrated by what family researchers Phil and Carolyn Cowan call the "pie chart." Over a period of nearly two years, the Cowans asked a large number of men to draw a circle and divide it up into sections that reflect how important each aspect of their life actually felt—not simply the amount of time in the role.

Over the duration of the study, "Men who remained childless showed a significant increase in the 'partner/lover' aspect," said the Cowans. "New fathers, however, were squeezing 'partner/lover' into a smaller space to accommodate the significant increase in the 'parent' piece of the pie."

The Ambivalent Father

Over the course of my writing career, I've written only a few things that I'm not sure I want my kids to see, and this section is one of them. But you can read it if you promise not to tell them.

Throughout this book (and the others in the series) we've talked a lot about the joys, anxieties, fears, and intense feelings of love that are all part of being a father. If you're like most men, the experience—despite the ups and downs—has been overwhelmingly positive, and you wouldn't trade it for anything. In fact, being a dad has become such an integral part of your life that you probably can't imagine *not* being one.

But one day, completely out of the blue, you'll look at your child and realize that the intense love you felt just the day before has been replaced by a numb, hollow feeling. And the delight you took in raising her and being part of her life has been supplanted by complete and utter ambivalence. You're feeling overburdened, underappreciated, and you can hardly remember the last time you had a conversation with someone who knows more than forty words. You feel like chucking this whole dad thing and starting a new life somewhere else, as far away from your kids as you can get.

Most of the time these feelings of ambivalence last only a few minutes or a few hours. Sometimes they go on for days or even weeks. But no matter how long they last, one thing is pretty much guaranteed: the instant after the ambivalence starts you'll get hit by feelings of guilt, guilt for having had the ambivalence in the first place. And it'll stick around long after the ambivalence is gone. After all, goes the internal monologue, if I'm not a completely committed father 100 percent of the time, I must not be cut out for the job at all.

Most mothers are quite familiar with this little ambivalence/guilt pattern. But because they are generally more willing to discuss their worries and concerns with other mothers, they learn rather quickly that it's perfectly normal. They still feel bad about it or maybe even scared, but at least they know they're not alone.

Men, on the other hand, don't learn this lesson. If we have a few other fathers with whom we can talk things over, we're incredibly lucky. But it's still pretty unlikely that we'll actually talk to them about *this.* It's already hard enough to ask for advice about diaper changing, discipline, or nutrition. But having ambivalent feelings is a serious weakness, perhaps a character flaw (or at least it sure seems like one). And we're certainly not going to expose any weaknesses or character flaws to another man who would just laugh anyway.

Hopefully just reading this section has been enough to convince you—at least a little—that your changing feelings toward your children are completely normal. If you're still worried, though, or if you need more reassurance, force yourself to spend a few minutes talking to someone about what you're feeling—a close friend, your clergyman, you therapist, even your partner (it's going to be harder to talk to her, but at least she'll know exactly what you're talking about). And remember this: you're going to have these feelings dozens of times throughout the course of your fatherhood. So you'd better start getting used to dealing with them now.

"How do you expect me to parent if you won't child?"

You and Your Baby

Identifying Your Parenting Style

So you've been a dad for almost two years, and you've probably noticed that the way you parent is quite a bit different from the way your parents parented. You may also do things much differently than your friends and perhaps even your partner. Sure, everyone has a unique parenting style. But according to Diana Baumrind, a sociologist at the University of California at Berkeley, almost all of them fall into three basic categories: authoritarian, authoritative, and permissive. The chart on pages 86–89 describes these three styles.

Discipline Ideas

- **Be firm.** Set reasonable limits, explain them, and enforce them.
- **Be consistent.** Your child will learn to adapt to inconsistencies between you and your partner; if you allow jumping on the bed but she doesn't, for example, the child will do it when he's with you and won't when he's with your partner (see pages 53–55 for more on dealing with disagreements). But if you allow jumping one day and prohibit it the next, you'll only

confuse your child and undermine your attempts to get him to listen when you ask him to do something.

- **Compromise.** Kids can't always tell the difference between big and little issues. So give in on a few small things once in a while (an extra piece of birthday cake at the end of a long day might avoid a tantrum). That will give the child a feeling of control and will make it easier for him to go along with the program on the bigger issues (holding hands while crossing the street, for example).
- **Be assertive and specific.** "Stop throwing your food now" is much better than "Cut that out!"
- **Give choices.** Kathryn Kvols, author of *Redirecting Children's Behavior,* suggests that if your child is, for example, yanking all the books off a shelf in the living room, you say, "Would you like to stop knocking the books off the shelf or would you like to go to your room?" If he ignores you, gently but firmly lead the child to his room and tell him he can come back into the living room when he's ready to listen to you.
- **Cut down on the warnings.** If the child knows the rules (at this age, all you have to do is ask), impose the promised consequences immediately. If you make a habit of giving six preliminary warnings and three "last" warnings before doing anything, your child will learn to start responding only the eighth or ninth time you ask.
- **Link consequences directly to the problem behavior.** And don't forget to explain—clearly and simply—what you're doing and why: "I'm taking away your hammer because you hit me," or "I asked you not to take that egg out of the fridge and you didn't listen to me. Now you'll have to help me clean it up."
- **No banking.** If you're imposing punishments or consequences, do it immediately. You can't punish a child at the end of the day for something (or a bunch of things) he did earlier—he won't associate the undesirable action with its consequence.
- **Keep it short.** Once the punishment is over (and whatever it is, it shouldn't last any more than a minute per year of age), get back to your life. There's no need to review, summarize, or make sure the child got the point.
- **Stay calm.** Screaming, ranting, or raving can easily cross the line into verbal abuse, which can do long-term damage to your child's self-esteem.
- **Get down to your child's level.** When you're talking to your child—especially to criticize—kneel or sit. You'll still be big enough for him to have no doubt who the boss is.
- **Don't lecture.** Instead, ask questions to engage the child in a discussion

PARENTING STYLE	AUTHORITARIAN (THE BOSS)
The parents . . .	♦ Are frequently uncompromising, dictatorial, strict, and repressive. ♦ Attempt to shape, control, and evaluate the behavior and attitudes of the child in accordance with some kind of absolute (often theologically motivated) standard.
The child . . .	♦ Must obey.
The power . . .	♦ Is with the parent.
Life at home can be . . .	♦ Tense ♦ Rigid ♦ Oppressive
Discipline tools	♦ Parents value obedience as a virtue and favor punitive, forceful measures to curb self-will at points when the child's actions or beliefs conflict with what parents think is correct conduct. ♦ yelling ♦ commanding ♦ ordering ♦ rewarding ♦ punishing ♦ bribing ♦ threatening

AUTHORITATIVE (THE GUIDE, THE LEADER)	PERMISSIVE (THE SERVANT, THE BYSTANDER)
♦ Are approachable, reasonable, and flexible. ♦ Attempt "to direct the child's activities but in a rational, issue-oriented manner," says Baumrind. ♦ Don't regard themselves as infallible or divinely inspired.	♦ Are often passive, weak, inconsistent, and yielding. ♦ Consult with the child too much about policy decisions and give too many explanations for family rules. ♦ Don't ask the child to clean or take on many household responsibilities. ♦ Allow the child to regulate his own activities as much as possible.
♦ Is encouraged to think and to be a participant in the family.	♦ Is subtly encouraged to control others. ♦ Is left to follow his own wants and instincts.
♦ Is shared between parent and child.	♦ Is firmly in the hands of the child.
♦ Relaxed ♦ Orderly ♦ Consistent	♦ Chaotic ♦ Uncontrollable ♦ Wild
♦ Parents exert firm control at points of parent-child divergence but do not hem the child in with restrictions. ♦ Parents use reason as well as power to achieve objectives. ♦ requests ♦ incentives ♦ consequences ♦ negotiation ♦ conflict resolution ♦ family councils	♦ Parents try not to exercise control and don't encourage the child to obey externally defined standards. ♦ Parents are tolerant and accepting toward child's impulses, using as little punishment as possible ♦ pleading ♦ waiting and wishing ♦ giving up and doing nothing

(continued on page 88)

(continued from page 87)

PARENTING STYLE	AUTHORITARIAN (THE BOSS)
The effect on the child	♦ Associated with low levels of independence and social responsibility as well as lower cognitive competence. ♦ Negatively associated with good grades. ♦ Child learns to obey out of fear of punishment. ♦ Child learns to subvert and manipulate underhandedly. ♦ Child is so used to being controlled that he doesn't learn to develop self-control, and as a result can often be unruly and uncooperative when parents aren't present.
The parent-child relationship	♦ Cold, rigid, and based on fear. ♦ Verbal interchange between parent and child is discouraged. Instead, children are taught to blindly accept the parents' word on the way things ought to be.

of the problematic behavior: "Is smoking cigars okay for kids or not?" "Do you like it when someone pushes you down in the park?"

- **Criticize the behavior, not the child.** Even such seemingly innocuous comments as, "I've told you a thousand times . . ." or "Every single time you . . ." gives the child the message that he's doomed to disappoint you no matter what he does.
- **Reinforce positive behavior.** We spend too much time criticizing negatives and not enough time complimenting the positives. Heartfelt comments, like "I'm so proud of you when I see you cleaning up your toys," go a long way.
- **Play games.** "Let's see who can put the most toys away" and "I bet I can put

AUTHORITATIVE (THE GUIDE, THE LEADER)	PERMISSIVE (THE SERVANT, THE BYSTANDER)
♦ Positively associated with independent, purposive, dominant behavior. ♦ Positively associated with good grades. ♦ Child develops self-discipline. ♦ Child is able to focus on the needs of the group.	♦ Associated with lack of impulse control and social responsibility, as well as low levels of independence and self-reliance. ♦ Negatively associated with good grades. ♦ Lower social and cognitive competence. ♦ Child becomes self-centered and demanding. ♦ Child doesn't learn the importance of consideration of others or of the needs of the group. ♦ Child develops little self-control.
♦ Close, respectful, and marked by sharing and communication. ♦ Parents encourage "verbal give and take, and share with the child the reasoning behind the policy." ♦ Encourages the child's independence and individuality. ♦ Recognizes the rights of both parents and children.	♦ Distant and often marked by resentment and manipulation. ♦ Parents make few demands for mature behavior and without limits the child can feel unloved and uncared for.

my shoes on before you can" are favorites. But be sure *not* to put away more toys or to put your shoes on first—kids under five have a tough time losing.

- **Avoid tantrums.** See pages 68–73 for some tips.
- **No spanking.** See pages 92–93.
- **No shaking.** It may seem like a less violent way of expressing your frustrations than spanking, but it really isn't. Shaking your baby can make his little brain rattle around inside his skull, possibly resulting in brain damage.
- **No bribes.** It's tempting to pay a child off to get him to do or not do something. But the risk—and it's a big one—is that he will demand some kind of payment before complying with just about anything.

- **Be a grown-up.** Biting your child or pulling his hair to demonstrate that biting or hitting is wrong or doesn't feel good will backfire. Guaranteed.
- **Offer cheese with that whine.** Tell your child that you simply don't respond to whining and that you won't give him what he wants until he asks in a nice way—and stick with it.
- **Set a good example.** If your child sees you and your partner arguing without violence, he'll learn to do the same. If he sees you flouting authority by running red lights, he'll do the same.

Discipline and Temperament

Naturally, not every approach to discipline will work equally well with every child. And one of the best ways to improve your chances of finding the right approach for your child is to take his temperament into consideration. Here are some of Jim Cameron's temperament-specific discipline tips:

- Energetic, slow-adapting kids need to have some areas in which they can practice their assertiveness. They need limits that are clear and consistent but reasonable and flexible (you may have to state the rule a few times, but he'll come around eventually). Too many limits will result in battles of will; too few will result in your being afraid of him all the time. It's especially tough for these kids to follow instructions in the evening, so keep them calm by reading or watching a video instead of wrestling.
- Slow-adapting kids are likely to protest just about everything you ask for, and it's awfully easy to interpret their foot-dragging as rebellion or as an attack on your authority. If you respond immediately with anger, your child will come to anticipate your anger and will resist even more. So instead, give several firm warnings, starting well in advance. Parents of slow-adapting kids sometimes just give in out of frustration or lash out with severe punishments, feel guilty, and become overly permissive again. "For slow-adapting children, loss of control over their own world [getting sent to their rooms] is the most effective punishment there is," says Cameron.
- Moderate-activity, moderate-frustration-tolerance kids have lots of tantrums. They want something, you don't give it to them, and they're off. . . . Their goal, of course, is to get you to give in. Don't. (See pages 68–73 for more on handling and preventing tantrums.)
- Moderate-activity, fast-adapting kids need to know exactly what the rules are and where the lines are drawn. Too many limits and they'll be frustrated by the lack of freedom. Too few and they'll run wild.
- Irregular, withdrawing kids are, not surprisingly, tough, and your expecta-

"Sure I'm bad. I'm a prisoner of my genes!"

tions are the key. Expecting your child to stay in his room at night is fine, but expecting him to stay in his bed or to go to sleep right away is a waste of time. The key here is to make repeated and firm requests for compliance. And try not to take your child's initial "deafness" as a personal affront.

Sexism and Punishment

It's all too easy to fall into the trap of treating boys and girls differently. And the way parents discipline their children is no exception. For example, boys are far more likely to be spanked, whereas girls are more likely to be sent to their rooms.

At the same time, parents—especially fathers—of girls are sometimes "overly involved with their daughters in ways that excessively protect them from experiences of failure, provide excessive direction, and generally inhibit their autonomy," says fatherhood researcher John Snarey.

You can take a major step toward reducing sexism by trying really, really hard to treat boys and girls the same way. This *doesn't* mean spanking your daughter or inhibiting your son's autonomy. In fact, you should do just the opposite—send your son to his room and give your daughter more freedom.

Spanking

A recent survey by *Child* magazine found that 37 percent of parents discipline their toddlers several times a day, and 27 percent discipline their child in public several times a week. It's not all that surprising, then, that 39 percent of parents spank their kids "often or sometimes" and 20 percent slap their kids' hands often or sometimes.

The big question, of course, is, "Does spanking do any good?" If you want to attract the child's attention in a hurry, the answer is yes. But if you're interested in any long-term positive effect, the answer is a resounding no. In fact, there's plenty of evidence that the long-term effect of spanking children is quite negative. (It's worth noting here that of the people polled in the *Child* magazine survey, only 4 percent felt that spanking was an effective way to get kids to be good.)

Basically, researchers confirm just what you might expect: spanking children does little more than teach them to resort to violence and aggression to solve their problems—not exactly the message most parents want to get across to their kids.

I still remember very clearly a scene that took place a few years ago at a bus stop not far from my house. A rather agitated woman was trying to keep her two kids—about five and seven years old—from fighting: "How many

Family Matters

The Old College Try

We all know it's going to cost a ton of money to send a child to college (realistic projections often exceed $200,000 for four years at a good school). But too many of us look at all those zeros and panic, thinking we're going to have to write a check to pay for the whole thing. My wife and I bought our house for about that amount (and in California, where $200,000 doesn't buy much) and never thought for a second of paying for the whole thing in cash.

So how *do* you finance your kid's education? Traditionally, parents have opened savings accounts in their children's names as a way of putting money aside for the child's education. However, according to financial author and counselor Eric Tyson, this is "usually a financial mistake of major proportions in the short- and long-term." The solution? Start socking away money—*into your own retirement account.* Sound a little counterintuitive? Well, here's a wonderful analogy Tyson uses to explain:

times," she said, smacking the older child, "do I have to [smack] tell you [smack] not to hit [smack] your brother [smack]?" Any guesses about where that little boy learned to hit his brother?

Author Doug Spangler suggests that fathers who spank their children are sending some very specific messages:

- It's okay to hit another person.
- It's okay to hit another person who is smaller than you.
- It's okay to hit someone you love.
- It's okay to hit someone when you feel angry and frustrated.
- Physical aggression is normal and acceptable under any circumstances.
- Daddy can't control himself or his temper.
- Fathers are to be feared.
- Children must always be quiet around their fathers.

Research also shows that children who get spanked are more likely to suffer from poor self-esteem and depression, and have a greater chance of accepting lower-paying jobs as adults. While this may not be a direct cause-and-effect relationship, there is clearly some correlation between being spanked and poor self-esteem.

If you were paying attention to the flight attendant before taking off on your last airplane trip, you'll remember that if those oxygen masks drop from the ceiling, you're supposed to put *yours* on first, *then* your child's, right? The idea is that if *you* can't breathe, you certainly won't be able to help anyone else. Tyson makes the same basic point about money: take care of *your* finances first—especially your IRA, 401(k), Keogh, or company-sponsored retirement—and your whole family will be better off.

But that still doesn't clear up the problem of how feathering your own personal retirement account instead of starting a college fund in your child's name will help put her through college. Well, here's how it works:

- Money you invest in your retirement accounts is often at least partially tax-deductible and always grows tax-free until you start withdrawing it. The dollars you invest in an account in your child's name are after-tax dollars and any interest and dividends may be taxable as income or capital gains.
- At the present time, financial-aid departments usually count just about everything you own as an asset—except your retirement accounts. They assume

"I wish you'd try harder to like school, Jeremy. It's costing Daddy a bundle"

that 35 percent of all the money held in your child's name will be available for educational purposes each year. Only about 6 percent of the money held in your name is considered available for education, and funds in your retirement accounts are not counted at all. Therefore, the less money you have in your child's name, the more financial aid you'll qualify for.

- Plenty of financial-aid options are available: student loans (usually available at below-market rates), grants, fellowships, work-study programs, and so forth.
- You can always borrow against the equity in your home.
- If you'll be over 59½ by the time your child starts college, you may be able to withdraw money from your IRA or other retirement account without incurring any penalties.

Wills and Trusts

By this time, hopefully, you've got your life insurance situation under control.

If You're Planning to Pay 100 Percent of Your Child's College Expenses

Despite all this sound financial advice, you may still be intent on paying cash for college. If you've got the money—and the desire—to do so, immediately disregard the above advice and start socking money away into an account in your child's name (with you as custodian). That way, you'll be able to save at least a little on taxes: until she's fourteen, the first $1,400 or so of your child's interest and dividends will be taxed at the (presumably lower) child's rate; the rest gets taxed at your rate. After age fourteen, however, *all* her income gets taxed at the rate for a single adult.

If not, put this book down right now and call your insurance agent. And while you're waiting for him to call back, you might want to review the section on insurance in *TNF I*, pages 191–96.

Knowing that your partner and kids will be financially secure in the event of your death should make you breathe a little easier. But don't relax completely—there are a few other things you have to worry about. For example, if, God forbid, you and your partner are killed tomorrow, who's going to take care of your kids? Who's going to make sure they get the kind of education and upbringing you want them to have? And who's going to get all your stuff?

The answers to these and other horrible-but-important-to-consider questions

Doing It Yourself

Without ever having gone to law school or earned a degree in accounting, you can probably write a will or set up a living trust by yourself. There are quite a few excellent books and software packages on the market that can take you through the whole process. Several excellent ones are listed in the Resources guide (page 217).

But don't be fooled. No lawyer can throw together a will or a trust in five minutes, and neither can you. It will take hours and hours of serious work and education. So if you have a lot of money or a complicated financial situation, or if you just feel more comfortable having a professional take care of things for you, your local or state bar association can give you referrals for attorneys in your area who specialize in wills and trusts. You should also talk to a good tax or probate lawyer if you aren't absolutely sure whether you need a will or a living trust or some other instrument.

Wills

ADVANTAGES

- You can distribute your assets exactly as you want.
- There is an automatic limit on how long someone has to challenge the terms of your will (varies from state to state). According to some estimates, one in three wills is contested, so this limit could be a very good thing.
- Creditors must make claims within a certain amount of time (again, varies from state to state).
- The activities of your executors, guardians, and trustees are supervised by the court.

DISADVANTAGES

- Probate. This is the name for the process through which everything in a will must go before it is completely straightened out. Probate can easily last as long as eighteen months. And until it's over, your heirs won't have access to most of the assets of your estate.
- Court fees, attorneys' fees, executor fees, accounting fees, and so forth can eat up 3 to 7 percent (or more) of the estate.
- In most cases, probate files are public records. This means that anyone can go down to the courthouse and take a peek at your will.

are up to you. They're outlined in a will or a trust, or both. Unfortunately, about half of all parents with young children don't have either a will or a trust.

If you die *intestate* (meaning without a will, trust, or other document that tells how you want your assets distributed), the details will be handled according to the laws of your state. In most cases, this means that a judge will appoint a guardian for your estate and another one for your children. Chances are, neither of these guardians will be the one you would have chosen.

So which is better? A will? A trust? Actually, the answer may be both. As a new parent, you absolutely, positively need a will to designate a guardian for your child. You can also use a will to distribute your assets, but many experts feel that setting up a *revocable living trust* is a better alternative. However, because of the time and expense involved, many decline to take advantage of the living trust alternative.

Some of the advantages and disadvantages of wills and living trusts are listed above and on the facing page.

As Long as You're Thinking about Depressing Things . . .

- Consider a *durable power of attorney.* This document (which you'll need an

Living Trusts

ADVANTAGES

- The costs and time delays of probate are largely avoided. After your death, your survivors should have control over your assets without involving the courts.
- The trust document is not public, so no one can see it unless you show it to them.
- Assets are distributed as you wish—either directly to your heirs upon your death or gradually over time.
- A living trust "not only allows your continued total control over your affairs during your lifetime, but provides a continuity in management and supervision in the event of your incapacity," says attorney Harvey J. Platt.

DISADVANTAGES

- Trusts generally cost more and take longer to set up than wills. It will also probably cost you a few dollars to transfer ownership of your assets from you personally to the trust. However, all the probate-related expenses that wills require can come to about the same amount as the cost of setting up a trust.
- Improperly prepared, a living trust can cause some serious problems. If the IRS feels that your trust was not properly executed, your estate could wind up in probate—the very situation you were hoping to avoid.
- Since all your assets are transferred during your lifetime from your name into the name of the trust, you are giving up personal ownership in a lot of what you own. This can be tough psychologically.
- Trusts may not reduce your tax liability.

attorney to help you prepare) gives someone you designate the power to manage your affairs if you become incapacitated. You can include a health-care directive, which covers such topics as whether or not you want to be kept on life support if things ever come to that.

- Consider making some gifts. You and your partner can each transfer up to $10,000 per year to each beneficiary tax free, thereby reducing the size of your estate as well as the amount of estate taxes that your heirs will have to come up with later. (Estate taxes, by the way, are usually due and payable within nine months of death.)

24–27 MONTHS

Off to School

What's Going On with the Baby

Physically

- Your two-year-old seems to "think with his feet"—wandering around almost aimlessly, spending a few seconds engaged in some activity or other, then moving on to something else.
- He's quite comfortable with his body and its capabilities; he can run without falling down, walk up and down stairs by himself, jump off a low step, and rock or march in time to music.
- His hand-eye coordination is getting much better, and he's now able to make use of his blocks to build structures that are more complex than towers: houses, forts, horse corrals, long walls.
- Nevertheless, he still has some problems using one hand independently of the other. "If he holds out an injured finger for bandaging, he tends also to hold out his matching uninjured finger," write child development experts Louise Bates Ames and Frances Ilg.
- As recently as six months ago, your toddler could only focus on things pretty much right in front of his face. Now he's developing peripheral vision. He's also becoming aware of faraway objects such as planes, birds, and distant houses.

Intellectually

- At this stage of his development, he's not able to separate the *goal* of his actions from the *process* of achieving it. In other words, *how* he does something is just as important as *what* he does. For example, if he decides to make a painting, he's not just interested in being creative. He's equally interested in making a mess and exploring the feel of paint brush on paper. And if he clambers to the top of a climbing structure, it's as much because he likes climbing as to conquer Everest.

- Your child may be exhibiting what you may interpret as more aggressive behavior. But according to Ames and Ilg, many seemingly aggressive kids are not actually aggressive. "It's just that children want what they want and, if necessary, hit, push, struggle to get it."
- For at least the next year, your child's primary concern will be satisfying his own needs and wants. The fact that your back is killing you and you need a break is of no concern to him if he wants you to lift him into the air for the 327th time. And he's outraged that you're tired of reading him the same book over and over.
- His feelings of power over his surroundings are reinforced by his burgeoning language skills. "He behaves as if the words give him control over the situation . . . as if he controls his own exits and entrances by means of the magic utterance," writes Fraiberg. Now that he can say "bye-bye," he doesn't seem to mind quite as much when you leave him alone. And he's more cooperative about going to bed when he's the one telling you "night-night."

Verbally

- Until now, your child learned about his world *physically:* he had to touch, feel, or taste things before he could truly understand them. But from here on out, *language*—questions, answers, explanations—begins to take over as the toddler's primary means of acquiring information.
- Your toddler's passive vocabulary (the words he understands) now includes 200 to 500 words. His active vocabulary (the words he uses), however, consists of only 20 to 100 words.
- He's now using verbs ("I go to the store") and adjectives ("I'm a good boy"). His favorite word, though, is probably "again."
- Ames and Ilg have found that despite your toddler's quickly increasing knowledge of the language, he talks mainly to himself; second most to you and other familiar adults; and little if any to other children. Most of what comes out of his mouth is self-initiated (as opposed to being in response to something you've said).
- *Note:* Some two-year-olds speak in short, 3-to-5-word sentences. Others still speak one word at a time. Unless your child doesn't understand simple questions and requests, there's nothing to worry about.

Emotionally/Socially

- The first few months of the third year are usually happy ones for both toddler and parents. He's having fewer tantrums and is generally more cooperative than even a few months ago.
- Although he's still not playing *with* other kids very much, he's getting more content to play alongside them. "Several may gather around a sandbox, each scooping up his own sand," write Ames and Ilg. "They may all be doing more or less the same thing, and playing with more or less the same kind of material, and may all be in much the same place, but without much interaction."
- He already had a rather short attention span, but thanks (in part, at least) to his widening peripheral vision, he's even more distracted than before—after all, there are so many interesting new things crossing his field of view.
- After playing with their genitals for a while, boys and girls are now establishing a budding gender identity, identifying with (and becoming more attached to) the parent of the same sex.
- He may tell you in advance when his bowel movements are about to occur, indicating that he's finally ready to begin potty training (see pages 103–6 for more on this).

What You're Going Through

Pride—or Disappointment—in Your Child's Accomplishments

One of the best things about being a parent is that it gives you a chance to go back and do all the things you loved to do as a kid, all the things you missed out on, and all the things you did but want to do again. It's like having a second childhood.

The problem is, however, that some parents forget whose childhood it really is. Too many parents "expect their child to be their ambassador out in the world," writes the Work and Family Institute's Ellen Galinsky, believing that "what the child does reflects upon them."

Barbara and Philip Newman agree. "Parents may experience intense emotional reactions to their child's behavior," they write. "They can make you feel warm, joyful, and proud. They can make you feel furious, guilty, and disgusted. Because of the deep commitment and love most parents feel for children, their emotional reactions to a child's behavior can be especially intense. It's one thing if someone else's child is rude or selfish. But if your own child is rude or

"Do that thing you do, Billy, but this time do it the way I taught you."

selfish, intense feelings of anger, disgust, or embarrassment may be stimulated. You may feel pleased by the successes of a neighbor's child, but the success of your own child gives rise to the peculiar parental emotion called 'gloating.'"

In addition, too many parents expect their children to live out all their unfulfilled dreams and expectations and to do as well as, if not better than, the parents themselves. Part of the reason for this is a fear of failing, a fear that the parent hasn't done a good enough job, or that he hasn't adequately prepared the child to be a good citizen.

The bottom line is that you need to relax. Your child's failures are *not* a referendum on your parenting skills. Taking failure too personally (including your child's failure to act like you want her to) puts way too much pressure on the child. You had your turn. Now move over and let someone else have a clear shot at being a child.

As simple as it sounds, your child is not an extension of you. You occupy "overlapping but not identical futures," say the Newmans. "Your children serve to connect you to the past, but they also free you from the past."

Thinking about Sexism

A few months ago, we talked about how easy it is for parents to fall into the trap of treating boys and girls differently. Given that kids learn most of what

"Just keep saying to yourself 'I'm not a sexist, I'm not a sexist . . .'"

they know from adults, it shouldn't come as much of a surprise that this kind of gender-based double standard works just as well the other way. In other words, kids treat men and women differently.

"Children learn the different roles that males and females play with children before the age of three," writes researcher Beverly Fagot. "And once this difference has been learned, the children will react to adults outside the home on the basis of this learned differentiation." Fagot found that in preschool classrooms, kids "elicited many kinds of play behavior from the male teachers; but when children needed materials or needed some caretaking, they approached female teachers."

So what can you do? Basically, just be a good role model. If you are a full participant in your home, and you love, nurture, and care for your children, they—boys and girls alike—will come to realize that men can be parents too. Second, make sure your children get the message that men and women and boys and girls are not locked into any particular roles or futures because of their gender. Your children should be free to dream of becoming whatever they want to. This means that besides telling our daughters that they can grow up to be doctors, we need to tell our sons that they can grow up to be nurses (an idea my older daughter still has a problem with, even though the father of one of her best friends is, indeed, a nurse anesthetist).

So if your daughters (like mine) demanded Matchbox cars for their birthdays, tore the heads off their Barbie dolls, and refused to be in the same room with a tutu, let them alone. And if your son wants to play with dolls or wear your partner's nail polish or lipstick, let him alone. A friend who has a particularly gentle, sweet little boy once confided that she was worried about her son's lack of physical aggressiveness and was concerned that he might be gay.

Forcing your child into a particular type of behavior—either to conform with or buck gender stereotypes—can scar them for life.

You and Your Baby

Potty Training: The Real Thing

The following steps were adapted from some of those suggested by pediatrician T. Berry Brazelton. Each one takes about a week, but if your child falters or loses interest, don't push. Take a break and pick up where you left off in a few days.

1. Leave a potty seat on the floor in the bathroom. Tell the child the little one is for him, the big one is for grown-ups.
2. After a week or so, have the child sit on the potty seat in his clothes while

Toilet Training Success Boosters

- Don't flush in front of the child. While some kids may be fascinated, others may be terrified, believing that a part of them is being flushed away (see pages 40–47 for more on fears).
- Minimize or eliminate liquids within an hour of bedtime. This will increase the chances that your child will wake up dry—something that will boost her confidence.
- Be positive, but not too positive. Too much excitement about the contents of a diaper can give the baby the idea that what she's produced is somehow valuable—a twisted notion that may result in her wanting to keep it for herself (inside her body if necessary).

you sit on yours (clothed or otherwise). You might want to read a story to keep him there.

3. After another week, ask the child once a day if you can take his diapers off so he can sit on his special toilet. You sit on your toilet as well and tell him that you, mommy, grandpa, grandma, and everyone else he knows does this every day. My younger daughter loved this stage and would sit on her potty seat for a few minutes shouting "peeeeeeee" (but without actually peeing).
4. A week later, take off the child's dirty diaper and dump the contents into the toilet. Emphasize that just like there's a special place for everything else, the toilet is the special place for urine and BM, and that that's where grown-ups put theirs. *Do not flush in front of the child* (see page 103).
5. Let the baby run around naked during the day for ten to twenty minutes. Tell him he can go to the potty anytime he wants to.
6. Over the course of a few days, leave the baby's diapers off longer and longer. Remind him every half-hour or so to go to the bathroom. If he has an accident, don't make a big deal about it—it happens to everyone.
7. Don't worry about night training for a while—at least until the child is regularly dry after waking from his naps and occasionally dry in the morning.

BOYS AND GIRLS DO IT DIFFERENTLY . . . AND SO DO THEIR PARENTS

Ninety percent of girls are bowel trained by 2 years, 7 months, while 90 percent of boys aren't bowel trained until 3 years, 1 month—a difference of 6 months. Ninety percent of girls are bladder trained by 3 years, 6 months, while 90 percent of boys take until 4 years 10 months—a difference of 16 months.

Although boys lag behind in toilet training, there is no significant biological reason for the delay. Some experts believe that the real reason girls are "trained" sooner is that women have traditionally done the training and girls have an easier time imitating their mothers than boys do. In addition, boys may not want to imitate their mothers.

It's completely normal for boys this age to start developing a male gender identity and rebel against their mothers (the same way girls this age start developing a female gender identity and rebel against their fathers). So a little boy may balk at sitting down when urinating (it's no fun to sit when you can stand), and may resist mom's instructions on how to grasp his penis—after all, she doesn't even have one!

"I think he's downloading."

Besides being done with potty training earlier, girls also have a much shorter time between bowel and bladder training (11 months) than boys (21 months). This difference may be the result of girls' not being taught to differentiate between the two functions. (Girls can't see either their urination or defecation and wipe after both, while boys can see their urine—and are encouraged to aim it—and wipe only after moving their bowels.)

Men and women traditionally have very different ways of teaching toilet training:

As you can see, "The female mode is compatible with and enhancing to the formation of a female gender identity," writes Moisy Shopper, who's done an exhaustive study of toilet training (don't ask why). "The child is encouraged to be like mother; by seeing mother's eliminative functioning, they have an intimacy with each other's bodies that fosters the girl's gender *and* sexual identity." Using the female mode to train boys "in no way enhances the boy's potential for further body differentiation or supports the sexual differences between him and his mother," writes Shopper. "In fact, in many ways it is antithetical to the boy's maturation."

THE TRADITIONAL MALE MODEL	THE TRADITIONAL FEMALE MODEL
♦ Urinary control is taught as a stand-up procedure with emphasis on skill, mastery, and fun.	♦ Sitting down for all elimination, wiping.
♦ Wipe only after bowel movements.	♦ Wiping after both kinds.
♦ Active participation and modeling by the father and/or other males.	♦ Use of the mother herself on the toilet as a model for imitation.
♦ Encouragement to touch and control the penis so as to aim the urinary stream.	♦ Discouragement from touching self.
♦ Greater tolerance for absence of bathroom privacy.	♦ Greater need for bathroom privacy.
♦ Control, function, and naming of urine is sharply differentiated from control, function, and naming of feces (boys tend to talk about "making pee pee" as opposed to "pooping").	♦ Minimal distinction between bladder and bowel training in vocabulary, timing, or technique (girls tend to talk about "going to the bathroom").

FOR BOYS ONLY

Basically, the primary role in toilet training boys should be yours. This, of course, does not mean that your partner can't toilet train your son (except for providing a model for how to urinate standing up, there's no reason she can't) or that you can't toilet train your daughter. Plenty of women support their sons' budding masculinity and encourage them to urinate standing up, holding on to their own penises.

A small number of mothers, however, won't allow their sons any autonomy, Shopper finds. And they feel "that *they* must hold their sons' penises as they pee. This is a rotten idea because your son may begin to question whether his penis belongs to him or to his mother, and that's just how serious sexual problems develop later in life."

When boys have a male model, they are much less conflicted about becoming toilet trained since training no longer carries the connotations of gaining their mother's love, submitting to her, and becoming like her.

Reading

CREATING A READING ENVIRONMENT

Having books and other reading materials readily available to your child will help her make books part of her daily life. And one of the best ways to do this is to be sure there are plenty of books on shelves or in racks that she can reach without having to ask for help.

The goal here is to have your child view reading as something she can do whenever she wants, without fear of being punished. So give her free and open access to board books and any other inexpensive or easily replaceable books you won't mind getting torn up or stuck together with drool. Keep the books you had as a child (and any others that you want to keep in one piece) far, far away and take them down only for special occasions.

SOME ADVANCED READING CONCEPTS

By now you've probably gotten into a nice, regular routine with your child, reading together in a quiet place at times when you won't be interrupted.

"Surely there must be a video of this?"

As you're reading (or planning your reading), make a conscious effort to keep the experience as interesting as possible for both you and your child. Here are some things to keep in mind:

- **Tone.** It's better to read stories that are slightly too advanced for your child (and explain a word or concept now and then) than ones that are too easy.
- **Variety.** Children's book illustrators use a huge variety of techniques: line drawings, photos, watercolors, charcoal, paint, collages, woodcut, needlepoint. Expose your child to as many approaches as possible and discuss what's unique about each of them.
- **Talk.** If your toddler interrupts the story to ask questions, follow her lead. You can interrupt the reading too. Questions like "How do you think he's feeling?" "Why did the bunny do that?" or "What's going to happen when she opens the closet door?" will help your child develop critical thinking skills and encourage her to be a more active participant.
- **Act out.** Instead of reading *Little Red Riding Hood* for the 639th time, assign roles.
- **Set an example.** Let her see you and your partner reading for pleasure.

Here are a few more books to check out from your local library or add to your collection:

Alfie Gets in First (and other Alfie books), Shirley Hughes, Bert Kitchen
Animals of the Night, Merry Banks
The Baby Blue Cat and the Smiley Worm Doll, Ainslie Pryor
Basket, Ella George Lyon
Bathwater's Hot (and others in the series), Shirley Hughes
Brown Bear, Brown Bear, What Do You See?, Bill Martin, Jr.
Carl, Alexandra Day
Changes, Changes (and others), Pat Hutchins
Corduroy (and others in the series), Don Freeman
Eat Up, Gemma, Sarah Hayes
The Elephant and the Bad Baby, Elfrida Vipont
Emma's Pet, David McPhail
First Words for Babies and Toddlers, Jane Salt
Follow Me (and many others), Nancy Tafuri
Freight Train, Donald Crews
General Store, Rachel Field
The Great Big Enormous Turnip, Alexei Tolstoy
In the Small, Small Pond, Denise Fleming
It Looked Like Spilt Milk, Charles Shaw

Kate's Car, Kay Chorao
Let's Make Rabbits, Leo Lionni
The Little Engine That Could, Watty Piper
Mary Wore a Red Dress and Henry Wore His Green Sneakers, Merle Peek
Millions of Cats, Wanda Gag
The Mitten, Jan Brett
Moon Game, Frank Asch
Moonlight (and many others), Jan Ormerod
Mr. Gumpy's Motor Car (and others in the series), John Burninghan
Peter Spier's Little Cats (and many others in the series), Peter Spier
Polar Bear, Polar Bear, What Do You Hear?, Bill Martin, Jr.
Pretend You're a Cat, Jean Marzollo
Rosie's Walk, Pat Hutchins
The Runaway Bunny, Margaret Wise Brown
Sheep in a Shop, Nancy Shaw
Shopping Trip (and others), Helen Oxenbury
The Tale of Peter Rabbit (and many others), Beatrix Potter
Up a Tree, Ed Young
Umbrella, Taor Yashima
A Very Busy Spider (and others), Eric Carle
A Very Special House, Ruth Krauss
Watching Foxes, Jim Arnosky
We're Going on a Bear Hunt, Michael Rosen
Where's My Teddy?, Jez Alborough
Who Said Red?, Mary Serfozo
Yellow Ball, Molly Bang

ESPECIALLY FOR OLDER SIBLINGS

These books deal in a particularly sensitive way with the special concerns of kids who suddenly (and usually against their will) are displaced from the center of the universe by a baby sister or brother. For more, see pages 110–12.

101 Things to Do with a Baby, Jan Ormerod
Dogger, Shirley Hughes
A New Baby at Your House, Joanna Cole
Tales of Oliver Pig (and others in the series), Jean Van Leeuwen

CONCEPTS

Alphabatics, Suse MacDonald
Anno's Counting House (and others), Mitsumasa Anno

26 Letters and 99 Cents, Tana Hoban
Color Zoo, Lois Ehlert
Colors (and other concept books), Jan Pienkowski
Of Colors and Things (and other photography books), Tana Hoban
Duck, David Lloyd

FOLK TALES
Little Red Riding Hood, James Marshall
The Three Little Pigs, Joseph Jacobs

GOING TO SCHOOL/DAY CARE
Going to Day Care, Fred Rogers
My Nursery School, Harlow Rockwell

POETRY/RHYMES
Egg Thoughts and Other Frances Songs, Russel Hoban
The Land of Nod and Other Poems for Children, Robert L. Stevenson
The Owl and the Pussycat, Jan Brett
Whiskers and Rhymes, Arnold Lobel

Family Matters

Family Planning

For a lot of couples, the question about whether to have another child isn't really a question; it's a given. For others, though, it's more complicated. Quite often one spouse wants a second (or third) child, while the other isn't nearly as excited about the prospect—for a variety of reasons. Although I wanted a second child quite a bit, my memories of the incredibly long and painful labor my wife endured delivering our first baby made it almost impossible for me to consider putting her through another similar experience.

Besides the pain aspect of pregnancy and childbirth, there are plenty of other factors that may affect your decision (or at least how you vote when you and your partner get around to discussing the issue):

- Do you really like being a parent? Is it as much fun as you thought it would be? Is it more—or less—work than you thought? Generally speaking, a second child is less stressful than the first; you'll feel like an old hand when the second baby does things that made you panic with the first one. As a result, you'll probably enjoy the second child's childhood more than the first one's.

AGE DIFFERENCE BETWEEN CHILDREN: 9 to 18 months

ADVANTAGES	DISADVANTAGES
• Because they're close in age, there's a better chance the kids will be great playmates. • Your first child will adjust to the change more easily than if he were older; he won't really know what's going on and won't feel quite as displaced.	• You may not like having two kids in diapers at the same time. • Your older child is still really a baby. He has plenty of baby needs and is going to have a tough time waiting for you to meet them. • "You can expect her to act very clingy at times, perhaps alternating with aggressive behavior towards you or others," says nurse practitioner Meg Zweiback. • Because they're close in age, they may compete with each other more.

AGE DIFFERENCE BETWEEN CHILDREN: 18 to 36 months

ADVANTAGES	DISADVANTAGES
• This is the most common age difference in the country, so some of your friends will probably have kids similarly spaced. • Your older child is now more capable of waiting a bit before having his needs satisfied. • The older child is more articulate and can entertain himself for limited amounts of time. • The older baby is mature enough to enjoy the new baby and also to enjoy time away from you without seeing it as a threat.	• The two kids are far enough apart to have very different schedules, activities, and interests. This means that if you're doing the driving you'll probably end up feeling like a taxi driver. • The older child is more likely to see the younger one as an invader. As a result, there's going to be more friction between the two.

AGE DIFFERENCE BETWEEN CHILDREN: 36+ months

ADVANTAGES	DISADVANTAGES
• The older child is even more articulate, more able to satisfy his own needs, and less likely to try to hurt the new child. • The older child can—and may very well want to—help out quite a bit.	• A child who has been an only child for so long may have a very difficult time sharing you and your partner with anyone else.

- Can you afford it? And if you can't, does it really make a difference? My parents, who were both starving grad students when I was born, claim that I spent my first two years sleeping in a dresser drawer.
- How are you and your partner going to divide the labor around the house? Are you both satisfied with the way things got handled the first time around? Two kids is going to be more than twice the work of one: each requires a certain amount of care and feeding, plus there's the additional job of keeping the two of them from killing each other.
- Do you have brothers or sisters, or were you an only child? How did you like growing up that way? Do you think your child would be better or worse off with a younger sibling?
- Do you think you'll be able to love the second baby as much as the first? This is one of the most common concerns of prospective second-time (and beyond) parents. The simple answer is that your capacity to love your children is infinite.
- The pregnancy is going to be different, especially for your partner. First, because the physical changes are familiar, she might not be as fascinated by what's going on inside her body. Second, many of the physical changes may happen sooner than they did the first time: she'll probably "show" sooner, she may gain more weight this time, and she may be more tired (being a parent is exhausting enough; trying to do it while you're pregnant is something altogether different).
- Try not to let the first baby's temperament influence your decision—it has *absolutely no* influence on how your next baby will turn out.

FILLING THE GAP

Once you make your decision to have another child, you will probably need to decide on how far apart to space them (see chart on page 111).

Looking for Preschools

During the first eighteen months of your child's life, he should be the focus of his caregiver's attention. "Without this confirmation of self-importance, the child may experience insecurity that, in turn, will encumber the emergence of creative behavior," says psychologist John Rosemond. But over the second eighteen months, your child's needs change, and he needs to be taught—gradually—that he isn't the center of the universe.

Most preschools begin taking kids at thirty-three months (two years, nine months). But in major metropolitan areas, good preschools fill up months, sometimes even years, before the start of the fall semester. So get your applications together now. (It may seem kind of absurd to have to *apply* to get into a preschool, but if Robert Fulgum is right, and you're really going to learn everything you'll ever need to know in kindergarten, maybe it's not so crazy after all.)

As with anything to do with education, preschools have lately become the subject of much controversy:

THE BAD	THE GOOD
• Full-time day care for babies is likely to damage their development, British parenting guru Penelope Leach has found.	• One study found that sixth graders who had entered a model full-time day-care program as toddlers posted higher math scores than their peers.
• Too much group day care can jeopardize infants' attachment to their parents, psychologist Robert Karen has determined.	• Kids who go to preschools tend to be more self-reliant and confident. But they're also more boisterous, competitive, or likely to fight, according to researcher John Bates. • There doesn't seem to be any evidence that day care for children *over* a year hurts their attachment to their parents. • Family problems such as stress and insufficient income are as much as twenty times more powerful than day-care problems.

Overall, the consensus is that three-mornings-a-week preschools are fine. The potential problems start when the discussion shifts to full-time day care: seven or eight hours a day, five (or more) days a week.

THE CHOICES

There are literally dozens of preschool opportunities in your community, most of which fall into one of the following categories:

- **Cooperative.** The parents help out a lot, volunteering in the classroom, organizing activities, creating the curriculum.
- **Orthodox.** The teachers are trained in a specific method or philosophy of educating young children. This may involve using certain equipment or teaching methods. Montessori is the most common.

Temperament and Preschool

TRAIT	SPECIAL CONSIDERATIONS
ENERGY LEVEL	
• High	• Your child will need lots of room to run around, plenty of indoor activities for rainy days, lots of ways to burn off excess energy. He will, however, need some moderately structured activities. Look for a program that has many kids his age or older: he'll admire their skills and want to emulate them. And make sure the teachers' energy level is at least as high as your child's.
• Low	• This child needs a quieter, smaller setting, and small groups.
• Moderate (especially those who are also a bit slow-to-warm)	• Your child will probably stick to the sidelines for a few days, watching and learning. He'll jump in after about a week. He likes more structure and predictability, and doesn't do well in large preschools, especially if there are a lot of more active kids his age—they can be frightening.
SENSORY THRESHOLD	
• Low	• Look for a fairly calm, subdued, relaxed environment. Lots of noise, colors, and activity can frighten your child.

- **Free-form.** The school may include the best (or the worst) of a variety of educational philosophies.
- **Academic.** Structured classes in traditional subjects (math, language). Many early childhood development experts think this may be too much too soon.

WHAT TO CONSIDER WHEN CONSIDERING PRESCHOOLS

Perhaps the most important factor is your child's temperament and how it meshes with what the school has to offer (see the chart above and on the facing page).

Another important factor is stability—particularly that of the children. "In child-care settings, the availability of a stable group of age-mates results in more complex, coordinated play," say Newman and Newman. "Children who

TRAIT	SPECIAL CONSIDERATIONS
ATTENTION SPAN	
• Short	• This child will need a constantly changing array of things to do and play with. Look for a staff that is large enough so that a teacher can spend extra time with your child to expose him to new things.
PREDICTABILITY	
• High	• This child will need a regular schedule, regular meal and nap times, and so forth.
• Low	• This child doesn't need much in the way of scheduling, but should have some anyway.
ADAPTABILITY	
• Slow	• Avoid schools with rigid schedules and highly structured activities. Also avoid unstructured schools. Look for teachers who will make a special effort to involve your child and introduce him to new materials slowly. Make sure you can stay with your child for a few minutes each morning (for at least the first week or so) to help ease his transition.
• Moderately slow-to-adapt, intense	• This child may occasionally bite or hit other children. This will fade as he becomes more articulate. He may be upset when you drop him off at school and just as upset when you come to pick him up.

have had many changes in their child-care arrangements are less likely to engage in complex social pretend play."

GENERAL GUIDELINES

Finding the right preschool will probably take a while, and you shouldn't give up until you've got exactly what you were looking for or have come as close as you possibly can. As a minimum, the day-care center you choose for your child should comply with your state's rules and regulations. But standards vary wildly from state to state, so licensing and accreditation are not necessarily the guarantees of quality that they ought to be. On the national level, however, the National Association for the Education of Young Children (NAEYC) accredits programs that meet their extremely high standards. They'll send you info on finding accredited providers in your area. Call (800) 424-2460 or write to NAEYC, 1509 16th Street NW, Washington, D.C. 20036-1426.

But accreditation isn't all there is. You should also keep the following general guidelines in mind (some of which were suggested by the NAEYC and the American Academy of Pediatrics):

RATIO

- The younger the kids allowed in the preschool, the lower the teacher-child ratio should be. In a typical preschool, kids' ages range from two and a half to five. Overall, there should be no more than seven kids to each adult caregiver, and the total size of the group (not including the teachers) shouldn't exceed twenty.

NUTRITION AND HEALTH

- No smoking on the premises.
- Proof of immunization required of each child.
- If the school provides meals and/or snacks, they should be varied, wholesome, and nutritious. Menus should be available in advance.
- Rest and nap times should be scheduled and each child should have a clean, individual place to sleep. There should also be special quiet activities for kids who don't nap.
- Teachers wear disposable gloves and wash hands with soap and water whenever changing diapers. They should also wash their hands after helping a child go to the bathroom and before touching food.
- Parents should be notified immediately of any accident or contagious illness, and there should be a clear policy for what to do (isolation, to start) with kids who get sick while at school.
- Teachers should give medication to children only with a parent's written permission.
- Emergency numbers should be clearly posted near a phone.
- At least one teacher (but all would be better) should have up-to-date first aid and CPR certifications.

GENERAL CLEANLINESS

- Hot running water, soap, and paper towels should be available—at kid level—and should be used after going to the bathroom and before all meals and snacks.
- The entire area—kitchen, tabletops, floors, sleep areas—should be clean. All garbage cans, diaper pails, and bathrooms should be cleaned thoroughly and regularly disinfected. So should toys that tend to end up in toddlers' mouths.

A Few Preschool Red Flags

As far as I'm concerned, any school that doesn't satisfy *all* the qualifications listed on these pages should be viewed with suspicion. Beyond that, though, here are a few things that should make you take a prospective preschool off your list completely and run the other way.

- Parents are not allowed to drop in unannounced. You need to call before visiting or coming to pick up your child.
- Your child is unhappy or scared after more than a few months.
- The staff seems to change every day.
- The staff ignores any of your concerns.
- You child reports being hit or mistreated, or you hear similar reports from other parents. Check this one out thoroughly, though. Kids have been known to fabricate stories.

SAFETY

- Outlets, heaters, and radiators are covered.
- Equipment is up-to-date and meets current safety codes.
- Cleaning fluids, medicines, and any other potentially dangerous substances are kept in places inaccessible to the children.
- There is an emergency plan, including regular fire drills. Fire extinguishers should be available as required.
- The school has a plan for dealing with violent children. While some hitting, pushing, and biting is pretty normal for kids this age, anything more serious (stabbing, hitting with large objects, or repeated, unprovoked attacks) are not.
- Children are not allowed to ride in any moving vehicle without a car seat.
- Children are not released to any adult whose name is not on a written list provided by you and your partner.
- Outdoor areas are safe from animal contamination (for example, the sandbox should be tightly covered).

PROGRAM

- To the extent possible, substitute teachers should be familiar to the kids.
- Children have daily opportunities to participate in a variety of active and quiet activities, including free play, art, music, and group and individual play.
- Children have adequate time to play outside every day, weather permitting. There should be plenty of space for active, physical play, such as climbing, running, and jumping.

- Indoor areas must be large enough to accommodate all the kids at one time. The area should be well organized so kids know where things go and what happens where. There should be a wide variety of age-appropriate toys, books, and materials. And there should be more than one of each toy so that the kids don't have to wait in long lines to play.
- Parents should be welcome at any time, without advance notice.
- Overall, the preschool should be a place you wish you could have gone to when you were a kid.

EASING THE TRANSITION

Several months before our older daughter's first day of preschool, my wife and I started trying to get her ready. The school principal had sent us a five-page handout on how tough this first big separation can be for kids, and my wife and I spent hours with our daughter reading books about other kids' first days, talking about who else would be at school, telling her about our own school experiences, and describing the fun things she would get to do. We bought her new clothes in her favorite colors and a Little Mermaid lunch box and reassured her over and over that we'd pick her up every day right after lunch and that, of course, we still loved her.

"Think of it as a brief interlude in, as opposed to a major disruption of, your life."

Even the school itself tried to help ease the transition. A few weeks before school started, one of the teachers came over to the house and spent hours playing with our daughter and getting to know her. She also brought along a Polaroid camera and left our daughter a snapshot of her with her new teacher. And on the morning of the fateful first day, we gave her honeycomb and cookies shaped like her favorite alphabet letters, to remind her that learning should be a sweet experience. By the time we got in the car for the drive to school on the first day, I felt pretty confident that we had prepared her both psychologically and emotionally for this milestone.

As soon as we got inside the building, I knew I was right. My daughter caught sight of a few of her friends and the teacher who had come to our house, and promptly disappeared, laughing and giggling. I shouted a good-bye (which she barely acknowledged), reminded her when I'd be back to pick her up, and walked out to the car.

Some kids won't even notice when you've gone on the first day of school. Others will freak out completely. Either way, here are some absolute musts (and must nots) for the first days:

- Prepare *yourself.* For more on this, see pages 177–79.
- No matter how well adjusted your child seems, never just drop her off on the first day. Go inside and get her settled.
- Never sneak out, even if she's deeply involved in some activity.
- Create a good-bye routine (kiss, do a quick drawing together, wave bye-bye through the window).
- Don't chastise your child for crying. Reassure her that you love her, that you'll be back.
- Don't be upset if your child comes home covered with dirt, paint, glue, sparkles, or even an occasional bruise. It means she's interacting with other people and having fun.

PASSING THE BUCK

Coincidentally, the same week that my older daughter was admitted to preschool, a friend of mine was admitted to the University of San Francisco's medical school. My friend was griping about how much her tuition cost and was surprised when I wasn't more sympathetic. But when I told her that my daughter's preschool was more expensive than med school, she stopped.

Naturally, not all preschools cost as much as medical schools, but it's not going to be cheap. If you have the money, great. But most of us could use (or wouldn't turn down) a little financial assistance. And asking your employer to help out a little may be your best bet. Here are a few alternatives:

- Direct financial assistance. Your employer pays for all or part of your expenses at the preschool of your choice.
- Negotiated discounts. Your employer—maybe in conjunction with other local employers—can negotiate group rates or discounts with a nearby preschool.
- Employee salary reductions or set-asides. You can have your employer put up to $5,000 of your pretax salary into a Dependent Care Assistance Plan (DCAP). This will enable you to reduce your preschool expenses by paying for them with before-tax dollars instead of after-tax ones. Your employer will save money too, since he or she won't have to pay social security tax or unemployment insurance on your DCAP money. (If your employee benefits department requests a reference, it's Section 129 of the 1981 Economic Recovery Tax Act.)

Of course, asking your boss for help—or anyone else, for that matter—isn't easy. In fact, the reason employees most often give for *not* asking their bosses to get involved in employee day-care problems is fear of losing their jobs. This may explain why fewer than six thousand of the nation's six million employers offer some kind of child-care assistance to their employees.

Nevertheless, it's worth a try. The first thing to do is to remind him or her that some assistance programs won't cost the company a cent (see above). Then read your employer this quote from the Child Care Action Campaign (CCAC): "Studies have shown that working parents' anxiety about their child care arrangements erodes their productivity—and directly affects employers' profit lines."

If those approaches don't work, follow the CCAC's advice and:

- Talk to other employees. Do any of them have trouble finding or paying for a good preschool? How do their worries affect their productivity?
- Find out what other employers in your field are doing about preschool. Some prospective employees are making decisions on which companies to work for based on benefits, and if the competition offers a more family-friendly environment, your company will have to follow suit.
- If you're in a union, speak to your union rep. Have other employers bargained for family-friendly benefits? You may be able to include some in the next contract negotiation.
- Encourage other employees to let management know about child-care problems.

The Child Care Action Campaign produces a variety of pamphlets that can help you approach your employer with your preschool questions and suggestions. Contact them for a catalog at 330 Seventh Ave, 17th floor, New York, NY 10001, or by calling (212) 239-0138.

27–30 MONTHS

Time for a Financial Tune-up

What's Going On with the Baby

Physically

- You may have noticed that your child looks different lately—less like a baby and more like a little kid. Her head doesn't seem so out of proportion to the rest of her body, and she's lost most of her baby potbelly.
- She's getting much better at dressing herself and is especially interested in shoes (although she's still more than a year away from being able to lace them up). She can, however, manipulate Velcro fasteners.
- Your child's emotions are more frequently expressed physically than verbally. When happy, she may jump up and down with glee; when angry, she may throw something down.

Intellectually

- "Self-control is still dependent upon factors outside himself, namely the approval or disapproval of his parents," writes Selma Fraiberg. Your child's still a long way away from developing a conscience or a true ability to regulate her own negative impulses. But this is an important first step.
- Another by-product of her improving memory is her new ability to imitate you when you *aren't* there with her. This signals the beginning of her ability to engage in fantasy play.
- She continues to choose less physical and more intellectual ways of solving problems. She does a lot less by trial and error and a lot more by thinking

things through. For example, rather than pull you over to the bookshelf and point to the book she wants you to get down, she may simply tell you to "bring me book."

- Your toddler's able to focus on incredibly tiny details—ones you probably would never notice. In the middle of the 400th read-through of *Goldilocks and the Three Bears,* my older daughter suddenly stopped me and pointed out that the artist had made an error: in a picture of the bears' breakfast table, both the daddy bear's porridge (which is supposedly too hot) and the mommy bear's porridge (supposedly too cold) were steaming. What an outrage.
- She's now able to distinguish a group of two objects from a group of more than two. She may not, however, have a word for the larger group.
- Although concepts such as "yesterday," "tomorrow," and "last week," are still beyond your toddler's grasp, she has a fairly good idea of what "pretty soon," and "in a minute" mean.

Verbally

- Your toddler is probably increasing her vocabulary by two to five words per day. She's so thrilled with the sound of her own voice that she'll repeat her new words over and over.
- She runs around naming every object she knows, and will accompany just about everything she does with a steady stream of chatter.
- She makes a lot of really cute (but extremely logical) grammatical errors ("I went to he's house," "Give the cup to she," are common). And she is still unclear on past and future tenses: "I go to store" can mean "I am going now," "I went," or "I will go."
- She still spends a lot of time talking to herself and would rather engage a grown-up in conversation than another child.
- Perhaps the most interesting language-related development is that at this age, according to Fraiberg, "language makes it possible for a child to incorporate his parents' verbal prohibitions, to make them part of himself." This isn't always 100 percent successful, though. You may find her sitting on the floor, eating sugar out of the box, and saying, "No, baby not eat sugar," between mouthfuls.
- In addition to "Whazzat?" your toddler now asks such questions as "Why?" and "Where is ____?" According to Ames and Ilg, your child will master more space words (in, out, up, down, in front of, behind, and so on) in the six-month period from two to two and a half than in any other six-month period of her life.

Emotionally/Socially

- Your toddler shows incredible pride in the things she's able to do, and actively seeks your approval. She will implore you a hundred times a day to "Look at me!!!" as she climbs up the stairs to the slide, fills up her bucket with sand, draws a straight line, or rides her trike.
- You might not be able to tell yet, but she's slowly becoming more interested in other kids. You'll realize it for yourself when, out of the blue, she starts making a strange noise or using a word she never had before—the same noise or word used a few days before by that two-year-old at the park, the one your child seemed to be ignoring completely.
- Another way she shows her interest in other kids is by physically exploring them. Unfortunately, this may entail some hitting, pushing, shoving, and hair-pulling. But remember, your child isn't intentionally being mean; she's still learning about the difference between animate and inanimate objects and is fascinated by cause and effect. As Ames and Ilg write, "A child may begin stroking another child's hair because he likes the way it looks, then may pull it to see how it feels."
- Marked by near-instant 180-degree mood swings and arbitrary mind changes, this can be an exceedingly demanding time for you and your child.

What You're Going Through

Taking a Long, Hard Look at . . . Yourself

I always feel proud when someone tells me how much my daughters look like me. And I feel tickled inside when my parents or other relatives tell me how much the girls act like I did as a kid. But I'm a little less enchanted when one of the girls spits out one of my "God damn its" when she can't tie her shoes.

When this kind of thing happens to you (and if it hasn't yet, it will very soon), you may suddenly find yourself imagining your child imitating some of your less savory and less cute behaviors. And you'll be horrified. "The honest and direct response of children to some 'bad habits' forces men to confront these behaviors and consider the consequences, not only for themselves but also for their children," says parenting educator Glen Palm. If, for example, you eat a lot of candy bars and potato chips, you may find yourself questioning the kind of example you're setting and quit.

Palm describes one of his clients, a smoker whose father had died of lung cancer. The man hadn't been able to bring himself to quit until his three-year-old began pretending he was smoking.

"Well then, do what I meant to say, not what I'm alleged to have done."

Emotional Changes

One of the most commonly heard complaints about men is that we are out of touch with our emotions or that we suppress them. A few years ago I think I might have agreed with this contention. But since becoming a father, I strongly disagree. Fathers—especially those who are actively involved with their children—feel tremendous joy, anger, affection, fear, and anxiety. The problem is that men in our society don't have places where they can safely express their feelings. "Society expects them to be the strong ones," say Phil and Carolyn Cowan. "And they worry that talking about their doubts and fears would only upset their wives."

As a result, men learn to regulate their emotions. But please remember: regulating is not the same as suppressing. "The ability to control one's own impulses in the service of caring for one's children and emotionally supporting one's spouse would seem to be an important marker of maturity," write the Cowans. Nevertheless, don't forget that *you* provide a crucial model for how your child learns to express his own emotions—fear, anger, disappointment, sadness, happiness, and excitement.

Besides regulating their emotions, fathers undergo a variety of other changes in the way they experience and react to the world around them:

- **Empathy.** "The desire for emotional intimacy with their children and the obvious responsibility of men to understand their children motivate them to think about their child's feelings," says Glen Palm. Learning to see the world from another person's perspective (in this case, your child's), is what empathy is all about.
- **Expressiveness.** "Parents learn to assist their child in expressing and understanding emotions," say Barbara and Philip Newman. And they frequently "develop strategies for helping children manage their fears and doubts." Seeing how emotionally expressive children can be often allows men to accept and express their own feelings more readily. "As fathers teach their children how to say 'I love you' or 'I'm sad because that hurt my feelings,' the fathers too learn to be more honest and open with their own emotions," adds Palm.
- **Selflessness.** Another major marker of maturity is the ability to take pleasure in doing something for someone else—without any hope of repayment.
- **Sensitivity.** Try to equate your child's bruised and unhappy feelings with physical bruises. This is exactly the approach taken by one father interviewed by parent-child communication experts Adele Faber and Elaine Mazlish. "Somehow the image of a cut or laceration helped him realize that his son required as prompt and serious attention for his hurt feelings as he would for a hurt knee," they write.
- **Outrage.** I know that before I was a father, I had seen plenty of parents hit or even abuse their children, and I'm sure it bothered me. But not like it bothers me now (see pages 171–74 for more on this).
- **Expansion.** Before becoming fathers, men are generally limited in the ways they express affection: kissing, hugging, holding hands, and sex. But having children frequently allows men to expand their repertoire, say the Newmans. Kissing, hugging, and holding hands are still appropriate affectionate gestures, but so are tickling, rocking, tumbling, snuggling, and stroking. Overall, fathers in the Cowans' studies reported that "having a child brought them more in touch with their feelings, and helped them learn how to be more comfortable expressing their emotions."
- **Patience.** "Learning patience is a primary goal of fathers—[this includes] controlling feelings of anger, improving the ability to listen, and coping with some of the tediousness of everyday parenting," says Palm.

You and Your Baby

More Computer Stuff: Getting Ready

Before you let your child sit down at the computer, there are a few things you should do to prepare for the big event.

- Don't allow anyone (even you) to bring food anywhere near the computer. Don't even do it when you're alone—you'll leave a dish next to the keyboard one night, and your child will remind you about it every day for the next six months.
- Get a plastic keyboard protector. Even if you do follow the no-food rule, a plastic protector also acts as a handy anti-slobber device.
- No fighting, kicking, running, or roughhousing near the computer. One good smack could destroy a lot of valuable stuff.
- If you are planning to share a computer with your child, you'll want to back up everything on your system first. Once you've done that, be sure to keep your personal files in an area of the computer your child won't be able to access. If you think you might be raising a future hacker, password-protect

"And always remember I'm here for you, son, at Dadman@connect.pop.net."

Picking Software

Basically, what you're looking for in a software package for your child are the following factors:

- ease of use (by the child)
- ease of installation (by you)
- age appropriateness
- ability to challenge the child
- degree to which the program is childproof
- the program's ability to educate
- the program's ability to entertain
- flexibility (can be used for kids of varying ages)

As you might expect, the ad copy on any box of software will tell you that besides satisfying all the above criteria, the program will also make you rich and your child smarter and more beautiful.

You could buy the program and test it out, but it's nearly impossible to return software these days. And unless you're a specialist in early childhood education, you probably won't be able to make a very informed decision about the program's appropriateness.

Fortunately, there are several reliable organizations that thoroughly test and evaluate children's software:

Children's Software Review, for ages 3–14, 6 issues for $24.00 / (313) 480-0040

High/Scope Buyer's Guide, ages 3–8, $19.95 plus shipping and handling / (313) 485-2000

your adult applications. The last thing you want is for your baby to start playing around with your tax returns.

- Put colored stickers on some of the more commonly used keys: Enter, Backspace, the letters of your child's first name, cursor keys. Use the stickers as a temporary crutch to help your child remember where they are. Do not start saying, "Push the red key"—your child's next computer probably won't have stickers on the keyboard.

A NOTE ABOUT HARDWARE

If you think you can get away with putting a child of the '90s in front of your old Apple II or your 8086, think again. Your child may actually need a newer system than *you* do, one that uses the most advanced graphics, sound, and animation capabilities. So if you have an old clunker lying around, donate it to your favorite charity and get a tax deduction while you still can.

ALL ABOUT SOFTWARE

All your hardware precautions and preparations will be entirely wasted if the software you're running is worthless.

According to researchers Susan Haugland and Daniel Shade, there are two basic types of software: nondevelopmental (also called "drill-and-practice"), which, according to Shade, is the "computer equivalent of flashcards and is not good for preschoolers"; and developmental (open-ended), which provides children with "the opportunity to explore an environment, make choices, and then find out the impact of these decisions."

Haugland recently tested four groups of children: the first used nondevelopmental software; the second used developmental; the third also used developmental, but supplemented it with additional activities; and the fourth group used no computers at all.

After eight months, the kids in the three computer groups all showed huge gains in self-esteem over the kids in the fourth group. Children who used the drill-and-practice software experienced an amazing 50-percent drop-off in their creativity—a drop not experienced either by the kids who used open-ended software or by those who had no computer exposure. "Clearly," write Haugland and Shade, nondevelopmental software may have a detrimental effect on children's creativity."

Kids who worked with the developmental (open-ended) software had "significant gains on measures of intelligence, nonverbal skills, structural knowledge, long-term memory, and complex manual dexterity."

Talk, Talk, Talk . . .

"The amount of live language directed to a child was perhaps the strongest single indicator of later intellectual and linguistic and social achievement," say Newman and Newman. Here's how to maximize the effect of what you say:

- **Explain.** Label everything you can, talk about what you're doing ("I'm taking your dirty diaper off, I'm wiping your butt, I'm putting a clean diaper on you") and where you're going.
- **Expand.** If your child says, "Truck drive," you say, "Yes, the truck is driving by." Or if he says, "Juice gone," say "That's right, the juice is gone because you spilled it on the floor."
- **Prompt.** When your child points to something he clearly doesn't know the

word for, tell him what it is. If he tries to pronounce something but makes a "mistake" ("baba" for bottle), say something like, "Yes, you're right. That *is* a bottle."

- **Don't make corrections.** Instead of correcting grammar or pronunciation mistakes, repeat the word or idea in a new, grammatically correct sentence.
- **Watch for some interesting word associations.** A friend once told me that whenever she recited "Wee Willie Winkie" to her son, she'd make a knocking gesture in the air during the "rapping at the windows" part. One day she was talking to the baby about wrapping birthday presents and she was surprised when the baby smiled and made the very same knocking gesture (Get it? rap/wrap).

LISTENING SO YOUR CHILD WILL TALK

Generally speaking, there's not really a lot of sense in talking if no one's listening. And the only way your child will ever learn how to be a good listener is if you show him the way. Here's how to do it:

- **Pay attention.** When your child wants to talk, face him and look him in the eye. Turn off the TV or radio, don't answer the phone, and disregard any other distractions. You may not even need to speak; sometimes all your child wants is for you to look at him. "One of the most important skills good listeners have is the ability to put themselves in the shoes of others or empathize with the speaker by attempting to understand his or her thoughts and feelings," writes Lilian Katz, director of ERIC, the Clearinghouse on Elementary and Early Childhood Education.
- **Allow your child to have her feelings.** Don't tell a kid who says she's sleepy (or hungry or sick or sad or angry) that she's not.
- **Keep things moving.** Asking questions whose answer is yes or no is the quickest way to end a conversation. Instead, pick up on something your child said and ask a question that restates or uses some of the same words your child used. "When you use children's own phrasing or terms, you strengthen their confidence in their conversational and verbal skills and reassure them that their ideas are being listened to and valued," says Katz.
- **Don't interrupt.** If you're having a discussion with your child, listen respectfully to his ideas—from beginning to end—before jumping in. You want him to afford you the same courtesy, don't you?
- **Be patient.** No matter how verbal he may be, your toddler still has a limited vocabulary and there may be occasional delays between what he's thinking and what actually comes out of his mouth. Let him struggle for a few seconds before you start filling in the missing words.

- **Get your child involved.** Asking your child for his vote about the dinner menu or weekend plans (and taking his advice once in a while), or asking for his opinion of a movie you saw together or on how to rearrange the furniture shows him you respect him and that what he says is important.
- **Acknowledge your child's feelings.** According to Faber and Mazlish, short, simple phrases like "Oh, I see," and "Hmmm," are much better for stimulating your child to talk than jumping in with advice.
- **Give your child's feelings a name.** If your child tells you he wants to smash a friend's face in, telling him, "I can see that you're really angry" is far better than telling him that he shouldn't talk that way about his friends. "Parents don't usually give this kind of response," say Faber and Mazlish, "because they fear that by giving a name to the feeling, they'll make it worse. Just the opposite is true. The child who hears the words for what he is experiencing is deeply comforted. Someone has acknowledged his inner experience." Lilian Katz adds, "Restating or rephrasing what children have said is useful when they are experiencing powerful emotions that they may not be fully aware of. . . . Your wider vocabulary can help children express themselves as accurately and clearly as possible and give them a deeper understanding of words and inner thoughts." But watch out: children usually hate it when you repeat their exact words back to them ("Daddy, I hate Bobby!" "It sounds like you really hate Bobby." Duh.)
- **Help them fantasize.** Rather than give a logical, rational response to your child's irrational request ("No, we can't go to Grandma and Grandpa's house for dinner—they live in Paris and it's too far to go right now."), jump in and fantasize ("I wish I could just snap my fingers and take us there right away.").
- **Watch for nonverbal cues.** Your child's mood, tone of voice, and energy level may tell you more about what he's feeling than what he actually says. Encourage your child to talk about his feelings.
- **Don't ask why.** Kids don't always know why they feel a particular way (do you?). "It's easier to talk to a grown-up who accepts what you're feeling," say Faber and Mazlish, "rather than one who presses you for explanations."

TALKING SO YOUR CHILD WILL PAY ATTENTION TO YOU

Once you and your child are able to communicate with each other verbally, you'll find that a lot of what you say to him is, in one form or another, an attempt to gain his cooperation. Here's how to improve the chances that your child will (a) hear what you say, and (b) respond the way you want him to:

- **Describe what you see, not what you think.** Instead of "You always take off your socks in the living room and dump sand on the rug. Do you have any idea how long it takes me to clean up after you every day?" try something like, "There's sand on the rug."

- **Give information.** Instead of "What on earth is the matter with you? I've told you seven hundred times to stop jumping on that couch!" try "Couches are not for jumping on."
- **Say it with a word.** Instead of "I've been telling you for the past hour and a half to put your crayons away, get your clothes off and get ready for bed," you'll probably have better luck with, "Pajamas!" This approach, by the way, works equally well with teenagers, who also don't like long-winded sermons.
- **Talk about *your* feelings.** Rather than criticize the child in a personal way ("You're really annoying me with your constant shouting and screaming, you're such a pain . . ."), keep the focus on you ("I get frustrated when you yell at me like that. I do much better when people speak to me in a nice way.").
- **Make specific—not general—requests.** "I want you to help me put your cars back in the box" is much better than "Clean up your stuff."
- **Be consistent.** Don't mumble "No" a few times and then forget about it. That only encourages your child to ignore you.
- **Give choices.** "Do you want an apple or an orange?" is far more likely to get a response than "What do you want to eat?" Offering choices in this way is just about guaranteed to reduce the number of adult-toddler power struggles.
- **Don't ask questions if you don't want answers.** "Can you help clean up your room, please?" only gives the child the (incorrect) impression that he has a choice.
- **Don't repeat yourself.** If he didn't listen the first six times, why would you think he'd listen the seventh?
- **Don't make idle threats.** Kids often take a threat as a challenge. Will you really carry through? If you don't, you've lost credibility. If you do, you might have to raise the ante every time you want your child to do something.
- **Admit your mistakes.** Your child will learn that it's okay to be wrong once in a while.
- **Keep your promises.** Your child may not have a very developed sense of time, but he'll never forget that trip to the zoo or that candy bar you promised in a weak moment. And if *you* do, you've lost a ton of credibility.
- **Whisper.** Kids hate to miss anything that might have anything to do with them. Speaking softly has been known to stop even the loudest child in his tracks.
- **Do your scolding in private.** Take your child into a separate room—it'll

be less embarrassing for both of you. It will also reduce your child's instinctive need to try to save face by flouting your authority in public.

- **Praise effectively.** Statements like "Great job" can become so automatic that they lose their meaning. Try to be more specific: "Wow! Did you ride your trike all the way around the block?" Besides being more satisfying, this type of praise encourages conversation.
- **Make a big deal out of good behavior.** As we've discussed elsewhere, your child craves your attention—any way he can get it. And if the only time you pay attention to him is when he's misbehaving, he'll misbehave as often as he can, feeling that behaving well is a waste of time since no one seems to notice.

Family Matters

Even More About Nutrition

Just a few months ago you may have been worried that your baby was eating only one food for days at a time. Well, at least he was eating. But now he may seem to be giving up food altogether.

And in a way, that's true. For the first two years of life your baby was storing body fat, and his weight was increasing about 9 percent every month. But now that he doesn't need all that fat, he's slowed way down, gaining only about 1 percent a month.

The good news is that your child isn't starving to death. He may go a day or two without eating much, but then the next few days he'll put away more food

Dealing with Desserts

Nutritionist Susan Kayman suggests putting all the food you'd like your child to eat on the plate at the same time—including dessert. The theory is that when dessert is no longer forbidden (and therefore less desirable), the child won't be any more attracted to a brownie than to a carrot.

But remember: although you're giving your child some control over his food intake, *you* pick the what and when, the child picks the whether and how much. So brownies don't have to be an option at all.

Oh, and by the way. For those of you who remember the four food groups, don't think you can get away with classifying marshmallows in the white group and chocolate in the brown.

than you would have thought possible. During those odd moments when your toddler *does* eat, he'll probably limit himself to only two or three foods.

The solution? Give your toddler some control over what he eats and when, says Jane Hirschman, author of *Solving Your Child's Eating Problems.* As we discussed on pages 47–50, your child's diet will probably balance out over the

Food and Your Child's Temperament

Researcher Jim Cameron has found that your child's eating habits—like just about everything else in his life—are greatly influenced by his temperament:

- The slow-adapting kid may consider your efforts to feed him intrusive and may try to get out of his high chair as if it were a straitjacket. He often rejects new foods, not because they taste bad but because they taste *new.* And old foods prepared in new ways may be rejected on principle.
- The intense kid may seem to exist only on five or six foods. Don't bother introducing a new food when your toddler is really hungry—he's probably tired and not in the mood for new things. His first reaction to new foods will be one of suspicion, so if you really want him to try something new, wait until he's a little hungry and not too tired. The more intense your child, the more problems you'll have trying to get him to stick to a strict eating schedule. The more you insist, the more likely your efforts will result in a tantrum.
- The energetic kid wants to be in complete control of his meals. He may refuse to be fed by anyone but himself, and may not eat if he can't hold the food (or at least the utensil it's supposed to be on). It's impossible even to guess how much he'll eat or when. If he's tired, he won't eat much, but you might get him to try an old favorite. If he's well rested, he'll eat even less (he'll want to run around instead). Have lots of snacks available for quick refueling and don't waste your time trying to get him into a high chair.
- The irregular, slow-to-warm kid may be the toughest of all. You can expect him to sit at the dinner table for a while, but don't expect him actually to eat anything. Instead, he'll want to eat on his own schedule; again, have lots of healthy snacks around for his swings through the kitchen.

The Dream Diet

Just in case you were wondering what an ideal toddler diet would look like, here it is:

- 1 serving of vitamin A foods every day (apricots, cantaloupe, carrots, spinach, yams)
- 1 serving of vitamin C foods every day (oranges, grapefruit, tomatoes)
- 1 serving of high-fiber foods every day (apples, bananas, figs, plums, pears, berries, peas, potatoes, spinach)
- Cruciferous vegetables a few times a week (broccoli, cauliflower, brussels sprouts, cabbage)

The fact is that getting a toddler to eat anything that remotely resembles the ideal diet is going to be a struggle. But here are a few things you can do to improve your chances:

- **Serve only 100 percent juice.** Anything that has the word *drink* in its name is probably more sugar than juice.
- **Limit fast foods.** Lunch meats, hot dogs, and many other processed fast foods contain sodium nitrates, which the American Cancer Society believes may cause cancer in children.
- **Limit candy and other junk food.** Kids between two and three consume about 1,500 calories a day, and a candy bar has about 200 calories—a pretty big chunk of the day's intake.
- **Limit caffeine.** A single can of Coke has the same effect on a toddler as drinking four cups of coffee does on you.
- **Set a good example.** If you stop at a convenience store for a candy bar, brush your teeth and don't leave the wrappers lying around. If your child doesn't smell the chocolate on your breath, he'll certainly recognize the empty packaging and know he's been left out.
- **Take things out of their original packages.** What's often most attractive about certain foods is the box they come in. Transferring cereals and other sugary things into a large jar or plastic container can make them a lot less attractive.

course of a few weeks. More important, says Hirschman, feeding your child on demand (within reason, of course) helps him learn to recognize when he's genuinely hungry (as opposed to being bored, bribed, or craving something just because he can't have it) and when he's full (rather than just going on a binge because he doesn't know when he'll get another chance to eat the food).

Giving your child some control over his own food intake will make him braver and more willing to try new things. He'll also end up eating more. Hirschman's theory—and it's a sound one—is that eventually, if he's not pressured, your child will come around to eating whatever everyone else in the house is eating.

If you're really worried about your child's eating habits, check with your pediatrician. Early signs of malnutrition include uncharacteristic constant crankiness, frequent illness, listless behavior, and little or no weight gain over a long period of time.

MINIMIZING FOOD FIGHTS

- **Relax.** If your child doesn't want to try a new food, leave him alone. And does he really have to eat in a high chair? Just put him someplace where

"Relax. The important thing is that he drinks his milk, not how."

he can't make a huge mess (or at least where his mess will be fairly easy to clean up).

- **Spy.** When your child is at someone else's house—especially one in which there are older kids to imitate—find out what he ate. He may try something at a friend's that he wouldn't touch if you gave it to him.
- **Keep foods far away from each other on the plate.** Kids this age like to keep everything in its own special place (just another way to exercise control), and mixing two foods—even if they're both favorites—could end up causing a tantrum. In a similar vein, kids like to have certain quantities of things and may ask for more milk in their glass even though there's already plenty there.
- **Peel foods with peels (apples, pears, plums).** Some kids are looking for any excuse not to eat something, and a tough-to-chew peel is a perfect pretext.
- **Grow a garden.** Even kids who don't like vegetables may be willing to eat something they planted, watered, and picked.
- **Get the child involved.** Have him set the table, decide on pizza toppings, make shopping decisions.
- **Have fun.** Even liver can look more appetizing if you cut it into the shape of a friendly animal or familiar cartoon character.
- **Encourage snacking.** Your child is burning tons of calories. Make sure he gets plenty to eat throughout the day, and if he wants some apple slices or a piece of cheese between meals, let him.

Giving Yourself a Financial Tune-up

Whether you're rich or poor, when it comes to money there are only three kinds of people:

- Those who spend less than they bring in and save the difference.
- Those who spend exactly what they earn and have nothing left over.
- Those who spend more than they earn and get deeper and deeper in debt.

If you're in the first category, congratulations! According to some studies, less than 20 percent of baby boomers are saving enough for their retirement, and 25 percent of adults ages 35–54 haven't even started saving.

If you're in either of the other two categories (or if you're in the first and want to make your financial situation even better), you're going to have to get under your financial hood and do a little tinkering. It's a simple process, really, with only two steps:

- Reduce your expenses (and your debts)
- Increase your savings

"I'd like to give you more, but I can't.
I'm restrained by an 'allowance cap.'"

REDUCING EXPENSES AND GETTING OUT OF DEBT ON THE WAY

Although starting a savings or investment plan sounds like a lot more fun than going on a financial diet, the truth is that you can't save money until you've got a good handle on your expenses. The first step is to take a hard look at your current spending. It may be a little scary, but trust me, it's important.

Gather together every money-related scrap of paper that's crossed your hands in the past four or five months. Categorize them by type of expense (housing, insurance, medical, food, and so forth). Using several months' worth of expenses will help you average variable expenses, such as gas and clothes, and include irregular expenses, such as auto repairs or major appliance purchases. Be sure to include the money—especially cash—you spend on lunch, dry cleaning, gifts, and the like.

Once you've got this done, go over each of the expense categories to see where you can do some cutting. Here are a few areas in which you can produce almost immediate, and often painless, returns:

- Food. Buy in bulk from Costco or other discount outlets, use coupons, and eat out less.
- Comparison shop. Prices vary widely on everything from refrigerators to long-distance carriers, so check three or four places before you buy anything. And don't forget to check out mail-order prices—they're often cheaper and tax-free (if you and the mail-order company are in different states).
- Buy a home instead of renting one (for more on this see pages 182–87).
- Make a sensible tax plan (for more on this see pages 144–45).
- Car pool. This can help you reduce many auto-related expenses, such as gas and oil, repairs, and insurance rates.
- Auto insurance. If your car is more than five years old, you can probably save some money by getting rid of your collision and comprehensive coverages. Check with your insurance agent.
- Health insurance. If you and your partner are both on employer-paid plans, your employer might be willing to refund some of the money they pay for you if you can prove that you're covered under your partner's plan. If you're self-employed and paying for your own plan, consider increasing your deductible or putting your child(ren) on a separate plan. Sometimes "family" coverage is much more than two separate policies—one for the adults, one for the kids.
- Use savings to pay off your debts. If you have $1,000 invested at 10 percent, you're earning $100 a year, which becomes $72 if you're in the 28 percent tax bracket. If you owe $1,000 on a 20 percent credit card, your interest payment is $200 a year, which, since you're using after-tax dollars, is really $278 if you're in the 28 percent tax bracket. Get the point? In this scenario, taking the money out of savings would save you more than $200 a year. That may not sound like a lot, but it's enough to pay for most of the clothes your child will go through in a year, or a good chunk of your annual health club membership, or a few sessions with your therapist. You'd have to earn roughly 30 percent (before taxes) on your investment to justify not using your savings to pay off your debt. And if some emergency comes up and you really, really need the money again, you can always get a cash advance on your credit card.
- Stop charging. Especially for things that lose their value, such as gas, clothing, cars, furniture, and meals out. If you can't afford to pay cash for these things, maybe you can't afford them at all. Making only the minimum pay-

ment pays off your balance in no less than three years. But if you keep buying stuff, you'll never get clean.

- If you still insist on charging, at least try to pay off your balance in full every month.
- Use a debit card instead. These cards look just like credit cards but take the money directly out of your checking account. Keeping that in mind might just scare you out of using the card altogether.
- Take charge of your credit cards. Get credit cards that charge low interest rates and no annual fees. A few years ago I called my own credit card

When Things Get Really, Really Out Of Control

Of course you want to pay what you owe. Just about everyone does. But sometimes, despite your best intentions, things just get to the point where they're no longer manageable. Fortunately, debtors' prisons went out with the nineteenth century. But that probably won't keep you from feeling helpless, humiliated, infuriated, frustrated, and, often, somehow less than a man. Men are supposed to know how to handle money, after all.

If you've gotten to this point and you're feeling completely overwhelmed by your debts and you're being hounded by creditors and collection agencies, you have three basic options.

- Keep on doing what you've been doing. But since that hasn't worked up to this point, why keep making yourself miserable?
- Get some professional help. A far more sensible approach. The Consumer Credit Counseling Service (CCCS) is a nonprofit group that helps people avoid bankruptcy and restructure their debts. They also have free workshops and seminars on debt management. You can find a local CCCS office at 800-388-2227. You might also want to contact your local chapter of Debtors' Anonymous; check your white pages.
- File for bankruptcy. Truly the option of last resort. Bankruptcy can essentially wipe out all debts from credit cards, auto loans, medical bills, utilities, and a few others. On the downside, though, it'll screw up your credit report for at least seven years. And even after you're done, you'll still owe any debts related to alimony and child support, taxes (in most cases), and student loans. Bankruptcy isn't for everyone. So if you're even considering it, get some sound advice first. *How to File for Bankruptcy* by attorneys Stephen Elias, Albin Renauer, and Robin Leonard is a good place to start.

company (which had been charging me $50 a year and 20 percent interest) and told them I'd take my business elsewhere if they didn't do something about their excessive rates. After working my way through several layers of "supervisors," I now pay no annual fee and about 8 percent interest.

- Take out a consolidation loan. Chances are that your bank or credit union offers loans at lower interest rates than those you're paying now. In many cases the lender may want you to cancel your credit cards (or at least turn the cards over to them). If you own your own home, consider taking out a home equity loan. The interest you pay on these loans may be tax deductible. Either way, you'll be able to pay off your bills faster and at far lower cost.

BOOSTING YOUR SAVINGS

Now that you've done everything you can to cut your expenses, you're ready for the fun stuff.

For most people, the first big question is, How much should I try to save? Well, the answer depends on your goals. Many experts feel that you should shoot for an income at retirement that's about 70 percent of your current income. If you're in your twenties and just starting to save, you'll be able to accomplish this goal if you sock away 4 to 6 percent of your take-home pay. If you're in your thirties, that goes up to 7 to 12 percent, and if you're in your forties, it's 15 percent or more.

"Now, where was I?"
"Return on equity, Pop."

DRIP a Little Savings into This

If you're going the do-it-yourself route and you're thinking about investing in stocks, here's a way to save yourself some real money.

Hundreds of companies now offer current shareholders dividend reinvestment plans (DRIPs) that allow them to buy stock directly from the company without having to pay a broker. Some make this service available to new investors as well. These plans almost always allow investors to reinvest dividends without commission. Many allow for automatic electronic purchases direct from your checking account, and several dozen actually allow DRIP participants to buy stock at a below-market rate. Finally, most plans will also let you sell your stock at rates far under what even a discount broker would charge.

So how can you find out about DRIPs? The hard way is to contact individual companies directly to find out whether they offer such programs. A much easier way is to check out the Direct Stock Purchase Plan Clearinghouse. Their phone number and web address is in the Resources section at the end of this book.

Whatever your situation, the most important thing is to save as much as you can as regularly as you can. Here are some things to keep in mind as you're getting started.

- **Out of sight, out of mind.** This means trying to have money taken out of your paycheck automatically—that way you'll miss it less than if you had to write a check out every month, and you'll be more inclined to do it regularly. Most employers have direct deposit and most financial institutions are more than glad to help you set up regular electronic withdrawals to a savings account of some kind.

The Best Investment

After paying off your credit cards, one of the most important—and safest—investments you can make is in yourself. If you never finished high school or college or grad school, get it done now. Over the course of your life, the increased salary you'll command and your increased self-esteem, confidence, and general level of happiness will more than pay for the cost of the increased education.

Picking a Financial Planner

Since most states don't have laws regulating or accrediting financial planners (who may also call themselves "advisors," "consultants," or "managers"), just about anyone can set up shop to dole out financial advice and sell products.

Most financial planners are paid on a commission basis, meaning that there's always at least the possibility of a conflict of interest. (In other words, whether or not your investments do well, the financial planner is assured his commission.) Commissions typically range from as low as 4 percent on some mutual funds to the entire first year's premium on a cash value life insurance policy. Others are paid on a fee basis and typically charge from $50 to $250 per hour.

This doesn't mean, of course, that fee-based planners are inherently better than their commission-based colleagues (although many experts believe that you'll be happier, and possibly richer, with someone who charges a fee). Your goal is to find someone you like and who you believe will have your best interests at heart. Here are a few things you can do to help you weed out the losers:

- Get references from friends, business associates, and so forth. Alternatively, the Institute of Certified Financial Planners (800) 282-7526 will give you some local references, and the National Association of Personal Financial Advisors (800) 366-2732 makes referrals only of fee-based (as opposed to commission-based) planners.
- Select at least three potential candidates and set up initial consultations (which shouldn't cost you anything). Then conduct tough interviews. Here's what you want to know:

- **Regularity.** Make your savings plan a habit for life. Making investments of the same amount each month is called "dollar cost averaging" and has some great benefits: when prices are up, you're buying a smaller number of shares. When prices are down you're buying more. On average, then, you'll be fine. This strategy also keeps you from falling into the trap of buying high (just to get on the bandwagon) and selling low (when the bottom has fallen out of the market).
- **Avoid temptation.** Don't put your long-term-savings money in any kind of account that has check-writing privileges. Making your money hard to get may increase the chances of your having it for a while.

◊ Educational background. Not to be snobby here, but the more formal the education—especially in financial management—the better. Watch out for fancy initials: many planners prominently display the letters CFP (for Certified Financial Planner) after their names. Forbes magazine recently called the CFP credential "meaningless."

◊ Level of experience. Unless you've got money to burn, let your niece break in her MBA on someone else. Stick to experienced professionals with at least three years in the business.

◊ Profile of the typical client. What you're looking for is a planner who has experience working with people whose income level and family situation are similar to yours.

◊ Compensation. If fee-based, how is the fee calculated? If commission, what are the percentages on each product offered? Any hesitation to show you a commission schedule is a red flag.

◊ Get a sample financial plan. You want to see what you're going to be getting for your money. Be careful, though: fancy graphics, incomprehensible boilerplate language, and expensive leather binders are often used to distract you from the report's lack of substance.

◊ References. How long have customers been with the planner? Are they happy? Better off? Any complaints or weaknesses?

♦ Check your prospective planner's record with state and federal regulators. You can call the federal Securities and Exchange Commission (202) 272-7450 or your state's equivalent to check on disciplinary action and to see whether your candidates have ever been sued.

♦ **Reinvest any interest and dividends.** It's almost like free money, so why take it out? Leaving earnings in the account also helps your balance grow faster.

♦ **Make a good tax plan** (see pages 144–45 for more on this).

♦ **Get an ESOP.** No, it's not a fable, it's an Employee Stock Ownership Plan, and it's offered by more than 10,000 employers across the country. Basically, these plans allow employees to purchase stock in their company without paying commission. Sometimes you can make your purchases with pre-tax dollars, sometimes with after-tax dollars. Some employers let you buy at below-market prices, and some even contribute extra money to your account, which vests (becomes yours) over time, usually five to seven years.

The next big question is, So what do I do with all the money I'm going to be saving? Again, there's no magic formula. Whether you put your money in government bonds or short the pork belly futures market will depend on your individual and family goals and how you feel about risk.

Correctly analyzing these things is a process that's far too complicated to cover here in a way that would be at all helpful. So unless you're already sophisticated financially, get yourself some help. It is, of course, possible to do it yourself, and if you think you want to try, Eric Tyson's *Personal Finance for Dummies* will walk you through the whole process. If you want a more personal touch, you'll need to get yourself a financial planner (see pages 142–43).

A Couple of Things about Tax Planning

Before (or at least at the same time as) you make any real changes to any part of your financial picture, you should be sure to talk to someone knowledgeable about the tax consequences. Your financial planner may be able to offer some help, but a good accountant would be a lot better.

One of the most important things to keep in mind is the changes in tax rates on capital gains (increase in an asset's value). Starting in July 1997, for example, if you've owned an asset (including shares of stock and mutual funds) for more than eighteen months, any capital gains are taxed at 20 percent, down from 28 percent under the old laws. If your taxable income is under $41,200 (for a married couple), your rate may be as low as 10 percent.

So why am I telling you this? Because it may have an effect on the way you invest your money. Because the capital gains tax rate is so much lower than regular income tax rates, you're probably going to want to move your high-yielding assets into something that allows you to defer your income for at least eighteen months (your IRA or other tax-deferred accounts, for example). Keep any lower-earning investments in your taxable accounts (checking or money market, for example). Of course, before you start moving things around, check with your accountant.

Here are a few other critical ways to save on your taxes:

- Immediately start a 401(k) if you're eligible for one through your employer. These plans offer participants a series of great benefits. First, since your contributions are taken out of your paycheck before you pay taxes, you reduce your taxable income. Second, the balance of the account grows tax-free until you start making withdrawals—sometime after age 59½ or so.

Sometimes there's a third benefit: your employer may match at least a portion of your contribution, giving you some free money that will also grow tax-free. Remember, though, that 401(k)s are not savings accounts. If you make withdrawals before age 59½, you'll have to pay at least a 10 percent penalty to the Feds and a smaller percentage penalty to your state. And then you'll get hit with a bill for income tax on the full amount withdrawn. That could eat up 50 percent of what you've saved—not the kind of return you were hoping for.

- Start an IRA. Starting with the 1997 tax year you and your partner (if you're married) can each contribute $2,000 to an IRA—even if one of you doesn't work for pay (this is up from a total of $2,250 for single-earner couples under the old laws). Like a 401(k), your taxable income is reduced by the amount you contribute to your IRA and the earnings grow tax-free until you start withdrawing it.
- If you or your partner is eligible for a company-sponsored retirement plan, you won't be able to deduct your IRA contributions. But make the contributions anyway; the earnings are still tax-deferred.
- Consider selling your house. If you're married and filing jointly, the first $500,000 in gain from the sale of your principal residence is now exempt from tax. If you're not filing jointly, the exemption is only $250,000. Either way, you can do this every two years.

Notes:

30–33 MONTHS

Hey, Who's In Charge Here?

What's Going On with the Baby

Physically

- There's almost nothing your two-and-a-half-year-old can't do on his feet. He can walk short distances on tiptoe, broad jump with both feet, make sudden starts and stops while running, turn sharp corners on the move, and even step over obstacles.
- His arms and hands are coming along nicely too. He can now differentiate between the two sides of his body (in other words, when pointing with one finger, he doesn't extend the same finger on the other hand). He can also draw an X on purpose and can consistently catch a large ball.

Intellectually

- Kids this age are still quite egotistical and have trouble controlling their impulses. Your toddler may have to pull the books out of the bookshelf 275 times before he's able to forgo his own pleasure in favor of parental approval.
- Symmetry, order, and patterns are especially important to your two-and-a-half-year-old. Half an apple (or a cookie with a bite taken out of it) is completely unacceptable. And if you forget to fasten your seatbelt before starting the car, you're likely to get a stern talking to.
- Band-Aids are your child's best friend, so you'd better stock up. Every single bump, scrape, or bruise—whether you can actually see it or not—can be "cured" instantly with a Band-Aid. "It's as if a leak in the container, the

body, is sealed up and his completeness as a personality is reestablished by this magic act," says Selma Fraiberg.

- Although he's just as physically active as before, he seems to be a bit more focused. Instead of doing things and going places for the simple pleasure of doing or going, he now has a specific goal in mind for each action.

Verbally

- Your toddler is not much of a conversationalist. He still initiates most verbal interactions but often doesn't respond when you speak to him.
- When you speak to him, he seems to understand just about everything you say. But he gets extremely frustrated if you don't understand what he's trying to say.
- He's the absolute master of the word *no.* And his negative reactions to you (or refusals to cooperate) are more likely to be verbal than physical.
- He talks, sings, and hums to himself while playing.
- He still hasn't mastered the concept of large chunks of time (yesterday, today, tomorrow), but he can express small pieces and sequences. "I get dressed now, *then* I have my cereal."
- Feeling pretty confident about his budding language skills, your toddler is now starting to play with language (in almost the same way as he plays with objects). He knows what words are "supposed" to sound like and laughs hysterically when you replace a few words of a familiar nursery rhyme with nonsense syllables. Soon he'll begin to imitate these language games and start giving silly-sounding names to objects he doesn't know.

Emotionally/Socially

- He's rebellious, defiant, negativistic, and exasperating; he doesn't know what he wants but he knows that he doesn't want to do most of the things you want him to do. Sound like a teenager? Could be, but it's also a description of the average child between the ages of two and three. Not surprisingly, psychologist Fitzhugh Dodson calls this period "first adolescence."
- He may drive you nuts with his seeming inability to make a decision and stick to it. If you're taking care of him, he'll demand his mother. If she is, he'll demand you. According to Ames and Ilg, the bottom line is that your two-and-a-half-year-old wants "*whatever* person is not available at the moment, and if everyone *is* available, his demand may change to 'Me do it myself.'"
- Being contrary and disobedient is an exhausting job for so young a child, and your toddler is likely to be tired a lot. Unfortunately, tiredness usually makes tantrums worse.

- For most toddlers, this is a fairly aggressive time, and violence is common. Fortunately, most aggressive behavior is still experimental and not intended to cause real harm. Ames and Ilg have found that it's "as if the child wonders what kind of response he will get. Thus, a child may hit, grab at, or push another child, then look closely to see what is going to happen."

What You're Going Through

Power Struggles

Here are perhaps the three most important words you will ever hear as a parent: *choose your battles.* Basically, this means that you should think carefully about whether it really matters that your child wants to wear one blue sock and one orange instead of a matched pair. As your child gets older, she becomes more independent. And the more independent she becomes, the more she tends to resist the limits you set. It's all part of growing up: your child needs to know how serious the rules are and how you'll react when they're violated.

I used to spend huge amounts of time arguing with my younger daughter, trying to get her to put her shoes on before getting in the car. I'd threaten, cajole, plead, and bribe, and gradually I'd wear her down and she'd put them on. But the moment she was strapped in her car seat and I was behind the wheel, she'd yank off her shoes and smirk at me in the rear-view mirror. Finally, I gave up, and we're both a lot happier. And for about six months my older daughter absolutely refused to sleep in her own bed. When my wife and I told her she couldn't sleep in ours, our daughter started sleeping on the floor, on the stairs, in the kitchen—anywhere but in her own bed. We argued with her for a while but eventually decided that since she was getting a good night's sleep, we'd leave her alone. A few days after we stopped complaining, our daughter retreated to her own bed.

A friend who lives in Chicago told me that his son suddenly began refusing to get into the family car unless he was stark naked. My friend and his wife made themselves and their son miserable for a few days before shrugging their shoulders and giving up. The three of them enjoyed several peaceful months, and when winter came their son rather sheepishly asked for some clothes.

Children, writes Ellen Galinsky, "have extremely accurate sensors and can tell when a parent is unsure of a limit and then will muster all of their force to dislodge it." Earlier we discussed the importance of setting firm, consistent limits for your child. But believe me, if you're prepared to go to the mat to enforce compliance with every request you make, you'll spend a lot of unnecessary time butting heads with your child. And you won't have the energy to enforce the rules that really matter, such as Don't go into the street unless you're holding hands with a grown-up.

The Mouth That Roars

In 1977 Art Linkletter wrote a book called *Kids Say the Darndest Things.* And boy, was he right. Every parent has dozens of stories about the shocking, embarrassing, horrifying, and hilarious things their innocent toddlers have said.

Has your child asked you (loudly, of course) whether that African-American woman in front of you is made of chocolate, or whether that obese man has eaten an elephant? He will.

I remember taking both my kids to a matinee a while back. The theater was crowded, so my older daughter had her own seat and the younger one, who had just turned two, sat on my lap. A few minutes into the movie, I felt something wet on my leg and instinctively put my hand on the baby's bottom to feel whether her diaper had leaked. Suddenly, at the top of her lungs, she screamed, "Get your hands out of my pants!" It was one of the more discomfiting (and funny) moments of my life.

"My dad says my mom is a Pagan because she serves burnt offerings for dinner"

Fortunately, not everything your child says will make you want to disappear down the nearest hole. But in many ways the nonembarrassing statements and the ordinary "Why . . ." questions are harder to deal with than the embarrassing ones. They'll make you think about the world in a way you never have before, and jar you into realizing just how little thought most of us give to what's going on around us. How, for example, do you explain homelessness, sickness, natural disasters, and violent crime?

When faced with tough questions, the best thing to do, it seems to me, is turn them into learning experiences (even questions about people made of chocolate can lead to a discussion of what it means to have your feelings hurt).

One of the greatest sources of educational topics is the newspaper (it's got enough pictures to spark the child's interest and is a lot easier to censor than the television). Both my daughters "read" the paper with me in the mornings and ask me to explain the articles that accompany interesting photos. The coverage of Senator Bob Packwood's sexual harassment problems led to fascinating discussions about personal privacy and the times when it's okay or not okay to touch someone else.

Reading the newspaper with a child is also a great reminder of how much basic information adults just take for granted. Try explaining elections, natural disasters, or AIDS to your child and you'll see what I mean.

You and Your Baby

Early Readers

According to reading expert Jim Trelease, studies of children who learned to read early have identified four characteristics of their homes. The first two are fairly obvious and you're probably doing them already: the child is read to on a regular basis, and there is a wide variety of printed materials—books, magazines, newspapers, comics—available in the home at all times.

The remaining factors are somewhat less obvious but may be even easier to implement than the first two.

1. Paper and pencil are available to the child. Most kids get curious about written language by watching their parents write things.
2. People in the home stimulate the child's interest in reading and writing by answering questions, praising the child's efforts at reading and writing, taking the child to the library frequently, buying books, writing down stories that the child dictates, and displaying the child's creations in a prominent place in the home.

"I don't want to see The Lion King *again, I want to read a book."*

HOME LIBRARY UPDATE

Here are the latest additions to your child's ever-growing library:

Blueberries for Sal (and others), Robert McClosky
Bread and Jam for Frances, Russel Hoban
Carl Goes to Daycare (and others), Alexandra Day
The Cat in the Hat, Dr. Seuss
Curious George (and others), H. A. Rey
Frog and Toad Are Friends (and others), Arnold Lobel
The Gingerbread Man, Paul Galdone
Happy Birthday, Moon, Frank Asch
Harry the Dirty Dog (and others), Gene Zion, Margaret B. Graham
Madeline (and others), Ludwig Bemelmans
Mike Mulligan and His Steam Shovel (and others), Virginia Burton
The Snowman, Raymond Briggs
The Snowy Day, Ezra Jack Keats
The Story of Babar, Jean de Brunhoff
The Story of Ferdinand, Leaf Munro
Strega Nona (and others), Tommie de Paola
When I Am Old with You, Angela Johnson
Where the Wild Things Are, Maurice Sendak

To Watch or Not to Watch—Television, That Is

There's one (or two or three or four) in every home, but reading expert Jim Trelease believes that watching television may have a serious negative impact on children. Here's why:

- Television is essentially the opposite of reading. A good book will hold a child's attention. But television—even *Sesame Street*—is sliced up into such tiny, disjointed pieces that it teaches a short attention span.
- TV is a passive, antisocial, or at least solitary experience, especially for young children. Reading, however, which among small kids often happens with another person, usually includes conversation.
- TV deprives the child of the most important learning tool: questions. There's no one to ask and no one to answer.
- Most of the programming aimed at young children requires little or no thinking. Trelease cites a recent study in which a group of three- to five-year-olds were shown a "Scooby Doo" cartoon whose soundtrack had been replaced by one from a "Fangface" cartoon. Only 12.5 percent of the kids realized that the soundtrack didn't match the video.
- TV discourages thinking. It's nearly impossible to show a character thinking through a problem on TV, and commercials tend to give the message that there is no problem that can't be solved by artificial means—by buying something.
- TV discourages creative play.
- The messages kids get from TV are flawed. Most fathers are portrayed as

CONCEPTS

How Many Snails, Paul Giganti
If You Look Around You, Testa Fulvio
Numbers (and others), John J. Reiss
Trucks You Can Count On, Doug Magee

FOLK TALES

Goldilocks and the Three Bears, Jan Brett
Jack and the Beanstalk, Joseph Jacobs
Stone Soup, Marcia Brown
Teeny Tiny, Jill Bennett
The Three Billygoats Gruff, Marcia Brown

clueless, incompetent boobs, and beer commercials send a message that the way to be popular is to drink.

In addition, some researchers have speculated that there may be a link between television watching and obesity—probably because kids have a tendency to snack in front of the tube and not exercise.

There are, of course, exceptions to the above-mentioned drawbacks, and you're probably not planning to toss your television out the window anytime soon. So if you are going to let your child watch, at least try to keep the following guidelines in mind:

- **Preview and monitor quality.** Watch the things your kid wants to watch and assess whether you think it's good. There actually are some good-quality programs on the air (PBS's *Reading Rainbow* and *Mister Rogers' Neighborhood* are both excellent).
- **Watch together.** Little kids can't always tell the difference between reality and what's happening on the screen and may become frightened or confused. So use whatever you're watching as the topic for a discussion.
- **Set some basic rules.** For example, no watching during meals or in the middle of a family time. And don't just leave the TV on as background noise; turn it off when your show is done.
- **Don't use the television (or VCR) as a baby-sitter.** From experience I can tell you that this is an incredibly easy trap to fall into, and one your child may not be in any hurry to get out of.

POETRY

All Small, David McCord
Blackberry Ink, Eve Merrian
I'll Be You and You Be Me, Ruth Krauss
Where the Sidewalk Ends, Shel Silverstein

GOING TO SCHOOL/DAY CARE

Molly, Ruth Shaw Radlauer
School, Emily McCully

ESPECIALLY FOR OLDER SIBLINGS

Babies!, Dorothy Hinshaw Patent

A Baby for Max, Christopher G. Knight (photographer)
Baby's Catalog, Janet Ahlberg, Allan Ahlberg
Julius, the Baby of the World, Kevin Henkes
Let Me Tell You about My Baby, Roslyn Banish
The New Baby, Fred Rogers
Peter's Chair, Ezra Jack Keats
Shadow's Baby, Margery Cuyler
The Very Worst Monster, Pat Huchins
When You Were a Baby, Ann Jonas

Play: Getting Physical

One of the biggest myths about play is that extremely active play, especially roughhousing, teaches kids to be violent. The evidence, however, supports the exact opposite conclusion:

- Physical play is a model for socially acceptable assertion but not necessarily aggression, according to John Snarey, who has spent several decades studying fathers' impact on their children. "Children who roughhouse with their fathers, for instance, usually quickly learn that biting, kicking, and other forms of physical violence are not acceptable."
- "Paternal engagement and physical play as well as maternal verbal interchange are generally positively associated with desirable attributes such as helpfulness, leadership, involvement, and clear communication skills," writes psychologist Ross Parke, "and negatively associated with undesirable attributes such as being apprehensive, being unable to get along with others, and an unwillingness to share."
- Physical play builds children's—especially girls'— confidence, assertiveness, and academic achievement. Several studies of successful women have shown that almost all of them had fathers who engaged in a lot of physical play with them.
- As we've discussed before, fathers and mothers have a strong tendency to play differently with their boys and girls. And this serves to reinforce children's "socially acceptable" (that is, stereotyped) sex-typed behavior, especially for boys. So if you're interested in reducing the chances that your child will end up trapped in a set of gender-based behaviors, play with him or her actively and frequently.
- Parke and his colleagues have also found that for girls, high levels of physical play are associated with such desirable social attributes as positive emotional expressiveness and clarity of communication as well as originality, novelty, and creativity.

A Special Note to Fathers of Girls

Somewhere along the line, people got the idea that girls are delicate and that they shouldn't be played with as roughly as boys.

Well, according to fitness expert Bonnie Prudden, girls are actually hardier than boys. Although more boys are conceived, more girls are born. They survive childhood illness better than boys and ultimately live an average of seven years longer. And in tests of general fitness, girls outperform boys every time.

The moral of the story? Treat your daughter like you'd treat your son (if you had one). She won't break. And, as the evidence I've cited in this chapter proves, she'll benefit enormously.

"Thanks dad, but I play catch on Monday, Wednesday, and Friday. Tuesday is my day to swing."

Sounds like throwing your kids around just about guarantees that they'll grow up confident, strong, and smart, doesn't it? Well, lots of physical play may increase the chances, but it's important not to force your children to play with you if they don't want to; it can do more harm than good. Research consistently shows that children whose fathers are overly "directive" (meaning they give too many commands) suffer: "Paternal directiveness . . . is associated with negative social attributes, such as being socially withdrawn, seldom being sought out by other children, being hesitant with other children, and being a spectator in social activities," says Parke.

Other Kinds of Fun

LARGE MOTOR SKILLS

- Taking a walk on a balance beam, along the curb, or even down a line on the sidewalk.
- Jumping over things (anything more than a few inches, though, will be too high for most kids this age).
- Throwing, kicking, rolling, and tossing balls of all sizes.
- Riding a trike.
- Spinning around 'til you drop.
- Pounding, pushing, pulling, and kicking.

SMALL MOTOR SKILLS

- Puzzles (fewer than twenty pieces is probably best).
- Clay or other molding substance.
- Finger paints.
- String and large beads.

THE BRAIN

- Matching games.
- Alphabet and number games (put colorful magnetic letters and numbers on the fridge and leave them low enough for the child to reach).
- Lots of dress-up clothes.
- Dolls of all kinds (including action figures).
- "Real" things (phones, computer keyboards).
- Sorting games (put all the pennies, or all the triangles, or all the cups together).
- Arranging games (big, bigger, biggest).
- Pattern games (small-big/small-big).
- Counting games (how many pencils are there?).

A FEW FUN THINGS FOR RAINY DAYS

- Pillow fights.
- A really, really messy art project.
- Cook something—kneading bread or pizza dough is especially good, as is roasting marshmallows on the stove (see pages 159–65 for more).
- Baby bowling (gentle tossing of the baby onto your bed).

- Other gymnastics (airplane rides: you're on your back, feet up in the air, baby's tummy on your feet, you and baby holding hands).
- Dancing to music.
- Hide and seek.
- A puppet show.

It's All in Their Heads

In the movie *Harvey*, Jimmy Stewart (in the lead role) had an imaginary friend (all right, a six-foot rabbit), and there's little doubt in our minds that he is more than just a bit nuts. But if your child has an imaginary playmate, there's nothing to worry about. In fact, as many as 65 percent of toddlers have imaginary friends.

According to Newman and Newman, imaginary companions serve several very important functions for toddlers:

- They take the place of other children when there are none around.
- They serve as a companion for pretend play.
- They serve as a confidant for children's private expression.

The existence of an imaginary companion may also help the child in his continuing struggle to draw a clear distinction between right and wrong. "Sometimes toddlers do things they know are wrong because they cannot stop themselves, and they find it difficult to accept responsibility for their misdeeds," writes Bruno Bettelheim. "They did not wish to be bad; they do not want to displease their parents; and the imaginary friend becomes a convenient scapegoat. Toddlers report that although they tried very hard to stop their friend, it went right ahead and did the 'bad' thing anyway. When children use an excuse of this kind, they are communicating that they understand the difference between right and wrong but are unwilling or unable to assume total responsibility for their misconduct."

While you should make every effort to go along with your child's claims about the existence of her imaginary buddy, don't let her imagination get the best of you:

- Don't let your child use the imaginary playmate to avoid dealing with the consequences of her actions.
- Don't use the imaginary companion to manipulate the real child (Maria cleaned up her room, so why don't you start cleaning yours?).
- Don't let the imaginary friend be your child's only friend.

- If it's not too cold, go outside, strip down to your underwear, and paint each other top-to-bottom with nontoxic, water-based paints.
- Otherwise, get bundled up and go for a long, wet, sloppy, muddy stomp in the rain.
- Get in the car and drive through puddles.

Group Activities

If you haven't already done so, it's a good idea to start getting your child involved in some regular group activities. Actually, it's a good idea for both of you: it'll give your child an opportunity to meet some new people and to practice her budding social skills. And while she's playing, you'll have a great opportunity to spend time with some adults who probably have many of the same questions and concerns you do.

If you're thinking about forming a regular play group, here are some things to consider:

- Find a place where you can easily keep an eye on the kids while you're talking to the grown-ups. A fenced park with benches can be great.
- Don't let the group get too large. Even if each adult keeps track of his or her own kids, any more than five or six is pushing it. And try to keep an even number so the little ones can pair off without excluding anyone.
- Meet regularly. As you well know, kids love routines.
- Bring some of your own toys. This should help reduce the amount of grabbing, shoving, and tears.
- Bring some food. Your child will probably prefer to eat someone else's, but some other kid will eat what you bring.
- Don't hover. Let the kids do what they want, as long as it's safe.
- Play with the other kids—but not too much. If the other little ones seem to be having too much fun with you, your child may get very jealous. Kids this age aren't too thrilled about sharing their daddies.
- Don't push togetherness. Kids may not want to play with each other all the time. They need plenty of time to play alone, too.
- Have a backup plan in case you get rained out of your regular place. Places like Chuck E. Cheese and Discovery Zone are hot foul-weather destinations. If your backup meeting place is your house, be prepared for a bit more friction than usual. Having to share his house *and* his toys may be more than your child bargained for.
- Keep your sick kid at home. Although chances are that whatever he's got has already been passed around, the other parents will be nervous anyway.

Music

During the last half of your child's third year, her language skills make a sudden, often dramatic spurt forward. You'll see this development in two distinct yet connected ways:

First, you'll notice that her imitation skills have become quite sharp: she can now repeat nearly any word or two-word phrase. She can also now tell when she's imitating something correctly and when she's not. Second, now that she's got a good grasp of the sounds that make up her native language, she'll begin using them as toys, amusing herself, and you, by making up her own "words." Musically, a similar development is taking place. "Once they've acquired a simple vocabulary of tonal patterns and rhythms, they can start creating their own songs," says music educator Edwin Gordon.

After a while she'll combine all these skills, and by her third birthday she may be able to sing all the words of a short song ("Happy Birthday to you . . .") or entire phrases of longer, familiar songs ("Baa, baa, black sheep, have you any wool? Yes, sir. Yes, sir. Three bags full," for example; she won't be able to sing the whole song for another few months). She may also make deliberate changes to songs she already knows ("Baa, baa, *blue* sheep . . .")—just for the fun of it.

Your child's sense of rhythm has also been developing nicely. Notice that now when she moves in response to the music she hears she's moving in time with the music (as opposed to making the seemingly random movements you saw just a few months ago).

This is a great time to try various imitation games with your child. Sing a note, then wait for her to repeat it. If she does that pretty well, try two notes, then three (a lot of kids can't do three-note patterns until well after they turn three, so don't get your hopes up too high). Also try tapping out various rhythms and asking your child to repeat them.

Cooking with Kids

Although it seems like a lot of trouble, cooking with your toddler can be a wonderful experience for both of you. Your child, of course, gets to make a huge mess for you to clean up. But besides that, here are a few things that Mollie Katzen, cookbook writer extraordinaire, says that kids get out of cooking:

- Confidence, self-esteem, and a feeling of accomplishment.
- Early math skills—measuring, counting, time sequences.
- Small motor skills.
- A greater understanding of cause and effect.
- An appreciation of the importance of following directions.
- Practice working as a team.

"I wouldn't go into the kitchen. It's become an area of unrest."

You, of course, benefit in very different ways. First of all, you get to use your time more efficiently—having fun *and* cooking dinner (or part of it) for the whole family simultaneously. It's not unlike taking a college course that satisfies a science requirement and a humanities requirement at the same time. Second, there's a good chance that your child will eat some of the food she makes, thereby expanding her food repertoire beyond plain pasta and white rice with soy sauce.

No matter what you're making, your child can participate in at least some part of the preparation. How long your child will actually stay in the kitchen with you usually depends on how much of a mess you'll let her make and whether or not what she's making is worth licking off a spoon. If you're willing to cooperate, just about any three-year-old can:

- Stir (my kids love this).
- Tear up leaves for salad (they hate salad but they love destroying things, so this works out nicely).
- Kneading and rolling out dough (my kids' absolute favorite kitchen activity).
- Break eggs (actually, this may be their favorite).

- Measure ingredients and dump them into bowls (if this isn't the favorite, it's certainly a close second, or third).
- Sprinkle toppings (Hmmm . . . that's a lot of favorites).

Here are some fun, simple, quick recipes that you and your child can make together. In fact, she can probably handle most of the tasks by herself if you let her. But a few things before you get started:

- Read the "Cooking Safety" section on page 163 very carefully.
- Don't force. If she doesn't want to do a particular step, let her alone.
- Have fun. Yes, she'll get flour all over the floor (and the walls and her clothes). And yes, she'll get broken eggshells into the batter. If you're not in the mood to deal with these things, save your cooking adventure for another day.

FRENCH TOAST

What you'll need:

4 eggs
1 cup milk
1 teaspoon vanilla extract (optional)
Pinch of cinnamon
6 to 8 slices of bread (Stale is fine; moldy is not. If you want to make this even more fun, cut the bread into animal shapes, cars, or faces before you start.)
1 tablespoon butter
Syrup, jam, sour cream, or any other kind of topping

1. Combine eggs, milk, vanilla, and cinnamon in a bowl.
2. Stir (or whisk, if you have one) until mixed thoroughly.
3. Pour the mixture into a pie pan or any bowl or dish that's large enough to hold a slice of bread.
4. Drop a slice of bread in the mixture, let it sit for a few seconds, flip it over, and do the same on the other side.
5. Heat a skillet and add some of the butter.
6. When the butter melts, spread it around and add a slice or two of the batter-soaked bread (as many as can fit on the surface of the skillet without overlapping).
7. Cook until light brown on the bottom. Be careful about this—most kids will refuse to eat anything that's anywhere close to being burned.

8. Flip over and cook until light brown on the other side (or somewhat less, if you happened to have overcooked the first side). Repeat until all slices are cooked.
9. Serve with your kids' favorite topping.

QUESADILLAS

What you'll need:

Cooking spray or 1 tablespoon butter or margarine
Two 6-inch tortillas (Wheat are usually softer, but if your child is allergic to wheat, corn is fine.)
Nice-sized handful of your child's favorite cheese, grated
Several tablespoons of refried beans (optional)
Several tablespoons of steamed rice
Several tablespoons of cooked fresh or frozen vegetables (optional)

1. Put the cooking spray, butter, or margarine in a skillet and place over medium heat.
2. Drop a single tortilla on the skillet and sprinkle some of the grated cheese all over it.
3. If you think your child will eat them, add the refried beans, rice, and/or vegetables.
4. Cover the first tortilla with a second one.
5. Cook for 30 to 45 seconds or until the cheese has melted enough to keep the two tortillas stuck together.
6. Flip over and cook for another 30 to 45 seconds. If you can flip the tortilla sandwich in the skillet, your child and all her friends will consider you the absolute coolest guy in the neighborhood. If you can't, practice.

MILKSHAKES

What you'll need:

1 cup milk
Large piece of your child's favorite fruit
Several ice cubes
1 to 2 drops vanilla extract (optional)
1 to 2 teaspoons chocolate syrup (optional)

1. Put all the ingredients in a blender.
2. Cover and blend until smooth.

Cooking Safety

Cooking with kids can be a huge amount of fun. But because it involves dealing with knives and flames, there's also the potential for getting hurt. Following these safety rules should help you get through the process with a minimum of bloodshed.

- Wash your hands before you start. No explanation necessary, right?
- Work at your child's level—either at the kitchen table or, better yet, at your child's very own table. This reduces the chances that she'll slip off the stool she's been standing on or that she'll pull a heavy bowl off the counter and onto her head.
- Keep pot and pan handles pointed toward the back of the stove. Again, this reduces the chances that hot things will get pulled off the stovetop.
- Remind your child about being careful about hot things. Electric stove coils stay hot even after they're turned off and so do pots and pans. Repeat the reminder every ten minutes, as necessary.
- Opening ovens, closing them, putting things into them, and taking things out are adult-only jobs. Don't even think about letting a three-year-old try any of these jobs.
- Dress appropriately. Long sleeves can get dragged through batter or yanked into blenders. Short sleeves are better. Topless is better still, and the most fun.

PRETZELS

What you'll need:

1 package yeast

1½ cups warm water

1 tablespoon sugar

1 tablespoon salt

4 cups flour

1 egg, beaten

1. Preheat the oven to 425°F.
2. Mix the yeast, water, sugar, and salt until everything is completely dissolved.
3. Stir in the flour.
4. Knead into a soft dough.
5. Roll into long ropes about the thickness of your finger.

6. Shape into pretzel shapes, numbers, letters, or anything your child feels like making.
7. Brush the beaten egg on the shaped dough.
8. Bake for 12 to 15 minutes.
9. Take out and let cool before eating.

POPCORN BALLS

What you'll need:

10 to 12 cups popped popcorn
1 cup corn syrup, OR 1 10-ounce package of marshmallows
¼ cup butter or margarine (only if you use the marshmallows instead of the syrup)
1 or 2 packages of gelatin, any flavor(s) you like

1. Half-fill several large bowls with the popcorn.
2. Put the corn syrup, or the marshmallows and margarine, in a pan and melt over low heat.
3. Add the gelatin. Stir until it's completely dissolved.
4. Remove the mixture from the heat and pour it over the popcorn. Stir quickly so that the popcorn gets covered evenly.
5. Shape the popcorn into baseball-sized balls.
6. Place the balls on a sheet of waxed paper and refrigerate until firm.

EVE'S CHOCOLATE LEAVES

What you'll need:

16-ounce package chocolate chips
New ¼-inch paintbrush
Cookie sheet covered with waxed paper
Some thick leaves with stems, gently washed and completely dry. (Check with your local garden shop to make absolutely sure they're not toxic; camellia and magnolia leaves are pretty widely available and are fine.)

1. Melt the chocolate chips over low to medium heat or in the top of a double boiler.
2. Paint the surface of the leaves with a thick coat of the melted chocolate.
3. Put the painted leaves on the waxed paper–covered cookie sheet.
4. When you've painted as many leaves as your child thinks is fun, put the cookie sheet into the refrigerator until the chocolate has hardened.

5. Hold the leaf chocolate-side down, and with your other hand *gently* pull up the stem and carefully remove the leaf from the chocolate.
6. Show your child the way the stem and vein pattern of the real leaf has been replicated in the chocolate.

Family Matters

Preparing the Older Sibling

BEFORE THE BIRTH

- Don't start too early. Wait until the child asks some questions about his mother's physical changes, about why you're moving furniture around, and so forth.
- Don't make too big a deal about how great it's going to be to become a big brother and don't try to force him to get excited about the prospect.
- Take the older child to the prenatal doctor visits. If he's interested, have him hold the Doppler to hear the baby's heartbeat; take him to see the ultrasound pictures. If he's not interested, leave him alone.
- Some hospitals offer older-sibling prep classes. In them kids learn: the basics of what their mothers are going to go through during the birth; the kinds of things they can and can't do with their new sibling; and that Dad and Mom still love them very much, even though they aren't going to be the center of the universe anymore.
- Expose him to other babies you know. If you don't know any, the nursery at the hospital should have plenty of extras. (Although with many hospitals tightening nursery security, it may be harder to visit babies that aren't your own.)
- If you're moving the older child out of a crib, moving to a new house, or making any other major changes, do it long before the baby arrives. Otherwise, the older child will think he's being moved out to make room for the new baby.

AFTER THE BIRTH

Handling your older children's reactions to their new baby brother or sister requires an extra touch of gentleness and sensitivity. Although kids are usually wildly excited (initially, at least) at their new status as big brother or big sister, when it hits them that the baby is going to be a permanent visitor, things change. Psychologist Henry Biller found that most kids show some negative reactions, "often involving an increase in disobedience, demandingness and other forms of regressive behavior."

For example, older children who are already toilet trained may start wetting themselves again (my older daughter did this). They may become clingy, start using "baby talk," or have crying jags for no reason at all. It's as if your older child is saying, "If all you wanted was a crying baby, why didn't you say so? I can cry."

These behavioral changes are perfectly normal and are really the result of the older child's feeling that the baby has stolen something that was exclusively hers: your love and affection.

Interestingly, Biller also found that "children who had a highly positive relationship with their father were much less likely to have severe and continuing adjustment problems after the birth of a new sibling."

Here are a few things you can do to ease the transition for your older kid:

- As soon as the new baby is born, call the older child and tell her first. Let *her* make the announcement that she is a big sister to the other members of the family.
- Have the older child come to the hospital right away (even if it's past her bedtime). Take a few pictures of her holding the baby.
- Don't expect your older child to love the baby instantly. It can take a long, long time. Really. A friend of mine told me that for years, every time he drove by the hospital the baby had been born in, his oldest son would ask, "So can we take her back yet?"
- Don't make a big fuss about the new baby in front of the older child—it will only make the older one feel left out, jealous, and resentful, advises pediatrician Barton White. It could also result in the older child's trying to hurt the baby. Have everyone who comes to visit the baby spend a few private minutes with the older child first.
- Don't blame yourself. Friction between your older and younger kids is normal. Saying, "If only I'd done . . . he'd love the baby" is a waste of time.
- Get some special gifts for the older child.
- Go through your photo albums, reminding the older child of what a wonderful baby she was.
- Encourage the older child to get involved. Let her help as much as possible with "her" baby—holding, feeding, diapering, clothing, singing or talking, and running errands around the house. And be sure to be extra appreciative.
- Teach the older child how to play with the baby. It might be fun to show the older child how to elicit reflex actions from the baby (see *TNF I*, pages 38–39).

But never leave the baby alone with your older child, not even for a second (unless, of course, your older one is over twelve). Your primary consideration is, of course, to keep the new baby alive and uninjured. And you'll need to remind the older child (dozens of times) that hurting the baby is simply not allowed. And make it clear that doing so will result in not being allowed to play with the baby for a while.

- Give the older child some space of her own that's completely off-limits to the baby.
- Allow her to have things she doesn't have to share at all. With toys that must be shared, be meticulous about giving each child equal time—set a timer with a loud beep.
- Give the older child plenty of opportunity to be out of the home regularly—sleepovers at friends' and grandparents', off with the baby-sitter, and so on. Otherwise, she'll feel in competition with the baby all day. Be careful, though, not to do too much of this—you don't want to give the child the impression that you're booting her out.
- Spend plenty of time alone with the older child doing special activities focused exclusively on her needs, showing her you still love her. Just saying so won't do the trick.
- Give the older child a few privileges—a later bedtime perhaps.
- Encourage the older child to express her emotions. Ask a lot of questions about how she feels. Keep the questions focused on her—not on the baby. She's probably tired of being asked how she likes being a big sister.
- Treat every vocal expression of pain or rage as positive, Biller recommends. You can't force a child to feel love if she doesn't feel it. And it's far better for her to *say* something hurtful than to express the idea physically. If she needs to burn off some hostility, make sure she gets plenty of exercise.
- Empathize. Vicky Lansky suggests expressing your own occasional annoyance with the baby's demands to your older child, but not so often that he or she gets the idea that the new sibling is a permanent nuisance. Express your joy, too. And talk about your own experience as an older child (if you were one).
- Look at the world from the older child's perspective. Imagine how it feels to your toddler when she sees her younger sister wearing a hand-me-down—even if she outgrew it long ago. To her it can seem like there's nothing left of her.
- For a child, the expression "it's not fair" really means "it's not the same." So get two of everything, and make sure the older child gets the first pick.

- Be prepared. When older children are forced not to hit younger siblings (life is tough, isn't it?), their aggression doesn't just disappear. It has to come out somewhere, and frequently it is reborn as a temper tantrum.

Those Pearly Whites

Although a few dentists think kids should have their first exam at about six months, almost all of them agree that you shouldn't wait any longer than three years before getting your child's teeth checked. By this time she should be brushing at least once a day and flossing (you'll have to help) daily.

Like most new things, the first trip to the dentist can be a scary experience. So start preparing your toddler several weeks in advance. Tell her you're going to a special doctor who is going to count her teeth and take some pictures of them. Have her practice opening her mouth with you, just to show her that there's nothing to fear.

If you have the time, take your child by the dentist's office to meet the staff a few days before the appointment so she can get familiar with the surroundings. Though you shouldn't ever lie to your child about what is going to happen at the dentist's office, make a special point to stay away from words that might frighten her, such as drill, needle, shot, and pain. And save all of your personal dental horror stories until she's a teenager.

LOOKING FOR MR. GOODBRUSH

Just as it's more appropriate to take your child to a pediatrician than to your internist, your child should have his teeth looked at by a pediatric dentist—someone who specializes in children—*not* the guy you've been going to for the past twenty years.

At my daughters' dentist, the waiting rooms are filled with toys and bowls of fruit. The furniture is all bright colors and kid-friendly patterns. In the examining room there are televisions mounted on the ceiling so the kids can watch videos while their teeth are being cleaned. And in the x-ray area, kids sit on a horse—complete with saddle and stirrups—instead of a regular chair. What I want to know is, where the hell were the pediatric dentists when I was a child?

Despite all the attempts to distract your child, she may still scream, squirm, and try to escape. Don't be embarrassed. Any good pediatric dentist and her staff see the same little show a hundred times a day.

Some dentists think it's a good idea to have parents in the examining room with their children; others think it's a rotten idea. Fortunately, you know your child better than anyone, so you know whether you need to hold her hand or do everyone a service by waiting in the car.

33–36 MONTHS

Learning to Let Go

What's Going On with the Baby

Physically

- If it wasn't already, it should be fairly clear by now whether your child is left- or right-handed.
- Her hand coordination is constantly improving. She tries to imitate your writing and can draw a pretty passable circle (or at least a swirl).
- She very neatly lays out her clothes for the next day the night before and has no trouble putting on her own pants, socks, T-shirt, and jacket. Buttons, snaps, and zippers may still give her some trouble.

Intellectually

- As she approaches her third birthday, your toddler will be quite comfortable with many short-term time concepts. She regularly uses "soon," "in a minute," and the endearing "this day" (instead of "today").
- She's also deepening her understanding of spatial relationships—she's mastered "in" and "out," but the more abstract "near" has eluded her until now.
- She's very concerned that every object has its own special place, and she may get quite upset if things aren't where they're supposed to be.
- She can now count up to three. (She may be able to say her numbers up to ten, but she doesn't really know what they mean.)

Verbally

- By her third birthday your child will understand the majority of the conversational language she'll use for the rest of her life. And about 80 percent of what she says can be understood, even by strangers.

- Boys' verbal skills and vocabularies are still lagging a bit behind girls'. Boys generally tell shorter stories whose main characters are usually themselves. Girls' stories are longer and their main characters are more likely to be adults.
- Your toddler is finally able to use tenses (although not always completely accurately). My mother fell down and tore a ligament in her knee, and we told my younger daughter about it the next day. For months afterward, she would look up and announce: "Grandma fell down boom and hurt her leg yesterday."
- Kids acquire most of their understanding of time words in the six months between ages two and a half and three.

Emotionally/Socially

- Like their teenage counterparts, "first adolescents" are incredible know-it-alls. But the veneer of confidence is pretty thin. "It helps to remember that the child is bossy not because he is sure, but actually because he is unsure," write Ames and Ilg. "The world still seems big and dangerous to him. If he can command even a small part of it (his parents), it helps him to feel secure." As your toddler's language skills improve, thus enabling her to gain some control over her impulses, the world will become (in her eyes) much less dangerous.
- Your "first adolescent" is still quite negative and contrary. But it's critical to keep in mind that her negativity is part of an important developmental stage. "The first step toward a positive self-identity and sense of selfhood is a negative self-identity, a negation of the values and desires of his parents," writes psychologist Fitzhugh Dodson. "A negative self-identity must precede positive self-identity."
- It's taken a while, but your toddler is finally beginning to interact regularly with her playmates. These interactions are not, however, as pleasant as we'd like them to be. "The dominant drive at this age," write Ames and Ilg, "tends to be the effort to try, either verbally or physically, to keep others away from their things."
- Although her sense of humor is getting more sophisticated, it's still the incongruous that gets the biggest laughs: try to put on her shoes or wear her pants on your head and you're likely to reduce your toddler to hysterical laughter. Other funny things: accidents (unless someone is injured), silly questions ("Where are your wings?"), and adults imitating baby talk.

What You're Going Through

Speaking Up

I was second in line to buy stamps at the post office when a young woman came into the lobby, dragging a three-year-old boy behind her. "Now just sit down over there and shut up," she snapped, pointing the boy to an empty seat on a nearby bench. But instead of sitting, the boy began to run around the lobby. And that's when his mother grabbed him. "I'm sick and tired of you," she said as she slapped his face, hard. "And you better quit that crying or I'll—" He didn't. She did, this time knocking him to the floor.

I was stunned. Whatever that little boy had done, it certainly didn't warrant the treatment he was getting. At first I wanted to say something to the woman, but I couldn't bring myself to do it. Then I looked around the post office, hoping

"Excuse me for sounding like a Jewish mother, but may I point out that your kid is getting wet."

that maybe someone else would say something. But everyone seemed to be concentrating on the return addresses on the envelopes they'd brought. The woman was still smacking her child when my turn came. I bought my stamps, exchanged helpless looks and shoulder shrugs with the clerk, and quickly left. I sat outside in my car for a while, furious—not only at that woman for hitting her child but also at myself and at everyone else in that post office. How could a bunch of adults have stood by silently?

Certainly, seeing an adult abuse a child is something that bothers just about everyone. But to parents concerned about the safety and welfare of our own children it's especially disturbing. Unfortunately, though, it happens all the time. And since we're likely to be spending time in places where there are other families around, we're likely to see more than our share.

WHY WE DON'T SPEAK UP

Most of us know what we'd do (or at least what we *think* we'd do) if someone tried to hurt our children. So why are we so hesitant to speak up when someone else's kids are being abused? Are we just uncaring and insensitive? "Not at all," says psychology professor Mark Barnett. "Historically, children have been regarded as personal property. And we still tend to believe that parents have the right to deal with them however they see fit."

Another reason we don't speak up when we see someone treating a child inappropriately is that most of us try to blend into our surroundings, hoping that someone else will take the lead. But when no one does, "We downplay our own reactions and convince ourselves that what we initially thought was abusive behavior really wasn't that bad after all," claims Dr. Ervin Staub. Staub refers to this extremely common phenomenon as "pluralistic ignorance."

But hesitating to "butt in" and taking one's cues from others are definitely not the only factors that keep us silent. Imagine this scenario: you're walking home alone at night, when you see a large man coming out the door of a house carrying a screaming child. He quickly stuffs her into the back seat and gets ready to drive away. He sees you staring suspiciously at him and glares back. Are you face to face with a violent kidnapper or just a frantic father taking a sick child to the hospital? If you play it safe and say nothing, you are probably experiencing one of the other feelings most likely to keep people from speaking up: fear of putting oneself in physical danger.

For better or for worse, passersby almost never have a *legal* obligation to do anything. (Doctors, dentists, teachers, social workers, and, in some states, the people who develop film at the local drugstore, however, are required to report suspected abuse to the proper authority.) But there are clearly times when all of us have a *moral* obligation to do something. Suzanne Barnard, a spokesperson for the Children's Division of the American Humane Society, suggests the following guidelines:

- If an adult is causing a child serious or life-threatening injury (hitting hard enough to leave a mark or actually drawing blood), do something.
- If a child has been abandoned or negligently left in a dangerous situation (locked in a car in hot weather with the windows closed), do something.
- If the child's actions make it reasonably clear that he or she is scared, or that the person doing the suspected abuse is a stranger to her, do something.

WHEN TO OPEN YOUR MOUTH

For some of us, confronting others is no problem. "I'd rather risk embarrassing myself to save a child," a friend of mine once told me, "than have to live with myself knowing that I could have done something but didn't." Of course, "confronting" doesn't have to mean "attacking." "If you can approach the parent in a non-judgmental way, there are things you can say that can help defuse the situation," says Barnard.

The National Committee for the Prevention of Child Abuse (NCPCA) endorses the following approach:

- Divert the *adult's* attention away from the child by sympathizing or by offering some praise for the child: "My child did the same thing just yesterday" or "He has the most beautiful eyes."
- Divert the *child's* attention by talking to her or pointing out something of interest.
- Say positive things—negative remarks or looks are likely to increase the parent's anger and could make matters worse.

For many of us, however, approaching a stranger—even to do something as simple as ask directions—is simply too embarrassing or daunting to do. So if you can't, don't feel guilty—you're not a wimp. You still can make an anonymous report to the appropriate authorities, who will check it out for you.

If you're in a store, contact the manager immediately and have him or her call the police (if the manager refuses, call the police yourself). If you're outside, try to get the adult's license plate number and then call 911. If you're concerned about a neighbor, call your county child protective services and give them the address.

THE FEAR OF MAKING A MISTAKE

But what should you do when the situation is not so clear-cut, or when you're seeing something that looks more like a flash of temper rather than a case of prolonged abuse? After all, as parents we've all come close to "losing it" on a particularly bad day. And what about that kid you know who's always covered with bruises?

Before calling the police, take a good, long look at the situation and make sure your suspicions are reasonable. As you well know, children are always having accidents and a few bruises and cuts are usually not an indication of abuse.

If you need help evaluating what you've seen, or if you want to know how to make a report in your area, call one of the following organizations and ask them how to get in touch with your county social services agency:

- CHILDHELP/IOF FORESTERS
  National Child Abuse Hotline
  1-800-4-A-CHILD or
  1-800-2-A-CHILD (TDP) for the hearing impaired
- The American Humane Association
  Children's Division
  Denver, CO
  (800) 227-4645

You and Your Baby

More on Sex Identity

A DIFFERENT KIND OF PLAYTIME

As you well know by now, the toddler years are the age of exploration, a time when your child explores her world and especially all the great things she can do with her body. The experts are essentially unanimous in saying that giving a child as much freedom as possible to explore her world is critical to the development of autonomy and self-confidence. And most parents are perfectly willing to let their children explore whatever they want to, until, that is, they start exploring their own genitals.

Genital self-exploration is a phase nearly all toddlers go through, and it is especially common right around the time they start making the transition from diapers to big-kid underwear. After all, when they were wearing their diapers all the time, their genitals were pretty hard to grab hold of. But now that they're accessible nearly all the time . . . (Reminds me a little of the old joke: Why do dogs lick their crotches? Because they can.)

Common or not, it's still a little discomfiting to watch a child play with his or her own genitals, and it's hard to resist pulling the child's hand away or shouting, "Stop that!" Maybe it's all those stories we heard about how masturbation causes blindness or hairy palms, or turns kids into perverts.

Whatever the reason, it's truly important that you resist the urge to step between your child and her genitals. Making a big deal out of it can give your child the message that that part of her body is dirty or that touching it is somehow wrong. For a little boy, "His penis is no more interesting than any other part of him," says Fitzhugh Dodson. "It is only when we react as though there is something bad or naughty about it that we teach him to become morbidly interested." The same obviously goes for little girls. The truth, of course, is that "our toddlers will only develop sex hangups if we teach them to," says Dodson.

At home, the best plan of action is neither to encourage nor to discourage genital exploration. In public places, however, gently redirect your child to another activity, telling her that private touching should be done in a private place, such as her own room in her own home. Here are a few more things you can do:

- Teach your child the correct names for human body parts—including penis, vagina, and rectum—just as you did for belly button, nose, and elbow.
- Explain physical differences between adults and children. Adults' pubic hair (and the hair on your chest, legs, back, and elsewhere) and adult-size genitals are of special concern to kids. The simple answer (one that's perfectly adequate for kids this age) is that as you get bigger, everything gets bigger and that when you get to be a grown-up you get hairier.
- Talk about touching. It's simply not okay for anyone (adult or child) to touch anyone else in his or her private area—except if the adult is a doctor or a parent bathing a child or changing her diaper. Bathroom privacy (closing the door, knocking) is also a good topic to bring up now.
- Stay away from intimate touching or sex in front of your child. But be warned: your child will walk in on you one day. And scrambling around trying to cover up may make your child think there's something wrong with your (and, by extension, her) body.

MODESTY VERSUS SHAME: WHY IT MAY BE TIME TO KEEP YOUR PANTS ON

At about the same time as your child develops an interest in her own body, she might become suddenly conscious of yours—and of the differences between yours and your partner's and between yours and hers (or his, if you've got a boy). This is most likely to come up if you have a habit of not wearing much clothing around the house.

Hyperactivity Alert

One of the most common—and least accurate—behavioral "diagnoses" these days is ADHD (attention deficit/hyperactivity disorder). While fewer than 5 percent of American children actually have ADHD, it is "diagnosed" far more frequently, often by people who have no business making a diagnosis of any kind. In my view, this overdiagnosis is a direct result of a combination of four factors:

- Teachers and day-care workers naturally prefer the kids who obey to those who don't. They also want children to be calmer—they're easier to care for that way.
- Research has shown that female teachers are less tolerant of physical activity than male teachers.
- Most day-care workers and preschool teachers are women.
- Since boys are perceived to be more active than girls, they are perceived to be "acting out," or hyperactive, seven to eight times more frequently than girls.

The natural consequence of this overdiagnosis is that it's becoming more and more common for kids to be drugged into submission. So if your baby-sitter, day-care provider, or preschool teacher tells you your child is hyperactive or suffers from ADHD, do not panic. Instead:

- Be skeptical. A lot of what is "diagnosed" as ADHD is nothing more than normal toddler behavior.
- Think about your child's temperament. Is he naturally active?
- If you're still worried, take your child to the pediatrician. Have him or her do an analysis of your child's diet—something that can have immediate impact on behavior.
- If your pediatrician suggests it, have your child tested by a qualified child psychiatrist.
- If the child psychiatrist suggests drugs, get a second opinion.

Generally speaking, there's nothing wrong with your child's seeing you or your partner naked. But how do you know when to be a little more modest around your child? The answer, of course, depends on many factors—your attitudes and comfort levels about nudity (do you think the human body is something to be proud of or something that should be kept completely private?), your child's awareness of the physical differences between you, and much more.

In my case, my daughters basically told me when to get dressed. I used to take baths with them, until one day, when the older one was about three, she decided to grab my penis in the bathtub—a pretty serious hint that I should either wear a swimsuit or she should bathe alone.

With my younger daughter the hint came a little earlier: one afternoon just after she'd turned two, she and I spent about half an hour talking about all the different kinds of tails animals have and why people don't have them at all. The next morning she strolled into the bathroom just as I was stepping out of the shower. We chatted for a second, but suddenly she gave me a stunned, betrayed look and pointed at my crotch. "Daddy has a tail," she announced. Clearly, she felt that I'd lied to her.

Just remember: your feelings about nudity (just like your feelings about everything else) rub off on your children. "In teaching and practicing modesty, we emphasize closeness, intimacy, and self-respect," writes child development expert Lilian Katz. "Shame, on the other hand, is generated by implying that curiosity about the body or nakedness is bad or by suggesting that feelings of sexual arousal experienced even by a young child (such as a young boy having an erection when he or someone else is naked) are in some way inappropriate or dirty. Scolding, teasing, or other strong reactions to curiosity, exploration, and exhibitionism (a child's deliberate act of running around naked) may make a young child feel guilty about early sexual feelings that are in fact quite natural and universal. It would help to respond to the child's feelings and curiosity by accepting and acknowledging them as understandable and at the same time by indicating that there's a time and place for everything."

More Adult Separation Problems

I don't think I'll ever forget the time I drove my older daughter a few blocks away from my house and abandoned her. Well, I didn't really abandon her, I just took her to preschool. But it was my first time, and somehow I felt I'd done something wrong.

When our first child was born, my wife and I both cut our work loads to three days a week so we could spend as much time as possible with her. And for the first two and a half years of her life, at least one of us was with her almost all the time. But as I sat in my car after dropping her off for her first day of preschool, I began to wonder what kind of parent I was, leaving her all alone with people I hardly knew. Would they read to her? Could anyone possibly teach her as well as my wife and I had? Who would encourage her? And who would love her? I was nearly overcome with a need to run back to the school, grab her, and take her home where she belonged.

After a few minutes of this sort of thinking, it became painfully clear that

"Soon you will be entering a phase son, in which you will no longer pay attention to anything I have to say. Please let me know when that changover occurs."

my wife and I had spent months preparing the wrong person for our daughter's first day of school.

Fighting the urge to go back to the school, I drove home and sat down in front of my computer. I tried to remind myself that up until then I had actually been looking forward to having my child in school, knowing I'd have a lot more time to write. But as I stared dumbly at the screen-saver, I kept thinking that maybe my priorities were in the wrong order. After all, what's more important, my getting to write a few articles or making sure my children get the best possible education? Eventually, though, I had to admit that school was clearly the best place for my daughter, especially a school taught by teachers all our friends agree are gifted.

What it really comes down to, I guess, is that I knew I was going to miss my daughter while she was at school. I'd miss the wonderful times we had—the rainy-day matinees and museums and the sunny-day outings, the hours spent cuddling on the couch reading the same book ten times in a row, or sitting at her table drawing. And most of all, I'd miss the long talks we had and the feeling of overflowing joy and pride I got from watching her learn new things and seeing how bright and articulate she'd become.

But missing her wasn't all there was. I was jealous, too. It just didn't seem fair that my daughter's teachers—people who hardly knew her—were going to be the beneficiaries of so much of her company. Oh sure, the two of us would still have plenty of afternoons together in the park, and we'd still make pizza dough, and soak each other with the hose while watering the garden, and hide under the covers in my bed, ready to scare my wife when she came home from work. But no matter how much time we'd spend together now, I knew it would never seem like enough because I'd always remember the time when I didn't have to share her with anyone.

She was still so small and helpless, but at the same time already off on her own. It really seemed like the end of an era.

I remembered then (and still do now) going into her room at night when she was a baby and marveling at her angelic, smiling face and her small, perfect body. It was always a struggle not to wake her up to play. Thinking about it now, I realize that I was jealous even of her dreams.

I guess I should have known what I was going to feel as I dropped her off on her first day of school. I remember going to pick her up at the park a few months before. I stood outside for a few minutes, watching her chat and play with her friends. She seemed so mature, so grown up, so independent. Until that moment, I'd felt that I knew her completely. I knew the characters she'd pretend to be, I knew what she liked and didn't like, and we told each other everything. But watching her interact with other people—sharing secrets I'd never hear—I realized that the process of separating from our parents doesn't begin by moving out of their house at seventeen or by joining the Marines. It really begins at three, in a park, digging tunnels in the sand with a friend.

Family Matters

Teaching the Kids about Money

For most parents, the thought of teaching our preschoolers about money is almost as scary as imagining having to teach them about sex. We know we're going to have to do it sometime, but we hope we can put it off for a while.

But think about it: there's really nothing in our lives that we use as frequently as money—from paying the rent and the electric bill to giving charity to a homeless family—and there's nothing that causes us so many problems. Money issues, for example, are a leading cause of divorce.

The point of this section, then, is to get you to start teaching your child about money—what it does and doesn't do—while she's still young. "If you don't know the real value of money, you can come to worship it too much," says Neale Godfrey, author of *A Penny Saved . . . : Teaching Your Children the Values and Life-Skills They Will Need in the Real World.* "Bad financial habits in childhood can lead to worse problems when you're grown up."

Your child probably knows a few more things about money than you think she does. For example, she knows in a general sort of way that one needs money to get things, and she knows (or thinks, anyway) that you always have some. Most kids absolutely refuse to accept "I don't have any money with me" as an excuse for not buying them whatever they want whenever they want it. "Why don't you just go get some out of one of those machines?" they say. If you're not careful about how you teach your children about money, says Godfrey, it can "take on a magical quality."

The best way to keep money from becoming too mysterious and alluring is to introduce the concept in a matter-of-fact way.

MAKING THE INTRODUCTION

- **Go to the store.** Stores provide a great opportunity to talk about lots of money-related things: how much things cost, how you know the prices, paying for things by check or credit card, the mechanics of making change. All these themes introduce the idea that things cost money.
- **Awareness.** Let your child look at the check in restaurants. Show him that the numbers on the check are (or should be) the same as the ones on the menu.
- **Identification.** Get four jars, label each with the name of a coin: penny, nickel, dime, quarter. Put a few of the appropriate coins in each jar. Then take a coin out of your pocket, tell the child what it is, and put it (or have him put it) in the correct jar.
- **Participation.** Let your child hand the money to the clerk and collect the change.
- **Counting games.** Have your child count out the forks and spoons when you're setting the table. Have him help you make recipes, scooping out the right number of spoonfuls of ingredients.
- **Equivalence games.** Using real coins, show your child that a nickel is the same as a stack of five pennies, that five nickels are the same as a quarter, or that two nickels are the same as a dime. Two dimes and a nickel for a quarter is too complex at this age.
- **Categorizing games.** As you're going up and down the aisles of the supermarket, have your child help you spot round things, red things, boxed

"That's it, start saving your money now. You'll never see a dime of Social Security."

things, and so forth. Being able to organize items into groups is a critical math and money-handling skill.

- **Comparisons.** Which products are a better bargain? If the store you're in sells three oranges for a dollar, and the other store you go to has two oranges for a dollar, which is a better deal? Why do you go to the other store at all?
- **Prioritizing.** Talk about which products your family needs and which ones you want.
- **Be patient.** It will take years for all these ideas to sink in.

THE FAMILY PAYROLL

There are four things you can do with money: get it, spend it, save it, and give it away. And since you need to do the first one before any of the others, Godfrey suggests that parents put their kids on the family payroll by giving them an allowance. (When the kids are older, you'll tie their allowance to the performance of certain household chores. But for now, start with an unconditional allowance.)

Since they turned three, my wife and I have paid each of our daughters their age in dollars—a veritable fortune to those us who had to make do on an extremely sporadic fifty cents a week. But don't worry, it doesn't all go straight into their pockets. Here's how it works:

You pay out the three dollars as ten quarters and ten nickels, and the first thing your child does is take 10 percent of her money (one nickel and one quarter) and put it into a jar marked "Charity." She gets to decide what to do with this money (either give it directly to a homeless person or combine it with some of your money and send it by check to a deserving organization).

She then divides the remaining coins into six neat piles—three with three quarters, three with three nickels. Next she takes a stack of each (ninety cents) and drops them into three different jars:

- The instant gratification jar. Bite your tongue. It's her money, so let her spend it however she wants—even if it's on candy. She'll learn awfully quickly that once it's gone, it's gone.
- The medium-term jar. This one gets saved up for a week or two and can then be cashed in for a larger toy or expense.
- The long-term jar. Basically, she'll never see this money again. Let it accumulate in the jar for a while, then take it (and your child) down to the bank and open up a savings account.

As wacky as this whole allowance scheme sounds, the opportunities for learning are amazing: counting, percentages, division, categorizing, the importance of helping others, the value of patience, the benefits of saving, and so much more.

To Rent or to Buy?

One of the most important choices you have to make as a parent is where you're going to live. If you're like most people, you'll base your decision on how close you are to friends and family; how far you are from your job; how good the schools and day-care centers are; the crime rate; the weather; and more. Once you've taken care of those important considerations, the next big question is whether to rent a home or an apartment or buy one.

Back in the 1980s, when homes were appreciating 10 to 15 percent or more a year, buying a house was the best option for just about everyone. But with inflation (and housing prices) stagnant, it's far from a slam-dunk kind of decision. There are clear advantages and disadvantages to both options.

If you already own a home, you're probably reasonably happy with your housing arrangements. But if you rent, you're probably feeling a little more unsettled. A recent survey by Fannie Mae (the Federal National Mortgage Association) found that 84 percent of renters feel that buying a home is better than renting. Nevertheless, most of them are still living in a rental. Here are the top five reasons why:

Renting

ADVANTAGES

- All you pay is rent (and utilities, unless they're included in the rent); no property taxes, no maintenance fees, no repair costs.
- If something needs repair or replacing, someone else will do it for you.
- You have nearly complete freedom to move almost anytime you want.

DISADVANTAGES

- You aren't building equity.
- You might have to deal with obnoxious neighbors on the other side of a thin wall or ceiling.
- You might have to deal with obnoxious landlords.
- Your rent will probably go up every year or two.
- You can be evicted.
- You don't have any real pride of ownership.

Homeownership

ADVANTAGES

- Pride of ownership: all that you survey is yours.
- You may be building equity.
- Real estate usually appreciates over time.
- There are some potentially large tax benefits: mortgage interest and property taxes are deductible, meaning that they reduce your taxable income and therefore the amount of taxes you pay.

DISADVANTAGES

- Sooner or later you're going to need to replace the roof or get some termite work done and it all comes out of your pocket.
- If the real estate market goes down you may actually lose money when you sell.
- Property taxes and homeowner's insurance costs usually rise every year.

- They can't find housing they can afford. Two-thirds of renters are in exactly this situation.
- They can't put together enough for a down payment.
- They can't find a house in the right neighborhood.
- They're bogged down by credit problems.
- They've received insufficient and/or confusing information about how to buy a house and obtain financing. In fact, only 45 percent of adults say they completely understand the home-buying process or are comfortable with it.

Doing the Numbers

One of the most important factors in the rent versus buy debate is the question of which option leaves you better off financially. Here's a worksheet that my accountant uses to help his clients work their way through this tough decision. It may help you do the same.

MONTHLY EXPENSES	RENT	BUY
Rent	______	
Payment (principal and interest—you can get this info from a local title company)		______
PMI (mortgage insurance charged by lenders if you make a down payment of less than 20 percent)		______
Insurance (fire, liability, contents, etc.)	______	______
Utilities	______	______
Repairs and maintenance	______	______
Major improvements	______	______
Total monthly expenses	______	______
Subtract the tax benefits of owning a home*		(______)
Actual monthly expenses to rent vs. to buy	______	______

If the Buy figure above is lower than the Rent one, skip the rest of this worksheet and buy your house. In most cases, though, it isn't, and you've got one more small calculation to go.

The difference between monthly rental and buy expenses, × 12 ______

Cost of your new home ______ × the expected annual appreciation ___ % ______

If the appreciation line is greater than the one above, you're better off buying. If not, you're not.

---

*Tax benefits to owning a home

- monthly mortgage interest ______
- monthly property taxes ______
- other deductible expenses (if buying a home now allows you to itemize your deductions, you can deduct your state income taxes, charitable contributions, and several other expenses that you couldn't have taken before) ______
- total deductions ______
- your tax bracket (federal and state) ___ %
- total monthly savings (total deductions × tax bracket) ______

IF YOU'VE DECIDED TO BUY

Before you start running around all over town looking at open houses, there are a few things you need to do.

First, sit down and take a look at your finances. Start with a thorough review of your income and expenses for the past twelve months. How much can you afford to pay? Actually, what you think you can afford and what your lender

Dealing with Down Payment Woes

Down payments are a crucial part of every home purchase. And they're the source of an enormous amount of worry. Here are the two biggest reasons why you might be pulling your hair out:

1. The opportunity cost is too high. In other words, you're worried that you'll have to take your down payment money out of some kind of account that is currently earning you some money, and you're concerned about losing that income. But imagine this: If your $35,000 down payment (20 percent on a $175,000 house) was earning 10 percent a year, you'd bring in $3,500 each year (less after you've paid your taxes on it). But if your house appreciates by 4 percent a year—the national average—you're picking up $7,000 the first year and more every year after that.
2. You don't have enough to make a down payment. This is a bit tougher to overcome. But there are some possibilities:
   - Try to save more. It's hard. Very hard. You might want to go back over some of the suggestions on pages 137–44.
   - Shop around for a low down-payment loan. The Federal Housing Authority (FHA) has some programs that allow first-time buyers to put down as little as 3 percent. In addition, a number of national and local mortgage companies offer loans for 100 percent of the value of the property. Restrictions, as they say, apply, so check with a reputable mortgage broker.
   - Get help from your family. As we discussed earlier (see page 97), each of your parents can give you $10,000 tax-free per year (for a total of $20,000, unless you have more than two parents). Besides helping you over the hump, this will reduce the size of their estate and, possibly, the amount of future estate taxes. If you do take money from your parents, though, be sure to get a letter from them explaining that what they've given you is a gift, not a loan.

thinks you can afford may well be two very different things. Generally speaking, lenders shoot for what they call a 28/36 debt ratio. This means that no more than 28 percent of your gross monthly income can go toward housing, and that your total monthly expenses combined (including housing) can't be more than 36 percent of your monthly income. Also, if your down payment will be less than 20 percent, the 28/36 ratio may drop to 25/33, a small but often significant difference.

Next, answer this question: How's your credit (and your partner's)? The best way to answer this question is to get yourself a copy of your credit report and look it over for yourself—before a potential lender has a chance to. Doing so will give you plenty of time to clear up any glaring errors or to come up with plausible excuses for why things aren't the way they should be. This may sound unnecessary, but it's amazingly easy to get your credit report screwed up and amazingly hard to get it unscrewed.

Many credit advisors suggest that as part of this process you cancel any credit cards or lines of credit that you no longer use. When calculating your debt ratios, many lenders take into consideration the available limits on your cards or lines of credit. So a card with a pristine $10,000 limit may look great to you, but to a lender it may be a potential liability and could end up reducing the size of the loan you can qualify for.

After you've gotten both of these steps out of the way, get a preapproval—not just prequalification—letter. This means that the lender has already checked your credit, verified your income, and nosed around in all your other financial affairs. They'll give you a letter saying exactly how much they'll actually lend you. (A prequalification letter, on the other hand, says only that based on your income, you *might* qualify for a loan in a particular amount—there's no guarantee that you'll actually get the loan, though.) If you qualify for a more expensive house than you're planning to buy, consider having the lender write your preapproval letter showing a smaller amount. This will keep your upper limit a secret when you get into a negotiation.

WHEN YOU SHOULDN'T BUY

Obviously, buying a home isn't for everyone. And here are three situations that should keep you out of the real estate market—even if you can afford it. Instead, figure out how much you'd be spending if you did buy and invest the difference between that and what you'll be spending on rent.

- You aren't planning to live in your new home for a minimum of five years. Commissions, transfer taxes, and other one-time fees will eat you alive if you don't give your house enough time to appreciate in value. This is especially true if you are in a job that requires you to move a lot. It isn't always easy to sell as quickly as you need to, and you might end up stuck with double house payments.

- You're in a very low income tax bracket. Many of the advantages of home ownership come in the form of tax deductions. So if you aren't paying much tax, you won't benefit nearly as much as someone in one of the higher brackets.
- If homes in the neighborhood you're thinking about buying into are either not appreciating or actually depreciating.

CONDOS AND CO-OPS

For those of us who want the benefits of homeownership without the hassles (the painting, the lawn mowing, the maintenance expenses), condos and co-ops may be the way to go. On the up side, the condo or co-op homeowners' association (or similar group) will handle all those things for you. But on the down side, they'll charge you quite a bit for it. Plus, you'll be assessed special fees for general expenses such as fixing the roof—even if you live five floors below it. In addition, condos and co-ops don't usually appreciate as fast as stand-alone homes.

More Communication Issues

As we've discussed throughout this book, you and your partner became parents at the same time but not in the same way. As a result, you and your partner have very different needs and expectations. Researcher Jay Belsky calls this phenomenon "His and Hers transitions."

YOU NEED YOUR PARTNER TO:

- Truly appreciate how hard it is to be an involved father today. She should also appreciate the commitment you've made to your family and the things you do for them—even if they aren't exactly what *she* wants.
- Understand that you and she will probably disagree on how you assess your level of support and involvement.
- Be patient. She needs to know that adults develop at different rates, just as children do. In many families the mother develops her skills faster, in others it's the father.
- Understand—and try to accommodate whenever possible—your desires for her attention and affection, your own space, time to see your friends, and a social life.
- Give you the freedom to do things your own way. "Many mothers, considering themselves the primary parent, have a difficult time watching their

husbands parent differently from themselves, and take over to 'do it right,'" writes psychotherapist Jerrold Shapiro. "If you are an active father, you will have your own way of parenting. It is likely to be just as 'right' as a mother's way and quite different. You may have to listen to your partner's preferences and discuss your own. If you allow her to determine how children are to be fathered, your family may well end up with a second junior mother and no father." In my opinion, your partner has the right to determine exactly how the children are to be mothered. She has no right to determine how they are to be fathered.

- Support you in your efforts to be a good parent. "If fathers sense that their involvement is not only desired but also expected and endorsed by their wives, they'll be more involved. If not, they won't," writes psychotherapist Brad Sachs. Researcher Pamela Jordan agrees. "The mother plays a critical role," she writes. "She can bring her mate into the spotlight or keep him in the wings. The most promoting mothers . . . brought their mates into the experience by frequently and openly sharing their physical sensations and emotional responses. They actively encouraged their mates to share the experience of becoming and being a father."
- Know you love her and the baby even if you don't show it the way she wants you to. Men and women have very different ways of expressing love. And according to Shapiro, sometimes a wink, a smile, a pat on the shoulder or the butt is just as effective a way of saying I love you as actually saying the words.

YOUR PARTNER NEEDS YOU TO:

- Be a full participant in your home, not just "mother's little helper." This means taking responsibility for things without having to be asked (housework, meal planning, shopping) and assuming a major role in child care (including caregiving, arranging playdates, and doing clothes shopping).
- Understand that although she may occasionally neglect your emotional and physical needs in favor of the baby's, she doesn't mean to hurt you.
- Listen to her carefully when she wants to talk about her doubts and anxieties. It's "more important to have our needs heard than it is to have them met," says Brad Sachs. "Though the specific needs may not be met, the more general and overarching one—the need for support and connectedness—will be."
- Not make her feel guilty when she makes mistakes. She wasn't born knowing how to parent any more than you were.
- Support her in her efforts to regain her prebaby body.

- Support her in her efforts to reconcile work and family.
- Understand that she may be feeling tremendous guilt at not being able to live up to society's expectations of her (to be a good wife, mother, executive).
- Be sympathetic to her daytime loneliness and desire for adult company if she's a stay-at-home mom.

PUTTING IT TOGETHER

Belsky says that the main thing couples can do to transform their separate transitions into an "our" transition is to try to "reconcile the conflicting priorities of their individual transitions." In other words, learn to focus on the things you have in common rather than on your differences (although being aware of your differences is critical). "Couples who are able to focus their attention on what unites them and produces mutual joy usually end up at the end of the transition with a better, happier marriage," says Belsky.

DAD, THE VENTRILOQUIST

Here, according to Belsky, are the things that can make a couple's transition to parenthood easier:

- Surrender individual goals and needs and work together as a team.
- Resolve differences about divisions of labor and work in a mutually satisfactory manner.
- Handle stresses in a way that does not overstress one partner or the entire marriage.
- Fight constructively and maintain a pool of common interests despite diverging priorities.
- Realize that however good a marriage becomes postbaby, it will not be good in the same way as it was prebaby.
- Maintain the ability to communicate in a way that continues to nurture the marriage. "Most couples do not know" write the Cowans, "that some conflict and tension are inevitable in any intimate relationship. Nor do they realize that the key to a satisfying marriage is not whether a couple has challenging problems or whether they always resolve them, but *how they talk to each other* about them."

It's a tall order, but one that, if you're willing to put in the time and effort, will change for the better the lives of everyone around you.

What to Do If Communication Breaks Down

If you and your partner have tried everything to save your relationship—talking with each other, talking with a therapist, trial separations—divorce may be the only remaining option. This, of course, is a topic I'd rather not be writing about at all, but given that about half of all marriages in this country end in divorce, it's truly necessary to understand what to do if you find yourself contemplating yet another change in identity: from "father" to "single father." It's also necessary to understand the devastating way divorce affects everyone—you, your partner, and especially your children.

With any luck, you and your soon-to-be-ex will be able to remain civil enough to reach some kind of equitable agreement on child custody—without expensive lawyers and court costs. In fact, this is the case in about 80 percent of divorces nationwide. But whether your breakup is civil or acrimonious, there are a few things you should know before you make any major decisions:

- **Your defenses are down.** You're under stress; there are a thousand intense and scary feelings running through your head and a million details you have to take care of. You want to avoid more conflict. That's natural.

A Good Alternative to Litigation

There's no question that divorces can be expensive—especially if you and your wife can't communicate any other way than through your lawyers and in front of a judge. But if the two of you are getting along okay (not well enough to be married, just civil to each other), and you think you can continue to do so for a while, you might want to consider mediation. This means that the two of you would split the expense of hiring one person (instead of two) to help the two of you arrange custody and divide up your property. With mediation, the process usually costs less, takes a lot less time, and is much less psychologically damaging for everyone, including the kids, than a knock-down, drag-out court battle.

But a lot of men facing divorce tend to lose track of what's good for them and make decisions they end up regretting forever.

- **You need a strategy.** Make the right moves now and you can save yourself not only a lot of grief but a lot of money as well. And most important, you can minimize the damage the breakup of your marriage will have on your child(ren).

Some of what I suggest below may seem a little aggressive, but it really isn't. It's all about looking out for your own best interests instead of abandoning them. And far more important than that, it's about looking out for the best interests of your children. Please keep in mind that what you're going to read here is not an exhaustive treatment of the subject. And remember that every case is different and there are no easy solutions.

GET A LAWYER—NOW

The minute you suspect there's going to be a divorce, get yourself a lawyer. "Don't even consider representing yourself unless you have no possessions, no income, and no interest in the outcome of your case," says Timothy J. Horgan, author of *Winning Your Divorce.* Get the point? One recent study found that fathers who were awarded sole custody had been represented by lawyers 92 percent of the time, and those who won joint custody had lawyers 90 percent of the time. In contrast, among fathers who failed to win any type of custody, only 60 percent had hired lawyers.

And don't share a lawyer with your ex, either. "It's unrealistic to think that an attorney can simply shift from side to side and represent each of you with

Gender Strategy

Despite what you may have heard ("judges are more sympathetic to women lawyers" or "men are tougher"), the gender of your attorney probably won't affect your case in any way. But it is important to pay attention to his or her views on custodial fathers. Many lawyers of both genders believe that mothers should get custody of the children. Get the best person you can afford who shares your views and who you think will put the best interests of your child first.

equal vigor," writes Harriet Newman Cohen, co-author of *The Divorce Book for Men and Women.*

If a friend of yours was recently divorced (and ended up with what he wanted), get a reference. Or check with men's or fathers' rights groups. But beware: while support groups can be a valuable source of contacts and comfort, they also can be a hunting ground for unscrupulous lawyers who prey on men who are at their most vulnerable.

Two excellent (and safe) resources are the Children's Rights Council in Washington, D.C., (202) 547-6227; and Fathers' Rights & Equality Exchange, headquartered in San Jose, California (1-500-FOR-DADS). Both these organizations are nonprofit and have chapters in every state. Whatever you do, don't let recommendations substitute for face-to-face interviews with the top prospects. Although it may cost you a little up front, finding the right lawyer can make the difference between feeling helpless and being in control.

Hiring a lawyer does not mean that you're heading for the courtroom—if you're lucky, you'll never even meet a judge. Nor does hiring a lawyer mean that you're expecting a confrontation with your soon-to-be-ex. What it does mean, though, is that you're getting someone involved who, without any unpleasant emotional attachments, will protect your interests and make sure that your concerns are properly addressed. Most divorce lawyers have seen dozens of cases just like yours and know exactly what to look out for. Do you? And finally, your lawyer can also help you draft fair property settlements and custody arrangements that will hopefully avoid conflict in the future.

During the interview, ask a lot of questions and be completely honest about your situation—financial and emotional. If you aren't, you're just going to complicate your own case. Ask the attorney about the strengths and weaknesses of your case, and find out what approach he or she would take to getting you what you really want. Also, be sure to find out how well the attorney knows local judges and other divorce attorneys. Each judge has his or her own prejudices, and having a lawyer who can maneuver within the system may be critical to your case. And don't worry: any conversation you have while interviewing an attorney—even if you don't ultimately hire him or her—is completely confidential.

Here are a few ways to cut down on how much you'll be paying for your initial consultation:

- Before your first appointment, sit down and make a detailed list of all your assets and debts (including account numbers), real estate, full names and social security numbers of everyone in the family (kids, too), and your wife's and your birthdays, driver's license numbers, and dates of marriage and separation. Also bring along your tax returns for the last four or five years. You're going to need all this information soon anyway, and there's no point in paying someone $100 or $200 per hour to sift through your wallet, tax records, and other documents.
- Don't confuse your attorney's interest in your case with friendship. Sure, she'll interrupt her day to let you stop by and cry on her shoulder. She'll also charge you for it. And with many attorneys billing in quarters of an hour, that thirty-second plea for sympathy could set you back $50.

DON'T MOVE OUT

In the old days, men facing a divorce would move out of the house—it was considered quite the chivalrous thing to do. Today, however, moving out may be the dumbest thing you could possibly do. Depending on the state, "If you move out of your house, you're essentially abandoning any possibility of getting custody of (or even any sort of meaningful visitation with) your children," says Timothy Horgan. In some states, your wife's attorney may be able to argue that since you left your children with your wife, you aren't interested in having a relationship with them, and your custodial rights should be severely limited.

Unfortunately, the judge is likely to agree. Most divorce attorneys find that the courts are generally quite reluctant to make any changes to the status quo in custody cases. That means that the one who's living in the marital home has a great advantage.

If there's no other alternative to moving out—for example, the judge orders you to—keep these things in mind:

- Get a place as close as possible to your former home so you'll be able to see the kids every day.

- Explain the situation to the children yourself, stressing that it's not their fault. (You may want to check with a mental health professional about the best way to broach this topic.)
- Be alert to what your wife is saying about you to the children. If she's bad-mouthing you, you'll need to make doubly sure that the children understand what your leaving does—and doesn't—mean. One important warning: never respond to anything your ex is saying about you in front of the children. You never want to put your kids in the middle.
- Consider taking your valuables with you. "If you move out and leave your possessions behind, don't count on seeing them again," writes Harriet Newman Cohen. Alternatively, make a written inventory of every item of value you're leaving behind. A videotape would be even better.

A word of caution: try not to let your refusal to move out escalate into a huge confrontation between you and your wife (She: "Get out!" You: "Screw you!"). Your anger may later be used as the basis for your wife getting a court order to throw you out.

GET CONTROL OF YOUR FINANCES

In most states, assets and other property that have both your names on them (particularly things like checking accounts and money-market accounts) are assumed to be owned equally by you and your wife. But since it's tough to tell whose half is whose, there's nothing to stop your wife from completely cleaning out the entire checking account, leaving you penniless. Every divorce lawyer I've ever spoken with had literally dozens of stories about divorcing men who came home one day to houses that had been stripped bare and to checking accounts that were in much the same condition.

To protect yourself (and to make sure you've got enough to live on and to pay your attorney with) do the following immediately:

- Get *half* the money and any liquid assets you can put your hands on out of the joint accounts and into a separate account—in your name only. If you don't already know which accounts are liquid, have your accountant or your lawyer help you figure it out.
- But be sure to check with your lawyer before taking anything out of any joint accounts. In some states, doing so without the permission of your wife can get you in serious hot water. And beware: taking more than half can put you in the uncomfortable position of having to explain to a judge why you cut your wife off without enough money to live on.
- Switch your automatic payroll deposits and put any other new deposits into

Community Property

In some states (California, for example) everything acquired from the day you got married until the day you get separated is considered "community property." Even if you have a bank or stock account in your name alone, your wife is still entitled to half and vice versa. Just about the only exception to the community property rules is money or assets you or your wife owned *prior* to the marriage or inheritances left solely to either one of you even during the marriage. Things like a personal stereo and an inheritance might fit into this category. This is pretty complicated stuff, so if you live in one of the nine community-property states (Arizona, California, Idaho, Louisiana, Nevada, New Mexico, Texas, Washington, and Wisconsin), check with your lawyer.

your new account; any money that comes into the old, joint account may be lost forever.

- Get all your important financial records out of the house as soon as possible. Before doing this, however, make a complete copy of these records for your wife; she's entitled to one and making her (or her lawyer) ask for it later will cost you. Documents such as bank and credit card statements, tax returns, and life insurance policies can be stored in a safety deposit box or at your lawyer's office. And don't forget to change the account address, so future statements don't go to your wife.
- Keep an extremely accurate accounting of all deposits into and withdrawals from the new account—you don't want anyone accusing you of frittering away half the marital assets in Vegas.

Besides sharing ownership of all assets with your wife, you each also "own" half of all debts—mortgages, credit card balances, and so forth. So the next thing to do is close all your joint credit card accounts and credit lines, even the ones from department stores and gas stations. Do this in writing and mention the fact that you're getting a divorce—that usually speeds things up. Until you close these accounts, you'll be responsible for half of any debts your wife incurs until the divorce is final. Actually, according to the law, after the date of your legal separation you are responsible only for anything *you* charge (your partner is responsible only for what she charges). Unfortunately, most creditors don't really care about the law; all they want is their money, and they're perfectly willing to trash your credit rating if that's what it takes to get it.

KNOW THE DETAILS OF YOUR KIDS' LIVES

If you didn't want to be an active, involved father, you probably wouldn't be reading this book. So I'm assuming that at the very least you're going to want to get shared physical custody of your child(ren). If so, be aware that you've got at least two major obstacles to overcome:

- The strong societal assumption that women are biologically better parents than men.
- The old stereotype that fathers are less important to children than mothers.

Psychologist Richard Warshak, author of *The Custody Revolution,* calls these two ideas (which many men who don't know any better also buy into) the "motherhood mystique" and feels that they are responsible for the fact that mothers get primary physical custody more than 80 percent of the time.

So how do you overcome the motherhood mystique? Perhaps the best way is to demonstrate that you have exceptional parenting skills. And the best way to do that is to make sure you're up-to-date on everything that's going on in your kids' lives. The bottom line is that very few things can destroy your custody case more quickly than showing the judge that you lack knowledge about your child. Here are a few important things you should be doing (if you aren't doing them already):

- Get up early and make the kids' breakfast and lunch. Take them to day care.
- Get to know your children's day-care provider, doctors, playmates (and their parents)—and make sure they know you. They will be crucial ammunition if your wife's attorney tries to demonstrate what an uninvolved father you are.
- Get involved in arranging birthday parties, arranging play dates, and so on.
- No matter how long your work hours are, be sure to schedule some quality time with the kids *every day*—you've got to demonstrate a deep and continuing interest in, and commitment to, the kids.

Whatever you do, be predictable. "People who do custody evaluations (and who pass their recommendations on to the judges, who in turn usually rubber-stamp them) believe that schedule and stability are the two key ingredients for raising children," says attorney Tom Railsback. Maintain a written schedule of everything you do with your children, and keep receipts (with your signature on them) of doctor visits, clothing purchases, and so forth. And pay attention to the details: know their clothing sizes, favorite foods, and all the other telling details that can demonstrate that your role in your kids' upbringing is critical. Remember, whether or not your wife knows the answers to these questions is irrelevant. The judge will assume she does, but you'll have to prove you do.

The Language of Separation

Before agreeing to any kind of custody arrangement, it's critical that you understand the terms. The parent with *legal* custody is the one who is legally responsible for making decisions about anything that affects the health, education, and welfare of the children. Ideally you should have *joint* legal custody (this is already the law in several states). *Physical* custody simply refers to the child's primary residence. Again, you should seek nothing less than *joint* physical custody. But watch out: it's possible to have joint physical custody and still have the child's primary residence be at one or the other parent's home.

Finally, keep your wife completely up-to-date on anything pertinent that happens while you've got the kids: if you bought clothes, tell her; if your child was injured and you took him to the doctor, tell her. Besides being the right thing to do, keeping your wife informed shows that you're trying to keep open the lines of communication.

WATCH OUT FOR ALLEGATIONS OF ABUSE

One of the ugliest weapons being used these days is the accusation of child abuse. If you are accused, you will be presumed guilty—unless you can disprove the charges. And that's not easy. By the time you first hear that you're accused, your child has probably been seen by a therapist or a child protective services officer who sees it as his or her role to "validate" the accusation. And things move pretty quickly from there. The instant you're accused of having molested your child, all your contact with the child will be cut off until the question gets heard in court, and that could be anywhere from a few days to a few months later.

Assuming you're innocent (if you're not, please close this book immediately and turn yourself in), you'll probably feel like strangling your ex and her lawyer. Needless to say, this won't help. Most attorneys agree that aggressive behavior will just make the judge more suspicious and negatively inclined toward you. It's critical, then, to be as cooperative as possible.

And as hard as it might be for you, try to give your ex the benefit of the doubt—she may have seen something she genuinely thought was a symptom of abuse. Try to imagine how you'd behave if you'd seen something suspicious. And remember, your goal should be to get the truth out, not to get revenge.

An accusation of domestic violence may have nearly the same effect as an accusation of sex abuse: no access to your child until a judge rules on the charge. But keep in mind that, as strange as it sounds, men are the victims of domestic violence at least as often as women. The problem is that men rarely see their wives' shoves, slaps, or thrown dishes as violence. Now's the time to change your thinking. If your wife has been violent toward you or the kids, file charges immediately.

This does two things: it helps protect the kids from further abuse, and it helps protect you if she attempts to bring charges against you.

If you think your wife is the type who might use this kind of weapon, there are a few things you can do to protect yourself in advance:

- Don't let yourself get suckered into a fight, particularly on the phone. Your wife and her lawyer are just looking for evidence that you're violent and unstable. Don't answer questions like, "Why did you touch Sally down there?" Categorically deny her accusations, and end the conversation immediately.
- Tape your conversations with her. But before you turn on your recorder, check with your lawyer to make sure doing so is legal in your state. It's a tricky area of the law, so be careful.
- Stay squeaky clean during the entire divorce process: don't drink, don't drive too fast, don't even stiff a waitress on her tip. A sharp lawyer (employed by your wife) can make something as innocuous as a speeding ticket into just another example of what an irresponsible brute you are.

YOU MIGHT WANT TO KEEP A LOG

Again, because men are at a disadvantage when it comes to custody battles, it's important to keep detailed notes about everything that happens. Be sure to include:

- Details of visits with the kids.
- Conversations with your ex, especially if she's threatening or baiting you.
- Phone calls with your kids.
- Details about what the kids are up to when you're *not* with them. This will demonstrate not only that you are actively involved when you're with your kids but that you are concerned about them *all* the time. Be extremely careful, though, not to grill the kids about what they're doing with mom. This can put them in a very uncomfortable position.

A few warnings: first, do not show your log to anyone except your lawyer—not your friends, not your co-workers, and especially not anyone remotely connected with your wife. It's the kind of thing that could be twisted into yet another example of your controlling, obsessive nature. Second, take a lesson

There's No Such Thing as Winning Custody

In case you were thinking that you could "win" a custody battle, think again. The fact is that everyone loses, especially the kids. If your wife gets sole or primary custody, your relationship with your children will suffer greatly, and your children will bear the many negative consequences associated with long-term father absence (poorer academic performance, poorer social skills, increased chance of abusing drugs or alcohol or of getting in trouble with the law, and a greater likelihood of starting sexual experimentation early). But if you get sole or primary custody, your ex will miss out on having a relationship with the kids. And while this may sound like the perfect way to hurt her, keep in mind that the negative consequences of mother absence are just as significant as those of father absence. The bottom line is that the best parent is both parents.

from Bob Packwood: *everything*—good and bad—that's in your log may become part of the record. So if you've been having particularly nasty thoughts about your wife, keep them to yourself.

GET SOME COUNSELING

Regardless of how well (or badly) you and your ex get along, the simple truth is that the two of you will be coparenting your child until the day you die. For this reason, it is to everyone's advantage—especially the child's—that the two of you get to a point where you can communicate civilly and reasonably and that you do it as soon as possible.

One of the best ways to accomplish this is to go to joint counseling, which comes in two basic flavors: *predivorce* counseling and *coparent* counseling. As you could probably guess, predivorce counseling takes place in the early stages of the divorce process, most likely before any kind of custody or separation arrangements have been finalized. Predivorce counseling is designed to help you and your wife dissipate some of the anger and hostility between you, and to help you build a better base of communication. Then, hopefully, you'll be able to make mature, informed, and rational decisions and not get tripped up by your own vindictiveness. And the more mature and rational you are, the better off your kids will be.

Coparent counseling is similar to predivorce counseling, except that it happens *after* initial custody and separation arrangements are in place. You and your wife may find that your counselor's office is a safe, neutral place where you can have discussions about the kids.

WHAT TO DO IF YOU DON'T GET THE CUSTODY ARRANGEMENT YOU WANT

Although most states now have some kind of "gender-blind" legislation specifically barring judges from granting custodial preference based solely on gender, our family law system still favors women by a huge margin. As mentioned earlier, mothers are awarded sole custody over 80 percent of the time. Only 11 percent of men get sole custody of their children, and just 7 percent have joint custody. Women are presumed to be "fit" parents. Men have to prove it.

Worse yet, nearly 40 percent of noncustodial fathers have no legal access or custody rights at all. And the men who do have court-ordered access (as well as many of those who have joint legal custody) are traditionally limited to visits every other weekend, on alternate holidays, and for a couple of weeks in the summer.

The bottom line is that your chances of getting the kind of custody arrangement you really want are not great (they can, however, be greatly improved by following the suggestions on pages 000–00).

If you end up with limited access to your children, it's hard not to get depressed—the constant good-byes are going to be incredibly painful, and in some cases, seeing the kids may be a stinging reminder of the loss of your marriage. According to several studies, these two factors are among the major reasons divorced fathers taper off contact with their kids. So, as in most things, try to think of your kids before deciding you can't deal with seeing them. Seeing them may be painful to you, but not seeing you will be much more painful to them.

Right now the most important thing you can do is try to make the transition from one family to two as smooth as possible. And the place to start is by trying to keep communication with your ex as civil as possible. You may not have been terribly successful before, but it's more crucial now than ever: the children who suffer the least when their parents split up are those whose parents have the lowest levels of conflict (or at least those whose parents keep their conflicts to themselves). This doesn't mean that you and your ex have to be best friends or even that you have to speak to each other very often. What it does mean, however, is that you both have to agree to keep your eyes on what's really most important: your child(ren).

Do Some Reading with Your Kids . . .

There are plenty of good children's books that deal with divorce and how it affects kids. Here are a few you might want to take a look at:

Ballard, Robin. *Gracie.* New York: Greenwillow Books, 1993.

Brown, Laurence Krasny, and Marc Brown. *Dinosaurs Divorce: A Guide for Changing Families.* Boston: Atlantic Monthly Press, 1986.

Christiansen, C. B. *My Mother's House, My Father's House.* New York: Atheneum, 1989.

. . . AND FOR YOURSELF

Here are just three excellent books on divorce and custody issues that can help you remember the priorities: kids first, everything else last:

Adler, Robert. *Sharing the Children: How to Resolve Custody Problems and Get on with Your Life.* Bethesda, Md.: Adler and Adler, 1988.

Hickey, Elizabeth, and Elizabeth Dalton. *Healing Hearts: Helping Children and Adults Recover from Divorce.* Carson City, Nev.: Gold Leaf Press, 1994.

Oddenino, Michael L. *Putting Kids First: Walking Away From a Marriage Without Walking Over the Kids.* Salt Lake City, Utah: Family Connections, 1995.

Next to the the death of an immediate family member, getting a divorce is one of the most painful experiences you'll ever go through. And you certainly won't be alone; it will be hard on your ex and hard on your children as well. Rest assured, though, you *will* pull through. The breakup of a family is almost always a tragedy in the short term. But in the long term it sometimes turns out to be the best thing for everyone involved.

Selected Bibliography

Books

Adler, Robert. *Sharing the Children: How to Resolve Custody Problems and Get on with Your Life.* Bethesda, Md.: Adler and Adler, 1988.

Ames, Louise Bates, and Carol Chase Haber. *Your One-Year-Old: The Fun-Loving, Fussy 12- to 24-Month-Old.* New York: Delta, 1982.

Ames, Louise Bates, and Frances L. Ilg. *Your Two-Year-Old: Terrible or Tender.* New York: Delta, 1980.

Belsky, Jay, and John Kelly. *The Transition to Parenthood: How a First Child Changes a Marriage: Why Some Couples Grow Closer and Others Apart.* New York: Delacorte, 1994.

Berman, Phyllis W., and Frank A. Pedersen. *Men's Transitions to Parenthood: Longitudinal Studies of Early Family Experience.* Hillsdale, N.J.: Erlbaum, 1987.

Bettelheim, Bruno. *A Good Enough Parent: A Book on Child-Rearing.* New York: Vintage, 1987.

———. *The Uses of Enchantment: The Meaning and Importance of Fairy Tales.* New York: Knopf, 1976.

Biller, Henry B. *Fathers and Families: Paternal Factors in Child Development.* Westport, Conn.: Auburn House, 1993.

Biller, Henry B., and Robert J. Trotter. *The Father Factor: What You Need to Know to Make a Difference.* New York: Pocket Books, 1994.

Blakey, Nancy. *Lotions, Potions, and Slime: Mudpies and More!* Berkeley, Calif.: Tricycle Press, 1996.

———. *The Mudpies Activity Book: Recipes for Invention.* Berkeley, Calif.: Tricycle Press, 1989.

Bluestine, Eric. *The Ways Children Learn Music: An Introduction and Practical Guide to Music Learning Theory.* Chicago: GIA Publications, 1995.

Bornstein, M. H., ed. *Handbook of Parenting.* Hillsdale, N.J.: Erlbaum, 1995.

Brazelton, T. Berry, and Bertrand Cramer. *The Earliest Relationship: Parents, Infants, and the Drama of Early Attachment.* Reading, Mass.: Addison-Wesley, 1990.

Britton, James. *Language and Learning: The Importance of Speech in Children's Development.* New York: Penguin, 1970.

Bronstein, Phyllis, and Carolyn Pape Cowan, eds. *Fatherhood Today: Men's Changing Role in the Family.* New York: John Wiley & Sons, 1988.

Brott, Armin. *The New Father: A Dad's Guide to the First Year.* New York: Abbeville Press, 1997.

Brott, Armin, and Jennifer Ash. *The Expectant Father: Facts, Tips, and Advice for Dads-to-Be.* New York: Abbeville Press, 1995.

Butler, Dorothy. *Babies Need Books.* New York: Atheneum, 1980.

Canfield, Dr. Ken. *The Heart of a Father.* Chicago: Northfield, 1996.

Cantor, Ruth F., and Jeffrey A. Cantor. *Parents' Guide to Special Needs Schooling: Early Intervention Years.* Westport, Conn.: Auburn House, 1995.

Caplan, Frank, and Theresa Caplan. *The Second Twelve Months of Life.* New York: Bantam, 1977.

Cath, Stanley H., et al., eds. *Father and Child: Developmental and Clinical Perspectives.* Hillsdale, N.J.: Analytic Press, 1994.

———. *Fathers and Their Families.* Hillsdale, N.J.: Analytic Press, 1989.

Chen, Milton. *The Smart Parent's Guide to Kids' TV.* San Francisco: KQED Books, 1994.

Cohen, Harriet Newman, and Ralph Gardner, Jr. *The Divorce Book for Men and Women: The Step-by-Step Guide to Gaining Your Freedom Without Losing Everything Else.* New York: Avon, 1994.

Cowan, Carolyn Pape, and Philip A. Cowan. *When Partners Become Parents: The Big Life Change for Couples.* New York: HarperCollins, 1992.

Cowan, Philip A., et al. "Mothers, Fathers, Sons, and Daughters: Gender Differences in Family Formation and Parenting Style." In *Family, Self, and Society: Toward a New Agenda for Family Research.* Philip A. Cowan, Dorothy Field, and Donald A. Hansen, eds. Hillsdale, N.J.: Erlbaum, 1993.

Cullinan, Bernice E., and Lee Galda. *Literature and the Child,* 3d ed. Orlando, Fla.: Harcourt Brace, 1994.

Dacyczyn, Amy. *The Tightwad Gazette III.* New York: Villard, 1996.

Dodson, Fitzhugh. *How to Father.* New York: Signet, 1974.

Eisenberg, Arlene, et al. *What to Expect the Toddler Years.* New York: Workman, 1994.

Elias, Steven, Albin Renauer, and Robin Leonard. *How to File for Bankruptcy.* Berkeley, Calif.: Nolo Press, 1997.

Faber, Adele, and Elaine Mazlish. *How to Talk So Kids Will Listen and Listen So Kids Will Talk.* New York: Avon, 1982.

Flint Public Library. *Ring a Ring O'Roses: Finger Plays for Pre-School Children.* Flint, Mich.: Flint Public Library, n.d.

Fraiberg, Selma H. *The Magic Years: Understanding and Handling the Problems of Early Childhood.* New York: Scribner's, 1959.

Galinsky, Ellen. *Between Generations: The Six Stages of Parenthood.* New York: Times Books, 1981.

———. *The Preschool Years.* New York: Times Books, 1988.

Godfrey, Neale, and Tad Richards. *A Penny Saved . . . : Teaching Your Children the Values and Life-Skills They Will Need in the Real World.* New York: Simon & Schuster, 1996.

Gordon, Edwin E. *A Music Learning Theory for Newborn and Young Children.* Chicago: GIA Publications, 1990.

Gould, Jonathan W., and Robert E. Gunther. *Reinventing Fatherhood.* Blue Ridge Summit, Pa.: TAB Books, 1991.

Greene, Ellin. *Books, Babies, and Libraries: Serving Infants, Toddlers, Their Parents, and Caregivers.* Chicago: ALA Books, 1991.

Greenspan, Stanley, and Nancy Thorndike Greenspan. *First Feelings: Milestones in the Emotional Development of Your Baby and Child.* New York: Penguin, 1985.

Grossman, Elmer R. *Everyday Pediatrics for Parents: A Thoughtful Guide for Today's Families.* Berkeley, Calif.: Celestial Arts, 1996.

Hass, Aaron. *The Gift of Fatherhood: How Men's Lives are Transformed by Their Children.* New York: Fireside, 1994.

Hanson, Shirley M. H., and Frederick W. Bozett. *Dimensions of Fatherhood.* Beverly Hills, Calif.: Sage, 1985.

Heddle, Rebecca. *Science in the Kitchen.* London: Usborne Publishing, 1992.

Hickey, Elizabeth, and Elizabeth Dalton. *Healing Hearts: Helping Children and Adults Recover from Divorce.* Carson City, Nev.: Gold Leaf Press, 1994.

Horgan, Timothy J. *Winning Your Divorce: A Man's Survival Guide.* New York: Dutton, 1994.

Katzen, Mollie, and Ann Henderson. *Pretend Soup and Other Real Recipes: A Cookbook for Preschoolers and Up.* Berkeley, Calif.: Tricycle Press, 1994.

Kohl, MaryAnn F., and Jean Potter. *Cooking Art: Easy Edible Art for Young Children.* Beltsville, Md.: Gryphon House, 1997.

Kropp, Paul. *Raising a Reader: Make Your Child a Reader for Life.* New York: Doubleday, 1996.

Kutner, Lawrence. *Toddlers and Preschoolers.* New York: William Morrow, 1994.

Lamb, Michael E., ed. *The Role of the Father in Child Development.* New York: John Wiley, 1981.

Lehane, Stephen. *Help Your Baby Learn: 100 Piaget-Based Activities for the First Two Years of Life.* New York: Prentice-Hall, 1976.

Leonhardt, Mary. *99 Ways to Get Kids to Love Reading. New York: Three Rivers Press,* 1997.

McCoy, Bill. *Father's Day: Notes from a New Dad in the Real World.* New York: Times Books, 1995.

Minnesota Fathering Alliance. *Working with Fathers: Methods and Perspectives.* Stillwater, Minn.: nu ink unlimited, 1992.

Monroe, Paula Ann. *Left-Brain Finance for Right-Brain People: A Money Guide for the Creatively Inclined.* Naperville, Ill.: Sourcebooks, 1996.

Newman, Barbara M., and Philip R. Newman. *Development Through Life: A Psychosocial Approach*, 6th ed. Pacific Grove, Calif.: Brooks/Cole Publishing, 1994.

Oddenino, Michael L., and Jeff Carter. *Putting Kids First: Walking Away from a Marriage Without Walking over the Kids.* San Diego: Family Connections Publications, 1994.

Ostermann, Robert, et al. *Father and Child: Practical Advice for Today's Dad.* Stamford, Conn.: Longmeadow Press, 1991.

Pagnoni, Mario. *Computers and Small Fries: A Computer-Readiness Guide for Parents of Tots, Toddlers and Other Minors.* Wayne, N.J.: Avery Publishing, 1987.

Parke, Ross. *Fathers*, rev. ed. Cambridge, Mass.: Harvard University Press, 1996.

———. "Fathers and Families." In *Handbook of Parenting.* M. H. Bornstein, ed. Hillsdale, N.J.: Erlbaum, 1995.

Platt, Harvey J. *Your Living Trust and Estate Plan: How to Maximize Your Family's Assets and Protect Your Loved Ones.* New York: Allworth Press, 1995.

Polly, Jean Armour. *Internet Kids Yellow Pages.* New York: Osborne McGraw-Hill, 1996.

Pruett, Kyle D. "The Nurturing Male: A Longitudinal Study of Primary Nurturing Fathers." In *Fathers and Their Families.* Stanley H. Cath, et al., eds. Hillsdale, N.J.: Analytic Press, 1989.

Ross, John Munder. *What Men Want: Mothers, Fathers, and Manhood.* Cambridge, Mass.: Harvard University Press, 1994.

Sachs, Brad E. *Things Just Haven't Been the Same: Making the Transition from Marriage to Parenthood.* New York: William Morrow, 1992.

Schiff, Donald, and Steven Shelov, eds. *American Academy of Pediatrics Guide to Your Child's Symptoms: The Official, Complete Home Reference, Birth Through Adolescence.* New York: Villard, 1997.

Sears, William, and Martha Sears. *The Baby Book: Everything You Need to Know about Your Baby—From Birth to Age Two.* New York: Little Brown, 1993.

———. *The Discipline Book: Everything You Need to Know to Have a Better-Behaved Child—From Birth to Age Ten.* Boston: Little Brown, 1995.

Shopper, Moisy. "Toiletry Revisited: An Integration of Developing Concepts and the Father's Role in Toilet Training." In Stanley H. Cath, et al., eds. *Fathers and Their Families.* Hillsdale, N.J.: Analytic Press, 1989.

Silberg, Jackie. *300 Three-Minute Games: Quick and Easy Activities for 2–5 Year Olds.* Beltsville, Md.: Gryphon House, 1997.

Snarey, John. *How Fathers Care for the Next Generation: A Four-Decade Study.* Cambridge, Mass.: Harvard University Press, 1993.

Spangler, Doug. *Fatherhood: An Owner's Manual.* Richmond, Calif.: Fabus, 1994.

Spock, Benjamin, and Michael B. Rothenberg. *Dr. Spock's Baby and Child Care.* New York: Pocket Books, 1992.

Steinberg, David. *Fatherjournal.* Albion, Calif.: Times Change Press, 1977.

Sullivan, S. Adams. *The Father's Almanac*, 2d ed. New York: Doubleday, 1992.

Trelease, Jim. *The New Read-Aloud Handbook.* New York: Penguin, 1989.

Tyson, Eric. *Personal Finance for Dummies.* Foster City, Calif.: IDG Books, 1995.

Ulene, Art, and Steven Shelov. *Discovery Play: Loving and Learning with Your Baby.* Berkeley, Calif.: Ulysses Press, 1994.

Warshak, Richard. *The Custody Revolution: The Father Factor and the Motherhood Mystique.* New York: Poseidon, 1992.

White, Burton L. *The New First Three Years of Life.* New York: Prentice Hall, 1995.

Wright, June L., and Daniel D. Shade, eds. *Young Children: Active Learners in a Technological Age.* Washington, D.C.: National Association for the Education of Young Children, 1994.

Zweiback, Meg. *Keys to Preparing and Caring for Your Second Child.* New York: Barron's Educational, 1991.

Journals

Bailey, William J. "A Longitudinal study of Fathers' Involvement with Young Children: Infancy to Age 5 years." *Journal of Genetic Psychology* 155, no. 3 (1994): 331–39.

———. "Psychological Develpoment in Men: Generativity and Involvement with Young Children." *Psychological Reports* 71 (1992): 929–30.

Ball, Jessica, et al. "Who's Got the Power? Gender Differences in Partner's Perceptions of Influence During Marital Problem-Solving Discussions." Typescript, 1993.

Baumrind, Diana. "Current Patterns of Parental Authority." *Developmental Psychology Monograph* 4, part 1 (January 1971): 1–101.

Cohn, Deborah A., et al. "Mothers' and Fathers' Working Models of Childhood Attachment Relationships, Parenting Styles, and Child Behavior." Typescript, 1997.

———. "Working Models of Childhood Attachment and Couple Relationships." *Journal of Family Issues* 13 (December 1992): 432–49.

Cooney, Teresa M., et al. "Timing of Fatherhood: Is 'On-Time' Optional?" *Journal of Marriage and the Family* 55 (February 1993): 205–15.

Cowan, Philip A., et al. "Parents' Attachment Histories and Children's Externalizing and Internalizing Behavior: Exploring Family Systems Models of Linkage." *Journal of Consulting and Clinical Psychology.* In press.

Daly, Kerry. "Reshaping Fatherhood: Finding the Models." *Journal of Family Issues* 14 (December 1993): 510–30.

DeLuccie, Mary F. "Mothers as Gatekeepers: A Model of Maternal Mediators of Father Involvement." *Journal of Genetic Psychology* 156, no. 1 (1994): 115–31.

Deutsch, Francine M., et al. "Taking Credit: Couples' Reports of Contributions to Child Care." *Journal of Family Issues* 14 (September 1993): 421–37.

Dornbusch, Sanford M., et al. "The Relation of Parenting Style to Adolescent School Performance." *Child Development* 58 (1987): 1244–57.

Fagot, Beverly I. "Sex Differences in Toddlers' Behavior and Parental Reaction." *Developmental Psychology* 10, no. 4 (1974): 554–58.

———. "Teacher and Peer Reactions to Boys' and Girls' Play Styles." *Sex Roles* 11, no. 708 (1984): 691–702.

Fagot, Beverly, and Richard Hagan. "Aggression in Toddlers: Responses to the Assertive Acts of Boys and Girls." *Sex Roles* 12, nos. 3–4 (1985): 341–51.

———. "Observations of Parent Reactions to Sex-Stereotyped Behaviors: Age and Sex Effects." *Child Development* 62 (1991): 617–28.

Gordon, Betty Nye. "Maternal Perception of Child Temperament and Observed Mother-Child Interaction." *Child Psychiatry and Human Development* 13 (Spring 1983): 153–65.

Grimm-Thomas, Karen, and Maureen Perry-Jenkins. "All in a Day's Work: Job Experiences, Self-Esteem, and Fathering in Working-Class Families." *Family Relations* 43 (1994): 174–81.

Hall, Wendy A. "New Fatherhood: Myths and Realities." *Public Health Nursing* 11, no. 4 (1994): 219–28.

Haugland, Susan W. "The Effect of Computer Software on Preschool Children's Developmental Gains." *Journal of Computing in Childhood Education* 3, no. 1 (1992): 15–20.

Heath, D. Terri. "The Impact of Delayed Fatherhood on the Father-Child Relationship." *Journal of Genetic Psychology* 155, no. 4 (1994): 511–30.

Herb, Steven, and Sara Willoughby-Herb. "Books as Toys." *Topics in Early Childhood Special Education* 5, no. 3 (1985): 83–91.

Jewett, Don L., et al. "A Double-blind Study of Symptom Provocation to Determine Food Sensitivity." *New England Journal of Medicine* 323 (August 16, 1990): 429–33.

Jordan, Pamela L. "The Mother's Role in Promoting Fathering Behavior." *Health Care for Women International.* In press.

Katzev, Aphra R., et al. "Girls or Boys: Relationship of Child Gender to Marital Instability." *Journal of Marriage and the Family* 56 (February 1994): 89–100.

Lovestone, S., and R. Kumar. "Postnatal Psychiatric Illness: The Impact of Partners." *British Journal of Psychiatry* 163 (1993): 210–16.

McBride, B. A., and G. Mills. "A Comparison of Mother and Father Involvement with Their Preschool-Age Children." *Early Childhood Research Quarterly* 8 (1993): 457–77.

MacDonald, Kevin, and Ross D. Parke. "Bridging the Gap: Parent-Child Play Interaction and Peer Interactive Competence." *Child Development* 55 (1984): 1265–77.

———. "Parent-Child Physical Play: The Effects of Sex and Age of Children and Parents." *Sex Roles* 15, nos. 7–8 (1986): 367–78.

McKenry, Patrick C., et al. "Predictors of Single, Noncustodial Fathers' Physical Involvement with Their Children." *Journal of Genetic Psychology* 153, no. 3 (1992): 305–19.

Marsiglio, William. "Contemporary Scholarship on Fatherhood: Culture, Identity, and Conduct." *Journal of Family Issues* 14 (December 1993): 484–509.

Newman, Philip R., and Barbara Newman. "Parenthood and Adult Development." *Marriage and Family Review* 12, nos. 3–4 (1988): 313–37.

Nicolson, P. "A Brief Report of Women's Expectations of Men's Behaviour in the Transition to Parenthood: Contradictions and Conflicts for Counselling Psychology Practice." *Counselling Psychology Quarterly* 3, no. 4 (1990): 353–61.

Palm, G. "Involved Fatherhood: A Second Chance." *Journal of Men's Studies* 2 (1993): 139–54.

Pearson, Jane L., et al. "Adult Attachment and Adult Child–Older Parent Relationships." *American Journal of Orthopsychiatry* 63 (October 1993): 606–13.

Power, Thomas G., et al. "Compliance and Self-Assertion: Young Children's Responses to Mothers Versus Fathers." *Developmental Psychology* 30, no. 6 (1994): 980–89.

Pruett, Kyle D. "The Paternal Presence." *Families in Society* 74, no. 1 (1993): 46–50.

Reis, Myrna, and Dolores Gold. "Relationship of Paternal Availability to Problem Solving and Sex-Role Orientation in Young Boys." *Psychological Reports* 40 (1977): 823–29.

Rubenstein, Carin. "That's My Baby." *Parenting,* April 1990, pp. 87–90.

Samuels, Andrew. "The Good Enough Father of Whatever Sex." Typescript, n.d.

Sorce, James F., et al. "Maternal Emotional Signaling: Its Effect on the Visual Cliff Behavior of One-Year-Olds." *Developmental Psychology* 21, no. 1 (1985): 195–200.

Starrels, Marjorie E. "Gender Differences in Parent-Child Relationships." *Journal of Family Issues* 15 (March 1994): 148–65.

Stayton, Donelda, et al. "Infant Obedience and Maternal Behavior: The Origins of Socialization Reconsidered." *Child Development* 42 (1971): 1057–69.

Thornburg, Kathy R., et al. "Parent as a Teacher Inventory: Factor Analyses for Fathers, Mothers, and Teachers." *Educational and Psychological Measurement* 49 (1989): 689–95.

Whaley, Kimberlee K. "The Emergence of Social Play in Infancy: A Proposed Developmental Sequence of Infant-Adult Social Play." *Early Childhood Research Quarterly,* no. 5 (1990): 347–58.

Whitehurst, G. J., et al. "Accelerating Language Development Through Picture Book Reading." *Developmental Psychology* 24, no. 4 (1988): 552–59.

Resources

This list of resources is by no means a comprehensive guide. Rather, it is designed to offer some immediate answers to your questions and needs and to steer you in the right direction.

A special note about the Internet addresses listed here: If you don't have a computer or access to the Net, don't worry. Your public library probably does and you can still tap into these valuable resources there.

Advice, General

PARENTSPLACE.COM has one of the largest clearinghouses of parenting advice on the Net.

http://parentsplace.com/

Their bulletin boards are especially interesting. You can get answers from other parents on just about any aspect of parenting.

http://www.parentsplace.com/genobject.cgi/talking.html

FAMILY.COM has a bunch of columnists who dispense advice on just about every topic you can imagine. The site is run by Disney so expect more than a little advertising, but it's a great source of info and support.

http://www.family.com/

PARENTSOUP is run by the same people who own ParentsPlace.com. There's some overlap, but this is still another great source of valuable info.

http://www.parentsoup.com/

POSITIVEPARENTING.COM offers on-line parenting classes and links to other good parenting sites.

http://www.positiveparenting.com/

At-Home Dads

"AT-HOME DAD" NEWSLETTER has just about everything a stay-at-home dad could want to know. Each issue of the newsletter also includes the At-Home Dad Network, a listing of more than 300 dads across the country looking to connect their families through playgroups.

Peter Baylies, Publisher
61 Brightwood Ave.
North Andover, MA 01845
Tel.: (508) 685-7931
e-mail: athomedad@aol.com
http://www.parentsplace.com/readroom/athomedad/index.html

Bankruptcy

CONSUMER CREDIT COUNSELING SERVICE is a nonprofit group that helps people avoid bankruptcy and restructure their debts. To find a local CCCS office, call their toll-free number.

Tel.: (800) 388-2227

Elias, Stephen, Albin Renauer, and Robin Leonard. *How to File for Bankruptcy.* Berkeley, Calif.: Nolo Press, 1977. If you can't find it in your local bookstore, call the publisher (Tel.: [800] 992-6656).

College Savings

COLLEGE SAVINGS PLAN NETWORK
P.O. Box 11910
Lexington, KY 40578-1910
Tel.: (606) 244-8175
Fax: (606) 244-8053
http://www.collegesavings.org

Computers

COMPUTERTOTS
10132 Colvin Run Road
Great Falls, VA 22066
(800) 531-5053
http://www.computertots.com

Pagnoni, Mario. *Computers and Small Fries: A Computer-Readiness Guide for Parents of Tots, Toddlers and Other Minors.* Wayne, N.J.: Avery Publishing, 1987. Nearly ancient at this point, this book still covers the basics quite well.

Wright, June L., and Daniel D. Shade, eds. *Young Children: Active Learners in a Technological Age.* Washington, D.C.: National Association for the Education of Young Children, 1994.

Cooking and Other Messy Things

Blakey, Nancy. *Lotions, Potions, and Slime: Mudpies and More!* Berkeley, Calif.: Tricycle Press, 1996.

Heddle, Rebecca. *Science in the Kitchen.* London: Usborne Publishing, 1992.

Katzen, Mollie, and Ann Henderson. *Pretend Soup and Other Real Recipes: A Cookbook for Preschoolers and Up*. Berkeley, Calif.: Tricycle Press, 1994.

Kohl, MaryAnn F., and Jean Potter. *Cooking Art: Easy Edible Art for Young Children.* Beltsville, Md.: Gryphon House, 1997.

Credit Reporting Agencies

If you've been denied credit within the past sixty days you may be able to get a copy of your credit report for free. Otherwise, it'll cost you about $8.00. The big three credit gathering companies are:

Experian (formerly TRW)—Tel.: (800) 682-7654

Equifax—Tel.: (800) 685-1111

Trans Union—Tel.: (312) 408-1050

Divorce

AMERICAN FATHERS COALITION
2000 Pennsylvania Ave. N.W.
Suite 148
Washington, D.C. 20006
http://www.americanfathers.com

CHILDREN'S RIGHTS COUNCIL has a well-stocked catalog of resources, including great books on the subject for kids and their parents.
http://www.vix.com/crc/catalog.htm

FATHERS' RIGHTS & EQUALITY EXCHANGE
701 Welch Rd., #323
Palo Alto, CA 94304
Tel.: (415) 853-6877
e-mail: shedevil@vix.com (Anne Mitchell)

SINGLE AND CUSTODIAL FATHERS NETWORK
http://www.single-fathers.org/

Adler, Robert. *Sharing the Children: How to Resolve Custody Problems and Get on with Your Life*. Bethesda, Md.: Adler and Adler, 1988.

Cohen, Harriet Newman, and Ralph Gardner, Jr. *The Divorce Book for Men and Women: The Step-by-Step Guide to Gaining Your Freedom Without Losing Everything Else.* New York. Avon, 1994.

Leving, Jeffery M. *Fathers' Rights: Hard-Hitting and Fair Advice for Every Father Involved in a Custody Dispute.* New York: Basic Books, 1997.

Oddenino, Michael L., and Jeff Carter. *Putting Kids First: Walking Away from a Marriage Without Walking over the Kids.* San Diego: Family Connections Publications, 1994.

Financial Planning

DIRECT STOCK PURCHASE PLAN CLEARINGHOUSE
Tel.: (800) 774-4177
http://servo.golden-tech.com/clearing/

DRIP INVESTOR
http://www.dripinvestor.com/

Monroe, Paula Ann. *Left-Brain Finance for Right-Brain People: A Money Guide for the Creatively Inclined.* Naperville, Ill.: Sourcebooks, 1996.

Tyson, Eric. *Personal Finance for Dummies.* Foster City, Calif.: IDG Books, 1995.

Fun Stuff

CREATIVE CREATIONS has a constantly changing list of twenty fun things to do with kids of all ages.
http://www.waidsoft.com/funkids.html

Ellen Davis has a web site listing a bunch of fun activities.
http://ucunix.san.uc.edu/~edavis/kids-list/crafts/easy-and-fun.html

Blakey, Nancy. *The Mudpies Activity Book: Recipes for Invention.* Berkeley, Calif.: Tricycle Press, 1989.

Silberg, Jackie. *300 Three-Minute Games: Quick and Easy Activities for 2–5 Year Olds.* Beltsville, Md.: Gryphon House, 1997.

General Fatherhood

THE FATHERHOOD PROJECT is a national research and educational project examining the future of fatherhood and ways to support men's involvement in child-rearing.
c/o Families and Work Institute
330 Seventh Ave
New York, NY 10001
Tel.: (212) 465-2044

FATHERNET provides information on the importance of fathers and fathering and how fathers can be good parents and parent educators. It includes research, policy, and opinion documents to inform users about the factors that support and hinder men's involvement in the lives of children.
12 McNeal Hall
1985 Buford Avenue
St. Paul, MN 55108
Tel.: (612) 626-1212
http://www.cyfc.umn.edu/Fathernet/index.html

FATHER'S RESOURCE CENTER offers parenting classes, support groups, and workshops geared toward helping fathers become more capable and involved parents so that fathers, mothers, children, and, subsequently, all society will benefit.

430 Oak Grove Street, Suite B3
Minneapolis, MN 55403
Tel.: (612) 874-1509
Fax: (612) 874-1014
e-mail: frc@visi.com
http://www.slowlane.com/frc/

FATHERS HOTLINE can refer you to local and state father-friendly organizations.

Tel.: (512) 472-DADS (3237)
e-mail: dads@fathers.org
http://www.menhotline.org

FATHERWORK is a new home page designed to encourage good fathering. The folks at FatherWork view fathering not so much as a social role men play, but as the work they do each day to care for the next generation.

http://fatherwork.byu.edu

NATIONAL CENTER FOR FATHERING (NCF) offers resources designed to help men become more aware of their own fathering style and then work toward improving their skills. Call for a free issue of NCF's quarterly magazine, *Today's Father.*

10200 West 75th Street, #267
Shawnee Mission, KS 66204-2223
Tel.: (800) 593-DADS (3237)
e-mail: ncf@aol.com
http://www.fathers.com

NATIONAL CENTER ON FATHERS & FAMILIES is a great source of research and data on fathers, father involvement, and the like.

c/o University of Pennsylvania
3700 Walnut Street, Box 58
Philadelphia, PA 19104-6216
Tel.: (215) 898-5000

NATIONAL FATHERHOOD INITIATIVE conducts public awareness campaigns promoting responsible fatherhood, organizes conferences and community fatherhood forums, provides resource material to organizations seeking to establish support programs for fathers, publishes a quarterly newsletter, and disseminates informational material to men seeking to become more effective fathers.

600 Eden Road, Building E
Lancaster, PA 17601
Tel.: (800) 790-DADS (3237)
http://www.register.com/father/

General Parenting

ERIC CLEARINGHOUSE provides more information on parenting than you could ever possibly go through.

Tel.: (800) 583-4135 or (217) 333-1386
e-mail: ericeece@ux1.cso.uiuc.edu
http://ericps.ed.uiuc.edu/ericeece.html

NATIONAL COUNCIL ON FAMILY RELATIONS

Minneapolis, MN
Tel.: (612) 781-9331

"SMART FAMILIES" is a great newsletter published by Family University.

P.O. Box 500050
San Diego, CA 92150-0050
Tel.: (619) 487-7099
Fax: (619) 487-7356
e-mail: FamilyU@aol.com

Health Concerns

KIDS HEALTH offers accurate, up-to-date information on issues ranging from child behavior and development to nutrition, general health, surgery, and immunizations.

http://kidshealth.org/

NATIONAL ORGANIZATION FOR RARE DISORDERS

P.O. Box 8923
New Fairfield, CT 06812-1783
Tel.: (800) 999-6673

NORTHWEST COALITION FOR ALTERNATIVES TO PESTICIDES (NCAP) publishes the *Journal of Pesticide Reform* as well as informational packets "Children and Pesticides" and "Planning for Non-chemical School Ground Maintenance."

P.O. Box 1393
Eugene, Oregon 97440
Tel.: (503) 344-5044
Fax: (503) 344-6923
e-mail: ncap@igc.apc.org

WEB DOCTOR will answer your specific questions on line.

http://www.parentsplace.com/readroom/health.html

Grossman, Elmer R. *Everyday Pediatrics for Parents: A Thoughtful Guide for Today's Families.* Berkeley, Calif.: Celestial Arts, 1996.

Schiff, Donald, and Steven Shelov, eds. *American Academy of Pediatrics Guide to Your Child's Symptoms: The Official, Complete Home Reference, Birth Through Adolescence.* New York: Villard, 1997.

Music

CENTER FOR MUSIC AND YOUNG CHILDREN produces tapes for children that adults enjoy as well. They also offer parent-child music classes.

66 Whitherspoon
Princeton, NJ 08542
Tel.: (800) 728-CYMC (2962)

Bluestine, Eric. *The Ways Children Learn Music: An Introduction and Practical Guide to Music Learning Theory.* Chicago: GIA Publications, 1995.

Gordon, Edwin E. *A Music Learning Theory for Newborn and Young Children.* Chicago: GIA Publications, 1990.

On-line Conferences, Mailing Lists, and Newsletters

FATHER-L is an e-mail conference dedicated to discussing the importance of fathers in kids' lives. Send an e-mail to listserv@vm1.spcs.umn.edu and write "subscribe father-l" in the body of the message. Send a message to father-l@tc.umn.edu if you need more info.

PARENTING-L is a great way to get fifty quick, informative answers to just about any nonemergency question you might have. To subscribe, send e-mail to listserv@postoffice.cso.usuc.edu with "subscribe parenting-l" in the subject line.

THE PARENTS' LETTER, published by a pediatrician, is filled with good, basic information on such topics as health maintenance, immunizations, illness, behavior, and parenting skills. To subscribe, send an e-mail to majordomo@pobox.com with a blank subject line and write "subscribe letter" in the body of the message.

OTHER PARENTING LISTS:
kids-newborn (0-2/3 months)
kids-infant (3 months-1 year)

To subscribe to one or more of the above, send an e-mail to listserv@vm.ege.edu.tr using the following format (substituting your own name for mine, of course):

sub kids-newborn Armin Brott
sub kids-infant Armin Brott

Reading and Other Media

CHILDREN'S LITERATURE provides reviews of the latest kids' books, videos, and computer games.

7513 Shadywood Road
Bethesda, MD 20817-9823
Tel.: (800) 469-2070 or (301) 469-2070 (yes, it's the same number)
Fax: (301) 469-2071

Chen, Milton. *The Smart Parent's Guide to Kids' TV.* San Francisco: KQED Books, 1994.

Kropp, Paul. *Raising a Reader: Make Your Child a Reader for Life.* New York: Doubleday, 1996.

Leonhardt, Mary. *99 Ways to Get Kids to Love Reading.* New York: Three Rivers Press, 1997.

Trelease, Jim. *The New Read-Aloud Handbook.* New York: Penguin, 1989.

Temperament

TEMPERAMENT TALK
1100 K Avenue
La Grande, OR 97850
Tel.: (541) 962-8836
Fax: (541) 963-3572

Travel

FAMILY WORLD HOMEPAGE offers calendars (broken down into four regions) that include information on all sorts of fun places for families to visit in different parts of the country.

http://family.com

Wills and Trusts

Platt, Harvey J. *Your Living Trust and Estate Plan: How to Maximize Your Family's Assets and Protect Your Loved Ones.* New York: Allworth Press, 1995.

For many more interesting web sites, check out Jean Armour Polly's *Internet Kids Yellow Pages* (Osborne McGraw-Hill, 1996). Despite the title, it's a wonderful source of resources for parents, too.

If you have any comments or suggestions about the topics discussed in this book, you can send them to

Armin Brott
P.O. Box 2458
Berkeley, CA 94702
e-mail: armin@pacbell.net

Index

F

G

H

I

CARTOON CREDITS

About the Author

Armin Brott, author of *The Expectant Father: Facts, Tips, and Advice for Dads-to Be* and *The New Father: A Dad's Guide to the First Year* and a contributing writer to *BabyTalk* magazine, has written on fatherhood for the *New York Times Magazine, Newsweek,* the *Washington Post, American Baby* magazine, *Parenting* magazine, and many other periodicals. His weekly radio show on parenting is carried by one of the largest radio stations in the San Francisco Bay area. He and his family live in Berkeley, California.

The New Father

A Dad's Guide to the First Year

Ooooglie oooglie googlie googlie...
Who is this person? Where's the one with the milk??
SIPRESS

The New Father

A Dad's Guide to the First Year

Armin A. Brott

Abbeville Press • Publishers
New York • London • Paris

To Tirzah and Talya,
without whom being a dad just wouldn't be the same

EDITOR: Jacqueline Decter
DESIGNER: Celia Fuller
PRODUCTION EDITOR: Leslie Bockol
PRODUCTION MANAGER: Lou Bilka

 Inquiries should be addressed to Abbeville Publishing Group, 22 Cortlandt Street, New York, N.Y. 10007. The text of this book was set in Bodoni Book. Printed and bound in the United States of America.

First edition
10 9 8 7 6

Cover photograph by Milton Heiberg. For cartoon credits, see page 239.

Library of Congress Cataloging-in-Publication Data
Brott, Armin A.
The new father : a dad's guide to the first year / Armin A. Brott.
p. cm.
Includes bibliographical references and index.
ISBN 0-7892-0275-1
1. Infants. 2. Infants—Care. 3. Father and infant. I. Title.
HQ774.B777 1997
649'.122—dc21 96-47489

Contents

Acknowledgments

I'd like to thank the following people (in alphabetical order), whose help has made this book far better—and far more accurate—than it otherwise might have been:

Jim Cameron and the folks at Temperament Talk, whose work on temperament changed my life; Phil and Carolyn Cowan and Ross Parke for their comments, suggestions, and inspiration; Jackie Decter, for her wisdom, insight, patience, sense of humor, and, above all, her sharp eye; Bruce Drobeck, Bruce Linton, and Glen Palm, who, completely independently of each other, have made major contributions to the literature on fatherhood and freely shared their research with me; Celia Fuller, for making me look good with yet another inspired design; Ken Guilmartin and Edward Gordon for their distinct but equally valuable contributions to the sections on music; Amy Handy, for her constructive criticism and for smoothing out the rough edges; Seth Himmelhoch, who more than once magically pulled out from his files precisely what I needed; Pam Jordan, for her wisdom, guts, and encouragement; Jim Levine, for getting everyone together with a minimum of bloodshed; the wonderful, compassionate, and completely selfless folks at the SIDS Alliance; Dawn Swanson, the incredible children's librarian at the Berkeley Public Library, for helping me select—and arrange developmentally—the best kids' books; Eric Tyson, for reviewing, commenting on, and adding to the sections on money and insurance; and finally, Andrea, who put our disagreements aside for the greater good and once again read every word; and my parents, for their hospitality, careful editing, and for not getting too upset when I griped about their parenting techniques—thirty years too late for them to do anything about it.

MAGAZINES
BOOKS
PARENTING
FATHERING
MOTHERING
BROTHERING
SISTERING
AUNTING
UNCLING
First Cousining
SIPRESS

Introduction

Nobody really knows how or when it started, but one of the most widespread—and most cherished—myths about childrearing is that women are naturally more nurturing than men, that they are instinctively better at the parenting thing, and that men are nearly incompetent.

The facts, however, tell a very different story. A significant amount of research has proven that men are inherently just as nurturing and responsive to their children's needs as women. What too many men (and women) don't realize is that to the extent that women are "better" parents, it's simply because they've had more practice. In fact, the single most important factor in determining the depth of long-term father-child relationships is opportunity. Basically, it comes down to this: "Having children makes you no more a parent than having a piano makes you a pianist," writes author Michael Levine in *Lessons at the Halfway Point.*

"In almost all of their interactions with children, fathers do things a little differently from mothers," writes researcher David Popenoe. "What fathers do—their special parenting style—is not only highly complementary to what mothers do, but by all indications important in its own right for optimum childrearing."

Not surprisingly, then, fathers have very different needs from mothers when it comes to parenting information and resources. But nearly every book, video, seminar, and magazine article on raising kids has been geared specifically to women and to helping them acquire the skills they need to be better parents. Fathers have been essentially ignored—until now.

How This Book Is Different

Because babies develop so quickly, most books aimed at parents of infants (babies from birth through twelve months) are broken down by month. The same goes here. But while the majority of parenting books focus on how babies develop during this period, the primary focus of *The New Father: A Dad's Guide to the First Year* is on how *fathers* develop. This is an approach that has rarely, if ever, been tried. Each of the chapters is divided into three major sections:

What's Going On with the Baby

This section is designed to give you an overview of the four major areas of your baby's development: physical, intellectual, verbal, and emotional/social. A lot of what a man experiences as a father is directly related to, or in response to, his children. So knowing the basics of their growth will help put your own growth into better perspective. Please remember, however, that all babies develop at different rates and that the range of "normal" behavior is very wide. If your baby isn't doing the things covered in the predicted month, don't worry. But if he is six months behind, check with your pediatrician.

What You're Going Through

Because the experience of fatherhood has largely been ignored in parenting books, many men think the feelings they are having are abnormal. In this section we examine at length what new fathers go through and the ways they grow and develop—emotionally and psychologically—over the course of their fatherhood. You're a lot more normal than you think.

You and Your Baby

This section gives you all the tools you need to understand and create the deepest, closest possible relationship with your child—even if you have only half an hour a day to spend with her. In this section we cover topics as diverse as play, music, reading, discipline, and temperament.

Family Matters

A number of the chapters feature a "Family Matters" section in which we discuss a variety of issues that will have a major impact not only on you but also on your family as a whole. Topics include dealing with crying, postpartum depression (which men get too!), childproofing, family finances, and finding appropriate child care.

Why Get Involved?

First, because it's good for your kids. "Everything we know shows that when men are involved with their children, the children's IQ increases by the time they are six or seven," says pediatrician T. Berry Brazelton. Brazelton adds that with the father's involvement "the child is also more likely to have a sense of humor, to develop a sort of inner excitement, to believe in himself or herself, to be more motivated to learn."

In contrast, a father's emotional distance can have a profound negative impact. "Research clearly documents the direct correlation between father absence and higher rates of aggressive behavior in sons, sexually precocious behavior in daughters and more rigid sex stereotypes in children of both sexes," writes Dr. Louise B. Silverstein of New York University.

Second, it's good for you. A mountain of research has shown that fathers who are actively involved with their children are more likely to be happily married and are more likely to advance in their careers. "Being a father can change the ways that men think about themselves," writes Ross Parke, one of the major fatherhood researchers. "Fathering often helps men to clarify their values and to set priorities. It may enhance their self-esteem if they manage its demands and responsibilities well, or alternatively, it may be unsettling and depressing by revealing their limitations and weaknesses. Fathers can learn from their children and be matured by them."

Third, being an involved father is good for your partner and for your marriage. Division of labor issues are the number one marital stressor, and the more support mothers get from their husbands, the happier they are in their marriages and the better they perform their parenting duties. Men whose partners are happy in their marriages tend to be happier themselves. And men who are happy in their marriages are generally more involved in their fathering role. It just never ends; and there's no reason why it should.

A Note on Terminology

He, She, It

In the not so distant past (the present, too, really) parenting books, in which the parent is assumed to be the mother, almost always referred to the baby as "he." While there's an argument to be made that in English the male pronoun is sort of a generic term, I'm pretty sensitive to issues of gender neutrality. And as the father of two girls, I wanted to see at least an occasional "she," just to let me know that what was being said might actually apply to my children. But as a writer, I find that phrases like "his or her," "he or she," and especially "s/he" make for cumbersome reading and awkward sentences. The solution? I decided simply to alternate between "he" and "she" as often as possible. Except in a few specific cases (circumcision, for example), the terms are interchangeable.

Your Partner in Parenting

In the same way that calling all babies "he" discounts the experience of all the "shes" out there, calling all mothers "wives" essentially denies the existence of the many, many other women who have children: girlfriends, lovers, live-in companions, fiancées, and so on. So, to keep from making any kind of statement about the importance (or lack of importance, depending on how you feel) of marriage, I refer to the mother of your child as your "partner," as we did in *The Expectant Father: Facts, Tips, and Advice for Dads-to-Be.*

If Some of This Sounds a Little Familiar . . .

If you read *The Expectant Father* (and if you didn't, it's not too late), you may notice that there's some overlap between the end of that book and the early part of this book. I assure you that this repetition of material is less the result of laziness on my part than of the necessity born of having to cover several of the same important topics in both books.

What This Book Isn't

While there's no doubt that this book is filled with information you can't get anywhere else, it is not intended to take the place of your pediatrician, financial planner, or lawyer. Naturally, I wouldn't suggest that you do anything I wouldn't do (or haven't done already). Still, before blindly following my advice, please check with an appropriate professional.

1 WEEK

Coming Home

What's Going On with the Baby

Physically

- Although most of your newborn's physical capabilities are run by a series of reflexes (see pages 38–43), she does have some control over her tiny body.
- She can focus her eyes—for a few seconds, at least—on an object held 8 to 10 inches from her face, and she may be able to move her head from side to side.
- She probably won't eat much for the first 24 hours, but after that, she'll want 7 to 8 feedings each day.
- She seems to be doing everything at an accelerated pace: at 33 breaths and 120 heartbeats/minute, her metabolism is moving about twice as fast as yours.
- Her intestines are moving even faster: she'll urinate as many as 18 times and move those brand-new bowels 4 to 7 times every 24 hours.
- Needing to recover from all that activity, it's no surprise that she spends 80 percent of her time asleep, taking as many as 7 to 8 naps a day.

Intellectually

- Right from birth, your baby is capable of making a number of intellectual decisions.
- If she hears a sound, she can tell whether it's coming from the right, left, or straight ahead.
- She can distinguish between sweet and sour (preferring sweet, like most of us).

- She also has a highly developed sense of smell. At seven days, she'll be able to tell the difference between a pad sprinkled with her own mother's milk and one from another mother.
- She prefers simple patterns to complex ones and the borders of objects (such as your jaw or hairline) to the inner details (mouth and nose).
- She can't, however, differentiate herself from the other objects in her world. When she grasps your hand, for example, her little brain doesn't know whether she's holding her own hand or yours.

Verbally

- At this point, most of the vocal sounds your baby produces will be cries or animal-like grunts and squeaks.

Emotionally/Socially

- Although she's alert and comfortable for only 30 or so minutes out of every 4 hours, your baby is already trying to make contact with you.
- When she hears a voice or other noise, she'll become quiet and try to focus.
- She's capable of showing excitement and distress, and will probably be quiet when you pick her up.

What You're Going Through

Comparing How You Imagined the Birth Would Go with How It Went

Let's face it: every expecting couple secretly (or not so secretly) hopes for a pain-free, twenty-minute labor, and nobody ever really plans for a horrible birth experience. Even in childbirth education classes, if the instructor talks at all about the unpleasant things that can happen, she usually refers to them as "contingencies"—a word that makes it seem as though everything is still under control.

If your partner's labor and delivery went according to plan, chances are you're delighted with the way things turned out and you're oohing and ahhing over your baby. But if there were any problems—induced labor, an emergency C-section, a threat to your partner's or your baby's life—your whole impression of the birth process may have changed. It's not unusual in these cases to blame the baby for causing your partner so much physical pain and you so much psychological agony. It can happen easily, without your really being aware of it.

So pay close attention during the first few weeks to how you're feeling about your baby. And if you find yourself being angry or resentful of her, or thinking or saying things—even in jest—such as "All the pain is the baby's fault," or (as I did) "The baby had jammed herself in there sideways and refused to come out," try to remember that no matter how brilliant and talented you think your baby is, she was a completely passive player in the entire process. Giving in to the temptation to blame your baby for *anything* at this point can seriously interfere with your future relationship together.

The Brief "Is This Really My Baby?" Phase

The first thing I did after both my daughters were born was make sure they had two arms and legs, and ten fingers and toes. Once all limbs and extremities were accounted for, I quickly looked over both my daughters to see whether they had "my" nose or chin.

Later on, I felt a little guilty about that—after all, shouldn't I have been hugging and kissing my daughters instead of giving them a full-body inspection? Maybe, but as it turns out, that's what almost all new fathers do within the first few minutes after the birth of their babies. "They immediately look for physical similarities to validate that the child was theirs," says researcher Pamela Jordan. And this happens for a reason: for almost all new fathers—regardless of how many of their partner's prenatal doctor appointments they went to, how many times they heard the baby's heartbeat or saw him squirm around on an ultrasound, and how many times they felt him kick—the baby isn't "real" until *after* the birth, when father and baby have a chance to meet each other face to face. "Seeing the infant emerge from his mate's body through vaginal or cesarean birth is a powerful experience for each father," writes Jordan. "Birth proved that this infant had been the growth within the mother's abdomen."

As it turns out, only one of my daughters has "my" chin, and it's looking like both of them will go through life without my nose (and, hopefully, the accompanying sinus problems). But what I really found disheartening at the time was that neither of them shared the Brott family webbed toes (it isn't all that noticeable, but it helps my swimming immeasurably).

Babies hardly ever look exactly as you imagined they would before they were born. And being disappointed about a nose, a chin, or even some toes is something you'll get over soon enough—especially when you discover in a few weeks that the baby does have something of yours (they always do).

But what if the baby has a penis or a vagina when you were expecting the opposite? Getting a boy when you expected a girl, or vice versa, can be a real shock. "When one's fantasy is not fulfilled, there is a period of regret for what might have been," writes Ellen Galinsky, head of the Work and Family Institute. "And this unhappiness can stand in the way of the parents' reaching out, accepting the baby."

Fortunately, things don't have to be this way. The conflict between fantasy and reality, says Galinsky, "can also be the trigger point for growth—one can either stay still, hang onto the old feeling, or one can change."

At Long Last, Reality

At some point not long after the baby is born, just about every new father gets hit with a sharp jolt of reality: he's a father, with new responsibilities, new pressures, new expectations to live up to. For some new fathers, this seemingly basic epiphany comes early, before they leave the hospital. For others, reality may not hit for a few days. But whenever it happens, a new father's realization that his life has changed forever can have some interesting results.

Only a day after the birth of his daughter, Hannah, Ken Canfield pulled into his driveway. "I . . . stared out through the windshield at the wooden steps leading up into our house," he writes in *The Heart of a Father.* "The steps were rickety. One board was a little rotten on one end, and the rusty nails had gouged their way to the surface. Another board had warped up off the supports. I had never given any thought to those steps before . . . but the thought occurred to me that in less than 48 hours, a new mother carrying a new baby would be climbing those rickety stairs. So, exhausted as I was, with blood-shot eyes and the aroma of my sleepless hospital visit about me, I got out the power saw, some wood, a handful of nails, a square, and a hammer. For the next three hours I built steps."

You and Your Baby

Getting to Know Each Other

"Most people make babies out to be very complicated," says comedian Dave Barry, "but the truth is they have only three moods: Mood One: Just about to cry. Mood Two: Crying. Mood Three: Just finished crying. Your job, as a parent, is to keep the baby in Mood Three as much as possible." With just a few days of fatherhood under your belt you may be inclined to go along with Barry's summary. But the real truth is that babies' moods are a bit more subtle.

In the previous book in this series, *The Expectant Father: Facts, Tips, and Advice for Dads-to-Be,* I discussed the six clearly defined behavioral states that are evident within moments of every baby's birth. "By recognizing them and realizing when they occur and what the expected responses are in each," write Marshall and Phyllis Klaus, authors of *The Amazing Newborn,* "parents not only can get to know their infants but also can provide most sensitively for their needs."

In my first few weeks of fatherhood, I found that learning about these six states was absolutely critical to my getting to know my babies. So I thought it would be worthwhile to go over them again. Here, then, is a summary of the six states, based on the Klauses' wonderful book.

QUIET ALERT

Babies in the quiet alert state rarely move—all their energy is channeled into seeing and hearing. They can (and do) follow objects with their eyes and will even imitate your facial expressions.

Within the first hour of life, most infants have a period of quiet alertness that lasts an average of forty minutes. During his or her first week, the normal baby spends only about 10 percent of any twenty-four-hour period in this state. It is in this state, however, that your baby is most curious and is absorbing information about his or her new world. And while the baby is in this state, you will first become highly aware that there's a real person inside that tiny body.

ACTIVE ALERT

In the active alert state, the baby will make small sounds and move his or her arms, head, body, face, and eyes frequently and actively.

The baby's movements usually come in short bursts—a few seconds of activity every minute or two. Some researchers say these movements are designed to give parents subtle clues about what the baby wants and needs. Others say these movements are just interesting to watch, and therefore promote parent–infant interaction.

CRYING

Crying is a perfectly natural—and for some, frequent—state (for more on this, see pages 39, 42–45). The infant's eyes may be open or closed, the face red, and the arms and legs moving vigorously.

Often just picking up the baby and walking around with him or her will stop the crying. Interestingly, researchers used to think that babies were soothed by being held or rocked in the upright position. It turns out, though, that what makes them stop crying is not *being* upright, but the movement that gets them there.

Keep in mind, too, that crying is not a bad thing—it not only allows the baby to communicate but also provides valuable exercise. So if your efforts to calm aren't immediately successful (and the baby isn't hungry or stewing in a dirty diaper), don't worry; chances are the tears will stop by themselves in a few minutes.

DROWSINESS

Drowsiness is a transition state that occurs as the baby is waking up or falling asleep. There may still be some movement, and the eyes will often look dull or unfocused. Leave the baby alone to drift off to sleep or move into one of the alert stages.

QUIET SLEEP

During quiet sleep the baby's face is relaxed and the eyelids are closed and still. There are no body movements and only tiny, almost imperceptible mouth movements.

When your baby is in this state, you may be alarmed at the lack of movement and be afraid she has stopped breathing. If so, lean as close as you can and listen for the baby's breath. Otherwise, gently put a hand on the baby's stomach (if she's sleeping on her back) or back (if she's sleeping on her stomach) and feel it rise and fall. (For information on back versus stomach sleeping, see page 69.) Try to resist the urge to wake the baby up—most newborns spend up to 90 percent of their first few weeks sleeping.

ACTIVE SLEEP

Eyes are usually closed, but may occasionally flicker open. The baby may also smile or frown, make sucking or chewing movements, and even whimper or twitch—just as adults do in their active sleep state.

Half of a baby's sleep time is spent in quiet sleep, the other half in active sleep, with the two states alternating in thirty-minute shifts. So, if your sleeping baby starts to stir, whimper, or seems to be waking up unhappy, wait a few seconds before you pick him up to feed, change, or hold. Left alone, he may well slip back into the quiet sleep state.

Newborn babies are capable of a lot more than crying, sleeping, filling their diapers, and looking around. Just a few hours out of the womb, they are already trying to communicate with those around them. They can imitate facial expressions, have some control over their bodies, can express preferences (such as for simple patterns over more complex ones), and have remarkable memories.

Marshall Klaus describes playing a game with an eight-hour-old girl in which he asked one colleague (who was a stranger to the baby) to stick out her tongue slowly while holding the baby. After a few seconds, the baby imitated the woman. Then Dr. Klaus took the baby and passed her around to twelve other doctors and nurses who were participating in the game, all of whom were told not to stick their tongues out. When the baby finally came back to the first doctor, the baby—without any prompting—immediately stuck out her tongue again. Even at just a few hours old, she had apparently remembered her "friend."

Interacting with the Baby

Although it may be tempting just to sit and stare at your baby, marveling at every little thing she does, you'll need to do a lot more than that if you're really going to get to know her. Here are some of the best ways to get to know your child:

- **Hold her.** Newborns love to be carried around, whether held in your arms or in a pack.
- **Talk to her.** No, she can't understand a word you're saying. In fact, she barely even knows you exist. But talk to her anyway—explain everything

you're doing as you're doing it, tell her what's happening in the news, and so forth—it will help her get to know the rhythm of the language.

- **Change his diapers.** It doesn't sound like much fun, but it's a great time to interact with the baby one on one, to rub his soft belly, tickle his knees, kiss his tiny fingers. For at least the first month or so, he needs to be changed every two hours—a baby's super-sensitive skin shouldn't stew in human waste—so there are plenty of opportunities. And don't worry: changing diapers is an acquired skill; in just a few days you'll be able to do it with your eyes closed (although you probably shouldn't). In the meantime, even if you don't do it right, baby stool washes right off your hands and won't stain your clothes. One hint, though: immediately after undoing the diaper, put something (such as a towel or cloth diaper) over baby for a few seconds. The sudden rush of fresh air on the baby's crotch can result in your getting sprayed.

A Note on Diapers and Wipers

It seems as though you can hardly do anything anymore without having to make choices—do you want the Tastes Great kind of beer or the Less Filling kind? do you want toothpaste with tartar control or with peroxide and baking soda? Fortunately, most of the choices we make are pretty easy. But some come with their very own built-in political controversy: Death penalty or life in prison? Smoking or non-smoking? Paper or plastic? Well, now that you're a parent, you can add "Disposable diapers or cloth?" to your list.

Americans throw away some eighteen billion disposable diapers a year, enough to constitute more than 1 percent of the nation's landfill. Disposables are made of plastic and will stay in their present form for about five hundred years. "Biodegradable" disposables are available in some places, but some environmentalists have complained that they use *more* plastic than the regular kind and take just as long to break down.

Cloth diapers, in contrast, are all natural. The problem is that they're made of cotton, which is taxing on farmland. And in order to sterilize cloth diapers properly, diaper services wash them seven times in near-boiling water, consuming huge amounts of power, water, and chemical detergents. The diapers are then delivered all over town in trucks that fill the air with toxic pollutants. One study concluded that "use of a diaper service appears to consume three times as much fuel and cause nine times as much air pollution as use of disposable diapers."

Tough choice, and it's all yours.

And let's not forget the cost factor:

- **Disposable diapers:** $8 to $9 for a package of forty-four newborn size. As your baby and his diapers get bigger, the number of diapers per package goes down, but the cost per package stays about the same. Since you'll be using 5 to 8 diapers a day, this option can get pretty pricey. But if you keep your eyes out for coupons (most parenting magazines have a bunch of them in every issue), you can save a lot. In addition, places like Toys "Я" Us have generic or house brands that are a lot cheaper and usually just as good.

  Some people say that kids who grow up with disposable diapers tend to become potty trained later than those who use cloth. Apparently, the disposable kind keep so much moisture away from the baby's bottom that the baby stays comfortable for a longer time.
- **Cloth diapers:** about $12 for a package of six. The availability and cost of diaper cleaning services vary greatly around the country. If you sign up with a diaper service, you'll probably start with about eighty diapers per week. If you're doing your own laundry, you should buy about forty.

  Even if you decide against using cloth diapers for the baby, buy a dozen anyway—they're great for drying baby bottoms on changing tables and for draping over your shoulder to protect your clothes when your baby spits up.

Whichever you choose, make sure you stay away from commercial baby wipes for the first few weeks; they contain too many chemicals for brand-new skin. Use warm, wet washcloths instead. If you're taking the baby out during this period, bring along some moistened disposable washcloths in a resealable plastic bag. Finally, skip the lotions for a few weeks (again, too many chemicals and potential allergens) and never, never use powders (besides being a carcinogen, powder can cause pneumonia if inhaled).

If you happen to have been raised in a family that doesn't think a baby is properly changed unless her bottom is covered in white powder, try using cornstarch. Some people find that corn starch (which doesn't have the same health hazards as traditional baby powder) absorbs moisture and reduces diaper rash. But remember, you're not baking a cake here: a little goes a long way.

What about Play?

During the first few weeks, forget about football and chess. But try to spend at least twenty minutes a day (in five-minute installments) doing something with the baby one on one. Chatting, reading aloud, rocking, making faces,

Different Isn't Bad, It's Just Different

From the moment their children are born, men and women have very different ways of handling them. Men tend to stress the physical and high-energy more, women the social and emotional. Your baby will catch on to these differences within days, and she'll begin to react to you and your partner very differently. When she's hungry, she'll be more easily soothed by your partner (if she's breastfeeding), but she'll be happier to see you if she wants some physical stimulation. Don't let anyone tell you that the "guy things" you do are somehow not as important as the "girl things" your partner may do (or want *you* to do). Ultimately your baby needs both kinds of interactions, and it's a waste of time to try to compare or rate them. Just be gentle.

experimenting with the baby's reflexes (see pages 38–43) or even simply catching her gaze and looking into her eyes are great activities. Here are a couple of things to remember:

- **Take your cues from the baby.** If she cries or seems bored, stop what you're doing. Too much playing can make your child fussy or irritable, so limit play sessions to five minutes or so.
- **Schedule your fun.** The best time for physical play is when the baby is in the active alert state; playing with toys or books is fine during the quiet alert state (see page 17). Also, choose a time when your full attention can be devoted to the baby—no phone calls or other distractions.
- **Be encouraging.** Use lots of smiles and laughter as well as verbal encouragement. Although the baby can't understand the words, she definitely understands the feelings. Even at only a few days old, she'll want to please you, and lots of reinforcement will help build her self-confidence.
- **Be gentle.** Because babies' heads are relatively large (one-quarter of their body size at birth versus one-seventh by the time they're adults) and their neck muscles are not yet well developed, their heads tend to be pretty floppy for the first few months. Be sure to support the head from behind at all times, and avoid sudden or jerky motions. *Never* shake your child. This can make their little brains rattle around inside their skulls, causing bruises or permanent injuries. Never throw the baby up in the air. Yes, your father may have done it to you, but he shouldn't have. It looks like fun but can be extremely dangerous.

Family Matters

Coming Home

Boy, has your life changed. You're still your partner's lover and friend, just as you were a few weeks ago, but now, of course, you're also a father. You may be worried about how you're going to juggle all your various roles, but for a few days the most important thing you can do is to be a solid support person to your partner. Besides her physical recovery (which we'll talk more about below), she's going to need time to get to know the baby and to learn (if she chooses to) how to breastfeed.

Your first days as a father will be awfully busy—mine sure were: cooking, shopping, doing laundry, fixing up the baby's room, getting the word out, screening phone calls and visitors, and making sure my partner got plenty of rest.

Recovery

As far as the baby is concerned, there's not much to do in the beginning besides feeding, changing, and admiring. But your partner is a different story. Despite whatever you've heard about women giving birth in the fields and returning to work a few minutes later, that's not the way things usually happen. Having a baby is a major shock—physically and emotionally—to a woman's system. And, contrary to popular belief, the recovery period after a vaginal birth is not necessarily any shorter or easier than the recovery period after a C-section. In fact, my wife—who has delivered both ways—says recovering from the C-section was a lot easier.

Physically, whatever kind of delivery your partner has, she'll need some time—probably more than either of you think—to recover fully. Fatigue, breast soreness, and lingering uterine contractions may not disappear for months, and vaginal discomfort, hemorrhoids, poor appetite, constipation, increased perspiration, acne, hand numbness or tingling, dizziness, and hot flashes may continue for weeks after delivery. In addition, between 10 and 40 percent of women feel pain during sexual intercourse (which they won't get around to for a few months anyway, so don't bother thinking about it), have respiratory infections, and lose hair for three to six months.

Emotionally, your partner isn't much better off. She's likely to be a little impatient at her lack of mobility, and while she's undoubtedly excited to be a mother and relieved that the pregnancy is finally over, she may well experience at least some postpartum depression (see pages 45–47). Now that the baby

Pets

Don't expect your pet to be as excited as you are about the birth of your baby; many dogs and cats do not appreciate their new (lower) status in your house. To minimize the trauma for your pet (and to minimize the chance your pet will do something to harm the baby), try to get your pet used to the baby as early as possible.

You can do this even before the baby comes home by putting a blanket in the baby's bassinet in the hospital, then rushing the blanket home to your pet. It'll give Rover or Fluffy a few days (or hours, at least) to get used to the interloper's smell.

"Homewrecker!"

is really here, she may feel a lot of pressure to assume her new role as mother and to breastfeed properly. Fortunately, as she and the baby get to know each other, her confidence will grow and a lot of her anxieties should disappear.

Here are some things you can do to make the recovery process as easy as possible and to start parenting off on the right foot:

- Help your partner resist the urge to do too much too soon.
- Take over the household chores or ask someone else to help. And if the house is a mess, don't blame each other.

Parents, In-Laws, Siblings, and Other "Helpers"

One of the most common questions you'll hear from people is whether they can help out in any way. Some people are serious; others are just being polite. You can tell one group from the other by keeping a list of chores that need to be done and asking them to take their pick.

Be particularly careful about accepting offers of help from people—especially parents (yours or hers)—who arrive on your doorstep with suitcases and open-ended travel arrangements. New grandparents may have more traditional attitudes toward parenting and may not be supportive of your involvement with your child. They may also have very different ideas about how babies should be fed, dressed, carried, played with, and so on.

The same can be said for just about anyone else who offers to move in with you for a few days, weeks, or months to "help out," especially people who have their own kids. With all your other responsibilities, the last thing you want to do is play host to a bunch of relatives. If someone does stay with you to help out after the birth, make sure he or she understands that although you appreciate their help and their suggestions, you and your partner are the baby's parents and what the two of you say ultimately goes.

- Be flexible. Expecting to maintain your normal, prefatherhood schedule is unrealistic, especially for the first six weeks after the birth.
- Be patient with yourself, your partner, and the baby. You're all new at this.
- Be sensitive to your partner's emotions. Her emotional recovery can take just as long as her physical one.
- Make sure to get some time alone with the baby. You can do this while your partner is sleeping or, if you have to, while you send her out for a walk.
- Control the visiting hours and the number of people who can come at any given time. Dealing with visitors takes a lot more energy than you might think. And being poked, prodded, and passed around won't make the baby very happy. Also, for the first month or so, ask anyone who wants to touch the baby to wash his or her hands first.
- Keep your sense of humor.

Feeding the Baby: Breast versus Bottle

At the time most of the people reading this book were born, breastfeeding was out of style and most women our mothers' age were given a wide variety of reasons (by their doctors, of course) not to breastfeed. But in the nineties you'd be hard-pressed to find anyone in the medical community who doesn't agree that breastfeeding is just about the best thing you can do for your child. Here's why:

FOR THE BABY

- Breast milk provides exactly the right balance of nutrients needed by your newborn. In addition, breast milk contains several essential fatty acids that are not found in baby formula.
- Breast milk adapts, as if by magic, to your baby's changing nutritional needs. Neither of our children had a single sip of anything but breast milk for the first seven or eight months of life, and they're both wonderfully healthy kids.

Just Because You Don't Have Breasts Doesn't Mean You Can't Help Breastfeed

Sounds strange, but *you* play a major role in determining how long—and how well—your partner will breastfeed. Several studies have shown that women breastfeed longer when their partners learn about breastfeeding (which you'll do as you read these pages). And English breastfeeding expert Sheila Kitzinger has found that besides learning, the father's support and confidence in his partner are decisive factors in the mother's desire and ability to breastfeed.

- Breastfeeding greatly reduces the chance that your baby will develop food allergies. If either of your families has a history of food allergies, you should withhold solid foods for at least six months.
- Breastfed babies are less prone to obesity in adulthood than formula-fed babies. This may be because with the breast it's the baby—not the parent—who decides when to quit eating.
- Breastfed babies have a greatly reduced risk of developing respiratory and gastrointestinal illness.
- Breastfeeding is thought to transmit to the infant the mother's immunity to certain diseases.

Just Because Your Partner Has Breasts Doesn't Mean She Knows How to Use Them

As natural as breastfeeding appears to be, your partner and the baby may need anywhere from a few days to a few weeks to get the hang of it. The baby won't immediately know how to latch on to the breast properly, and your partner—never having done this before—won't know exactly what to do either. This initial period, in which cracked and even bloody nipples are not uncommon, may be quite painful for your partner. And with the baby feeding six or seven times a day, it may take as long as two weeks for your partner's nipples to get sufficiently toughened up.

Surprisingly, your partner won't begin producing any real milk until two to five days after the baby is born. But there's no need to worry that the baby isn't getting enough food. Babies don't eat much the first 24–48 hours, and any sucking they do is almost purely for practice. Whatever nutritional needs your baby has will be fully satisfied by the tiny amounts of colostrum your partner produces. (Colostrum is a kind of premilk that helps the baby's immature digestive system get warmed up for the task of digesting real milk later.)

Overall, the first few weeks of breastfeeding can be very stressful for your partner. If this is the case, do not be tempted to suggest switching to bottles. Instead, be supportive, praise her for the great job she's doing, bring her something to eat or drink while she's feeding, and encourage her to keep trying. You also might ask your pediatrician for the name of a local lactation consultant (what a job!).

FOR YOU AND YOUR PARTNER

- It's convenient—no preparation, no heating, no bottles or dishes to wash . . .
- It's free. Formula can cost a lot of money.
- It gives your partner a wonderful opportunity to bond with the baby. In addition, breastfeeding will help get your partner's uterus back into shape and may reduce her risk of both ovarian and breast cancer.
- In most cases, there's always as much as you need, and never any waste.
- Your baby's diapers won't stink. It's true. Breastfed babies produce stool that—especially when compared to formula stools—doesn't smell half bad.

What If Your Partner Doesn't Breastfeed

JUICE

If you and your partner decide not to breastfeed or decide to supplement breastfeeding with a bottle, don't fill it with juice. A recent study found that children who drink large quantities of fruit juice—especially apple juice—suffer from frequent diarrhea and, in the worst cases, may fail to grow and develop normally. The problem is that babies love juice so much that, if you give them all they want, they'll fill up their tiny stomachs with it, leaving no room for the more nutritious foods they need. The American Dietetic Association recommends that parents refrain from giving their babies juice until they're at least six months old, and then restrict juice intake until age two.

FORMULA

Prices vary. You can use powdered, full-strength liquid, or liquid concentrate. But when you start checking formula prices, your partner may decide to keep breastfeeding a while longer. When we weaned our older daughter, we put her on the powdered formula; I made a pitcher of it every morning and kept it in the refrigerator.

A Few Cosmetic Details

SKIN

Before my first daughter was born, I'm pretty sure that I believed that she—even right after her birth—would look radiant and have clear, glowing skin. Well, chalk up another victory for the ad execs. The fact is that in most cases, babies' skin isn't radiant or clear. But before you panic and call a dermatologist, here are some of the more common, and perfectly normal, newborn skin conditions you should know about:

- **Acne.** These cute little pimples are usually confined to the baby's face and are either the result of your partner's hormones continuing to swim through the baby's system or of his underdeveloped pores. Either way, don't squeeze, poke, pick at, or scrub these pimples. Just wash them with water a few times a day, pat them dry, and they'll go away in a few months.
- **Blisters.** Pictures taken of babies in utero have shown that long before birth, they frequently suck their thumbs—or any other part of their body they can reach. Sometimes they suck so hard they raise blisters.
- **Jaundice.** If your baby's skin and/or the whites of his eyes seem a little yellow, he may have jaundice. This condition is the result of the baby's liver being unable adequately to process bilirubin, a yellowish by-product of red blood cells. It affects about 25 percent of newborns (and a higher percentage of preemies), appears within the first five days of life, and is usually gone a few days later.
- **Splotches, blotches, birthmarks.** They can be white, purple, brown, or even yellow with white bumps in the center, and they can appear on the face, legs, arms, back. In most cases, they'll go away on their own if you just leave them alone. But if you're really worried, check with your pediatrician.
- **Cradle cap.** Also called seborrheic dermatitis, cradle cap looks like flaky, yellowish, sometimes greasy dandruff. It usually shows up on the head, but can also work its way into baby's eyebrows. It isn't a serious condition and will bother you much more than it does the baby. Frequent shampooing with a baby shampoo will help it go away.

CLEANING

Your baby's umbilical cord stump will drop off anywhere from one to three weeks after she's born. Until then, limit your baby-washing efforts to sponge baths. Keep the stump as dry as possible and clean it with rubbing alcohol on a cotton swab every time you change her diaper. Folding down the front of the diaper exposes the stump to more air and speeds up the falling-off process.

Until your baby starts moving around by herself, don't bathe her any more often than three times a week. (You may take a shower every day, but until she starts crawling, she's unlikely to do anything that would get her terribly dirty.) Any more than that could unnecessarily dry her skin. A few exceptions: it's okay to clean the baby's face every day, and be sure to carefully clean everything covered up by her diapers every time you change one.

For Boys Only

I'm assuming that by now, you and your partner have already made your decision about whether or not to circumcise your son. Whatever your choice, your son's penis requires some special care.

THE CIRCUMCISED PENIS

The penis will be red and sore for a few days after the circumcision. Until it's fully healed, you'll need to protect the newly exposed tip and keep it from sticking to the inside of his diaper (a few tiny spots of blood on his diapers for a few days, however, is perfectly normal). Ordinarily, you'll need to keep the penis dry, and the tip lubricated with petroleum jelly or antibiotic ointment and wrapped in gauze to protect it from urine, which is very irritating. The person who performed the circumcision or the hospital nursing staff will be able to tell you how long to keep the penis covered and how often to change the bandages.

THE UNCIRCUMCISED PENIS

Even if you elect not to circumcise your son, you'll still have to spend some time taking care of his penis. The standard way to clean an uncircumcised penis is to retract the foreskin and gently wash the head of the penis with mild soap and water. However, 85 percent of boys under six months have foreskins that don't retract, according to the American Academy of Pediatrics. If this is the case with your son, do not force it. Check with your pediatrician immediately and follow his or her hygiene instructions carefully. Fortunately, as boys get older, their foreskins retract on their own; by age one, 50 percent retract, and by age three, 80 to 90 percent.

Notes:

1 MONTH

Getting to Know You

What's Going On with the Baby

Physically

- Most of your baby's physical movements are still reflexive. But sometime this month, while flailing his arms around he'll accidentally stick his hand into his mouth. After getting over the initial shock, your baby will realize that sucking—even when there's no milk involved—is downright fun. By the end of the month, he'll probably be able to get his hand in his mouth—on purpose—fairly regularly.
- Lying on his tummy, he's now able to lift his head just enough to turn it so his nose won't be smashed into the mattress.
- If you put him in a sitting position, he'll try to keep his head in line with his back, but he won't be able to hold it steady for more than a second or two without support.
- Waste production is way down: 2 to 3 bowel movements and 5 to 6 wet diapers per day.

Intellectually

- Your baby is already beginning to express an interest in finding out what's new in the world—he'll stare at a new object for much longer than a familiar one.
- According to psychiatrist Peter Wolff, an object exists for a baby only as "something to suck, or something to see, or something to grasp, but not as something to grasp *and* to see at the same time."

Verbally

- As his vocal chords mature, your baby will be able to expand his collection of animal sounds to include some small, throaty, and incredibly cute noises.
- He is already beginning to differentiate between language and the other kinds of noise he hears all day.
- Still, his main form of using his vocal chords will be to cry—something he'll do for a total of about three hours a day.

Emotionally/Socially

- Don't expect many hints from your baby about what he's thinking—most of the time his expression is pretty blank.
- Not quite ready for the cocktail circuit, your baby is probably sleeping 16 to 20 hours a day. In fact, he may use sleep as a kind of self-defense mechanism, shutting down his systems when he gets overstimulated.

What You're Going Through

Bonding with the Baby

In one of the earliest studies of father-infant interaction, researcher Ross Parke made a discovery that shocked a lot of traditionalists: fathers were just as caring, interested, and involved with their infants as mothers were, and they held, touched, kissed, rocked, and cooed at their new babies with at least the same frequency as mothers did. Several years later, Dr. Martin Greenberg coined a term, *engrossment,* to describe "a father's sense of absorption, pre-occupation, and interest in his baby."

Over the years a number of other researchers have confirmed these findings about father-infant interaction and have concluded that what triggers engross-ment in men is the same thing that prompts similar nurturing feelings in women: early infant contact. "In sum," writes Dr. Parke, "the amount of stimulatory and affectional behavior depends on the opportunity to hold the infant."

Not surprisingly, Parke and others have found that men who attended their babies' birth bonded slightly faster than those who didn't. But if you weren't able to be there for the birth, don't worry. "Early contact at birth is not a magic pill," writes Ellen Galinsky. "It does not guarantee attachment. Neither does lack of contact prevent bonding."

But What If I Don't Bond Right Away?

If you haven't established an instant bond with your baby, there's absolutely nothing wrong with you. In fact, in a study by psychiatrists Kay Robson and

Remesh Kumar, 25 to 40 percent of new parents—mothers *and* fathers—admitted that their first response to the baby was "indifference." Putting it in slightly stronger terms, researcher Katherine May says, "This bonding business is nonsense. We've sold parents a bill of goods. They believe that if they don't have skin-to-skin contact within the first fifteen minutes, they won't bond. Science just doesn't show that."

This really makes more sense than the love-at-first-sight kind of bonding you hear so much about. And anyway, there's no evidence whatsoever that your relationship with or feelings for your child will be any less loving than if you'd fallen head over heels in love in the first second. So, just take your time. Don't pressure yourself, and don't think for a second that you've failed as a father.

In addition, there's a lot of evidence that parent-child bonding comes as a result of physical closeness. So if you'd like to speed up the process, try carrying the baby every chance you get, taking him with you whenever you can, and taking care of as many of his basic needs as possible.

My Baby Doesn't Love Me

For about the first six to eight weeks of life, your baby probably won't give you much feedback about how you're doing as a father: he won't smile, laugh, or react to you in any noticeable way. In fact, just about all he will do is cry. This can result in your feeling unloved and, surprisingly often, feeling a need to "get even" with the baby by deliberately withholding your own love.

As the grown-up, it's your job to nip this destructive cycle in the bud. "The relationship between parent and child is interactive," writes Ellen Galinsky. "What the child does affects what the parent does, which in turn affects what the child does." So if you find yourself feeling unloved or unappreciated by your newborn, here are a few things to keep in mind:

- Although your baby can express preferences for sounds, tastes, or patterns (see pages 13–14, 19), he is not yet capable of expressing love.
- Your baby's needs and wants are fairly limited at this stage—feed me, change me, hold me, put me in bed—and he has a different way of letting you know which one he wants. If you pay close attention, you'll soon be able to figure out what he's "telling" you. Getting to know your baby in this way will make you feel less anxious and more confident as a parent, which will make the baby more comfortable with you, which in turn will make your mutual attachment more secure.
- Another important way to get to know your baby is by carefully reading the "What's Going On with the Baby" sections of this book. Knowing what your baby is capable of—and what he isn't—at various stages can go a long way

Attachment and Bonding Are *Not* the Same Thing

While there's no question that bonding with your baby is an important goal, it is essentially a one-way street: you establish a relationship with the infant and don't get much back. But attachment is more of a two-way street: you and the baby establish relationships with each other.

In our attachment relationships with adults (including our partners), both players have "relatively equal positions in providing an emotionally satisfying relationship with each other," write Barbara and Philip Newman of Ohio State University. But the attachment you have with your baby is not—by any stretch of the imagination—equal. It is, however, balanced in very interesting and delicate ways.

Basically, it works like this: as you learn to read your baby's signals and satisfy his needs in an appropriate way, he learns to view you as a reliable and responsive person—someone he can count on in times of trouble. And he'll find some way (babies always do) to get you the message that you're needed and wanted.

This exchange of information is what psychologist Bertrand Cramer and pediatrician T. Berry Brazelton call "synchronous communication." And according to them, parents who have synchronous communication with their babies "experience their own competence. . . . When they achieve it for themselves, the most insecure parents can feel a sense of control, over their baby's vulnerabilities and over their own."

Meanwhile, babies who have synchronous "chats" with their parents come to prefer them over any of the other adults around who might be able to satisfy a need or two. Over time, this kind of preference (based on feelings of security and the parents' reliability) develops into self-confidence and becomes the foundation for all of the growing baby's future relationships.

toward helping you understand your baby's behavior and establish reasonable expectations.

- Change your perspective a little. The fact that your baby often stops crying when you pick him up and that he loves to fall asleep on your chest are signs that he feels close to you and trusts you—critical steps on the way to the love you want him to feel. Allow yourself the pleasure of stroking his incredibly soft skin, of admiring his tiny fingers, and of filling your lungs with his clean, new baby smell. If that doesn't hook you, nothing will.

Bonding, Attachment, and Adoptive Parents

It's extremely common for adoptive couples—particularly those who adopted because of infertility—to feel insecure or inadequate as parents. They often believe that the process of bonding and forming an attachment with a baby comes "naturally" to birth parents, and that since they weren't with the baby from the beginning, they'll never be as close to their child as a biological parent would.

The good news is that this isn't true. "Most infants, if adopted before the age of nine months," write adoption psychotherapists Judith Schaffer and Christina Lindstrom, "will take to their new parents as if they were born to them, developing an attachment to them as they would have done to their birth parents."

There are things, of course, that can interfere with adoptive parent-child attachment. Among the most common are the feelings of inadequacy discussed above, and the age and physical health of the child at adoption. But remember: as we've discussed earlier in this chapter, the processes of bonding and attachment don't happen automatically. They take time—and often a lot of work—to develop. In all but the rarest cases, the desire for attachment to a child can overcome even the most formidable obstacles.

So if you're worried for any reason about your abilities as a parent or about anything else that might get in the way of your relationship with your adopted child, call the National Adoption Information Clearinghouse, at (301) 231-6512, or The National Adoption Center, at (800) TO-ADOPT. Either of these organizations can refer you to resources—including support groups and counseling services—in your area. A few other adoption-related resources are listed in the Resources appendix of this book.

The Incredible Shrinking Baby

In their first week or so of life, most babies lose some weight—often as much as 25 percent of their birth weight. This can be pretty scary, especially since babies are generally supposed to get bigger over time, not smaller. This shrinking baby thing is perfectly normal (in the first few days the baby isn't eating much), and your baby will probably regain his birth weight by the time he's two weeks old. After that, the rate of growth—for the next few months, at least—is phenomenal: about an ounce a day and an inch per month. Doesn't sound like much, but if he continued growing at this rate, by his eighteenth birthday your baby would be nearly twenty feet tall and weigh in at about 420 pounds.

During every visit to the pediatrician your baby will be weighed, his overall length and head circumference will be measured, and the results will be given not only in inches (or centimeters) but in *percentile.* (If your baby is in the 75th percentile for weight, that means that he's heavier than 75 percent of babies the same age.) Try not to get too caught up with these numbers. As with most things, bigger isn't necessarily better; more important, it's normal for different parts of a baby's body to grow at different rates. Both my daughters, for example, were built like nails—90th percentile for both height and head size, but 40th percentile for weight.

Keep in mind also that the numbers on these charts generally apply to formula-fed babies, who tend to bulk up a little more quickly than their breastfed agemates.

You and Your Baby

The most important thing you can do for your baby is to make him feel loved and cared for. And the best way to do this is to continue to do the activities listed on pages 19–20, only more so.

Reading

At this age, you can read just about anything to your baby—even *War and Peace* or those *New Yorker* profiles you're so behind on. "What is important . . . is that the child becomes accustomed to the rhythmic sounds of your reading voice and associates it with a peaceful, secure time of day," writes Jim Trelease, author of *The New Read Aloud Handbook.* So set up a regular reading time and place. And as with most baby-related things, your baby will let you know whether she's interested or not, so don't force her to sit through the end of a chapter.

Toys and Games

Giving your baby a rattle, stuffed animal, or anything else that needs to be grasped is a total waste of time. She simply isn't interested in toys right now. That doesn't mean, however, that she doesn't want to play. If you pay close attention, you'll soon figure out when she's telling you she wants to play. "She'll look you straight in the eye and 'talk' to you," write Drs. Art Ulene and Steven Shelov. "The talk may be only a syllable or two, or it may be a

"You have the right to remain silent . . ."

prolonged cooing, but you'll know from the tone and intensity whether she's in a good mood or a bad."

It's even more important that you learn to recognize the clues your baby gives you when she wants to quit. "At first she'll look away," say Ulene and Shelov. "Then she may become glassy-eyed or look right through you. She may move her body to physically turn away or simply go limp. Finally, if all else fails, she may wail for escape. By getting to know and respect your baby's early warning signals, you can spare both of you a lot of needless discomfort."

Visual Stimulation

Since your baby still isn't capable of grabbing hold of much of anything, she's doing most of her learning with her eyes. Here are a few ways to stimulate your baby visually:

- Fasten an unbreakable mirror securely to the inside of the baby's crib.
- Make sure the baby has a lot of different things to look at. For the first few months, infants are particularly responsive to high contrast, so black-and-white toys and patterns are often a big hit.
- Have your baby show you what she prefers. Hold up different patterns

12 to 18 inches from the baby's face for a few seconds. Which ones does she stare at intently? Which ones does she turn away from?

- Play some visual tracking games. With the baby on his back, hold a small object 12 to 18 inches from his nose. Move the object slowly to one side. Does the baby follow the object with his eyes? Does he move his head? Do the same thing for the other side.

Whatever games you're playing with the baby, keep in mind that your baby is not a trained seal and that these activities are games, not college entrance exams.

Mobiles

Mobiles are among the most popular furnishings in almost any baby's room. And this is the perfect time to put some up: one over the bed and perhaps another, smaller one over the changing table. When considering mobiles, keep these ideas in mind:

- Get mobiles that allow you to change the figures. As your baby gets older his taste will become more sophisticated and you'll need to keep up. My wife and I found that mobile characters were quite expensive; we could have bought a year's worth of clothes for the baby with what it would have cost us to buy five or six sets of mobile characters. The solution? Make your own.
- When buying or making mobile characters, keep in mind that the baby will be looking at them from underneath. Quite a number of manufacturers produce mobiles that are gorgeous when viewed from the parents' perspective, but from the baby's perspective they're essentially blank.
- At this point, your baby is still interested in simple lines: stripes, large squares, and the outlines of things. Intricate patterns or complicated designs are not appropriate now.
- Keep the mobile 6 to 18 inches above the baby's face and put it slightly to the side; babies don't like to look straight up for long.

Fun with Reflexes

"The newborn is faced with two fundamental and simultaneous challenges during the first weeks of life," writes child psychiatrist Stanley I. Greenspan. "The first is self-regulation—the ability to feel calm and relaxed, not overwhelmed by his new environment. The second is to become interested in the world about him."

Unfortunately, babies can't do much to accomplish either of these goals on their own. That's your job. And you'll do it by caring for and responding to your baby, and by providing him with a stimulating environment. But because your baby can't be expected to sit around waiting for you, he came fully equipped with a wide range of reflexes to get him started.

Yes, all that wild, seemingly random arm and leg flailing really has a purpose: "Many reflexes are designed to help infants to survive and lead them on to more complicated sequences of voluntary behavior," write the Newmans. "The sucking reflex is a good example. At birth, inserting something in an infant's mouth produces the sucking reflex. This reflex helps infants gain nourishment relatively easily before sucking behavior is under voluntary control."

Understanding these reflexes can give you greater insight into your baby's behavior. And by keeping track of when they disappear, you'll be able to monitor his development. Best of all, they're a lot of fun—for you as well as the baby.

In addition to these reflexes, there are a few more that the experts haven't yet figured out what to do with. For example, babies seem able to determine the path of an oncoming object; they will take defensive action (leaning back hard, turning away, closing eyes, bringing arms up in front of the face) if the object is going to hit them. But if the object isn't on a path that will hit the baby, he'll ignore it. If you want to try this, strap your baby into his car seat and, from a few feet away, move a ball or other fairly large object straight at his head and again past him.

If you want to experiment with any of these reflexes, the best time is during your baby's active alert stage (see page 18). Remember to be extra careful of the baby's head and to respect his desire to quit.

Family Matters

Crying

Since the moment your baby was born she's been trying to communicate with you. That's the good news. The bad news is that she settled on crying as the way to do it. It will take you a while to teach her that there are more effective, and less annoying, ways of getting your attention. In the meantime, though, if she's like most babies, she's a real chatterbox: 80 to 90 percent of all babies have crying spells that last from twenty minutes to an hour every day.

Of course, not all of your baby's tears mean that she is sad, uncomfortable, or dissatisfied with something you've done. Nevertheless, holding an inconsolably crying baby can bring out a range of emotions, even in the most seasoned parent, running from pity and frustration to fury and inadequacy.

Exploring Your Baby's Reflexes

IF YOU	THE BABY WILL
♦ Tap the bridge of your baby's nose (gently, please), turn on a bright light, or clap your hands close to his head	♦ Close his eyes tightly
♦ Make a sudden, loud noise or give the baby the sensation of falling	♦ Fling legs and arms out and back, throw head back, open eyes wide, and cry
♦ Straighten the baby's arms and legs	♦ Flex arms and legs
♦ Pull baby up to a sitting position (be sure to support baby's head while doing this)	♦ Snap eyes open, tense shoulders, try (usually unsuccessfully) to right head
♦ Stand baby up (while holding under the arms) on a solid surface; works just as well holding baby against a wall (but be sure to support her head)	♦ Lift one leg, then the other, as if marching
♦ Put baby on tummy on flat surface or support baby's chest on a water surface (if trying in water, *do not let go*—baby can't really swim); *never do this on a beanbag or other soft surface—baby can suffocate*	♦ Turn head to side and lift it slightly; wiggle arms around as if swimming
♦ Stroke back of hand or top of foot; gently poke sole	♦ Withdraw hand or foot and arch it
♦ Stroke leg or upper body	♦ Cross opposite leg or hand to push hand away
♦ Stroke palm or sole of foot	♦ Grasp with hand or foot; hand grasp may be strong enough to allow you to pull baby to sitting position (be sure to support head)

WHAT IT MEANS	HOW LONG UNTIL IT'S GONE
♦ Protects baby's eyes from being injured by an object or a harsh light	♦ 1–2 months
♦ A fairly primitive way for the newborn to call for help	♦ Called the Moro or startle reflex, disappears within 3 or 4 months
♦ Probably the body's attempt to resist being held down	♦ 3 months
♦ Attempts to get self upright	♦ Called the China Doll reflex, disappears within 1–2 months
♦ Baby can protect herself by kicking away potentially dangerous things; has absolutely nothing to do with real walking	♦ About 2 months
♦ A way for the baby to protect self against smothering	♦ 2–4 months
♦ Protection against pain	♦ 2–4 months
♦ Protection against pain	♦ 3–4 months
♦ Encourages baby to start understanding the shape, texture, and weight of whatever she's grasping	♦ 2–4 months

(continued on next page)

Exploring Your Baby's Reflexes *(continued from pages 40–41)*

IF YOU	THE BABY WILL
♦ Stroke cheek or mouth	♦ Turn head toward side being stroked, open mouth and start sucking
♦ Place an object over baby's face (be *very careful* while doing this)	♦ Open and close mouth vigorously, twist head, flail arms
♦ Place baby on his back and turn his head to one side (don't force anything)	♦ Straighten arm on the side he is looking, bend arm and leg on other side

Fathers are likely to experience these feelings—especially inadequacy—more acutely than mothers. As with so many mother/father differences, the culprit is socialization: most men come into fatherhood feeling less than completely confident in their own parenting abilities, and a baby's cries are too easily seen as confirmation that daddy is doing a less-than-adequate job.

As difficult as crying can be to deal with, you obviously don't want your baby to be completely silent (in fact, if your baby doesn't cry at least several times a day, have a talk with your pediatrician). Fortunately, there are a few things you can do to make your baby's crying a less unpleasant experience for both of you:

- **When (not if) your child starts to cry, resist the urge to hand him or her to your partner.** She knows nothing more about crying babies than you do (or will soon enough). Since each of you instinctively has a different way of interacting with the baby, your hanging in there through a crying spell will double the chances you'll find new ways to soothe the baby.
- **Learn to speak your baby's language.** By now, you can almost always tell your baby's cry from any other baby's, and you can probably recognize her "I'm tired," "Feed me now," and "Change my diaper" cries. And while the language she speaks isn't as sexy or as vocabulary-rich as French, your baby has added a few more "phrases" to her vocabulary, including "I'm as uncomfortable as hell," "I'm bored out of my mind," and "I'm crying because I'm mad and I'm not going to stop no matter what you do." Responding promptly when your baby cries will help you learn to recognize which cry is which. You'll then be able to tailor your response and keep your baby happy.
- **Carry your baby more.** The more you hold them (even when they're not

WHAT IT MEANS	HOW LONG UNTIL IT'S GONE
♦ Called rooting reflex, helps baby get ready to eat	♦ 3–4 months
♦ Attempt to keep from suffocating	♦ 5–7 months
♦ Called the tonic neck reflex or fencer's pose, encourages baby to use each side of body and to notice own hands	♦ 1–3 months

crying), the less likely they are to cry. In one study, researchers found that a two-hour increase in carrying time per day resulted in a 42 percent decrease in crying time.

- **Get to know your baby's routine.** Keeping a diary of when your baby cries, how long the crying spells last, and what (if anything) works to slow them down can really help. Some babies like to thrash around and cry a little (or a lot) before going to sleep; others don't.
- **If your partner is breastfeeding, watch what she eats.** This is especially important if the baby suddenly and inexplicably deviates from her normal crying routine. Broccoli, cauliflower, brussels sprouts, and milk, when consumed by nursing mothers, often result in gastrically distressed (and weepy) babies.

After you've tried soothing, feeding, changing the diaper, checking for uncomfortable clothing, and rocking, the baby may still continue to howl. Sometimes there's really nothing you can do about it (see the section "Coping with Crying," pages 44–45), but sometimes all it takes is a new approach. Here are a few alternatives you might want to try:

- **Hold the baby differently.** Not all babies like to be held facing you; some want to face out so they can see the world. One of the most successful ways I've learned to soothe a crying baby—and I've tried this on many kids besides my own—is to use Dave's Magic Baby Hold. (Dave, the father of a close friend, supposedly used the Hold to calm his own three children.) Quite simply, have the baby "sit" in the palm of your hand—thumb in front, the other fingers on the baby's bottom. Then have the baby lie face down on the inside of your forearm, with his or her head resting on the inside of your elbow. Use your other hand to stroke or pat the baby's back.

- **Distraction.** Offer a toy, a story, a song. If the baby is diverted by a story or song, you'd better be prepared to repeat it over and over and over. . . .
- **Give the baby something to suck on.** Just take a guess why they call them "pacifiers." If you don't approve of pacifiers, you can either help the baby suck on his or her own fingers, or loan out one of yours (for more on pacifiers, see page 137).
- **Give the baby a bath.** Some babies find warm water soothing. Others freak out when they get wet. If you do decide to try bathing a crying infant, don't do it alone. Holding onto a calm soapy baby is no easy chore. Keeping a grip on a squirming, screaming, soapy baby takes a team of highly trained specialists.
- **Invest in a frontpack.** No matter how strong you think you are, carrying a baby around—even a newborn—is rough on the arms and back.
- **Take the baby for a walk or a drive.** A word of caution: this doesn't work for all babies. When she was an infant, my elder daughter would fall asleep in the stroller or the car in a heartbeat. But my younger daughter hates riding in the car, especially when she's tired, and cries even more when she's put in her car seat. If you don't feel like going out, try putting the baby on top of a running washing machine or dryer. There's also a special device called SleepTight that, when attached to the baby's crib, simulates the feel (and sounds) of a car going fifty-five miles an hour. Call 1-800-NO-COLIC for more information.

Coping with Crying

If you've tried everything you can think of to stop the baby from crying but to no avail, here are some things that may help you cope:

- **Tag-team crying duty.** There's no reason why both you and your partner have to suffer together through what Martin Greenberg calls "the tyranny of crying." Spelling each other in twenty-minute or half-hour shifts will do you both a world of good. Getting a little exercise during your "time off" will also calm your nerves before your next shift starts.
- **Let the baby "cry it out."** If the crying has gone on for more than twenty minutes, you might put the baby in his crib and give yourself a break. If the baby doesn't stop screaming in ten minutes, pick him up and try to soothe him some other way for fifteen more minutes. Repeat as necessary. Note: The "crying it out" approach should be used only after you've tried everything else. Generally speaking, you should respond promptly and

"See what Daddy has for you, if you stop crying?"

lovingly to your baby's cries. Several studies show that babies who are responded to in this way develop into more confident youngsters.

- **Get some help.** Dealing with a crying child for even a few minutes can provoke incredible rage and frustration. And if the screams go on for hours, it can become truly difficult to maintain your sanity, let alone control your temper. If you find yourself concerned that you might lash out (other than verbally) at your child, call someone: your partner, pediatrician, parents, baby-sitter, friends, neighbors, clergy person, or even a parental-stress hotline. If your baby is a real crier, keep these numbers handy.
- **Don't take it personally.** Your baby isn't deliberately trying to antagonize you. It's all too easy to let your frustration at this temporary situation permanently interfere with the way you treat your child. "Even if your powerful feelings don't lead to child abuse," write the authors of *What to Expect the First Year,* "they can start eroding your relationship with your baby and your confidence in yourself as a parent unless you get counseling quickly."

Dealing with Postpartum Blues and Depression

About 70 percent of new mothers experience periods of mild sadness, weepiness, moodiness, sleep deprivation, loss of appetite, inability to make decisions, anger, or anxiety after the baby is born. These postpartum blues, which many

Colic

Starting at about two weeks of age, some 10–20 percent of babies develop colic—crying spells that, unlike "ordinary" crying, can last for hours at a time. Although many colicky babies limit their crying to certain times of the day, many others cry all day or all night. The duration and intensity of crying spells peaks at about six weeks, and usually disappears entirely within three months.

Since there's no real agreement on what causes colic or on what to do about it, your pediatrician probably won't be able to offer a quick cure. Some parents, however, have been able to relieve (partially or completely) their colicky infants with an over-the-counter gas remedy for adults. Talk to your doctor about whether he or she thinks taking this medication would benefit your child. Here are a few other approaches to dealing with colic (or crying babies in general).

- Use the methods described in the "Crying" and "Coping with Crying" sections.
- If you're bottle-feeding the baby, try taking her off cow's milk. Some pediatricians feel that colic may be linked to a milk intolerance and suggest switching to a non–cow's milk formula.
- Hold the baby facing you, with his head over your shoulder and your shoulder pressing on his stomach.
- Hold the baby a little *less*. One school of thought maintains that some babies cry because their nervous systems aren't mature enough to handle the stimulation that comes with being held and stroked and talked to. But don't do this unless your physician advises you to.
- Put a hot water bottle on your knees, place the baby face down across it to warm his tummy, and stroke his back.
- Baby massage (see pages 59–60).
- Try swaddling. Being enveloped in a blanket may make the baby feel more comfortable.
- See the section on anger (pages 199–202).

believe are caused by hormonal shifts in a new mother's body, can last for hours or days, but in most cases they disappear within a few weeks. If you notice that your partner is experiencing any of these symptoms, there's not much you can do except be supportive. Encourage her to get out of the house for a while and see to it that she's eating healthily.

In a small number of cases, postpartum blues can develop into postpartum depression. According to the American College of Obstetricians and Gynecologists, postpartum depression, if not recognized and treated, may become worse or last longer than it needs to. Here are some symptoms to watch out for:

- Postpartum blues that don't go away after two weeks, or feelings of depression or anger that surface a month or two after the birth.
- Feelings of sadness, doubt, guilt, helplessness, or hopelessness that begin to disrupt your partner's normal functioning.
- Inability to sleep when tired, or sleeping most of the time, even when the baby is awake.
- Marked changes in appetite.
- Extreme concern and worry about the baby—or lack of interest in the baby and/or other members of the family.
- Fear of harming the baby or thoughts of self-harm.

Again, most of what your partner will go through after the birth is completely normal and nothing to worry about. If you're really concerned, however, encourage your partner to talk with you about what she's feeling and to see her doctor or a therapist.

Even Guys Get the Blues

Although postpartum blues or depression are almost always associated with women, the fact is that many men also get the blues after their babies are born. Men's blues, however, are not hormonally based like their partner's. The feelings of sadness, the mood swings, and the anxiety you may be experiencing are more likely the result of coming face to face with the reality of your changing life.

"The hearty congratulations at work last a few days," writes S. Adams Sullivan, author of *The Father's Almanac,* "but then your status as a celebrity wears off and you begin to notice that you're coming home every night to a demanding baby and a distraught wife, and the bills are piling up. . . . You look at your wife and . . . the healthy, radiant glow that made her beautiful while she was pregnant has disappeared, and you're tempted to agree with her when she gripes about her looks . . . you're getting maybe four and a half hours of sleep, total, and that's broken up into hour-and-a-half naps, so that you're nodding off every day at work and falling behind."

Fortunately, most men (and women, for that matter) don't suffer from any kind of postpartum depression. But if you do, you can take some comfort in knowing that it will eventually pass: you'll get caught up at work, the baby will settle into a routine, you'll get more sleep, and your wife's body will somehow get back to looking pretty much the way it did before she got pregnant.

Safety First

It may seem strange to talk about safety at a time when the baby is practically immobile and probably can't get into any serious trouble. But even at this age babies can do the most surprising things. Here are a few precautions you should take now to start making your home a little safer:

- Avoid beanbags. Most beanbag chairs and baby rests have been taken off the market, but there are still plenty of them in garages all over the country. There is more than a coincidental link between beanbags and suffocation deaths.
- Never leave the baby's car seat—with the baby in it, of course—balanced on anything. A flailing arm or leg, even a sneeze, might move the car seat enough for it to tip over.
- Put together a good first aid kit. You can find a list of items on page 140.
- Take an infant CPR class. Instruction is usually available at your local Red Cross or YMCA.
- Take a quick look at the safety measures described in later chapters (pages 138–41, for example). Start putting together the materials you'll need and get into the habit of doing such things as pointing pot handles toward the rear of the stove.

Notes:

2 MONTHS

First Smiles

What's Going On with the Baby

Physically

- By the end of this month, most of your baby's innate reflexes will have disappeared. Sad but true. Nevertheless, she still holds her arms and legs away from her body, and there's plenty of twitching to go around.
- Lying on her tummy, she can now hold her head at a 45-degree angle for a few minutes. And when she's sitting (a position she probably prefers by now), she's getting a lot better at keeping her head straight.
- Your baby is now beginning to reach for objects. Grasping, which was once purely a reflex action, is now becoming voluntary. She even may be able to hold small objects for a few minutes at a time.
- Although her vision is still limited to what's directly in front of her face, just about everything is now in focus. And because you're such an interesting sight, she'll follow you with her eyes everywhere you go.

Intellectually

- As her brain develops, your baby will prefer more complex patterns. Instead of the simple, relatively motionless outline of your face, she now prefers your eyes and mouth, which are constantly changing shape.
- If you touch her cheek now, she probably won't start sucking—an indication that she can now tell the difference between your finger and a milk-bearing nipple.
- She is also now able to accommodate herself to various situations. If you're

holding her upright against your shoulder, she'll hold herself differently than if you're resting her on your knees.

- She gets excited when she sees familiar objects, but she has no sense of "object permanence" (which means that as far as the baby is concerned, anything she can't see simply doesn't exist).

Verbally

- Leaving behind the grunting and squeaking, your baby is adding to her repertoire some delightful cooing (a combination of a squeal and a gurgle), as well as some impressive oohs, ohhs, and ahhs.
- Crying, however, is still one of her favorite ways of communicating.

Emotionally/Socially

- And now, the moment you've been waiting for: your baby is finally able to smile at you (sorry, but until now those things you thought were smiles were probably just gas).
- As she becomes more and more interested in learning about her world (a process that hopefully won't stop for the rest of her life), your baby will really enjoy regular changes of scenery; she's also very capable of expressing excitement—and distress.
- She's awake about 10 hours a day; although she's stimulated more by touch than by social interaction, she'll stay awake longer if there are people around to amuse her.

What You're Going Through

Thinking about Sex

Most OB/GYNs advise their patients to refrain from intercourse for at least six weeks after giving birth. But before you mark that date on your calendar, remember that the six-week rule is only a guideline. Resuming intercourse ultimately depends on the condition of your partner's cervix and vagina, and, more important, on how you're both feeling. Many couples begin having sex again in as little as three or four weeks, but it's not at all uncommon for couples to take as long as six months to fully reestablish their prepregnancy sex life.

Many factors—both physical and psychological—influence when and how a couple decides to resume their sex life. Here are a few:

- When you had sex with your partner before, she was the woman you loved. Now she's also a mother—a thought that may remind you of your own

> **Nonsexual and Almost Nonsexual Affection**
> Professors Phil and Carolyn Cowan have found that many couples need practice finding sensual ways to please each other short of intercourse. Hand-holding, back rubs, hair stroking while watching TV, or even gentle, nonsexual kissing are good for those times one of you isn't in the mood. If you're not in the mood but want to give—or receive—some nonsexual affection, tell your partner up front that there are no strings attached. Researchers have found that men and women who don't want sex are frequently afraid that the kiss or hug they need from, or want to give to, their partners will be misinterpreted as a sexual overture.

mother and can be a big turn-off. At the same time, in your new capacity as parent, you may remind your partner a little too much of her own father. She may also find it tough to reconcile her roles as lover and mother, and may see herself as unsexual.

- Your partner may not have fully recovered from her episiotomy or C-section.
- Your partner may be embarrassed if milk flows from her breasts when she's aroused.
- A lot of men find leaking breasts erotic. But if you don't—and she senses your feelings—she may worry that you don't find her desirable anymore.
- Some men have "emotional difficulty being sexual with the part of their wives that produced their children," says psychologist Jerrold Shapiro. And a lot of women find it difficult to think of their vaginas as sexual organs after seeing babies come out of them.
- You may resent your baby's unlimited access to your partner's breasts and feel that your partner is focusing more on the baby than on you.
- Your (or your partner's) motivation to have sex may have changed since your baby was born. If, for example, you or she were motivated to have sex because you really wanted to be a parent, sex after having a baby may feel a little anticlimactic, so to speak.
- Now that you have concrete proof (the baby) of your virility, you may feel more intimate with your partner than ever before.

When You and Your Partner are Out of Sync

Just as you and your partner can't always agree on what movie you want to see or what you want to have for dinner, you can't expect that you'll both feel sexually aroused at the same time. She might want to make love at a time when

The First Time . . . Again

When you do finally get around to making love, you should expect the first few times to be a period of tentative rediscovery for both of you. Her body has changed, and she may respond differently than she used to. Some studies have shown that after giving birth women experience a slightly decreased interest in vaginal stimulation and an increased interest in clitoral and breast stimulation. Also, women who experienced multiple orgasms before giving birth are less likely to do so, or will do so less frequently, now.

She may also be worried that having sex will hurt, and you may be afraid of the same thing or that those extra pounds she hasn't lost yet will interfere with her pleasure. Go slowly, take your cues from her, and give yourselves plenty of time to get used to each other again.

Sex researchers William Fisher and Janice Gray found that nursing mothers generally resume their sexual lives sooner than women who don't breastfeed. This is a little odd, considering that nursing mothers produce lower levels of ovarian hormones, which are responsible for producing vaginal lubrication. As a result, if your partner is nursing, her vagina may be much drier than before, making intercourse painful. Obviously, this doesn't mean she isn't aroused by you; it's simply a common postbirth condition. In situations like these, a little K-Y Jelly, Astroglide, or other over-the-counter lubricant will go a long way.

you're simply too tired to move. Or you might want to have sex when she's feeling "touched out," having spent an entire day with a baby crawling all over her, sucking her breasts.

The months right after the birth of a baby are a particularly vulnerable time for your sex life. "If you had a good sex life before and during the pregnancy, it is important to be intentional about keeping a positive sex life after the birth of your child," says Dr. William Stayton, a professor of human sexuality at the University of Pennsylvania. "If you did not have a good sex life before the pregnancy, then it is very likely that it will not get better after the birth of your child unless you intentionally give time and energy to your sexual relationship." Here are a few suggestions that might help smooth over some of the rough spots you'll invariably encounter:

- Figure out what, exactly, is motivating you to want to have sex. "Sex can be an expression of monogamy, intimacy, love, or even an affirmation of one's sexual identity ('I'm a man and this is what men do')," says Linda Perlin

Alperstein, an associate professor at the University of California, San Francisco. "It can also be the only way some of us ever get held and touched lovingly in our culture." And for some people (this is pretty rare, though) sex is thought of exclusively as a way to reproduce.

- Talk. "Unless the couple can talk about their sex life, their entire relationship may suffer, and that in turn will compound their sexual problems," write psychologists Libby and Arthur Colman.
- Negotiate. If you really want to have sex and she doesn't, ask her—without putting a lot of pressure on her—what, if anything, she'd be willing to do. Would she, for example, be willing to masturbate you? Would she hold you in her arms or let you touch her breasts while you stimulate yourself? It goes without saying (or at least it should) that you should be prepared to reciprocate. The object here is not to convince her to have sex with you; the two of you should be working toward creating an environment in which you both feel safe expressing your desires and in which each of you can turn the other down without fear of causing offense or hurting feelings.
- Be completely honest. If you and your partner agree that you'll hold each other like spoons and kiss, but that you won't touch each other's genitals, don't go over the line. Doing so will only make her tense and not trust you.
- Change your attitude. A lot of men have the idea that every erection has to be paired up with an ejaculation. "But the truth is that just being aroused can be nice—and quite enjoyable," says Linda Alperstein. "So rather than have no sexual life if you can't have the one you fantasize about, enjoy what you can have; just enjoy the fact that you can get aroused again. You don't have to actually reach an orgasm to experience pleasure."
- Take it easy. "While a positive sexual relationship is a very nice and important component of an enduring and happy marriage," writes psychologist Brad Sachs, "it will not, by itself, ensure one."
- Ask for—and give your partner—some nonsexual affection (see page 51).

Not Ready to Be a Father

One of the most consistent findings by researchers is that new fathers almost always feel unprepared for their new role. Personally, I would have been surprised if it were otherwise. As writer David L. Giveans says, "It is both unfair and unrealistic to expect a man . . . to automatically 'father' when his life experiences have skillfully isolated him from learning how."

When most of our fathers were raising us, a "good father" was synonymous with "good provider." He supported his family financially, mowed the lawn, washed the car, and maintained discipline in the home. No one seemed to care

"You're not real experienced at this father business, are you?"

whether he ever spent much time with his children; in fact, he was *discouraged* from doing so, and told to leave the kids to his wife, the "good mother."

Yesterday's "good father" has now retroactively become an emotionally distant, uncaring villain. And today's "good father," besides still being a breadwinner, is expected to be a real presence—physically and emotionally—in his kids' lives. This, in a nutshell, is exactly what most new fathers want. Most of us have no intention of being wait-till-your-father-comes-home dads and want to be more involved with our children than our own fathers were. The problem is that we just haven't had the training.

The solution? Quit complaining and jump right in. The "maternal instinct" that women are supposedly born with is actually acquired on the job. And that's exactly where you're going to develop your "paternal instinct."

Confusion

If there's one thing that set my first few months of fatherhood apart from the next few years, it was the confusing and often conflicting emotions I felt:

- On the one hand, I had a sense of incredible virility, power, and pride at having created a new life. On the other, I often felt helpless when I couldn't understand—let alone satisfy—the baby's needs.

- Most of the time I felt the most powerful kind of love for my tiny child. But sometimes I also felt ambivalent. And once in a while I felt a powerful anger—one that seemed to come out of nowhere—at the very same baby.
- Most of the time I felt particularly close to my wife—especially when we would admire our children together. But every so often I'd get suspicious that she loved them more than she did me.

Apparently I wasn't the only confused new dad around. "Almost all new fathers express some level of confusion," says psychologist Bruce Linton, who runs workshops for expectant and new fathers. But as if feeling confused isn't bad enough, Linton has found that new fathers "consistently express anxiety and concern that there's something wrong with them or that they're abnormal because they're confused."

Before you go off and check yourself into a mental hospital, there are a few things you should know. First, being confused isn't abnormal at all. After spending the day in Linton's workshop discussing their concerns with other men, new fathers are greatly relieved to find out that their feelings aren't all that different from those of any other new father. (And anyway, doesn't it seem logical that if almost everyone thinks he's abnormal, then being abnormal must really be the norm?) Second, this state of confusion—and the accompanying suspicions about your sanity—usually disappear by the end of the third month.

Fears—Lots of Them

The combination of feeling unprepared and confused at the same time can be rather frightening, and the first few months of fatherhood are riddled with fears. Here are some of the most common:

- Fear of not being able to live up to your own expectations.
- Fear of not being able to protect your children from physical harm as they grow and develop.
- Fear of not being able to deal with the most basic parenting responsibilities: feeding, clothing, earning enough money, dealing with the baby's illnesses.
- Fear of not being able to shield your child from some of the more abstract horrors of modern life: poverty, war, disease, the destruction of the environment . . .
- Fear of simply not being "ready" to assume the role of father.
- Fear of picking up the baby because you think you might hurt him.
- Fear of your anger at the baby.

Don't Panic

Taken together, the feelings of unpreparedness, the fears, and the confusion so many new fathers experience can be overwhelming. Unfortunately, some men respond to this turmoil by running away—emotionally, physically, or both—from their kids and their partners. If you're feeling unable to deal with your anxieties and your feelings, do *not* run. Find yourself a more experienced father about your age and ask him to help you sort things out (see pages 133–35 for information on fathers' groups). If you can't find another father, talk to your partner. And if none of those alternatives work, find a good therapist, preferably one with experience dealing with men's concerns. There *is* help out there; you just have to find it.

- Fear of not being able—or willing—to love the baby enough.
- Fear of not being in control (see pages 73–74).
- Fear of repeating the mistakes made by your own father (see pages 71–72).
- Fear that if you discuss your fears with your partner, she'll misinterpret them and think you don't love her or the baby.

Some fears—such as fear of poverty and war, or of not being ready—you just can't do anything about. But others you can. For example, fear of not being able to handle the little things can be overcome by practice; fear of hurting the baby can also be overcome by spending more time carrying, stroking, picking up, and holding him—babies are not nearly as fragile as they look; and the fear of discussing things with your partner can be cured (to a certain extent) by taking a deep breath and telling her what you feel. She's going through many of the same things you are and will be relieved to find that she's not alone. Guaranteed.

Whatever your fears, you need to start by admitting to yourself that they exist and remembering that all new fathers are afraid sometimes. In his book *Fatherjournal,* David Steinberg eloquently describes coming to terms with himself and his fears. "I was going to be the perfect father: loving, caring, nurturing, soft. . . . I was going to do it right. . . . Tonight I see how scared I am. There is so much to do for this little creature who screams and wriggles and needs and doesn't know what he needs and relies on me to figure it out. . . . I need to accept my fear, my reluctance, my instinct to flee. I have to start from where I am instead of where the model new-age father would be."

Rethinking What It Means to Be a Man

There are two major reasons why so many of us would prefer to drive ten miles down the wrong road rather than stop and ask for directions. First, from the time we were little boys, we've been socialized to associate knowledge with masculinity—in other words, real men know everything, so admitting to being lost is a sign of weakness (and, of course, a lack of masculinity). Second, and even worse, we've also been socialized to be strong, independent, and goal-oriented, so asking for help is a sign of weakness (and, again, a lack of masculinity).

Nothing in the world can bring these two factors into play faster than the birth of a baby. Because of the near-total absence of active, involved, nurturing male role models, most new fathers can't seriously claim that they know what to do with a new baby (although never having cooked before didn't prevent my father from insisting he could make the best blueberry pancakes we'd ever taste; boy, was he wrong).

Getting help seems like the obvious solution to the ignorance problem, but most men don't want to seem helpless or expose their lack of knowledge by asking anyone. Now toss in a few more ingredients:

- The confusion and fears we've been feeling lately.
- The prevailing attitude that a man who is actively involved with his children—especially if he's the primary caretaker—is not as masculine as his less-involved brothers.
- Psychologist Henry Biller's observation that "too many men get caught up in the idea that to be an effective parent they must adopt a more maternal or mothering role."

It's easy to see how the whole experience of becoming a father can lead so many new fathers to wonder secretly (no one would ever *openly* admit to having these thoughts) whether or not they've retained their masculinity. All too often the result of this kind of thinking is that fathers leave all the child-rearing to their partners and thereby leave their kids essentially without a father. As Biller writes, "Children are at a particular disadvantage when they are deprived of constructive experiences with their fathers. Infants and young children are unlikely to be provided with other opportunities to form a relationship with a caring and readily available adult male if their father is not emotionally committed to them."

So you have a choice. Either accept the hardest yet most rewarding challenge you'll probably ever face by becoming an actively involved father and taking on a significant share of the responsibility for raising your children, or take the easy way out and leave it all to someone else. What would a "real" man do?

You and Your Baby

Awakening the Senses

Your baby was born equipped with the same five basic senses you were. And although his senses would probably develop pretty well without any additional help, there's a lot you can do (while having fun at the same time) to encourage development by exposing him to a broad range of sensory stimulation.

TASTE

By putting drops of various foods (in liquid) on babies' tongues, researchers have proven that babies have definite likes and dislikes. You're not going to try this, of course. At this age, your baby has no business eating anything but breast milk or formula. Save the experiments with real taste sensations for when you wean your baby (see pages 205–7). In the meantime, give the baby lots of different objects to put in his mouth. But be extremely careful that none of them is small enough to be a choking hazard or has removable pieces or sharp edges.

SMELL

Offer the baby a wide variety of things to smell:

- If you're cooking, let her smell the spices and other ingredients.
- If you're out for a walk, let her smell the flowers.
- Try some experiments to see whether she prefers sweet smells to sour ones.
- Be careful, though. Make sure she doesn't get any of these things in her mouth, and don't experiment with extremely strong smells. Also, stay away from ammonia, bleach, gasoline, paint thinner, pool or garden chemicals, and any other toxic materials you may have around the house.

SIGHT

- Experiment with the baby's sight. Regularly change the patterns and keep track of which ones he prefers. Over the course of the next few months he'll advance from simple shapes and patterns to more complex ones.
- Show him mirrors, pictures, and photographs.
- Take the baby out for a walk and let him see what's going on in the world.

TOUCH

Expose the baby to as many textures as possible: the satin edges of his blanket; the plastic (or cloth) on his diaper; the family dog; a window; your computer keyboard. Let the baby feel each object for as long as he's interested. And don't

No Baby Talk, Please

Whenever you talk to your baby, pay close attention to your voice. Your natural, conversational voice is best because it exposes the baby to English as it is actually spoken. For some reason I've never been able to understand, many people can't bring themselves to speak naturally to a baby. Instead, they smile the biggest fake smile they can and say things like "Cootchie-cootchie widduw baby-poo, can I pinchy-winchy your cheeky-weeky?" Is that really the way you want your baby to learn how to speak? Need I say more?

limit yourself to the baby's hands; you can gently rub objects on the baby's cheeks, arms, or legs. (From a very young age, both my daughters loved me to rub the bottoms of their feet on my two-day beard growth.) Again, use common sense here. Be gentle and don't leave any objects with the baby.

HEARING

- Expose the baby to as wide a variety of sounds as possible: the radio; any musical instruments you have around the house; construction sites (if they're not too loud). Does your baby seem to prefer one kind of noise—or music—over another?
- For fun, take a small bell, hold it behind the baby, and ring it gently. Does he try to turn around? Now move the bell to one side. Did the baby notice the change?
- Don't forget about your own voice. Make sounds, changing the pitch of your voice; sing; and even have leisurely chats (okay, monologues) with the baby.
- Play imitation games. Make a noise (a Bronx cheer is always a good place to start) and see whether the baby responds. It may take a few minutes or even a few days to get a reply. Once you do, try the same noise a few more times and then switch roles, having the baby initiate the "conversation" so you can imitate her.

Baby Massage

Many parents in Africa, Asia, and India massage their babies every day. But in the United States this idea is just catching on. And in the eyes of some, it's about time. According to researcher Tiffany Field, massage:

- Facilitates the parent-infant bonding process and the development of warm, positive relationships.

Massage for Preemies

Over a dozen researchers have seriously explored the question of whether baby massage could help preterm infants. One study found that preemies who had daily ten-minute sessions of neck, shoulder, back, and leg massage, and five minutes a day of gentle limb flexing gained 47 percent more weight than preterm babies who got no massage, even though the two groups did not differ in calorie intake. In addition, massaged infants were awake and active a greater percentage of the time, developed more quickly, and required six fewer days of hospitalization.

- Reduces stressful responses to painful procedures like vaccines (at least for the baby).
- Reduces pain associated with teething and constipation.
- Reduces colic.
- Helps induce sleep.
- Makes parents feel good while they're massaging their infants.

Sounds like it's at least worth a try, doesn't it? Here's how to do it:

1. With your fingertips, gently massage the baby's forehead, nose, and mouth.
2. Starting in the middle of your baby's chest, use a flat hand to stroke outward.
3. Do the same thing on his back—start from the middle and stroke outward.
4. Take one of the baby's feet with one hand. With the other, hold the baby's ankle like a baseball bat and slide your hand toward the thigh. Repeat with the other foot.
5. Do the same thing for the arms: start at the wrist and move toward the shoulder.

The best time to massage is when the baby is calm. You might want to rub a little baby oil or lotion on your hands before you start, and be sure to use a combination of straight and circular strokes.

It's especially important to keep the pressure gentle yet firm. Babies respond negatively to a very light touch, which they perceive as tickling. If at all possible, try to do some massage every day (or split the duties with your partner). If you're interested in learning more about baby massage, several books on the subject are probably available at your local library. One of the best is Vimala McClure's *Infant Massage: A Handbook for Loving Parents.*

The Importance of Squirming Around

Most two-month-old babies are not really mobile. They can raise their heads about 45 degrees, but rolling over is still a ways away. Nevertheless, it's a good idea to let your baby exercise her muscles. Here are a few ways to do this:

- Stop swaddling (if you haven't already). Your baby needs to practice using her arms and hands, something she won't be able to do if she's all bundled up in a blanket.
- When putting the baby down, alternate among front, back, left side, and right side. This encourages the baby to use as many different muscles as possible. Babies who spend all day on one side (including front or back) generally don't learn to lift their heads as quickly as those who are shifted from side to side.

Introducing the Doctor

If you went to all your partner's prenatal doctor visits, the schedule of visits to your baby's pediatrician will seem quite leisurely—only eight (usually called well-baby checkups) the entire first year. Whether or not you got into

Vaccinations

There has been a lot of controversy lately about vaccinations (Are the vaccines themselves dangerous? Are the risks worth the rewards?), and a small but growing number of people are electing not to have their children inoculated. On pages 62–65 you'll find a chart listing the vaccines, the possible side effects, and what might happen to someone who's not inoculated. If you're thinking of skipping the vaccinations, keep these points in mind:

- Almost all public schools, and many private ones, require proof of vaccination before admitting a child.
- Not vaccinating your kids can be a viable option only if everyone else's kids *are* vaccinated, thus reducing the chance that your child will be exposed to health risks. This is known as "herd immunity": if enough people are immune, they'll protect the rest of the "herd." Imagine what would happen if everyone decided not to vaccinate.

VACCINE	RISKS (👎) / REWARDS (👍)
Diphtheria, Pertussis, Tetanus (DPT) or Diphtheria, Tetanus (DT) or DTaP: same as above, minus pertussis part for babies who have: ♦ history of seizures ♦ suspected or known neurological disease ♦ reactions to previous shot	👍 almost all protected after 3 doses plus booster 👎 you'll need to observe baby carefully for 72 hours after shot 👎 some fussiness, drowsiness, soreness, or a lump at injection site 👎 fever for 24 hours after the shot is common 👎 irritation of the brain occurs in 1 in 100,000 kids, and rarely (1 in 310,000), permanent brain damage results. *Note:* Most of the risks are associated with the pertussis component. The only risk associated with the diphtheria and tetanus parts is local (injection site swelling)
Hepatitis B: a noninfectious vaccine produced from cultures	👍 almost all children protected after 3 doses 👎 no adverse reactions, but occasional fussiness 👎 possible soreness at injection site, low-grade fever, or headache
Haemophilus (HiB)	👍 90–100 percent protection rate after the full series of shots 👎 soreness and/or lump at the injection site 👎 fever (rarely above 101 degrees) for 12–24 hours after shot
Measles	👍 over 95 percent protected after one dose 👎 10–20 percent have mild fever or rash 10 days after shot 👎 1 in 1,000,000 may develop a brain disorder

WHAT IT PREVENTS	RISKS IF YOU GET THE DISEASE
Diphtheria	♦ extremely contagious ♦ attacks the throat and nose, interferes with breathing, and causes paralysis ♦ damages heart, kidneys, nerves ♦ 10–35 percent death rate
Pertussis (whooping cough): prior to the invention of this vaccine, pertussis caused as many deaths as all other contagious diseases combined	♦ can cause brain damage, pneumonia, and seizures ♦ can cause death (1–2 percent) ♦ most severe in young babies
Tetanus (lockjaw), caused by dirt getting in cuts	♦ causes painful muscle contractions ♦ 20–60 percent of kids die
Hepatitis B	♦ important cause of viral hepatitis ♦ complications include cirrhosis, chronic active hepatitis, and liver cancer
Haemophilus Influenza type B, bacterial infection of children under 5	♦ causes 12,000 cases of meningitis and 8,000 cases of deep-seated infections (bones, joint, heart, lungs, throat) each year ♦ 5 percent mortality rate
Measles	♦ a most serious, common childhood disease ♦ high fever (103–105 degrees) and rash for up to 10 days ♦ may cause pneumonia or ear infection ♦ 1 in 100 kids becomes deaf or develops brain disorders

(continued on next page)

(continued from pages 62–63)

VACCINE	RISKS (👎) / REWARDS (👍)
Mumps	👍 99 percent protected after one dose 👎 rare fever, rashes, and swelling of glands after vaccination
Rubella	👍 over 95 percent protected after one dose 👍 getting it now protects future fetuses of girl babies 👍 children of pregnant women can be vaccinated without risk to mother 👎 1 percent of young children will have temporary leg, arm, joint pain
MMR measles, mumps, rubella vaccines	👍 protection is as good as when vaccines are given separately 👍 side effects are same as when given separately
Oral Polio (OPV): three kinds of polio virus—your child needs all 3 vaccines to be protected	👍 drops, not shots 👍 95 percent receiving all 3 doses are protected 👍 no common reactions 👎 1 in 4 million chance of paralysis 👎 1 in 12 million chance of actually getting polio

the doctor-visit habit before the baby was born, make every effort to go to as many well-baby visits (and not-so-well-baby visits) as you can. Your doing so is good for everyone, says James Levine, head of the Fatherhood Project at the Families and Work Institute.

- Your baby will know that he can turn to you for help and that you'll be there to comfort him when he needs it.
- Your doctor will be able to get some of *your* family history to apply to the

WHAT IT PREVENTS	RISKS IF YOU GET THE DISEASE
Mumps	♦ causes fever and swelling of salivary glands ♦ may cause irritation of heart, pancreas, or thyroid ♦ can cause permanent deafness and temporary brain disorder
Rubella (German measles)	♦ can cause birth defects in fetus of pregnant women ♦ symptoms are mild, often missed
Mumps, Measles, Rubella	
Polio	♦ causes paralysis of arms and legs ♦ interferes with breathing ♦ 1 in 10 kids with polio dies

baby. And since most of what pediatricians know about their young patients comes from what the parents tell them, your input doubles the amount of information the doctor can use to make a diagnosis.

- You'll be more in touch with your child and more involved in his life.

Most doctor visits will be pretty much the same: the nurse will try to convince the baby to lie flat enough to be measured, and to sit still on a scale long enough to get weighed. Then the doctor will poke the baby's stomach, measure his head, and ask you a series of questions about the baby's health. The big events at most doctor visits for the first several years are the vaccinations.

We'll discuss some specific medical questions in later chapters. But for now, here's a fairly typical schedule of well-baby checkups and the vaccinations your baby will receive at each visit:

AGE AT TIME OF VISIT	VACCINATION(S) GIVEN
birth–2 weeks	Hepatitis B
2 months	DPT and Hepatitis B
3 months	OPV and Haemophilus Influenza B
4 months	DPT and Hepatitis B
5 months	OPV and Haemophilus Influenza B
6 months	DPT and Hepatitis B
8 months	OPV and Haemophilus Influenza B
12 months	MMR and TB test

Notes:

3 MONTHS

Let the Games Begin

What's Going On with the Baby

Physically

- As more and more of his reflexes disappear, your baby's body is changing. He can now keep his hands open (instead of balled up in tiny fists), and when you put him down on his tummy, he extends his legs instead of automatically rolling up into a little ball like a pill bug.
- But he can't yet tell one side of his body from the other, and he moves both legs or both arms together.
- When you pull him from a reclining position, he'll try to stand up, pressing his feet against whatever he was lying on.
- His head is bobbing around a lot less, and if you can get him into a sitting position, he can probably sit fairly well for a few seconds (he'll still need plenty of support). He may also be able to clap his hands.
- Your baby is getting much better at grasping things—a development some experts feel is a new reflex, designed to develop your baby's hand-eye coordination. "Everything that the child grasps is brought to the eyes and everything he sees evokes an effort to grasp," says Dr. Wolff.

Intellectually

- Moving objects are a source of nearly endless fascination. Your baby will follow with his eyes and head an object moving from one side of his head to the other.
- One day your baby will catch sight of his own hand on its way into his

mouth. Until this very moment, he had no idea that the thing he's been sucking on for the past few months actually belongs to him. Best of all, he now realizes that objects (or at least his hand) can exist for at least two reasons at the same time: to look at *and* to suck on.

- As a result of this startling, and incredibly important, revelation, your baby will spend as much as 15 minutes at a stretch intently staring at his squiggling fingers and then shoving them into his mouth. He'll repeat the process over and over and over.
- The baby is now able to tell the difference between various objects; he prefers circular shapes to stripes.
- He is also able to make associations between certain objects and qualities linked to them. For example, he may associate your partner with food and you with play, and will react differently to each of you.

Verbally

- Although most of your baby's vocalizing is crying, he's making some delightful, soothing, single-syllable sounds.
- He's now beginning to use his vocalizing for a purpose—if you listen carefully, you should be able to tell the difference between his "I'm hungry," "I'm tired," and "Change my diaper" cries.
- He's now also attentively listening to all the sounds around him and distinguishes speech from any other sound.

Emotionally/Socially

- At this point your baby's schedule of eating, sleeping, diaper filling, and being alert is fairly regular.
- When it comes to people, he has strong likes and dislikes, crying or calming down depending on who holds him. He'll also smile at familiar people, stare at strangers.
- He'll stare, absorbed with his surroundings, for up to 30 minutes at a time.

What You're Going Through

Worried about SIDS

Every year seven thousand children die of SIDS (Sudden Infant Death Syndrome). Striking one out of every thousand babies, it is the most common cause of death of children between one week and one year old.

Although government and private agencies spend millions of dollars each year in the fight against SIDS, scientists have been unable to figure out what, exactly, causes the disease. And there's no medical test to determine which babies are at the greatest risk. Here is what scientists *do* know:

- SIDS is most likely to strike infants two to four months old.
- Ninety percent of deaths happen by six months, but SIDS still strikes children up to one year old.
- It is more likely to occur to boys than girls, to preterm babies, to multiple-birth babies, and to babies from families in which a parent or caretaker smokes or bottle-feeds.
- The disease is more common in cold weather, when respiratory infections and overheating are more common. Both have been linked to SIDS.

Although two-thirds of all SIDS babies have no risk factors, there are a few things you can do to minimize the risk:

- Make sure your baby sleeps on his back. When my older daughter was born in 1990, the then-current wisdom was that babies should not sleep on their backs because of the risk of choking if the baby spit up. But by the time my second was born in 1993, the spit-up theory had been debunked. If your baby has been sleeping on his stomach, it's not too late to change (sure, he's been doing it all his life, but still, it's been only three months). After four months, making the stomach-to-back shift is far less critical.
- Don't smoke and don't let anyone else smoke near the baby.
- Don't overdress the baby (see the section on dressing, pages 79–80).
- Have your baby sleep on a firm mattress: no pillows, fluffy blankets, cushiony sofas, waterbeds, thick rugs, or beanbags. Make sure the mattress fits snugly into the crib so that the baby can't slip between the mattress and the crib frame. And take out of the crib all the plush animals, extra blankets, and other things that might accidentally cover the baby.
- Breastfeed.
- Don't panic. Although SIDS is a horrible, devastating experience for any parent, remember that 999 out of 1,000 babies *don't* die of it.

What to Do If You Lose Your Baby to SIDS

The loss of a child is a terrible thing, something that will affect you and your partner for the rest of your lives. Too often SIDS affects couples who haven't been together very long, and the strain can be especially taxing to their new relationship. But no matter how long a couple has been together, the loss of a child will have a devastating effect on their relationship.

"Surviving grief does not mean escaping from it," says Amy Hillyard

Grief: Not for Women Only

For better or worse, men and women are socially and culturally conditioned to behave in certain ways in certain situations. We could spend a lot of time arguing about the advantages and disadvantages of our socialization, but one thing we can all agree on is that men, generally, aren't allowed to experience or express grief in a way that is healthy to themselves or to those who love them.

Women are more likely to talk about their grief—they have more intimate friends and are more willing to ask for help. They're also more likely to get offered help. Men, however, are less likely to talk about their grief, preferring to internalize it and remain silent. They have fewer intimate friends and avoid asking for help. They also get offered a lot less help.

Men have some very specific needs when it comes to grieving. Here are some wonderful suggestions from the SIDS Alliance in Baltimore:

- Talk to your family—especially your wife. "Grief is the stone that bears one down, but two bear it lightly," said William Hauff in the nineteenth century. Let people know you're doing as much as you can and let them know how they can help you.
- Have quality "alone" time. You need time to sort through all

Jensen, author of *Healing Grief.* "Grief itself is the healing process and you must go through it. Grief will change you, but you have some control over whether the changes are for better or for worse."

Marion McNurlen of the Minnesota SIDS Alliance suggests that grieving couples do as many of the following as possible:

- Don't assume the other doesn't know what you're feeling or what you're going through.
- Schedule some time to talk to each other. You and your partner have experienced the same physical loss, but you won't grieve at the same pace, or at the same time. You need to check in with each other often.
- Have other people to talk to. Your partner can't be there for you (nor you for her) all the time. Call your friends, clergy person, or therapist.
- Touch each other. Often, the completely normal feelings of blame (either of yourself or of your partner) lead to not wanting to touch or be touched. At the same time, though, you and your partner may be nearly screaming inwardly for the other's touch, but you're afraid to ask, afraid of burdening

the questions running through your brain. Think about keeping a journal.

- Decrease your social activities. Many men seek out new hobbies or other activities, but these only detract from the grieving you really need to do.
- Cry. It's just about the hardest thing to do for most of us, but don't try to keep down that lump in your throat or swallow your tears. Crying releases some tension and can actually make you feel better.
- Get angry. Anger is a natural part of the grieving process and holding it back or ignoring it won't make it disappear. There's nothing wrong with being angry; it's what you do with the feeling that counts, so find a way to express your anger that won't hurt others. Exercise is perhaps the best outlet for it.
- Find a support system. For many men, asking for help is even tougher than crying. But research has shown that what men find most helpful is a caring listener, someone patient, someone, perhaps, who is going through (or has recently gone through) the same experience. Local hospitals are an excellent source of referrals to support groups. So is the SIDS Alliance, which has counselors available twenty-four hours a day. You can reach them at (800) 221-SIDS (7437).

the other with your own needs. Physical closeness may be more important now than at any other time in your relationship.

- Try to have some fun. "It is common for grieving parents to have a strong sense that it is disrespectful of their child for them to laugh," says McNurlen. "But laughter is very healing, you can deeply miss your child and have fun once in a while."

Examining Your Relationship with Your Father

As you continue to grow and develop as a father, you may find yourself spending a lot of time thinking about your own father. Was he the kind of father you'd like to use as a role model, or was he exactly the kind of father you don't want to be? Was he supportive and nurturing, or was he absent or abusive? Like it or not, it is the relationship you had with your father when you were young that sets the tone for your relationship with your own children.

Depending on your perspective, this is either good news or bad news. If you are satisfied with your relationship with your dad and you'd like to be the kind

Well, Dad, I'll tell you: Every time I face a dilemma about parenting, I ask myself, "What would Dad do?"... And then I do the opposite.
SIPRESS

of father he was, you don't have much to worry about. "A cohesive boyhood home atmosphere in which the father and mother worked together," writes researcher John Snarey, "predicts that the boy who grew up in it will provide more care for his own children's social-emotional development in adolescence."

But if your relationship with your father was not everything it should have been, you may be afraid that you are somehow destined to repeat your father's mistakes. And you may have started to act accordingly. Psychologist Bruce Linton has observed that if a man's father was abusive, he may begin to withdraw or disengage from parenting his own infant out of "an unconscious or conscious desire to protect his child from his own fear of being abusive." And when the son of an absent father becomes a father himself, says Linton, "He often carries a deep grief or longing for the father he never had, and this feeling is activated as he experiences his own infant."

If you're finding yourself doing—or not doing—things with your baby out of fear, you can relax. At least a little. Dr. Snarey found that new fathers seem to take the good from their fathers and throw away the bad. In fact, many new fathers are able to turn to their advantage the example of a less-than-perfect relationship with their fathers. Here are some common scenarios:

- Men whose fathers were distant or non-nurturant often provide high levels of care for their children's social-emotional and intellectual-academic development in adolescence.

- Men whose fathers provided inconsistent or inadequate supervision tend to provide high levels of care for their children's physical-athletic development in childhood.
- Men whose fathers used or threatened to use physical punishment that instilled fear in them as boys generally provide high levels of care for their own children's physical-athletic development in childhood.

Taking On More Responsibility

Nearly two-thirds of the men in Dr. Bruce Drobeck's research studies stated that the biggest change in their lives since they became fathers was that they had taken on more responsibility. Drobeck doesn't say where "taking on more responsibility" ranked for the remaining third, but I can't imagine any new father not experiencing at least *some* increase. Then again, it depends on how one defines the term.

If you think, for example, that "taking on more responsibility" means only that you are spending the same amount of time on child care as your partner, you may not view those two extra dinners you plan and prepare or the three extra loads of laundry you now do each week as an increase. But I do. One new father, a man who had been out of work for four years, became more responsible when he started looking more realistically at his employment situation. "I just have to lower my sights," he said. "I can't hold out for the exact position I want." Sounds quite responsible to me.

Whatever definition of responsibility you settle on, you'll undoubtedly find that you're focusing much more on your family now, and you're spending more time thinking about the consequences of your actions. "A D.W.I. would put a hardship on the family," said one new father who quit having a few drinks before driving home from the golf course.

For me, being more responsible meant obeying the speed limits (or trying to) and not accelerating at yellow traffic lights. For you, however, it might mean anything from giving up bungee jumping or alligator wrestling to reducing the aggressiveness of your investments.

So whether you call it "taking on more responsibility," "changing your priorities," or "putting your family first," these completely normal behavioral changes all have at least one thing in common. Each, in Bruce Drobeck's words, gives the new father "a positive motivation for personal improvement and growth."

Losing Your Grip

"The baby cries, the parent answers," writes Ellen Galinsky. "The baby is hungry, the parent provides food. The baby is awake most of the night, so is the parent. Parents feel as if their old life, their ability to plan, to have a reliable pattern to their days, is slipping away. . . . They don't know how to gauge themselves. The chores, the repetitious cycles of feeding, changing, putting the baby to sleep, seem endless. Night blurs into day. Time and their ability to control it, even count on it, seem far beyond their grasp, perhaps forever." Sounds like a horror story, doesn't it?

Of course, no one wants to lose control. But the feeling of losing one's grip on one's own life is particularly hard for men. Although there aren't any guaranteed cures for feeling out of control, there are two deceptively simple things you can do to at least take the edge off the feeling:

- Sit down with your partner and schedule some regular breaks for each of you: from the baby, from each other, from the house. You'll be amazed at how rejuvenated you'll feel after even just a couple of hours alone, doing something non-baby-related. This isn't a one-shot deal—try to schedule breaks once a week or more often, if you need to.
- Learn to accept that some things are within your control and that some things aren't. Babies—at least at this age—aren't.

You and Your Baby

Let the Games Begin

Playing with your baby is one of the most important things you can do for him. Researchers have found that early parent-child play can speed up the attachment process. In addition, kids who are played with a lot as babies are more attentive and interactive as they grow up, and end up with higher self-esteem than kids who weren't played with as much.

But before you mount that basketball hoop, remember that at this stage of life babies have literally just discovered themselves, and watching and experimenting with their own little bodies are quite enough to keep them occupied for a big chunk of their waking time.

At this age, the first "game" you play with your baby starts off with nothing more than his giving you a smile. If you respond nicely, he'll smile at you again. After repeating this a few times (it may even take a few days), your baby will learn that what *he* does can lead to a response from *you*. That seemingly simple realization is the basis for any kind of meaningful interaction your baby will have with other people.

Nuts and Bolts

For now, most babies have no idea what to do with rattles, keys, or anything else that needs to be grabbed. This doesn't mean, however, that you shouldn't make regular attempts to introduce some objects into the baby's life. Just don't take it personally if your gesture is completely ignored.

You don't really need any more equipment or supplies than last month. However, you might want to hang a few more pictures of faces where the baby can see them easily. Also, be sure to review the "Awakening the Senses" section, pages 58–59.

A fun experiment: tie one end of a ribbon loosely to the baby's ankle and the other to a mobile. Make the ribbon taut enough so that if the baby moves his leg, he'll also move the mobile. After a few minutes, most (but definitely not all) babies at this age will begin to see a cause and effect relationship developing and will begin to move the tied leg more than the other. Move the ribbon to the other leg, then to the arms, and see how well the baby adapts. A note of caution: never leave the room—even for a minute—with the baby tied to the mobile.

Music

While it's way too early to introduce your baby to music in any serious way, it's not too early to acclimate him. And if you pay attention, you'll notice that he already has a rudimentary sense of rhythm. Lay him on the floor and turn on the stereo (not too loud, please). Notice how he moves his arms and legs rhythmically—not in *time* to the music, but definitely in *response* to it. Try different types of music. Do his movements change as you change the style?

Here are a few things to keep in mind as you're thinking about introducing your baby to music:

- Kids are surrounded by language from their first days (in fact, there's plenty of research showing that kids respond to linguistic rhythms and patterns they heard even before they were born).
- Kids learn music in much the same way as they do language: they start off by listening and absorbing. And remember: "It is not possible to harm a child by allowing her to listen to too much music," says music education researcher Edwin Gordon.
- Play a wide variety of music. Major or minor keys, fast or slow tempos, simple or complex rhythms, and the types of instruments are not important at this stage.
- Select music you like too (after all, you'll be listening as well).

- Some babies this age may try to imitate tones they hear. This is, however, extremely rare.

Reading: From Birth through Eight Months

Feeling a little silly about the prospect of sitting down and reading to your baby? Consider this: "When children have been read to, they enter school with larger vocabularies, longer attention spans, greater understanding of books and print, and consequently have the fewest difficulties in learning to read," writes Jim Trelease, author of *The New Read Aloud Handbook.* And in 1985, a U.S. Department of Education report stated, "The single most important activity for building the knowledge required for eventual success in reading is reading aloud to children."

Still not convinced? How about this: 60 percent of prison inmates are illiterate, 85 percent of juvenile offenders have reading problems, and 44 percent of adult Americans do not read a *single* book in the course of a year. Clearly, reading is an important habit to develop, and it's never too early to start.

What to Read When

For the first few months of your baby's life, your reading probably won't seem to be having much effect on him. Sometimes he'll stare at the book, sometimes not. Once in a while a flailing arm might hit the book, but it's completely accidental. It doesn't really matter what you read at this stage, just as long as you do it. It's a great opportunity for you and the baby to snuggle together and for him to get to know the rhythm and feel of our language.

At about three months, your baby may start holding your finger while you read to him. While it doesn't seem like much, this tiny gesture is a clear indication that he's starting to become aware of the book as a separate object and that he likes what you're doing. Look for books with simple, uncluttered drawings as well as poetry and nursery rhymes.

At four months, your baby will sit still and listen attentively while you're reading. He may even reach out to scratch the pages of the book. Don't get too excited, though, he's a while away from being able to identify anything on the page. Nursery rhymes, finger plays (this little piggy went to market and so on), and books with pictures of other babies are big hits at this stage.

At about five months most babies are just starting to respond to your pointing. There are two ways to take advantage of this new development: first, watch your baby's eyes, then point to and talk about what he is already focusing on. Second, point to something and encourage the infant to look where you're pointing.

At six months babies will respond to what you're reading by bouncing up and down or chuckling before you get to a familiar part of the story. If you've been reading regularly to your baby for a few months, you may notice that he has developed clear preferences for books and will let you know which one he wants you to read. A word of warning: at this age babies have an irresistible need to put everything into their mouths, and books are no exception. But first they'll want to scratch, tear, pat, rub, hit, and get into a serious tug-of-war with you over the book. To avoid these problems before they start, give your baby something else to put in his mouth while you're reading to him, and try to distract him with noise books (the cow says "moo," the airplane goes "whooosh").

At about seven months your baby's grabbing and tearing are now slightly more purposeful, and you may notice an occasional attempt to turn pages. It will be another month or two, though, until he's actually able to do so. Plot is pretty well wasted on babies this age. But he'll like books with brightly colored pictures of familiar objects, as well as those that encourage you to make different sounds.

READY, SET . . .

Here are a few things to keep in mind when you're getting ready to read:

- Select a regular place for reading.
- Set aside a regular time, when you will be able to devote your full attention to the baby and the book. Just before or just after a nap is usually good.
- Try to read for at least fifteen minutes each day. Be prepared: you may have to do this in several installments. Kids' attention spans average only about three minutes at this age, but vary widely (my older daughter would sit in my lap for an hour at a time, whereas my younger couldn't sit still for more than three seconds).
- Reading to your child is for *her,* not for you. So if she arches her back, squirms, lurches forward, or does anything to let you know she's not happy, stop immediately—you're wasting your time. If you don't, the baby will begin to associate reading with discomfort.
- Don't read things that are developmentally inappropriate. "The difference between whether kids enjoyed it or not," say researchers Linda Lamme and Athol Packer, "was whether or not the parents adjusted their bookreading behavior to the developmental levels of their infants."

A list of appropriate titles follows. This is by no means a definitive list. With about five thousand new children's titles published each year, the pool of good books never stops growing. I strongly urge you to get to know your local librarians, who are always up to date, or to subscribe to *Children's Literature*, a wonderful newsletter that reviews current children's books (the address is in the resource guide at the end of the book).

. . . GO!

GENERAL INTEREST FOR THE FIRST SIX TO EIGHT MONTHS

Baby Animal Friends, Phoebe Dunn (board book)
The Baby (and others), John Burningham
Baby Farm Animals, Garth Williams
Baby's Book of Babies, Kathy Henderson
Baby's First Words, Lars Wik
Baby's First Year, Phyllis Hoffman
Baby's Home, Tana Hoban
First Things First, Charlotte Voake
Hand Rhymes, Marc Brown
Happy Baby, Angie and Sage
I See (and others), Rachel Isadora
Pat the Bunny, Dorothy Kunhardt
Pat the Cat, Edith Kunhardt
Peek-a-Boo!, Janet and Allan Ahlberg
Spot's Toys, Eric Hill
This Is Me, Lenore Blegvad (board book)
Ten Little Babies, Debbie MacKinnon (board book)
Trot Trot to Boston: Play Rhymes for Baby
Welcome, Little Baby (and others), Aliki
What Do Babies Do? Debby Slier (board book)
What Is It? Tana Hoban (board book)

MOTHER GOOSE, LULLABIES, POETRY AND SONGS, FINGERPLAYS

These are great for kids of all ages. Start now and return to them as often as you like.

The Baby's Bedtime Book, Kay Chorao
A First Caldecott Collection: The House That Jack Built and *A Frog He Would A-Wooing Go*
A Second Caldecott Collection: Sing a Song of Sixpence and *Three Jovial Huntsmen*
A Third Caldecott Collection: Queen of Hearts and *The Farmer's Boy*
The House that Jack Built, Janet Stevens

The Mother Goose Treasury, Raymond Briggs
Old Mother Hubbard, Alice and Martin Provensen
The Random House Book of Mother Goose, Arnold Lobel
Read-Aloud Rhymes for the Very Young, selected by Jack Prelutsky
Ring a Ring O-Roses, Flint Public Library
Sing a Song of Popcorn: Every Child's Book Of Poems, selected by Beatrice S. De Regniers et al.
The Complete Story of the Three Blind Mice, John Ivimey
Three Little Kittens, Lorinda Cauley
Singing Bee! A Collection of Favorite Children's Songs
Tail Feathers from Mother Goose: The Opie Rhyme Book, Iona and Peter Opie
Tomie De Paola's Mother Goose, Tomie De Paola
A Week of Lullabies, Helen Plotz
Wendy Watson's Mother Goose, Wendy Watson

Hittin' the Road

Despite what your mother or mother-in-law might tell you, you can take your baby out at any age. The trick is in knowing how to dress him.

One of the great myths about babies is that you have to bundle them up like Nanook of the North every time you take them out of the house. Here's the truth: overdressed babies are at risk of getting heat stroke, which can result in abnormally high fevers and even convulsions. This risk is especially high if you're taking the baby out in a sling, backpack, or frontpack, where he'll be even hotter.

Of course, underdressing can be a problem, too. The answer is to dress your baby just as you would dress yourself (except that you're probably not going to wear any of those cute little booties). When the weather's cold, it helps to dress the baby in various layers rather than one or two very heavy items. That way you can remove a layer or two if the baby gets overheated.

Most important, because you're the grown-up, you're going to have to pay close attention. If you underdress your baby, he'll probably let you know about it; babies usually complain loudly when they're too cold. Babies who are too hot, though, tend *not* to complain, preferring, instead, to lie there listlessly.

SUMMER

For the first six months, your baby should be kept far away from direct sunlight. Because babies' skin is at its thinnest and lightest during this period, even a little sun can do a lot of damage. This applies to babies of all races and skin tones.

When you go out, dress your baby in lightweight and light-colored long-sleeved shirts and long pants. From the time they were a few months old, neither of my kids would let me put any kind of hat anywhere near them. But if you can get your baby to wear a cute hat with a wide brim, so much the better. And if you're brave enough to try putting sunglasses on her, get the kind that shield her eyes from UVA and UVB rays. For extra protection, consider getting a parasol or sunshade for your stroller and try to stay indoors during the hottest parts of the day (about 11 A.M. to 3 P.M.).

When you're putting together your supplies for an outdoor summertime excursion, throw in a sweater and some warm pants for the baby. Sounds a little strange, but if you step into any kind of air-conditioned building (such as a supermarket or your office building) after having been outside for a while, you're going to feel awfully cold—and so will the baby.

Oh, and by the way, if you were thinking that your baby can't get a sunburn on a cloudy or overcast day, think again. Studies have shown that 60 percent of the sun's UV rays make their way down here, regardless of clouds, fog, or anything else.

Skin Problems

SUN

Despite all your precautions and good intentions, your baby may still end up with a minor sun-related condition:

- **Sunburn.** If it's minor, cover the affected area with a cool compress. If there are blisters, if the baby is running a fever, or if he's listless or nonresponsive, call your doctor immediately.
- **Prickly heat (heat rash).** A direct result of overdressing, prickly heat looks like tiny red blisters on a flushed area. It occurs anywhere sweat can build up: where the neck meets the shoulders, under the arms, inside elbows and knees, inside diapers. If your baby has heat rash, try to keep him as cool as possible. Lotions and creams probably won't help much, but putting a cool, damp washcloth or some cornstarch on the affected area may make your baby more comfortable.

INSECTS

The sun isn't the only potentially dangerous element that comes out in the summer. Here are some tips for preventing your baby from being consumed by insects:

- Don't use any kind of scented powders, lotions, or even diaper wipes. Bugs love them.

Sunscreen

Until she's six months old, don't use any sunscreen on your baby at all (that's why it's so important to keep infants out of the sun). Because they are usually so filled with chemicals, sunscreens frequently cause allergic reactions.

After six months, the risk of an allergic reaction from sunscreen is much lower, but stick with one that's unscented, alcohol- and PABA-free, and hypoallergenic, or made specially for infants. Hawaiian Tropic, Johnson & Johnson, and Water Babies all make acceptable formulas.

Lube your baby up with sunscreen about half an hour before going outside, and add some more every three hours or so. Pay special attention to feet, hands, legs, and arms—even if they're completely covered. Socks can roll down, and sleeves and pant legs can hike up all by themselves, exposing baby's skin to the elements.

- Avoid insect repellent if at all possible. A long-sleeved shirt and long pants can provide just about the same level of protection and are a lot easier on infant skin.
- Stay away from clothes with floral patterns: most bugs aren't smart enough to tell the difference between a real flower and your equally delicious flower-covered child. Light colors are far less attractive to bugs than dark colors.

DIAPER RASH

In the pre-disposable-diaper era, when a baby urinated the moisture stayed right there against her skin. Partly because of the acid in urine and partly because it's uncomfortable to sit in something wet, the baby would soon start complaining. And if she made what my older daughter used to call "a big dirty" (a bowel movement), her discomfort was greater, and her complaints voiced sooner. This raised the chances that she'd get changed fairly quickly.

But with disposables, a lot of the moisture is whisked away from the baby (just like in the commercials) and converted into some kind of nonliquid gel. Still, the digestive acids in the baby's waste, especially in her stool, continue to irritate her skin until—voilà!—diaper rash. But because the baby isn't uncomfortable enough to complain, her diapers somehow don't manage to get changed quite as often.

Unlike sunburn or insect bites, no matter what you do or how hard you try, one of these days your baby is going to get diaper rash. Just about the only thing you can do to keep it to a minimum is to check your baby's diapers every few hours and change them even if they're only slightly wet. Also:

- If you're using cloth diapers, don't use rubber or plastic pants. Your baby's bottom needs good air circulation.
- When diaper rash develops, let your baby frolic for a few minutes sans diaper (on a towel, perhaps, just in case . . .). The extra air circulation will help.
- Apply some diaper cream with each change, but be especially gentle: irritated skin doesn't like to be rubbed. A piece of advice: after you've applied diaper rash cream to the baby's bottom, wipe any residual cream on your fingers onto the inside of the diaper. If any of the cream gets onto the plastic fasteners of a disposable diaper, they won't stick to the diaper.

Notes:

4 MONTHS

Born to Be . . .

What's Going On with the Baby

Physically

- Lying on her back, she can now track moving objects, coordinating the activities of her eyes and head as well as an adult can.
- She's making better use of her hands, using them to finger each other, and to grasp small objects (most of which immediately end up in her mouth). But she hasn't yet figured out what to do with her opposable thumb. So, for the next few months at least, she won't be using it much, making her grasping a little clumsy.
- By the end of this month, though, she will have figured out that the two sides of her body are separate—a discovery she's glad to demonstrate by passing things back and forth between her hands.
- While on her tummy, she can lift her head 90 degrees and prop herself up on her forearms.
- She may be able to roll from her tummy to her side, and may occasionally make it onto her back.
- She still tries to stand when you pull her up, and when she's sitting, her back is straight and her head hardly wobbles.

Intellectually

- Your baby is developing a physical sense of her body, recognizing that her hands and feet are extensions of herself. And she'll spend a great deal of time every day using her hands to explore her face, her mouth, and whatever other parts of her body she can reach.

- She can retain objects in her hands voluntarily.
- She's beginning the long process of understanding cause and effect relationships. If she accidentally kicks a toy and it squeaks, she may try to kick it again, hoping to get the same reaction.
- She's begun to draw small distinctions between similar objects. She can clearly tell the difference between a real face and a picture of one, and she can distinguish nearby objects from distant ones.
- She is also starting to differentiate herself from some other objects in her world. She may, for example, find a special toy particularly soothing.

Verbally

- The amount of time your baby spends crying has decreased dramatically and she's just about ready to hold up her end of a conversation.
- When she hears a sound—especially a voice—she actively searches for it with her eyes.
- And if you wait a few seconds after saying something to her, she may "answer" you, making ample use of her expanding vocabulary of squeals, chuckles, chortles, giggles, and clicks.
- She's trying as hard as she can to imitate one or two sounds and, if she's got something on her mind, may take the initiative and start a "conversation" with you.

Emotionally/Socially

- Overall, your baby is a pretty happy kid, smiling regularly and spontaneously and anticipating pleasurable encounters by vigorously kicking her arms and legs.
- She's also so anxious to socialize that she can actually suppress other interests in order to play. If you talk to her while she's eating, for example, she'll gladly stop for half an hour or so to chat.
- She now tries to extend her playtime by laughing or holding her gaze on a desired object, and she may protest loudly if you stop doing what she wants you to.
- Despite this hedonistic streak, she's still got clear preferences among playmates. Some will be able to soothe her, others won't.
- This is an extremely busy developmental time for your baby, and you may notice some interruption in her sleep patterns as she wakes up in the middle of the night to practice her new tricks.

What You're Going Through

Reevaluating Your Relationship with Your Job

Remember the shift in focus and priorities we talked about last month—from self to family? Well, once that shift has begun, the very next thing most new fathers do is take a long, hard look at their jobs.

In a small number of cases, fathers make a renewed commitment to their jobs—longer hours, increased productivity, more responsibility—motivated by a need to provide for their growing families. A far more common scenario, however, is the one Bruce Drobeck found in his research. Most new fathers, he says, "were looking for ways to reduce or restructure their work hours in order to achieve a balance between work and family."

This, of course, flies in the face of a lot of the stereotypes we often hear about fathers. But if you don't believe me, consider the results of a few national polls:

- 65 percent of fathers in one national poll said they believe they are being asked to sacrifice too much family time for the workplace.
- 57 percent of the men surveyed at one major corporation (up from 37 percent five years earlier) wanted work-schedule flexibility that would allow them to spend more time with their families.
- A recent survey by *Forbes* magazine found that 30 percent of fathers with kids under twelve had personally turned down a job promotion or transfer because it would have reduced the time they spend with their families.

Based on these statistics, it shouldn't come as much of a surprise that, as researcher John Snarey found, "a majority of husbands now experience fathering as more psychologically rewarding . . . than their occupations."

However, lest you think that all this is just a bunch of optimistic rhetoric, here's an example of the lengths to which some new fathers will go in order to spend more time with their families. A recent study by the Families and Work Institute stated that "some men had told friends at work they were going to a bar when in fact they were going home to care for their children."

Coming to Terms with Breastfeeding

Before their babies are born, nearly all expectant fathers feel that breastfeeding is the best way to feed a baby and that their partners should do so as long as possible. After the baby comes, new fathers still feel that breast is best, but many are also feeling a little ambivalent.

Most new fathers feel that breastfeeding "perpetuates the exclusive relationship the mother and infant experienced during pregnancy," writes Dr. Pamela Jordan, one of the few researchers ever to explore the effects of breastfeeding on men.

Given all this, says Dr. Jordan, a new father is likely to experience:

- A diminished opportunity to develop a relationship with his child.
- A sense of inadequacy.
- A feeling that the baby has come between him and his partner.
- A feeling that nothing he does to satisfy his child can ever compete with his partner's breasts.
- A sense of relief when his partner weans the baby, giving him the opportunity to "catch up."
- A belief in what Jordan calls the "hormonal advantage theory"—the idea that women are born with certain knowledge and skills that give them an advantage in parenting, including guaranteed success with breastfeeding.

Whether or not you're experiencing these or any other less-than-completely-positive feelings, there's a good chance that your partner is having a few ambivalent feelings of her own about breastfeeding. Here are some of the things she may be feeling:

- Exhaustion. It may look easy and relaxing to you, but nursing a baby is tough work.
- Despite the images of smiling, happy nursing mothers, your partner simply may not be enjoying the experience. And if she isn't, she may be feeling guilty or inadequate. (Just goes to show you that fathers aren't the only ones boxed in by socialization.)
- She may resent the way nursing interferes with some of the other things she'd like to do.
- She may want to run as far away from the baby as possible. If so, she's also likely to feel guilty or selfish (socialization again . . . mothers are always supposed to be happy to be with their children).
- She may not be interested in answering your questions about the process. (I had a million for my wife: How does it feel? How much comes out in each feeding? Does the milk come out from one hole or more than one?)

"Preparing a meal and feeding someone is a powerful symbolic act," writes

Dr. Jordan. "Feeding the infant is often perceived by parents as the most important aspect of infant care, the most meaningful interaction." If your partner is breastfeeding, there's no question that you're at a bit of a disadvantage when it comes to feeding the baby. There are, however, a few ways you can help your partner and yourself make breastfeeding as pleasant an experience as possible for everyone:

- You can bottle-feed your baby with breast milk if your partner is willing to express some. But don't insist on this. Many women find expressing milk—manually or with a pump—uncomfortable or even painful.
- Don't take it personally if your baby doesn't seem interested in taking a bottle from you. Some babies need a few days to get used to the idea of sucking on a plastic nipple instead of a real one. Other babies, like my younger daughter, simply refuse to take a bottle at all. But don't give up without a fight. Plastic nipples—like real ones—come in all sorts of shapes and sizes. So you may have to do a little experimenting before you and your baby discover the kind she likes best (which may or may not have anything in common with the kind you like best).
- Make sure you get some private time with your baby for activities that provide regular skin-to-skin contact, such as bathing, cuddling, playing, putting to bed, and even changing diapers. According to Dr. Jordan, establishing rituals like these with your baby may help you feel that "the mother does not have exclusive rights to a special relationship." It can also help your partner by giving her some needed time off.
- Compare notes with other men whose partners breastfed their babies.

For Women Only (you can read this, but only if you promise to show it to your partner when you're done)

"The breastfeeding mother has the control of parenting and must realize that she has the power to invite the father in or exclude him," writes Dr. Pamela Jordan. "She can play a vital role in establishing exclusive father-infant time, often while simultaneously meeting her own needs for time away and alone. Just as the father is viewed as the primary support of the mother-infant relationship, the mother is the primary support of the father-infant relationship . . . supporting the father during breastfeeding may help improve his, and consequently, the mother's, satisfaction with breastfeeding, the duration of breastfeeding, and the adaptation of both parents to parenthood."

Worried That Your Life Will Never Be the Same Again (It Won't)

Before my kids were born, just about everybody my wife and I knew with kids pulled us aside and tried to warn us that our lives would change forever once we became parents. They told us about how hard it is to shift from worrying about only ourselves to being responsible for the safety and well-being of a completely helpless little person. They told us that we'd lose a lot of sleep and even more privacy. And they told us that we'd better go to a lot of movies and read a stack of books because we might not have another chance for a while. Everything everyone said was absolutely correct, but none of it really prepared us for our transition to parenthood.

What I often find most interesting about the changes I underwent when I became a father is the way my memories of my prefatherhood past have been subtly altered. It's not that I can't or don't remember life before children, it's just that that life, in retrospect, seems somehow incomplete.

I have clear, fond memories of taking long walks on the beach by myself, sleeping in all day, and going out at midnight for a beer with friends—things I haven't done much since becoming a father. It's as though those things happened to someone else, however. I don't really miss my other life, but in a way I wish I could have shared it with my children (not the beers, perhaps, but the walks on the beach and the sleeping in).

You and Your Baby

Your Baby's Temperament

About forty years ago a husband-and-wife team of psychiatrists, Stella Chess and Alexander Thomas, theorized that children are born with a set of nine fundamental behavioral and emotional traits they called "temperamental qualities." These qualities, which experts now believe remain fairly consistent throughout life, combine differently for each child and determine, to a great extent, a child's personality and whether he will be "easy" or "challenging." In addition, Chess and Thomas found that a child's temperament has a major influence on his parents' behavior and attitudes.

Over the past few decades, Chess and Thomas's original research in temperament has been expanded, refined, and improved upon. Here, then, are the nine temperament traits, adapted from Chess and Thomas, the Temperament Program at the Center for Parenting Excellence, and the work of Jim Cameron, head of The Preventive Ounce, a nonprofit mental health organization for children.

The Nine Temperament Traits of Babies

APPROACHING	WITHDRAWING
♦ separate easily from parents ♦ are excited to meet and interact with new people ♦ greet new foods eagerly ♦ seem perfectly "at home" in new situations	♦ are usually shy, cling to their parents in new situations or around strangers ♦ have difficulty separating from parents ♦ need time to warm up to new experiences ♦ may be extremely picky eaters and spit out food with new taste sensations
FAST ADAPTING	**SLOW ADAPTING**
♦ fall asleep easily and without fussing, no matter where they are ♦ don't mind changes in routines ♦ can be fed easily by different people ♦ don't mind being handled by different people or passed around ♦ smile back quickly when talked to	♦ may refuse to fall asleep in a strange place (or even a moderately familiar one like grandma and grandpa's) ♦ are slow to get back to sleep after being awakened ♦ don't like being picked up and held by strangers ♦ take a long time to warm up to new situations, and once upset, may take a long time to calm down
LOW INTENSITY	**HIGH INTENSITY**
♦ display their emotions, but are often hard to read ♦ have subdued moods ♦ seem fairly nonchalant	♦ react strongly (positively or negatively) to strangers, loud noises, bright lights ♦ do everything—shrieking with delight or crying—so loudly it hurts your ears
POSITIVE MOOD	**NEGATIVE MOOD**
♦ laugh and smile at just about everything ♦ are happy even when having their diapers changed ♦ seem genuinely happy to see you	♦ cry when being changed ♦ are fussy or cranky most of the time ♦ whimper or cry a lot, sometimes seemingly for no reason ♦ complain during hair brushing
LOW ACTIVITY	**HIGH ACTIVITY**
♦ seem content to lie still while nursing or getting changed ♦ will sit calmly in the car seat ♦ prefer less physical play (swings instead of wrestling)	♦ move around a lot while sleeping, frequently kicking their blankets off ♦ move around a lot while awake, and are hard to dress, change, bathe, or feed ♦ often reach physical developmental milestones earlier than lower-activity kids

PREDICTABLE ♦ get hungry, tired, and move their bowels at about the same times every day ♦ love regular eating and bedtime schedules ♦ struggle with changes in eating and sleep routines	**UNPREDICTABLE** ♦ may or may not take naps ♦ have frequent sleep problems and get up several times during the night ♦ may not be hungry at mealtimes and may want to eat at different times every day ♦ have irregular bowel movements
HIGH SENSORY THRESHOLD (OBLIVIOUS) ♦ love loud events (basketball games, circuses, bands . . .) ♦ aren't bothered by wet or dirty diapers ♦ are emotionally stable ♦ don't seem to be able to differentiate between two voices ♦ aren't bothered by clothing labels or scratchy fabrics ♦ don't seem bothered by pain	**LOW SENSORY THRESHOLD (VERY AWARE)** ♦ are easily overstimulated ♦ are awakened easily by gentle touch or by turning on lights ♦ may get extremely upset at loud noises ♦ notice tiny variations in the taste of food ♦ are extremely uncomfortable in wet or dirty diapers ♦ are very sensitive to fabrics, labels, and the fit of their clothes
LOW DISTRACTIBILITY ♦ are quite hard to soothe ♦ seem completely oblivious to interruptions (noise, familiar voices) when involved in something important (like nursing)	**HIGH DISTRACTIBILITY** ♦ have short attention spans ♦ are easily distracted while nursing ♦ are easily soothed when upset
HIGH PERSISTENCE ♦ are able to amuse themselves for a few minutes at a time ♦ like to practice new motor skills (like rolling from back to front) for a minute or more ♦ pay close attention (for more than a minute) to rattles and mobiles ♦ pay close attention to other children when playing ♦ cry when you stop playing with them	**LOW PERSISTENCE** ♦ can't amuse themselves for very long in crib or playpen ♦ have short attention spans and are frustrated easily, even by simple tasks ♦ quickly lose interest in playing, even with favorite toys ♦ won't spend much time working on new skills (rolling over, sitting up)

1. Approach/Withdrawal: Your child's usual *initial* reaction to a new experience, such as meeting a new person, tasting a new food, or being in a new situation.
2. Adaptability: Similar to Approach/Withdrawal, but deals with your child's longer-term reactions to changes in routines or expectations, new places, and new ideas.
3. Intensity: The amount of energy a child commonly uses to express emotions—both positive and negative.
4. Mood: Your child's general mood—happy or fussy—over the course of a typical day.
5. Activity level: The amount of energy your child puts into everything he does.
6. Regularity: The day-to-day predictability of your baby's hunger, sleeping, and filling diapers.
7. Sensitivity: Your baby's sensitivity to pain, noise, temperature change, lights, odors, flavors, textures, and emotions. Note: it's quite possible for your baby to be highly sensitive to one sensation (bright lights, for example) but not at all sensitive to others (noise).
8. Distractibility: How easy is it to change the focus of your baby's attention.
9. Persistence: Similar to Distractibility, but goes beyond the initial reaction and concerns the length of time your baby will spend trying to overcome obstacles or distractions.

Now that you know what to look for, spend a few minutes rating your baby on the following scale. And have your partner do it, too.

TRAIT	RATING						
Approach/Withdrawal	Approaching	1	2	3	4	5	Withdrawing
Adaptability	Fast	1	2	3	4	5	Slow
Intensity	Low	1	2	3	4	5	High
Mood	Positive	1	2	3	4	5	Negative
Activity Level	Low	1	2	3	4	5	High
Regularity	Predictable	1	2	3	4	5	Unpredictable
Sensitivity	Oblivious	1	2	3	4	5	Very Aware
Distractibility	Low	1	2	3	4	5	High
Persistence	High	1	2	3	4	5	Low

If you have a lot of 1s and 2s, you're one lucky guy. You've got an "easy" child (about 40 percent of parents do), and having an easy child is, well, easy. The baby's always smiling and happy, sleeps through the night, eats at the same time every day, and loves playing and meeting new people. When he does get upset or fussy, you can usually calm him down almost immediately. You're madly in love with your baby and you're feeling confident about your parenting skills.

But if you ended up with a lot of 4s and 5s, you most likely have a "challenging" child (only about 10 percent of parents do), and things are not nearly as rosy. She doesn't sleep through the night, has trouble eating, freaks out at the slightest noise or change in her surroundings, cries for hours at a time (and nothing you try seems to make it any better), and is generally fussy. Meanwhile, you're exhausted and depressed, angry at the baby for her "malicious" behavior, embarrassed at the way people stare at your unhappy child, guilty about your unparental feelings, and jealous of your friends and their easy babies. In short, you're not finding your parenting experience very satisfying, you're discouraged and frustrated, and you think you must be a complete failure as a father. You may even feel trapped and fantasize about running away.

As bad as it sounds, there are some things you can do to help you overcome a lot of your frustration and negative feelings:

♦ Recognize that challenging children are challenging because of their innate makeup. Their temperament exists at birth. It's not their fault, it's not your fault, and it's not your partner's fault. It's just the way things are.

- Stop blaming yourself, your partner, or your baby. There's probably nothing wrong with any of you. The problem is that the way you're interacting with your child simply isn't working.
- Get to know your child's—and your own—temperament and look for similarities and differences. If you're both Highly Distractible, you may never get through that book you're reading—and neither of you will care. But if you're Highly Approaching and the baby is Highly Withdrawing, you may have some real problems taking her to meet your boss for the first time.

At the very least, these steps will enable you to modify your approaches to your child's behavior and to anticipate and avoid conflicts before they occur. The result will be a far happier, more loving, and more satisfying relationship with your child. Guaranteed.

Putting Your Knowledge of Temperament to Good Use

Following are some of the most common, difficult-to-handle traits you're likely to encounter during your baby's first year, along with some suggestions for how to handle them, loosely based on the work of researchers Stanley Turecki and Leslie Tonner.

INITIAL WITHDRAWAL/SLOW ADAPTABILITY

Just because your baby initially spits out new foods and refuses to play with new toys doesn't mean he'll never change. Before you give up, try gently introducing new foods a few times at different meals, and give the baby a chance to "meet" a new toy from a distance before letting him touch it. (This process will help you figure out whether your child is Withdrawing and Slow-Adapting or has a Low Sensory Threshold.)

Your Withdrawing/Slow-Adapting baby will probably begin experiencing *stranger anxiety* (see pages 149–50) earlier—and it will last longer—than more Approaching and Fast-Adapting babies. Tell new visitors, and even those the baby knows a little bit, not to approach too quickly, not to try to pick him up right away, and not to take it personally if the baby reacts negatively.

One warning: Think about your baby's temperament before making any major changes in your appearance. Shaving your beard, getting a haircut, or even replacing your glasses with contact lenses can trigger a strong, negative reaction. When my older daughter was six months old, her baby-sitter—whom she absolutely adored—got a haircut, and it took her more than a week to recover.

HIGH INTENSITY

Short of leaving the room or getting ear plugs (both of which are perfectly reasonable approaches), there's not much you can do about your High-Intensity baby.

NEGATIVE MOOD

Not much can make you happier than going out with a smiling, happy baby. But a baby who isn't a smiler, and who whimpers and cries all the time, can be a real challenge to your self-confidence. It's hard to take pleasure in a baby with a Negative Mood, or even to feel proud of her. And it's certainly tempting to think that if the baby doesn't smile at you all the time, she doesn't love you.

If you're feeling this way, resist the urge to get angry with your baby for her whining, or to "get even" with her by withholding your love. (I know it sounds silly, but it happens.) The truth is that the lack of a smile doesn't necessarily mean there's a lack of love. And the whining *will* subside as your baby's verbal skills improve, enabling her to get your attention in more productive ways.

HIGH ACTIVITY

Because your High-Activity baby will spend his sleeping moments doing laps in his crib, it's important to install some big, soft bumpers (pads designed to protect babies' heads from banging into the bars). You'll also need to make sure there's nothing in the crib (or nearby) that could fall on top of the baby's head. And, if your house tends to be a little cold at night, dress the baby in something thick so he'll be warm when he kicks the covers off.

Never, never leave your baby unattended—even for a second—on a changing table or bed; she could very well roll off. Once, when my older daughter was seven months old, I was tickling her in her bassinet when the phone (located about three feet away) rang. I stepped over, said "Hello," and heard a loud thump behind me: my daughter, who had never given any indication that she could pull herself up, had done exactly that, and toppled over the side of the bassinet. No harm was done, but we never used that bassinet again.

UNPREDICTABILITY

Since your Unpredictable baby seems to be eating, sleeping, and filling his diaper at random, it's up to you to try to establish a regular schedule. Although he may not want to eat, try to feed him something at times that are more convenient for you. If you schedule meals at the same times every day, you may be able to help him create a modified routine.

When it comes to getting your baby to sleep, establishing a routine is also important. When you go into his room at night, don't turn on the lights, don't pick him up, don't play, and get out as soon as you can. Once you stumble on a getting-back-to-sleep routine, stick with it. If your baby's sleep irregularities are truly serious, you and your partner should divide up the night, each taking a shift while the other sleeps. If that doesn't help, talk with your pediatrician about a mild sedative. For the baby, not you.

LOW SENSORY THRESHOLD

For the first few months of a Low-Sensory-Threshold baby's life, you'll never know what's going to set her off. Sounds, smells, and sensations you might hardly notice can cause her to explode into tears: turning on the car radio, the crowd applauding at a basketball game (yes, you can take babies to basketball games), even too many toys in her crib.

One way to make your baby's life a little less jarring is to modify the amount and type of stimulation in her environment. Avoid neon colors when decorating her room, get opaque drapes to keep daytime light out during nap time, and don't play actively with her right before bedtime. When dressing your baby, stay away from tight clothes, brand-new clothes (they're often too stiff), wool, synthetic fabrics, or anything with a rough texture. Cotton blends usually offer the best combination of washability and softness. And be sure to clip off scratchy labels and tags.

HIGH DISTRACTIBILITY AND LOW PERSISTENCE

These traits are usually not much of a problem for you or your baby at this stage.

For most readers, this discussion of temperament should be sufficient to identify and begin to deal with their child's behavior patterns. But if you're seriously concerned about your child's temperament, or would be interested in exploring the subject in greater detail, I suggest you contact Temperament Talk, in Portland, Oregon, or Jim Cameron at The Preventive Ounce.

Family Matters

Sleeping Tight

We all love our children, but let's face it, sometimes we want them to go to sleep—and stay that way for a while. There are all sorts of factors (many of which are beyond your control) that influence whether your child will be a "good" sleeper or a "bad" one. Fortunately, though, there are a few rules of thumb that can help tilt the odds in your favor:

"And so the big bad wolf ate Little Red Riding Hood, Hansel and Gretel, Cinderella, and the three little pigs, and that was the end of fairy tales forever. Now good night!"

- Don't become the baby's sleep transition object. Baby's last waking memory should be of her crib or something familiar in it (blankie, toy, a picture on the wall). That way, if she wakes up in the middle of the night, she'll see the familiar object and be able to associate it with sleep. If you were the last thing she saw before dropping off, she'll want you again, even if you happen to be sleeping.
- It's perfectly natural for babies to fuss or be restless for fifteen or twenty minutes after being put down. (Please remember that fussing is one thing, screaming is another. If the baby begins to really wail, pick her up and soothe her, but try to get her back in her crib while she's still awake. It's absolutely impossible to spoil a baby by picking her up or soothing her in the first three or four months of life.)
- Keep nighttime activity to a minimum. Whether your baby is sleeping with you or not, she needs to learn that nighttime is for sleeping, not for playing.
- Don't turn on the lights. If the baby wakes up for a middle-of-the-night breast or bottle, do it in the dark.
- Don't change diapers unless you absolutely have to (such as when you're trying to treat a particularly nasty case of diaper rash). In most cases, your baby will be perfectly fine until the morning.
- Establish a routine. You'll need to make up your own, depending on what

works best for you. Here's a fairly simple routine that is good for babies this age as well as for toddlers: change diapers, get sleepsuit on, read a story or two, go around the room and say "goodnight" to all the toys and animals, give a kiss goodnight, and into bed.

- When your baby is about six months old, start leaving the door to her room open. Kids this age get scared if they feel they're trapped in a small space, especially if they aren't sure you're just outside the door.
- In case of nightmares or other middle-of-the-night scares, respond promptly and be as reassuring as possible. Unless your child is hysterical with fear, try to keep things brief and resist the urge to take the baby out of the crib. You can do a lot of soothing by rubbing the baby's back or head—all from your side of the bars.
- During the day, gently wake up—and entertain—your baby if she tries to nap more than two or three hours at a stretch. The idea is to make her longest sleep of the day occur at night.

But What about Those Middle-of-the-Night Wake-Ups?

The most common reason babies wake up in the middle of the night is that they want to eat. If your partner is breastfeeding, do everything you can to stay in bed and let her handle things. I realize that this sounds positively insensitive, but the truth is that there's really nothing you can do to help out. If your partner wants some adult company (and who wouldn't?), try not to give in. Instead, offer to give her a few extra hours of sleep while you handle the early-morning child-care shift (which usually lasts a lot longer than a 2 A.M. feeding).

Of course, if you're bottle-feeding your baby (either with formula or expressed breast milk), you should do your fair share of the feedings. And since there's no sense in both you and your partner getting up at the same time, you

Naps and Sleep Schedules

At four months your baby has probably only recently settled into a regular sleep routine. Every baby has her own sleeping schedule, but a typical one for a baby this age might include a ten-hour stretch at night plus, if you're lucky, two two-hour naps—one midmorning, the other midafternoon.

Keep an eye on these naps, however; if they get too late, they may start upsetting the night-sleeping routine. You can't expect a baby to take a nap from 4 to 6 P.M. and then go to bed for the night at 7.

should be able to negotiate breakfast in bed (or at least a couple of hours of sleep) on those days when you do the 2 A.M. feeding.

Sometimes, no matter what you do, your baby is going to wake up at two or three in the morning for no other reason than to stay awake for a few hours and check things out. As with the feeding situations, try to split the entertainment duty as much as you can (unless one of you really needs to catch up on TV reruns or order a slicing, dicing, memory-improving, income-boosting workout machine).

No matter what it is that gets your baby (and you) up at three thirty in the morning, be sure to keep your middle-of-the-night encounters as boring as possible. Until they're old enough to have sex, kids need to know that nighttime is for sleeping.

Sleeping Arrangements

As hard as it may be to imagine, there exists a rather basic parenting issue that regularly generates even more controversy than the disposable versus cloth diapers debate: whether or not to have your child sleep in the same bed as you and your partner.

The argument goes something like this: Proponents of the "family bed" say that kids are being forced to be independent too early, that human evolution simply can't keep pace with the new demands our culture is placing on its children. "Proximity to parental sounds, smells, heat, and movement during the night is precisely what the human infant's immature system expects and needs," says James McKenna, an anthropologist and sleep researcher. They also add that in most countries (comprising about 80 percent of the world's population), parents and children sleep in the same bed.

Opponents of the family bed, however, say that what works in other countries doesn't always work here. In America early independence is critical, and babies should therefore quickly learn to be away from their parents, especially if both work and the children have to be in day care.

Fortunately (or unfortunately, depending on where you stand on the issue), there's absolutely no consensus on which of these two opposing views is the "right" one. And just to make sure that there's no real way to decide this issue once and for all, there's no serious scientific data supporting either position.

Our older daughter slept in a bassinet in our room for a month or so until we moved her into her own room. Our younger daughter, however, slept in bed with us for six months before being asked to leave. Personally, I kind of liked being able to snuggle up with a warm, smooth baby, but after being kicked in the head, stomach, back, face, and chest every night for six months I was glad to go back to an adults-only sleeping arrangement.

Here are some of the most common issues that come up in discussions of the family bed:

- **Independence.** Critics of family sleeping claim that parents who let their kids sleep with them are spoiling their children, who will grow up clingy and dependent. "Sleeping alone is an important part of a child's learning to be able to separate from his parents without anxiety and to see himself as an independent individual," writes Dr. Richard Ferber, one of the most well-respected anti-family-bed people around. Proponents of family sleeping, however, make nearly the opposite claim, maintaining that before a child can become independent she must feel that the world is a safe place and that her needs will be met. Kids who sleep in a family bed, proponents argue, turn out to be more independent, more confident, and more self-assured than those who don't.
- **Sleep: the baby's.** Despite what you might think, co-sleeping children tend to sleep more lightly than children who sleep alone (blankets rustling and parents turning over in bed wake them up). But light sleeping isn't necessarily a bad thing. In fact, there seems to be a correlation between lighter sleep and a lower incidence of SIDS.
- **Sleep: yours.** It's perfectly normal for even the soundest-sleeping kids to wake up every three or four hours for a quick look around the room. The vast majority (about 70 percent) soothe themselves back to sleep after a minute or two. But about 30 percent will spot something they just have to play with (you or your partner, for example), and they're up for hours.
- **Safety.** Many parents are afraid that they'll accidentally roll over their sleeping child if the whole family is sharing the same bed. While this is a perfectly legitimate concern, most adults—even while asleep—have a highly developed sense of where they are. It's probably been quite a while since you fell out of bed in the middle of the night. However, a recent study published in the *New England Journal of Medicine* found that adult overlying (non-alcohol and non-drug-related) was the probable cause of death in almost 20 percent of infants whose death had initially been attributed to SIDS.
- **Sexual spontaneity.** No kidding. But there are plenty of other places to make love besides your bed.
- **Breastfeeding.** There's no question that it's a lot easier for a nursing mother to reach across her bed for the baby than to get up and stagger down the hall. Problems arise, however, when fathers feel (and they often

do) displaced by the nursing baby and decide that the only place to get a good night's sleep is on the couch.

- **Think before you start.** Once your baby has been sleeping in your bed for six to eight months, it's going to be awfully hard to get her out if you change your mind.

A Few Things to Consider If You're Thinking about Sharing Your Bed with Your Child

- Keep politics out of your decision-making. Sleep with your child because you and your partner want to, not because you feel you have to.
- Don't be embarrassed. You're not being soft, negligent, or overindulgent—it's a choice made by millions of fine parents.
- Make sure your bed is large enough to accommodate everyone. (But no waterbeds—baby could roll between you and the mattress.) Put the bed against the wall and have the baby sleep on the wall side, or get a guard rail if she's going to sleep on the outside edge. And remember, overly soft mattresses and pillows may pose a risk of suffocation.
- Make sure everyone's toenails are trimmed.
- Rethink your decision right now if you're obese, you drink or take any medication that might make you hard to wake up, or if you're generally such a sound sleeper that you're worried you might roll on top of your baby without noticing.

A Few Things to Consider If You're Thinking about Not Sharing Your Bed with Your Child

- Don't feel guilty. You're not a bad or selfish parent for not doing it.
- There is absolutely no evidence that sleeping with your child will speed up the bonding/attachment process.
- It's okay to make an occasional exception, such as when a child is ill or has had a frightening experience.
- If you're making your decision because of safety issues, you may be able to compromise by setting up the baby's crib in your bedroom.

5 MONTHS

Work and Family

What's Going On with the Baby

Physically

- This month's big discovery is, yes, toes. And just as your baby spent hours fondling and sucking his own fingers, he'll repeat the process with his lower extremities.
- He's getting a lot stronger and is now able to roll from his stomach to his back at will. He can also get himself from his tummy to his hands and knees. Once there, he may rock back and forth as if anxious for some kind of race to begin.
- When you pull him to a standing position, he'll try to help you out by leaning his head forward and bending at the waist. Once standing, he may stamp his feet up and down.
- He's almost able to sit without support and can now pick up objects while sitting.
- His hands continue to get more coordinated. He now plays with a toy in either hand and can turn his wrist (it's harder than it sounds), thus enabling him to get a better look at what he's picked up.
- There are now longer and more regular intervals between feedings and bowel movements.

Intellectually

- For the past four months, your baby's world has been "a series of things that mysteriously disappear and reappear," writes child development expert Frank Caplan. But now he's no longer content to sit back and stare at objects, nor is he satisfied when you put something in his hand. In an attempt to actively engage in his world, he's starting to reach for things. Watch carefully as he looks back and forth between an object and his hand—inching the hand slowly toward the object. As mundane as it sounds, reaching is a critical intellectual stage, introducing the baby to the idea that, says Caplan, "things are beyond and apart and, therefore, separate" from him.

- Handling and turning an object teaches the baby that even though something looks different from different angles, its shape remains the same.
- With these newfound skills, the baby will now anticipate (and get excited by) seeing only a small part of a familiar object and will try to move small obstacles out of his way. He's also learning that objects can move, and he may lean over to find a toy he's dropped instead of staring at his hand. But if the object is out of his sight for more than just a few seconds, it ceases to exist and he forgets about it.

Verbally

- It's finally happened: your baby is babbling. Besides the vowel sounds *(eee, aaa, ayy)* he's been making, he's added a few consonants *(bbb, ddd, mmm)* to the mix.
- He's found his voice's volume switch and will practice modulating his voice.
- Although he's still trying to imitate more of the voice sounds you make to him, the noises he produces sound nothing like actual language.
- He's so delighted with his newfound language skills that he'll babble for 20 to 30 minutes at a stretch. Don't worry if you're not there to enjoy it—he's perfectly content to talk to his toys or, in a pinch, to himself.
- He may understand, and respond to, his name.

Emotionally/Socially

- He's capable of expressing a growing number of emotions: fear, anger, disgust, and satisfaction. He'll cry if you put him down and calm down if you pick him up.
- He also has—and readily expresses—strong preferences for toys and people. And he deliberately imitates faces and gestures.
- If he feels you're not paying enough attention to him, he'll try to interrupt whatever you're doing with a yelp or a cry. If he does start crying, you can usually stop his tears just by talking to him.

- He knows the difference between familiar people and strangers, and associates friends with his pleasure.
- Unfortunately, he doesn't remember that his friends started off (to him, at least) as strangers. Consequently, he's a little slow to warm to new people.
- He may spend some time trying to soothe himself—either by talking to himself or by clutching a favorite toy.

What You're Going Through

Worried about Doing Things Wrong

Just a few months ago your baby didn't make very many demands, so satisfying them wasn't all that tough. But now his needs are far more complex, and at times you may feel that it's nearly impossible to react promptly and appropriately.

With so much to respond to, it's perfectly normal to worry that you're not reading your baby's signals correctly and that you're doing everything wrong. These feelings, of course, are made worse by a baby who won't stop crying (a reflection of inadequate fathering skills?) or by a dissatisfied or seemingly hostile look on the baby's face (possibly a reproach that you've made some terrible mistake).

Perhaps the best way to overcome your worries is to spend more time with the baby. The more practice you get, the better you'll be at understanding the baby's "language" and the more confident you'll be in responding.

Also, learn to go with your gut feelings. There's almost always more than one solution to a given problem, and you'll undoubtedly settle on a good one. Even if you make a few mistakes, they aren't likely to have any long-term effects. After all, just because your partner burps the baby over her shoulder doesn't mean you can't do it with the baby sitting on your knees.

Of course, if you're really sure you're making *serious* mistakes, ask for some help. But spending too much time analyzing things and worrying that you've done something wrong can get you into trouble. According to psychiatrist Stanley Greenspan, excessive worrying can destroy your self-confidence and lead to doing nothing at all or to adopting a hands-off attitude toward the baby. (That way, the twisted logic goes, at least you won't make any *more* mistakes.) This, of course, can have a decidedly negative effect on your baby's development—and on your development as a father.

Finally, before you toss in the towel, consider this: If you think you're having trouble reading your baby's signals, how can you be so sure that his crying and odd looks mean all the horrible, negative things you think they do?

Striking a Balance Between Work and Family

Most new fathers, writes author David Giveans, are "torn between the need to provide economically for the family and the desire to be a nurturing father." And finding the right balance between these two seemingly mutually exclusive options is something you'll be working on for the rest of your life.

As mentioned in the previous chapter (pages 85–86), most men place a high value on their family life and claim that they're willing to make sacrifices to spend more time with their children. But by six months after their children's birth, about 95 percent of new fathers are back working full-time. (Phil and Carolyn Cowan found that at the same point in time only 19 percent of women are employed full-time, and another 36 percent are working part-time.)

At first glance it seems that there's a major contradiction between what men say and what they do. But researcher Glen Palm found that the work/family trade-off isn't nearly so cut-and-dried. Many new fathers, Palm says, are "taking time off from friendships, recreation, and sleep to devote to their children, while they continue the time commitment to a full-time job."

Clearly there's something keeping fathers from spending less time at the office. One explanation, of course, is financial. Since the average working woman makes less than the average working man, if one parent is going to take time off from work, many families conclude that they can better survive the loss of the woman's salary.

Another important explanation is that in our society men and women have very different choices about the relative value of career in their lives. According to Dr. Warren Farrell, author of *Why Men Are the Way They Are,* women can choose between having a full-time career, being a full-time mother and homemaker, or some combination of the two. Men's choices, says Farrell, are a bit more limited: career, career, or career.

While this may be a bit of an exaggeration, the truth is that we simply expect men to show their love for their families by providing for them financially. "To many people, 'working mother' means conflict," says the Fatherhood Project's Jim Levine. "But 'working father' is a redundancy."

Perhaps the most interesting explanation (and my favorite) for why we keep fathers tied to their jobs and away from their families is offered by anthropologist Margaret Mead: "No developing society that needs men to leave home and do their thing for society ever allows young men in to handle or touch their newborns . . . for they know somewhere that if they did the new fathers would become so 'hooked' they would never go out and do their thing properly." Hmmmm.

Just because most fathers are trapped at the office doesn't mean that they aren't affected by what's going on at home. Radcliffe professor Rosalind Barnette found that men are just as likely as women to worry about family problems at the office. And according to researcher Joseph Pleck, 36 percent of fathers (and 37 percent of mothers) say work/family conflicts have caused them "a lot of stress." Pleck also says that "when stress occurs it has more negative consequences for men than for women."

Making Some Changes

Although you may never be able to resolve your work/family conflicts completely, there are a few ways you can maximize your time with your family, minimize your stress, and avoid trashing your career.

SCHEDULE CHANGES

"One of the conditions for men to become and stay highly involved in childrearing is for their work hours to be and continue to be flexible," writes John Snarey. Here are a few rather painless flexible scheduling options to run by your employer:

- Work four ten-hour days instead of five eight-hour days.
- Work from 5:00 A.M. to 1:00 P.M. (or some other schedule) instead of the usual 9:00–5:00.
- Consider a split shift, for example, work from 8:00 A.M. to noon and from 5:00 P.M. to 9:00 P.M.

"It's your husband. The baby won't burp for him.'

WORKING LESS THAN FULL-TIME

If you can afford to, you might want to consider one of the following options:

- Job sharing. You and another person divide up the responsibilities of the job. You would probably use the same office and desk. A typical job-share schedule might have you working two days one week and three days the next, while your workplace partner does the opposite. One warning: be very careful to negotiate a continuation of your health benefits. Many employers drop them for less-than-full-time employees.
- Switch to part-time, which is more or less the same as job sharing, except you probably won't have to share a desk with someone else.
- Become a consultant to your current employer. This can be a great way for you to get a lot of flexibility over your workday. There are also lots of tax advantages, particularly if you set up a home office (see more on this in the next section). At the very least, you'll be able to deduct auto mileage and a percentage of your phone and utility bills. But be sure to check with an accountant first; the IRS uses certain "tests" to determine whether someone is an employee or a consultant. If, for example, you go into the office every day, have a secretary, and get company benefits, you are an employee. Also, remember that if you become a consultant, you'll lose your benefit

package. So be sure to build the cost of that package (or the amount you'll have to pay to replace it) into the daily or hourly rate you negotiate with your soon-to-be-former employer.

WORKING AT HOME (TELECOMMUTING)

Far too many managers believe in the importance of daily "face time" (actually being seen at the office). The truth is that face time is highly overrated and often unnecessary. In all the years I've been writing, I've worked for dozens of magazines and newspapers, most of which are several thousand miles from my home. And in most cases I've never even met my bosses.

I'm certainly the first to admit that being a writer isn't a typical job. But millions of Americans do work that doesn't require their physical presence in any particular place at any particular time (engineers, computer programmers, and just about anybody else who sits at a desk). If you're not a construction worker or a retail salesman, you might be a prime candidate for telecommuting.

If You're an Employer (or a Supervisor)

"Companies compete to woo skilled women," says *Wall Street Journal* columnist Sue Shellenbarger. "But many still assume that men will continue to work regardless of how they are treated as fathers." The ultimate responsibility for changing this Neanderthal attitude and helping men get more involved with their families rests at the top—with you.

- Change your own schedule. Many of your male employees will be reluctant to approach you with proposed schedule changes. So if you know someone has just become a father, raise the issue with him first. Chances are he'll be grateful.
- Make some changes. If you have enough employees, organize classes and support groups for new parents. Even if you don't have many employees, you can still offer free (or subsidized) on-site or near-site child care. You can also encourage your employees to take advantage of part-time, job-sharing, or flexible scheduling options. Overall, your company's policies should recognize that *all* parents (as opposed to just mothers) are responsible for their children's care and development.
- Don't worry about the cost. Companies with family-friendly policies find that the costs of implementing such programs are more than compensated for by increased morale and productivity, reduced absenteeism, and lower turnover. They're also a great recruiting tool.

Now don't get too excited: it's not as if you and your boss will never see each other again. Most telecommuters are out of the office only a day or two a week. And if it's going to be a workable option at all, telecommuting is something you'll have to ease yourself (and your employer) into. Like the other flexible work options discussed in this chapter, telecommuting is designed to give you more time with your family. But if you think you'll be able to save money on child care or have your baby sit on your lap while you crunch numbers, you're sorely mistaken.

If you want to give it a try, here's what you'll probably need:

- A computer (compatible with your employer's system)
- An additional phone line or two
- A modem
- A fax machine (or a send/receive fax/modem)
- A quiet place to set things up

Besides the convenience aspect, one of the major advantages of telecommuting is that you don't have to shave and you can work in your underwear. There are, however, a few disadvantages. Primary among them is lack of human contact: you may hate that train ride into the city or the annoying guy in your carpool, but after a few months alone in your house, you might actually miss them. You might also miss going out to lunch with your co-workers or even just bumping into them in the halls. And if you have a tendency to be obsessive about your work (as I do), you'll have to train yourself to take frequent breaks. I can't tell you how many times I've realized—at ten o'clock at night—that I haven't eaten all day and that the only time I went outside was to take the newspaper in from the porch.

Putting It All Together

No matter how you try to keep your work life separate from your family life, there's going to be plenty of spillover between the two. This isn't necessarily a bad thing. In his four-decade-long study of fathers, John Snarey found that, "contrary to the stereotype of rigid work-family trade-off, a positive, reciprocal interaction may exist between childrearing and bread-winning."

Other researchers have come to similar conclusions. "Before they became fathers, men did not appear to be conscious that home and work life often require different personal qualities," writes Phil Cowan. After becoming fathers, however, many men "described new abilities to juggle conflicting demands, make decisions, and communicate quickly and clearly both at home and at work. . . . Some described themselves as more aware of their personal relationships on the job, and more able to use some of their managerial skills in the solution of family problems."

You and Your Baby

Time for Solids

When I was a baby, the current wisdom about introducing solid foods was to do it as early as possible, often as soon as five or six weeks. One of the explanations was that babies who ate solid foods supposedly slept longer than those on bottles (almost no one was being breastfed then). Today, people are more interested in the baby's health than in whether he sleeps through the night (which eating solid food doesn't affect anyway), and most pediatricians now recommend that you delay introducing solids until your baby is anywhere from four to six months old. The recommended delay may be even longer if you or your partner has a history of food allergies (for more on food allergies, see page 112).

Even if you're tempted to start solids earlier than four to six months, resist. "Introducing solids to the younger baby can interfere with his desire to suck," says Frances Wells Burck, author of *Babysense*. "Solids may also crowd out room for milk without making up for its nutritional loss." According to Burck, there are a few other reasons to keep your baby off solids until he's truly ready:

- Because younger babies' digestive systems are immature, solid food—along with their nutrients—passes undigested through their systems.
- Babies' young kidneys have to work harder to process solid foods than they do for milk or formula.
- Delaying especially allergenic foods (see page 113) can reduce the likelihood of developing allergies later on.
- Breast- and bottle-feeding is a great opportunity for parents to cuddle with their babies, although it's nearly impossible for *you* to cuddle the baby while your partner is breastfeeding.
- With breasts, there's nothing to clean up; with bottles, only the bottle. But with solids, you have to wash spoons, dishes, high-chair trays, bibs, and perhaps even the floor and nearby walls.

Here's how you can tell if your baby is really ready for solids:

- Her weight has doubled since birth (indicating that she's getting plenty of nutrition).
- She's very underweight for her age (indicating that she's not getting enough nutrition).

- She's drinking more than a quart (32 ounces) of formula or breast milk per day.
- She chews on nipples (either your partner's or the bottle's) while sucking.
- She pays close attention when you're eating.

Remember, introducing solids does not mean that breast- or bottle-feeding will end (see pages 205–8 for information on weaning). In fact, most of your baby's nutrients will still come from milk or formula for a few more months.

Getting Started

Getting your baby to eat solid foods isn't going to happen overnight. For starters, he'll probably take a few days to get used to the strange new taste and texture. Then he's got to figure out how to move it from the front of his mouth to his throat (liquids kind of know where to go by themselves), where he can swallow it. Here's the way to do it:

- Your baby's first food should be a single-grain cereal (no, not Cheerios)—oatmeal, barley, or rice. For the first few days, add breast milk or formula—but *not* cow's milk—to make the cereal especially liquidy. If you're buying packaged baby cereal, get the kind that's iron fortified.
- Offer new foods at the beginning of the meal, when the baby is likely to be at his hungriest.
- Three days after you actually manage to get some cereal down the baby's throat, start adding vegetables—one at a time, three to five days apart. Make sure the baby gets a good mix of yellow (carrots, squash) and green (peas, spinach, zucchini) veggies. Many people prefer to make bananas baby's first noncereal food. The problem with bananas is that they are fairly sweet, and babies may become so fond of them that they won't be interested in any other foods you may introduce thereafter.
- After a week or so on vegetables, introduce the bananas and some other noncitrus fruits (again, one at a time, three to five days apart). Until he's a year old, your baby can't digest raw apples, but applesauce is okay. Hold off on the oranges for a few more months.
- If you absolutely must give your baby juice (see page 28 for a few reasons not to), be sure to dilute it fifty-fifty with water.
- When your baby is about seven months old, introduce yogurt. It's an important source of protein and can easily be mixed with other foods. Although most babies like yogurt, mine didn't, and we had to trick them into eating it by putting a blueberry (always a favorite food) at the back of the spoon.
- Breads and cereals (yes, Cheerios are okay now) are next.

Allergies and Intolerances: What They Are and How to Prevent Them

Despite the claims of about 25 percent of American parents, fewer than 5 percent of children under three are truly allergic to any foods. True allergies are abnormal responses by the immune system to ingested proteins. The most common symptoms are nasal congestion, asthma, skin rashes (eczema and hives), chronic runny nose or cough, vomiting, and severe mood swings. In contrast, symptoms such as headaches, excess gas, diarrhea, or constipation are generally caused by intolerances, which are usually the result of an enzyme deficiency.

While you may be tempted to say, "What's the difference? A reaction is a reaction," the distinction between an allergy and an intolerance is critical and subtle. Allergies often begin in infancy and get progressively worse with each encounter with the offending food. Intolerances don't. Fortunately, most kids—except those allergic to peanuts and fish—usually outgrow their allergies altogether by age five. (Only about 2 percent of children over five have true food allergies.)

The consensus among pediatricians is that the way to deal with allergies and intolerances is to prevent them before they happen. Complete prevention, of course, is impossible. But here are a few things you can do to better the odds:

- Breastfeed your baby and withhold solid foods for at least four to six months.
- If your partner has a history of true allergies, she should reduce or completely eliminate high-risk foods (see page 113) while breastfeeding.
- Introduce only one new food at a time. That way, if your baby has a reaction, you'll know right away what caused it.
- After introducing a new food, wait three to five days before introducing another.
- If your baby has any of the negative reactions mentioned above, eliminate the food right away and call your pediatrician. He or she will probably tell you to take the baby off the food and reintroduce it in six months. By then, your baby may have built up the necessary defenses.

MOST ALLERGENIC FOODS	LEAST ALLERGENIC FOODS
♦ Egg whites	♦ Rice
♦ Wheat and yeast	♦ Oats
♦ Milk and other dairy products	♦ Barley
♦ Citrus fruits	♦ Carrots
♦ Berries	♦ Squash
♦ Tomatoes	♦ Apricots
♦ Chocolate	♦ Peaches
♦ Nuts	♦ Apples
♦ Shellfish	♦ Lamb

- At about one year, your baby can eat almost any kind of food, but in small pieces. Some foods, such as grapes, raw carrots, nuts, and hot dogs, can still present choking hazards.
- One big warning: Do not give your baby honey or corn sweeteners for at least the first year. They often contain tiny parasites that an adult's digestive system exterminates with no problem. But the baby's still-immature system won't be able to handle the chore.

I Wanna Do It Myself

When your baby is ready to feed himself, he'll let you know, usually by grabbing the spoon from your hand (babies are quicker than you'd think) or mushing around anything that's dropped on to the high-chair tray. When this happens, prepare yourself; in the course of the next few weeks, your baby will discover the joys of sticking various kinds of food in his nose and eyes, under his chin, behind his ears, and in his hair. And it won't be much longer until he learns to throw.

One way to minimize the mess is to put a large piece of plastic under the high chair; a large trash bag cut open along the side is good. But don't relax yet; your baby will soon learn to use his spoon as a catapult to launch food beyond this protective boundary. There's really nothing you can do about this, so avoid wearing your best clothes while the baby is eating.

Making Your Own

You can, of course, buy pre-prepared baby food in those tiny jars. But they're expensive and often filled with preservatives, chemicals, and other nasty stuff. Some companies, such as Earth's Best, offer organic, pesticide- and preservative-free foods. They're even more expensive.

Two Small Warnings

First, when you begin giving your baby solids, she's going to make an incredible array of faces: horror, disgust, fear, betrayal. Try not to take them personally. Your baby is probably reacting to the new and unknown and not criticizing your cooking.

Second, don't make a ton of food the first few times. You'll probably end up feeding the baby the same spoonful over and over again (you put some in her mouth, she spits it out; you scrape it off her cheek and put it in her mouth again . . .). This can be frustrating, but try to remember what comedian Dave Barry says: "Babies do not take solid food through their mouths. . . . Babies absorb solid food through their chins. You can save yourself a lot of frustrating effort if you smear the food directly on your baby's chin, rather than putting it in the baby's mouth and forcing the baby to expel it on to its chin, as so many uninformed parents do."

The solution: be patient and keep your video camera ready at all times.

By far the cheapest alternative is to make your own. After all, the major ingredient of most baby food is cooked vegetables. You can even do it in bulk. All you have to do is boil some vegetables, mash them up, and put the mash into an ice-cube tray. Whenever you need to, just pop out a cube, thaw, and serve.

A word of caution: Microwaves heat food unevenly, leaving hot spots right next to cold ones. So if you're using a microwave, make sure you stir well and test anything you're planning to give the baby.

Notes:

6 MONTHS

Gaining Confidence

What's Going On with the Baby

Physically

- By the end of this month she'll probably be able to sit by herself in "tripod position" (feet splayed, hands on the floor in between for balance). She may even be able to right herself if she tips over.
- She can turn herself from back to front or front to back at will, and may even be able to propel herself short distances (usually backward at first) by creeping or wiggling. Be prepared, though: she'll be demonstrating a lot of these new moves when you're trying to change or dress her.
- She can probably get herself to her hands and knees and will spend hours rocking back and forth, picking up an arm here, a leg there—all in preparation for crawling.
- She can clap her hands and bang two objects together. And whatever isn't being banged is sure to be in her mouth.

Intellectually

- With so many new things to do and learn, your baby is now awake about 12 hours a day and spends most of that time finding out about her environment by touching, holding, tasting, and shaking things. According to Frank Caplan, this is proof that "the need to learn is at least as important as pleasure-seeking in determining behavior."
- The idea that she is separate from other people and other objects is slowly sinking in. But she still thinks she has absolute control over all she sees or

touches. As if to rub it in, she'll endlessly drop toys, dishes, and food from her high chair and revel in the way she can make you pick them up.

- Another way your baby demonstrates her complete power over the world and everything in it (especially you) is to cry for attention whether she needs any or not.
- Both these activities show that your baby is able to formulate plans and can anticipate the consequences of her actions.

Verbally

- She's now more regularly adding consonants to vowels and creating single-syllable "words" such as *ba, ma, la, ka, pa.*
- She's getting pretty good at imitating sounds and also tries—with some success—to imitate your inflections.
- She's getting so familiar with language that she can easily tell the difference between conversational speech and any of the other noises you make. She might, for example, laugh when you start making animal noises.
- She's also learning to like other sounds; music in particular will cause her to stop what she's doing and listen.

Emotionally/Socially

- Until this month, your baby really didn't care who fed her, changed her, played with her, or hugged her, just as long as it got done. But now, for about 50–80 percent of babies, *who* satisfies their needs is almost as important. You, your partner, and perhaps a few other very familiar people may now be the only ones your baby will allow near her without crying. This is the beginning of *stranger anxiety.*
- She'll wave her arms to let you know to pick her up, cling to you when you do, and cry if you take away a toy or stop playing with her.
- Despite all this, she's still incredibly curious in new situations, and will spend as much as ninety minutes taking in her surroundings.
- Her desire to imitate what you do has led to an interest in eating solid food.

What You're Going Through

Growing Up

There's nothing quite like having a kid to make you realize that you're a grown-up. It also makes you realize that besides being a son, you're also a father. That may sound like a painfully obvious thing to say, but you'd be

surprised at how many men have a hard time with the concept. After all, we've spent our whole lives looking at our fathers as fathers and at ourselves as sons.

Here's how a friend of mine describes becoming aware that he had made the transition: "One day I slipped my arm into the sleeve of my jacket and my father's hand came out the other side."

Feeling Like a Father

According to Bruce Drobeck, a large percentage of men see the fatherhood role as that of a teacher of values and skills. Until they can actually communicate with their children, these men don't quite feel that they've become fathers. And since it's hard to communicate with a helpless and essentially nonresponsive baby, caring for one doesn't seem very fatherly.

But by the time your baby is six months old, she's no longer unable to communicate. She turns her head when you call her, she gets excited when you walk into the room. And when you wrestle with her, build a tower together, or tickle her, she'll give you a smile that could melt steel—a smile that's only for you. You're starting to feel confident that your baby needs you and that you're playing an important and influential role in her young life. You're finally starting to feel like a father; and the more you and your baby interact, the more you'll feel that way.

Jealousy

"The single emotion that can be the most destructive and disruptive to your experience of fatherhood is jealousy," writes Dr. Martin Greenberg in *The Birth of a Father.*

There's certainly plenty to be jealous about, but the real question is: Whom (or what) are you jealous of? Your partner for her close relationship with the baby and the extra time she gets to spend with her? The baby for taking up more than her "fair share" of your partner's attention and for having full access to her breasts while they may be "too tender" for you to touch? The baby-sitter for being the recipient of the baby's daytime smiles and love—tokens of affection you'd rather were directed at you? Or maybe it's the baby's carefree life. The answer, of course, is: All of the above.

Like most emotions, a little jealousy goes a long way. Too much can make you feel competitive toward or resentful of your partner, the baby-sitter, even the baby. Do you feel you need more attention or emotional support from your partner? Do you need more private time with the baby? Whatever or whomever you're jealous of, it's critical to express your feelings clearly and honestly and to encourage your partner to do the same. If for some reason you feel you can't discuss your feelings on this issue with your partner, take them up with a male friend or relative. You'll be surprised at how common jealousy is. Jealousy's "potential for destruction," writes Greenberg, "lies not in having the feelings but in burying them."

Gaining Confidence

I don't remember every day of my children's childhoods, but there's one day in particular—when my older daughter was about six months old—that I recall quite clearly.

It really wasn't all that different from any other day. I gave her a bottle and dressed her. When she threw up all over her clothes, I dressed her again. Five minutes later she had an explosive bowel movement that oozed all the way up to her neck, so I cleaned her up and dressed her for the third time. Over the course of the day I probably changed five more diapers and two more outfits, gave her three bottles, calmed her from crying four times, took her in and out of the car eight times as I drove all over town doing errands, put her down for two successful naps during which I managed to do a few loads of laundry and wash the dishes. I even managed to get some writing done.

All in all, it wouldn't have been a very memorable day if it weren't for what happened at the end of it. As I sat in bed reading, I remember thinking to myself, "Damn, I'm really getting a pretty good handle on this dad stuff." The truth is that I was. And by now, you probably are too.

Things that would have had you panicking a few months ago now seem completely ordinary. You've learned to understand your baby's cues, you can predict the unpredictable, and those feelings of not being able to do things right are nearly gone. You probably feel more connected and attached to your baby than ever before. The feeling is one of confidence and stability, and signals that you've entered what some sociologists and psychologists refer to as the "honeymoon period" with your baby.

For many men, feelings of confidence as fathers lead them to feel more confident in their relationships with their partners as well. A majority of men in fatherhood researcher Bruce Linton's studies felt that their relationships with their partners had gotten "easier" and described a sensation of connection and attachment to both baby and partner—kind of "bonding as a family."

You and Your Baby

Playing Around

As your baby develops her reaching, grabbing, and shoving-things-into-her-mouth skills, she'll gradually lose interest in face-to-face play and become more focused on the objects around her (or at least the ones she can reach) and on exploring her environment.

The first, and perhaps most important, lesson your baby will learn about objects is that she can, to a certain extent, control them. Of course, this startling epiphany comes about as a complete accident: you put a rattle in her hand and after swinging her arms around for a while, she'll notice that the rattle makes some noise. But over the course of several months, your baby will learn that when she stops flailing, the rattle stops rattling and that she can—just because she wants to—get it to rattle again, and again, and again.

Your baby will learn quite a bit about objects all by herself. But if you're interested, there are a number of games you can play with your baby that, besides being fun, will encourage object awareness and perception.

REACHING GAMES

To encourage your baby to reach and to expand her horizons, try holding attractive toys just out of her reach: above her head, in front of her, to the sides. See how close you have to get the toy before she makes her move. Remember, the object here is not to tease or torture the baby, it's to have fun.

TOUCHING GAMES

Try this: Let your baby play with a small toy without letting her see it (you might want to do this in the dark or with her hands in a paper bag). Then put that toy together with several other toys she's never played with. Many babies this age will pick up the familiar toy. Although this may sound fairly easy, it isn't. You're asking your baby to use two senses—touch and vision—at the same time. If your baby isn't ready for this one, don't worry. Just try it again in a few weeks.

IF . . . THEN . . . GAMES

There are thousands of things you can do to reinforce cause-and-effect thinking. Rattles, banging games, rolling a ball back and forth, and splashing in the pool are excellent. So is blowing up your cheeks and having the baby "pop" them. Baby gyms—especially the kind that make a lot of noise when smacked—are also good, but be sure to pack them up the moment your baby starts trying to use the gym to pull herself up; they just aren't sturdy enough.

Give the Kid a Break

Don't feel that you have to entertain your baby all the time. Sure it's fun, but letting her have some time to play by herself is almost as important to her development as playing with her yourself. And don't worry; letting her play alone—as long as you're close enough to hear what she's doing and to respond quickly if she needs you—doesn't mean you're being neglectful. Quite the opposite, in fact. By giving her the opportunity to make up her own games or to practice on her own the things she does with you, you're helping her learn that she's capable of satisfying at least some of her needs by herself. You'll also be helping her build her sense of self-confidence by allowing her to decide for herself what she'll be playing with and for how long.

GOOD TOYS	BAD TOYS
♦ Blocks ♦ Dolls with easy-to-grasp limbs ♦ Real things: phones, computer keyboards, shoes, etc. ♦ Toys that make different sounds and have different textures ♦ Musical toys ♦ Balls ♦ Sturdy books	♦ Anything made of foam—it's too easy to chew off pieces ♦ Anything small enough to swallow or that has detachable parts ♦ Anything that could possibly pinch the baby ♦ Anything that runs on electricity ♦ Stuffed animals and other furry things that might shed (stuffed animals that *don't* shed are fine) ♦ Toys with strings, ribbons, elastic—all potential choking hazards

OBJECT PERMANENCE

When your baby is about six or seven months old, the all-important idea that objects can exist even when they're out of sight slowly starts sinking in.

- Peek-a-boo and other games that involve hiding and finding things are great for developing object permanence. Peek-a-boo in particular teaches your baby an excellent lesson: when you go away, you always come back. This doesn't sound like much, but making this connection now lets her know she can count on you to be there when she needs you and will help her cope with *separation anxiety* (see pages 154–55).
- Object permanence develops in stages. If you're interested in seeing how, try this: Show your baby a toy. Then, while she's watching, "hide" it under a pillow. If you ask her where the toy is, she'll probably push the pillow out of the way and "find" it. But if you quickly move the toy to another hiding place when she's not looking, the baby will continue to look for it in the first hiding place.

TRACKING GAMES

Hold an object in front of the baby. When you're sure she's seen it, let it drop out of your hand. At five or six months, most babies won't follow the object down. But starting at about seven months, they'll begin to anticipate where things are going to land. When your baby has more or less mastered this skill, add an additional complication: drop a few objects and let her track them down. Then hold a helium balloon in front of her and let it go. She'll look down and be rather stunned that the balloon never lands. Let her hold the string of the balloon and experiment.

Again, if your baby doesn't respond to some, or any, of the activities suggested here, don't worry. Babies develop at very different rates, and what's "normal" for your baby may be advanced—or delayed—for your neighbor's.

Family Matters

Finding Quality Child Care

Most parents instinctively feel (and there's plenty of research to back them up) that to have one or both of them care for their baby in their own home would, in a perfect world, probably be the best child-care option. But most couples can't afford the traditional dad-goes-to-work-while-mom-stays-at-home option or the less-traditional mom-goes-to-work-while-dad-stays-at-home scenario. So chances are that, sooner or later, you'll need to consider some form of day care for your child. Here are some of the options, along with their advantages and disadvantages.

IN-HOME CARE

Unless you work at home, in-home care is probably the most convenient option for parents. You don't have to worry about day-care schedules, and your baby can stay in the environment to which he or she has become accustomed. In addition, your baby will receive plenty of one-on-one attention, and, if you stay on top of the situation, the caregiver will keep you up to date on your child's development. Finally, by remaining at home, your child will be less exposed to germs and illness.

Leaving your child alone with a stranger can be daunting and traumatic, especially the first time. On the one hand, you might be worried about whether you really know (and can trust) the caregiver. You might also be worried—as I was—that no one will be able to love or care for your child as well as you and your partner. On the other hand, you might experience what psychologist and parenting guru Dr. Lawrence Kutner calls the "natural rivalry" between parents and caregivers. "As parents, we want our children to feel close (but not too close) to the other adults in their lives. We worry that, if those attachments are too strong, they will replace us in our child's eyes."

Fortunately, no one will ever be able to replace you—or your love. But

Au Pairs

Au pairs are usually young women who come to the States on yearlong cultural exchange programs administered by the United States Information Agency (USIA). Legally, au pairs are nonresident aliens and are exempt from social security, Medicare, and unemployment taxes (see below for more on taxes and payroll).

What an au pair provides is up to forty-five hours per week of live-in child care. In exchange, you pay a weekly stipend (currently about $155) as well as airfare, insurance, an educational stipend, program support, and full room and board. On average, having an au pair will set you back about $12,000 for the full year.

You can hire an au pair through one of only eight USIA-approved placement agencies. You could hire one through a non-USIA agency, but the au pair would be subject to immediate deportation and you to a $10,000 fine.

Having an au pair can be a wonderful opportunity for you and your baby to learn about another culture. One drawback, however, is that they can stay only a year; then it's *au revoir* to one, *bonjour* to another. In addition, it's important to remember that from the young woman's perspective, being an au pair is a cultural thing. In theory she's supposed to do a lot of child care and other work, but in reality she may be far more interested in going to the mall with her new American friends or hanging out with your neighbor's teen-age son.

there are many wonderful caregivers out there who can give your baby the next best thing. You just need to know how to find them.

HOW TO FIND IN-HOME CAREGIVERS

The best ways to find in-home caregivers are:

- Agencies
- Word of mouth
- Bulletin boards (either caregivers respond to your ad, or you respond to theirs)

The first thing to do is to conduct thorough interviews over the phone—this will enable you to screen out the obviously unacceptable candidates (for example, the ones who are only looking for a month-long job, or those who don't drive if you need a driver). Then invite the "finalists" over to meet with you, your partner, and the baby in person. Make sure the baby and the prospective caregiver spend a few minutes together, and pay close attention to how they interact. Someone who approaches your baby cautiously and speaks to her reassuringly before picking her up is someone who understands, and cares about, your baby's feelings. And someone who strokes your baby's hair and strikes up a "conversation" is a far better choice than a person who sits rigidly with your baby on her knee.

Another good "test" for potential caregivers is to have them change your baby's diapers. Does the applicant smile or sing or try some other way to make getting changed interesting and fun for the baby, or does she seem disgusted by the whole thing? And be sure that she washes her hands when she's done.

When you've finally put together your list of finalists, get references—and check at least two (it's awkward, but absolutely essential). Ask each of the references why the baby-sitter left his or her previous jobs, and what the best and worst things about him or her were. Also, make sure to ask the prospective caregiver the questions listed below.

When you make your final choice, have the person start a few days before you return to work so you can all get to know each other, and, of course, so you can spy.

WHAT TO ASK THEM

Here are a few good questions to ask prospective in-home caregivers. You may want to add a few more from the sections on other child-care options.

- What previous child-care experience have you had (including caring for younger relatives)?
- What age children have you cared for?
- Tell us a little about your own childhood.
- What would you do if . . . ? (Give several examples of things a child might do that would require different degrees of discipline.)
- When would you hit or spank a child? (If the answer is anything other than "Never," find yourself another candidate.)
- How would you handle . . . ? (Name a couple of emergency situations, such as a gushing head wound or a broken arm.)
- Do you know baby CPR? (If not, you might want to consider paying for the caregiver to take a class.)
- What are your favorite things to do with kids?
- Do you have a driver's license?

- What days/hours are you available/not available? How flexible can you be if an emergency arises while we're at work?
- Are you a native speaker of any foreign language?

OTHER IMPORTANT ISSUES TO DISCUSS

- Compensation (find out the going rate by checking with other people who have caregivers) and vacation.
- Telephone privileges.
- Complete responsibilities of the job: feeding, bathing, diapering, changing clothes, reading to the baby, and so on, as well as what light housekeeping chores, if any, will be expected while the baby is sleeping.
- English-language skills—particularly important in case of emergency (you want someone who can accurately describe to a doctor or 911 operator what's going on).
- Immigration/green card status (more on this and other legal complications below).

You might want to draw up an informal contract listing all of the caregiver's responsibilities—just so there won't be any misunderstandings.

LIVE-IN HELP

Hiring a live-in caregiver is like adding a new member to the family. The process for selecting one is similar to that for finding a non-live-in caregiver, so you can use most of the questions listed above for conducting interviews. After you've made your choice, try out your new relationship on a non-live-in basis for a few weeks, just to make sure everything's going to work out to everyone's satisfaction.

To Grandmother's (or Grandfather's) House We Go

If your parents, in-laws, or other relatives live in the neighborhood, they may provide you with a convenient, loving, and low-cost child-care alternative. According to a recent survey by the U.S. Census Bureau, about 16 percent of children under five years old are being cared for by their grandparents while their parents are working—half of them in their grandparents' homes. Other relatives account for an additional 8 percent of all child-care arrangements for preschoolers.

FAMILY DAY CARE

If you can't (or don't want to, or can't afford to) have someone care for your child in your home, the next best alternative is to have your child cared for in someone else's home. Since the caregiver is usually looking after only two or three children (including yours), your baby will get the individual attention he needs as well as the opportunity to socialize with other children. And since the caregiver lives in his or her own house, personnel changes are unlikely; this gives your baby a greater sense of stability.

Be sure to ask potential family-day-care providers what kind of backup system they have to deal with vacations and illness (the provider's). Will you suddenly find yourself without child care or will your baby be cared for by another adult whom both you and your baby know?

GROUP DAY CARE

Many people—even those who can afford in-home child care—would rather use an out-of-home center. For one, a good day-care center is, as a rule, much better equipped than your home, or anyone else's for that matter, and will undoubtedly offer your child a wider range of stimulating activities. But remember, "There is absolutely no relationship between the amount of money a child-care center charges and the quality of care your baby will receive," writes Lawrence Kutner. "The best child-care centers invest in hiring and retaining the best people, not buying the most toys."

Many parents also prefer group day care because it usually offers kids more opportunities to play with one another. In the long run, most parenting experts agree that being able to play with a variety of other kids helps children become better socialized and more independent. The downside, of course, is that your child won't get as much individual attention from the adult caregivers; and since your six-month-old won't really be playing with other kids for a while longer, adult-baby contact is more important. In addition, interacting with other kids usually means interacting with their germs: children in group day care tend to get sick a lot more often than those cared for at home (whether yours or someone else's).

Where to Find Out-of-Home Caregivers

You're most likely to find out of home child care facilities through word of mouth or by seeing an ad in a local parenting newspaper. Perhaps the easiest (and safest) alternative is through Child Care Aware, a nationwide campaign created to help parents identify quality child care in their communities. Contact them at 1-800-424-2246.

However you find out about a potential child-care facility, there's no substitute for checking it out for yourself in person. Here are some of the things Child Care Aware suggests you keep in mind when comparing child-care facilities:

ABOUT THE CAREGIVERS

- Do they seem to really like children? And do the kids seem to like them?
- Do they get down on each child's level to speak to the child?
- Are the children greeted when they arrive?
- Are the children's needs quickly met even when things get busy?
- Are the caregivers trained in CPR, first aid, and early childhood development?
- Are they involved in continuing education programs?
- Does the program keep up with children's changing interests?
- Will the caregivers always be ready to answer your questions?
- Will they tell you what your child is doing every day?
- Are parents' ideas welcomed? Are there ways for you to get involved if you want to?
- Are there enough caregivers for the number of kids? (One adult for four kids is the absolute maximum ratio you should accept; if there are two or more infants the ratio should be less.)

ABOUT THE FACILITY

- Is the atmosphere bright and pleasant?
- Is there a fenced-in outdoor play area with a variety of safe equipment?
- Can the caregivers see the entire playground at all times?
- Are there different areas for resting, quiet play, and active play?
- What precautions are taken to ensure that kids can be picked up only by the person you select? Do strangers have access to the center?
- Are there adequate safety measures to keep children away from windows, fences, and kitchen appliances and utensils (knives, ovens, stoves, household chemicals, and so forth)?

ABOUT THE PROGRAM

- Is there a daily balance of play time, story time, and nap time?
- Are the activities right for each age group?
- Are there enough toys and learning materials for the number of children?
- Are the toys clean, safe, and within reach of the children?

ABOUT OTHER THINGS

- Do you agree with the discipline practices?

Taxes and Government Regulations

If you hire an in-home caregiver or family day-care provider, here are some of the steps you have to take to meet IRS, INS, and Department of Labor requirements:

- Get a federal ID number (you may be able to use your social security number)
- Register with your state tax department
- Register with the Department of Labor
- Calculate payroll deductions (and, of course, deduct them)
- File quarterly reports to your state tax board
- Calculate unemployment tax
- Get a worker's compensation policy and compute the premium (usually a percentage of payroll rather than a flat fee for the year)
- Prepare W-2 and W-4 forms
- Demonstrate compliance with Immigration and Naturalization Service guidelines

If the prospect of doing all this doesn't make you want to quit your job to stay home with the baby, nothing will. There is, however, an alternative: get in touch with Alan L. Goldberg, president of NannyTax, Inc. (phone: 212-867-1776; fax: 212-867-2045). His organization takes care of all these matters and any other pesky details that may arise.

- Do you hear the sounds of happy children?
- Is the program licensed or regulated? By whom?
- Are surprise visits by parents encouraged?
- Will your child be happy there?

Try to visit each facility more than once, and after you've made your final decision, make a few unannounced visits—just to see what goes on when there aren't any parents around.

A FEW THINGS TO GET SUSPICIOUS ABOUT

- Parents are not allowed to drop in unannounced. You need to call before visiting or coming to pick up your child.
- Parents dropping off kids are not allowed into the care-giving areas.
- Your child is unhappy after several months.

- There seem to be new and unfamiliar caregivers almost every day.
- You don't get any serious response when you voice your concerns.

Finding a good child-care provider is a lengthy, agonizing process, and it's important not to give up until you're satisfied. "Half to three-quarters of parents who use daycare feel they have no choices and must settle for what they can find," writes Sue Shellenbarger, author of the Work & Family column for the *Wall Street Journal.* The result? Most infants get mediocre care. A recent study by the Work and Families Institute (WFI) found that only 8 percent of child-care facilities were considered "good quality," and 40 percent were rated "less than minimal." According to WFI's president, Ellen Galinsky, 10 to 20 percent of children "get care so poor that it risks damaging their development." So be careful.

Notes:

7 MONTHS

A Whole New Kind of Love

What's Going On with the Baby

Physically

- He's getting so good at sitting that he doesn't need his hands for balancing anymore. Instead, he can—and will—use them to reach for things.
- He can get himself to a sitting position from his stomach.
- He's starting to crawl, but don't be surprised if he goes backward at least some of the time, or, instead of crawling, scoots around on his bottom, using one arm to pull, the other to push.
- If you hold him upright, supported under the arms, he can bear some weight on his feet and will stamp and bounce up and down.
- He now uses his opposable thumb almost like you do, and is able to pick up what he wants confidently and quickly. He still prefers objects he can bang together and, of course, put into his mouth.

Intellectually

- As his brain develops, so does his ability to make associations. He recognizes the sound of your approaching footsteps and starts getting excited even before you come into his room.
- If confronted with blocks of different sizes, he will pick each one up, manipulate them a bit, then line them up to compare them to one another.
- He's so thrilled with his newfound ability to pick up and hold objects, he just can't get enough. He spends a lot of time examining objects upside

down and from other angles. And if he's holding a block in one hand, he'll reach for a second one and eye a third—all at the same time.

- The idea that objects may exist even when he can't see them is just beginning to take shape. If he drops something, he no longer thinks it's gone forever. Instead, he'll grope around for it or stare intently at the place it disappeared from, hoping to bring it back. But if it doesn't show up within 5 to 10 seconds, he'll forget about it.

Verbally

- A few months ago, your baby was capable (with practice) of producing any sound that a human can produce. But since he spends all his time trying to make the sounds *you* make, he's forgetting how to make the ones you don't (like rolled Rs or the clicks of the African bush people).
- In English, though, your baby's babbling is shifting from single-syllable to multisyllable (*babababa, mamamama, dadadada* . . .). He's able to modulate the tone, volume, and speed of his sounds and actively tries to converse with you, vocalizing after you stop speaking and waiting for you to respond to him.
- Your baby's passive language skills are also improving. He now turns when he hears his own name and understands several other words.

Emotionally/Socially

- Although he's fascinated with objects, your baby really prefers social interactions and one-on-one activities, such as chasing and fetching.
- He can now tell the difference between adults and children, and may be interested in playing with (actually, alongside) kids his own age.
- He recognizes, and reacts differently to, positive and negative tones of voice and happy or sad facial expressions.
- Shyness or anxiety around strangers continues.
- Continuing on his mission to imitate everything you do, your baby now wants to finger-feed himself or hold his own bottle or cup.

What You're Going Through

A New and Different Kind of Love

Sooner or later, almost every writer takes a crack at trying to describe love. And for the most part, they fall short. The problem is that there are so many different kinds. The love I feel for my wife, for example, is completely different from the love I feel for my sisters, which is different from the love I feel for my parents. And none of those seems even remotely similar to the love I have for my children.

I usually describe my love for my children in fairly happy terms, but periodically I experience it in a completely different way—one that sometimes frightens me.

Here's how it happens: I'm watching one of my daughters (either one will do) play in the park, her beautiful, innocent face filled with joy. All of a sudden, out of nowhere, I begin to imagine how I would feel if something terrible were to happen to her. What if she fell and broke her neck? What if she got hit by a truck? What if she got horribly sick and died? The loss is almost palpable, and just thinking about these things is enough to depress me for the rest of the day.

And there's more. Sometimes my imagination goes a step further and I wonder what I would do if someone, anyone, tried to hurt or kidnap or kill one of my children. At the very instant that that thought pops into my head, my heart suddenly begins beating faster and so loudly I can almost hear it, my breathing quickens, and my teeth and fists clench. I haven't hit another person outside a Karate studio for more than twenty-five years. But during those brief moments when my imagination runs loose I realize that I would be perfectly capable of killing another human being with my bare hands and without a moment's hesitation.

Feeling Isolated

When my older daughter was still quite young, she and her baby-sitter spent several mornings a week at Totland, a nearby park that had become something of a Mecca for caretakers and children. Most afternoons I'd come to pick up my daughter at the park, and I'd stay for an hour or so watching her play with the other kids.

The other caregivers—almost all of whom were women—would be gathered in groups of four or five, chatting, sharing information, and learning from each other. And newcomers—as long as they were female—were quickly welcomed into these groups. But despite the nodding relationships I had developed with a few of the women, I was never made completely welcome. "It's strange being a man in this woman's place," writes David Steinberg, describing a trip to the park with his baby. "There is an easy-going exchange among the women here, yet I am outside of it. . . . Maybe it's all in my head, just me being uncomfortable about integrating this lunch counter. Whatever it is, it leaves me feeling strange and alone."

Once in a while another father would come to the park with his child, and we'd nod, smile, or raise our eyebrows at each other. We probably had much in common as fathers, shared many of the same concerns, and could have learned a lot from each other. But we didn't. Instead, we sat ten yards apart; if we ever spoke, it was about football or something equally superficial. Each of us was afraid to approach the other for fear of seeming too needy, too ignorant, or not masculine enough. What a couple of idiots.

Unfortunately, the majority of new fathers in the same situation would do exactly the same thing. "Most men," says Bruce Linton, "turn to their wives, not to other men, to help them understand their feelings about fatherhood." That approach, however, is often less than completely satisfying. Even if their wives are supportive, most men report that "there's something they are not 'getting,'" says Linton. The result is that many new fathers feel isolated; they have all sorts of concerns, worries, and feelings they don't completely understand, and they think there's no one else they can share their experience with. Fatherhood, it seems, can be a lonely business at times.

Getting Together with Other Men

One of the best ways to overcome your feelings of isolation or loneliness as a father is to join or start a fathers' group. Even in California, where there are so many support groups that there are support groups for people who belong to too many support groups, the idea of being involved in a fathers' group still sounds a little risky. But according to Doug Spangler, author of *Fatherhood: An Owner's Manual,* there are many important reasons to do it:

- Education. Women get a ton of parenting (and other) advice from other women: where to buy the best used children's clothes, places to take the kids on rainy days, surefire cures for illnesses, ways to soothe crying babies, finding and hiring baby-sitters. You'd be surprised how much you already know, and how much you'll be able to help other men.
- Perspective. It won't take long for you to learn that you're not the only father who is having the feelings or thoughts you are. Yet because each of us has a different way of looking at or doing things, you'll have plenty of unique insights to contribute to the other guys in the group.
- Opportunities for sharing. Like most men, you probably have a few things you just can't talk about with your wife. When those issues arise, you need a couple of guys who are—or have been—experiencing some of the same things you have.
- Encouragement. If you're having a tough time with something, or you need help making a decision, you'll be able to tap into the collective wisdom of other men who have made fatherhood a priority in their lives.

"Gotta go, guys. I've had about all the male bonding I can take for today."

- Accountability. The other fathers in your group will support you, but because they're guys, they'll also let you know if you're screwing up.

Finding other fathers to join a group probably won't be easy. But if you put the word out you're sure to get some responses. Here are some likely sources of new (or existing) fathers:

- Your church or synagogue
- The hospital where your baby was born
- Your partner's OB/GYN
- Your pediatrician
- Leaders of mothers' groups

If you aren't comfortable joining a group (and there are plenty of us who aren't), it's still important to make regular contact with other fathers. You can do this one-on-one with another father, or, if you've got a computer, by logging on to the Internet. There are discussion groups, lists, and Web pages dealing with just about every aspect of parenting: some for both mothers and fathers, some just for fathers. Almost all of these services are available for free. There's a listing of good Internet addresses in the Resources appendix at the end of this book.

According to Bruce Linton, "A father's need for friendships with other fathers is critical to his continued development." In addition, there's plenty of research indicating that fathers who join support groups are generally happier. So don't think you can handle by yourself every fatherhood-related matter that comes up. You can't. And trying to do so will only hurt your kids and yourself.

You and Your Baby

A (Very) Brief Introduction to Discipline

"Discipline is the second most important thing you do for a child," says pediatrician T. Berry Brazelton. "Love comes first." There's no question in my mind that Brazelton is absolutely right. But before we go any further, let's clarify one thing: Discipline does *not* mean "punishment"; it means "teaching" and "setting limits."

According to pediatrician Burton White, there is absolutely no need to discipline kids under seven months. There are two main reasons for this. First, your child simply isn't capable of understanding that she's doing

"Your father and I have come to believe that incarceration is sometimes the only appropriate punishment."

something wrong. She has no idea at this point what "right" and "wrong" mean. Second, babies under about seven months have very short memories. So by the time you've disciplined the baby, she's already forgotten what she did to get you so upset.

Starting at about seven months, though, White suggests slowly beginning

Your Baby's Teeth

Although your baby's little chompers started forming when your partner was four months pregnant, they probably won't make their first appearance ("eruption" in dental lingo) until about six or seven months. And it's not at all uncommon for a child to be toothless until his first birthday. One thing you can count on, though: whenever your baby's teeth show up, they'll be followed immediately by plaque. Yes, the same stuff that your dentist has to chip off your teeth with a chisel.

It's way too early to start taking your child to a dentist, but you should use a small piece of gauze to clean each of his teeth once a day. When he's a year old, use a toothbrush with a very soft bristle. Flossing won't be necessary for a while.

TEETHING

There are two important things to know about teething. First, your baby's teeth start showing up in a fairly predictable order: first the two lower central incisors, then the two top central incisors, and then the ones on either side. Most kids will have all eight incisors by the end of their first year.

Second, teething isn't usually much fun for your baby or for anyone else nearby. Most kids experience at least some discomfort around the tooth for a few days before it breaks through the gum. For many, those pre-eruption days are marked by runny noses, loose stools, a low-grade fever, and some general crankiness.

Fortunately, teething discomfort doesn't last long and is relatively easily dealt with. Most babies respond quite well to acetominophen (ask your pediatrician how many drops to give and don't waste your time rubbing it on the baby's gums—it doesn't work). Teething rings are also helpful, especially the kind that are water filled and can be frozen, and so, for that matter are frozen bagels (although if you go the bagel route, you'll be finding crumbs all over your house for a month).

Pacifier Safety

Generally speaking, there's nothing wrong with giving your baby a pacifier. A lot of babies have a need to suck that can't be satisfied by breastfeeding or shoving their own (or even your) fingers into their mouths. And don't worry about damaging your baby's soon-to-be-dazzling smile; most dentists agree that sucking on a pacifier isn't a problem until about age four.

Thumbs, on the other hand, are a bit more problematic. First of all, because thumbs don't conform to the shape of your baby's mouth as well as pacifiers do, there's a greater chance that thumbsucking will damage your baby's teeth (although not until he's five or so). And if your baby is a constant thumbsucker, there's a chance it will have an impact on the way he speaks. Finally, most illness-causing germs get into our bodies from our hands. Need I say more?

There are, however, some potential dangers involved in using pacifiers. Here's what to do to avoid them:

- Nipples should be made of a single piece of nontoxic material.
- The shield (the part that stays on the outside of the baby's mouth) should be nondetachable and have several holes for saliva.
- Check the nipple for holes, tears, or other signs of wear. If you find any, replace the pacifier immediately—you don't want baby to chew off pieces and swallow them.
- Never, never, never tie the pacifier around your baby's neck or use string to attach the pacifier to your baby—it can pose a serious strangulation risk. But if you're tired of picking the pacifier up off the floor thirty-eight times a day, buy yourself a clip-on holder, one that detaches easily.

to set limits. Nothing rigid—just some basic guidelines to get your baby used to the idea.

The best way (in fact, it's really the only serious option at this age) to discipline and set limits for your baby is to distract him; take advantage of his short memory while you still can. So if he's gotten hold of that priceless Van Gogh you accidentally left on the floor, give him a teddy bear; and if he's making a break for the nearest busy street, pick him up and turn him around the other way. Chances are, he won't even notice. And even if he does, he'll be disappointed for only a few seconds.

Walkers

I had a walker when I was a baby and both my kids did too. But there's a lot of controversy about whether walkers are safe or not. Supposedly, 15,000 emergency room visits per year are attributed to them. This has less to do with the actual walker and more to do with falling down the stairs. So if you keep your stairs securely gated, walkers shouldn't be a problem.

Another common complaint about walkers is that babies can build up some real speed and fly around the house smacking into everything in sight—fun for them, not so fun for you. In addition, they can be a source of great frustration for the baby: he may have a hard time going over thresholds or making the transition from smooth floor to carpet; and because walkers are usually fairly wide, babies always seem to be getting stuck behind the furniture.

If you're worried, most of the potential problems can be resolved by buying a "jumper"—essentially a walker with a bouncy seat and no wheels.

Childproofing Your House

Once your baby realizes that he's able to move around by himself, his mission in life will be to locate—and make you race to—the most dangerous, life-threatening things in your home. So if you haven't already begun the never-ending process of childproofing your house, you'd better start now.

The first thing to do is get down on your hands and knees and check things out from your baby's perspective. Don't those lamp cords and speaker wires look like they'd be fun to yank on? And don't those outlets seem to be waiting for you to stick something in them?

Taking care of those enticing wires and covering up your outlets is only the beginning, so let's start with the basics.

ANYWHERE AND EVERYWHERE

- Move all your valuable items out of the baby's reach. It's not too early to try to teach him not to touch, but don't expect much compliance at so young an age.
- Bolt to the wall bookshelves and other freestanding cabinets (this is especially important if you live in earthquake country); pulling things down on top of themselves is a favorite baby suicide attempt.

- Don't hang heavy things on the stroller—it can tip over.
- Get special guards for your radiators and raise any space heaters and electric fans off the floor.
- Install a safety gate at the bottom and top of every flight of stairs. After a few months, you can move the bottom gate up a few steps to give the baby a low-risk way to practice climbing.
- Adjust your water heater temperature to 120 degrees. This will reduce the likelihood that your baby will scald himself.
- Get a fire extinguisher and put smoke alarms in every bedroom. If you want to be extra cautious, consider a carbon monoxide detector.
- If you have a two-story house (or higher), consider getting a rope escape ladder.
- Take first aid and CPR classes; they're usually offered by the local Red Cross, YMCA, or hospital.
- Put together a first aid kit (see page 140 for the ingredients).

ESPECIALLY IN THE KITCHEN

- Install safety locks on all but one of your low cabinets and drawers. Most of these locks allow the door to be opened slightly—just enough to accommodate a baby's fingers—so make sure the kind you get also keeps the door from *closing* completely as well.
- Stock the one unlocked cabinet with unbreakable pots and pans and encourage your baby to jump right in.
- Keep baby's high chair away from the walls. His strong little legs can push off the wall and knock the chair over.
- Watch out for irons and ironing boards. The cords are a hazard and the boards themselves are very easy to knock over.
- Get an oven lock and covers for your oven and stove knobs.
- Use the back burners on the stove whenever possible and keep pot handles turned toward the back of the stove.
- Try to keep the baby out of the kitchen when anyone is cooking. It's too easy to trip over him, drop or spill something on him, or accidentally smack him with something.
- Never hold your baby while you're cooking. Teaching him what steam is or how water boils may seem like a good idea, but bubbling spaghetti sauce or hot oil hurts when it splashes.
- Put mouse and insect traps in places where your baby can't get to them. Better yet, set them after he's asleep and take your kill to the taxidermist before he gets up.

What Every Good First Aid Kit Needs

- ace bandages
- acetaminophen (Tylenol) drops and tablets
- adhesive strips
- adhesive tape
- antibiotic ointment
- antiseptic ointment
- antibiotic wash
- butterfly bandages
- clean popsicle sticks (for splints)
- cleansing agent to clean wounds
- cotton balls (sterile if possible)
- cotton cloth for slings
- disposable instant ice packs
- disposable hand wipes (individual packets)
- emergency telephone numbers
- gauze rolls or pads (sterile if possible)
- mild soap
- syrup of ipecac (to induce vomiting, if necessary)
- tweezers (for splinters and the like)
- pair of clean (surgical) gloves
- scissors with rounded tip
- sterile 4 × 4-inch bandages

It's also a good idea to have an emergency treatment manual around the house. Here are a few good ones:

- *Emergency Treatment: Infants* (for kids birth–12 months), $7.95.
- *Emergency Treatment: Children* (for kids 1–9 years), $7.95.
- *Emergency Treatment: Infants, Children, and Adults* (for the whole family), $12.95. Available in English and Spanish from Mosby/EMT, 200 North La Salle Street, Chicago, IL 60601. (800) 767-5215.
- *The American Medical Association Handbook: First Aid/Emergency*, $10.00 plus $4.00 shipping and handling. Available from Random House Ordering Department, 400 Hahn Road, Westminster, MD 21157. (800) 733-3000.

- Use plastic dishes and serving bowls whenever you can—glass breaks, and, at least in my house, the shards seem to show up for weeks, no matter how well I sweep.
- Post the phone numbers of the nearest poison control agency and your pediatrician near your phone.

ESPECIALLY IN THE LIVING ROOM

- Put decals at baby height on all sliding glass doors.
- Get your plants off the floor: more than seven hundred species can cause

illness or death if eaten, including such common ones as lily of the valley, iris, and poinsettia.

- Pad the corners of low tables, chairs, and fireplace hearths.
- Make sure your fireplace screen and tools can't be pulled down or knocked over.
- Keep furniture away from windows. Babies will climb up whatever they can and may fall through the glass.

ESPECIALLY IN THE BEDROOM/NURSERY

- No homemade or antique cribs. They almost never conform to today's safety standards. Cribs with protruding corner posts are especially dangerous.
- Remove from the crib all mobiles and hanging toys. By five months, most kids can push themselves up on their hands and knees and can get tangled up in (and even choke on) strings.
- Keep the crib at least two feet away from blinds, drapes, hanging cords, or wall decorations with ribbons.
- Check toys for missing parts.
- Toy chest lids should stay up when opened (so they don't slam on tiny fingers).
- Don't leave dresser drawers open. From the baby's perspective, they look a lot like stairs.
- Keep crib items to a minimum: a sheet, a blanket, bumpers, and a few *soft* toys. Babies don't need pillows at this age and large toys or stuffed animals can be climbed on and used to escape from the crib.
- Don't leave your baby alone on the changing table even for a second.

ESPECIALLY IN THE BATHROOM

- If possible, use a gate to keep access restricted to the adults in the house.
- Install a toilet guard.
- Keep bath and shower doors closed.
- Never leave water standing in the bath, the sink, or even a bucket. Drowning is the third most common cause of accidental deaths among young children, and babies can drown in practically no water at all—even an inch or two.
- Keep medication and cosmetics high up.
- Make sure there's nothing your baby can climb up on to gain access to the medicine cabinet.
- Keep razors and hair dryers unplugged and out of reach.
- Never keep electrical appliances near the bathtub.
- Use a bath mat or stick-on safety strips to reduce the risk of slipping in the bathtub.

8 MONTHS

Perpetual Motion

What's Going On with the Baby

Physically

- At this stage, your baby is in motion just about every waking minute. She's an excellent crawler and will follow you around for hours.
- Having mastered crawling, she's now working on getting herself upright.
- She'll start by pulling herself up to a half-standing crouch and letting herself drop back down. Sometime in the next few weeks, though, she'll pull herself up to a complete standing position.
- If she's really adventurous, she'll let go with one hand or even lean against something and release both hands. Either way, she'll be shocked to discover that she can't get down.
- She now uses a "pincer grip" to pick things up and, because of her increased dexterity, becomes fascinated by tiny things.
- If she's holding a toy and sees something new, she'll drop what she's got and pick up the second. She may even retain the first toy and pick up the second with her other hand.
- Her finger-feeding and bottle- or cup-handling skills are improving fast.

Intellectually

- Your baby's increased mobility has opened a new range of possibilities for exploration and discovery. She now gets into drawers and cabinets and can empty them amazingly quickly.
- Her mobility also lets her get better acquainted with some of the objects

she's heretofore seen only from afar. Crawling around on the floor, for example, a baby will stop underneath a chair and examine it from every possible angle. Then, writes child psychologist Selma Fraiberg, "Upon leaving the underside of the chair, he pauses to wrestle with one of the legs, gets the feel of its roundness and its slipperiness and sinks his two front teeth into it in order to sample flavor and texture. In a number of circle tours around the chair at various times in the days and weeks to come, he discovers that the various profiles he has been meeting are the several faces of one object, the object we call a chair."

- Now able to pick up a different object in each hand, your baby will spend a lot of time comparing the capabilities of each side of her body.

Verbally

- She now babbles almost constantly, using your intonation as much as she can.
- She can also use sounds to express different emotions.
- She continues to concentrate on two-syllable "words"; *b*, *p*, and *m* are her favorite consonants.
- Her name is not the only sound she knows. She'll also turn her head in response to other familiar sounds, such as a car approaching, the phone ringing, the television "speaking," and the refrigerator opening.

Emotionally/Socially

- With so much to keep her busy during the day, your baby may feel she doesn't have time for naps anymore. The lack of sleep, together with the frustration at not being able to do everything she wants with her body, may make her cranky.
- When she's in a good mood, she really wants to be included in socializing; she may crawl into the middle of a conversation, sit up, and start chattering.
- She can anticipate events and will, for example, wriggle her entire body when she thinks you're getting ready to play with her.
- She may actually be frightened by the developing idea that she and you are separate, and may cling to you even more than before. At the same time, her fear of strangers is peaking.

What You're Going Through

Learning Flexibility and Patience

Before my older daughter was born, I was incredibly anal about time; I always

"Hey, would you kids mind holding down the quality-time racket?"

showed up wherever I was supposed to be exactly when I was supposed to, and I demanded the same from others. But as you now know, going on a simple trip to the store with baby in tow takes as much planning as an expedition to Mt. Everest. And getting anywhere on time is just about impossible.

It took a while, but eventually I learned that trying to be a father and Mr. Prompt at the same time just wasn't going to work. And somehow, simply accepting that fact made me a lot more forgiving of other people's lateness as well.

Interestingly, this new flexible attitude about time began to rub off on other areas of my life. Overall, since becoming a father I think I'm far more tolerant of individual differences and can more easily accept other people's limitations, as well as my own.

Whatever you're most rigid and impatient about, you can bet that your baby will figure it out and push all your buttons. That leisurely walk in the park you planned might have to be cut short when the baby panics and won't stop crying after a friendly dog licks her face. Or you might end up having to stay a few extra hours at a friend's house so as not to wake the baby if she's sleeping or, if she's awake, not to upset her nap schedule by having her fall asleep in the car on the way home.

"As soon as I get oriented to one of Dylan's patterns, he changes and a whole new pattern begins to evolve," writes David Steinberg about his son. "It's like standing up in a roller coaster. I'm finding that the more I accept this constant change, the more I can enjoy the dynamics of it, the constant growing. Dylan is deepening my sense of change as a way of life."

Not everyone, however, finds change as pleasant or as easy to accept as David Steinberg. For some, any sort of deviation from an orderly schedule, or any lack of continuity, can be very discombobulating. If you're in this category, you've got a rather Zen-like choice to make: you can bend or you can break. Babies are, almost by definition, irrational and not at all interested in your timetables. "I can't impose my rules on Dylan," writes Steinberg. "All the persuasive skills I use to get other people to do things my way are totally irrelevant to him. I am forced to accept the validity of his rules, and then to learn to integrate that with my real needs. The trick is to become less of a control freak without entirely sacrificing myself." True, true, true.

Thinking about How Involved You Are

Before I became a father, I don't think I had ever held an infant. I babysat two or three times when I was a teenager, but only when my young charges were fast asleep. And I certainly had never changed a diaper, filled a bottle, or pushed a stroller.

Whenever I imagined myself with a child of my own, she was always two or three years old and we were walking on the beach holding hands, wrestling, playing catch, telling stories. The thought that babies start off as tiny, helpless infants never really crossed my mind, and I wouldn't have been able to describe what I—or anyone else, for that matter—would do with a baby.

Most fathers-to-be know just about as much about babies as I did. But despite our ignorance, we spend a lot of time thinking about how we want to be involved with our kids. In his research, Bruce Drobeck found that although "being involved" means different things to different people, most men agreed that they:

- Don't want their partner to raise the kids alone.
- Don't want to be stuck in the role of the "wait-till-your-dad-comes-home" disciplinarian they may have grown up with.
- Want to be more open and communicative than their fathers were with them.
- Want to be involved with their children in a meaningful manner, from the earliest stages of development.

So how are you doing? Are you as involved with your baby as you want to be? As you planned to be? As we discussed earlier, new fathers generally do less child care than either they or their partners had predicted during pregnancy (to review the reasons why, see pages 105–6). Jay Belsky describes one study in which 74 percent of new fathers said that child care should be shared equally. But when asked whether or not they actually shared child care with their partners, only 13 percent said yes.

If you're in that 13 percent, you're probably feeling pretty proud of yourself, and you have every right to. But many new fathers—especially those who have to return to work sooner than they'd like, or have to work longer hours to bring in extra money—experience a profound sadness and longing for their families.

It's Hard to Make Up for Lost Time

There's nothing like a long day at the office to make you realize just how much you miss your baby. And when you get home, you might be tempted to try to make up for lost time by cramming as much active, physical father/baby contact as you can into the few hours before bedtime (yours or the baby's). That's a pretty tall order, and just about the only way you'll be able to fill it is to be "overly controlling, intrusive, and hyperstimulating," writes psychiatrist Stanley Greenspan. So before you start tickling and wrestling and playing with the baby, spend a few minutes reading or cuddling with her, quietly getting to know each other again—even at eight months, a day away from you is a looooong time for your baby. You'll both feel a lot better if you do.

Besides making you miss your baby, a long day at the office can also make you feel guilty about the amount of time you're away from her. Now a little guilt is probably a good thing, but far too many parents let their guilt get out of hand. And the results are not good at all. "In order to make the emotional burden easier," writes Greenspan, "they distance themselves from their children."

Although there's no practical way for you to make up for lost time, it's important that you find some middle ground between being overly controlling and distancing yourself from your baby. The best way to do that is to make sure that whenever you're with your child, you're there 100 percent. Forget the phone, forget the newspapers or the TV, forget washing the dishes, and forget eating if you can. You can do all those things after the baby goes to sleep.

He Says, She Says

Remember the story about the five blind men and the elephant? Each of them approaches an elephant and bumps into a different part—the leg, the tail, the ear, the trunk, the side—and then authoritatively describes to the others what he thinks an elephant *really* looks like. The moral of the story, of course, is that two (or more) people looking at exactly the same object or situation may see very different things.

The same moral applies when couples are asked to rate the husband's level of involvement in the home: men are more likely to be satisfied with their contribution and women are more likely to be disappointed. The problem here is not one of blindness, however. Instead, it's that men and women, according to Jay Belsky, are using different yardsticks to measure.

"A wife measures what a husband does against what she does. And because what a man does looks small . . . the woman often ends up . . . unhappy and disgruntled," writes Belsky. "The man, on the other hand, usually measures his contribution to chores against what his father did." And because he's sure to be doing more, he ends up feeling "good about himself and his contribution."

Another factor that Belsky feels contributes to a new father's tendency to overrate his participation is that ever since the baby was born, he has probably been the main, even the sole, breadwinner. And since he's been socialized to equate breadwinning with parenting, going to work "makes the 20 percent he does at home seem like 200 percent," says Belsky.

Circumstances may make it impossible for you to make any changes in the time you can spend with your family. But if you have any flexibility at all, take another look at the work/family options on pages 106–9. On his deathbed, no father ever wishes he'd spent more time at the office.

You and Your Baby

Reading

At eight to nine months of age, children who have been read to regularly can predict and anticipate actions in a familiar book and will mimic gestures and noises. So at this age it's a good idea to involve your baby more actively in the

"The weasel represents the forces of evil and the duck the forces of good, a surrogate for American air and naval superiority."

reading process. Talk about the things on the page that aren't described in the text and ask your baby a lot of identification questions. If you can, show your baby real-life examples of the objects pictured in her books.

At around ten months, your baby may be perfectly content to sit with a book and turn pages—probably two or three at a time. Don't worry if she seems not to be paying any attention to what she's "reading"; she's learning a lot about books' structure and feel. If you put a book upside down in front of your baby she'll turn it the right way. Singing, finger plays, and rhythmic bouncing while reciting nursery rhymes are still big hits.

At eleven months, your baby may be able to follow a character from page to page. This is also the age at which she may start demanding that you read specific stories or that you reread the one you just finished. Board books and sturdy flap books are great for this age.

By the time she's a year old, your baby may be able to turn the pages of her books one at a time. She will point to specific pictures you ask her to identify and may even make the correct animal sounds when you ask her, "What does a . . . say?" Be sure to respond positively every time your baby makes any attempt to speak—animal noises included.

As you've probably noticed already, reading provides you and your baby with a wonderful opportunity for close physical contact. The best position I've found (it's the one with maximum snuggle potential) is to put the baby on your lap and, with your arms around her, hold the book in front while you read over her shoulder.

When considering the next few months' reading, look for books with bright, big, well-defined illustrations, simple stories, and not too much text. Besides your baby's current favorites (which you should keep reading for as long as she's interested), you might want to check out a few of these books:

Baby Animals (and many others), Gyo Fujikawa
The Baby's Catalog, Janet Ahlberg, Allan Ahlberg
Baby's Bedtime Book, Kay Chorado
The Ball Bounced (and many others), Nancy Tafuri
Daddy, Play with Me (and many others), Shigeo Watanabe
Dressing (and many, many others), Helen Oxenbury
Goodnight Moon, Margaret Wise Brown
"More, More, More," Said the Baby: 3 Love Stories, Vera B. Williams
"Paddle," Said the Swan, Gloria Kamen
Sam's Bath (and other books in the Sam series), Barbro Lindgren
Sleepy Book, Charlotte Zolotow
Step by Step, Bruce McMillan
Spot Goes Splash (and many other Spot books), Eric Hill
Tickle; All Fall Down; Say Goodnight; Dad's Back (and many others), Jan Ormerod
What Sadie Sang; Sam Who Never Forgets (and others), Eve Rice
Wheels on the Bus, adapted by Paul O. Zelinsky
Who Said Meow? Maria Polushkin

CONCEPTS
The ABC Bunny, Wanda Gag
Clap Hands (and many others), Helen Oxenbury
First Words for Babies and Toddlers, Jane Salt
Ten, Nine, Eight, Molly Bang

Dealing with Stranger Anxiety

At about seven or eight months, you'll probably notice a marked change in your baby's behavior around strangers. Only a few weeks ago, you could have handed him to just about anyone and he would have greeted the new person with a huge smile. But now, if a stranger—or even someone the baby has seen before—comes anywhere near him, he'll cling tightly to you and cry. Welcome to *stranger anxiety,* your baby's first fear.

What's happening is that your baby is just beginning to figure out that he and you (and his other primary caretakers) are separate human beings. It's a scary idea, and he's simply afraid that some person he doesn't like very much might take you—and all the services you provide—away.

Stranger anxiety affects 50–80 percent of babies. It usually kicks in at around seven or eight months, but sometimes not until a year. It can last anywhere from a few weeks to six months.

Your baby is more likely to experience stranger anxiety if he's withdrawing, slow-adapting, or has low sensory threshold (see the "Temperament" section on pages 89–96). He'll be less likely to be affected if he's approaching or fast-adapting or if he's been exposed to a steady flow of new people since early infancy.

Here are a few things you can do to help your baby (and yourself) cope with stranger anxiety:

- If you're getting together with friends, try to do it at your own house instead of someplace else. The baby's reaction will be less dramatic in a familiar place.
- Hold your baby closely whenever you enter a new environment or anyplace where there are likely to be other people.
- When you enter a new place, don't just hand the baby off to someone he doesn't know. Let him cling to you for a while and use you as a safe haven.
- Warn friends, relatives, and strangers not to be offended by the baby's shyness, crying, screaming, or overall reluctance to have anything to do with them. Tell them to approach the baby as they might any other wild animal: slowly, cautiously, with a big smile, talking quietly, and perhaps even offering a toy.
- Be patient with your baby. Don't pressure him to go to strangers or even to be nice to them. And don't criticize him if he cries or clings to you.
- If you're leaving the baby with a new sitter, have her or him get to your house at least twenty minutes before you have to leave. This will (hopefully) give baby and sitter a few minutes—with you nearby—to get to know each other.
- If your partner stays at home with the baby while you're at work, you need to understand that your baby might lump you in with the people she considers strangers. Don't take it personally. Just follow the steps above on how strangers should approach the baby, and be patient.

Family Matters

Money

Without a doubt, money is the number one issue couples fight about. And financial squabbles are especially common during the early parenthood years, while both parents are getting settled.

Many factors contribute to quarrels over money. Here are some of the most common:

- **Frustration.** Women who have put their careers on hold to take a more active role at home may resent having their income (and the associated power) reduced. This goes double for men because of the still-lingering "good provider" pressures.
- **Your childhood.** The way you were raised can have a big impact—positive or negative—on the way you raise your own kids. If you grew up in a poor family, you may feel weird spending money on anything more than the bare necessities. Or you may feel obligated to give your child all the things you never got—at least the ones that money can buy. And if your parents were big spenders, you may be inclined to bury your baby in gifts, or you may be afraid of spoiling your child and cut way back. Whatever your overall attitude toward money, if your partner's differs considerably from yours, look out.
- **Differences in spending habits.** You like Cheerios and eating lunch out; your partner wants you to buy the generic brand and bring lunch from home. She makes long-distance calls in the middle of the day; you want her to wait until the rates go down.
- **Differences in definitions.** My wife loves to get things "half off"; the way I figure it, half off of something that costs three times more than it should is still no deal.
- **Gender differences.** Generally speaking, fathers and mothers have different ideas about money and what should be done with it. Fathers tend to worry about enhancing the family's long-range financial outlook and to be more concerned than mothers about savings. "Often for women new baby clothes represent a sensible economic choice because they advance another of the new mother's priorities: social presentation," says Jay Belsky. "This is the name given to her desire to present her baby—her creation—to the larger world of family and friends for admiration and praise." The big problem here is that your partner may interpret your not wanting to spend money on clothes as a sign that you don't love your baby (and, by extension, that you don't love her either).

Avoiding Money Problems, or at Least Learning to Live with Them

- Be realistic. Having a baby can have a major impact on your financial life. Food, clothing, medical expenses, and day-care or preschool tuition all add up pretty quickly.
- Make a budget (there are plenty of good budgeting software packages, Quicken being among the best). Keep track of everything coming in and going out—even your cash expenditures.
- Hold regular monthly meetings to discuss your financial situation. Listen to each other's concerns and remember that whatever your differences, you both have the best interests of your family at heart. No blaming or yelling, and stay away from discussion-killing phrases like "You always" and "You never."
- Rearrange your priorities. Take care of the absolute necessities—food, clothing, shelter—first. If there's anything left over, start saving it for ice cream cones, vacations, private school education.
- Negotiate and compromise. You give up Cheerios and take a brown bag to lunch; she makes her long-distance calls after 11 P.M. or before 8 A.M. And remember, there are plenty of ways to cut back without having to skimp. Why pay full price for a pair of pants your child is going to outgrow in a few months when you can get a perfectly good used pair for less than three bucks?
- Make a plan. Set realistic and achievable savings goals, and make sure you're adequately insured.

Notes:

9 MONTHS

The Building Blocks of Development

What's Going On with the Baby

Physically

- As if recovering from the frantic developmental pace of the past two months, your baby will probably not add many new skills this month. Instead, he'll spend his time perfecting the old ones.
- By the end of this month he'll be such a confident crawler that he'll be able to buzz around the house grasping a block or other toy in one hand. He'll be able to crawl backward and may even make it up a flight of stairs.
- He easily pulls himself to an upright position and can stand (briefly) while holding your hand. He can cruise (sidestep) along furniture and walls, and when he's done, he no longer has any trouble unlocking his knees and sitting down.
- Now able to move his fingers separately, he has discovered that the house is filled with holes and cracks that are just big enough to accommodate his index finger.
- The biggest development this month (and this is pretty important) is that your baby is now coordinated enough to build a "tower" of two or three blocks (which he'll knock down immediately).

Intellectually

- In previous months your baby would learn a new skill and then repeat it endlessly. At this point, though, he'll begin to experiment with new ways of doing things. For example, instead of repeatedly dropping his spoon off his high-chair tray, he may start with the spoon, then drop his bowl off the other side, and finish up by tossing his cup over his shoulder.

- He's just beginning to come to terms with the idea that he is not the power behind everything that happens. He may, for example, bring you a wind-up toy to wind up.
- He's also beginning to shake his if-I-can't-see-it-it-doesn't-exist attitude, but just barely. Now if he watches you hide a toy, he will look for it. But if you hide the same toy in a second hiding place, he will continue looking in the first hiding place. In his mind, something out of his sight can exist, but only in one specific place.
- He's also learning about actions and their consequences. If he sees you putting on a coat, he'll know you're going outside and he may cry.
- As his memory gets better, you'll be able to interrupt him in the middle of an activity and he'll go back to it a few minutes later.

Verbally

- He's developing a distinctive "voice" in his babbling and may identify certain objects by the sound they make (*choo-choo* for train, *moo* for cow).
- Besides recognizing his name, your baby now understands and responds to other words and phrases, such as "No" and "Where's the baby?" He also understands and might even obey simple commands such as "Bring me my pipe."
- Although he's several months away from saying anything truly understandable, your baby already has a good grasp of the rhythm and sound of his native language. German researcher Angela Friederici found that even at this young age, babies are sensitive to the structure of words in their own language and can listen to a string of speech and break it down into wordlike units.

Emotionally/Socially

- This baby loves to play. He'll shout if he thinks you should be paying more attention to him and imitates such acts as blowing out candles, coughing, and sneezing.
- He may be able to get you to understand—by pointing, grunting, squealing, or bouncing up and down—that he needs something specific.
- Preferences are becoming more distinct, and he'll push away things (and people) he doesn't want.
- Perhaps a little scared of the new world he's discovering, he clings to

you more than ever and cries if you leave him alone; it's the beginning of *separation anxiety* (different from the stranger anxiety of the past few months).

What You're Going Through

Feeling More Attached to Your Baby

As your baby gets older and becomes more and more responsive and interactive, your attachment to her will deepen. As we discussed earlier, however, parent-child attachments are a little bit lopsided: "It is fairly obvious," write psychologists Barbara and Philip Newman, "that soon after a child's birth the parent's attachment to the child becomes quite specific, that is, the parent would not be willing to replace his or her child with any other child of similar age."

But what the Newmans and I—and you, too—really want to know is, "At what point does the child make this kind of commitment to the *parent*?" The answer is somewhere between six and nine months. By that time, the baby has developed the mental capacity to associate you with having his needs and wants satisfied and can summon up a mental image of you to keep him company when you're not there.

But don't think that this means you needn't bother trying to establish an attachment to your baby right away. On the contrary. Attachment doesn't just happen overnight; it's a gradual process that takes months to develop, and the sooner you get started, the better. "A healthy attachment in infancy is likely to turn out a healthier adult," write the husband-wife/pediatrician-nurse team of William and Martha Sears. And the way you react and respond to your baby will have a great influence on the kind of attachment you and she eventually establish.

As you might imagine, the single most successful strategy for forming lasting, secure attachments with your children is to spend time with them one-on-one, doing everything you possibly can together, from the mundane to the exciting. "The earlier the father can feel involved with the infant," says Henry Biller, "the more likely will a strong father-child attachment develop."

Attachment theories were first developed in the 1950s by researchers John Bowlby and Mary Ainsworth, who conducted detailed studies of the interactions between several hundred parents and their children. Bowlby and Ainsworth concluded that there are two basic types of attachment: *secure,* meaning that

Attachment Basics

ATTACHMENT	TWELVE-MONTH-OLDS
Secure (about ⅔ are securely attached, but that doesn't mean they won't have any problems when they grow up)	♦ Are confident that their parents will be there when needed. ♦ Know they can depend on their parents to respond to their pain, hunger, and attempts at interaction. ♦ Readily explore their environment using parents as bases. ♦ Don't cry much and are easy to put down after being held.
Avoidant (⅙)	♦ May avoid physical contact with parents. ♦ Don't depend on parents to be secure base. ♦ Don't expect to be responded to caringly. ♦ Learn not to act needy no matter how much they may want to be held or loved.
Ambivalent (⅙)	♦ Cry a lot but don't know whether their cries will get a response. ♦ Are afraid of being abandoned physically or emotionally. ♦ Are worried and anxious, easily upset. ♦ Cling to parents, teachers, other adults. ♦ Tend to be immature and mentally scattered.

the child feels confident that the parent will respond appropriately to her needs; and *insecure,* meaning that the child is constantly afraid her needs *won't* be met by the parent. They further divided the insecure category into two subcategories: *avoidant* and *ambivalent.* (See the chart above for a more detailed explanation.)

TODDLERS	PARENTS
♦ Are independent and trusting. ♦ Learn early how people treat other people. ♦ Are open to having their behavior redirected. ♦ Mix well with all age groups. ♦ Become social leaders. ♦ Are curious and eager to learn.	♦ Respond to children sensitively and consistently. ♦ Pick up the baby when he cries, feed him when he's hungry, hold him when he wants to be held.
♦ Are less curious. ♦ Are frequently distrusting. ♦ Can be selfish, aggressive, manipulative. ♦ May have few friends.	♦ Deny their (and others') feelings and needs. ♦ Believe children should be independent early. ♦ Don't like to cuddle with the baby or pick him up when he cries. ♦ Can be emotionally cold.
♦ Lack self-confidence. ♦ May experience uncontrolled anger. ♦ May either overreact emotionally or repress feelings. ♦ Are frequently less adaptable.	♦ Are wildly inconsistent and unpredictable in their parenting. ♦ Are frequently self-involved. ♦ Hope to get from the baby the love that they never had from their own parents and that they may not be able to get from each other.

Based on the information they gathered by observing babies in their first months of life, Bowlby and Ainsworth were able to predict accurately the specific behavior patterns those same babies would exhibit as they grew. Bowlby's and Aisworth's theories are just as applicable today as they were when articulated nearly fifty years ago.

In Case You Thought You Were Alone . . .

There isn't a single animal species in which the female doesn't produce the eggs. But eggs aren't worth much without the male's sperm to fertilize them. In most cases, once the eggs are laid, neither parent sticks around to watch it hatch or to meet their babies. Sometimes, though, eggs need more specialized care or they'll all perish. In these cases, one or both parents are required to pitch in. Here are just a few examples of some of the dozens of species of animals in which the father plays an important role in carrying, raising, protecting, and educating his young.

Long before the male three-spined stickleback has even met his mate, he sets to work building an attractive little house out of algae. When he's finished, he hangs out in front and makes a pass at the first female who happens by. If she's interested, the male invites her in, but, not being much of a romantic, he asks her to leave after she's laid her eggs, which he quickly fertilizes as soon as she's gone. For the next few weeks, the father guards his nest, keeping it well ventilated and repairing any damage. Until his babies hatch, the father never leaves the nest, even to eat.

Like the stickleback, the male giant water bug does everything he possibly can to attract females. If one shows any interest, he fertilizes her eggs. The female then climbs onto her lover's back and lays nearly a hundred eggs, securing each to his back with a special glue. For the next two weeks the father is completely responsible for the eggs' safety and well-being. When they finally hatch, the babies stick close to dad until they feel confident enough to swim away.

Unlike the stickleback, a cichlid (pronounced SIK-lid) doesn't need a nest. As soon as the female lays the eggs, the male scoops them up into his mouth. Because his mouth is so full, the father can't eat until the babies hatch—sometimes up to two weeks. And after they're born and can swim by themselves, dad still protects his children by carrying them in his mouth. He spits them out when it's time to eat, get some air, or just have a little fun. And when play time is over (or if danger is lurking), he sucks them back in again.

Frogs are famous for having involved fathers. After the eggs of the two-toned poison-arrow frog hatch, the tadpoles crawl onto their father's back, where they hang on with their suckerlike mouths as dad carries them through the jungle. Darwin's frogs take things one step further. Just as his tiny, jelly-covered eggs are about to hatch, the future father snaps them up with his tongue and slides them into a special pouch inside his body. The eggs hatch and the tiny tadpoles stay inside the pouch until they lose their tails and jump out of their father's mouth.

Among birds and mammals, there is a high rate of co-parenting. For example, male and female geese, gulls, pigeons, woodpeckers, and many other birds work as a team to build their homes, brood (sit on the eggs to keep them warm), and feed and protect the young after they're born. In a similar fashion, the male California mouse is responsible for bringing food into the nest and for huddling with the young to keep them warm (the babies aren't born with the ability to regulate their own body temperatures). These mice have at least two things in common with human parents. First, they are both generally monogamous. Second, the presence of an involved father has a major impact on the babies: pups weigh more, their ears and eyes open earlier, and they have a greater survival rate than pups who are separated from their fathers.

"They're hatching! Quick, Albert, get the camcorder!"

The Generational View

Like it or not, the type of attachment you establish with your baby will be influenced (not set in stone, just *influenced*) by your own attachment experience with your parents. So as you read this section, spend some time thinking about *your* childhood. Doing so may help you understand a few things about yourself and your parents. More important, it may help you avoid making some of the same mistakes with your own children that your parents made with you.

Your attachment with your child may also be influenced by your relationship with your partner. Dozens of studies confirm that the better the couple relationship, the more secure the parent-child relationship (see pages 210–12 for more on couple relationships).

The Father-Child Connection

Although the vast majority of research on attachment has focused on mothers and children, some researchers are now beginning to study father-child attachment. Their findings confirm what active, involved fathers have known in their hearts for years—that the father-child bond is no less important than the mother-child bond. Here's what the experts have to say:

- Researcher Frank Pedersen and his colleagues found that the more actively involved a six-month-old baby has been with his father, the higher the baby's scores on mental and motor development tests.
- Fatherhood pioneer Ross Parke found that "the more fathers were involved in the everyday repetitive aspects of caring for infants (bathing, feeding, dressing, and diapering), the more socially responsible the babies were and the better able they were in handling stressful situations."
- Researcher Norma Radin found that greater father involvement leads to increased performance in math. She also found that active fathering contributed to better social adjustment and competence, to children's perception that they were masters of their own fates, and to a higher mental age on verbal intelligence tests.

There are also factors that may interfere with father-child attachments, and researcher Glen Palm has identified several of them:

- Many fathers experience some tension in their relationships with their children because they feel excluded by the mother-infant bond, or because they feel that they have to compete with their partners to form a relationship with the child. Others say it's hard to form a close relationship because they feel they are unable to comfort their children adequately.

"Really, Howard! You're just like your father."

A lot of these fathers were able to form close attachments only after their children were weaned.

- Fathers who have to be away from home a lot during the week find that "re-attaching" with the kids on the weekends takes a lot of time and energy.
- Temperament. No matter how much you love your child, you'll find it easier to attach to an "easy" child than to a "difficult" one. (See pages 89–96 for more on temperament.)
- A small but significant percentage of fathers feel that their in-laws are overprotective of their adult daughters and get in the way too much.
- There is a glaring lack of information and support for new fathers.

You and Your Baby

Playing Around . . . Again

For the first seven or eight months of your baby's life, he had to be content with staring at things from across the room and waiting for you to bring them to him. But now that he's mobile, he's going to try to make up for lost time. He's incredibly curious about his world, and no obstacle can stand between him and something to touch, squeeze, gum, or grab. (If your baby *isn't* very curious, however, let your pediatrician know. But don't be alarmed if you catch the baby staring off into space once in a while. According to Burton White, babies this age spend about 20 percent of their waking time soaking up information visually.)

Although our society doesn't value play nearly as highly as some other parent-child pastimes such as feeding and diaper changing, it is, nevertheless, critical to your baby's development. "Many children who do not have much chance to play and who are only infrequently played with suffer severe intellectual arrest or setbacks," writes developmental psychologist Bruno Bettelheim.

One of your major goals should be to expose your baby to the most varied, enriching play environment possible. But perhaps even more important is your basic philosophy about play. "Parents' inner attitudes always have a strong impact on their children," says Bettelheim. "So the way parents feel about play, the importance they give it or their lack of interest in it, is never lost on their child. Only when parents give play not just respect and tolerance but also their personal interest, will the child's play experience provide a solid basis upon which he can develop his relation to them and further to the world."

Brain Builders

These games and exercises can stimulate your baby's capacity to use different skills at the same time (seeing, hearing, thinking, and remembering, for example):

- Get two toys that are nearly identical except that they react in different ways (one might need to be squeezed to make noise, the other shaken). Let the baby play with one of them for a few minutes, then switch. Did he get confused?
- Ring a bell, squeeze a toy, or shake a rattle. When the baby looks to see what made the sound, put the toy into a group of things he's familiar with. Will he go for the one that made the noise or will he get sidetracked by the other toys?
- More hiding games. A few months ago you discovered that if you hid a toy under a pillow or towel, your baby would push the obstacle out of the way

Vive la Différence!

As we've discussed earlier, fathers and mothers generally have distinctive but complementary styles of playing with their children: fathers tend to be more physical; mothers, less. But besides the physical nature of play, there are some other male-female differences you should be able to see now.

Fathers tend to encourage their children to do things for themselves, take more risks, and experience the consequences of their actions. Mothers, in contrast, tend to want to spare their children disappointment, be more protective of them, and steer clear of encouraging risk-taking.

To see how these differences might play out, imagine that your baby is building a tower that is just about to collapse. You'll probably let the tower fall, hoping your baby will learn from his mistakes. Your partner, though, will probably steady the tower as it teeters.

Many researchers have found that the differences in father-child and mother-child play styles can have a significant impact on the child. "There were indications that children's intellectual functioning was stimulated more in families with high father involvement," writes researcher Norma Radin. "We attribute this effect to the fact that fathers appear to have a different way of interacting with children; they tend to be more physical, more provocative, and less stereotyped in their play behavior than mothers."

to "find" the toy (see page 121). Now that he's a little older and more sophisticated, you can up the ante a little by hiding an interesting toy under three or four towels. The look on his face when he pulls the first towel off and doesn't see what he was expecting will be priceless. Until he's about a year old, he'll probably get confused by the extra obstacles and forget what he was looking for in the first place.

- Imitating and pretend games. According to Bettelheim, engaging in this type of activity is an important developmental milestone. When our children imitate us, they're trying to figure out who we are and what we're doing. "When they imitate an older sibling or friend, they're not only trying to understand them, but they're figuring out what it's like to be older," he writes. When playing with blocks, for example, be sure to include some nonblock things such as people, cars, trucks, animals.
- Show him that objects can have more than one function. Envelopes, for example, can be shredded or used to contain other things.
- Encourage him to use tools. For example, tie a string around a toy that is well out of reach. Will he crawl to get the toy or will he pull the string to bring it closer? What happens if you demonstrate what to do? A word of caution: once your baby has mastered the idea that there are new and exciting ways to get hold of things, watch out for low-hanging tablecloths and other dangling stuff.

Exercises for the Major Muscle Groups

It's taken a while, but your baby is finally getting around to discovering that he has control over his feet. And over the next few months, he'll be making more and more use of his feet by learning to walk. He'll do this all by himself, of course, but helping him build up his muscles and coordination can be great fun for both of you:

- Put some toys near his feet and see if he'll kick them.
- Roll a ball far enough out of your baby's reach so he has to crawl to get it.
- Supervised stair climbing is great. But stay nearby and be extremely careful. This is a good time to start teaching your baby to come down stairs backward. But be prepared to demonstrate yourself and to physically turn your baby around a few dozen times a day.
- Play alternating chasing games: you chase him; he chases you. At the end, "reward" him with a big hug and—if he doesn't protest—a little wrestling. Besides being fun, these kinds of games teach your baby a valuable lesson: when you go away, you always come back. The more that idea is reinforced, the less he'll be impacted by separation anxiety (see pages 154–55).

Crawling
Although you may be in a hurry to see your baby walk, be patient. Crawling (which includes just about any type of forward movement, such as slithering, "hopping" along on the butt, or "rowing" forward with one leg) is a major developmental stage, and you should encourage your baby to do it as much as possible. There's also some evidence that makes a connection between crawling and later proficiency in math and sciences. Kids who don't crawl apparently don't do as well in those fields.

Getting Those Little Hands and Eyes to Work Together

There are plenty of activities you and your baby can do that stimulate hand-eye coordination:

- Puzzles. The best ones for this age are made of wood, have a separate hole for each piece, and a peg for easy lifting.
- Nesting and stacking toys. These help improve gentle placement skills.
- Things to crush, tear, or crinkle—the noisier the better.
- Weave some string between baby's fingers or tape two of his fingers together. Can he "free" himself?
- Stock your bathtub with toys that squirt or spin.
- Get toys that can be used in the bathtub or a sandbox to pour stuff back and forth. Measuring cups and spoons are also good.
- When you're shopping, have the baby help you put things in the grocery cart.
- If you're brave, let the baby change channels on your stereo or TV (supervised, of course).
- Play hand-clapping games.

More Experiments from the Land of Consequences

The idea that different actions produce different effects is one that can't be reinforced often enough. Here are a few ways that are especially appropriate for your nine-to-twelve-month-old.

- Jack-in-the-boxes—especially the kind with four or five doors, each opened by a push, twist, poke, or some other action. These are also good for hand-eye coordination. Be cautious the first few times, though; some babies may be frightened.
- Balls are a big hit. They roll, they bounce off things, they can knock over other things. For your baby's protection (and to reduce the chance of breaking your good dishes) make sure the balls you use are soft.

The Building Blocks of Development

There are literally dozens of cutting-edge, high-tech (and expensive) toys and games that claim to be essential to your baby's physical and mental development. Some are worthwhile, others aren't. But there's one toy—just about the least cutting-edge, lowest-tech, cheapest thing going—that truly is an essential part of every nursery: blocks. Here's why:

- They help your baby develop hand-eye coordination as well as grasping and releasing skills.
- They teach your baby all about patterns, sizes, categories (big ones with the big ones, little ones with the little ones); gravity, balance, and structure. These brief lessons in math and physics lay the foundation for your baby's later understanding of how the world works.
- They teach good thinking skills. "Taken from a psychological viewpoint," wrote Albert Einstein, "this combinatory play [erector sets, blocks, puzzles] seems to be the essential feature in productive thought—before there is any connection with logical construction in words or other kinds of signs which can be communicated to others."
- They can help babies grasp the difference between things they have control over and things they don't. "In building a tower, a child has had to deal with the laws of gravity, size, balance, etc.—laws he cannot control," says Bruno Bettelheim. "And when he knocks the tower down, he is trying to regain control over the situation."
- They teach perseverance. Building a tower—or anything else—out of blocks can be an excruciatingly frustrating experience for a baby. But along the way, he'll learn that if he keeps working on something long enough, he'll eventually succeed.

- Pots, pans, xylophones, or anything else the baby can bang on. He'll learn that different things make different noises when smacked and that hitting something hard sounds different from hitting something soft.
- Doors (and anything else with a hinge)—provided you're there to make sure no one gets pinched. Books operate on the same basic principle. (If you've been reading to your baby lately, you've probably noticed that he's more interested in turning the pages than in looking at what's on them.)

The bigger your baby's world gets, the more interested he'll become in objects and the less interested in you. And why not? After all, you always

Success and Failure
Whatever your baby is doing, be sure to praise his *efforts* as well as his *accomplishment.* Kids need to learn that trying to do something can often be just as important as actually doing it. Confining your praise and happiness only to successful completion of a project can make your baby less likely to take risks or try new things for fear of failing.

seem to be around, but one of those exciting new toys might disappear before he gets a chance to grab it.

Giving up the number one position in your baby's heart and mind can be tough on the ego, especially if you're being replaced by a stuffed animal or a toy car. But instead of pouting, take a more aggressive, if-you-can't-beat-'em-join-'em attitude: if you're having trouble keeping your baby interested in playing with you, use a toy to get his attention. But don't be in a hurry; wait until the baby has begun to lose interest in whatever (or whomever) he's playing with before replacing it with something new.

Family Matters

The Division of Labor

About 90 percent of new parents experience an increase in stress after their babies are born. And the number one stressor—by a huge margin—is the division of labor in the home.

Oh, How Much Work Could a Baby Really Be?

Before your baby was born, you and your partner probably anticipated that having a baby would increase the amount of household work you'd both have to do. But I'll bet you were *way* off on your estimates.

Psychologist Jay Belsky found that for most new parents, dishwashing increased from once or twice a day to four times, laundry from one load a week to four or five, shopping from one trip per week to three, meal preparation from two times a day to four, and household cleaning from once a week to once a day.

And that's just the nonbaby areas of your life. When you factor in all the baby-related stuff, things really start to get out of control. "On average, a baby needs to be diapered six or seven times and bathed two or three times per day, soothed two or three times per night and often as many as five times per day,"

writes Belsky. In addition, the baby's helplessness makes just about every task, from going to the bank to getting dressed in the morning, take five times longer than it used to.

One woman in Belsky's studies summed up the discrepancy between her prebirth workload estimate and the postbirth reality as essentially the difference between "watching a tornado on TV and having one actually blow the roof off your house."

And Who's Going to Do It?

Another thing you and your partner may have agreed upon before your baby was born was that you'd both be sharing responsibility for all the extra work the baby would require. That was a good thing: the more equitably domestic tasks are divided up, the happier couples are with their marriages. Unfortunately, though, you were most likely wrong about this one too.

"Women ended up doing more of the housework than before they were mothers," write Phil and Carolyn Cowan. "And men did less of the baby care than they or their wives predicted." Researcher Ross Parke confirmed these findings: "The birth of a baby seems to bring even egalitarian parents back to traditional roles," he writes. "There was a marked return to the customary division of labor for a variety of functions."

Everyone Knows that Women Do More Around the House, Right?

It seems that every few months or so there's a new study telling us that although women have dramatically increased the hours they work outside the home, men have barely changed the number of hours they spend working *inside.* The most widely quoted figure for men's contribution to child care, for example, is twelve minutes a day.

Pretty incriminating, eh? Well, it's not nearly as bad as it sounds. The twelve-minutes-a-day figure comes from data analyzed by Arlie Hochschild in her book *The Second Shift: Working Parents and the Revolution at Home.* And to call Hochschild's conclusions "flawed" would be charitable. Here's why:

- Hochschild based her findings on data gathered in 1965, although there was much more recent, and accurate, data available.
- When tallying *men's* hours, Hochschild "neglected" to include weekends, times when men are more likely to be actively involved with their kids.
- She also didn't include the hours men spend playing with their kids as child care. So if your partner is cooking dinner and you're playing with the baby, her hours are counted as household work, yours aren't. Doesn't seem very fair, does it?
- Even if she had counted weekends and playtime, Hochschild failed to make a distinction between *accessibility* (being on duty and available) and *engagement* (active involvement with a child). Most kids don't need or want to be entertained every second of the day, but an adult still needs to be around.

Here's what happens to Hochschild's twelve minutes a day when her errors of omission are corrected:

- Researchers McBride and Mills found that fathers were *accessible* an average of 4.9 hours per day on weekdays and 9.8 hours per day on Saturday and Sunday.
- McBride and Mills found that fathers were *engaged* with their children

an average of 1.9 hours on weekdays and 6.5 hours per day on Saturday and Sunday.
- In the 1960s and 1970s fathers spent one-third as much time engaged with and half as much time accessible to their children as their partners. These numbers went way up in the 1980s and 1990s, to 40 percent as much time engaged and two-thirds as much time accessible. One study found that fathers were engaged 83 percent as much as mothers and accessible 82 percent as much as mothers.

That's a very different story. Of course, researchers can come up with statistics to back up just about any claim. Still, no matter how you crunch the division-of-labor numbers, the bottom line is that women do a greater share of the household and child-related work.

What's important to remember, though, is that in most cases this inequity is *not* a function of men's lack of interest in their families. Phil and Carolyn Cowan have identified five significant barriers that prevent men from taking on a completely equal role in the home:
- Both men and women can't seem to shake the age-old idea that child-rearing is women's work and that breadwinning is men's work. Many men, therefore, are afraid of committing career suicide by openly expressing a desire to spend more time with the family and less at work.
- Mothers step in quickly to take over when either the father or the baby looks a little uneasy. At the same time, men—who hate feeling incompetent and who expect their wives to be competent with babies right from the start—are all too glad to hand over the baby to the "expert." Jay Belsky adds that "a woman's significant biological investment in the child can make her so critical of her husband's parenting that, without intending to, she drives him away." As a result, says Belsky, "men who find themselves continually criticized for their inadequate diapering, bathing, and dressing skills . . . feel humiliated and often conclude that the best (and safest) policy to adopt vis-à-vis child-care chores is a hands-off policy."
- The roles available to men are considered second-rate and discourage male involvement. As discussed on pages 86–88, feeding the baby—something women generally have a lock on—is considered the most important task, whereas soothing the baby and changing her diapers—tasks available to men—don't seem nearly as important.
- The more men attempt to take an active role in the care of their children, the more mixed or negative feedback they receive from their own parents. During my first few years as a father, my own parents, for example, would

wonder—just loud enough for me to hear—when I'd be going back to work, or whether taking so much time off would have a negative effect on my career.

- The economics of the workplace and the lack of quality child care encourage fathers to work and mothers to stay home while the children are young.

The Cowans recognize that some men are willing to buck the traditional roles and do whatever it takes to get more involved. "Unfortunately, they are swimming upstream," write the Cowans, "fighting off a formidable array of forces as they try to make their way forward."

As a result, far too often *both* parents give up and adopt a more traditional division of labor. That, in turn, can lead to a decline in marital satisfaction.

Notes:

10 MONTHS

Forming an Identity

What's Going On with the Baby

Physically

- Unless you have a very active baby, the slowdown in motor learning that began last month will continue this month, says Frank Caplan. But don't be deceived: she's "really gathering strength to carry herself through that big step of walking."
- She may be able to get herself to a standing position from a crawl and, once upright, can stand with little support.
- She can "cruise" (sidestep while holding on to something) just about everywhere, and if you hold both her hands, she'll walk and walk and walk.
- She's getting to be a fairly confident climber as well, getting up and down from couches and chairs almost without fear.
- She's also getting much better at manipulating her hands now, and can grasp two objects in one hand.
- She is beginning to discover that each side of her body can be used differently. And she may even be exhibiting an early "handedness" preference. She can, for example, use one hand for picking up and manipulating toys, the other for holding.
- If both hands are full, she may put down one object in order to pick up a third.
- Although she's quite graceful in her grasping, her releasing is still fairly clumsy.

Intellectually

- Although she still isn't completely convinced that things she can't see do exist, she's starting to suspect as much. This month, she'll look for a toy she sees you hide. If she's seen you move the toy to a second hiding place, she'll look for it there as well.
- She now understands that objects of different sizes need to be treated differently. She'll approach small objects with her fingers, but large ones with both hands.
- She's also intrigued by the idea that objects can exist for several reasons at the same time (they have properties as well as functions). Paper, for example, can be chewed, crumpled, and torn. And crayons can be held, eaten, and, best of all, used to scribble on things. This ability enables the baby to organize things into two categories ("things I can chew on" and "things that are too big to get into my mouth")—a realization that gives her a bit of control and predictability in her life.
- As her memory improves, she's getting more persistent. It's harder to distract her from whatever she's doing, and, if you manage to turn her attention to something else, she'll go right back to her original activity as soon as you quit bugging her.
- She's now capable of *symbolic thinking* (associating something you can see with something you can't). For example, a few months ago, your baby would probably cry when seeing the nurses at her pediatrician's office. She associated nurses with shots. But now she may recognize the doctor's office from the street and will start crying as soon as you pull into the parking lot.

Verbally

- Although she's been saying "dada" and "mama" for a while, she really didn't know what those words meant. But now "dada," "mama," "bye-bye," "no," and possibly a few others have a definite meaning that she uses deliberately.
- She now understands what she hears and may actually cooperate (but probably not in front of friends you're trying to impress) in a game of Identify the Baby's Body Part ("Where's your belly button?").
- She's also able to combine words and gestures: a head shake with "no," a hand wave with "bye-bye."
- She listens actively to adult conversation and will frequently butt in with a few "words" of her own.

Emotionally/Socially

- With physical development on hold for this month, says Frank Caplan, your baby is spending most of her energy on social and personal growth.
- Her mimicking skills are growing by leaps and bounds, and she'll now try to imitate just about everything you do: rubbing her hands together under running water, saying "brr" and shivering after getting out of the bath, and talking on the phone.
- When she cries (which she does much less frequently than a few months ago), it's less to get you to come running and more out of fear—of unfamiliar places or things, or of separation from you.
- She's becoming more sensitive to your emotions and is better able to express her own. If you're happy, she will be too. But if you scold her, she'll pout; if you do something she doesn't like, she's capable of genuine anger; and if you leave her alone for too long (only she knows how long that is), she may "punish" you by clinging and crying at the same time.

What You're Going Through

Feeling Irreplaceable

You've been a father for most of a year now, and, as we briefly discussed a few months ago (pages 118–19), you should be feeling pretty good about your fathering skills. If you're lucky, your partner, your friends, and your relatives have been telling you what a great father you are. But there's one person whose opinion of your abilities probably means more to you than anyone else's: the baby.

As a grown man, you'd think you wouldn't need to have your ego stroked by a baby. But the fact is that there is absolutely nothing in the world that will ever make you feel better, more powerful, or more loved than the feeling of being needed by your own child. "In the family, children send a message that you are really irreplaceable—no one has the meaning and value to your child that you do," write Barbara and Philip Newman. "The feeling that your life has meaning because of your role as a parent makes an important contribution to your sense of psychological well-being."

A Sense of Fulfillment

If feeling needed and appreciated by your boss and co-workers can give you a sense of self-worth and security at the office, feeling needed and appreciated as a father has the same result at home. In fact, nearly half the men in Bruce

"I've never once demanded respect from you simply because I'm your father. You should respect me for that."

Drobeck's studies described fatherhood "as giving them more of a sense of fulfillment and/or purpose in their lives."

For some, becoming a father was the achievement of their fondest dreams and long-term goals. One man said, "I finally feel like I'm where I want to be and doing what I want to be doing." Another added that having a baby "kind of puts a reason to everything."

A New Kind of Feeling Left Out, or Mr. Baby's Father

It's hard for any father to discuss his children objectively, but you're just going to have to take me at my word when I tell you that my older daughter has always been exceptionally well behaved, good-tempered, and social (my younger is pretty much the same, but this story's not about her). From the time she was just a few months old, people would stop me on the street to tell me how gorgeous and engaging she was. Even in France, the Parisians, who I'm convinced share W. C. Fields's legendary love for children (he preferred them fried), were enraptured by her easy smile and made special trips across the Champs Elysées to tickle her under the chin.

Having a baby who attracts this kind of attention (and we all do, of course) has some interesting side effects. The most common is the feeling of being completely ignored by the people who come over to gawk at your baby. This can be especially disconcerting if you actually want to meet the people who don't seem to have noticed that you're alive.

A few years ago I had a rather intense exposure to these feelings while visiting the set of *The Linguini Incident,* a movie written by one of my sisters and starring David Bowie and Roseanna Arquette. My sister had written a small scene for my wife, my daughter, and me, and the three of us had flown to L.A. for our fifteen minutes of celluloid fame.

Over the course of our twelve hours on the set, Roseanna Arquette must have taken my daughter away from me ten times, each time muttering under her breath, "Oh, my womb, my aching womb." We hardly saw our daughter all day.

At nearly midnight, we finally finished shooting, and Roseanna began saying her good-byes. She hugged the director and then came over to the table my wife, baby, and I were sitting at. Again, she took my daughter out of my arms, told her that she'd miss her, that she'd been a great little baby, that she was the best, the cutest . . . all the time kissing and kissing her. After about two minutes, Roseanna handed my baby back, said a flat "Goodnight" to me and left.

There is a strange, if false, sense of closeness that one establishes with someone who has held one's child. Roseanna had held my baby for hours, she'd told me about her womb, and I felt that we'd shared something that day—forged a kind of bond. So when I didn't get a goodnight kiss, I felt slighted.

A few months later, at the preview screening of the movie, I approached Roseanna to say hi. She gave me an icy stare and walked away. But a few minutes later she was back, smiling almost apologetically, "Oh, you're that incredibly gorgeous baby's father, aren't you?" she said. "How is she?"

You and Your Baby

Exposing Your Child to Music

By the time your baby started babbling verbally, she had already been babbling *musically* for several months—cooing happily, adjusting her pitch up or down to match yours. You'd sing or coo back and the two of you would have a little "duet."

For your baby, there is little if any difference between musical and verbal babbling. But for most parents, the difference is enormous. And the minute parents get even the slightest hint that their babies are beginning to understand language, the cooing and singing stops and they focus their attention on developing the baby's verbal skills. "Consequently," says Ken Guilmartin, president of Center for Music and Young Children, "the singing form is not reinforced and becomes developmentally delayed, or even atrophies completely."

Even if you and your partner don't have any particular musical talent, there's no reason why you can't stimulate your baby's musical potential. Now before you protest that you can't carry a tune to save your life, keep in mind that "potential" and "achievement" are *not* the same thing. Unfortunately, this is a distinction that far too many parents fail to make. And the result, says music education researcher Edwin Gordon, "can be fatal to a child's music development."

According to Gordon, every child is born with at least some musical aptitude: 68 percent have perfectly average aptitude; 16 percent well above; and 16 percent well below. "Just as there are no children without intelligence," he says, "there are no children without musical aptitude."

Good, bad, or indifferent, your baby's musical aptitude is greatly affected by the environment you provide. Even if you're so tone deaf that you're embarrassed to sing in the shower, you can easily provide your baby with a rich musical atmosphere—and you'll probably enjoy yourself in the process. Here's how:

- As you started when your baby was three months old (see pages 75–76), continue exposing her to a wide variety of musical styles. But now try to choose recordings that have frequent changes in rhythm, tempo, and dynamics (loudness/softness). At ten months your baby's attention span is still quite short and these contrasts will hold her interest longer and more easily, says Guilmartin.
- Never force your baby to listen to music. Your goal here is not to teach her (just like you won't be teaching her how to speak, crawl, or walk); rather, it is to guide and encourage her and let her develop at a natural pace.
- Don't turn off the music if the baby doesn't seem to be paying any attention. "There is little doubt that young children derive as much from listening to music when they appear not to be paying attention as when they appear to be paying attention," says Dr. Gordon.
- Try to avoid songs with words. Because your baby is rapidly developing her language skills, she may pay more attention to the words than to the music.
- Sing. Whenever and wherever you can. And don't worry about being in

tune—your baby doesn't care. As above, use nonsense syllables—dum-dee-dum kinds of things—instead of real words.

- Listen to music *you* like. Your baby will be paying close attention to the way you react to the music and will know if you've selected some "good-for-you" piece that you hate.
- Watch your baby's reaction to the music. She's moving much more actively than a few months ago. Her arm and leg movements may seem (to adults, anyway) to have no connection to the music, but they are actually internally rhythmic.
- Be patient. "The process of learning music is much the same as the process of learning language," write Gordon and his associates Richard Grunow and Christopher Azzara. Here are the steps they've identified:
  - Listening. From birth (and before), you absorbed the rhythm and inflections of your language—without any expectation of response.
  - Imitating. You weren't too successful at first, but you were encouraged to babble even though no one understood a single "word" you said.
  - Thinking (understanding). As you got more proficient with language, you were able to decipher the muddle of sounds coming out of people's mouths into meaningful words and phrases.
  - Improvising. You made up your own words and phrases and sometimes other people actually understood them.
  - Reading and writing. But not until you'd been listening, imitating, improvising, and thinking for more than five years.

Don't try to mess with the order—it's set in stone. If your parents had insisted on trying to teach you to read before you could speak, you might never have learned to do either.

Your Role in Molding Your Kids' Sexual Identity

Everyone knows that little girls are sugar and spice and all that's nice, while little boys are frogs and snails and puppy-dogs' tails, right? Well, as with most stereotypes, there is, at the core, a kernel of truth there: girls and boys *are* different and they *do* seem to behave differently, even in early infancy. Girls tend to respond to sights and sounds earlier and more intensively than boys, and they also learn to talk earlier. Boys tend to cry more and are somewhat more physical and aggressive. But what accounts for these differences—biology (nature) or the way boys and girls are treated by their parents (nurture)?

Without going into all the gory details of the debate, suffice it to say that the generally accepted view is that "sex differences in infant behavior are more a function of differential treatment than of innate biological predispositions," writes psychologist Henry Biller. "Parents may exaggerate relatively minor sex differences by talking to their girls more and handling their boys more vigorously."

Well, that was easy. But here's a much more provocative question: are the differences we see in boys' and girls' behavior—however they got there—real, or are we just imagining them?

Researchers John and Sandra Condry showed a group of more than two hundred adults a videotape of a nine-month-old baby playing. Half were told that they were watching a boy, half that they were watching a girl. Although everyone was viewing the exact same tape, the descriptions the two groups gave of the baby's behavior were startlingly different. The group that was watching a "boy" saw more pleasure and less fear in the baby's behavior than the group that was watching a "girl." And when the baby displayed negative emotions, the boy group saw anger; the girl group saw fear.

So do these imagined differences affect the way adults interact with children? The Condrys think so. "It seems reasonable to assume," they write, "that a child who is thought to be afraid is held and cuddled more than a child who is thought to be angry."

Other researchers have confirmed that adults do indeed behave differently with (perceived) boys than with (perceived) girls. Hannah Frisch conducted essentially the same experiment as the Condrys, except that in hers the adults actually played one-on-one with two different children. One time the adults were told they were playing with a boy, one time with a girl. "The general picture which emerges," writes Frisch, "is one in which adults are playing in masculine ways with children whom they think are boys and in feminine ways with children whom they think are girls."

In another study, Beverly Fagot found that by treating boys and girls differently adults may inadvertently reinforce sex stereotypes. For example, parents tend to react more positively to their daughters' attempts to communicate and more negatively to similar attempts by their sons, thus "confirming" that girls are more verbal than boys. Parents also react more positively when their sons engage in physical play and more negatively when their daughters do, thus "confirming" that boys are more physical than girls. So do boys play with trucks and girls with dolls because *they* want to or because that's what their parents want them to? Think about that the next time you're looking for a gift for your baby.

Although mothers and fathers generally treat their sons and daughters in

"I gotta go play with my doll now, so that I'll be a really great Dad someday."

the same sex-stereotyped ways—pushing girls to be more "feminine" and boys to be more "masculine"—fathers have a greater tendency to do it. "Fathers are likely to cuddle infant daughters gently but to engage in rough-and-tumble activities with sons," writes Biller. In addition, Biller has found that "fathers are more apt to accept a temperamentally difficult male infant but to withdraw from a female infant who presents similar problems (see pages 89–96 for more on temperament).

Biller warns, however, that fathers are not always discriminating when treating boys and girls differently. "The child's reaction can be a major factor; in general, infant sons may actually display more positive emotional reactions than daughters do when fathers engage them in physically stimulating play."

The whole point of this section is to get you to see how easy it is to fall into sex-stereotype traps. Sure, you'll still probably treat girls a little differently from boys; that's normal. But hopefully, now that you're a bit more aware of the dynamics, you'll be able to avoid the larger problems and give your kids a richer childhood experience.

If you have a boy, encourage him to communicate as much as he can. Don't discourage him from crying or from playing with dolls, and teach him that asking for help isn't a bad (unmanly) thing. If you have a daughter, encourage

"We're calling her Fred, after her father."

her to play physically and teach her that assertiveness and independence aren't unfeminine.

But whether you have a boy or a girl, make sure you aren't forcing your child into a type of behavior that doesn't fit his or her character or temperament. "Trying to force a boy or a girl into a straightjacket conception of appropriate sex-role behavior is certainly not in the child's best interests," writes Biller. "But neither is trying to pressure a child into behaving in a so-called nonsexist manner when he or she naturally appears comfortable with more traditional expectations." The bottom line is that some boys, if you give them a Barbie to play with, will tear her head off and use her legs as a double-barreled shotgun; and some girls are going to want to wear lace everywhere they go.

11 MONTHS

Planes, Trains, and Automobiles

What's Going On with the Baby

Physically

- Your baby is still conserving a lot of his physical energy in preparation for taking his first steps.
- He can nevertheless get himself to a standing position by straightening his legs and pushing off from his hands, and may even be able to stand up from a squatting position.
- He may be able to stand without any support and will try to do two activities at the same time, such as standing and waving. He may even try to squat down to pick up a toy.
- He can climb up stairs holding on to a railing and can walk holding on to only one of your hands.
- He adores rough play—wrestling, rolling around on the floor, being held upside down, and bouncing on your knees.
- He can turn the pages of a book, but not as accurately as he'd probably like to.
- He still can't release grasped objects exactly when and how he wants to.

Intellectually

- One day this month, your newly upright baby will be leaning against a chair and he'll accidentally make it move a little. He'll immediately understand that *he's* the one responsible and will do it again. And again. He may, in fact, spend the rest of the day (and the month, for that matter) pushing the chair around the house.

- Imitation reaches new heights this month. But rather than mimicking specific actions, he's now able to imitate *concepts,* or even a series of actions. He'll now hide things and get you to look for them, feed you, and try to brush his own teeth and get himself dressed.
- He'll spend a lot of time this month dropping small objects into larger containers, learning the difference between big and small, container and contained, "in" and "out."
- He's also expanding his knowledge about symbols. He's fascinated by books but doesn't really know what to make of them. He'll poke at the pictures in a book, intrigued by the idea that he can *see* an object but can't pick it up.
- Although still convinced that he's running the world, he's discovering that his body has certain limitations. If some precious object is out of reach, he'll push you toward it, trying to get you to reach it for him, thus using you as a tool.

Verbally

- Although his vocabulary is growing, he's nowhere near being able to put together sentences. But he'll babble in long "paragraphs" and toss in an occasional recognizable word.
- Interestingly, the sounds he uses in his babbling are specific to his native language, and he can no longer produce some of the ones he could even a few months ago.
- Whenever he learns a new word, he'll repeat it to himself dozens of times.
- He recognizes the symbolic use of words: he'll say "yum" if you're talking about ice cream, "meow" if you point out a cat.
- He's developed an incredible ability to hear what he wants to: he'll completely ignore a shouted "get away from that stove," but will stop whatever he's doing and rush to your side if you whisper "ice cream" from another zip code.

Emotionally/Socially

- Besides happy and sad, your baby is now capable of other, more sophisticated emotions. If you play with another baby, for example, he'll become jealous and protest loudly. He's also getting much more demonstrative, and will show genuine tenderness and affection to you as well as to his stuffed animals.
- He also understands approval and disapproval. When he cleans his plate, he'll joyously shout for you to come look, and he'll beam with pride at

having done something good. If he's done something he shouldn't have, though, he knows it and will bow his head sheepishly in anticipation of a few sharp words. Generally, he wants to please you, but he also needs to displease you to learn how you'll react.

- He may also be afraid of growing up and may regress emotionally as well as physically to a time when he was a baby and you took care of him.
- Strange as it sounds, your baby is already beginning to establish his or her own sexual identity. Girls begin to identify with their mother and other females and do what they do, while boys will identify with you and other men and want to do what you do.

What You're Going Through

Fear of Sexual Feelings

This may very well be the most controversial section in this book. So before you continue, you've got to promise that you'll keep an open mind and read all the way to the end.

Imagine this: you're rolling around on the floor with your baby, having the time of your life, or you're standing by your sleeping child's bed, stroking his beautiful, perfect cheek. Then, without warning, you get, well, aroused.

Now before you throw this book down and report me to the police, keep in mind that the overwhelming majority of mental health professionals say that it is *perfectly normal* for a parent to experience brief sexual feelings toward his or her child. "Most parents feel physical pleasure toward their babies," writes psychiatrist Stanley Greenspan. "For some, these pleasures are translated into fleeting sexual feelings."

Normal or not, feeling sexual desire—even briefly—for a child can be especially terrifying for men. You might be afraid that someone will accuse you of being a child molester, or that you actually are one and won't be able to control your unnatural "urges." Or that you might have to be locked up to protect your children. Or that you're completely insane.

Despite everything we hear about the "epidemic of sexual abuse," the truth is that well over 99 percent of parents never abuse anybody. So the odds are pretty slim that you'll do anything even remotely improper. Nevertheless, many men (and women as well) are so afraid and feel so guilty about their feelings that they withdraw from their children and stop playing with them, picking them up, or cuddling with them.

If you find yourself reacting in this way, stop it right now. "If you withdraw

"I did ask her and she said to ask you where I came from."

your physical displays of affection," says clinical psychologist Aaron Hass, "your child may believe there is something wrong with being affectionate in that manner. And if you stop hugging your child, you will miss the opportunity to enhance, in a very primal way, the bond between the two of you."

By reading this section you have, without even being aware of it, taken a very important step toward understanding and dealing with your momentary sexual feelings. Simply being aware of how normal these feelings are, says Dr. Greenspan, can "inhibit you from acting inappropriately" and "keep your special relationship with your baby from being dominated by fear."

Of course, if you're seriously worried that your feelings toward your child are inappropriate, and/or if you're having trouble managing them, get some professional help quickly. And don't worry, telling your therapist about your feelings will not get you arrested.

More Worries about the Baby's Health

For the first few months of your baby's life, you depended on your doctor to keep you informed as to how the baby was doing. And had there been any major problem (neurological defects, Down syndrome, and so on), or anything amiss with your baby's growth or development, you would have heard about it by now.

But most problems that affect children aren't easy to spot. And now that your baby is older and his well-baby checkups are farther apart, your pediatrician will rely more on you and your daily observations about your baby's behavior to make any diagnoses. Here are the kinds of things you should be looking out for:

- Is the baby having trouble manipulating objects or moving around? Delays in developing sensory/motor skills can cause delays in language development as well.
- Is the baby using her body fairly symmetrically? Does she use one hand (or foot, or eye) more than the other?
- Is the baby having trouble eating or swallowing food? Besides resulting in nutritional deficiencies and general health problems, these problems may interfere with your baby's using his jaw, lips, and tongue. Once again, language and cognitive skills can be seriously (negatively) affected.
- Has your baby lost previously attained skills? Did he used to babble and coo but suddenly stop? Does she no longer react when people come and go? This could be an indication of a hearing problem, which, again, can affect language development.
- Is the baby not achieving, within a month or two, the milestones described in the "What's Going On with the Baby" sections in this book?
- Does the baby seem uninterested in exploring his surroundings?
- Has your baby undergone a major change in temperament? (See pages 89–96.) But remember: difficult temperament by itself is *not* an indication of any kind of disability.

In most cases, the "problem" behaviors you identify will turn out to be perfectly normal. But that doesn't mean you should stop paying attention. Here are some things you can do to reassure yourself:

- Spend some time studying the "What's Going On with the Baby" sections of this book. The more you know about what your baby is and isn't capable of, the less you'll worry.
- Don't worry that your doctor—or your partner—will think you're asking too many questions or becoming overly concerned. You (or your insurance company) are paying your doctor more than enough for him or her to listen respectfully to any questions you might have.
- If, after talking to your doctor, you're still not satisfied (or you think you're being ignored), get another opinion.
- Keep a detailed log of things your child does (or doesn't do) that concern you, when they happen, and under what circumstances.

- Men have a tendency to ignore their own health concerns either because they hope whatever's worrying them will go away or because they're afraid the doctor will confirm their worst suspicions. If you want to ignore something that's been bothering you, that's your own prerogative. But don't apply the same standard to your baby. You may not be the most experienced parent in the world, but your gut reactions about what ails your children are usually pretty good and should be acted on. Of course, this doesn't mean bringing the baby into the emergency room every day, but an occasional call to your doctor's advice nurse is fine. If there is something to worry about, you're better off knowing sooner than later, when the problem will be much harder to deal with.

You and Your Baby

Planes, Trains, and Automobiles

When my older daughter was only six months old, my wife and I decided it was about time to take that honeymoon trip we'd been putting off since we'd gotten married. So we traded in a few years' worth of frequent-flier miles, and the three of us took off on a month-long trip to New York, France, Israel, and Phoenix. All in all, it was a great trip.

While your first trip with your baby is not likely to be as big an expedition as ours, sooner or later you're going to want to pack up the family and go somewhere.

What to Do Before You Go

- Spend some time planning your itinerary. You can take babies under about seven months just about anywhere anytime. After your baby has learned to walk, however, it's best to limit your destinations. Seven cities in four days is hard for even the most seasoned adult traveler.
- If possible, pick destinations that won't be terribly crowded; large groups of unfamiliar people may spook babies and toddlers alike.
- Get your tickets in advance. There's no sense standing in lines if you don't have to.
- Travel during off-peak times. Christmas Day, New Year's Day, and Thanksgiving Day (as opposed to the days before or after), for example, are good. If you're driving, there'll be less traffic on the road; if you're traveling some other way, you'll find a lot more empty seats, meaning more room to stretch out or run around.

- Red-eye flights may increase the chances your baby will sleep on the plane, and can also help get the jet-lag acclimation process under way.
- Prepare for jet-lag/time differences before you leave. You can keep the kid up late, put him to bed early, and so forth. Also adjust meal times.
- Prepare your child for the upcoming trip by talking about it regularly. Make it sound like it's going to be the most fun anyone has ever had.
- Schedule a doctor's appointment (for your child) for a few weeks before you leave. Tell your pediatrician where you're going and ask for the names of a few good local doctors. Also ask him or her to suggest any medical supplies you should bring along. If your child is taking any medication and will come anywhere near running out while you're on the road, get an extra prescription.

What to Bring

No matter where you go, the trick to making things run smoothly on a trip away from home is to surround your baby with as many familiar things as possible. This will help minimize the shock of the new routine and scenery. Whatever your destination, then, you'll probably need most of the following:

- Eating utensils and bibs.
- If you're traveling overseas and will be using powdered formula, plan on bringing some bottled water.
- Car seat. Doubles nicely as a high chair if you really need to restrain your baby while she's eating.
- A good backpack. It'll free up both your arms so you can schlep the six tons of other baby-related stuff you'll be needing.
- A portable crib. Or, if you'll be staying in a hotel, call ahead to reserve one.
- A first aid kit (see page 140 for the ingredients).
- A stroller that collapses compactly enough so you can take it on the plane.
- Lots of familiar toys, stuffed animals, favorite foods.
- Bring only what you're absolutely sure you'll need. If you aren't going trekking in the Himalayas, for example, there's really no sense taking along a large number of disposable diapers—they're available just about anywhere. The first thing my wife and I did when we arrived in New York was get a huge cardboard crate and ship home about half of the stuff we'd brought.

Once You Get There

- Keep up the routines you've established at home. Read, sing, play at the same times if you can. This is especially important for predictable babies (see page 91).

- Don't overbook activities. One or two excursions a day is plenty.
- Pick up local parenting publications (they're usually free) in whatever city or cities you're going to. You can order copies of these publications before you go by contacting Parenting Publications of America, 12715 Path Finder Lane, San Antonio, TX 78230-1532, (210) 492-3886, 492-3887 (fax); parpubs@aol.com.
- Keep a sharp eye on baby/relative contact. If friends and relatives haven't seen the baby for a while or are meeting him for the first time, they'll all want to hold, squeeze, cuddle, and entertain. This can freak out even the calmest of babies. Be especially sensitive if your baby is going through a period of stranger or separation anxiety.
- If you're planning to leave the baby with a sitter or a relative, have her or him come early so the two of them can get to know each other for a few minutes.
- Stay away from meats, fish, eggs, and dairy products. If you're going to get food poisoning on the road, it'll probably come from one of those food groups. And if you're traveling overseas, stay away from water, milk, juice, raw foods, and anything served by street vendors.

Traveling by Car

- For short trips, try to leave an hour or so before your baby's usual nap time and, once he falls asleep, drive as far as you can while his nap lasts.
- For longer trips, consider doing your driving from 4 P.M. to midnight. That way, you'll only have a few hours of entertainment and stops for feedings before baby goes to sleep for the night.
- If you need to drive during the day, you or your partner should ride in the back seat with the baby in hour or two-hour shifts to keep him amused and awake. Car travel tends to knock babies out and can really screw up their sleep schedules.
- Take lots of breaks and make sure everyone has plenty of opportunity to stretch, unwind, and relax. Stop at interesting places, pet the cows, watch the road-repair crews, point out new sights (forests, cloud shapes, and so forth), sing songs, read stories. Going through an automatic car wash can be a thrill for some kids, but for others it can be terrifying. Whatever you do, have fun.
- Put the car seat in the middle of the back seat; it's safest there.
- Lock car doors from the inside.
- Never, never leave your child alone in a car. Babies can suffocate a lot faster than you might think.

GOOD THINGS TO BRING IN THE CAR

- Lots of food and drink.
- Lots and lots of books.
- Stickers, markers, crayons, paper, and other art supplies.
- Magnetic puzzles.
- A battery-operated tape recorder (if you don't have one in the car) and a good selection of music. Make sure to bring some you like as well.

One warning: if you have to slam on your brakes at sixty miles an hour, every object you have in your car is a potential projectile. So before you bring anything into the car, think about whether you'd like to be hit in the head by it.

Traveling by Plane

- Get to the airport early. Let the baby run around and tire himself out. This may make the flight a little easier on everyone.
- Try to get bulkhead seats (usually the first row)—they generally offer a little more room, and you won't have to worry that your child will kick the seat of the people in front of you. Also, ask to be seated next to an empty seat if possible. Be sure to hold your absolutely adorable baby in your arms while you're asking—this can improve your chances of getting what you want.
- *Don't* board early. Instead, send your partner on with the carry-on stuff while you stay out in the lounge, letting the kids run themselves ragged until the last minute. Why spend any more time cooped up in the airplane than you absolutely have to?

The All-Purpose Travel Bag

If there's ever any danger of getting separated from your luggage (even if most of it is just in the trunk of your car), you should have a well-stocked bag with the necessary "emergency" supplies:

- Diapers and wipers.
- Toys (one for each hour of travel time); mirrors and suction-cup rattles are big hits with babies.
- Food.
- Something to suck on (pacifiers, teething rings, and so forth).
- A few books.
- Some favorite comfort items (blankets, teddy bears, and so on).

- If you're going on a long trip and your child is particularly restless or active, schedule a stopover or two to give you all a chance to get off the plane, stretch, and run around.
- Every child under two years old should suck on something—breast, bottle, or pacifier—on the way up and the way down. This will counteract the pressurization and reduce the chances of painful earaches.
- Make sure your child drinks a lot on board. Airplane travel can dry out your baby's (and your) mucous membranes, making her more susceptible to colds or sinus infections.
- Check as many bags as you can, but carry on the all-purpose travel bag (see page 190).

WHAT TO BRING

- Same as for cars (see page 190).
- Some extra food. The meals you ordered might not show up, or, if you're taking a short flight, there might not be any food at all.

DEALING WITH JET LAG

- If you're traveling for only a few days, keep baby doing things at the time he would be doing them at home. This will make it easier to return to your regular schedule when you get back home.
- Spend time outside. Natural light helps acclimate people to new time zones more quickly.

Family Matters

Life Insurance

Becoming a parent does some interesting things to your mind and to your outlook on life. On the one hand, having a child makes you want to live forever and not miss a single second with your child. On the other hand, watching your child grow older is like a hard slap in the face; it makes you realize that no matter how much you want to, you're not going to live forever.

Simply put, the purpose of life insurance is to make sure that after your death at least some of your survivors' financial needs are taken care of. But according to the National Insurance Consumer Organization, more than 90 percent of Americans have the wrong kind of insurance coverage and in the wrong amounts.

Unfortunately, there really aren't any hard-and-fast rules or secret formulas

"Greetings, stockholders."

to help you determine how much insurance you need. But spending some time thinking about the following questions will put you in the top 10 percent (it's really not that hard) of insurance consumers:

- Do you need or want to pay off your mortgage? Could your partner make the full payment on what she makes?
- Do you have a lot of debts you want to pay off?
- Do you need or want to leave an estate large enough to pay fully for your kids' college education?
- How many years of your income do you want your insurance to replace?
- What do you expect your tax situation to be? If you have a huge estate, your heirs will have to come up with a tidy sum to cover inheritance taxes.

There are two basic ways to make sure your insurance needs are properly taken care of:

- Read a few good personal finance guides (or at least sections of them). Despite what you might think, it's not all that complicated. Eric Tyson's *Personal Finance for Dummies* (IDG Books) is one of the best.
- Get yourself a financial planner (see pages 194–95 for some helpful tips).

Either way, you should at least be aware of your insurance options. Basically, there are two types of life insurance on the market: term and cash value; each is further divided into several subcategories. Here's a brief overview:

TERM

There are three types of term insurance, and they all share these features:

- Fairly low cost, especially in the early years.
- Premiums increase over time as your odds of dying go up.
- Policies are in effect only for a specified period of time.
- No cash value accumulation.

Here are your basic term insurance choices:

- Renewable term. You can renew the policy annually. Death benefit generally remains level, while premiums increase over time.
- Level premium. The death benefit and the premium remain the same for a specified period of time, usually five, ten, or twenty years.
- Decreasing premium. The death benefit decreases each year, while premiums remain the same.

CASH VALUE

There are an increasing number of cash value insurance products available. Despite their differences, they all share the following features:

- These policies are essentially a combination of term insurance and a savings plan. A portion of your premium pays for pure term insurance. The balance is deposited into some kind of side fund on which you can earn interest or dividends.
- These policies tend to offer—initially—very competitive interest rates. The rate is usually guaranteed for a year, but then drops to whatever the market is paying.
- You can pay pretty much whatever you want to. But if your payment isn't enough to cover the insurance cost, the balance is taken out of your side fund, reducing your cash value.
- The cash benefit accumulates tax-free, and you can borrow against it or withdraw from it during your lifetime.
- If properly placed in trust, the entire cash and accumulated savings can go to your heirs free of income tax.

Here are your cash value choices:

- Whole life. Locks in a death benefit, cash values, and premium. The side fund is invested by the insurance company.

Picking a Financial Planner

Since most states don't have laws regulating or accrediting financial planners (who may also call themselves "advisors," "consultants," or "managers"), just about anyone can set up shop to dole out financial advice and sell products.

Most financial planners are paid on a commission basis, meaning that there's always at least the possibility of a conflict of interest. (In other words, whether or not your investments do well, the financial planner is assured his commission.) Commissions typically range from as low as 4 percent on some mutual funds to the entire first year's premium on a cash value life insurance policy. Others are paid on a fee basis and typically charge from $50 to $250 per hour.

This doesn't mean, of course, that fee-based planners are inherently better than their commission-based colleagues (although many experts believe that you'll be happier, and possibly richer, with someone who charges a fee). Your goal is to find someone you like and who you believe will have your best interests at heart. Here are a few things you can do to help you weed out the losers:

- Get references from friends, business associates, and so forth. Alternatively, the Institute of Certified Financial Planners (800) 282-7526 will give you some local references, and the National Association of Personal Financial Advisors (800) 366-2732 makes referrals only of fee-based (as opposed to commission-based) planners.
- Select at least three potential candidates and set up initial consultations (which shouldn't cost you anything). Then conduct tough interviews. Here's what you want to know:

- Universal life. Similar to Whole life, except that you can change the premium payment and death benefits anytime. And since the side fund is invested in fixed-income home securities (bonds and so forth), your cash values can fluctuate.
- Variable life. Similar to Universal, except that you have a bit more input into how your side fund is invested. Your choices usually include money markets, government securities, corporate bonds, growth, fixed-income, or total-return portfolios.

So how can you possibly make a choice between term and cash value?

- ◊ Educational background. Not to be snobby here, but the more formal the education—especially in financial management—the better. Watch out for fancy initials: many planners prominently display the letters CFP (for Certified Financial Planner) after their names. Forbes magazine recently called the CFP credential "meaningless."
- ◊ Level of experience. Unless you've got money to burn, let your niece break in her MBA on someone else. Stick to experienced professionals with at least three years in the business.
- ◊ Profile of the typical client. What you're looking for is a planner who has experience working with people whose income level and family situation are similar to yours.
- ◊ Compensation. If fee-based, how is the fee calculated? If commission, what are the percentages on each product offered? Any hesitation to show you a commission schedule is a red flag.
- ◊ Get a sample financial plan. You want to see what you're going to be getting for your money. Be careful, though: fancy graphics, incomprehensible boilerplate language, and expensive leather binders are often used to distract you from the report's lack of substance.
- ◊ References. How long have customers been with the planner? Are they happy? Better off? Any complaints or weaknesses?

- ♦ Check your prospective planner's record with state and federal regulators. You can call the federal Securities and Exchange Commission (202) 272-7450 or your state's equivalent to check on disciplinary action and to see whether your candidates have ever been sued.

Financial author and counselor Eric Tyson has some fairly strong views on the subject: "Cash value insurance is the most oversold insurance and financial product in the history of the industry," he writes. His solution?

Unless you have a high net worth, get yourself a term insurance policy with the following features:

- ♦ Guaranteed renewable (you don't want to be canceled if you get sick).
- ♦ Level premiums for five to ten years (that way you won't need to get a physical exam every year).
- ♦ A price you can live with. Costs for the very same policy can vary by as much as 200–300 percent, so shop around. (Since a rather big chunk of

your premium is going to some agent in the form of commission, you can cut your costs way down by buying a "no load" or "low load" policy.)

WHEN YOU SHOULD BUY CASH VALUE INSURANCE

- Currently, an individual can leave up to $600,000, and a couple can leave up to $1,200,000 to beneficiaries *without* having to pay federal estate taxes. If you aren't worth this much, or don't expect to be when you die, stick with term.
- If you own a small business that's worth more than $1 million, cash value insurance makes sense, unless you have enough in liquid assets to pay off the estate taxes your heirs will owe.

Notes:

12 MONTHS

There Now, That Wasn't So Bad, Was It?

What's Going On with the Baby

Physically

- Still building toward walking, your baby can now get to a standing position from a squat and can lower herself gracefully from standing to sitting.
- She's also getting more confident about combining standing and walking. She can turn 90 degrees, stoop to pick things up, and walk holding on to you with one hand while clutching a favorite toy (or two or three) in the other. She might even experiment with taking a few backward steps.
- If your baby does take a few steps this month, she'll still use crawling as her main means of transportation.
- She can take simple covers off containers (but probably not screw-tops), and she'll help you dress and undress her (well, at least she *thinks* she's helping . . .).
- She's finally mastered her opposable thumb and can now pick up tiny objects between her thumb and pointing finger.
- She's also expressing a strong preference for "handedness," using one hand for grasping, the other for manipulating. If you put an object in her "passive" hand, she'll transfer it to the "active" one.
- She's now learned to store objects. If she's holding one thing in each hand and you offer her a third, she now wants to get control of all three; she'll transfer the contents of one hand to her mouth or armpit and *then* pick up the third object with the free hand.

Intellectually

- One of the most important intellectual accomplishments of your baby's first year is her ability to retain a visual image of an object she has seen before but that is currently out of sight.
- By the end of this month, your baby will be able to demonstrate this ability by searching—in more than one place—for objects she has seen but that she didn't see you hide.
- In another major intellectual leap this month, your baby will begin using trial and error to solve her problems and overcome obstacles.
- As annoying as it may get, it's important to recognize that your baby's constant banging, building and knocking over, and putting things in and dumping them out are important learning activities that are teaching her more about the multiple properties of the objects in her world. Adding water to sand changes the way the sand feels (and tastes); dropping marbles into a metal can produces a much different sound than dropping them into a plastic box; and dumping them onto the living room rug isn't nearly as much fun as watching them bounce and roll around after dumping them on the vinyl kitchen floor.

Verbally

- She probably has a vocabulary of six to eight real words, as well as five or six more sound words, such as *moo, woof,* or *boom.*
- Her passive vocabulary is significantly larger, and she'll gleefully identify quite a few of her body parts, as well as such familiar objects as you and your partner, her bottle, and her crib.
- She still doesn't know much about the symbolic use of words. If you point to a book at a friend's house and say, "Look at the book," your baby may be confused. In her world, the word *book* applies only to the ones at home.

Emotionally/Socially

- She actively tries to avoid doing things she knows you don't like, and loves your applause and approval.
- She's not always cooperative and will regularly test your limits (and your patience). She also is developing a basic sense of right and wrong and shows guilt when she does something wrong.
- She's developing a sense of humor and finds incongruities most entertaining. If you tell her a dog says "moo," or if you crawl or pretend to cry, she'll laugh hysterically.
- In her home, where she feels most secure, your baby will play with other

kids and may share some of her toys with them. In less secure environments, however, she's not nearly as sociable and will not stray far from you.

- She's got some pretty firm ideas of what she wants and will do what she can (cry, have a tantrum, smile sweetly) to influence your decisions.

What You're Going Through

Anger

While my wife was pregnant with our first child, I spent a lot of time thinking about the things I would never do once I became a father. First on my list was No Hitting the Kids. Then I thought about all those parents (including my own) I'd seen over the years scream at their children in the grocery store or

"If you ask me, this kid isn't lost. His parents just made a run for it."

the post office. "How weak," I remember thinking to myself. "If people can't control themselves any better than that, they really shouldn't be parents." I quickly and rather smugly added No Yelling at the Kids to my list.

One afternoon my daughter woke up from her nap crying like she never had before. I knew she wasn't tired, so I checked to see if her diaper was full (it wasn't), whether her clothes were binding her (they weren't), and even took her temperature (normal). She didn't respond to my comforting words or my requests to stop crying and tell me what was wrong (at six months, why should she?), and she continued howling. I was alone in the house, and after half an hour I'd had enough. I was frustrated and angry. So angry, in fact, that I felt like throwing my baby out the window and driving away.

Almost immediately, though, I was nearly overcome with feelings of embarrassment and disappointment for having let my emotions get away from me. I also felt like a complete failure as a father for having had such horrible thoughts about my own baby. It's no wonder that, in the words of psychologist Lawrence Kutner, "Anger—no, fury—is among the 'dirty little secrets' of parenthood."

"While parents talk about and glorify their feelings of love and protectiveness, their normal and often predictable moments of rage toward their children are seldom brought into the open," writes Kutner. "It is as if acknowledging the intensity of their anger is an admission of inadequacy or failure. If we deny it, perhaps it will go away, or we can convince ourselves that it never happened at all."

COPING WITH ANGER

"The conflicts that trigger the most intense responses often tell us more about ourselves than about our children," says Kutner. "Our most dramatic reactions to our children's behavior often come when we're feeling hurt. The child most likely to set off that strong, emotional response is the one who is most like us—especially when that child reminds us of things we don't particularly like about ourselves."

In addition, of course, things like job pressures, financial difficulties, health problems, or even car trouble can be redirected toward our kids and make us lash out at them. Whatever the reason for your anger, remember that there's nothing wrong with *feeling* it—even when it's directed at your kids. It's what you *do* with your anger, however, that can be a problem. Here are some suggestions that will help you understand, and better deal with, your anger.

- **Change your perspective.** Although your child may periodically do something deliberately to annoy you, many of his actions are really beyond his control. "A child's ability to bring out anger in his parents is usually

If You Lose Control . . .

Even parents with the best intentions accidentally lose control. If you do:

- Apologize. Explain to your child that you lost your temper. Make sure she knows that it was her *behavior* you didn't like, not her as a person, that you love her, and that you'll never hit her again.
- Don't go overboard, though. Resist the urge to punish yourself for your mistakes by being extra lenient with your child. You're only human, so lighten up.

Remember, anger can be just the first step in a vicious circle: something angers you enough that you lose control; feeling out of control makes you angrier; and feeling angry makes you feel even more out of control.

Unchecked, this process can escalate into physical and emotional abuse (which, besides screaming, can include insulting, humiliating, or withholding love). If you're worried that you might lose control again, get some help immediately: call a friend, a therapist, your child's pediatrician, or even a local parental-stress hotline (see also some of the suggestions for dealing with crying on pages 44–45). And if you're worried that your partner might prove to be violent, suggest she do the same.

a sign of normal development," says Kutner. "A toddler who is testing the limits of her independence will reject her parents occasionally, ignoring their pleas."

- **"Keep your sense of humor,"** says Ellen Galinsky. It may be a pain to clean up, but drawing on the walls with lipstick can be funny—if you let it.
- **Take regular breaks.** This can help keep minor annoyances from accumulating and boiling over. Make sure your partner gets plenty of time off too.
- **Give yourself a time-out.** Remove yourself from the situation and your child *before* you do something you'll regret for a long, long time.
- **Watch what you say.** Don't insult or humiliate your child. If you must criticize her, do it in private. Contrary to the old adage "Sticks and stones may break my bones, but names will never hurt me," calling your baby names can, in fact, have greater long-term negative impact than hitting.
  - Use "I" messages: "*I* don't like it when you scratch me—it hurts," is a much more effective message than "*You're* a bad girl because you scratched me."
  - Saying things like "You always . . ." or "You never . . ." can fill a child

with a sense of futility, a conviction that she'll fail no matter what she does or how hard she tries.

◊ Avoid mixed messages. Yelling at your child to stop yelling will probably not do you a lot of good.

- **Watch what you do.** "Children learn as much or more about the expression of anger from watching their parents when they are angry as they do from verbal explanations or punishment," say Barbara and Philip Newman. So don't let your toddler see you vent steam in a physical way; he won't be able to understand your anger and might even be afraid that you'll turn on him. He could also try to imitate you, and might hurt himself, someone else, or someone's property.
- **Get physical.** Taking a long jog, punching a pillow, and taking a boxing class are good ways to let off some steam. If there are any batting cages nearby, try them out—if you squint, slow-moving softballs can look an awful lot like a human head . . .

You and Your Baby

Discipline Update

When I was a kid, one of my father's favorite sayings was, "You're free to swing your arms around any way you want. But that freedom ends right where someone else's nose begins." In a nutshell, teaching your child this lesson—to be respectful of other people's noses—is the primary goal of discipline.

A few months ago this was a concept your baby couldn't possibly have grasped. And the only way for you to control his evil impulses was to distract him with a toy and hope he'd forget about whatever it was he shouldn't have been doing. But your baby's memory has been improving every day, and by the time he's a year old one toy just won't do the trick anymore; now you'll need two or three. And pretty soon, toys won't work at all.

When this happens, you'll face two major challenges, say the Newmans: making a smooth transition from "nurturing protector to the force for law and order," and combining "empathic caring" with "firm protectiveness."

The first step toward accomplishing these goals is to set reasonable, consistent limits. Here are a few things that will make this a lot easier:

- Limit potential risks. Basically, this means childproofing the hell out of your house and keeping anything you really want to stay in one piece as far away from the baby as possible. (To minimize problems elsewhere, ask your parents and in-laws to take similar preventive measures.)

- Give the baby a safe place to explore.
- Have plenty of substitutes available: old phones and remote controls, spare computer keyboards, and so on. But be prepared: some kids can tell instinctively that what you're giving them isn't the real thing, and they won't be amused.
- Stop dangerous behavior immediately, but *subtly.* If your baby is pounding on a plate-glass window with his toy hammer and you scream, drop your coffee, and leap across the room to wrestle him to the ground, he'll find your reaction so much fun that he'll be sure to repeat exactly the behavior that provoked it the first time.
- Be tolerant of your baby's "negativity." Your baby's "no's" are an important part of his developing identity. Giving your baby some decision-making control will help him accept the limits you set.
- Spend some serious time trying to figure out what the baby needs. Researcher Donelda Stayton and her associates found that early obedience (in nine-to-

YOU'VE BEEN A BAD BOY, JIMMY. AND I'M GOING TO PUNISH YOU IN A WAY YOU'LL NEVER UNDERSTAND UNTIL YOU'RE MY AGE.
MUELLER

twelve-month-olds) was related to the sensitivity of responsiveness to infant signals, *not* to the frequency of commands or forcible interventions.

While setting limits is important, it's really only half the battle. "If children are to correct their own behavior," write the Newmans, "they must know what acts are considered appropriate as well as how to inhibit their inappropriate acts." And the way your child will learn these lessons is by watching you. "Parental modeling and reinforcement of acceptable behavior are significant in the development of internal control," write the Newmans.

Biting and Hitting

For some strange reason, right around their first birthdays, almost all babies go through a phase when they bite and/or hit people—strangers and loved ones alike. If (when) your baby starts, the first thing you need to do is find out why. Your baby may be biting or hitting because she's:

- Trying to express affection (you probably nibble gently on her and she may simply be trying to imitate you).
- Frustrated that she can't express herself verbally.
- Teething and trying to relieve her discomfort.
- Simply conducting an experiment to see how others will react.
- Tired, overstimulated, or frustrated.
- Trying to defend herself or her property.
- Imitating an older friend or sibling.

Fortunately, the hitting-and-biting phase usually lasts no longer than a few months (although, when you're getting bitten a few times a day, that can seem like a very long time). Here, however, are a few dos and don'ts that may make this painful period a little shorter:

- Don't get angry; it will only make her defensive.
- Don't slap or spank.
- Don't bite back or have the baby bite herself "to show her what it feels like"; this sets a rotten example and will only reinforce the behavior by implying that it's really okay.
- Do remove the baby promptly. If she's sitting on your lap and bites you, put her down for a minute (no longer); if she's hit or bitten someone else, take her away from that person for a minute.
- Don't say, "You're bad" or any variation on that theme. Instead say, "*Biting* is bad."
- Don't insist on an apology. There's almost no chance that your baby has

Keep Your Mouth Running

There's plenty of evidence that talking to your baby can have some very positive long-term effects. So as you go through the day, identify everything you can, tell the baby what you're doing, where you're going, what's going on outside, what the weather's like, who won last night's baseball games, and so on.

According to pediatrician Burton White, parents who raised babies who turned out to be gifted or at least bright did the following things to build their children's language skills from infancy:

- They identified the things their children were interested in and talked about them a lot.
- They engaged in fifteen to twenty verbal interchanges each hour, most lasting between twenty and thirty seconds.
- They rarely "taught" or lectured children. Instead, they spoke casually and conversationally.
- They spoke in full sentences, using words slightly above the child's apparent level of comprehension.
- They read picture books and stories from infancy, even though most of the kids didn't seem to be paying much attention until they were two.

any idea what regret is or that biting really hurts (babies this age are completely incapable of imagining anything from any other perspective than their own).

- Don't overreact. The baby might find your reaction so amusing that she'll bite or hit again just to get your attention.
- Do spend some time trying to figure out why your baby is biting or hitting. Is it happening at certain times of the day (right before nap time, for example)? Does she do it only to certain people?
- Do rethink your discipline policies. You may be setting so many limits that your baby may be trying to bite her way to freedom.

Weaning Your Baby from Breast or Bottle

Most pediatricians today agree that new mothers should breastfeed their babies for as long as possible—generally between six months and a year. What to do after that, however, is the source of far less agreement.

So should you stop breastfeeding completely now or gradually phase it out? Should you transition your baby from breast to bottle, or skip the bottle and go directly to cups? And if you've been bottle-feeding from the start, when should you stop? The answers, of course, are up to you, your partner, and your baby.

We're assuming here that your baby is eating at least *some* solid foods in addition to her breast- or bottle-feeding. Eventually, she'll get all her food via cup and utensils, but the process of weaning her completely can take months or even years. (My wife nursed our older daughter for nine months and our younger for two years.)

Why to Wean the Baby from the Breast (or at Least Cut Back Some)

- By one year, the baby's gotten most of the long-term health benefits from breastfeeding. At this point, breastmilk alone can't satisfy all the baby's needs and may, in fact, suppress her appetite for solids.
- Babies who fall asleep with a breast in their mouth (and many do), often leave their teeth soaking in a pool of milk—this can lead to tooth decay.
- Most babies nurse in some kind of reclining position. This allows fluid from the mouth back up into the Eustachian tubes and can cause ear infections.
- The baby may start (or may already be) using the breast as a comfort or sleep aid, thus delaying development of the ability to comfort herself or fall asleep by herself.
- You may be feeling that enough is enough: your partner's breasts have been at least partially off-limits for a year, and it's time to unlatch that baby. You may see your wife's refusal to do so as a kind of slap in your face.

Why to Wean the Baby from the Bottle (or Start Cutting Back)

- Babies tend to let formula or juice slosh around in their mouths for a while. Little teeth that soak up too much can rot.
- Your baby may fill herself up on liquids so much that she will lose interest in all those solid foods she needs for a well-balanced diet.
- By about fifteen months your baby may begin forming an emotional attachment to her bottle (just as she might to a blanket, thumb, or favorite stuffed animal). Emotional attachments are nice, but breaking an attachment to a bottle will be a lot easier now than in a few months, when the baby starts getting stubborn and contrary.
- Some experts believe that overdependence on the bottle can interfere with physical and mental developmental milestones and advise giving it up entirely by eighteen months.

Introduction to Potty Training

Have you heard the one about the kid who was toilet-trained at eight months? If you haven't, you soon will. But prepare yourself: it isn't a joke—or, at least, it isn't *supposed* to be one. People will tell you all sorts of things about the babies they knew who were out of diapers before they could walk. But no matter what anyone says, or how much you might want to believe the stories, they just aren't true.

First of all, there's no such thing as potty training; your child will learn to use the toilet on her own only when she's ready. And at eight months or even a year, she's simply incapable of controlling her bowels or bladder. Sure, she may grunt and groan while producing a bowel movement, and everyone in the house (except her, of course) will be able to smell it, but she has no idea there's any connection between the feeling she gets when she's filling a diaper and the actual contents. If anybody's being "trained" at this age it's the parents, who may have learned to recognize their baby's signals and rush her to the toilet. But rest assured, the baby can't do it on her own.

At about fifteen months your baby will begin associating what's in her diaper with herself and may announce from time to time that she's produced something. But only after the fact. At eighteen months she may occasionally announce that she is *about* to do something, but she still hasn't learned how to hold it in long enough to get to a toilet. For the best results, unless your child is extremely interested, wait until she's at least two before seriously starting to toilet "train" her.

In the meantime, however, you can help increase your child's awareness of what's going on in her diapers by talking about the process as it's happening. As you're changing her, show the baby what she's done, but don't emphasize the yuckiness of it. Instead, say something admiring, like "Hey, that's a pretty impressive load—someday you'll do this in the toilet like me and mommy."

♦ A hint for easing the process of giving up the bottle: If the baby protests her missing bottle, offer her some solid food first. The theory here is that if she's full before starting the bottle, she won't be as interested in it and will miss it less when it's gone.

Perfectly Good Reasons to Continue Limited Breastfeeding

- The baby likes it.
- Your partner likes it, likes the contact and connection with the baby, and doesn't want to give it up.
- It's more natural, cheaper, and more convenient than prepared food.

Making the Switch

On one occasion while my wife was still nursing, she got held up in meetings and couldn't get home to feed the baby. If our daughter had been used to taking a bottle, this wouldn't have been a problem. But I'd only tried once or twice to get her to take a bottle and hadn't put up much of a fight when she'd spit it out. My punishment for having been so lax was that I had to drive

Temperament Tidbits

How well your baby makes the transition from breastfeeding to bottle-feeding or cups may depend more on his temperament than on any other factor. According to temperament researcher Jim Cameron:

- Extremely active toddlers with high-frustration tolerance (they aren't easily frustrated) usually wean themselves. They prefer bottles to breast because of the convenience.
- Highly active, slow-to-adapt kids also like the independence and convenience of a bottle or cup during the day. But they'll still want to nurse in the morning and at night.
- Active kids who don't tolerate frustration as well, however, know that parents are quite helpful in overcoming frustration. To them, giving up nursing means giving up support and help from parents and they won't be in any hurry to do it.
- Slow-adapting kids see the breast as security and won't want to give it up without a fight, especially at night. A gradual phase-out is particularly important for these kids.
- Moderately high-energy, high-adjustability kids wean themselves naturally.
- Kids who are moderately high in activity level and moderately low in frustration tolerance are fairly ambivalent about weaning. They'll generally take their direction from you and your partner.

twenty miles to my wife's office—with the baby screaming at the top of her lungs—so she could nurse. The moral of the story is: start getting the baby used to taking a bottle as early as possible (but not before she's completely comfortable with the breast). Here are some things you can do to get even the most committed breastfeeder to give the bottle a try:

- Use smaller bottles and nipples. Keep experimenting until you find a size and style the baby likes. If she's got a pacifier, try a bottle nipple that is shaped like the one on her pacifier.
- When introducing the bottle, hold the baby in the position she's in for breastfeeding.
- Ease the transition by filling bottles or cups with expressed breast milk. Some women find pumping very painful, so leave this one up to your partner.
- Go slow. Introduce the bottle for a few minutes at first, then add a minute or two every day.
- Phase out gradually. Kids tend to be more attached to the morning and evening feedings, so start by eliminating your baby's midday feeding(s) first. If that goes well for a few days, drop the morning feeding next. Of course, exceptions can be made: we dropped the evening feeding first because our daughters were getting up at five in the morning to eat anyway. So why not nurse (and hope the baby goes back to sleep again), rather than get out of a warm bed.
- A tip: Make sure your partner is out of the house (or at least out of sight in another room) when you're trying to give the baby a bottle. If your partner (actually, her breasts) are within smelling distance, your baby may refuse the bottle.
- A warning: The American Academy of Pediatrics suggests not starting your baby on cow's milk until after the baby's first birthday.

When *Not* to Wean Your Baby

No matter how old your baby is or how long he's been breast- or bottle-feeding, there are a few really rotten times to try to wean him:

- Any impending or recent major transition that might make the baby feel vulnerable, out of control, and in need of extra parental support. Moving to a new home, the birth of a younger sibling or the announcement of pregnancy, a new baby-sitter, and starting day care are good examples.
- If the baby has been sick.
- If you or your partner are under some kind of extreme pressure.
- If the baby is teething.

Family Matters

Ch-Ch-Ch-Changing Relationships

Considering how small and helpless babies are, it's sometimes surprising just how much of an impact they can have on the lives of the adults around them. Just think, for example, about how different things are for you now compared to your prefatherhood life.

Babies create new relationships in people's lives simply by being born: you and your partner have gone from being children to being parents, your parents are now grandparents, your brothers and sisters are uncles and aunts, and so on. And naturally, those relationships (as well as the rights and responsibilities that go with them) will take some getting used to.

But perhaps babies' greatest power is their ability to change profoundly the relationships that had existed long before they were born.

Your Changing Relationship with Your Partner

"Most couples approach parenthood imagining the new baby will bring them closer together, giving them a new and deeper sense of 'us,'" writes researcher Jay Belsky. For most families, things ultimately work out this way. But Belsky found that in the early stages of parenthood a new baby "tends to push his mother and father apart by revealing the hidden and half-hidden differences in their relationship."

Not surprisingly, says Phil Cowan, "differences between partners lead to feeling distant, that feeling distant tends to stimulate conflict, and that increased conflict, in turn, affects both partners' feelings about the marriage."

Some of the differences are aggravated because, although their feelings about their relationship with each other are very similar, men and women rarely feel the same thing at the same time. Many women, for example, tend to experience a major drop in their level of satisfaction with the marriage within six months of the baby's birth. Among the common reasons for this are a woman's feelings about her postbirth body, her perception that her partner is less interested in her, and her dissatisfaction with the workload around the house.

Many men, too, go through a decline in satisfaction with their marriages, but usually not until twelve to eighteen months after the baby's birth. This is when financial issues, fears about not being loved by the baby, and feelings of being left out by their partners are uppermost in their minds.

Although declining satisfaction with a marriage sounds bad, Phil Cowan believes it doesn't necessarily have to be so. "Given that men's and women's

Baby's First Birthday Party

Let's get one thing straight: your baby's first birthday party is really more for you than for her. She won't help you put together the guest list, is too little to play Pin the Tail on the Donkey or to bob for apples, and will probably be more interested in the wrapping paper than in what's inside it.

Here are a couple of first birthday dos and don'ts:

- Don't knock yourself out planning special activities. At this age your baby will prefer the familiar to the new almost every time.
- Don't invite too many kids—two or three is plenty. And limit the adults to six or seven. Any more and you run the risk of overwhelming the baby.
- Don't make a huge cake (unless the adults plan to eat it). And remember: no nuts, honey, or cow's milk.
- Save the clowns and masks for next year or the year after. Kids under two or three are more often scared by masks than entertained.
- Keep the party short (no more than an hour) and try not to have it conflict with nap or sleep times or any other time when your baby tends to be cranky.
- Don't go overboard on gifts. And don't demand or even expect wild declarations of thanks or any other great performances for the cameras. It's just not going to happen.
- Give identical party favors to any other child guests. Make sure your baby gets one as well.
- Get presents (smaller ones) for any older or younger siblings.
- Keep a list (or have someone else do it) of who gave what so you can send thank-yous later.

energies are not infinitely expandable," he writes, "it may be adaptive for some energy to be diverted from the couple relationship in the service of attending to the needs of the infant or young child. . . . Those who can adopt the perspective that placing the marriage on the back burner is a regrettable but temporary state of affairs may be able to return to enhanced relationship satisfaction and quality in the future."

Here are a few of the very positive ways the baby can affect your life and your relationship with your partner.

- You may feel a sense of gratefulness to the baby for enabling you to feel what it's like to be loved and to love more deeply than you ever have before.

- For some men having a baby is like having a great new toy and may give you a chance to relive certain parts of your childhood.
- The baby may bring you and your partner closer together and may make the two of you feel more deeply committed to the marriage and to making it work. You now also have someone to pass along new and old family traditions to.
- The baby may give you and your partner a sense of tremendous pride at having jointly created something absolutely amazing.

Parent/Grandparent Relationships

THE GOOD . . .

- After becoming parents, most men feel closer to their parents, especially their fathers. Even those who don't feel closer are usually at least willing to end, or put behind them, long-running family disputes.
- Seeing your parents in action with your child may bring back happy memories of your own childhood. You may also be pleasantly surprised at how

"Do you remember any of those things people said we'd tell our grandkids someday?"

your parents have changed since you were young. The father who may not have had much time for you, for example, may now spend hours with his grandchild. And the mother who limited your junk food intake to half a stick of sugarless gum a week may be a little more relaxed now.

- Now that you know exactly how much work it is to be a parent, you may be feeling a bit more appreciative of what your own parents did—and sacrificed—for you.
- After all these years of being a child, you're in charge now; if they want to be with the baby, they'll have to do things *your* way.
- You'll develop a closer relationship with your in-laws.

THE BAD . . .

- Seeing your parents in action with your child may bring back unhappy memories of your own childhood. And if your parents are treating the baby differently than they treated you, you may be jealous, feeling that the love your baby is getting should really be yours.
- Your parents may not be supportive or accepting of your increased role in your child's life.
- They may want to assume a role in your child's life—either too involved or not involved enough—that you aren't happy with. Grandparents are free to love their grandchildren without any of the restrictions of parenthood, says psychologist Brad Sachs.
- There may be some friction between your parenting style and that of your parents, between the way you react to the baby's needs and the way they do. It's not uncommon to hear from one's parents statements such as: "I did a pretty good job of raising my own kids, so don't tell me how to . . ." or "Don't you think it's time she [your partner] stopped nursing that child?"
- If you think they did a lousy job as parents, you may be afraid of repeating their mistakes.
- If your parents live nearby, they may always be "in the neighborhood," and you might be seeing them more than you really care to.
- There may be disputes and power struggles between your parents and your partner's about their grandparental roles.

However your relationship with your parents and/or in-laws changes, remember this: "A loving and vigorous bond between the grandparent and grandchild," writes Sachs, "is not just related to, but *essential* to, the emotional health and stability of *all three generations.*"

Other Relationships

Without really thinking about it, you and your partner will find that your relationships with friends and other nonimmediate family members have changed.

- You may be interested (or at least more interested than you were before becoming a parent) in getting together with relatives your own age, especially those with kids, so that the next generation can get to know their cousins.
- Your circle of closer friends will gradually change to include more couples, especially couples with kids.
- While your child is young, she'll be happy to play with whomever you introduce her to, and her first friends are most likely going to be *your* friends' kids. But as she gets older and starts meeting other kids on her own in parks and preschools, your child will take on a more active role in the family social committee, and all of a sudden you'll find yourself socializing with *her* friends' parents.
- Relationships between you and other adults may continue longer than they otherwise might because the kids like getting together.
- Relationships can be affected by competition: whose kid walks, talks, reads, or even sings first. As minor as it sounds, this can have a dramatic effect on your friendships. My wife and I used to get together fairly regularly with a couple whose two kids were just a few months older than ours. We all had a lot in common and got along fine, but the woman couldn't stop comparing her kids to ours—usually right in front of them—and hers, surprisingly, always came up on the short end. It was all very nice to hear how great our kids were, but after a while my wife and I couldn't stand it any more and the friendship eventually fizzled out.

Going Public with Fatherhood

In the concluding chapter of *The Expectant Father* I painted a rather gloomy portrait of the ways men and women—both individually and collectively as a society—actively discourage men from getting involved with their children. Sadly, in the several years since the publication of that book, little has changed. Men still don't get the support and encouragement they so sorely need to assume a greater nurturing role.

Fortunately, though, more and more men are expressing their dissatisfaction with this Neanderthal status quo. And we're just now starting to see the results of a modest revolution that's been going on quietly for more than twenty years.

Today, some 90 percent of fathers (even those who don't or won't live with their kids) are present at their children's births—more than triple the percentage in 1974. Seventy-five percent of men say their jobs conflict with their family responsibilities—up from only 12 percent in 1977; 74 percent say they'd give up their fast-track job for a "daddy-track" job that would allow them to spend more time with their families; and 30 percent reported actually having turned down a job promotion or transfer for the same reason.

Of course, some of these dramatic changes may have been born out of economic necessity: more and more mothers are entering the workplace and someone else has to step in to share the child-care burden. But in my view, the more significant reason for the nurturing-father revolution has to do with men themselves.

Most men, especially those whose fathers were physically or emotionally absent, instinctively know what they missed when they were young. And just as they know they were deprived of a relationship with their fathers, they know that their fathers were deprived of relationships with them.

More than turning down a job promotion or transfer, the real measure of a man's commitment to a new kind of relationship with his kids is how he feels about being a father and about the impact fatherhood is having on his life.

In one major study, researchers found that fathers generally see fathering as an important and satisfying experience. They disagree that only mothers should be responsible for discipline or for caring for a sick child; rather, they consider parenting a partnership experience to be shared equally with their wives.

Clearly, things are changing for fathers—perhaps not as quickly as we would like, but they are changing. "Discussion is growing on on-line computer networks. Men's centers and private-practice therapists are beginning to offer fathers' groups," writes Steven Harris, editor of *Full-Time Dad* magazine. "Fathers are tentatively pushing their way into play-groups and other informal gatherings, once the domain of mothers exclusively. The life of the father is expanding, slowly but surely."

Still, far too many men continue to devalue the importance of the role they play in their children's lives. Too many children have missed having a relationship with their fathers, and too many fathers have missed having relationships with their children.

As a new father, you are in a unique position to break this cycle and to make the word *fatherhood* as synonymous with childrearing and nurturing as *motherhood.* And there's no better time to start than right now.

For most new fathers, the last few months of their first year as parents are a time of relative calm. They've dealt with the big emotional, professional, and personal hurdles of fatherhood and are now comfortably juggling their

"My father wakes up the sun every morning. What does your father do?"

roles as husband, father, provider, and son. In short, they're finally feeling "like a family," and are entering what Bruce Linton calls the "community phase" of fatherhood.

As a result, says Linton, at this stage many new fathers feel ready to socialize—along with their partners and children—with other families, and use their fatherhood as a way to participate more actively in the public domain. They typically take on a more active role in their churches or synagogues, and they experience a heightened sense of *public* responsibility. Issues such as the quality of schools, city planning and zoning, the environment, and public safety become much more pressing than before.

Other researchers have confirmed Linton's theory. "Parenting brings new levels of insight and social commitment," write Barbara and Philip Newman, "that contribute in positive ways to the overall evolution of the culture."

In the introduction to this book, I quoted author Michael Levine, who said that "having children makes you no more a parent than having a piano makes you a pianist." Well, at this point you may not be any closer to being a pianist than you were a year ago. But there's no doubt that you're a parent. And a pretty good one at that.

Selected Bibliography

Books

Ames, Louise Bates, and Carol Chase Haber. *Your One Year Old: The Fun-Loving, Fussy 12- to 24-Month-Old.* New York: Delta, 1982.

Barry, Dave. *Bad Habits.* New York: Henry Holt, 1985.

Belsky, Jay, and John Kelly. *The Transition to Parenthood: How a First Child Changes a Marriage: Why Some Couples Grow Closer and Others Apart.* New York: Delacorte, 1994.

Berman, Phyllis W., and Frank A. Pedersen. *Men's Transitions to Parenthood: Longitudinal Studies of Early Family Experience.* Hillsdale, N.J.: Erlbaum, 1987.

Bettelheim, Bruno. *A Good Enough Parent: A Book on Child-Rearing.* New York: Vintage, 1987.

Biller, Henry B. *Fathers and Families: Paternal Factors in Child Development.* Westport, Conn.: Auburn House, 1993.

Biller, Henry B., and Robert J. Trotter. *The Father Factor: What You Need to Know to Make a Difference.* New York: Pocket Books, 1994.

Bluestine, Eric. *The Ways Children Learn Music: An Introduction and Practical Guide to Music Learning Theory.* Chicago: GIA Publications, 1995.

Bornstein, M. H., ed. *Handbook of Parenting.* Hillsdale, N.J.: Erlbaum, 1995.

Brazelton, T. Berry, and Bertrand Cramer. *The Earliest Relationship: Parents, Infants, and the Drama of Early Attachment.* Reading, Mass.: Addison-Wesley, 1990.

Bronstein, Phyllis, and Carolyn Pape Cowan, eds. *Fatherhood Today: Men's Changing Role in the Family.* New York: John Wiley & Sons, 1988.

Britton, James. *Language and Learning: The Importance of Speech in Children's Development.* New York: Penguin, 1970.

Brott, Armin, and Jennifer Ash. *The Expectant Father: Facts, Tips, and Advice for Dads-to-Be.* New York: Abbeville Press, 1995.

Butler, Dorothy. *Babies Need Books.* New York: Atheneum, 1980.

Canfield, Ken. *The Heart of a Father.* Chicago: Northfield, 1996.

Caplan, Frank, ed. *The First Twelve Months of Life.* New York: Grosset & Dunlap, 1973.

Cath, Stanley H., et al., eds. *Fathers and Their Families.* Hillsdale, N.J.: Analytic Press, 1989.

———. *Father and Child: Developmental and Clinical Perspectives.* Hillsdale, N.J.: Analytic Press, 1994.

Cowan, Carolyn Pape, and Philip A. Cowan. *When Partners Become Parents: The Big Life Change for Couples.* New York: HarperCollins, 1992.

Cullinan, Bernice E., and Lee Galda. *Literature and the Child,* 3d ed. Orlando, Fla.: Harcourt Brace, 1994.

Cutchins, Judy, and Ginny Johnston. *Parenting Papas: Unusual Animal Fathers.* New York: Morrow Junior Books, 1994.

Drobeck, Bruce. "The Impact on Men of the Transition to Fatherhood: A Phenomenological Investigation." Dissertation, 1990.

Eisenberg, Arlene, et al. *What to Expect the First Year.* New York: Workman, 1989.

Flint Public Library. *Ring a Ring O'Roses: Finger Plays for Pre-School Children.* Flint, Mich.: Flint Public Library, n.d.

Fraiberg, Selma H. *The Magic Years: Understanding and Handling the Problems of Early Childhood.* New York: Scribner's, 1959.

Galinsky, Ellen. *Between Generations: The Six Stages of Parenthood.* New York: Times Books, 1981.

Gordon, Edwin E. *A Music Learning Theory for Newborn and Young Children.* Chicago: GIA Publications, 1990.

Greene, Ellin. *Books, Babies, and Libraries: Serving Infants, Toddlers, Their Parents, and Caregivers.* Chicago: ALA Books, 1991.

Greenspan, Stanley, and Nancy Thorndike Greenspan. *First Feelings: Milestones in the Emotional Development of Your Baby and Child.* New York: Penguin, 1985.

Hanson, Shirley M. H., and Frederick W. Bozett. *Dimensions of Fatherhood.* Beverly Hills, Calif.: Sage, 1985.

Hass, Aaron. *The Gift of Fatherhood: How Men's Lives Are Transformed by Their Children.* New York: Fireside, 1994.

Hochschild, Arlie. *The Second Shift: Working Parents and the Revolution at Home.* New York: Viking, 1989.

Jacob, S. H. *Your Baby's Mind.* Holbrook, Mass.: Bob Adams, 1991.

Jordan, Pamela L. "The Mother's Role in Promoting Fathering Behavior." In *Becoming a Father: Contemporary Social, Developmental, and Clinical Perspectives,* J. L. Shapiro, et al., eds. New York: Springer Publications, 1995, pp. 61–71.

Karen, Robert. *Becoming Attached: Unfolding the Mystery of the Infant-Mother Bond and Impact on Later Life.* New York: Warner Books, 1994.

Kitzinger, S. *The Experience of Breastfeeding.* Middlesex, England: Penguin, 1987.

Kropp, Paul. *Raising a Reader: Make Your Child a Reader for Life.* New York: Doubleday, 1996.

Kutner, Lawrence. *Your School-Age Child.* New York: William Morrow, 1996.

Lamb, Michael E., ed. *The Role of the Father in Child Development.* New York: John Wiley, 1981.

Leach, Penelope. *Babyhood.* New York: Knopf, 1974 (1983).

Lehane, Stephen. *Help Your Baby Learn: 100 Piaget-Based Activities for the First Two Years of Life.* New York: Prentice Hall, 1976.

Linton, Bruce. "The Phases of Paternal Development: Pregnancy Through Twelve Months Post-Partum." Dissertation, 1991.

Marino, Jane, and Dorothy F. Houlihan. *Mother Goose Time: Library Programs for Babies and Their Caregivers.* New York: H. W. Wilson, 1992.

Marzollo, Jean. *Fathers and Babies.* New York: HarperPerennial, 1993.

Minnesota Fathering Alliance. *Working with Fathers: Methods and Perspectives.* Stillwater, Minn.: nu ink unlimited, 1992.

Newman, Barbara M., and Philip R. Newman. *Development Through Life: A Psychosocial Approach,* 6th ed. Pacific Grove, Calif.: Brooks/Cole Publishing, 1994.

Pagnoni, Mario. *Computers and Small Fries: A Computer-Readiness Guide for Parents of Tots, Toddlers and Other Minors.* Wayne, N.J.: Avery Publishing, 1987.

Parke, Ross D. *Fathers,* rev. ed. Cambridge, Mass.: Harvard University Press, 1996.

———. "Fathers and Families." In *Handbook of Parenting,* M. H. Bornstein, ed. Hillsdale, N.J.: Erlbaum, 1995.

Parke, Ross D., and Barbara R. Tinsley. "The Father's Role in Infancy: Determinants of Involvement in Caregiving and Play." In *The Role of the Father in Child Development,* Michael Lamb, ed. New York: Wiley, 1981.

Platt, Harvey J. *Your Living Trust and Estate Plan: How to Maximize Your Family's Assets and Protect Your Loved Ones.* New York: Allworth Press, 1995.

Pleck, Joseph H. "Are 'Family Supportive' Employer Policies Relevant to Men?" In *Men, Work, and Family,* Jane C. Hood, ed. Newbury Park, Calif.: Sage, 1993.

Pruett, Kyle D. "The Nurturing Male: A Longitudinal Study of Primary Nurturing Fathers." In *Fathers and Their Families,* Stanley Cath et al., eds. Hillsdale, N.J.: Analytic Press, 1989.

Sachs, Brad E. *Things Just Haven't Been the Same: Making the Transition from Marriage to Parenthood.* New York: William Morrow, 1992.

Schaffer, Judith, and Christina Lindstrom. *How to Raise an Adopted Child.* New York: Crown, 1989.

Sears, William, and Martha Sears. *The Baby Book: Everything You Need to Know about Your Baby—From Birth to Age Two.* New York: Little Brown, 1993.

Snarey, John. *How Fathers Care for the Next Generation: A Four-Decade Study.* Cambridge, Mass.: Harvard University Press, 1993.

Spangler, Doug. *Fatherhood: An Owner's Manual.* Richmond, Calif.: Fabus, 1994.

Spock, Benjamin, and Michael B. Rothenberg. *Dr. Spock's Baby and Child Care.* New York: Pocket Books, 1992.

Steinberg, David. *Fatherjournal.* Albion, Calif.: Times Change Press, 1977.

Sullivan, S. Adams. *The Father's Almanac,* rev. ed. New York: Doubleday, 1992.

Trelease, Jim. *The New Read-Aloud Handbook.* New York: Penguin, 1989.

Tyson, Eric. *Personal Finance for Dummies.* Foster City, Calif.: IDG Books, 1995.

Ulene, Art, and Steven Shelov. *Discovery Play: Loving and Learning with Your Baby.* Berkeley, Calif.: Ulysses Press, 1994.

White, Burton L. *The First Three Years of Life: The Revised Edition.* New York: Prentice Hall, 1985.

Journal Articles

Bailey, William T. "Fathers' Involvement and Responding to Infants: 'More' May Not be 'Better.'" *Psychological Reports* 74 (1994): 92–94.

———. "Psychological Development in Men: Generativity and Involvement with Young Children." *Psychological Reports* 71 (1992): 929–30.

Barrett-Goldfarb, Minna, and Grover J. Whitehurst. "Infant Vocalizations as a Function of Parental Voice Selection." *Developmental Psychology* 8, no. 2 (1973): 273–76.

Baumrind, Diana. "Current Patterns of Parental Authority." *Developmental Psychology Monograph* 4, no. 1, part 1 (1971): 1–101.

Cohn, Deborah A., et al. "Working Models of Childhood Attachment and Couple Relationships." *Journal of Family Issues* 13, no. 4 (1992): 432–49.

Condry, John, and Sandra Condry. "Sex Differences: A Study of the Eye of the Beholder." *Child Development* 47 (1976): 812–19.

Condry, John, and David F. Ross. "Sex and Aggression: The Influence of Gender Label on the Perception of Aggression in Children." *Child Development* 56 (1985): 225–33.

DeLuccie, Mary F. "Mothers as Gatekeepers: A Model of Maternal Mediators of Father Involvement." *Journal of Genetic Psychology* 156, no. 1 (1994): 115–31.

Deutsch, Francine M., et al. "Taking Credit: Couples' Reports of Contributions to Child Care." *Journal of Family Issues* 14, no. 3 (1993): 421–37.

Dickstein, Susan, and Ross D. Parke. "Social Referencing in Infancy: A Glance at Fathers and Marriage." *Child Development* 59 (1988): 506–11.

Fagot, Beverly I. "The Influence of Sex of Child on Parental Reactions to Toddler Children." *Child Development* 49 (1978): 459–65.

———. "Sex Differences in Toddlers' Behavior and Parental Reaction." *Developmental Psychology* 10, no. 4 (1974): 554–58.

Fagot, Beverly, and Richard Hagan. "Aggression in Toddlers: Responses to the Assertive Acts of Boys and Girls." *Sex Roles* 12, nos. 3–4 (1985): 341–51.

———. "Observations of Parent Reactions to Sex-Stereotyped Behaviors: Age and Sex Effects." *Child Development* 62 (1991): 617–28.

Field, T., S. Schanberg, et al. "Tactile/Kinesthetic Stimulation Effects on Preterm Neonates." *Pediatrics* 77, no. 5 (1986): 654–58.

Frisch, Hannah L. "Sex Stereotypes in Adult-Infant Play." *Child Development* 48 (1977): 1671–75.

Gambill, Lionel. "Can More Touching Lead to Less Violence in Our Society?" *Human Touch* 1, no. 3 (1985): 1–3.

Goldbloom, Richard B. "Behavior and Allergy: Myth or Reality?" *Pediatrics in Review* 13, no. 8 (1992): 312–13.

Gordon, Betty Nye. "Maternal Perception of Child Temperament and Observed Mother-Child Interaction." *Child Psychiatry and Human Development* 13, no. 3 (1983): 153–65.

Hall, Wendy A. "New Fatherhood: Myths and Realities." *Public Health Nursing* 11, no. 4 (1994): 219–28.

Haugland, Susan W. "The Effect of Computer Software on Preschool Children's

Developmental Gains." *Journal of Computing in Childhood Education* 3, no. 1 (1992): 15–20.

Jewett, Don L., et al. "A Double-Blind Study of Symptom Provocation to Determine Food Sensitivity." *New England Journal of Medicine* 323, no. 7 (1990): 429–33.

Jordan, Pamela L. "Laboring for Relevance: Expectant and New Fatherhood." *Nursing Research* 39, no. 1 (1990): 11–16.

Jordan, Pamela L., et al. "Breastfeeding and Fathers: Illuminating the Darker Side." *Birth* 19, no. 4 (1990): 210–13.

———. "Supporting the Father When an Infant is Breastfed." *Journal of Human Lactation* 9, no. 1 (1993): 31–34.

Krupper, Jan C., and Ina C. Uzgiris. "Fathers' and Mothers' Speech to Young Infants." *Journal of Psycholinguistic Research* 16, no. 6 (1987): 597–614.

Lamme, Linda, and Athol B. Packer. "Bookreading Behaviors of Infants." *Reading Teacher* 39, no. 6 (1986): 504–9.

Lovestone, S., and R. Kumar. "Postnatal Psychiatric Illness: The Impact of Partners." *British Journal of Psychiatry* 163 (1993): 210–16.

McBride, B. A., and G. Mills. "A Comparison of Mother and Father Involvement with Their Preschool Age Children. *Early Childhood Research Quarterly* 8 (1993): 457–77.

MacDonald, Kevin, and Ross D. Parke. "Parent-Child Physical Play: The Effects of Sex and Age of Children and Parents." *Sex Roles* 15, nos. 7–8 (1986): 367–78.

McKenna, James J., and Sara Mosko. "Evolution and Infant Sleep: An Experimental Study of Infant-Parent Co-Sleeping and Its Implications for SIDS." *ACTA Paediatrica: An International Journal of Paediatrics* 82, supplement 389 (June 1993): 31–35.

Medoff, David, and Charles E. Schaefer. "Children Sharing the Parental Bed: A Review of the Advantages and Disadvantages of Cosleeping." *Psychology: A Journal of Human Behavior* 30, no. 1 (1993): 1–9.

Newman, Philip R., and Barbara Newman. "Parenthood and Adult Development." *Marriage and Family Review* 12, nos. 3–4 (1988): 313–37.

Nicolson, P. "A Brief Report of Women's Expectations of Men's Behaviour in the Transition to Parenthood: Contradictions and Conflicts for Counselling Psychology Practice." *Counselling Psychology Quarterly* 3, no. 4 (1990): 353–61.

Palm, G. "Involved Fatherhood: A Second Chance." *Journal of Men's Studies* 2 (1993): 139–54.

Palm G., and Bill Joyce. "Attachment from a Father's Perspective." *Typescript*, 1994.

Papousek, Mechthild, et al. "Didactic Adjustments in Fathers' and Mothers' Speech to Their 3-Month-Old Infants." *Journal of Psycholinguistic Research* 16, no. 5 (1987): 491–516.

Power, Thomas G., et al. "Compliance and Self-Assertion: Young Children's Responses to Mothers Versus Fathers." *Developmental Psychology* 30, no. 6 (1994): 980–89.

Power, Thomas G., and Ross D. Parke. "Patterns of Early Socialization: Mother- and Father-Infant Interactions in the Home." *International Journal of Behavioral Development* 9 (1986): 331–41.

———. "The Paternal Presence." *Families in Society* 74, no. 1 (1993): 46–50.

Reis, Myrna, and Dolores Gold. "Relationship of Paternal Availability to Problem Solving and Sex-Role Orientation in Young Boys." *Psychological Reports* 40 (1977): 823–29.

Sampson, Hugh A., et al. "Fatal and Near-Fatal Anaphalyctic Reactions to Food in Children and Adolescents." *New England Journal of Medicine* 327, no. 6 (1992): 380–84.

Sorce, James F., et al. "Maternal Emotional Signaling: Its Effect on the Visual Cliff Behavior of 1-Year-Olds." *Developmental Psychology* 21, no. 1 (1985): 195–200.

Stayton, Donelda, et al. "Infant Obedience and Maternal Behavior: The Origins of Socialization Reconsidered." *Child Development* 42 (1971): 1057–69.

Whaley, Kimberlee K. "The Emergence of Social Play in Infancy: A Proposed Developmental Sequence of Infant-Adult Social Play." *Early Childhood Research Quarterly* 5, no. 3 (1990): 347–58.

Whitehurst, G. J., et al. "Accelerating Language Development Through Picture Book Reading." *Developmental Psychology* 24, no. 4 (1988): 552–59.

Resources

Adoption

NATIONAL ADOPTION CENTER offers a great list of questions to ask adoption agencies; addresses tax issues, single-parent issues, and legal issues; provides photos of kids waiting to be adopted, book reviews, lists of state and local contacts, and links to other adoption-related organizations.

1500 Walnut Street, Suite 701
Philadelphia, PA 19102
Tel.: (215) 735-9988
e-mail: nac@adopt.org
http://www.inetcom.net/adopt/nac/nac.html

Advice

FAMILY PLANET has a stable of columnists who dispense advice on just about every topic you can imagine.

http://family.starwave.com/experts/index.html

PARENTSPLACE.COM has one of the largest clearinghouses of parenting advice on the Net.

http://parentsplace.com/

At-Home Dads

"AT-HOME DAD" NEWSLETTER has just about everything a stay-at-home dad could want to know.

Peter Baylies, Publisher
61 Brightwood Ave.
North Andover, MA 01845
Tel.: (508) 685-7931
e-mail: athomedad@aol.com

NATIONAL AT-HOME DADS ASSOCIATION. A resource for all at-home dads who are the primary care providers to their children, this association is designed to help at-home dads connect with one another. NAHDA sponsors a national network for at-home dads and offers an extensive and growing resource list. Contact them for details at:

P.O. Box 1876
Coppell, TX 75019-1876
e-mail: fulltdad@aol.com

or write to Curtis Cooper, founder of the NAHDA, at:
120 Ashbrook Lane
Roswell, GA 30075
Tel.: (770) 643-6964

Babies

FAMILY INTERNET'S BABYCARE CORNER

http://www.familyinternet.com/babycare/babycare.htm

PARENTS' PAGE

http://members.aol.com/AllianceMD/parents.html

Two fact-filled resources written by pediatricians for parents of infants who need basic information fast (treating diaper rash, growth patterns, immunizations, introducing solid foods).

Computers

COMPUTERTOTS

Tel.: (800) 531-5053

Death and Grief

AMERICAN SUDDEN INFANT DEATH SYNDROME (SIDS) INSTITUTE

6065 Roswell Road, Suite 876
Atlanta, GA 30328
Tel.: (800) 232-7437
Fax: (404) 843-0577
e-mail: prevent@sids.org
http://www.sids.org/#Bereavement

SIDS NETWORK
9 Gonch Farm Road
Ledyard, CT 06339
http://sids-network.org/net.htm

Both organizations offer great resources, information, references, and support to help parents and other surviving family members deal with the tragedy of the death of a child.

Divorce

CHILDREN'S RIGHTS COUNCIL has a well-stocked catalog of resources, including a listing of great books on the subject for kids and their parents.
http://www.vix.com/crc/catalog.htm

SINGLE FATHERS HOMEPAGE
http://www.pitt.edu/~jsims/singlefa.html

Fun Stuff

BRITE has quite a comprehensive line of parenting aids, child development tools, phonics programs, and teaching ideas.
http://users.aol.com/clintg777/private/brite.html

CREATIVE CREATIONS has a constantly changing list of twenty fun things to do with kids of all ages.
http://www.waidsoft.com/funkids.html

ELLEN DAVIS also offers a bunch of fun activities.
http://ucunix.san.uc.edu/~edavis/kids-list/crafts/easy-and-fun.html

KIDS CRAFTBASE has great suggestions, advice, and products for doing art with kids of all ages.
http://www.vistek.com/kidcraft.htm

PARENTSPLACE.COM is the parents' resource center on the World Wide Web. It offers a constantly growing collection of articles, advice, and links to other great sites, as well as a newsletter.
http://www.parentsplace.com

General Fatherhood

FATHER TO FATHER is a wonderful source of information, referrals, and support.

12 McNeal Hall
1985 Buford Avenue
St. Paul, MN 55108
Tel.: (612) 626-1212
http://www.cyfc.umn.edu/FatherNet.htp

FATHERS HOTLINE can refer you to father-friendly organizations in your state or community.

Tel.: (512) 472-DADS (3237)
e-mail: dads@fathers.org

FATHER'S RESOURCE CENTER offers parenting classes, support groups, workshops, legal clinics, and reading lists, and publishes the quarterly newsletter "FatherTimes."

430 Oak Grove Street, Suite 105
Minneapolis, MN 55403
Tel.: (612) 874-1509
e-mail: frc@freenet.msp.mn.us
http://freenet.msp.mn.us/org/frc/index.html

FATHERWORK is a new home page designed to encourage good fathering. The folks at FatherWork view fathering not so much as a social role men play, but as the work they do each day to care for the next generation.

http://fatherwork.byu.edu

NATIONAL CENTER FOR FATHERING has resources designed to help men become more aware of their own fathering style and then work toward improving their skills. Call for a free issue of NCF's quarterly magazine, "Today's Father."

10200 West 75th Street, #267
Shawnee Mission, KS 66204-2223
Tel.: (913) 384-4661
Fax: (913) 384-4665
e-mail: ncf@aol.com
http://www.fathers.com

NATIONAL CENTER ON FATHERS & FAMILIES is a great source of research and data on fathers, father involvement, and so forth.
c/o University of Pennsylvania
3700 Walnut Street, Box 58
Philadelphia, PA 19104-6216
Tel.: (215) 898-5000

NATIONAL FATHERHOOD INITIATIVE offers membership that includes the quarterly newsletter "Fatherhood Today"; updates on family issues and political/legislative developments; the Fatherhood Resource Catalog of books, videos, and audio tapes, offering a discount on all items; and updates on activities and events.
600 Eden Road, Building E
Lancaster, PA 17601
Tel.: (800) 790-DADS or (717) 581-8860
Fax: (717) 581-8862

General Parenting

ERIC CLEARINGHOUSE. More information on parenting than you could ever possibly go through.
Tel.: (800) 583-4135 or (217) 333-1386
e-mail: ericeece@ux1.cso.uiuc.edu
http://ericps.ed.uiuc.edu/ericeece.html

FAMILY PLANET offers links, articles, and resources on just about everything from stranger anxiety to child safety.
http://family.starwave.com/resource/pra/Table_of_Contents.htm

NATIONAL COUNCIL ON FAMILY RELATIONS
Minneapolis, MN
Tel.: (612) 781-9331

"SMART FAMILIES" is a great newsletter published by Family University.
P.O. Box 500050
San Diego, CA 92150-0050
Tel.: (619) 487-7099
Fax: (619) 487-7356
e-mail: FamilyU@aol.com

Health Concerns

NATIONAL ORGANIZATION FOR RARE DISORDERS
P.O. Box 8923
New Fairfield, CT 06812-1783
Tel.: (800) 999-6673

NORTHWEST COALITION FOR ALTERNATIVES TO PESTICIDES (NCAP) publishes the *Journal of Pesticide Reform* as well as the information packets "Children and Pesticides" and "Planning for Non-chemical School Ground Maintenance."
P.O. Box 1393
Eugene, OR 97440
Tel.: (503) 344-5044
Fax: (503) 344-6923
e-mail: ncap@igc.apc.org

WEB DOCTOR will answer your specific questions on line.
http://www.parentsplace.com/readroom/health.html

Music

ADVENTURE KIDS MUSIC AND STORIES
http://www.rmii.com/dreamweaver/colors.gif

CENTER FOR MUSIC AND YOUNG CHILDREN
217 Nassau Street
Princeton, NJ 08542
Tel.: (609) 924-7801

MUSIC FOR PEOPLE
David Darling
Tel.: (203) 672-0275

On-line Conferences, Mailing Lists, and Newsletters

FATHER-L is an e-mail conference dedicated to discussing the importance of fathers in kids' lives. Send e-mail to listserv@vm1.spcs.umn.edu and write "subscribe father-l" in the body of the message. If you need more info, send a message to father-l@tc.umn.edu

PARENTING-L is a great way to get fifty quick, informative answers to just about any nonemergency question you might have. To subscribe, send e-mail to listserv@postoffice.cso.usuc.edu with "subscribe parenting-l" in the subject line.

THE PARENTS' LETTER is published by a pediatrician and filled with good, basic information on such topics as health maintenance, immunizations, illness, behavior, and parenting skills. To subscribe, send e-mail to majordomo@pobox.com with a blank subject line and "subscribe letter" in the body of the message.

OTHER PARENTING LISTS:

kids-newborn (0–2/3 months)
kids-infant (3 months–1 year)

To subscribe to one or more of the above, send e-mail to
listserv@vm.ege.edu.tr using the following format (substituting your own name for mine, of course):
sub kids-newborn Armin Brott
sub kids-infant Armin Brott

Reading and Other Media

CHILDREN'S LITERATURE provides reviews of the latest kids' books, videos, and computer games.

7513 Shadywood Road
Bethesda, MD 20817-9823
Tel.: (800) 469-2070 or (301) 469-2070 (yes, it's the same number)
Fax: (301) 469-2071

Temperament

TEMPERAMENT TALK

1100 K Avenue
La Grande, OR 97850
Tel.: (541) 962-8836
Fax: (541) 963-3572

Toys

VTECH has a wonderful array of high-tech toys for kids six months and older. For a catalog, write or call:

101 E. Palatine Road
Wheeling, IL 60090
Tel.: (800) 521-2010

Travel

FAMILY WORLD HOMEPAGE offers calendars (broken down into four regions) that include information on all sorts of fun places for families to visit in different parts of the country.

http://family.com

Twins

TWINLINE parenting consultation.

http://www.parentsplace.com/readroom/twins/twinline.html

For many more interesting web sites, check out Jean Armour Polly's *Internet Kids Yellow Pages* (Osborne McGraw-Hill, 1996). Despite the title, it's a wonderful source of resources for parents too.

If you have any comments or suggestions about the topics discussed in this book, you can send them to

Armin Brott
P.O. Box 2458
Berkeley, CA 94702
e-mail: armin@pacbell.net

Index

C

I

J

K

L

M

N

CARTOON CREDITS

© 1997 George Abbot from The Cartoon Bank,™ Inc.: pp. 15, 199; © 1997 Donna Barstow from The Cartoon Bank,™ Inc.: p. 159; © 1997 Frank Cotham from The Cartoon Bank,™ Inc.: pp. 24, 37; © 1997 Joseph Farris from The Cartoon Bank,™ Inc.: p. 107; © 1997 Ed Frascino from The Cartoon Bank,™ Inc.: pp. 175, 180, 185, 192, 212, 216; © 1997 Anne Gibbons from The Cartoon Bank,™ Inc.: p. 168; © 1997 William Haefeli from The Cartoon Bank,™ Inc.: pp. 26, 54; © 1997 John Jonik from The Cartoon Bank,™ Inc.: p. 120; © 1997 Arnie Levin from The Cartoon Bank,™ Inc.: p. 161; Robert Mankoff © 1986 from The New Yorker Magazine, Inc.: p. 134; © 1997 Peter Mueller from The Cartoon Bank,™ Inc.: pp. 93, 203; © 1997 J. P. Rini from The Cartoon Bank,™ Inc.: p. 85; © 1997 David Sipress from The Cartoon Bank,™ Inc.: pp. 2, 8, 72, 87, 104, 117, 160; © 1997 Peter Steiner from The Cartoon Bank,™ Inc.: p. 135; © 1997 Mick Stevens from The Cartoon Bank,™ Inc.: p. 181; © 1997 Jack Ziegler from The Cartoon Bank,™ Inc.: pp. 45, 97, 144, 148.

About the Author

Armin Brott, author of *The Expectant Father: Facts, Tips, and Advice for Dads-to Be* and a contributing writer to *BabyTalk* magazine, has written on fatherhood for the *New York Times Magazine, Newsweek,* the *Washington Post, American Baby* magazine, *Parenting* magazine, and many other periodicals. His weekly radio show on parenting is carried by one of the largest radio stations in the San Francisco Bay area. He and his family live in Berkeley, California.

Brenda + Jeff
Hewitt

The Expectant Father

Facts, Tips, and Advice for Dads-to-Be

"Just as your wife suspected, Mr. Sanders. You have a very little boy growing inside you."

The Expectant Father

Facts, Tips, and Advice for Dads-to-Be

Armin A. Brott and Jennifer Ash

Abbeville Press • Publishers
New York • Paris • London

To Tirzah and Talya,
who make the world a better place.—A.A.B.

For Joe, Clarke, and my parents, Clarke and Agnes Ash,
with love and affection.—J.A.

EDITOR: Jacqueline Decter
DESIGNER: Celia Fuller
PRODUCTION EDITOR: Abigail Asher
PRODUCTION MANAGER: Lou Bilka

Inquiries should be addressed to Abbeville Publishing Group, 22 Cortlandt Street, New York, N.Y. 10007. The text of this book was set in Bodoni Book. Printed and bound in the United States of America.

First edition
20 19 18 17 16 15 14 13 12 11 10

Cover photograph by Milton Heiberg. For cartoon credits, see page 215.

Library of Congress Cataloging-in-Publication Data
Brott, Armin A.
The expectant father : facts, tips, and advice for dads-to-be / Armin A. Brott and Jennifer Ash.
p. cm.
Includes bibliographical references and index.
ISBN 1-55859-690-9 (pb).—ISBN 0-7892-0417-7 (hc)
1. Fathers—Psychology. 2. Pregnancy—Psychological aspects.
I. Ash, Jennifer. II. Title.
HQ756.B76 1995
649'.1'0242—dc20 94-41096

Contents

Acknowledgments

Many people had a hand in creating this book and all deserve much gratitude. In particular, I'd like to thank David Cohen and Jackie Needleman, and Douglas and Rachel Arava for their careful reading of the manuscript and for their thoughtful, insightful comments and suggestions; and Michael Feiner and Jenny Shy, and Matthew and Janice Tannin for sharing their anecdotes, advice, and recipes.

Thanks also to Jackie Decter for her savvy advice and editing acumen, to Jim Levine and Arielle Eckstut for thinking of me at the right time, and especially to Jennifer Ash, whose idea made this project possible.

But by far the biggest thanks goes to my wife, Andrea Adam Brott, who read every draft, helped hone my ideas (while adding some of her own), and even managed a chuckle about the irony of our having to hire a babysitter so I could have enough time to write a book about how men can get more involved with their children. Without Andrea's love, encouragement, and support, this book wouldn't exist, and I would never have been able to enjoy the kind of relationship I now have with my children.

Armin A. Brott
November 1994

While awaiting the arrival of our first baby, I vowed to read every piece of printed advice on pregnancy and motherhood. It quickly became apparent that nine months wasn't sufficient time to digest all that was available for expectant mothers. However, my husband's bedside table remained bare, not for lack of interest but for want of resources. A heartfelt thanks to Joe, who convinced me men do want to know more about pregnancy and thus encouraged me to embark on this project. I'm also grateful to my brothers, Eric and Jim, and to the many friends who candidly discussed impending fatherhood and made insightful suggestions. Virginia Webb's and Esther Williams's advice about newborns was invaluable.

Sincere thanks to everyone at Abbeville, especially Alan Mirken, who supported this project from the onset. The enthusiasm of Bob Abrams and Mark Magowan kept it on track. Jackie Decter deftly guided the book to completion and her friendship made the journey a joy. Thanks to Armin Brott for agreeing to provide the narrative, which breathed male life into the book. Laura Straus made the inclusion of cartoons possible, and Celia Fuller's inspired design brought all of this to life.

Jennifer Ash
November 1994

J. GREER

Introduction

When my wife and I got pregnant in July 1989, I was the happiest I'd ever been. That pregnancy, labor, and the birth of our first daughter was a time of incredible closeness, tenderness, and passion. Long before we'd married, my wife and I had made a commitment to share equally in raising our children. And it seemed only natural that the process of shared parenting should begin during pregnancy.

Since neither of us had had children before, we were both rather ill-prepared for pregnancy. Fortunately for my wife, there were literally hundreds of books designed to educate, encourage, support, and comfort women during their pregnancies. But when I began to realize that I, too, was expecting, and that the pregnancy was bringing out feelings and emotions I didn't understand, I couldn't find any books to turn to. I looked for answers in my wife's pregnancy books, but information about what expectant fathers go through (if it was discussed at all) was at best superficial, consisting mostly of advice on how men could be supportive of their pregnant wives. And to make things worse, since my wife and I were the first couple in our circle of close friends to get pregnant, there was no one else I could talk to about what I was going through, no one who could reassure me that what I was feeling was normal and all right.

Until fairly recently, there has been precious little research on the man's emotional and psychological experiences during pregnancy. The very title of one of the first articles to appear on the subject should give you some idea of the medical and psychiatric communities' attitude toward the impact of pregnancy on men. Written by William H. Wainwright, M.D., and published in the July 1966 issue of the *American Journal of Psychiatry,* it was called "Fatherhood as a Precipitant of Mental Illness."

But as you'll soon find out, an expectant father's experience during the transition to fatherhood is not confined simply to excitement—or mental illness; if it were, this book would never have been written. The reality is that men's emotional response to pregnancy is no less varied than women's; expectant fathers feel everything from relief to denial, fear to frustration, anger to joy. And for anywhere from 22 to 79 percent of men, there are physical symptoms of pregnancy as well (more on this on pages 53–55).

So why haven't men's experiences been discussed more? In my opinion it's because we, as a society, value motherhood more than fatherhood, and we automatically assume that issues of childbirth and childrearing are women's issues. But as you'll learn—both from reading this book and from your own experience—this is simply not the case.

Who, Exactly, Has Written This Book?

When Jennifer Ash approached me about collaborating with her on *The Expectant Father,* we agreed that our goal was to help you understand and make sense of what you're going through during your pregnancy. That's an important goal, but one that is clearly dependent on your partner's *being* pregnant. A good understanding of your *partner's* perspective on the pregnancy—emotional as well as physical—is essential to understanding how *you* will react. It was precisely this perspective that Jennifer, whose son was born only a few days after my second daughter, provided. Throughout our collaboration she contributed valuable information and comments not only about what pregnant women are going through but also about the ways women most want men to stay involved.

A Note on Structure

Throughout the book, Jennifer and I try to present straightforward, practical information in an easy-to-absorb format. Each of the main chapters is divided into four sections as follows:

What She's Going Through

Even though this is a book about what you as an expectant father are going through during pregnancy, we felt it was important to summarize your partner's physical and emotional pregnancy experience as well.

What's Going On with the Baby

This section lets you in on your future child's progress—from sperm and egg to living, breathing infant.

What You're Going Through

This section covers the wide range of feelings—good, bad, and indifferent—you'll probably experience at some time during the pregnancy. It also describes the *physical* changes you may go through, as well as the ways the pregnancy may affect your sex life.

Staying Involved

While the "What You're Going Through" section covers the emotional and physical side of pregnancy, this section gives you specific facts, tips, and advice on what you can *do* to make the pregnancy yours as well as your partner's. For instance, you'll find easy, nutritious recipes to prepare, information on how to start a college fund for the baby, valuable advice on getting the most out of your birth classes, and tips about how to be supportive of your partner and stay included in the pregnancy.

The book covers more than the nine months of pregnancy. Jennifer and I have included a detailed chapter on labor and delivery and another on Cesarean section, both of which prepare you to understand and help your partner through the birth itself. Perhaps even more important, these chapters prepare you for the often overwhelming emotions you may experience when your partner is in labor and your child is born.

We've also included a special chapter that addresses the major questions and concerns you may have about caring for and getting to know your child after you bring him or her home. And finally, we've included a chapter called "Fathering Today," in which you'll learn to recognize—and overcome—the many obstacles contemporary fathers are likely to encounter.

As you go through the book, remember that each of us brings different emotional baggage to our pregnancies, and that none of us will react to the same situation in the same way. You may find that some of the feelings described in the "What You're Going Through" section in the third-month chapter won't really ring true for you until the fifth month, or that you have already experienced them in the first month. You may also want to try out some of the ideas and activities suggested in the "Staying Involved" sections in a different order. Feel free.

A Note on Terminology

Wife, Girlfriend, Lover . . .

In an attempt to avoid offending anyone (an approach that usually ends up offending *everyone*), we've decided to refer to the woman who's carrying the baby as "your partner."

Hospitals, Doctors . . .

We realize that not everyone who has a baby delivers in a hospital or is under the care of a medical doctor. Still, because this is the most frequent scenario, we've chosen to refer to the place where the baby will be born as "the hospital" and to the people attending the birth (besides you, of course) as "doctors," "nurses," "medical professionals," or "practitioners."

As a rule, today's fathers (and prospective fathers) want to be much more involved with their children than their own fathers were able to be. It's our belief that the first step on the road toward full involvement is to take an active role in the pregnancy. And it's our hope that when you're through reading *The Expectant Father*—which is the book Jennifer wishes she could have bought for her husband when she was pregnant and I wish I'd had both times my wife and I were pregnant—you'll be much better prepared to participate in this important new phase of your life.

The First Decisions

The first major questions you and your partner will face after learning you are pregnant are *Where are we going to have the baby?*, *Who is going to help us deliver it?*, and *How much is it all going to cost?* To a certain extent, the answers will be dictated by the terms of your insurance policy, but there are nevertheless a range of options to consider.

Where and How

Hospital Birth

For most couples—especially first-time parents—the hospital is the most common place to give birth. It's also the safest. In the unlikely event that complications arise, most hospitals have specialists on staff twenty-four hours a day and are equipped with all the necessary machinery and medications. And in those first hectic hours or days after the birth, the on-staff nurses monitor the baby and mother and help both new parents with the dozens of questions that are likely to come up. They also help fend off unwanted intrusions.

Many hospitals now have labor and delivery rooms that are decorated to look less like a hospital and more like a bedroom at home. The cozy decor is supposed to make you and your partner feel more comfortable. But with nurses dropping by every hour or so, and with tables full of sophisticated monitoring equipment and cabinets full of sterile supplies, it's hard to forget where you are.

Home Birth

With all their high-tech efficiency and stark, impersonal, antiseptic conditions, hospitals are not for everyone. So, if you don't feel particularly comfortable in

Risks of Home Birth

Things can happen during your pregnancy that might make a home birth unnecessarily risky: if your partner develops preeclampsia (pregnancy-induced hypertension, a fairly rare condition, but one that can have serious complications if not detected and treated early) or goes into labor prematurely, or if you find out that the baby is breech (feet down instead of head down) or that you're having twins (or more), you'll probably want to reconsider the hospital.

You also might want to reconsider the hospital if your partner suffers from diabetes, has a heart or kidney condition, has had hemorrhaging in a previous labor (a quick blood transfusion can be conducted at the hospital), has had a previous Cesarean section, or smokes cigarettes regularly. While plenty of people with these and other conditions have delivered perfectly healthy babies at home, the chances that complications can develop are significant, and you and your partner should make every effort to ensure the safest possible delivery.

hospitals, and you're not anticipating any complications during pregnancy, home birth can be a more relaxed option to consider.

But be prepared. Having a baby at home is quite a bit different than it's made out to be in those old westerns—you're going to need a lot more than clean towels and boiling water. If you are considering a home birth, contact a nurse-midwife who, at the very least, will be able to provide a list of the things you'll need.

My wife and I thought about a home birth for our second baby but ultimately decided against it. While I don't consider myself particularly squeamish, I just couldn't imagine how we'd avoid making a mess all over the bedroom carpet. What really clinched it for us, though, was that our first child had been an emergency Cesarean section; fearing that we might run into problems again, we opted to be near the doctors.

Natural Birth vs. Medicated

In recent years giving birth "naturally"—without drugs, pain medication, or any medical intervention—has become the most desirable method of delivery. But just because it's popular doesn't mean it's for everybody. Labor and delivery are going to be a painful experience—for both of you—and many couples elect to take advantage of the advances medical science has made in relieving the pain and discomfort of childbirth.

Be flexible. You may be planning a natural childbirth and conditions could develop that necessitate intervention or the use of medication (see pages 151–55). On the other hand, you may be planning a medicated delivery but could find yourself snowed in someplace far from your hospital and any pain medication.

Who's Going to Help?

At first glance, it may seem that your partner should be picking a medical practitioner alone—after all, *she's* the one who's going to be poked and prodded as the pregnancy develops. But considering that more than 90 percent of today's expectant fathers are present during the delivery of their children, and that the vast majority of them have been involved in some significant way during the rest of the pregnancy, *you're* probably going to be spending a lot of time with the practitioner as well. So if at all possible, you should feel comfortable with the final choice, too.

Private Obstetrician

If your partner is over twenty, she probably has been seeing a gynecologist for a few years. And since many gynecologists also do obstetrics, it should come as no surprise that most couples elect to have the woman's regular obstetrician/gynecologist (OB/GYN) deliver the baby.

Private OB/GYNs are generally the most expensive way to go, but your insurance company will usually pick up at least part of the bill. Private OBs also give their patients the most personal attention. Make sure, though, that you arrange to meet the other doctors in your OB's practice, in case the baby is born on a day when your doctor is not on call. Labor and delivery are going to be stressful enough without having to deal with a doctor you've never met before.

Midwife

Even if your partner has a regular OB, you might want to consider having a midwife deliver your baby. Midwives are specially trained in coaching women during labor and in delivering babies. Because of this training, many midwives—a good number of whom are also registered nurses—actually have more experience delivering babies than OB/GYNs.

Although midwives are not as common in the United States as they are in Europe, they're becoming increasingly popular. Many standard OB/GYN

What to Ask Your Prospective Practitioner

Before making a final decision about who's going to deliver the baby, you should get satisfactory answers to the following questions:

ESPECIALLY FOR OB/GYNS

- Do you allow family members and/or coaches to attend delivery?
- Do you recommend any particular childbirth preparation method (Lamaze, Bradley, and so on)?
- At which hospital do you deliver your babies?
- Are you board certified?
- Do you have any specialties or special training?
- How many partners do you have and how often are they on rotation?
- How many sonograms do you routinely recommend?
- Do you perform amniocentesis yourself?
- What percentage of your deliveries are Cesarean?
- Do you permit fathers to attend Cesarean sections?
- Do you routinely order medications, IV, enemas, fetal monitoring, or do you judge each situation individually?
- What is your policy on inducing labor?
- Do you usually perform an episiotomy?
- Can the mother lift the baby out herself if she wishes?

practices, recognizing that some of their patients might want to have a midwife in attendance at the birth, now have one or more on staff. Officially, then, your partner is still under the care of an M.D.—whose services can be paid for by insurance—but she'll still get the kind of care she wants. It's important to remember, though, that midwives are generally not trained to deal with birthing complications and must refer their "patients" to an M.D. if anything unusual or dangerous arises.

Many states strictly regulate the midwife's role, and midwives are frequently not allowed to do the actual delivery of the baby. If you're considering using a midwife, the American College of Nurse Midwives (see page 18) can put you in touch with one in your area and fill you in on any applicable regulations.

- Can the father?
- Do you routinely suction the baby during delivery?
- Do you usually hand the naked baby straight to the mother?
- Do you allow the mother or father to cut the umbilical cord?

ESPECIALLY FOR MIDWIVES

- Are you licensed?
- How many babies have you delivered?
- What M.D.s are you associated with?
- What position do most of the women you work with adopt for the second stage of labor?

FOR BOTH OB/GYNS AND MIDWIVES

- What are your rates and payment plans?
- What insurance, if any, do you honor?
- What percentage of your patients had natural, unmedicated births in the past year?
- Are you willing to wait until the umbilical cord has stopped pulsating before you clamp it?
- Can the baby be put to the breast immediately after delivery?
- Are you willing to dim the lights when the baby is born?

Family Physician

Your family doctor has probably delivered a few babies in his or her time. But since obstetrics isn't the focus of a family physician's practice, he or she probably doesn't know the support staff or the hospital procedures as well as the OB/GYN whose office is across the street and who delivers three babies a week there. In addition, many hospitals won't allow anyone but "recognized" OBs or midwives to admit patients to the delivery ward.

Nevertheless, if your doctor has delivered other babies in your family and you want him or her to deliver yours, it may be possible to make special arrangements. But if you go this route, make sure an OB will be around for the actual birth—just in case.

For More Information about Prenatal and Family Medical Care

American Academy of Pediatrics
141 Northwest Point Blvd.
Elk Grove Village, IL 60009
(708) 228-5005

American College of Nurse Midwives
818 Connecticut Avenue, N.W.
Washington, DC 20006
(202) 728-9860

American College of Obstetricians
and Gynecologists
409 12th Street, S.W.
Washington, DC 20024
(202) 638-5577

American Red Cross
17th & D Streets
Washington DC, 20006
(202) 737-8300

International Childbirth Education Association
8060 26th Avenue South
Bloomington, MN 55425
(612) 854-8660

Maternity Center Association
48 East 92nd Street
New York, NY. 10128
(212) 369-7300

Bills

Having a baby isn't cheap. Even if you have good insurance, the 20 percent (plus your deductible) that most policies make you pay can still add up in a hurry. In the sections that follow, you'll get an idea of how much a typical—and a not-so-typical—pregnancy and childbirth experience might cost. It's a

"Listen, are you absolutely sure *you want to have kids?"*

good idea to look over your insurance policy, find out about how much it will be picking up, and start putting together a budget now.

Pregnancy and Childbirth

Most doctors will charge one flat fee for your partner's care during the entire pregnancy. This should cover monthly visits during the first two trimesters, biweekly visits for the next month or so, and then weekly visits until delivery. But don't make the mistake of thinking that that's all you'll pay. Bills for blood and urine tests, ultrasounds, hospital fees, and other procedures will work their way into your mailbox at least once a month. Here's what you can expect to pay (before your insurance pays its part) for having your baby:

OB/GYN

$2,500 to $6,500 for general prenatal care and a problem-free vaginal delivery. Most doctors will meet with you to discuss their rates and the services they provide. For a list of important questions to ask, see pages 16–17. In addition, be sure to discuss which insurance plans, if any, they participate in;

whether they'll bill your insurance company directly or will want you to make a deposit (usually about 25 percent of the anticipated bill) up front; whether you can make your payments in installments; and whether they expect their fee to be paid in full *before* the delivery.

MIDWIFE

The average cost of a delivery by a midwife is $1,200.

Lab and Other Expenses

- Blood: Over the course of the pregnancy, you can expect to be billed anywhere from $100 to $700 for various blood tests.
- Ultrasound: At least $200 each. In an ordinary pregnancy, you'll have between none and three.

Prenatal Testing

If you and/or your practitioner decide that you're a candidate for amniocentesis or any other prenatal diagnostic test, you can expect to pay $800–1,200. In most cases genetic counseling is required beforehand, and that costs an additional $300–500. If you're having any prenatal testing done just because you'd like to find out the sex of the baby or want reassurance of its well-being (and not because you're in a high-risk group), your insurance company may not pay for it.

At the Hospital

- For a problem-free vaginal delivery and a twenty-four-hour stay, hospital charges will run anywhere from $1,000 to $2,500.
- If you're planning to spend the night in the hospital with your partner, hospitals will add about $200 per day extra to your bill.
- Anesthesiologists charge from $750 to $1,500 for an epidural, more for a spinal block, even more for a Cesarean section.

If Your Partner Has a Cesarean Section

If your partner requires a C-section, all bets are off. This is major surgery, and it is expensive. The operation, which your OB/GYN will perform, is not included in his or her flat fee, and you'll have to pay for at least two other doctors to assist, plus a pediatrician, who must be in attendance to care for the baby. In addition, a C-section entails a longer recovery period in the hospital—usually four to five days, as well as extra nursing care, pain medication, bandages, and other supplies. If the baby is in good health, he or she may be taken home, but chances are you will want him or her to stay with your partner, especially if she is breastfeeding. The baby's additional time in the nursery costs more, too. In our case, by the time all the bills had been paid, we (actually, mostly our insurance company) had shelled out more than $15,000 for the birth of our first child. That alone was just about enough to make us decide on a home birth for the second one (although we ultimately opted against it).

An Important (and Possibly Profitable) Word of Advice

Make sure that you and your partner check your birth-related bills *very* carefully. Hospitals can make mistakes, and they are rarely in your favor. After we'd recovered from the shock of the C-section bills (which started off at closer to $17,000), we asked a doctor friend to go over them with us. He found that we'd been charged for a variety of things that didn't happen and overcharged for a lot of the things that did. For example, we'd been billed $25 for a tube of ointment that the hospital's own pharmacy was selling for $1.25. And for the second pregnancy, our nit-picking review of the bills cut about 20 percent off the total.

Now here's the "profitable" part. Since your insurance company will probably be paying for most of your bills, they'll be ecstatic if your review ends up saving them money. In fact, some insurers are so thrilled that they'll actually give you a percentage (sometimes as much as half) of the money they save. Naturally, though, you'll have to ask for your reward. So, read your policy carefully and, if you still have questions, talk to your agent or one of the company's underwriters.

And while you're reading your insurance policy, here are a few other things to look out for:

- **How long before the birth does the insurer need to be notified about the pregnancy and estimated due date?** Not complying with the carrier's instructions could mean a reduction in the amount they'll pay for pregnancy and birth-related expenses.
- **When can the baby be added to the policy?** Until the baby is born, all pregnancy- and birth-related expenses will be charged to your partner. After the birth, however, your partner and the new baby will be getting separate checks (all baby-related expenses, such as medication, pediatrician's exams, diapers, blankets, and various other hospital charges, will be charged to the baby). Some carriers require you to add the baby to your (or your partner's) policy as far in advance as thirty days before the birth; others give you until thirty days after the birth. Again, failing to carefully follow the insurer's instructions could result in a reduction of coverage.

Your Rights to Free and Subsidized Medical Care

- Many state health departments operate free health clinics.
- Hospital emergency rooms are required by federal law to give you an initial assessment—and any required emergency care—even if you can't afford to pay.

Low-Cost Alternatives

Obstetrical Clinics

If you live in a city where there is a large teaching hospital, you may be able to have your baby at its obstetrical clinic. If so, you'll spend a lot less than you would have for a more traditional hospital birth. The one drawback is that your baby will probably be delivered by an inexperienced doctor or a medical student. This isn't to say that you won't be getting top-quality care. Clinics are often equipped with state-of-the-art equipment and the young professionals who staff them are being taught all the latest methods by some of the best teachers in the country—some of whom will be in the room supervising.

Notes:

THE 1ST MONTH

Salad Days

What She's Going Through

Physically

- Morning sickness (nausea, heartburn, vomiting)
- Food cravings—or aversions
- Headaches
- Fatigue
- Breast changes: tenderness, enlargement

Emotionally

- Thrilled that she's pregnant
- A heightened closeness to you
- Apprehension about the nine months ahead
- Mood swings and sudden, unexplained crying

What's Going On with the Baby

It's going to be a busy first month. About two hours after you had sex, the egg is fertilized, and after a full day or so there is a tiny bundle of quickly dividing cells. By the end of the month the embryo will be about ¼-inch long and will have a heart (but no brain), as well as arm and leg buds.

What You're Going Through

Thrills

I still have the white bathrobe I was wearing the morning my wife and I found out we were pregnant the first time. I stood nervously in the kitchen, the countertop cluttered with vials of colored powders and liquids, droppers, and the small container filled with my wife's "first morning urine." (Even as

Morning Sickness

About half of all pregnant women experience morning sickness. Despite the name, the nausea, heartburn, and vomiting traditionally associated with morning sickness can strike your partner at any hour of the day. Fortunately, for most women morning sickness disappears after about the third month. Until then, here are a few things you can do to help your partner cope with morning sickness:

- Help her maintain a high-protein, high-carbohydrate diet.
- Encourage her to drink a lot of fluids—especially milk. You might also want to keep a large water bottle next to the bed. She should avoid caffeine, which tends to be dehydrating.
- Be sensitive to the sights and smells that make her queasy—and keep them away from her.
- Encourage her to eat a lot of small meals throughout the day, and to eat *before* she starts feeling nauseated. She should try to eat basic foods like rice and yogurt, which are less likely to cause nausea than greasy foods.
- Make sure she takes her prenatal vitamins.
- Put some pretzels, crackers, or rice cakes by the bed—she'll need something to start and end the day with, and these are low in fat and calories.
- Be aware that she needs plenty of rest and encourage her to get it.

recently as 1989, do-it-yourself pregnancy detection kits were a lot more complicated than they are today.) Feeling like a Nobel prize–winning chemist on the edge of making a discovery that would alter the course of the entire world, I carefully dropped several drops of the urine into one of the vials of powder. I stirred the mixture with the specially provided swizzle stick, rinsed it, and slowly added the contents of the other vial.

In all honesty, the results we got twenty minutes later weren't a complete surprise. But that didn't make it any less thrilling. I'd always wanted to have children, and suddenly it seemed that all my dreams were finally going to come true.

Relief . . . and Pride

At the same time, I was filled with an incredible feeling of relief. Secretly, I'd always been afraid that I was sterile and that I'd have to be satisfied with

"Young kids today don't know how good they have it . . . I remember the old days before home pregnancy tests."

taking someone else's kids to the circus or the baseball game. I also felt a surge of pride. After all, I was a man, a fully functional man—all right, a stud, even. And by getting my wife pregnant, I'd somehow lived up to my highest potential.

Irrational Fears

At some point after the initial excitement and sense of relief, a surprising number of men find themselves experiencing an irrational fear that the child their partner is carrying is not theirs. Psychologist Jerrold Lee Shapiro interviewed more than two hundred men whose partners were pregnant, and found that 60 percent "acknowledged fleeting thoughts, fantasies, or nagging doubts that they might not really be the biological father of the child." The majority of these men don't actually believe their partners are having affairs. Rather, Shapiro writes, these feelings are symptoms of a common type of insecurity—the fear many men have that they simply aren't capable of doing anything as incredible as creating life, and that someone more potent must have done the job.

Staying Involved

Exercise

If your partner was already working out regularly before the pregnancy, she won't need any extra encouragement to exercise, and if her doctor approves, she can probably continue her regular physical fitness routine. Some health clubs will ask a pregnant woman to provide a letter from her doctor.

If she wasn't physically active before pregnancy, this isn't the time for her to take up rock climbing. That doesn't mean, however, that she should spend the entire pregnancy on the sofa. Getting sufficient exercise is critical. It will help improve her circulation, thereby ensuring that the baby has an adequate blood supply, and it will keep her energy level high. One way to help her get the exercise she needs is to work out with her. The key is to start easy and not to push her if you see she's feeling tired or winded.

If your budget doesn't permit joining a health club, a pregnancy exercise course is a less expensive alternative. There are also a number of pregnancy workout videotapes on the market.

Workout No-Nos

- **High-impact sports** There's a lot of disagreement about whether or not it's possible to induce a miscarriage by falling. Dr. Robert Bradley, who has delivered over 30,000 babies, says that he has "never known a mother to have harmed a baby by any external trauma." Still, most high-impact activities should be avoided.
- **Scuba diving and water skiing** Highly pressurized water can be squeezed through the vagina and cervix into the uterus.
- **Skiing** Unless you're an expert, and even then take it easy. My wife skiied when she was seven months pregnant but avoided the most challenging runs where she'd have risked a fall.
- **Hot tubs/steam baths/saunas** Research indicates that raising a pregnant woman's body temperature by more than two degrees could be dangerous to the fetus. To cool itself, the body moves blood away from the internal organs—including the uterus—and toward the skin.

Exercises and Sports to Do Together

- Speed walking
- Swimming
- Noncompetitive tennis
- Easy weight lifting
- Golf
- Yoga
- Paddle tennis

Before starting *any* kind of workout program, discuss the details with your practitioner and get his or her approval.

Nutrition

The principles of good nutrition haven't changed all that much since you learned about the four basic food groups (or, if you're younger, the pyramid of food) in sixth grade. But now that she's pregnant, your partner will need about 300 more calories a day than before. (Of course, if she was underweight before the pregnancy or is pregnant with twins, she might need a little more.)

If she was overweight before getting pregnant, this is *not* the time to go on a diet. At the same time, the fact that she's "eating for two" is *not* a license to eat anything she wants. Your practitioner will undoubtedly suggest a diet for your partner to follow, but here are a few important nutritional basics to keep in mind:

PROTEIN

The average woman needs 45 grams of protein a day, but your pregnant partner should take in 75 to 100 grams per day. When the fetus is eight weeks old, it has about 125,000 brain-cell neurons. By the end of the nineteenth week, there are about 20 billion—the most he or she will *ever* have. Obstetrician F. Rene Van de Carr has found that a high-protein diet—especially during the first nineteen weeks of pregnancy—supports this surge in brain-cell growth in the baby. Lean proteins are always the best bet. Good sources are skinless chicken, lean meats, low-fat cheese, and cooked fish. Eggs (stay away from the raw ones) are another excellent source of protein; hard-boiled, they travel well and make a convenient between-meal snack.

IRON

If your partner doesn't get enough iron, she may become anemic and begin to feel exhausted. Spinach, dried fruits, beef, and legumes are all good sources, but since much of your partner's iron intake is being used to manufacture the fetus's blood, she may need still more. If so, her doctor will prescribe some over-the-counter supplements. If possible, she should take the tablets with a glass of orange juice—it helps the body absorb the iron. One warning: iron supplements frequently cause constipation.

CITRUS (AND OTHER FOODS HIGH IN VITAMIN C)

Vitamin C is critical to the body's manufacture of collagen, the stuff that holds tissue together. It also helps ensure the baby's bone and tooth development. An inadequate level of vitamin C may weaken your partner's uterus, increasing the likelihood of a difficult labor. Your partner should have at least two servings a day of citrus.

CALCIUM

Calcium is critical to the manufacture of the baby's bones. And since so much of your partner's intake of calcium goes directly to the baby, she needs to make sure she's getting enough for herself. The best sources of calcium are milk and other dairy products. But if your partner is allergic to milk, she should stay away from it—especially if she's planning to breastfeed (her milk allergy could be passed to the baby). Good alternate sources of calcium include pink salmon (canned, with soft bones, is okay), tofu (soybean curd), broccoli, calcium-fortified orange juice, eggs, and oyster shell calcium tablets.

GREEN AND YELLOW VEGETABLES

Besides helping form red blood cells, green and yellow vegetables (which, strangely enough, include cantaloupe and mango) are excellent sources of vitamins A and B, which will help your partner's body absorb all that extra protein she'll be eating. Vitamin A may also help prevent bladder and kidney infections. The darker the green, the better it is for your partner. She should try to have a serving or two per day.

GRAINS AND OTHER COMPLEX CARBOHYDRATES

Grains (including breads and cereals) are basically fuel for your partner's body, and she should have at least four servings a day. Since her body will burn the fuel first, if she doesn't get enough there may not be enough for the baby. Grains are generally low in calories and high in zinc, selenium, chromium, and magnesium—all essential nutrients. They're also high in fiber, which will help your partner combat the constipating effect of iron supplements. Good sources includes whole-grain breads (keep her away from white bread for a few months), brown rice, fresh potatoes, peas, and dried beans.

Nutritional and Chemical No-Nos

- **Cigarettes** When a mother-to-be inhales cigarette smoke, her womb fills with carbon monoxide, nicotine, tar, and resins that inhibit oxygen and nutrient delivery to the baby. Cigarette smoking increases the risk of low-birth-weight babies and miscarriage.
- **Alcohol** Complete abstinence is the safest choice (although your partner's practitioner may sanction a glass of wine once in a while to induce relaxation). One binge, or even just a few drinks at the wrong time (such as when the baby's brain is developing) can cause Fetal Alcohol Syndrome, a set of irreversible mental and physical impairments. And even moderate social drinking has been linked to low-birth-weight babies, learning impairments, and miscarriages in the early stages of pregnancy.
- **Fasting** Unless she has the doctor's approval, your partner should *never* go twenty-four hours without eating—especially in the first nineteen weeks of pregnancy, when the baby's brain is developing.
- **Over-the-counter or prescription drugs** Consult your doctor before taking *any* medication, including aspirin, ibuprofen, and cold medicines—especially those containing alcohol or codeine.

"Is it organic?"

- **Illegal/recreational drugs** Abstain during pregnancy—unborn children can be born addicted to illegal drugs.
- **Raw meats and fish** These may contain *Toxoplasma gondii*, which can blind the fetus or damage its nervous system. Practitioners do disagree, however, on the magnitude of the risk involved. My wife's first OB/GYN was Japanese; he was not worried about her eating sushi.
- **Cat feces** Although cat feces don't have much to do with nutrition, they do contain high quantities of the same parasite found in some raw meats. So if you have a cat, you should take over the duty of cleaning the litter box for the duration of the pregnancy.
- **Insecticides, weed killers, and the like** Prolonged and repeated exposure to such toxic substances is thought to be linked to birth defects. So, after you change the litter box, do the gardening. And while you're at it, you might as well switch to organic fertilizers and pesticides.
- **Hair dyes** Although no link to birth defects has been proven, the chemical solutions in hair dyes can be absorbed through the scalp into the bloodstream. So it is recommended to avoid dyeing hair during pregnancy. Vegetable dyes are an alternative; they don't last as long, but they look as good as, and in some cases even better and less artificial than, the chemical variety.

WATER

As if she doesn't have enough to do already, your partner should try to drink eight 8-ounce glasses of water a day. This will help her to replace the water she loses when she perspires (something she'll do more during pregnancy), and to carry away waste products.

FATTY FOODS

Your partner will be getting most of the fat she needs in the other things she's eating during the day. And while she'd be better off eating cheese than an order of fries, remember this: a candy bar once in a while probably never hurt anybody.

A WORD ABOUT A VEGETARIAN DIET

If your partner is a vegetarian, there's no reason why she and the baby can't get the nutrition they need—especially if she eats eggs and milk. But if your partner is a strict vegan, you should check with your doctor for special guidance.

A FINAL NOTE ON NUTRITION

Helping your partner eat right is one of the best things you can do to ensure that you'll have a healthy, happy baby (and a healthy, happy partner). But don't be too hard on her—an occasional lapse is not going to cause any serious problems. Finally, be supportive. This means that you should try to eat as healthily as she does. If you absolutely must have a banana split, do it on your own time (and keep it to yourself).

The Hunger Campaign

One of the things I constantly underestimated while my wife was pregnant was how incredibly hungry she would get, and how quickly it would happen. Even though she might have had a snack before leaving the office, by the time she got home she was ravenous.

If you've been doing most of the cooking at your house, things probably won't change much during the pregnancy. But if your partner has been doing most of the cooking, there are a few things you can do to simplify her life a great deal.

- **Learn to cook simple, quick meals.** There are plenty of cookbooks specializing in meals that can be made in less than thirty minutes (*The 15-Minute Vegetarian Gourmet* is an example). In addition, most major newspapers run columns featuring easy-to-cook meals using local and

"Why have you brought me here?"

Stocking Up

If you keep the following items on hand you should be able to create a healthy meal or snack any time.

- Unsweetened cereals
- Whole-wheat pasta
- Tomato or vegetable juice
- Whole-grain bread
- Skim milk
- Nonfat cottage cheese
- Low-fat, naturally sweetened yogurt
- Fresh eggs
- Natural peanut butter
- Pure fruit jams
- Bottled water
- Crackers
- Fresh vegetables that can be eaten raw, including carrots, cucumbers, celery, and tomatoes
- Fresh fruit
- Frozen berries and grapes
- Raisins and other dried fruits

seasonal produce. Significantly more expensive alternatives are to stock up on healthy microwavable dinners or order take-out meals.

- **Plan a few meals.** This means you'll have to spend some time reading cookbooks, looking for things that sound good. As you're reading, be sure to write down the ingredients you'll need. Although meal planning doesn't sound all that difficult, it's time-consuming.
- **Do the shopping.** Even if you aren't planning or cooking meals, doing the shopping can spare your partner an hour or so a week of walking around on floors that are tough even on nonpregnant people's feet. In addition, many women who have severe morning sickness find that being in a grocery store, surrounded by so much food, is just too much to stomach. If your partner did the shopping before the pregnancy, ask her to make a *detailed* list of the items she usually bought.
- **Make her a nutritious breakfast shake.** Let her spend a few more precious minutes relaxing in bed in the morning (see page 34 for a good recipe).

Recipes

Power Shake

$\frac{1}{2}$ cup skim milk
1 banana
12 strawberries
juice of 2 oranges

Combine ingredients in a blender or food processor and serve over crushed ice or straight up chilled.

Basic Quick Snacks

- Peel and slice carrots and celery the night before for your partner to take to work for lunch.

Reading the Small Print

Getting healthy food isn't always as easy as it might seem, and most food manufacturers aren't about to do you any favors. So as you're pushing your cart around the grocery store, be sure to read the labels carefully. In particular, watch out for the following:

- **Ingredients** The first ingredient on the list is always the one there's the most of—no matter what you're buying. So, if that healthy ingredient (OAT BRAN!!!) splashed all over the front of the box turns out to be at the bottom of the ingredients list, try something else.
- **Sugar—and all the synonyms** Watch out for fructose, corn syrup, corn sweeteners, sucrose, dextrose, and even honey. They're just fancy ways of saying "sugar."
- **Words like "drink," "flavored," or "cocktail"** Despite the healthy-looking label, most fruit "drinks" or fruit-"flavored" drinks contain less actual juice than you might guess—often as little as 10 percent, with the rest usually water and sugar.
- **Servings** This is one of the most potentially deceptive areas in food labeling. In most cases, the number of calories, grams of fat and protein, and other nutritional information, is given *per serving*. That's all

- Boil eggs (for about 10 minutes—get an egg timer) and shell them.
- Mix up some GORP (dried fruits, nuts, raisins, sunflower seeds).

Open-Face White Mexican Omelet

3 egg whites
1 teaspoon cilantro, finely chopped
1 small tomato, chopped
¼ cup green and/or red pepper, chopped
¼ cup red onion, diced
black pepper to taste

Separate eggs and discard yolks. Whisk egg whites in a bowl or measuring cup and pour into a medium nonstick frying pan. Turn heat on low. As egg whites begin to cook, add all other ingredients. Simmer until egg becomes firm, and slide omelet onto plate for serving.

very nice, except that manufacturers don't all use the same serving size. For example, I recently saw an 8-ounce package of fairly healthy frozen lasagna. The calories, protein, and fat all seemed okay—until I noticed that the serving size was actually only 6 ounces. This means that since one person would eat the entire 8 ounces, there was really 33 percent more fat and calories than expected.

- **Percentage of calories from fat** Most nutritionists agree that pregnant women should keep their percentage of calories from fat to about 30 percent. Manufacturers are now required by law to make this calculation for you. But there's a fairly simple way to figure it out for yourself: just multiply the number of grams of fat by 10. So, if you're buying something that has 100 calories and 5 grams of fat per serving, the percentage of calories from fat is 50 percent (5 grams × 10 = 50).
- **A word about additives** When it comes to ingredients, if you can't pronounce it, don't eat it. And while your partner is pregnant, keep her away from saccharine (a popular sweetener), nitrates and nitrites (preservatives commonly found in lunch meats and bacon), and monosodium glutamate (MSG—a flavor enhancer especially popular in Asian food). All of these may have negative effects on your unborn child.

Microwave Oatmeal

1/3 cup oats (you can use 1-minute, 5-minute, quick, or regular)
2/3 cup water
1/2 banana, sliced
dash cinnamon
1/8 teaspoon vanilla extract
milk
1 tablespoon wheat germ

Put the oats in a 1-quart microwave-safe bowl. Stir in the water, banana, cinnamon, and vanilla. Microwave on high for 2 to 3 minutes, or until the concoction starts steaming or bubbling. Take out and stir again. Add milk to taste. Sprinkle with wheat germ for extra vitamins and protein.

Chocolate Banana Pancakes

1/2 cup white flour
1/2 cup whole wheat flour
2 teaspoons baking powder
1/4 teaspoon cinnamon
pinch salt
1/2 tablespoon white sugar
1/2 tablespoon brown sugar (if you're missing either kind of sugar, just use a whole tablespoon of the one you have)
1 egg
1 teaspoon vanilla extract (optional, but great)
1 tablespoon vegetable oil
a bit less than 1 cup milk
1/2 cup chocolate chips
1 tablespoon butter or margarine
3 bananas, sliced

Mix the dry ingredients in a large bowl. Add the egg, vanilla, oil, and milk. Mix into a smooth batter. Add the chocolate chips and mix again. Melt the butter on a heated griddle. Pour the batter onto the griddle in large spoonfuls. Then quickly place several banana slices on each pancake. When the bubbles that form on the surface of the pancakes pop, flip them over. Cook until the second side is as brown as the first, and remove from griddle.

Any of the following salads can be served as a main course for lunch or as a side dish for dinner.

Tomato and Basil Salad

The combination of these 2 ingredients makes a refreshing salad. When available, use fresh basil and local tomatoes for the best flavor.

2 vine-ripened tomatoes
6 to 8 basil leaves
4 tablespoons balsamic vinegar
4 tablespoons extra virgin olive oil
freshly ground black pepper to taste

Slice tomatoes and arrange on serving plate. Shred basil leaves and sprinkle over tomatoes. Cover with the vinegar and oil. Add freshly ground pepper. Cover and refrigerate for at least 1 hour. Remove from refrigerator a half-hour before serving.

Mixed Green Salad with Balsamic Vinaigrette

Combining different types of greens, such as Boston, red leaf, radicchio, arugula, and endive, makes a green salad more interesting. Raw cucumbers, snow peas, French beans, shredded carrots, and cooked beets also add to the flavor, color, and nutrition of a mixed salad. Stay away from croutons, which are high in calories and low in nutrition.

Thoroughly wash and dry greens, place each serving on a flat plate, and arrange whatever selection of vegetables you like on top. Just before serving, pour about three tablespoons of balsamic vinaigrette dressing (see recipe below) over each salad.

BALSAMIC VINAIGRETTE
2 cloves crushed garlic
⅔ cup balsamic vinegar
1 teaspoon Dijon mustard
½ teaspoon chopped parsley
½ teaspoon chopped chives
½ teaspoon chopped basil
⅓ cup oil
salt and pepper

Mix garlic, vinegar, mustard, and herbs together. Whisk oil into the vinegar mixture. Add salt and pepper to taste.

Cucumber Salad

2 large cucumbers, sliced
1 medium Bermuda onion, diced
1 cup cider vinegar
½ cup nonfat plain yogurt
1 teaspoon fresh dill, chopped

If the cucumbers are not waxy, leave the skin on. Slice the cucumbers thinly (a food processor does the job best). Combine the diced onion with the cucumber slices in a large bowl that can be refrigerated. Pour the vinegar and yogurt over the mixture, cover, and leave in the refrigerator overnight. Serve cold as a side dish, garnished with the dill.

Low-Calorie Pizza

Create your own combination of toppings, including artichokes, olives, and squash, and use an assortment of cheeses, such as blue, cheddar, Swiss, and even low-fat cottage cheese.

4 soft tortillas (found in grocery freezer)
2 fresh plum tomatoes, sliced
3 cloves garlic, minced or crushed
1 cup mushrooms, sliced and sautéed
1 medium onion, chopped and sautéed
6 teaspoons fresh herbs (oregano, thyme, and basil), minced
(or 3 teaspoons dried)
½ cup shredded cheese or low-fat cottage cheese

Preheat oven to 350°F. Place tortillas on a lightly greased cookie sheet. Cover with tomatoes, garlic, mushrooms, onions, and herbs. Add cheese. Bake for 20 minutes or until tortilla is crisp. Serve hot.

Low-Calorie Cream of Zucchini Soup

This recipe can be varied by substituting carrots, potatoes, or celery for zucchini.

3 medium-size zucchini, seeded and cut into ¼-inch slices
1 medium white onion, diced
1 small chicken bouillon cube (optional; bouillon cubes usually
contain MSG)
1 cup nonfat plain yogurt

1 tablespoon fresh dill
salt and pepper

Put zucchini, onion, and bouillon cube in a saucepan. Add just enough water to cover. Bring to a boil and cook until soft (about 10 minutes). Let cool. Transfer to a blender or food processor, add yogurt and dill, and blend until smooth. Add salt and pepper to taste.

Quick and Easy Vegetarian Spaghetti Sauce

2 large onions, chopped
4 tablespoons olive oil
½ pound mushrooms, thinly sliced
2 16-ounce jars meatless spaghetti sauce
2 14.5-ounce cans stewed tomatoes
1 4-ounce can tomato paste
1 pound tofu, diced into ½-inch cubes
1½ teaspoons dried basil
generous pinch of cayenne pepper
1 bay leaf
salt and pepper to taste
1 teaspoon sugar
½ teaspoon garlic powder
1 tablespoon rice vinegar

In a small saucepan, sauté onions in the olive oil over medium heat until they're translucent. Add mushrooms, and sauté for 5 more minutes (until the mushrooms begin to release their liquid). Add all the other ingredients and simmer for 40 minutes. If sauce won't be used immediately, let cool, pour into two-serving containers, and store in freezer. Defrost as needed.

Spa Potato Chips

3 baking potatoes, peeled and thinly sliced
nonstick cooking spray
paprika to taste

Preheat oven to 350°F. Slice potatoes as thinly as possible (a food processor is best). Spray a cookie sheet with nonstick cooking spray. Spread out potatoes evenly in pan. Sprinkle with paprika and bake for about 15 minutes, or until crisp.

Spicy Peanut Butter Pasta

1 pound angel hair pasta
1 tablespoon sesame oil
4 tablespoons peanut or safflower oil
6 cloves garlic, minced
1 generous pinch (⅛ teaspoon) red pepper flakes
10 scallions, thinly sliced
½ cup creamy peanut butter
6 tablespoons rice wine vinegar
6 tablespoons soy sauce
4 teaspoons white sugar
1 cucumber, peeled, seeded, and diced (optional)
cilantro to taste (optional)

Cook pasta according to directions on package. Drain and drizzle with the sesame oil. Set aside. Sauté garlic and pepper flakes in the peanut or safflower oil in a large frying pan. Add scallions. Turn to high heat and stir for one minute. Turn off. Add remaining ingredients and use a wire whisk to thoroughly mix into a thick sauce. Pour over noodles while sauce is still warm. Garnish with cucumber and/or cilantro, if desired.

Garlic Roasted Chicken

1 roasting chicken (3 to 4 pounds)
5 garlic cloves
1 carrot, sliced
2 celery stalks, sliced
4 small white onions
2 teaspoons olive oil
½ cup white wine (optional)
¼ cup water

Preheat oven to 450°F. Clean chicken and rinse thoroughly with water. Pat dry. Using fingers, make pockets under skin and stuff with garlic cloves. Place chicken in a deep baking dish. Stuff cavity of chicken with carrot and celery slices and onions. Drizzle olive oil on top of chicken. Pour wine and water over chicken. Bake chicken at 450°F for ten minutes to sear. Then reduce heat to 350°F and cook for 30 to 40 minutes, or until the juices run clear when the thigh is pierced with a fork.

Rack of Lamb

A festive, delicious dish that is easy to prepare.

¼ cup bread crumbs
3 cloves garlic, crushed
2 teaspoons parsley flakes
salt and pepper to taste
1 rack of lamb (ask the butcher to crack the rack, remove excess fat, and French-cut the ribs)
5 teaspoons Dijon mustard

Preheat oven to 450°F. In a small bowl, mix the bread crumbs, garlic, parsley, and salt and pepper. Place rack of lamb in a baking pan, meat side up. Spread mustard on top and bake for 10 minutes. Remove from oven. Using a fork, press the bread crumb mixture into mustard, reduce heat to 350°F, and cook for about 20 more minutes, or until medium rare.

Fruit Salad with Creamy Yogurt Dressing

A refreshing, low-calorie dish for breakfast, lunch, or dessert. As a side dish or dessert, this recipe serves four. As a main course for lunch, it serves two.

1 green apple, cored and diced
1 banana, sliced
juice of 1 lime
1 small bunch of red or green seedless grapes
5 strawberries, halved
1 seedless navel orange (or other citrus fruit), sectioned
2 kiwis, peeled and sliced
1 cup low-fat vanilla yogurt (or nonfat plain yogurt)
1 teaspoon cinnamon
½ cup shredded coconut (optional)
4 to 8 fresh mint leaves (optional)

In a large mixing bowl combine banana and apple, pour lime juice over them, and mix. Add remaining fruit and mix again. In a separate bowl combine yogurt and cinnamon. Just before serving, mix the yogurt dressing and coconut into the fruit. If fresh mint is available, garnish each serving with one or two leaves.

THE 2ND MONTH

The Doctor Will See You Now

What She's Going Through

Physically

- Continuing fatigue
- Continuing morning sickness
- Frequent urination
- Tingly fingers and toes
- Breast tenderness

Emotionally

- Continued elation and at the same time some ambivalence about being pregnant
- Inability to keep her mind on her work
- Fear you won't find her attractive anymore
- Continuing moodiness
- Fear of an early miscarriage

What's Going On with the Baby

During this month, the baby will change from an embryo to a fetus. By the end of the month, he or she (it's way too early to tell which) will have stubby little arms (no fingers yet), eyes (without eyelids) on the side of the face, ears, and a tiny, beating heart (on the outside of the body). If you bumped into a six-foot-tall version of your baby in a dark alley, you'd run the other way.

What You're Going Through

The Struggle to Connect

Just about every study that's ever been done on the subject has shown that women generally "connect" with their pregnancies sooner than men do. Although they can't feel the baby kicking inside them yet, the physical changes they're experiencing make the pregnancy more "real" for them.

For most men, however, pregnancy at two months is still a pretty abstract concept. For me—as excited as I was—the idea that we were really pregnant was so hard to grasp that I actually forgot about it for several days at a time.

Excitement vs. Fear

But when I remembered we were pregnant, I found myself in the midst of a real conflict—one that would plague me for months. On the one hand, I was still so elated that I could barely contain myself; I had visions of walking with my child on the beach, playing, reading, helping him or her with homework, and I wanted to stop strangers on the street and tell them I was going to be a father. On the other hand, I made a conscious effort to stifle my fantasies and to keep myself from getting attached to the idea of being pregnant. That way, if we had a miscarriage or something else went wrong, I wouldn't be devastated.

Increased or Decreased Sexual Desire

It was during the times when I let myself get excited about becoming a father that I noticed that my wife's and my sex life was changing. Perhaps it was because I was still reveling in the recent confirmation of my masculinity, or perhaps it was because I felt a newer, closer connection to my wife. It may even have been the sense of freedom resulting from not having to worry about birth control. Whatever the reason, sex in the early months of the pregnancy became even more passionate and erotic than before.

But not all men experience an increase in sexual desire during pregnancy. Some are turned off by their partner's changing figure; others are afraid of hurting the baby (a nearly impossible task at this stage of the game). Still others may feel that there's no sense in having sex now that they're pregnant. Whatever your feelings—about sex or anything else for that matter—try to talk them over with your partner. Chances are she's feeling—or soon will be—the same way.

Staying Involved

Going to the OB/GYN Appointments

The general rule that women connect with the pregnancy sooner than men has an exception: men who get involved early on and stay involved until the end have been shown to be as connected with the baby as their partners. And a surefire way to get involved is to go to as many of your partner's OB/GYN appointments as possible.

Going to a doctor wasn't something I ever looked forward to. And going to someone else's doctor was even lower down on the list. But over the course of two pregnancies, I think I missed only two of my wife's medical appointments. Admittedly, some of the time I was bored out of my mind, but overall it was a great opportunity to have my questions answered and to satisfy my curiosity about just what was going on inside my wife's womb.

Theoretically, it's possible to get at least some basic questions answered by reading a couple of the hundreds of pregnancy and childbirth books written for women. But there are other, more important reasons to go to the appointments. First, you will become more of a participant in the pregnancy and less of a spectator. Second, it will demystify the process and make it more tangible. Hearing the baby's heartbeat for the first time (in about the third month), and seeing his or her tiny body squirm on an ultrasound screen (in about the fifth month) bring home the reality of the pregnancy in a way that words on a page just can't do. Third, as the pregnancy progresses, your partner is going to be feeling more and more dependent on you, and she'll need more signs that you'll always be there for her. And while going to her doctor appointments may not seem quite as romantic as a moonlit cruise or a dozen roses, being there with her is an ideal way to tell her you love her and to reassure her that she's not going to be alone.

If you do decide to go to your partner's checkups, you'd better get your calendar out: most women see their health care provider at least once a month for the first seven months, twice in the eighth month, and once a week thereafter. Of course, taking time off from work for all these appointments may not be realistic. But before you write the whole thing off, check with your doctor—many offer early-morning or evening appointments.

Testing

Pregnancy, besides being a time of great emotional closeness between you and your partner, is also a time for medical testing. Most of the tests, such as the monthly urine tests for blood sugar and the quarterly blood tests for other problems, are purely routine. Others, though, are less routine and sometimes can be scary.

The scariest of all are the tests to detect birth defects. One of the things you can expect your partner's doctor to do is take a detailed medical history—from both of you. These medical histories will help the practitioner determine whether or not you are at risk of having a child with severe—or not so severe—problems.

Prenatal Testing

If you are in one of the high-risk categories, your doctor may suggest prenatal testing. You should know that, with the exception of ultrasound and blood tests, each of the other prenatal diagnostic tests involves some potential risks either to your partner or to the baby. Ask your doctor about them and make sure the benefits of taking the test outweigh the potential risks.

ULTRASOUND (SONOGRAM)

This noninvasive test is painless to the mother, safe for the baby, and can be performed any time after the fifth week of pregnancy. By bouncing sound waves around the uterus, the procedure will give you a pretty clear picture of your baby. In the first trimester, your doctor will probably recommend an ultrasound if your partner has experienced any bleeding, if there's any doubt as to the number of fetuses, or if he or she suspects an ectopic pregnancy (a pregnancy that takes place outside the uterus). In the second trimester, you may have an ultrasound to determine the sex of the baby (if you want to), to get a more accurate estimate of the due date, or just because you're curious about what the baby looks like. During the last part of the pregnancy—and especially if the baby is overdue—your partner's doctor may order additional ultrasounds to determine the baby's position, to make sure the placenta is still functioning, or to confirm that there's still enough amniotic fluid left to support the baby.

ALPHA-FETOPROTEIN TESTING (AFP)

This simple blood test is conducted when your partner is 15–18 weeks pregnant. It screens for a variety of neural-tube defects (defects relating to the brain or spinal column), the most common of which are spina bifida and anencephaly (a completely or partially missing brain). The results are available within a week or two. But because AFP is considered quite inaccurate, most obstetricians won't recommend the test unless you or your partner has a family history of neural-tube defects.

OTHER BLOOD TESTS

A variety of genetically transmitted birth defects affect some ethnic groups more than others. So, based on your family histories, your partner's doctor may order one or both of you to get additional blood tests. Among the most common ethnically linked defects are:

- Sickle-cell anemia. If you're African American, you should be tested.
- Tay-Sachs. If you're both Jewish, and your families are of Eastern European origin, at least one of you should be tested.

AMNIOCENTESIS

This test is usually performed at 15 to 18 weeks, and involves inserting a needle through the abdominal wall into the amniotic sac. A small amount of fluid is collected and analyzed to detect chromosomal and developmental abnormalities. Amnio is extremely accurate and test results are usually available in three to four weeks. Unless your partner is considered at high risk (see page 47) or you want to know everything there is to know about your baby, there's no real reason to have this test. The chances that a woman under thirty will give birth to a baby with a defect that an amnio can detect are less than 1 in 400. The chances that the procedure will cause a miscarriage, however, are 1 in 200. But for a woman over thirty-five, amnio begins to make statistical sense: the chances of having a baby with abnormalities are 1 in 192 and rise steadily as the woman ages.

CHORIONIC VILLI SAMPLING (CVS)

Generally this test is performed at 9 to 11 weeks to detect chromosomal abnormalities and genetically inherited diseases. A catheter is threaded through the vagina and cervix into the uterus, where small pieces of the chorion—a membrane with the identical genetic makeup as the fetus—are snipped off or suctioned into a syringe and analyzed. The risks are slightly higher than with an amnio (the chances of miscarriage are about 1 in 100), but because CVS is potentially much more accurate and can detect a wider range of abnormalities, it is expected to replace amnio in the future.

PERCUTANEOUS UMBILICAL BLOOD SAMPLING (PUBS)

This test is usually conducted at 18 to 36 weeks to confirm possible defects detected through amnio. The procedure is virtually the same as an amnio, except that the needle is inserted into a blood vessel in the umbilical cord; practitioners believe this makes the tests more accurate. Results are avail-

Reasons You Might Be Considered High Risk for Having a Baby with Birth Defects

- You or your partner has a family history of birth defects.
- You are a member of a high-risk ethnic group (African Americans, for example, are at risk for sickle-cell anemia; Jews of Eastern European descent are considered at high risk for Tay-Sachs).
- Your partner is thirty-five or older.

Other Reasons for Prenatal Testing

Prenatal testing is also available to people who, while not considered at risk, have other reasons for wanting it done. Here are some of the most common reasons:

- Peace of mind. Having an amniocentesis or a Chorionic Villi Sampling (CVS) test can remove most doubts about the health of your child. For some people, this reassurance can make the pregnancy a much more enjoyable—and less stressful—experience. If the tests do reveal problems, you and your partner will have more time to prepare yourselves for the tough decisions ahead (for more on this, see pages 49–50).
- To find out the sex of the baby.

able within about three days. In addition to the risk of complications or miscarriage resulting from the procedure, PUBS also slightly increases the likelihood of premature labor or clotting of the umbilical cord.

Dealing with the Unexpected

For me, pregnancy was like an emotional roller coaster ride. One minute I'd find myself wildly excited and dreaming about the new baby, and the next I was filled with feelings of impending doom. I knew I wanted our babies, but I also knew that if I got too emotionally attached and anything unexpected happened—like an ectopic pregnancy, a miscarriage, or a birth defect—I'd be crushed. So, instead of allowing myself to enjoy the pregnancy fully, I ended up spending a lot of time torturing myself by reading and worrying about the bad things that could happen.

ECTOPIC PREGNANCY

About 1 percent of all embryos don't embed in the uterus but begin to grow in the fallopian tube, which is unable to expand sufficiently to accommodate it. If undiagnosed, an ectopic pregnancy would eventually cause the fallopian tube to burst, resulting in severe bleeding. But the vast majority of ectopic pregnancies are caught and removed by the eighth week of pregnancy—long before they become dangerous.

MISCARRIAGES

The sad fact—especially for pessimists like me—is that miscarriages happen fairly frequently. Some experts estimate that as many as one pregnancy out of five ends in miscarriage. In fact, almost every sexually active woman will have one at some point in her life. (And in most cases the miscarriage occurs before a couple ever knew they were pregnant—whatever there was of the tiny embryo is swept away with the woman's regular menstrual flow.)

Before you start to panic, remember two things: first, over 90 percent of couples who experience a miscarriage get pregnant—and have a baby—later. Second, many people believe that miscarriages—most of which happen within the first three months of the pregnancy—are "a blessing in disguise." The authors of *What to Expect When You're Expecting* sum up this feeling quite well: "Early miscarriage is generally a natural selection process in which a defective embryo or fetus (defective because of environmental factors, such as radiation or drugs; because of poor implantation in the uterus; because of genetic abnormality, maternal infection, random accident, or unknown reasons) is discarded before it has a chance to develop." But if you and your partner have a miscarriage, you probably won't find either of these explanations particularly reassuring.

Until very recently, miscarriage, like the pregnancy it ends, has been considered the exclusive emotional domain of women. This is simply untrue. While men don't have to endure the physical pain or discomfort of a miscarriage, their emotional pain is just as severe as their partner's. They still have the same hopes and dreams about their unborn children, and they still feel a profound sense of grief when those hopes and dreams are dashed. And many men, just like their partners, feel tremendous guilt and inadequacy when a pregnancy ends prematurely.

Some good friends of mine, Philip and Elaine, had a miscarriage several years ago, after about twelve weeks of pregnancy. For both of them, the experience was emotionally devastating, and for months after the miscarriage they were besieged by sympathetic friends and relatives—many of whom had found out about the pregnancy only after it had so abruptly ended. They asked how Elaine was feeling, offered to visit her, expressed their sympathy, and often shared their own miscarriage stories. But no one—not even his wife—ever asked Philip what *he* was feeling, or expressed any sympathy for what *he* was going through, or offered *him* a shoulder to cry on.

Psychologists and sociologists have conducted many studies on how people grieve at the loss of a fetus. But the vast majority of these studies have dealt only with women's reactions. The ones that have included fathers' feelings generally conclude that men and women grieve in different ways. Dr. Kristen Goldbach found that "women are more likely to express their grief openly, while men tend to be much less expressive, frequently coping with their grief in a more stoical manner." This doesn't mean that men don't express their grief at all. Instead, it simply highlights the fact that in our society men, like my friend Philip, have virtually no opportunity to express their feelings.

BIRTH DEFECTS

If one of the tests discussed earlier in this chapter indicates that your baby will be born deformed or with any kind of serious disorder, you and your partner have some serious discussions ahead of you. There are two basic options for dealing with birth defects in an unborn child: keep the baby or terminate the pregnancy. Fortunately, you and your partner won't have to make either of these decisions on your own; every hospital that administers diagnostic tests has specially trained genetic counselors who will help you sort through the options.

When a pregnancy ends unexpectedly or prematurely, it's critical that you and your partner seek out the emotional support you are entitled to. While there's nothing that can be done to prepare for or prevent a miscarriage, telling your partner how you feel—either alone or with a member of the clergy, a therapist, or a close friend—is very important. And don't just sit back and wait for her to tell you what *she's* feeling. Take the initiative—be supportive and ask a lot of questions.

If you're considering terminating the pregnancy for genetic reasons, remember that communicating clearly and effectively with your partner is probably the most important thing you can do during this stressful time. The decision you make should not be taken lightly—it's a choice that will last a lifetime—and you and your partner must fully agree before proceeding with either option.

Don't feel that the two of you have to handle your grief by yourselves: counseling and support are available to both women *and* men who have lost a fetus through miscarriage or genetic termination. Going to a support group can be a particularly important experience for men—especially those who aren't getting the support they need from their friends and families. Many men who attend support groups report that until they joined the group, no one had ever asked how they felt about their loss. The group setting can also give men the chance to stop being strong for their partners for a few minutes and grieve for themselves.

If you'd like to find a support group, your doctor or the genetic counselors can refer you to the closest one—or the one that might be most sympathetic to men's concerns.

Some men, however, are not at all interested in getting together with a large group of people who have little in common but tragedy. If you feel this way, be sure to explain your feelings tactfully to your partner—she may feel quite strongly that you should be there with her and might feel rejected if you aren't. If you ultimately decide not to join a support group, don't try to handle things alone—talk to your partner, your doctor, your cleric, or a sympathetic friend. Keeping your grief bottled up will only hinder the healing process.

Notes:

THE 3RD MONTH

Spreading the Word

What She's Going Through

Physically

- Fatigue, morning sickness, breast tenderness, and other early pregnancy symptoms beginning to disappear
- Continuing moodiness
- Thickening waistline

Emotionally

- Heightened sense of reality about the pregnancy from hearing the baby's heartbeat
- Continuing ambivalence about the pregnancy
- Frustration and/or excitement over thickening of waistline
- Turning inward—beginning to focus on what's happening inside her
- Beginning to bond with the baby

What's Going On with the Baby

By now, the little fetus looks pretty much like a real person—except that he or she (an ultrasound technician might be able to tell you which) is only about two or three inches long and weighs less than an ounce. Teeth, fingernails, toenails, and hair are developing nicely, and the brain is not far behind. By the end of this month, the baby will be able to curl its toes, turn its head, and even frown.

What You're Going Through

A Heightened Sense of Reality

During the third month, the pregnancy begins to feel a little more tangible. By far the biggest reality booster for me was hearing the baby's heartbeat, even though it didn't sound anything like a real heart at all (more like a fast hoosh-hoosh-hoosh). Somehow, having the doctor tell us that what we were hearing was really a heartbeat—and a healthy one at that—was mighty reassuring.

Feeling Left Out

While becoming more aware of the reality of the pregnancy is certainly a good thing, it's not the only thing that you'll be feeling at around this point in the pregnancy. Toward the end of this first trimester, your partner will probably begin to spend a lot of time concentrating on what's happening inside her body, wondering whether she'll be a good enough mother, and establishing a bond with the baby. She also may start internalizing her feelings about these processes and may become a little self-absorbed. And if she has a close relationship with her mother, the two of them may develop a deeper bond as your partner tries to find good role models.

Everything she's going through at this point is completely normal. The danger, however, is that while your partner is turning inward or bonding with her own mother, *you* may end up feeling left out, rejected, or even pushed out of the way. This can be particularly painful. But no matter how much it hurts, you should resist the urge to "retaliate" by withdrawing yourself. Be as comforting as you can be, and let her know—in a nonconfrontational way—how you're feeling (see the "Your Relationship" section, pages 60–63). Fortunately, this period of turning inward won't last forever.

Excluded—or Welcomed—by Your Partner's Doctors

For some men—especially those who are feeling left out by their partners—the joy they experience at the increasing reality of the pregnancy is outweighed by the bitterness they feel at the way they're treated by their partner's doctors. Researcher Pamela Jordan found that most men felt that their presence at the prenatal visits was perceived as "cute" or "novel," and that their partners were considered the only patients. If they were talked to at all, it was only to discuss how they could support their partners. The fact that they had needs and concerns didn't seem to occur to anyone.

Fortunately, this was not my experience at all. During both pregnancies, my wife's OBs went out of their way to include me in the process. They made a special point of looking at me when talking about what was happening with my wife and the baby, encouraged me to ask questions, and answered them thoroughly. Our first OB even invited me to take a look at my wife's cervix. I was a little put off by the idea, but getting to see the cervix—through which our baby would emerge just six months later—somehow made the pregnancy seem less mysterious and made me feel much more a part of the whole thing. If your OB doesn't offer you a look, ask for one—I highly recommend it. But be sure to ask your partner first.

Physical Symptoms: Couvade

Although most of what you'll be going through during your pregnancy will be psychological, don't be surprised if you start developing some *physical* symptoms as well. Various studies estimate that anywhere from 22 to 79 percent of expectant American fathers experience *couvade* syndrome (from the French word meaning "to hatch"), or "sympathetic pregnancy." Couvade symptoms are typically the same as those traditionally associated with pregnant women —weight gain, nausea, mood swings, food cravings—as well as some *not* associated with pregnant women: headaches, toothaches, itching, and cysts. Symptoms—if you're going to have them at all—usually appear in about the third month of pregnancy, decrease for a few months, then pick up again in the month or two before the baby is born. In almost every case, though, the symptoms "mysteriously" disappear at the birth.

Considering that our society generally denies the importance (if not the very existence) of what expectant fathers go through during pregnancy, it's not surprising that some men express their concerns and feelings by developing physical symptoms. Among the most common reasons an expectant father might develop couvade symptoms are:

SYMPATHY OR FEELINGS OF GUILT FOR WHAT THE WOMAN IS GOING THROUGH

Men have traditionally been socialized to bite the bullet when it comes to pain and discomfort. And when our loved ones are suffering and we can't do anything to stop it, our natural (and slightly irrational) instinct is to try to take their pain away—to make it *ours* instead of *theirs*. The father of a good friend of mine, for example, had splitting headaches for the last month of all three of his pregnancies.

"Just as your wife suspected, Mr. Sanders. You have a very little boy growing inside you."

JEALOUSY

There's no question that your partner is going to be getting a lot more attention during the pregnancy than you are. And a lot of men who develop couvade symptoms do so in a subconscious attempt to shift the focus of the pregnancy to themselves. My father, who was pacing the waiting room while my mother was in labor with me, suddenly got a gushing nosebleed. Within seconds the delivery room was empty—except for my mother—as three nurses and two doctors raced out to take care of my poor, bleeding father. I'm sure he didn't do it on purpose, but for one brief moment during the delivery, Dad was the complete center of attention.

A LITTLE HISTORY

Most researchers today agree that in Western societies couvade symptoms appear unconsciously in those expectant fathers who experience them. But as far back as 60 B.C.E. (and continuing today in many non-Western societies), couvade has been used *deliberately* in rituals designed to keep fathers involved in the experience of pregnancy and childbirth. Not all these rituals, however, have been particularly friendly to women. W. R. Dawson writes that in the first century mothers were routinely ignored during childbirth, while their husbands were waited on in bed. And more recently, in Spain and elsewhere, mothers frequently gave birth in the fields where they worked. They then returned home to care for the baby's father.

But in some other cultures, men tried to do the same thing they try to do today: take their partner's pain away by attracting it to themselves. In France and Germany, for example, pregnant women were given their husband's clothes during labor in the belief that doing so would transfer the wives' pains to their husbands. The eighteenth-century Scots believed that a nurse could use witchcraft to transfer the pain of childbirth from the wife to the husband.

Perhaps the most interesting aspect of ritual couvade is the importance attached to the supernatural bond between the father and the unborn child. Whatever the fathers did during the pregnancy was believed to have a direct impact on the unborn child. In Borneo expectant fathers ate nothing but rice and salt—a diet said to keep a new baby's stomach from swelling. In other countries a man who hammered a nail while his wife was pregnant was said to be dooming her to a long, painful labor, and if he split wood, he would surely have a child with a cleft lip. Afraid of making his own child blind, an expectant father wouldn't eat meat from an animal who gave birth to blind young. He also avoided turtles—to make sure that his child would not be born deaf and anencephalic (with a cone-shaped head).

While it's pretty doubtful that couvade rituals actually reduced any woman's childbirth pains or prevented any deformities, they do illustrate an important point: men have been trying to get—and stay—involved in pregnancy and childbirth for thousands of years. As Bronislav Malinowski noted in his 1927 book, *Sex and Repression in Savage Society:*

> Even the apparently absurd idea of couvade presents to us a deep meaning and a necessary function. It is of high biological value for the human family to consist of both father and mother; if the traditional customs and rules are there to establish a social situation of close moral proximity between father and child, if all such customs aim at drawing a man's attention to his offspring, then the couvade which makes man simulate the birth-pangs and illness of maternity is of great value and provides the necessary stimulus and expression for paternal tendencies. The couvade and all the customs of its type serve to accentuate the principal of legitimacy, the child's need of a father.

Staying Involved

Spilling the Beans

Another thing (this month anyway) that will make the pregnancy more real is getting to tell people. By the end of the third month, I'd pretty well gotten over my fears of miscarriage or other pregnancy disaster and we'd decided it was safe to spill the beans to our family and close friends. Somehow just saying the words "My wife's pregnant" (I switched to "*We*'re pregnant" a while later) helped me realize it was true.

The decision about when to let other people in on your pregnancy is a big one. Some people are superstitious and opt to put off making the announcement for as long as possible. Others rush to the phone as soon as they get out of bed. Even if you're in the first category, sooner or later you're going to have to start spreading the word—and the end of the third month is a pretty good time.

Whom you decide to tell, and in what order, is your own business. But there are a few guidelines you might want to keep in mind.

FAMILY

Unless you have some compelling reason not to, you should probably tell your family first. Your close friends will forgive you if they hear about the pregnancy from your Aunt Ida; if it happens the other way around, Aunt Ida may take real offense. There are a few cases, however, when telling your family first might not be a great idea. One couple we know, Lawrence and Beth, kept their pregnancy a secret from their friends for five months—and from their family for longer—hoping that Lawrence's brother and sister-in-law, who had been trying to get pregnant for years, would succeed in the interim.

FRIENDS

If you do decide to tell your friends first, make sure you swear them to secrecy—good news travels a lot faster than you might think. As in the case of relatives, be considerate of friends who have been trying but who haven't been as successful as you.

THE OFFICE

You'll probably want to tell your coworkers and your boss (if you have one) at about the same time as you tell your friends. But you should remember that society has some pretty rigid work/family rules for men, so be prepared for a less-than-enthusiastic response from some people (see the "Work and Family" section, pages 88–93, for a complete discussion). Whatever you do,

Trying to Keep the Secret

Despite your attempts to control the flow of information, if you're not careful about what you do, people—especially your close friends—are going to guess. If you're serious about not wanting anyone to know, here are a couple things to keep in mind:

- **Stay away from expressions like "in her condition" or "I think she really needs to rest."** That's exactly how I inadvertently leaked the news to a friend who had asked how we liked working out on the Stairmaster machine at the gym.
- **Be unobtrusive if you change your habits.** If your partner used to drink or smoke before she got pregnant, you might want to think a little about how your friends and family will react to her new, vice-free life-style. When my wife was pregnant with our second daughter, we agreed to meet some good friends at a bar one Saturday night. No one really noticed that my wife was drinking mineral water instead of her usual beer. But when she ordered an ice cold glass of milk, the jig was up.

though, don't wait until the last minute to tell the folks at work—especially if you're planning to take some time off or to make any work schedule changes after the birth.

YOUR OTHER CHILDREN

If you have other children, give them plenty of time to adjust to the news. But do *not* tell them until after you want everyone else to know. Until they're over six, kids don't understand the concept of "keeping a secret." One of our four-year-old's big thrills in life is to whisper in people's ears things that are supposed to be secrets.

You should also make a special effort to include your other children as much as possible in the pregnancy experience. Our older daughter came with us to most of the doctor appointments and got to hold the doppler (through which you hear the fetus's heartbeats) and help the doctor measure my wife's growing belly. Finally, keep in mind that it's perfectly normal for expectant siblings to insist that they, too, are pregnant—just like Mommy. Insisting that they're not may make them feel excluded and resentful of the new baby. This is *especially* true for little boys.

ANNOUNCING YOU'RE PREGNANT

♦ ♦ ♦

No matter how or when you do it, telling people you're expecting will open a floodgate of congratulations and advice; after a few weeks, you may wonder what anyone used to talk about at parties before. Just about everybody has something to say about what you should and shouldn't do now that you're pregnant. You'll hear delightful stories, horror stories, and just plain boring stories about pregnancy and childbirth. You'll probably also have to endure endless "jokes" about your masculinity, speculation about who the "real" father is, and questions about what the mailman or the milkman looks like—mostly, unfortunately, from other men. With attitudes like these, is it any wonder that 60 percent of men have at least fleeting doubts as to the true paternity of their children?

Immediately after breaking the news to our friends and family, my wife and

What If You're Not Married?

Even in the last few years of the twentieth century, when it's the norm for couples to live together before getting married, having a child out of wedlock still raises a lot of eyebrows. Your most liberal-minded friends and relatives might surprise you by suggesting that you "make an honest woman of her" before the baby comes. Try to keep your sense of humor about these things. You and your partner are grown-ups and capable of making the decisions you think best. And anyway, most unmarried parents-to-be find that their relatives' joy at the prospect of a new little niece, nephew, or grandchild frequently overshadows those same relatives' disappointment over your lack of a marriage certificate.

I began to feel some slight changes in our relationship with them. What had once been our private secret was now public knowledge, and just about everyone wanted to share it with us. People would "drop in" unannounced, usually bearing either gifts or advice—just to "see how things were going"—and the phone never stopped ringing.

After a few days, you and your partner may start to feel a little claustrophobic. If this happens, don't hesitate to establish some ground rules. For example, you might want to ask your friends and families to call before coming over, or you might set up—and let everyone know about—specific visiting hours.

You should also prepare yourself for the possibility that you may feel a little left out. Most people are going to be asking how your partner is feeling, what she's going through, and so on. Few, if any, will ask the same questions of you. If you start feeling that you're being treated more like a spectator than a participant in the pregnancy, there are three basic solutions. First, you can just ignore the whole thing—no one's deliberately trying to exclude you; it just doesn't occur to most people that pregnancy, at least at this stage, affects men all that much. Second, you can sulk. This (although sometimes satisfying) will probably not get you the kind of attention you're craving. Third, you can take a proactive role and volunteer information about how the pregnancy is affecting you. Tell people about how excited you are; confide your hopes and fears to your friends—especially those who already have kids and can offer advice. If you're lucky, they'll then start asking you for updates.

"You're entirely too touchy. My saving grace is my ability to laugh at myself."

Your Relationship

COMMUNICATING WITH EACH OTHER

Pregnancy is not only a time of great joy and anticipation, it's also a time of great stress. And even though you and your partner are both pregnant at the same time, you're not experiencing the pregnancy in exactly the same way or at the same pace. This can lead to an increasing number of misunderstandings and conflicts between you and your partner.

As Dr. Shapiro writes, when a couple becomes a family, "generally all the things that are good get better, and all the things that are bad get worse." As your pregnancy continues, then, it's critical to learn to talk—and listen—to each other, and to find ways to help each other through this marvelous, but emotionally bumpy, experience.

As men, we've been conditioned to try to protect our partners from harm. And when our partners are pregnant, protecting them may include trying to minimize the levels of stress in their lives. One way men do this is by not talking about their own concerns. Researchers Carolyn and Philip Cowan write that men fear that mentioning their own worries may not only cause stress to their partners but also expose their own vulnerability at a time when they're expected to be strong for their wives.

The Cowans also found that this overprotective, macho attitude has some very negative side effects. First, because we never give ourselves the chance to talk about our fears, we never learn that what we're going through is normal and healthy. Second, our partners never get the chance to find out that we understand and share *their* feelings.

DANGEROUS ASSUMPTIONS

When I was in the Marines, one of my drill instructor's favorite comments was "Never assume anything. 'Assuming' makes an **ass** out of **u** and **me**." The sergeant's spelling problems notwithstanding (he also thought habitual thieves were called hypochondriacs and that Italians ate bisgetti), he was right about the dangers of making assumptions.

Here are a few important things you may have assumed were no problem. Not all these issues are important to everybody, but if you haven't discussed them already, do it now.

- **Your involvement in the pregnancy** Dr. Katharyn Antle May has found that there are three basic styles of father involvement during pregnancy. The *Observer Father* maintains a certain emotional distance and sees himself largely as a bystander; the *Expressive Father* is emotionally very involved and sees himself as a full partner; the *Instrumental Father* sees himself as the manager of the pregnancy and may feel a need to plan

"Me carrying the baby and you having the cravings is not *my idea of shared responsibility!"*

every medical appointment, every meal, and every trip to the gym. Whatever your style is, make sure to talk it over with your partner. After all, she's pregnant, too.

- **Your involvement in family tasks** How much child care are you planning to do when the baby comes? How much is your partner expecting you to do? How much are you expecting her to do? Several studies have shown that to some extent, women control their partners' involvement at home. If a woman wants her partner to take an active role in child care, he generally wants the same thing. But if she wants to keep these activities to herself, he usually expects to be less involved. In addition, the Cowans have found that men who take a more active role in running their households and rearing their children "tend to feel better about themselves and about their family relationships than men who are less involved in family work."
- **Religion** Both you and your partner may never have given a thought to the religious education—if any—you plan to give your child. If you have thought about it, make sure you're both still thinking along the same lines. If you haven't, this might be a good time to start.
- **Discipline styles** How do you feel about spanking your children? Never? Sometimes? How does she feel about it? How you were raised and whether your parents spanked you will have a great deal to do with how you raise your own children.
- **Sleeping arrangements** It's never too early to give some thought to where you want the baby to sleep: In your bed? In a bassinet next to you? In a separate room?
- **Work and child-care expectations** Is your partner planning to take some time off after the birth before going back to work? How long? Would *you* like to be able to take some more time off? How long? What types of child-care arrangements do you and she envision?
- **Finances** Do you need two paychecks to pay the mortgage? If you can get by on one, whose will it be?

And throughout the pregnancy, don't forget:

- **Your feelings—good, bad, or indifferent** Talk about your excitement about having a child, your dreams, your plans for the future, your fears, worries, and ambivalence, and how satisfied you are with your level of involvement during the pregnancy. But don't forget to ask your partner what she's feeling about the same things. Have these discussions regularly—what you and your partner are thinking and feeling in the third month may be completely different from what you'll be thinking and feeling in the fourth, sixth, or ninth months. As difficult as it may seem, learning to communicate with each other now will help you for years to come.

Getting Time Alone

There may be times when you find the pressures of the pregnancy so overwhelming that you need just to get away from it for a while. If so, take advantage of the fact that you don't have a baby inside you, and take some time off. Go someplace quiet where you can collect your thoughts or do something that will give you a break from the endless conversations about pregnant women and babies. Before you go, though, be sure to let your partner know your plan of escape. And whatever you do, don't rub it in: she'd probably give anything to be able to take a breather from the pregnancy for a couple hours.

Here are a few things you might want to do with your free time:

- Hang out with some childless friends.
- Start a journal about what you're feeling and thinking during the pregnancy.
- Go to the batting cages and let off a little steam.
- Go for a long drive or for a walk on the beach or in the woods.
- Be a kid for a while—blow some quarters on a video game.

Notes:

THE 4TH MONTH

Money, Money, Money

What She's Going Through

Physically

- Nipples darkening
- Increasing appetite as morning sickness begins to wane
- Clumsy—dropping and spilling things
- She may be able to feel some slight movements (although she probably won't associate them with the baby unless she's already had a child)

Emotionally

- Great excitement when she sees the sonogram
- Worries about miscarriage are beginning to fade
- Concerned about what it really means to be a mother
- Continuing forgetfulness and mood swings
- Increasingly dependent on you—needs to know you'll be there for her, that you still love her

What's Going On with the Baby

During this month, the baby will grow to about four inches long. His or her heart will finish developing and will start pounding away at 120–160 beats per minute—about twice as fast as yours. The baby can now tell when your partner is eating sweet things or sour things. He or she can also react to light and dark—if you shine a strong light on your partner's abdomen, the baby will turn away.

What You're Going Through

Increasing Sense of the Pregnancy's Reality

By the time the fourth month rolls around, most men are still in what Dr. Katharyn May calls the "moratorium phase" of pregnancy—intellectually we know she's pregnant, but we still don't have any "real" confirmation. Oh, sure, there was the pregnancy test, the blood test, the doctor's pelvic exams, her swelling belly and breasts, the food cravings, and hearing the baby's heartbeat a month before, but even with all that, I had the lingering suspicion that the whole thing was an elaborate, Mission: Impossible–style fake.

But the day my wife and I went in for the ultrasound, everything began to change. Somehow, seeing the baby's tiny heart pumping and watching those bandy little arms and legs squirm convinced me that we might really be pregnant after all.

Can We Really Afford This?

Besides being fun, seeing the ultrasound filled me with a wonderful sense of relief. After counting all the fingers and toes (not an easy task, considering how small they were and how fast they were moving), I felt I could finally stop worrying about whether our baby would be all right.

But my newfound sense of ease didn't last long. I suddenly became possessed by the idea that we couldn't possibly afford to have a baby—not an uncommon thought among expectant fathers.

American society values men's *financial* contribution to their families much more than it does their *emotional* contribution. And expressing strong feelings, anxiety, or even fear is not what men are expected to do—especially when their wives are pregnant. So, as the pregnancy progresses, most expectant fathers fall back on the more traditionally masculine way of expressing their concern for the well-being of their wives and little fetuses: they worry about money.

Some men express their financial worries by becoming obsessed with their jobs, their salaries, the size of their homes, even the rise and fall of interest rates. Expectant fathers frequently work overtime or take on a second job; others may become tempted by lottery tickets or get-rich-quick schemes. Insurance agents and financial advisors sometimes try to take advantage of an expectant father's concerns about money by encouraging him to buy insurance policies he doesn't need or make investments he and his family can't afford. Clearly, a new baby (and the decrease in household income while the mother is off work) can have a significant impact on the family's finances. But as real as they are, write Libby Lee and Arthur D. Colman, authors of *Pregnancy: The Psychological Experience,* men's financial worries "often get out of proportion to the actual needs of the family. They become the focus because they are something the man can be expected to handle. The activity may hide deeper worry about competence and security."

Safety—Your Partner's and the Baby's

As if worrying about finances weren't enough, many expectant fathers find themselves preoccupied with the physical health of the other members of their growing family (but not their own—studies have shown that men go to the doctor much less frequently than usual when their partners are pregnant).

I'd seen the ultrasound and knew that the baby was fine. And I'd already read that at this point in the pregnancy, there was very little chance of a miscarriage. But still, I worried. I quizzed my wife about how much protein she was eating; I reminded her to go to the gym for her workouts; I even worried about the position she slept in. (Sleeping on the back is a bad idea; the baby-filled uterus presses on the intestines, back, and a major vein—the inferior vena cava—and could cause hemorrhoids or even cut off the flow of oxygen or blood to both your partner and the fetus.) All in all, I was a real pain.

A word of advice: If you're feeling overly concerned and protective of your partner and your baby, be gentle and try to relax a little. Your partner probably has the same safety concerns you do. If you're still worried, discuss your concerns with her practitioner at your next appointment.

Staying Involved

Focus on Her

Although every pregnant woman will need and appreciate different things, there is a lot more common ground than you might imagine. Basically, she

Ways to Show Her You Care

Here are some ideas that will make you popular around the house (and make your wife the envy of all of her friends—pregnant and otherwise):

- Offer to give her back rubs and foot massages.
- Suggest activities that might be harder to do when the baby comes, like going to movies or concerts.
- Bring home roses for no reason at all.
- Vacuum the house—even under the bed—without being asked.
- Give your wife lots of hugs; research shows that the more she is hugged, the more she will hug the baby.
- Buy her a moisturizing bubble bath.
- If you're traveling on business, arrange to have a friend take her to dinner.
- Offer to pick up a pizza on your way home from work—and surprise her with a pint of her favorite frozen yogurt, too.
- Offer to run errands (pick up cleaning, shop, go to the drug store, and so forth).
- Do the laundry before it piles up.
- Tell her you think she's going to be a great mother.
- If she arrives home after you, have a candlelight dinner on the table, complete with sparkling cider.
- Write her a love letter and send it to her in the mail.
- Buy a toy or outfit for the baby, have it gift-wrapped, and let her unwrap it.

- Buy her a pretty maternity dress.
- Go on a long walk with her.
- Learn baby CPR.
- Offer to give her a back rub—again.
- If you smoke, stop.
- Tell her she's beautiful.
- Pay extra attention to making sure she has enough to eat—pack some snacks for her before the two of you go out for an evening or for a hike.
- Keep a list of your favorite names or buy her an interesting name book.
- Paint a picture for or write a letter to your unborn baby.
- Offer to set up interviews with potential child-care people.
- Buy her a Mother's Day gift.
- Keep a journal (either written, tape-recorded, or videotaped) of what you're thinking and feeling during the pregnancy.
- Subscribe to parenting magazines.
- Take her to visit the nursery at your local hospital.
- Help her address envelopes for the birth announcements.
- Learn easy recipes (see pages 34–41).
- Invite her to go swimming somewhere beautiful.
- If you already have children, take them to the park and let your partner have time alone to relax or run an errand she's had to put off.
- Surprise her with breakfast in bed on a lazy Sunday. Or, on a workday, get up five minutes earlier and surprise her with a power shake.
- Give other expectant mothers seats on trains and buses.
- Make a donation to a children's hospital.
- Make a donation to a school.
- Discuss your fears with your wife and listen to hers. Be certain not to belittle her fears—no matter how small they may seem to you.
- Paint or wallpaper the baby's room.
- Help put together the changing table and crib.
- Install smoke detectors in your house.
- Make a new will that includes your baby.
- Join a health club together.
- Clean out closets to make room for baby things.
- Call her on the phone during the day—just to tell her you love her.
- Offer to carry her bags.
- Buy a few tapes of her favorite music to listen to in the labor room.

needs three things from you now—and for the rest of the pregnancy—more than ever before: expressions of affection, admiration, and support (both verbal and physical) for *her;* sensitivity to her changing physical condition (hunger, fatigue, muscle pains, and so on); and expressions of affection and excitement about the *baby* and your impending parenthood.

Finances

PLANNING A COLLEGE FUND

It may seem hard to imagine now, but in eighteen years or so the baby you haven't even met yet is going to be graduating from high school and heading off to college. And so, at the risk of reinforcing the old stereotype that a father's role in his children's lives is primarily financial, it's time to talk about money.

From the mid-1970s to the mid-1990s, college tuition and expenses, such as room and board, rose about 5 to 8 percent a year. Experts project that these costs will continue to rise by about 6 to 7 percent a year. This means that by the year 2015 a *single year* at a public college will cost more than $36,000; at a private college, costs will exceed $77,000.

If you're not independently wealthy, this may sound like an exorbitant amount of money—especially when you consider that you'll have to come up

"I just found out what braces cost."

with the same amount four years in a row. But if you establish a well-thought-out college fund now, things won't be as bad as you think. And if you're lucky, you might even be able to afford to have another kid.

Within the scope of this book it would be impossible to cover the full range of educational investment possibilities. So we've chosen to focus on a few of the most common alternatives. After you've considered what we have to say, we recommend that you get yourself a stockbroker or a financial planner and make sure that the education fund you're considering fits in with your overall financial objectives. But be wary of those who recommend that you do all of your investing through them. You should also have your accountant take a look at what you're planning.

ZERO COUPON BONDS are bonds issued by the U.S. Government and by corporations that you purchase for a small fraction of what they'll be worth when they mature (face value). You could, for example, pay $200 today for a bond that would be worth $1,000 by the time your child enters college. The price you pay now, and what the bonds will be worth at maturity, depend on current interest rates (the higher they are, the less you pay now) and when they mature (the longer you hold them, the less you pay).

The advantages of zeros are:

- You can pick any maturity date, from next year to thirty years in the future.
- You can lock in current interest rates until maturity.
- You know exactly what they'll be worth when they mature.
- There's an active market for zeros. So if you have a financial emergency, you can sell the bonds for whatever they're worth at that time.
- With government-issued zeros there's absolutely no risk of default.

The disadvantages of zeros are:

- You can't take advantage of changes in interest rates (if rates rise after you've bought a bond, you're out of luck).
- Even though you don't actually receive any money until the bond matures, you have to pay taxes on the interest earned each year. (You can, however avoid this problem by buying tax-exempt zero coupon municipal bonds.)
- If you don't hold the bonds to maturity, you may lose some of your principal.

SERIES EE SAVINGS BONDS are a type of zero coupon bond issued by the U.S. Government that, like zero coupon bonds, you purchase at a fraction of their face value.

The advantages of EE bonds are:

- Unlike zeros, they pay an adjustable rate of interest (a guaranteed 85 percent of the average market yield on five-year Treasury securities) if you hold them at least five years.
- No taxes are due until the bonds are cashed. This means you get to keep more of the interest you earn, which means that you get more interest on your interest, which means that you'll have more money at maturity.
- They may be *entirely* tax-free if you cash them in only for your child's education.

The disadvantages of EE bonds are:

- You can invest a maximum of $15,000 per year in EE bonds.
- Unlike zeros, there's no market for these bonds. All you can do is cash them in. You won't have to pay a commission, however.
- If you and your partner earn over $60,000 combined (the IRS will adjust this amount every year for inflation), the "entirely tax-free" advantage noted above doesn't fully apply.

PREPAID TUITION PLANS Some states have plans that allow you to prepay all or part of your child's state college tuition costs. How much you pay depends on when you expect your child to start college, and on current interest rates. Some private colleges offer similar programs.

The advantages of prepaid tuition plans are:

- These plans usually offer good value for the money.
- Tuition is fully paid.

The disadvantages of these plans are:

- If your child doesn't end up going to the college you selected eighteen years before, all you'll get back is the principal you put in—the interest you would have earned will be lost.
- You may have to pay taxes on the difference between what you pay today and what tuition costs eighteen years from now.

MUTUAL FUNDS save you the trouble of trying to put together your own stock or bond investment program. There are more than four thousand different mutual funds available—ranging from high-risk to low-risk—enabling you to pick the one that most closely matches your needs. Over the past ten years, mutual funds have increased an average of about 13 percent a year—significantly more than the rate of inflation.

HOW OFTEN TO INVEST

If you have the money, the best way to finance your child's college education is to invest an amount equal to four years of today's private-school tuition and fees right now. As the cost of education goes up, so will the value of your investment. Thus, by the time your child reaches college age, the entire cost of his or her education will be covered.

If you don't have the money now, you should invest as much as you feel you can afford, as often as you can afford to. The best way to do this is through a system called "dollar cost averaging." This means that on a regular basis—weekly, monthly, quarterly—you contribute a fixed amount to the same mutual fund or other investment. When prices are up you're buying fewer shares; when prices are down, you're buying more. A stockbroker friend says that dollar cost averaging is by far the best overall long-term investment strategy.

The problem with this or any other regular savings plan is remembering to do it. If things get tight—as they have plenty of times at my house—the education checks can get "overlooked" or "rescheduled." Fortunately, most brokerage houses allow you to have your specified investment automatically deducted from your checking or savings account, effectively creating a forced savings plan.

A NOTE ON TAXES

Whatever investment program you're considering, remember one thing: put it in your child's name. The first $500 of income earned by a child under fourteen is tax-free each year. The next $500 is taxed at 15 percent, which is probably less than your tax rate. Income over $1,000 a year is taxed at your rate.

What this means is that as soon as your child's investment account begins to earn over $1,000 a year, you ought to consider putting any future investments into tax-free zeros or mutual funds. That way, the tax liability will be kept to a minimum. Another option is to invest in aggressive-growth funds that will bring in the highest returns, and pay the taxes you'll owe along the way.

One final note: before you can start an investment program in your child's name, you'll have to have his or her Social Security number, which means you'll have to wait until he or she is born. So take advantage of the next few months and spend some time talking over with your partner what your educational objectives are, how much you have to invest, how much risk you're willing to tolerate, and how many children you're planning to have.

INSURANCE

LIFE INSURANCE While you may not think that this is the time to be talking about life insurance, you couldn't be more wrong. Because there are so many different kinds of life insurance, and because each of them is right only in certain circumstances, we're not going to go into much detail here. Suffice it to say that you and your partner should get life insurance if you don't have any, or meet with your agent to discuss if and how your new baby will change your insurance needs. The point is that if, God forbid, either of you dies unexpectedly, the survivor shouldn't have to worry about having to get a better job just to keep up the mortgage or private-school tuition payments.

LIFE INSURANCE FOR CHILDREN This one is pretty simple. In most cases, taking out a life insurance policy on a child is a complete waste of money. The one exception is if you're getting a policy that builds cash value.

Choosing a Financial Planner, a Stockbroker, or an Insurance Broker

- The safest way to start your search for a representative is to ask trusted friends and family members for their recommendations.
- Every family is different. You need a representative who's willing to take the time to get to know you and your goals for the future. You also need someone who is willing to answer every question you have, no matter how basic.
- Check the person out. This means asking for personal and professional references and following up on them. Some highfalutin-sounding certifications are nothing more than alphabet soup and mean only that the person paid a few hundred bucks to join an organization.
- Things change fast. So get together with your representative to review your overall financial plan once a year.

But if your aim is to build cash value, you'd probably get a higher return by putting the money into a mutual fund or other investment.

DISABILITY As long as you've got insurance on your mind, you really should take a long, hard look at disability coverage. If your employer offers a long-term disability policy, sign up now. If not, explore the subject of getting one of your own through your broker. In many cases, a long-term disability could be more devastating to your family's finances than death.

GETTING PROFESSIONAL ADVICE

Over the course of the next twenty years or so, you're probably going to be spending a lot of your hard-earned money on health, life, and disability insurance; college investment plans; and retirement plans. The way you spend all that money will have a powerful—and long-lasting—effect on you and your family. So, unless you're a financial planner, stockbroker, or insurance agent yourself, you've probably got no business making major financial decisions without advice. The problem, of course, is how to get the best advice (see page 73).

Notes:

THE 5TH MONTH

The Lights Are On and Somebody's Home

What She's Going Through

Physically

- Can feel the baby's movements—and she knows what they are
- May have occasional painless tightening of the uterus (Braxton-Hicks contractions)
- Continuing darkening of nipples, appearance of dark line from belly button down the abdomen

Emotionally

- Very reassured by the baby's movements and less worried about miscarriage
- Developing feeling of bonding with the baby
- Sensitivity about her changing figure
- Increase in sexual desire
- Increasingly dependent on you
- Feelings of jealousy (after all, it was her private pregnancy until now)

What's Going On with the Baby

The baby can now close his or her eyes and is beginning to grow eyelashes and hair on the head. He or she is about nine inches long and kicks, punches, grabs at the umbilical cord, and can even suck his or her thumb. Best of all, he or she can now hear what's going on outside the womb.

What You're Going Through

Oh My God, I'm Going to Be a Father

I have to admit that even after seeing the baby on the sonogram, I still found it hard to believe I was really going to be a father (the technology to fake a sonogram must exist, right?). But when my wife grabbed my hand, placed it on her belly, and I felt that first gentle kick, I knew the whole thing was true. And as usual, after the initial excitement passed, I found something to worry about.

More Interested in Fatherhood

After that first kick, I suddenly became consumed with the idea that I just wasn't ready to be a father. I still wanted children—nothing had changed there—but I suddenly realized that in only four months I would face the biggest challenge of my life, and I didn't know a thing about what I was getting into. I felt as though I were about to attempt a triple back flip from a trapeze—without a safety net.

I had already done a lot of reading about pregnancy and childbirth, but I felt I still didn't know what fathers really *do*. Doesn't it seem a little strange—scary, really—that you need to have years of training and take loads of tests before you can get most jobs, but there are absolutely no prerequisites for the far more important job of being a father?

Feeling the baby's first kicks may make you much more interested in reading about pregnancy, if you haven't been doing so already. You may also find yourself wanting to spend more time with friends or relatives who have small kids or just watching how other men interact with their children.

Turning Inward

You've had a lot to think about lately—your family's finances, your new role as a father, your partner's (and your baby's) safety. So don't be surprised if you begin to become preoccupied with your own thoughts—sometimes to the exclusion of just about everything else, even your partner.

Although this sort of "turning inward" is perfectly normal, make every effort to keep from distancing yourself from your partner. If you can, tell her what's on your mind; it'll probably make you feel a lot better. (If you're having a tough time opening up, you might want to review the "Your Relationship" section on pages 60–63.)

At the same time, though, remember that she may be feeling insecure and need to be reassured that you aren't going to leave her. She may also be feeling emotionally needy and crave confirmation of your love for her. Pay close attention to her subtle (or not so subtle) hints and make sure she gets the attention she needs. If she doesn't, she may think you don't care. As Arthur and Libby Colman write, "A man who ignores his partner's anxieties may find they escalate rather than abate with a condescending 'Everything is going to be all right, dear.'"

Staying Involved

Prenatal Communication

As we've discussed elsewhere, good communication is a critical part of your pregnancy. But what about communicating with your unborn child? While the very idea may sound a little wacky, research has shown that months before they are born, fetuses are extremely responsive to what's happening "on the outside."

For your partner, communicating with your unborn child is quite a bit different—or at least more convenient—than it is for you. After all, she and the fetus are physically connected; and she can talk to it, sing to it, or rub it through her belly any time of day or night. But just because your access to the baby is comparatively limited doesn't mean you can't communicate with it.

There's no question that unborn babies can hear. In one study, an obstetrician inserted a microphone into a woman's uterus while she was in labor (after her water had broken), and recorded the external sounds that could be heard from the inside. He got clear recordings—not only of voices and the mother's internal body sounds but also of Beethoven's Ninth Symphony, which was being played in the delivery room.

Hearing is one thing, but are babies actually affected by what they hear from within the womb? Absolutely. Researcher Anthony DeCasper asked sixteen women to make a tape of themselves reading a poem called "The King, the Mice, and the Cheese," and two different tapes of Dr. Seuss's *The Cat in the Hat.* Then, during the last six and a half weeks of their pregnancies, the women were instructed to choose only one of the stories they'd recorded (roughly a third of the women chose each story) and play it three times a day for their unborn child.

When the babies were three days old, DeCasper offered them a choice between the story they'd heard over and over or one of the other stories. Since three-day-old babies aren't real good about speaking up, DeCasper used a "suck-o-meter" (a specially rigged pacifier that enabled the babies

A Few Things to Remember about Prenatal Communication

- Respect your partner. You've got a right to speak with your child, but she's got a right to privacy.
- Try to overcome the feeling that what you are doing is absolutely ridiculous.
- Don't whisper. Speak to the fetus loudly enough so that a person standing across the room could hear you clearly.
- Don't do it when you're feeling bored. The fetus will pick up on your tone of voice.
- Don't get your expectations too high. There's very little you or anyone else can do to guarantee that your child will be a genius.
- Have fun.

to determine which story they'd get to hear merely by changing their sucking speed) to allow the children to express their preferences. Fifteen out of the sixteen babies chose the story they'd heard while in the womb. If nothing else, this research ought to convince you that even before they're born, babies' lights are on and there's somebody home.

So why should *you* try to communicate with your growing fetus? First of all, because it's kind of fun. In the evening, I used to place my hands on my wife's belly and tell the current resident all about what I'd done during the day. Sometimes I'd even do "counting" exercises with them: I'd poke once and say (loudly), "One." Most of the time, I'd get an immediate kick back. A few seconds later, I'd poke twice and say, "Two." Frequently, I'd get two kicks back.

The second reason to try some prenatal conversations is that they can help you establish a bond with your baby before the birth. It may even help make the pregnancy seem a little more "real." I've got to admit that in the beginning, the idea of talking to a lump in my wife's belly seemed silly. But after a while I got used to it and began to feel a real closeness with the baby. Another father felt that by communicating extensively with his unborn daughter, he was able to establish a loving relationship with her while she was still inside. And when she finally was born, he described their first meeting as "like meeting someone face to face with whom you had only spoken on the telephone."

In addition, communicating with your unborn child will help him or her develop a bond with *you*. Many fathers are jealous of the immediate bond newborn children have with their mothers. It seems, though, that this bond may have more to do with the mother's voice (which the baby has heard every day for nine months) than anything else. Dr. DeCasper, in another suck-o-meter study, found that nine out of ten newborns selected a story recorded by their own mother over the same story recorded by another woman. By getting your baby used to your voice, he or she will be able to begin bonding with you immediately.

A third reason to try prenatal communication is that there's some evidence that you can influence the type of person your child turns out to be. Boris Brott (yes, he's a relative, but I've never met him), a famous Canadian orchestra conductor, traces his interest in music to the womb:

> As a young man, I was mystified by this ability I had to play certain pieces sight unseen. I'd be conducting a score for the first time and, suddenly, the cello line would jump out at me: I'd know the flow of the piece before I turned the page of the score. One day, I mentioned this to my mother, who is a professional cellist. I thought she'd be intrigued because it was always the cello line that was so distinct in my mind. She was; but when she heard what the pieces were, the mystery quickly solved itself. All the scores I knew sight unseen were ones she had played when she was pregnant with me.

In an effort to harness the power of prenatal communication, several physicians and obstetricians have developed organized communication systems. Psychiatrist Thomas Verny says that by singing and talking to the fetus, "parents create a positive intrauterine environment, reducing the level of anxiety-producing hormones that lead to frenetic activity and even ulcers in the unborn." Going one step further, Dr. Rene Van de Carr says that his program, the Prenatal Classroom, provides systematic stimulation that may "actually help the growing fetus' brain become more efficient and increase learning capacity after birth." Perhaps the most fantastic claims, though, are made by psychiatrist Brent Logan. Logan, who uses what he calls the "cardiac curriculum" to pump a set of increasingly complex heartbeatlike sounds into the mother's womb, says his "graduates" frequently learn to talk as early as at five or six months and to read at eighteen months (most kids don't usually talk until they're at least a year old, or read until they're five or six).

For more information about prenatal learning, I recommend reading Rene Van de Carr's and Thomas Verny's books, both of which may be available in your local public library (see bibliography).

Sex

Pregnancy can do funny things to your libido. Some expectant fathers are more interested in sex and more easily aroused than ever before. Others are repelled by the very idea. Whether you're feeling either of these ways or something in between, rest assured that it's completely normal.

In this section, we'll talk about the sexual issues that may come up in the first six months of your pregnancy. Late-pregnancy sexual issues are covered on pages 114–15.

WHY YOU AND/OR YOUR PARTNER MIGHT BE FEELING *INCREASED* SEXUAL DESIRE

- After about the third month, her nausea and fatigue are probably gone, making sex more appealing.
- You may find her pregnant body (with its larger breasts and fuller curves) erotic.
- Your partner may be proud of her more ample figure and may be feeling sexier.
- You may be turned on by the feeling of power and masculinity at having created life.
- Your partner may be turned on by the confirmation of her femininity and by the awe at what her body is doing.
- Throughout pregnancy, you both may experience a newfound feeling of closeness that frequently manifests itself sexually.

WHY YOU AND/OR YOUR PARTNER MIGHT BE FEELING *DECREASED* SEXUAL DESIRE

- In the first trimester, your partner may be too nauseated or tired to be interested in sex. In the second trimester, she may feel too uncomfortable or too awkward to want to have sex (about 25 percent of pregnant women feel this way).
- She may think that you don't find her attractive and don't want to have sex with her.
- You may *not*, in fact, be attracted to a woman whose body has been transformed from fun to functional.
- You may think your partner isn't feeling attractive and wouldn't be interested in sex.
- You or your partner may be afraid that sex will hurt her—or the baby. In fact, there's nothing to be afraid of. The baby is safely cushioned by its amniotic fluid–filled sac, and, unless your doctor feels there are exten-

uating circumstances, sex during pregnancy is no more dangerous for your partner than at any other time. You (and your partner) may find this information reassuring. If you do, great; if not, now may be the time to talk about and try some different sexual positions (lying on your sides or with your partner on top, for example) and different ways of bringing each other to orgasm (oral sex, vibrators, and so on). Often simply making a few such changes can go a long way toward alleviating your fears.

- Although in most cases sex is required to become a parent, you and your partner may feel, as it gradually sinks in that you are about to become parents, that parents aren't supposed to be sexual. (Even though we are all living proof that our parents had sex at least once, it's somehow hard to imagine the two of them, in bed, naked . . .)
- You or your partner may feel that sex serves only one purpose: creating children. And once you've done that, there's no more need for sex—until you want more kids.

WHAT THE EXPERTS SAY

As you can see, the range of feelings about sex is broad. But if you still aren't convinced that you're not the only one feeling the way you do, here are a few interesting things researchers have found out about expectant couples' sexuality during pregnancy:

- According to psychologists Wendy Miller and Steven Friedman, expectant fathers generally underestimate how attractive their partners feel, and expectant mothers consistently underestimate how attractive their partners find them. (The bottom line is that most men find their pregnant partners' bodies erotic, and most pregnant women feel quite attractive.)
- According to the Cowans, expectant fathers have more psychological inhibitions about physical intimacy during pregnancy than their partners do.
- The old myth that pregnancy somehow desexualizes women is just that—a myth. In fact, Miller and Friedman found that there are no significant differences in the level of sexual desire or sexual satisfaction between expectant men and women.

WHEN YOU AND YOUR PARTNER ARE OUT OF SYNC

Of course, you and your partner may not always be on the same wavelength. She may feel like having sex just when you're feeling put off by her Rubenesque figure. Conversely, you may want to have sex at a time when she's simply not interested. Here are a few suggestions that might help:

- **Talk.** At these and so many other times during your pregnancy, communicating with your partner is essential. As Arthur and Libby Colman so wisely write, "Unless the couple can talk about their sex life, their entire relationship may suffer, and that in turn will compound their sexual problems."
- **Try some nonsexual affection,** such as snuggling, touching, or just hugging each other. And say up front that that is what you're interested in doing, because it isn't as easy as it sounds. Professors Cowan and Cowan have found that many couples need practice finding sensual ways to please each other short of intercourse. And both men and women hesitate to make affectionate overtures if they aren't sure they're ready to progress to intercourse and are worried they'll be misinterpreted.
- **Be nice to each other.** Being critical of her figure will make her feel self-conscious, less attractive, and less interested in sex.

Notes:

THE 6TH MONTH

Work and Family

What She's Going Through

Physically

- Period of greatest weight gain begins
- Increased sweating
- Increased blood supply gives her that pregnant "glow"
- Increased fetal activity

Emotionally

- Moodiness is decreasing
- Continued forgetfulness
- Feeling that the pregnancy will never end
- Increased bonding with the baby
- Still very dependent on you

What's Going On with the Baby

The baby is now covered with vernix, a thick, waxy protective coating. The movements of the now foot-long two-pounder are getting stronger, and he or she can hear, and respond to, sounds from outside the uterus.

What You're Going Through

Reexamining Your Relationship with Your Father

As the reality of your prospective fatherhood unfolds, you'll probably find yourself spending a lot of time contemplating how you'll reconcile the various roles—parent, provider, husband, employee, friend—that will make up your paternal identity. As mentioned in earlier chapters, you may be spending more time reading about childhood and watching how your male friends, or even strangers, juggle these roles.

But eventually you'll realize that your own father—whether you know it or not—has already had a profound influence on the kind of father you'll be. You also may find yourself nearly overcome with forgotten images of childhood—especially ones involving your father. Just walking down the street, I'd suddenly remember the times we went camping or to the ballet, how he taught me to throw a baseball in the park, and the hot summer afternoon he, my sisters, and I stripped down to our underwear in the backyard and painted each other with watercolors. There's nothing like impending paternity to bring back all the memories and emotions of what it was like to be fathered as a child.

Not all childhood memories of fathers are positive. Many men's images of their fathers are dominated by fear, pain, loneliness, or longing. Either way, don't be surprised if you find yourself seriously reexamining your relationship with your father. Was he the kind of man you'll want to use as your role model? Was he the perfect example of the kind of father you *don't* want to be like? Or was he somewhere in between? Many men, particularly those who had rocky, or nonexistent, relationships with their fathers, find that the prospect of becoming a father themselves enables them to let go of some of the anger they've felt for so long.

Don't be surprised if you start having a lot of dreams about your father. Dream researcher Luis Zayas found that an expectant father's uncertainty about his identity as father, his actual role, and the changed relationship with his wife and family are "among the psychic threads of fatherhood" that are fundamentally related to the man's relationship with his own father and are frequently present in his dreams.

So, whether you're awake or asleep, as you're thinking about your father, remember that what's really going on is that you're worried about what kind of a father *you* will be when your baby arrives.

A Sense of Mortality

Although I've always been more than just a little fascinated by death, it wasn't until my wife got pregnant the first time that death became more than a mere abstraction. Suddenly it occurred to me that my death could have a serious impact on other people.

This realization had some interesting and fairly immediate results. The first thing that happened was that I became a much better driver—or at least a safer one. Overnight, yellow lights changed their meaning from "floor it" to "proceed with caution." I began to leave for appointments a few minutes earlier so I wouldn't have to hurry, I wove in and out of traffic less, and I found myself not quite so annoyed with people who cut me off in traffic. But besides becoming a better driver, I began to look back with horror at some of the risky things—parachuting, scuba diving—I'd done before I'd gotten married, and I began to reconsider some of the things I'd tentatively planned for the near future—bungee jumping, hang gliding. After all, now there were people counting on me to stay alive.

My preoccupation with my own mortality had other interesting consequences as well. I found myself strangely drawn to my family's history; I wanted to learn more about our traditions, our history, our family rituals, the wacky relatives no one ever talked about. I even bought a family-tree computer program and began bugging my relatives about their birth dates. Apparently it's quite common for expectant fathers to experience a heightened sense of attachment to their relatives—both immediate and distant—even if they weren't particularly close before.

This really isn't so unusual, especially when you consider that one of the main reasons we have kids in the first place is so that a little piece of us will live on long after we're gone. I guess the hope is that one day seventy-five years from now, when my great-grandson is expecting a child, he'll start to explore his roots and want to get to know more about me.

Feeling Trapped

As we've already discussed, you and your partner probably aren't feeling the same things at the same time. Earlier on in the pregnancy, your partner may have turned inward, preoccupied with how the pregnancy was affecting *her.* You may have felt a little (or a lot) left out. By now, though, your partner may be "coming out"—concentrating less on herself and the baby, and more on you.

Meanwhile, you may have just begun the process of turning inward. You're going to be a father in less than four months, and you've got a lot of things to think about, many of which you need to work through on your own. The potential problem here is that just as you begin to focus on yourself, your partner is becoming increasingly dependent on you. She may be afraid that you don't love her anymore and that you're going to leave her. Or she may be worried—just as you are—about your physical safety. Although being doted upon is nice, it can sometimes get out of hand. And your partner's increased dependence on you may cause you to feel trapped. As the Colmans found, a pregnant woman's "sudden concern may make a man feel over-protected, as though his independence is being threatened." If you are feeling trapped, it's important to let your partner know in a gentle, nonconfrontational way. At the same time, encourage her to talk about what she's feeling and what she wants from you.

Staying Involved

Having Fun

Besides being a time of great change—physical as well as emotional—pregnancy can be a fun time, too. Here are a few ways to amuse yourselves:

- **Take lots of pictures.** I took regular shots of my wife—from the front and the side, with emphasis on the belly—holding a mug-shot-style card labeled "Pregnant Woman Number 1 (2, 3, and so on)." For another series of photos, she stood up while I lay on my back between her legs and took pictures of her soft underbelly. If you don't have a camera that marks the date right on the prints, you'll want to take note of the critical day the belly completely blocks your view of your partner's face. Take pictures at least once a month until the eighth month, then once a week after that.
- **Get some special clothes.** His and hers "Yes sir, that's my baby" T-shirts, and "Father-to-bee" hats (featuring a picture of a bumble bee) are favorites.
- **Get some exercise—together.** Taking a water aerobics or swimming class together can be a lot of fun. You'll be amazed at how agile pregnant women can be when they're floating in water. Unless you're quite confident about your partner's sense of humor, it's best to stifle your comments about whales—beached or otherwise.
- **Start a clipping file for the baby.** Just before our older daughter was born, my wife started putting together a file with newspaper and magazine photos of the hot fashions of the day; lists of the top ten movies, books, and records of the year; articles on the pressing political and social issues of the day; pictures of the house we live in and the baby's room—before and after we fixed it up; and ads—showing the prices, of course—for a variety of items (houses for sale in our neighborhood, computers, food, movie and theater tickets, and so on).
- **Go shopping for baby announcements.** Or, you can design your own. See pages 101–2 for more details.

- **Make a plaster belly cast.** Believe it or not, this is my all-time favorite. It's a little complicated, but well worth the trouble. Long after the baby is born, you, your partner, and your friends will be absolutely amazed that your partner was ever that big (and the baby that small). If you're interested in trying it, Francine Krause (P.O. Box 1024, Guerneville, CA 95446 [707] 869-3925) sells a wonderful kit that includes all the materials you'll need. An important warning: Don't even *think* about making a cast of your partner's belly using any kind of plastic, rubber, or resin. No matter what anybody tells you, these products can be extremely harmful to both your partner and the baby.

Work and Family

FAMILY LEAVE

Let's face it: for a man, staying involved with the fetus is possible only a few hours a week—a little before work, a bit more after work, on weekends. But what about *after* the pregnancy? Is a few hours a day going to be enough time to spend with your child? If it were, you probably wouldn't be reading this book.

Contrary to the common stereotypes, most fathers want to spend a lot of time with their families. Consider the results of a few recent studies:

- One major corporation found that 57 percent of men (up from 37 percent five years earlier) wanted work-schedule flexibility that would enable them to spend more time with their families.
- A *Los Angeles Times* poll found that 39 percent of men say they would quit their jobs and stay home with the kids.
- Three out of four fathers consider family to be the most important aspect of their lives.
- Eighty percent of fathers want to take more of a role in parenting than their own fathers did and expect to make parenting a fifty-fifty proposition with their wives.

Despite contemporary fathers' good intentions, however, only about *1 percent* of men ever take advantage of their companies' family-leave options when they have the chance. So what accounts for the contradiction between what men *say* and what they actually *do*? First of all, the vast majority of family-leave plans (including the recently enacted Family and Medical Leave Act of 1993) are unpaid. Since the average working woman still makes less than the average working man, if one person is going to take time off from work, many families conclude that they can better survive the loss of the woman's salary.

The Family and Medical Leave Act of 1993

The Family and Medical Leave Act of 1993 is not a simple document to understand. You can (and should) get a free copy from your senator or congressional representative. Here's a summary of what it means for fathers:

- **Who can take the leave?** Any person who works for a company that employs fifty or more people, has been employed by that company for at least twelve months, *and* has worked at least 1,250 hours.
- **How much leave can you take?** Eligible employees can take up to twelve work weeks of leave at any time during the twelve-month period that starts the day your child is born. Be careful, though: if you and your wife are employed by the same company, you are entitled to a *total* of twelve weeks between you.
- **Is it paid?** Employers are not required to pay you your salary while you're on leave. But say your employer pays for six weeks of family leave, you're still entitled to take another six without pay.
- **What about benefits?** Your employer must maintain your coverage under the company's health plan for the duration of your leave.
- **Is your job protected?** In most cases, yes. Your employer cannot fire or replace you while you're on leave unless he or she can prove that your being gone has caused "substantial and grievous economic injury to the operations of the employer."
- **Do you have to give notice?** Under the act, you're required to give your employer at least thirty days' notice before taking your family leave. But the more notice you give, the more time everyone will have to get used to the idea.

Check with your state's employment department to see whether it offers family-leave benefits that are more liberal than those of the federal program. In California, for example, companies that employ twenty-five or fewer people are required to offer their employees family leave (as opposed to the federal program's fifty-employee minimum).

Family Leave If You're an Employee

- **Take the leave.** Every man I interviewed who took family leave told me he'd do it again. One even told me he thought that men who *didn't* take family leave were "nuts."
- **Know your rights.** Find out whether you're eligible for family leave under the Family and Medical Leave Act of 1993 (see page 89), your company's voluntary plan, or any other government- or state-mandated program.
- **Start talking to your employer *now*.** If you're covered by a leave plan, start working out the details in a nonthreatening, nonconfrontational way. If you're *not* covered by a leave plan, you may be able to arrange for some time off anyway.

Family Leave If You're an Employer (or Supervisor)

- **Take the leave yourself.** The ultimate responsibility for helping men get more involved with their families rests at the top—with male managers. If you set an example and take family leave yourself, everyone else will see that it's okay and follow your lead.
- **Encourage other men to take the leave.** Most of your male employees will be reluctant to approach you with their family-leave plan. If you know they're pregnant, raise the issue with them first. Chances are, they'll be grateful. At Los Angeles Water and Power, employee turnover dropped drastically after the Doting Dads program started.
- **Don't worry about the cost.** Companies with liberal family-oriented benefits have found that the costs incurred to keep a job open for a man on leave or to redistribute his workload while he's gone are more than made up for in improved morale and increased productivity.

But financial pressure isn't the only reason men don't take family leave. Even when their companies offer *paid* paternity leave (less than 2 percent of all employers), men still don't participate. Why not? A lot of men have a deep-rooted conviction that getting on the "daddy track" will hurt their careers. Tom, an attorney friend of mine who elected not to take advantage of his firm's paid

"Adorable, Kravitz, but from now on baby pictures will suffice."

family-leave plan, told me: "I wanted to take the leave, but I knew I'd never make partner if I did. All the male associates knew it would be career suicide."

Unfortunately, Tom's fears are not unfounded. Dr. Joseph Pleck, of Wellesley College, says that "because employers don't understand or accept the idea of child-care leave for anyone, they find the concept of paternity leave incomprehensible, or simply frivolous." It's not surprising, then, that many companies send their male employees mixed messages about whether or not it's okay to take family leave. A few years before the Family and Medical Leave Act was signed, one major study found that most firms that voluntarily offered gender-neutral family-leave plans didn't advertise that they could be taken by fathers. And when the researchers asked more than 1,500 human resources directors and CEOs how much time they thought would be reasonable for men to take as paternity leave, 63 percent said, "None." Even at companies that did offer paternity leave, 41 percent said *no* amount of paternity leave was reasonable. Sadly, even today, when most larger employers are required by law to grant family leave to men, the prevailing attitude hasn't changed.

Some companies, however, are bucking old conventions; having decided that simply offering paternity leave isn't enough, they're *encouraging* their male employees to take it. For example, in 1991 the Los Angeles Department of Water and Power (78 percent of whose employees are men) started a complete fathering program called Doting Dads. The highly publicized program includes a four-month paternity-leave plan, a father mentorship program, child-care referral services, and even breastfeeding classes for both spouses. Between 1980 and 1990 (before the program started), a total of only three or four men took paternity leave. But after Doting Dads came into being, the number of men taking paternity leave has grown to about thirty each year. A few other large employers have begun to notice a small increase in the number of men who take family leave. The numbers are still minuscule—especially when compared to the number of women who take additional time off after the disability portion of their maternity leave has run out—but it's progress.

LONG-TERM WORK-SCHEDULE CHANGES

So far we've talked about taking a few weeks off just after the birth of your child. But what about after that?

Not long after our first daughter was born, my wife left her big, downtown law firm and found a less stressful, three-day-a-week job closer to home. Almost everyone we knew applauded. But when I made the announcement that I, too, would be cutting back to three days a week, the reaction was quite a bit different. At work, I was hassled repeatedly by my boss and coworkers, and a lot of my friends and relatives began to whisper that if I didn't go back to work full-time, my career might never recover.

For the most part, flexible schedules, job sharing, part-time work, or working-at-home options have been considered "women's issues." But they're not. As a new (or a veteran) father, you're probably going to want to spend more time with your children than your own father did, and just about the only way you'll get to is to make some changes in your work schedule.

I'm not suggesting that everyone should cut back their work schedules to three days a week. Clearly, that just isn't practical for most people (although it sure would be nice, wouldn't it?). But there are a few other ways to increase the amount of time you spend with your family.

JOB SHARING

More and more companies are recognizing that their employees—at least their female ones—need more flexibility than a traditional job can provide. One solution is to have two people share a job—and a desk—at the office. For example, one person might work in the mornings, the other in the afternoons.

WORKING AT HOME (TELECOMMUTING)

While many managers feel they have to see their employees on a daily basis to supervise them, this just isn't the case. Years ago, when I was a commodities trader, I used to spend eight or nine hours a day on the phone haggling with people—most of whom I never met—about grain prices. My coworkers were similarly occupied, and my boss was two thousand miles away. Realistically, there was no reason I couldn't have been working at home.

Granted, commodities trading is not a typical job, but the fact is that many Americans do work that doesn't require their physical presence in any particular place at any particular time. If you're not a construction worker or a retail salesman, you might be a prime candidate for telecommuting.

Now before you start to panic, I'm not suggesting that you rent out your office to someone else—most telecommuters work only a day or two a week at home. The point is that being able to telecommute is just another option that can allow you a little more time with your family. Remember, though, that telecommuting is *not* meant to be a substitute for child care.

If you think you might want to try telecommuting, here's what you'll probably need:

- a computer (compatible with your employer's system)
- an additional phone line or two
- a modem
- a fax machine (or a send/receive fax/modem)
- a quiet place to set things up

As great as working at home is, there are still a few disadvantages. Some of my friends began to think that since I was always at home, I wasn't really doing anything, and since I wasn't doing anything, I could run errands for them. If this happens to you, you're going to have to learn to say no. Working at home can also get a little lonely—you might miss hanging out around the water cooler and schmoozing with your buddies at work.

Notes:

THE 7TH MONTH

Entering the Home Stretch

What She's Going Through

Physically

- Increasing general physical discomfort (cramps, dizziness, abdominal achiness, heartburn, and so forth)
- Itchy abdomen
- Some increased clumsiness
- Learning to walk in a new, awkward way
- Some thick, white, vaginal discharge (it's called *leukorrhea*, and is completely normal)
- Increased Braxton-Hicks (false labor) contractions

Emotionally

- Decreased moodiness
- Dreaming/fantasizing about the baby
- Concerned about work—not sure she'll have the energy to go back, and concerned about how to balance roles of mother, wife, employee . . .
- Fear about the labor and delivery

What's Going On with the Baby

The baby's lungs are maturing and he or she can now move in rhythm to music played outside the womb. Weighing in at three pounds and measuring fifteen inches long, he or she is starting to get a bit cramped in the uterus and may spend a lot of his or her free time sucking a thumb.

What You're Going Through

Increasing acceptance of the pregnancy

As we've discussed earlier, for most expectant fathers the process of completely accepting the pregnancy is a long one—with the baby becoming progressively more real over the course of the nine months. "It's like getting the measles," said one man interviewed by researcher Katharyn May. "You get exposed, but it takes a while before you realize that you've got it." Another researcher, Pamela Jordan, found that despite seeing the fetus on a sonogram many men don't really experience their children as real until they meet them face-to-face at birth.

Visualizing the Baby

The growing reality of the pregnancy is reflected in men's dreams as well. Researcher Luis Zayas has found that in expectant fathers' dreams in the early and middle stages of the pregnancy "the child is not represented as a person. Instead, symbols of the child are present." But as the pregnancy

"I want kids. He wants children."

advances to the final stage, expectant fathers—consciously and unconsciously—produce clearer images of their children.

If you're discussing this with your partner, keep in mind that women typically begin visualizing their children very early in pregnancy. These visions, which occur both in daydreams and night dreams, undoubtedly have something to do with the physical link the woman has with the fetus, as well as with the fact that many women—thanks largely to socialization—readily view themselves as mothers. In addition, pregnant women generally dream and fantasize about *babies,* while their partners imagine themselves with three- to five-year-old children. This was certainly true for me. In almost every dream or fantasy involving children that I had while my wife was pregnant, I was holding hands, leaving footprints on the beach, or playing catch—all things you can't do with an infant. My wife, in contrast, dreamed of a palm-sized, hairless baby who talked to her like an adult.

Speculating about Gender

Like it or not, our society is fixated on gender. So it's not surprising that most parents (if they don't already know) eventually—or constantly—speculate about the sex of their unborn baby. Is your partner carrying the baby high? Wide? Low? Are the baby's kicks hard enough to move your hand, or are they more gentle? Is your partner's complexion clear, or does she have a little acne? There are literally hundreds of absolutely, positively surefire ways of determining what flavor your baby will be—and before your baby is born, you'll hear every one of them.

But before you start believing any of the stories you hear, there are a few things you might find interesting:

- Most expectant fathers express a preference for boys.
- Most women claim to have no preference.
- More women than men call the unborn baby "it." However, both men and women prefer to call the baby by some kind of nickname.

In our case, the nicknames we gave our in-utero daughters stuck with them long after they were born. We called our older "The Roo"—as in kanga—because she kicked so hard she could knock an open book off my wife's belly. And we called our younger "Pokey" because, unlike her sister, she preferred to jab and poke.

If you have a preference for the gender of your child, you might think about keeping it to yourself. If your child turns out to be of the "wrong" gender, chances are he or she will eventually find out about it (probably from

an unthinking friend or relative whom you once told). The feeling of being inadequate, of "letting you down," and even of being secretly rejected or loved less, may haunt the child for many years, especially in adolescence, when self-confidence is often at a low. So even if you have such a preference in your heart of hearts, there is little to gain—and plenty to lose—by spreading the word.

Some expectant fathers are actually afraid of getting a child of the "wrong" gender, feeling that if they do, they won't be able to have the parenting experience they'd imagined. For many men, their images of themselves as parents are closely linked to the gender of their children. As boys, we spent a great deal of our childhood engaging in physical activities such as running, jumping, wrestling, and playing football. So it's natural to imagine ourselves doing the same things with our own children. Yet some men feel uncomfortable with the idea of wrestling with their daughters, believing that playing physically with girls would somehow be inappropriate. The truth of the matter is that not only is it safe and appropriate to play physically with girls, it may also be quite beneficial for them in some unexpected ways (see pages 185–87 for more on this).

Fear of Falling Apart During Her Labor

Men are supposed to be strong, right? Especially while their wives are pregnant. And any sign of weakness could be taken as an indication of, well, weakness. Perhaps it's those old societal pressures that make most men dread labor—not only because they aren't looking forward to seeing their partners in pain, but because they're afraid that they'll simply fall apart. And everybody knows that real men don't crack under pressure.

If you're worried about how you'll perform during your partner's labor, do yourself two favors:

- Read the "Classes" section on pages 102–10—especially the "What If You Feel Like You Don't Want to Be in the Delivery Room at All?" section at the end.
- Remember that it rarely happens. Dr. Jerrold Shapiro interviewed more than two hundred expectant fathers, none of whom fell apart during his partner's labor.

Staying Involved

Choosing a Name

Naming a child may sound like an easy task, but it's harder than you think. And you'd better start thinking about it soon, because the second question you're going to hear after the baby comes (the first being "Boy or girl?") is "What's the baby's name?" Here are a few things you might want to keep in mind as you begin your search:

- Think about the future. That cute name you're considering if you have a girl might sound pretty ridiculous when she turns out to be a Supreme Court justice.
- According to the author of *The Best Baby Name Book in the Whole Wide World,* boys who have peculiar names (Armin, for instance) have a higher incidence of mental problems than boys with common ones, and than girls with peculiar ones.
- Do you need—or want—to honor a relative?
- Do you want a name that indicates your ethnic or religious background?
- Do you want something unique yet manageable?
- Do you want something easy to spell and/or pronounce?
- How do you feel about the nicknames that go with it?
- How does it sound with the last name? How would the nicknames sound with the last name?
- No, you can't use numbers. (There was a real-life court case a while back about a guy in Minnesota who tried to change his name to a number. He lost.)

HOW TO PICK 'EM

Start by making a list of the ten boys' and ten girls' names you like best. Exchange lists with your partner and cross off all the ones on her list you couldn't possibly live with. She'll do the same to your list. If there are any names left, you're in business. If not, keep repeating the process until you come up with names acceptable to you both. Some couples who absolutely cannot agree on two names decide instead to let one partner choose the name if it's a boy and the other choose the name if it's a girl (and let the loser choose the next child's name).

Not only is this little exercise fun, but it will also give you and your partner some interesting insights into each other's minds. My wife, for example, had never really taken my interest in mythology seriously until the names Odin (the chief god in Norse legends) and Loki (the Norse god of mischief and evil) showed up on my top-ten list. I don't know what I'm more grateful for, that both those choices were vetoed or that both our children are girls.

If you need a little help, here are a few books—each containing thousands of names and their meanings—you might want to check out:

- *The Best Baby Name Book in the Whole Wide World,* by Bruce Lansky (Meadowbrook, 1984), offers 13,001 possibilities.
- *Name Your Baby,* edited by Lareina Rule (Bantam, 1986), claims to have over 10,000 suggestions.
- *20,001 Names for Baby,* by Carol McD. Wallace (Avon, 1992).
- *Proud Heritage,* by Elza Dinwidde-Boyd (Avon, 1994), offers 11,001 names for African-American babies.
- *Multicultural Baby Names,* by M. J. Abadie (Longmeadow Press, 1993), offers 5,000 African, Arabic, Asian, Hawaiian, Hispanic, Indian, and Native American names.
- *The New Age Baby Name Book,* by Sue Browder (Workman, 1987) has 10,000 possibilities and is filled with other really great information.
- *Beyond Jennifer and Jason,* by Linda Rosenkrantz and Pamela Satran (St. Martin's Press, 1994). If you're moving to England, pick up *Beyond Charles and Diana,* by the same authors (St. Martin's Press, 1992).

It might seem as though these books pretty well cover all the bases, but out of the 174,003 names my wife and I looked at, we came up with only four that worked for us (a first and middle for each daughter).

Another approach—albeit an odd one—to picking names is offered by Albert Mehrabian in his book *The Name Game* (Signet, 1992). Mehrabian surveyed two thousand people, asking them to judge several thousand first names and rate them according to success, morality, health, warmth, cheerfulness, masculinity/femininity. Not surprisingly, Mehrabian found that certain names evoke certain stereotypes. Bunny, for example, scored high on femininity, but low on morality and success. Ann and Holly were highly rated in all categories. For boys, Grover and Aldo were big losers in all categories, while Hans (go figure) was rated highly across the board.

So what does all this mean? No one knows. Some onomasticians (people who study names) claim that a child's name has a direct and profound effect on the kind of a life, and successes, he or she will have. Some cite a study in which fifth- and sixth-grade teachers were asked to grade identical essays called "What I Did Last Sunday." The essays "written" by Michael and David were given one full grade higher than those "written" by Elmer and Hubert. Similarly, Karen and Lisa outperformed Bertha by one and a half grades. Other studies have shown that, contrary to popular opinion, unusual names may actually have a *positive* effect for college women.

FAMILY PRESSURES/TRADITIONAL CUSTOMS

In many cultures (or families), your choice of names may be severely limited by tradition.

- Among the Kikuyu people of Africa, the family's first son is named after the father's father; the second son, after the father's grandfather; the first daughter, after the father's mother; and so on.
- In Burma, each day of the week is assigned a different letter of the alphabet and children's names must begin with the letter of the day on which they were born.
- In Thailand, the parents may ask a nearby priest—or even a fortune-teller—to give their child just the right name.
- Jews of Eastern European extraction generally don't name babies after living people because of the traditional fear that the Angel of Death might take the baby instead of the older namesake.
- If there is someone on either side of a family who absolutely has to be honored with a name for the sake of family peace, you may be able to find a reasonable compromise. Harry Truman's parents, for example, gave him the middle initial *S*—no name, no period, just the initial—to satisfy both grandfathers (whose names were Solomon and Shippe).

THE LAST-NAME GAME

If you and your partner already have the same last name, you haven't got anything to worry about; if you don't, there could be a few complications.

Perhaps we've lived in Berkeley too long, but my wife and I have various friends who have done all of the following when they had kids:

- Given the kids the man's last name (common enough)
- Given the kids the woman's last name (less common)
- Given the kids a hyphenated last name (but when Benjamin Brandt-Finnell marries Sarah Rosenberg-Wohl, what will *their* children's last name be?)
- Made up a completely new last name
- Given the boys the man's last name, and the girls the woman's

Birth Announcements

WHEN TO ORDER

Since you don't know the exact weight, height, and (in most cases), gender of the baby before he or she is born, there's not much sense in having birth announcements printed until then. But running around trying to decide on birth announcements is about the last thing you're going to want to do after the baby is born. So now is a good time to pick out the kind you want.

There are three basic types of birth announcements: the preprinted kind with blanks for you to fill in; the custom-made variety; and those you design yourself. Fill-in-the-blank and custom-made announcements are available at most stationery and card shops. If you're ordering custom-made announcements, you can select the design you want in advance and then call in the baby's vital statistics as soon as you know them. Whatever type you choose, try to get the envelopes now and address them while your lives are still relatively calm.

WHAT TO INCLUDE

As medical science becomes more exact, birth announcements will probably contain your baby's IQ and future profession. But for now, most standard birth announcements include the baby's name, date and time of birth, weight, length (since they can't stand up, babies don't usually have "height"), and the names of the parents.

WHOM TO SEND ANNOUNCEMENTS TO

Family and friends are the obvious recipients. When it comes to more casual acquaintances and business associates, however, exercise restraint. Many people will feel obligated to send a gift if they receive a birth announcement, so don't send one to anyone from whom you wouldn't feel comfortable getting a gift. Exceptions include people who request an announcement as a memento,

Baby Showers

Not too long ago, baby showers—like so many other baby-related activities—used to be considered "for women only." But today, if your partner's relatives or friends organize a shower for her, there's a good chance you'll be invited, too. (It's still pretty unlikely that your friends or relatives will plan one especially for you.)

The vast majority of baby showers take place several weeks or months before the baby is born, and the idea behind them is obvious: give the new parents a selection of baby clothing, furniture, and toys so the soon-to-be newborn can come home to a well-stocked nursery. If your relatives and friends are so inclined, enjoy—a shower can be a wonderful way to share your excitement about the coming event with others. And don't forget to keep track of who gave what—after the birth, when you get around to those thank-you notes, all those yellow sleepers can look disconcertingly similar.

For some, however, the idea of having a baby shower before there's a baby seems kind of creepy—after all, what if, God forbid, something were to happen to the baby? If you fall into the anti-shower camp, you may find that some people might be offended by your not wanting one. In such cases, you might want to steer them toward a post-birth shower instead (call it a "Welcome Baby" or "Baby Birthday" party if you want to stay away from the word "shower"). Be firm. Stressing how much more fun it will be for the guests to get presents for a baby whose name and gender are known may also make the no-shower news easier to swallow.

employers or employees who have already given you and/or your partner a baby gift and/or shower, and people your parents and in-laws ask you to send announcements to.

Classes

Until the late 1960s, there really was no such thing as childbirth education. Basically, all you had to know to have a baby was where the hospital was located. And all that expectant parents did to prepare for the arrival of their baby was set up a nursery. Women checked into the hospital, labored alone in stark, sterile rooms, received general anesthesia, and woke up groggy and tender, not even knowing the sex of the child they'd delivered. Meanwhile, men were left to pace anxiously in hospital waiting rooms until a nurse came to give them the happy news. Fathers who tried to buck their nonrole in the birth of their children were in for a real surprise. Dr. Robert Bradley, in *Husband-Coached Childbirth,* cites the 1965 case of a man who was arrested and fined for having "gained unauthorized admission to a hospital's delivery room in an attempt to witness the birth of his second child."

Today, however, the situation is radically different. It's hard to find a man who didn't already, or isn't planning to, attend the birth of his children (according to recent statistics, 90 percent of fathers-to-be are present at the birth) and just about everyone involved in the process—from parents to doctors—has given the word *preparation* a whole new meaning. Mothers and fathers frequently attend prenatal OB/GYN visits together, and many embark on a reading program reminiscent of cramming for college exams. In addition, an increasing number of expectant couples are signing up for childbirth preparation classes. When my wife and I got pregnant for the first time, one of the first things we did was read everything we could get our hands on. By the time the baby was born, we'd probably read enough magazine and newspaper articles, books, and pamphlets to qualify for a degree in prenatal education. But unlike my various "real" degrees, which were fairly useless once I got out into the real world, my education in childbirth and child raising has served me quite well.

SELECTING A BIRTHING CLASS

When the first childbirth preparation classes appeared in the late 1960s, the emphasis was on how to have a natural, unmedicated childbirth. Recently, however, the focus has changed somewhat. While natural childbirth is still the goal of most classes today, the overriding principle is that the more you learn about pregnancy and the birth process—from good nutrition and exercise to the types of pain medications most frequently given to laboring women—the less you have to fear and the more in control you'll feel.

Most classes are taught in groups and give you an opportunity to ask questions about the pregnancy in a less hurried environment than your practitioner's office. They also allow you to socialize a little with other pregnant couples and compare notes. But, depending on the class and the other couples, you may not get as much out of the socializing part as your wife does. When my wife and I took our birthing classes, for example, the teacher lectured most of the time; the socializing consisted of the women discussing how much weight they'd gained, how painful their backs were, and how many times a night they had to get up to go to the bathroom. What was helpful for me was the class itself. And by the time we'd finished, I felt that whatever

I THOUGHT YOU SAID "LE MANS" CLASS.
J. GREER

happened, whether we had a "natural" birth or a medicated one, whether my wife had a C-section or an episiotomy (an incision to enlarge the vaginal opening), I'd know what was happening at every stage and what to do.

What distinguishes one childbirth method from another is the approach each takes to relaxation and coping with pain. Here's a little about the most common methods:

LAMAZE On a trip to Russia, Dr. Ferdinand Lamaze learned of an approach to pain called *psychoprophylaxis,* which held that pain was a learned reflex and that if a woman were given something else to focus on, her pain would be relieved. The Lamaze method uses the woman's breathing patterns as the object of focus. In addition, Dr. Lamaze incorporated extensive education in anatomy and physiology in the belief that the more a mother knew, the more she could concentrate on what was happening instead of on the pain she was feeling.

BRADLEY Instead of trying to distract the woman's attention from her pain, Dr. Robert Bradley believes that she should just "go with it." If she feels like groaning, she's encouraged to groan; if she feels like screaming, she's encouraged to scream. The Bradley method also devotes a lot of attention to exercise and nutrition. Over 90 percent of Bradley graduates have "natural" births. Bradley was the original "husband-coached" childbirth method and does more to include the father than any of the other methods.

KITZINGER PSYCHO-SEXUAL British-born educator Sheila Kitzinger believes that pleasurable sexual sensations can be aroused during the birth process and that these sensations can be used to relax laboring women. Kitzinger also believes that the home birth is the best way to go since birth is a family process and everyone should be involved.

LEBOYER Hospital delivery rooms are usually bright, noisy places. Dr. Leboyer, a French obstetrician, contends that these circumstances are quite stressful and upsetting for a newborn. Leboyer babies are generally born in dimmed rooms, with the mother fully or partially submerged in warm water.

"Coach"—Don't Use That Word

Almost all of the most common childbirth methods refer to the man as the childbirth "coach"—a term that seems to have been coined by Dr. Robert Bradley, the founder of the Bradley method. Today most expectant fathers (at least those who take childbirth classes) and their partners view themselves in those terms, but I agree with Professor Katharyn May that there are some very compelling reasons to erase the word from your nonsports vocabulary.

- The coach concept focuses attention on the father's role only during the brief period of labor and delivery, and minimizes the important role he plays during the entire pregnancy and beyond.
- The coach concept reinforces the sexist stereotype of the father as a prop, and dehumanizes him as a unique individual in the process of sharing a challenging life experience with his partner. It also places too much pressure on the father by implying that he should be providing direction if things go badly during labor and birth.

So, if anyone calls you "coach," tell them you're not—you're the child's *father.*

DICK-READ This method was developed by an English obstetrician named Grantley Dick-Read. He believed pain in labor was caused by images women learned through their culture. His classes comprise three main components:

- Learning the anatomy and physiology of childbirth to dispel the idea that birth must be painful.
- Physical relaxation, physical conditioning, and breathing exercises.
- A therapeutic relationship between the mother and the doctor that gives the mother faith in the doctor, allaying her fear and making it easier for her to relax.

Childbirth classes usually run five to nine weeks (if you're really short on time, you may be able to find an intensive two- or three-day program) and typically cost $75 to $100 for the whole course. Your practitioner or the maternity ward of the hospital in which you're planning to deliver are good sources for information on where childbirth classes meet and how to sign up.

Baby CPR

Another class you should try to fit in this month is baby CPR (if you wait until after the baby comes, you'll never get around to it). Hopefully, you'll never have to use the skills you'll learn, but it's important to learn them—for your own peace of mind and for your baby's safety. You can find out where to sign up from your birth class instructor, your baby's pediatrician (if you've picked one already), the hospital where the baby will be born, or your local American Red Cross Community Education Center.

GETTING THE MOST OUT OF THE CLASS

While you should definitely take a birthing class, there's one essential thing you should know about them: the focus is exclusively on your partner—what *she's* going through, what *she's* feeling, and what you can do to help her. All these things are very important, but you might still reasonably ask, "What about me?" Reading this book will help you prepare yourself for the emotional and physical experiences you'll be going through during pregnancy and birth. But while you and your partner are actually going through labor, you are *both* in a state of trauma. You're *both* under pressure and you *both* need support—physical as well as psychological.

Each time my wife was in labor, I tried to do everything they'd taught me

What Childbirth Classes Don't Teach You

While childbirth education classes are an important part of the birthing experience, there are a few things you probably won't learn there.

- **Ask a lot of questions.** No matter how much you've read or how thorough your class is, something you don't understand is bound to happen during the labor or delivery. When it does, don't let the hospital staff steamroller you. Have them explain everything they're doing, every step of the way. If you miss something the first time, have them explain it again.
- **Stand up for your rights.** Most couples have a tendency to step back and let the practitioners take control of their labor or delivery, especially when something unusual happens. They feel out of place and unsure of their rights. Don't. This is your partner's and your labor and delivery—not the doctor's or the nurse's—and you have the right to have things done the way you want them done.
- **Don't take no for an answer.** Often, the first thing out of a doctor's or nurse's mouth when you ask for something is "No"—not because it's the right answer, but because it's the easy answer. If you want the lights dimmed for the delivery and the staff refuses, dim them yourself. If you want to videotape the birth and the doctor won't let you, demand an explanation. If you don't get a good one, do what *you* feel you should do.

in the classes we'd taken: I reassured her, held her, told her stories, massaged her back and legs, mopped her brow, and fed her ice chips. But there was no one to reassure me or hold me when I was feeling frightened. And neither this nor any other book can do that for you.

Fortunately, however, there *is* a way to help ease the burden—both yours and hers—of the trauma of labor and delivery: get yourselves a *doula.*

WHAT IS A *DOULA?*

Doula is a Greek word that means "a woman caregiver of another woman." Most doulas have had children of their own, and all of them go through an intensive training period in which they are taught how to give the laboring woman *and* her partner emotional and physical support throughout labor, as well as information about the delivery.

Doulas—Some Basic Q's and A's

- **What do doulas charge?** Most doulas charge a flat fee ranging from $200 to $600.
- **Will my insurance company pay for a doula?** There's no hard and fast rule about this. But more and more insurance companies are finding that paying for a doula can significantly reduce their other birth-related costs.
- **Where can I find one?** Your OB, hospital, or local chapter of the LaLeche League should be able to help you locate one. You also can contact Doulas of North America, 1100 23rd Avenue East, Seattle, WA 98112. Fax (206) 325-0472.

According to Dr. Marshall Klaus, the doula concept is not new. For hundreds of years, pregnant women in more than 125 cultures have gone through labor with another woman at their side the whole time. This used to be the case in the United States as well. But in the 1930s women began to have their children in hospitals instead of at home, and everyone but the laboring woman and her doctors was barred from the delivery room. In 1980, however, Dr. Klaus and his colleagues reintroduced the doula concept in the U.S. and gave it its name.

I've got to confess that when I met with Dr. Marshall Klaus, my first reaction was: no way. I've got too much invested in this pregnancy, and nobody is going to come between me and my wife during this critical stage. But as I continued talking to Dr. Klaus and reading the research on doulas, I began to change my mind.

I learned that the presence of a doula can have some rather dramatic effects on the length of a woman's labor (25 percent shorter), as well as on the odds of her needing pain medication (reduced by up to 47 percent), forceps delivery (reduced by 35 to 82 percent), or a Cesarean section (reduced 34 to 67 percent). Considering my wife's history of long, painful labor, I began to feel that having a doula around the next time might be the way to go.

But what would a doula do for *me*? Wouldn't she just push me out of the way? "The doula is there to help parents have the type of birthing experience they want," says Dr. Klaus. "She will never take over or attempt to control the birth. We make the mistake of thinking that a father can take a birthing class and be prepared to be the main source of support and knowledge for the entire labor. That's just unreasonable. A doula can reach out to the man, decreasing his anxiety, giving him support and encouragement, and allowing him to interact with his partner in a more caring and nurturing fashion."

Many men, even after taking birthing classes, still feel unsure about how they'll "perform" during the labor. Others feel they'd like to be fully involved in the pregnancy, but that labor and delivery are experiences that women are simply better equipped to handle. If you fit into either of these categories, or if you think it might be reassuring to have someone knowledgeable and supportive at your side during labor, consider a doula.

WHAT IF YOU FEEL LIKE YOU DON'T WANT TO BE IN THE DELIVERY ROOM AT ALL?

Years ago, no one expected men to be involved in their partners' pregnancy or to be there for the birth of their children. But today, men who aren't enthusiastically involved are generally regarded as insensitive Neanderthals. "There's a fine line between finding options for father participation, and pressuring men to adopt levels of involvement which may be unwanted or inappropriate for them," says Katharyn May. The truth of the matter is that not all of us feel the same need to be involved, and the *last* place some men should be is in the delivery room.

You may be squeamish during medical procedures or worried about losing control during labor. You may not want to see your partner in pain, or you may simply be feeling ambivalent about the pregnancy. You may even be feeling resentful about the pressure other people are putting on you to get involved. It's important to remember that these—and any other feelings you might have for just not wanting to be there—are not only completely normal, but they're shared by more men than you might think.

If you're feeling less than overjoyed about being involved in the labor and delivery, you might want to consider some of the following suggestions:

- **Talk to other fathers.** Hearing what other men have been through may help you get over some of your concerns. You might also find that you're not alone.
- **Understand what your partner's thinking.** Instead of trying to understand *why* you're feeling the way you do, your partner may interpret your apprehensiveness as a sign that you don't care about her or the baby.
- **Talk to your partner.** Let her know what you're feeling and why. At the same time, reassure her about your commitment to her and to the baby.
- **Do it for her.** No matter how well you explain it to your partner, your desire to miss the birth or to miss the classes is probably going to hurt her. If you can stomach it at all, at least try to take the class—it will

help her feel more understood, and you might just learn what it is that's been bothering you.

- **Consider a doula.** See pages 107–9 for information about doulas.
- **Don't feel that you're a failure.** You're not. As many as half of all expectant fathers have at least some ambivalence about participating in the pregnancy and childbirth. Being forced into a role that isn't comfortable for you will do you—and your partner—more harm than good.
- **Don't give in to the pressure.** If, after everything is said and done, you still don't feel comfortable participating, don't. But be prepared: your family, friends, and medical practitioner will probably suggest that you just quit pouting and do what you're "supposed to."
- **Don't worry about how your child will turn out.** While there's plenty of evidence about the positive impact on children of early paternal bonding, your not being there for the actual birth will *not* cripple your children—you'll still be able to establish a strong relationship with them. Just get there as soon as you feel comfortable, and take as active a role as you can handle.

Notes:

THE 8TH MONTH

Making a List and Checking It Twice

What She's Going Through

Physically

- Even stronger fetal activity
- Heavier vaginal discharge
- General discomfort getting more severe
- Frequent urination
- Sleeplessness
- Increased fatigue
- Shortness of breath as the baby takes up more room and presses against her internal organs
- Water retention, and swelling of the hands, feet, and ankles
- More frequent Braxton-Hicks contractions

Emotionally

- Feeling special—people are giving her their seats on buses or in crowded rooms, store clerks go out of their way to help her
- Feeling a bond with others, like a member of a secret club (strangers keep coming up to tell her about their own pregnancy experiences or to touch her belly)
- Feeling exceptionally attractive—or ugly
- Worried about what she's going to do with the baby once it arrives
- Worried about whether her body will ever get back to normal
- Afraid her water will break in public

What's Going On with the Baby

At this point, most babies will have assumed the head-down position that they'll maintain for the rest of the pregnancy. He or she is getting big and fat—eighteen inches long, five pounds—and his or her movements are so powerful that you can frequently tell which part of the baby's body is doing the poking. The baby can now open his or her eyes and responds differently to your and your partner's voices.

What You're Going Through

Dealing with the "Public" Nature of Pregnancy

As intensely private as pregnancy is, it is also inescapably public. Your partner's growing belly can bring out the best—and the worst—in people. Perfect strangers will open doors for her, offer to help her carry things, give up their seats in crowded subway cars and buses. In some ways, people's interest in pregnant women and in the process of creating life is heartwarming. But there may come a point at which this outpouring of interest in her status and concern for her comfort begins to feel like an invasion of privacy.

People would come up to my wife and start talking to her even when she was standing in the check-out line at the grocery store. The "conversations" would usually start out fairly innocuously, with questions like, "So, when are you due?" or pronouncements about the baby's gender. But after a while the horror stories would inevitably come out—tales of debilitating morning sickness, ten-month pregnancies, thirty-hour labors, emergency C-sections, anesthesia that didn't work, and on and on. And as if that weren't enough, people would, without even asking, start touching, rubbing, or patting her belly.

Perhaps the strangest thing about the public nature of pregnancy is that many women seem to take it all in stride. I kept waiting for my wife to bite some belly-rubber's hand off, but she never did. For some men, however, this touching business can bring out feelings of anger: "Nobody touches my woman!" If this happens to you, it's best to take your cues from your partner. If she doesn't mind, try to relax.

Panic

Just about six weeks before our first daughter was born, I suddenly had a great epiphany: our childless days were about to be over. It wasn't that I was worried about becoming a father—I already felt confident and prepared for my new role: I'd read a lot of material about becoming a parent, my wife and I had been taking childbirth classes, and we'd thoroughly discussed our concerns and fears.

What had struck me was much more superficial: once the baby came, it would be a long time before we'd be able to go to movies, plays, or concerts (or just about anyplace where you might have to be quiet), or even stay out late with our friends.

As it turned out, my wife was feeling the same thing at about the same time, so during the last two months of the first pregnancy, we ate out more often, went to more movies, saw more plays, and spent more late evenings with friends than in the next three years combined.

In addition to trying to pack a lot of fun activities into the last few months of the pregnancy, you might want to consider cramming in a few practical things as well: when you (or your partner) are preparing food, try to double or even triple the recipes and freeze what's left over in two-person servings. Believe me, during that first postpartum week, defrosting some frozen spaghetti sauce is a lot easier than making a new batch from scratch.

Nesting

After morning sickness and 2 A.M. cravings for pickles, perhaps the most famous stereotype about pregnancy is a woman's "nesting instinct." Most women, at some point in their pregnancies, become obsessed (often unconsciously) with preparing the house for the new arrival: closets and cupboards are cleaned, and furniture that hasn't been budged for years suddenly has to be swept under.

Although much has been made of the *woman's* instinct, a variety of studies have shown that almost all expectant fathers experience some sort of nesting

instinct themselves. Besides worrying about finances, many men spend a lot of time assembling—or even building—cribs, changing tables, and other baby furniture; shopping for baby supplies; painting and preparing the baby's room; rearranging furniture in the rest of the house; and even trying to find a larger living space for their growing families.

For some men, these activities are a way to keep busy and to avoid feeling left out. But for others, they represent something much more fundamental. As Pamela Jordan writes, "These nesting tasks may be the first opportunity the father has to do something for the baby rather than his pregnant mate."

Sex—Again

Whereas the second trimester is frequently a time of increased sexual desire and activity, during the third trimester a decrease in sexual relations is not unusual. The most common reasons for this are:

- A mutual fear of hurting the baby or your partner.
- Fear that your partner's orgasm might trigger premature labor.
- Your partner's physical discomfort.
- Your partner's changing body makes the "usual" sexual positions uncomfortable.
- Your sense of changing roles. Soon your partner will no longer be only your partner; she's going to be a mother—someone just like your own mother. Remember that as she begins to see you as a father, your partner may have similar (subconscious) thoughts.

Unless your partner's doctor has told you otherwise, sex should pose no physical risk to the baby or to your partner. As discussed on page 81, if you're both still interested in sex, now would be a good time to try out some new and different positions. Again, if you and your partner aren't in sync, sexually speaking, it's critical to talk things through.

Several researchers have noted that a small number of expectant fathers have affairs during the late stages of their partners' pregnancies. But these "late pregnancy affairs" rarely happen for the reasons you might think. Dr. Jerrold Shapiro found that most men who have had a late-pregnancy extramarital affair share the following characteristics:

- They felt extremely attracted to their partners and were very interested in "affectionate sexual contact" with them.
- They felt particularly excluded from the pregnancy and birth process.
- The affair was with a close friend or relative of the woman. (This would indicate that the person with whom the man had the affair

was also feeling excluded from the pregnant woman's life during the pregnancy.)

Expectant mothers also have affairs during their pregnancies. In fact, Dr. Shapiro suggests that women are just as likely to have affairs as men. Couples who suddenly find themselves with no sexual outlet—and are feeling pushed away or misunderstood by their partners—may be tempted to satisfy their needs elsewhere.

Birth Plans

The notion that an expectant couple has some choice in the labor, delivery, and the immediate postpartum-period procedures is a fairly recent one. And while you may be tempted just to "leave things up to the professionals" at the hospital, you'll have a much better—and less stressful—birthing experience if you and your partner spend some time thinking about what you really want, and writing up a *birth plan.*

A birth plan is a good way for you and your partner to make decisions and set goals for the labor and delivery while you still have clear heads. Remember, though, that things rarely, if ever, go the way they're supposed to. So, be flexible. Also, be sure to discuss your plan with your practitioner and with the

Sample Birth Plan

This birth plan outlines our desires for this labor, birth, and postpartum period. These plans can be revised for medical reasons, should some complication arise, after informed consent has been well established.

- Mother will be free to move during labor and birth to any position she prefers or finds helpful to the birthing process.
- We would prefer that no pain medication be routinely offered. If the mother wants something, she'll ask for it.
- No episiotomy will be performed; a tear is acceptable if unavoidable.
- The baby will be given directly to the mother after birth.
- The baby will be with at least one of his or her parents at all times.
- Father would like to "catch" the baby as he or she emerges.
- Father will cut the cord, but not until it stops pulsing.

We would like to thank everyone involved for their support and cooperation during this birth.

hospital. There may be certain policies that can't be breached. Here are some topics you may want to cover in your plan:

- **Pain medication.** Do you want the hospital staff to offer it if they feel your partner could use some? Or do you want them to wait for her to ask for it?
- **Staying together.** Do you and your partner want to remain together for the entire labor and delivery?
- **Freedom of movement.** Will you be able to labor in the hallways (or in the shower), or will your partner have to stay in bed?
- **Labor.** Do you want to be able to select your own positions? If labor slows down, do you want to be offered oxytocin or other drugs to speed it up?
- **Shaving.** Does your partner want her pubic area shaved or left alone? (There's no real reason to shave her if she doesn't want it done.)
- **Pictures and videos.** Do you want to take them? Do you want someone else to? Do you want to be able to take them even if there's a C-section?
- **Fetal monitoring.** Does your partner want to be hooked up to machines throughout her labor, or would she prefer that monitoring be done only when necessary?
- **The birth.** Do you want the doctors to try forceps or suction to speed up the delivery, or do you want to hold out for a while longer? Do you want any other people (friends, relatives, midwife, other children) to attend the birth? Will a mirror be available (so your partner can get a better view of the birth)?

- **Episiotomy.** Do you want the OB to do one as a preventative measure, or is a small tear preferable?
- **Cesarean section.** In case of a C-section, can you stay with your partner, or will you have to be separated? Will you be separated only for the spinal anesthesia, or for the entire procedure? Where will you be allowed to stand?
- **The baby.** Who will cut the cord, and when? Do you want the hospital staff to take the baby away for cleaning and testing right after birth, or would you like him or her handed to you first?
- **After the birth.** Do you want the baby to breastfeed right away, or will you be bottle feeding? Do you want the baby with one of you all the time, or would you rather have him or her kept in the hospital's nursery? What about circumcision?
- **Going home.** Do you want to stay for as long as the hospital will let you, or do you want to go home as soon as possible?

Should Your Older Children Attend the Birth?

Having older children attend the birth of the new baby can be a tricky thing. In general, it's probably okay to have children present both during labor and immediately *after* the birth. But for a variety of reasons, children—especially those under five—probably shouldn't be there for the birth itself.

- They may be frightened that their mother is being hurt, and that all of the blood and moaning might mean she is dying.
- Even well-prepared children can have unpredictable reactions, and you and your partner won't want to have to be distracted by anyone else's needs but yours (and the new baby's).
- The older child might be jealous of all the attention paid to the new baby.

If you're still thinking about having an older child there for the birth of his or her new sibling, be sure to discuss the idea with your doctor first. Then, get yourselves some visual aids—books, movies, or pictures of births, for example—and plan on having some long discussions with the child. *Birth: Through Children's Eyes,* edited by Sandra Van Dam Anderson and Penny Simkin (P. T. Pennypress, 1981), is a good resource.

Birth instructor Kim Kaehler suggests that you keep the following points in mind when writing your plan:

- In the opening paragraph, indicate your flexibility should a medical emergency arise. But also stress the importance of informed consent.
- Try not to make it sound like a legal document. That will make a doctor or other health-care provider very nervous and defensive.
- Try to word your desires in a positive way. Avoid beginning every statement with "No" or "Do not."
- Refrain from including things in your plan that are not part of your birthplace's normal procedures. (If your hospital doesn't routinely do fetal monitoring, there's no need to mention it.)
- Be sure to thank everyone for their cooperation and support.
- After you and your partner have hammered out a draft of your birth plan, show it to your doctor. Let him or her go over it and make suggestions.

Making Final Plans

REGISTERING AT THE HOSPITAL

Despite what you've seen on TV and in the movies, getting to the hospital doesn't have to be a frantic exercise at breakneck speed. Fortunately for men (but not nearly as fortunately for our partners), the onset of labor and the delivery itself are usually hours (if not days) apart, so if you plan carefully, there should be plenty of time to get everything done. And once you've got your bags packed and ready to go (see pages 121–22 for details), the next most pressing concern is registering at the hospital.

Most hospitals will allow—or may even require—you to register up to sixty days before the anticipated birth of the child. This doesn't mean that you're making a reservation for a particular day. All it means is that when you do show up at the hospital, you won't have to waste time signing papers while your partner is having contractions. So check with your hospital's or clinic's administrative offices as soon as you can. Doing so is particularly important because besides making you fill out 785 forms, the hospital will have to get a verification of coverage and eligibility from your insurance company. And that can take some time.

FINDING A PEDIATRICIAN

During their first year, both my daughters saw their pediatrician nine times—and they were both healthy. You can expect visits every two weeks for the first month, monthly or every other month until six months, once in the ninth month, and again in the twelfth month. Clearly, since you're going to be spending a lot of time with your child's doctor, you should select someone you think you can get along with. It's perfectly acceptable to interview several prospective pediatricians, and if you do, here are some questions you should ask:

- **What insurance plans do you participate in?**
- **What is your philosophy about vaccinations?** Although the vast majority of pediatricians advocate routine vaccination, there is a vocal minority that doesn't. The debate is interesting but beyond the scope of this book.
- **How many doctors are in your practice?** You may think that male and female doctors are the same, but your child may not agree. When she was about two, my older daughter absolutely refused to see her regular (male) pediatrician, and insisted on seeing a "girl doctor." Don't worry about offending your pediatrician—about 75 percent of kids prefer to see a doctor of their own gender.
- **Where is your lab work done?** It's a lot faster and cheaper when most routine tests are done right in the office.
- **What about emergencies?**
- **What about nighttime and weekend hours?**
- **What about non-life-threatening emergencies?** During business hours, the practice we go to has a special, free phone line staffed by pediatric nurses who have successfully diagnosed at least 80 percent of the problems we've called about. At about $50 per visit to the doctor, I can't tell you how much money this has saved us.

GETTING TO THE HOSPITAL

Sooner or later—unless you're planning to have a home birth—you and your partner are going to have to get to the hospital. There are several ways of getting there, each with its own advantages and disadvantages:

- **Walking** If you live close enough to the hospital, walking may be the best option. You won't have to worry about any of the disadvantages of driving yourself or getting a ride (see below). You will, however, have to deal with the possible embarrassment of having people stare at you as your partner leans up against the side of a building every three minutes and groans. But your partner may actually like this option since walking can help make the contractions of early labor easier to cope with.

  If you're walking, be sure to bring enough cash to take a cab—just in case things don't go the way they should.

- **Driving yourself** No matter how much you've prepared, when labor really starts, you're going to be a little nervous, and that could be dangerous when you're behind the wheel of a car. You could get lost, get caught speeding, or even cause an accident. And worst of all, if your eyes and mind are on the road, they can't be where they really ought to be—with your partner. Then, when you finally get to the hospital, you'll have to deal with parking—and later retrieving—the car.

  If you're driving, make sure you have a full tank of gas, that you know the route (and several alternatives) well, and that you allow enough time to get there. Also, check with the hospital parking lot (if they have one) to find out their rates and hours of operation.
- **Getting a ride—taxi, friend, or relative** If you're in the back seat of someone else's car, you'll at least be able to tend to your partner. Problems might arise, however, if your partner goes into labor at 2 A.M. and your friends or in-laws take more than a minute or two to roll out of bed. In addition, since most people have never driven a pregnant woman to the hospital, they'll be at least as nervous (probably more) than you would have been. And watch out for potholes; my wife assures me they're hell for a laboring woman.

  If you're taking a taxi, have the phone numbers of at least three companies who can get a cab to your door within minutes, at any hour of the day or night. Also, be sure to have enough money for the fare. If you're planning on having someone else do the driving, make sure you have a few backups.

WHAT IF YOU HAVE OTHER KIDS?

If you have other kids—especially young ones—getting to the hospital can be doubly stressful and requires extra planning.

Toward the end of my wife's second pregnancy, we decided that we'd take a cab to the hospital. We also decided that if my wife went into serious labor in the middle of the night, we'd signal our friends who had agreed to take care of our older daughter by calling them, letting their phone ring once, hanging up, calling again, and letting it ring three times.

So, at one in the morning, we made the phone calls, got into the cab, and arrived at our friends' house, where, holding thirty-five pounds of sleeping deadweight, I pounded on the door for five minutes before giving up (our friends had apparently slept through the secret signals). Fortunately, we'd made a backup plan, and when we got to the hospital, we called my parents and had them take their grandchild to their house.

AND FINALLY, SOME LAST-MINUTE DETAILS

- Keep your doctor's number by the phone.
- Keep your gas tank full. Have an extra set of keys stashed someplace, or cash for a cab ready.
- Make sure you've checked to see whether there are any road closures or construction projects along your route to the hospital.
- Get ready at work. Labor usually starts without warning and can last a long time—sometimes more than a day. Be sure you've delegated urgent matters to a coworker or supervisor, and that your time-off plans are in order. (See pages 88–93 for more on work/family concerns.)

Packing Your Bags

FOR HER

- A favorite picture on which to focus during labor.
- Tape player and some favorite tapes to help you both relax during labor.
- A bathrobe she won't mind getting covered with blood.
- A large gym bottle (you know, the kind with the built-in straw) for sipping clear liquids.
- Warm socks and/or old slippers (again, ones she won't mind getting bloody).

- Change of clothes to go home in—*not* what she was wearing before she got pregnant. Sweats or maternity pants are particularly good.
- Nursing bra.
- Her toiletries bag. Don't forget things like mouthwash, toothbrush and toothpaste, contact lens paraphernalia, hairbrush or comb, and a hair ribbon or two.
- Box of heavy-duty maxi-pads (unless your partner doesn't mind the kind with the belt, which is what she'll get at most hospitals).

FOR YOU

- Comfortable clothes.
- Some magazines or a collection of your partner's favorite short stories to read to her.
- A swimsuit (you might want to get into the shower with your partner, and the nursing staff might be surprised at the sight of a naked man).
- Camera *and* film.
- This book.
- A cooler filled with snacks. You're not going to want to leave your partner, midcontraction, to run down to the hospital cafeteria. If you have some extra room, a small birthday cake and maybe even some champagne will add a festive touch.
- Cash. Depending on the hospital, you may have to leave a cash deposit for phone or television rental. You'll probably need to pay for parking your car or for the taxi ride. You might also need a supply of quarters if you have to use a pay phone.
- Phone numbers of the people you'll want to tell the news to right away.
- Phone company credit card.
- Tennis balls for back rubs.
- Toothbrush, extra underwear, shaving kit, and the like. You'll probably end up staying at least one night.

FOR THE BABY

- An infant car seat (if you don't have one, the hospital won't let you leave).
- A little outfit to go home in—a sleeper or sleep-sac is fine. (It's a good idea to wash *all* new clothes before putting them on the baby.)
- Diapers (and pins or diaper wraps if you're using cloth).
- Several receiving blankets, weather-appropriate.

The Nursery: Everything You Need and What It Costs

When acquiring anything for your baby, safety should be your primary concern. So before you spend a fortune on Queen Victoria's original bassinet or drag out the crib that you (or your parents or grandparents) slept in as a kid, consider this: your baby will do just about everything possible to jeopardize

Essentials to Have Waiting at Home

FOR THE BABY

- Enough diapers to last for at least a week (you're not going to want to go shopping)
- Baby soap and shampoo
- Thermometer (digital is easiest)
- An ear bulb (These are usually used for rinsing adults' ears, but for babies, they're used for suctioning mucous from their noses. Well, what do you expect? They can't do it themselves!)
- Nail scissors (essential: a baby's nails are like tiny razors and grow like Jack's beanstalk)
- Cotton swabs and alcohol for umbilical cord dressing
- Three or four undershirts
- Three or four sleepers
- Three or four coveralls with snaps
- Sun or snow hat
- Snowsuit (as needed)
- Bottles and formula—even if breastfeeding, just in case . . .
- Three or four baby blankets

FOR YOUR PARTNER

- Nursing pads
- More maxi-pads (she may need these for weeks)
- Any medication or dressing materials needed in the event of a C-section or episiotomy
- Milk and vitamins, especially if she is nursing
- Flowers, and favorite chocolates or other foods she might have avoided during pregnancy
- A good book about your baby's first year of life

his or her own life, from sticking his head between the bars of a crib to burying herself under a pile of blankets left in the corner.

New baby furniture must comply with the most recent safety standards. For some guidance on the safest—and best-quality—deals, consult the *Consumer's Guide to Baby Products.*

There are literally hundreds of things you could buy for your newborn's nursery, but here are some of the items you'll need to get the soonest. The prices are retail; you can probably save up to 80 percent by buying these things at garage sales, from friends, or at used furniture stores. But before you get *anything* secondhand, make sure it meets with the safety considerations outlined below.

BABY FURNISHINGS

CRIB: $100 to $600. There's nothing that says *baby* quite like a crib. And so it's no surprise that this is one of the first pieces of baby furniture an expectant couple thinks about. Here are some safety tips:

- Get rid of corner posts. Babies can accidentally strangle themselves if their clothes become caught on a post. New cribs are constructed without them, but if you have your heart set on using a vintage model, you should unscrew or saw off the posts.
- Slats or bars should be spaced no more than 2⅜ inches apart, and none should be broken or missing.
- Never place your crib near draperies, blinds, or anything else that has long, wall-mounted cords. Babies can tear these down or become entangled in them.

CRIB MATTRESS: $100 to $150. Couples are often surprised that mattresses are usually sold separately from the crib. The theory is that some babies prefer firm mattresses while others prefer softer ones. Don't skimp on mattresses—there's no reason why the one you buy now shouldn't last you through several kids. Just make sure you get a plastic mattress protector.

A few safety tips:

- The firmer the better. Studies have shown that there is an increased risk of SIDS (Sudden Infant Death Syndrome) if the mattress is too soft. For the same reason, pillows should never be placed in cribs.
- The mattress must fit tightly into the crib (no more than two fingers' width between the edge of the mattress and the side of the crib).

CRIB ACCESSORIES

- Crib sheets: $20 to $60.
- Bumper: $100 (optional). Even though they can't move very well, babies somehow manage to ram their heads against the sides of the crib—hard enough to leave an impression of the slats or bars on their foreheads. It supposedly reminds them of the feeling of having their heads smashed up against your partner's pubic bone for the last month or two of pregnancy.
- Dust ruffle: $80 (optional).
- Comforter: $80.
- Mobile: $35 to $90 (optional). Some of the most beautiful (and most expensive) mobiles are made to be looked at from the side—where the person who bought it is standing. So remember whom the mobile is really for, and think about whether your baby is really going to be interested in looking at the bottom of a bunch of cars or the underside of a group of jungle animals. In fact, infants can't make out specific shapes for quite some time; experts believe, however, that they can distinguish bold, contrasting colors, and that is why black-and-white mobiles seem to please them the most.

BASSINET: $80 to $150. For the first few months of your baby's life, you may want him or her to sleep in the bedroom with you. If nothing else, this arrangement will make breastfeeding a lot more convenient.

Bassinets can generally accommodate a baby until he or she is about three months old. They come in a variety of styles (wheels, no wheels, handles, no handles, rocking, nonrocking).

CAR SEAT: $40 to $100. A car seat may be the most indispensable baby item. (Again, you won't be able to take your baby home from the hospital without one.) You may want to consider getting two car seats—a small one (perhaps with handles so you can carry the baby around with you) that can be used until the baby reaches twenty pounds, and a larger one for later.

CHANGING TABLE: $70 to $200. Changing tables come in an unbelievable variety of sizes and configurations. Some have drawers so that they can be used as a dresser when your child no longer needs to be changed. The problem with drawers, however, is that you have to remember to take out what you need *before* you get started; when you're in the middle of changing the baby, the last thing you want to be doing is fumbling around blindly for a clean outfit. Be sure to get a foam pad for the top of the table and a couple of washable pad covers. You also should stock your changing table with a good supply of the following:

- Diapers
- Baby wipes
- Diaper rash ointment, such as A&D or Desitin
- Cotton swabs and alcohol for cleaning the umbilical cord stump
- Baby shampoo and soap (a mild one like Neutrogena or Dove is best)

Note: Stay away from baby powder. Most pediatricians believe that the dust could be harmful to babies.

PORTABLE PLAYPEN: $80 to $150. This is perfect for children less than thirty-four inches tall and lighter than about thirty pounds. Not only does it fold up compactly enough to check as luggage when you're traveling, but it can also be used at home. Some of our friends' children essentially lived in their playpens for the first eighteen months of their lives.

STROLLER: $100 to $600. A good stroller can make life worth living, and you shouldn't waste your time or your money on one that won't last. We took our older daughter and her stroller all over the world, and the stroller is still in perfect condition. Getting a quality stroller doesn't mean you have to buy the one with every available option. Stick to the basics, such as weight, ease of folding, brakes, and balance (you don't want the thing tipping over backward with your baby in it). Finally, make sure the handles are long enough for *you* to push the stroller when you're standing up straight. Most strollers are made to be used by women, which means that if you're over 5′7″ or so, you'll have to stoop a little to push. You might not notice it at first, but after a while, your back may give you trouble. Handle extenders cost about $20 and are a great investment. City dwellers who do a lot of traveling on subways or buses will want a sturdy but collapsible stroller—preferably one that you can fold with one hand while holding the baby with the other. Otherwise, it's next to impossible to get onto public transportation (at least without annoying everyone behind you).

BATHTUB: $20. A small plastic washbasin is best for newborns because a sink is too big and can be dangerous. When the baby outgrows the basin, you can soak his or her little formula-stained clothes in it.

DIAPERS: A few years ago, no one would have thought that diapers would become a political issue or that something so insignificant could make or break friendships, but they have. Here are the basic arguments:

Disposable diapers account for more than 1 percent of the nation's landfill. They're made of plastic and will stay in their present form for thousands of years. "Biodegradable" diapers, which break down after only five hundred years, are available in many cities.

Cloth diapers, in contrast, are all natural. The problem is that they're made of cotton, which is taxing on farmland. And in order to sterilize them properly, diaper services wash them seven times (it's true) in near-boiling water, thereby consuming a tremendous amount of power, water, and chemical detergents. The clean diapers are then driven all over town in trucks that fill the air with toxic pollutants.

The choice is yours.

My wife and I started out by using cloth diapers for our older daughter. But I noticed that every time my daughter filled one up, it had a nasty tendency to siphon the contents immediately away from the baby and onto my pants—not pleasant—and that meant even more laundry! It's possible that this phenomenon was the fault of my poor diapering technique. But I'm convinced that disposables, which have elastic around the leg openings, do a better job of keeping the contents in place.

- **Disposable diapers:** $8 to $9 for 50. Since you'll be using 5 to 8 diapers a day, this option can get pretty pricey. But if you keep your eyes out for coupons (most parenting magazines have a bunch of them in every issue), you can save a lot. In addition, places like Toys "Я" Us have generic or house brands that are a lot cheaper and usually just as good.

  Some people say that kids who grow up with disposable diapers tend to become potty trained later than those who use cloth. Apparently, the disposable kind keep so much moisture away from the baby's bottom that the baby stays comfortable for a longer time.
- **Cloth diapers:** about $12 for a package of six. The availability and cost

of diaper cleaning services vary greatly around the country. If you sign up with a diaper service, you'll probably start with about eighty diapers per week. If you're doing your own laundry, you should buy about forty.

Even if you don't end up using cloth diapers for the baby, you should still buy a dozen anyway—they're great for drying baby bottoms on changing tables and for draping over your shoulder to protect your clothes when your baby spits up.

FORMULA: Prices vary. You can use powdered, full-strength liquid, or liquid concentrate. But when you start checking formula prices, your partner may decide to keep breastfeeding a while longer. When we weaned our daughters, we put them on the powdered formula—I made a pitcher of it every morning and kept it in the refrigerator.

Notes:

"Dear, It's Time..."

What She's Going Through

Physically

- Some change in fetal activity—the baby is so cramped that instead of kicking and punching, all he or she can do is squirm
- Increased sleeplessness and fatigue
- A renewed sense of energy when the baby's head "drops" into the pelvis and takes some of the pressure off
- Just plain miserable—increased cramping, constipation, backache, water retention, and swelling of the feet, ankles, and face

Emotionally

- More dependent on you than ever—afraid you won't love her after the baby is born (after all, she's not the same woman you married)
- Impatient: can't wait for pregnancy to be over
- Short-tempered: tired of answering "So when's the baby coming?" questions—especially if she's overdue
- May be afraid she won't have enough love to go around—what with loving you, and all
- Fear she won't be ready for labor when it comes
- Increasing preoccupation with the baby

What's Going On with the Baby

Over the course of this last month of pregnancy, your baby will be growing at a tremendous clip. Before he or she finally decides to leave the warm uterus, he or she will weigh six or seven pounds, if not more, and be about twenty inches long—so big that there will be hardly any room for him or her to kick or prod your partner. Fingernails and toenails are frequently so long they have to be trimmed right after birth.

What You're Going Through

Confusion

Well, it's almost over. In just a few weeks, you're finally going to meet the child you've talked to and dreamed about, and whose college education you've planned. But be prepared; the last month of pregnancy is often the most confusing for expectant fathers. At times you may be almost overcome with excitement and anticipation. At other times you may be feeling so scared and trapped that you want to run away. In short, all the feelings—good and bad—that you've experienced over the last eight months are back. But now, because of the impending birth, they're more intense than before. Here are a few of the contradictory emotional states you may find yourself going through during the final stages of the pregnancy:

- On the one hand, you may be feeling confident about your readiness to be a father. On the other, you may be worried and unsure about whether you'll be able to handle your dual roles as husband and father.

- If you've taken on a second job or increased responsibilities at work, all you'll probably want to do at the end of the day is go home and relax. But with your partner less and less able to handle physical tasks, you may be greeted at the door with a list of chores that need to be done.
- You and your partner may be feeling an exceptionally strong emotional bond with each other. At the same time, your sex life may have completely disappeared.
- As your partner gets more and more uncomfortable, she may feel less and less like going out with friends, so the two of you may be spending a lot more time together. This may be the last chance you have to enjoy some quiet, private time before the baby comes. But it may also be an unwelcome opportunity to get on each other's nerves.
- You may find yourself spending a lot more time with friends and family members who have small children, or you may find yourself avoiding families with kids.

Increased Dependency on Your Partner

By this time your attention—and that of your friends and family—is focused squarely on your partner and the baby. Since you're the person she's closest to and sees most often, your partner is going to be increasingly dependent on you—not only to help her physically, but to get her through the last-month emotional ups and downs. At the same time, though, you are going to be increasingly dependent on her as you get onto the last-month roller coaster.

Your partner's increased dependency is considered a "normal" part of pregnancy. But thanks to the ridiculous, gender-specific way we socialize people in this country, men are supposed to be independent, strong, supportive, and impervious to emotional needs—especially while their partners are pregnant. So, just when you are feeling most vulnerable and least in control, your needs are swept under the rug. And what's worse, the one person you most depend on for sympathy and understanding may be too absorbed in what's going on with herself and the baby to do much for you.

This results in what Dr. Luis Zayas calls an "imbalance in interdependence," which leaves the father to satisfy his own emotional needs *and* those of his partner. In addition, in many cases this imbalance essentially becomes a kind of vicious circle that "accentuates the stress, intensifies feelings of separation, and heightens dependency needs." In other words, the less response you get to your dependency needs, the more dependent you feel.

Feeling Guilty

Especially in the last month or so of the pregnancy, many men begin to feel guilty about what they think they've been putting their partners through. Yes, you're the one who got her pregnant, and yes, she's uncomfortable as hell. But strange as it might seem to you, your partner does not blame you for what she's going through. She understands and accepts—as you should—that this was her idea, too, and that (at least short of surrogate motherhood or adoption) there's simply no way to have a baby without going through this. So quit torturing yourself—there are a lot more productive things you can be doing with your time during these last few weeks.

Staying Involved

Sensitivity

The bottom line is that during the last few weeks of her pregnancy, your partner is likely to be miserable and uncomfortable. And although there's not a whole lot you can do to ease her burden, here are a few suggestions that might make the final stretch a little more bearable—for both of you:

- Answer the phone. If you have an answering machine, you might consider changing the recording to something like: "Hi. No, we don't have a baby yet, and yes, Jane's fine. If you're calling about anything else, please leave a message and we'll call you back." That may sound a little snotty, but believe me, it's a lot less snotty than *you* would be if you were really answering the same questions twenty times a day.
- Stay nearby whenever you can. Try to come home a little earlier from work, give away those basketball tickets, and postpone that long business trip.
- Stay in touch. A couple of quick calls to her every day can make her feel loved and important. They'll also reassure her that *you* are all right. If you need to be away from the phone, consider getting a pager or a cellular phone.
- Stay as calm as you can. She'll be nervous enough for both of you.
- Be patient. She may do some pretty bizarre things, and the best thing you can do is bear with her. If the house has already passed the white-glove test and the car has been waxed twice, and she wants it all done over again, do it—she needs the rest.
- Review the breathing, relaxation, and any other techniques you plan to use during labor.
- If she wants it, give her some time to herself. And if she wants time with you, make sure you're there for her.

In addition, now would be an appropriate time to reread the "Ways to Show Her You Care" section on pages 67–68.

What If She's Overdue?

There's nothing more frustrating than starting the tenth month of a nine-month pregnancy. You've already given up answering the phone, afraid it's another one of those "What are *you* doing at home? I was sure you'd be at the hospital by now" calls. And you're sick of ending every conversation at the office with, "Now if I'm not in tomorrow, don't forget. . . ." The empty bassinet looks forlorn, and you're just dying to meet the baby face to little wrinkled face.

In most cases, however, couples who think they're late really aren't. When doctors tell a pregnant woman her due date, they often neglect to add that it's only a ballpark figure based on an assumed twenty-eight-day menstrual cycle. If your partner's cycle is long, short, or irregular, her "official" due date could be off by as much as three weeks. And even if her cycle is like clockwork, it's nearly impossible to tell exactly when you conceived. The

Labor: Real or False

By now, your partner has probably experienced some Braxton-Hicks contractions, often called "false labor." Such contractions essentially warm up the uterus for the real thing. Sometimes, however, these practice contractions may be so strong that your partner may feel that labor has begun.

The bottom line is that when *real* labor starts, your partner will probably know it. (This may sound strange, especially if she is carrying her first child. Nevertheless, the majority of mothers I've spoken to have told me it's true.) But until then, you—and she—may not be sure whether the contractions and other things she's feeling are the real thing or not. So before you go rushing off to the hospital, take a few seconds to try to figure things out.

FALSE LABOR

- Contractions are not regular, or don't stay regular
- Contractions don't get stronger or more severe
- If your partner changes position (from sitting to walking, or from standing to lying down), the contractions usually stop altogether or change in frequency or intensity
- Generally, there is little or no vaginal discharge of any kind
- There may be additional pain in the abdomen

REAL LABOR

- Contractions are regular
- Contractions get stronger, longer, and closer together with time
- There may be some blood-tinged vaginal discharge
- Your partner's membranes may rupture (the famous "water" that "breaks" is really the amniotic fluid that the baby has been floating in throughout the pregnancy)
- There will undoubtedly be additional pain in the lower back

bottom line is that "70 percent of post-term [late] pregnancies are due to miscalculations of the time of conception," according to the authors of *What to Expect When You're Expecting.*

While going past the due date by a week or so is usually not a problem, being truly overdue *can* have serious consequences:

- The baby can grow so large that he or she will have problems passing through the birth canal, thus increasing the chances of a difficult delivery or a C-section.

- After a certain point the placenta gets so old that it can no longer provide adequate nourishment for the baby. This can result in the baby's losing weight in the uterus, increasing the risk of fetal distress.
- There may no longer be enough amniotic fluid to support the baby.
- There may be inadequate room for the umbilical cord to perform properly.

If your doctor feels the baby is overdue, he or she will most likely prescribe some tests to make sure the baby is still okay. The most common tests are an ultrasound (to determine the level of amniotic fluid as well as to get a general idea of how the baby is doing) and a nonstress test, which monitors changes in the baby's heart rate and movement in reaction to certain stimuli.

If the baby "passes" the tests, the doctor will probably send you home, telling you to repeat the test in a week if the baby hasn't come by then. Otherwise, he or she may suggest that you schedule a date for labor to be induced.

If all of this starts getting you down, remember the words of obstetrician J. Milton Huston of New York Hospital, "In all of my years of practice, I've never seen a baby stay in there."

What If It's a Boy?

If you haven't made up your mind about circumcision yet, now's the time to do so. You may already have strong feelings on the subject. If so, feel free to skip this section. But if you're still undecided, the pros and cons of circumcision are summarized below.

WHY YOU MIGHT WANT TO CONSIDER CIRCUMCISION

- **Religious reasons.** Circumcision is a traditional, ritual practice for Jews and Muslims.
- **Health.** A 1989 study commissioned by the American Academy of Pediatrics (AAP) found that circumcision may reduce a boy's risk of developing urinary tract infections or cancer of the penis, and may reduce his future partner's chance of developing cancer of the cervix. In addition, circumcision completely prevents *phimosis,* a condition in which the foreskin can't be retracted. Generally, the cure for phimosis (which affects about 10 percent of males) is circumcision, a procedure that gets a lot more painful with age.

- **Hygiene.** A circumcised penis is a lot easier to clean—both for the parents and for the boy himself.
- **Conformity.** If you've been circumcised, your son will probably want to look like you. And because circumcision is so popular in the United States, he'll look more like the other boys in the locker room.

WHY YOU MIGHT WANT TO CONSIDER *NOT* CIRCUMCISING YOUR SON

- **Pain.** No matter how you look at it, getting circumcised is painful. The circumcision cut will take about three days to heal fully.
- **Other risks.** Complications, while extremely rare, can occur. The AAP found that there is about a 1 in 500 chance of bleeding or local infection due to circumcision, and that death is almost never a risk. In 1979, for example, there was only one circumcision-related death in the entire United States.
- **Is it necessary?** Some claim that many of the health risks thought to be reduced by circumcision may in fact be reduced simply by better hygiene—something that *can* be taught.
- **Conformity.** As above, if you haven't been circumcised, your son will probably want to look like you.

CARE OF THE CIRCUMCISED PENIS

Your son's penis will be red and sore for a few days after the circumcision. And until it's fully healed, you'll need to protect the newly exposed tip and keep it from sticking to the inside of his diaper (a few tiny spots of blood on his diapers for a few days, however, is perfectly normal). Ordinarily, you'll need to keep the penis dry, and the tip lubricated with petroleum jelly and wrapped in gauze. The person who performed the circumcision or the hospital nursing staff will be able to tell you how long you'll need to keep the penis covered and how often to change the bandages.

CARE OF THE UNCIRCUMCISED PENIS

Even if you elect not to circumcise your son, you'll still have to spend some time taking care of his penis. The standard way to clean an uncircumcised penis is to retract the foreskin and gently wash the head of the penis with mild soap and water. However, 85 percent of boys under six months have foreskins that don't retract, according to the AAP. If this is the case with your son, *do not force it.* Check with your pediatrician immediately and follow his or her hygiene instructions carefully. Fortunately, as boys get older, their foreskins retract on their own; by age one, 50 percent retract, and by age three, 80 to 90 percent.

Dealing with Contingencies

PRETERM LABOR/PREMATURE BIRTH

In the vast majority of pregnancies, labor doesn't start until after the fortieth week. However, a small but significant number of babies (7 to 10 percent) are born prematurely—meaning sometime before the thirty-seventh week. The symptoms of premature labor are exactly the same as those of real labor—they just happen before they're supposed to.

If your partner has any of the following symptoms, she may be considered high risk for premature labor. If you haven't already done so, be sure to let your doctor know whether

- She has an "incompetent cervix"—meaning that the cervix is too weak and may open, allowing the baby to be born too soon. Diagnosed early enough, an incompetent cervix can be "corrected" (and premature births prevented) by sewing the opening of the cervix shut.
- She's had any kind of surgery during pregnancy.
- She's carrying twins (or more).
- She is (or has been recently) a smoker.
- She was exposed to Diethylstilbestrol (DES) while her mother was pregnant with her (many of the daughters of women who took DES to prevent miscarriage were born with abnormalities of the reproductive tract).
- She's had a previous premature labor.
- She's carrying an unusually small fetus.

In most cases, babies born prematurely grow up healthy, but every additional day spent in the uterus significantly increases the chances of survival. Therefore, if your partner shows signs of being in real labor (see page 134 and pages 141–48), call your doctor immediately. If caught early, premature labor can be arrested (usually with the help of intravenous drugs), and the fetus will be able to stay where it belongs for a few more weeks.

After an arrested premature labor, your doctor will most likely order your partner to stay in bed for the rest of the pregnancy. She may even be put on a home fetal monitor to keep an eye on the baby. If this happens, be prepared to step in and take over all of the household responsibilities, as well as responsibility for other children if you have them. If you aren't in a position to do this, you may have to hire someone or ask friends or relatives to help out.

PLANES, TRAINS, AND AUTOMOBILES

It seems like half the births you see in the movies take place on the back seat of a taxi, in a snow-bound cave, or in an airplane bathroom. While those sorts of images may sell movie tickets, the reality is that about 99 percent of babies are born in hospitals, according to the American College of Obstetricians and Gynecologists (ACOG). (And many of the nonhospital births were *planned* that way.) Nevertheless, at some point, just about every pregnant couple starts worrying about giving birth unexpectedly.

EMERGENCY BIRTHS

Emergency births fall into two general categories: either you have a lot of time to prepare (you're snowed in, trapped in your basement because of an earthquake, or shipwrecked—you know you're not going to get to a hospital for a while), or you have little or no time to prepare (you're caught in traffic or your partner's labor was extremely short). Either way, there's very little you can do to get ready.

If you have time, make sure that your partner is in the most sheltered area of wherever you happen to be, and that she's as comfortable as possible. If you have facilities available, boil a piece of string or a shoelace and a pair of scissors or a knife. Then, all you can do is sit tight and let nature take its course.

If you don't have time, try to stay cool. Handling a birth is not as difficult

An Emergency Kit

It's extremely unlikely that your partner will give birth anywhere but in the hospital. However, if you want to make sure all the bases are covered, here's a list of supplies to keep at home, in the car, or anyplace else you and your partner are likely to be spending a lot of time during the last month or so of the pregnancy:

- Chux pads (large, sterile pads) for absorbing blood, amniotic fluid, and so forth. They're available at medical supply stores. If you can't find Chux pads, newspapers are fine—don't worry, a little ink won't hurt anything.
- Clean string or shoelaces for tying the umbilical cord, if necessary (see page 140).
- Clean scissors or knife for cutting the cord, if necessary (see page 140).
- Some towels to warm the baby and mother after the birth.

as you might think. Doctors who do it for a living, in fact, usually show up just a few minutes before the birth and are there primarily in case any complications arise. Fortunately, full-term babies who seem to be in a hurry to come out usually do so without any complications.

Whether you have time to prepare or not, once the baby starts to come, the procedure for performing a delivery is the same. And you'll know the process has started when

- Your partner can't resist pushing.
- The baby's head—or any other body part—is visible.

For the rest of this chapter, we'll describe what you should do if there's no way to avoid delivering the baby yourself. The information isn't intended to replace the years of training your doctor or midwife has. So don't try this at home—unless you absolutely have to.

STEP ONE: PREPARATION. Call for help if a phone is available. Try to keep your partner focused on the breathing and relaxation techniques. Put a pillow or some clothing under her buttocks in order to keep the baby's head and shoulders from hitting a hard surface.

STEP TWO: THE HEAD. When the head begins to appear, *do not pull it.* Instead, support it and let it come out by itself. If the umbilical cord is wrapped around the baby's neck, *slowly* and *gently* glide it over the head. Once the head is out, try to remove any mucus from the baby's nose and mouth (although the baby's passage through the birth canal is usually enough to do the trick).

STEP THREE: THE REST OF THE BODY. Holding the baby's head, encourage your partner to push as the baby's shoulders appear. After the head has emerged, the rest of the baby's body should slide out pretty easily.

Immediately place the baby on your partner's chest and encourage her to begin breastfeeding right away. (Breastfeeding makes the uterus contract, which helps expel the placenta and reduces the chances of excessive bleeding.) And don't worry— the umbilical cord is generally long enough to allow the baby to nurse while still attached.

STEP FOUR: THE PLACENTA. Don't think your delivery job is over as soon as the baby's out—the placenta is still to come. *Do not pull on the cord* to "help" things along. After a while the placenta, which is surprisingly large

Cutting the Cord

If you know you can get to a hospital within about two hours, *do not cut the cord.* If you're more than two hours away, however, follow these instructions:

- Using a sterilized piece of string (or, if you have no string, a clean shoelace), tie a tight knot in the cord at least six inches away from the future sight of the baby's navel.
- Tie a second tight knot about two inches farther away.
- Cut the cord *between* the knots with a sterilized pair of scissors or sharp knife.

Things to Remember During an Emergency Birth

- Try to relax. Do everything carefully, thoughtfully, and slowly.
- Call for help as soon as possible.
- Keep the area where the baby will be delivered as clean as possible.
- Baby CPR. If you haven't taken a baby CPR class already, you should really consider it—just in case.

and meaty (it kind of reminds me of a hefty chunk of liver), will emerge on its own. When it does, wrap it up in something clean—but *do not throw it away;* your doctor will want to take a look at it as soon as possible.

After the placenta is out, gently massage your partner's lower abdomen every few minutes. This begins the important process of returning her uterus back to its original shape.

Notes:

Labor and Delivery

What She's Going Through

Labor is generally divided into three stages. The first stage consists of three phases.

STAGE 1

PHASE 1 (EARLY LABOR) can last anywhere from a few hours to several weeks. Your partner can't always feel the contractions. But if she can, they're generally irregular (often 30–40 minutes apart, measured from the time one starts to the time the next one starts) and will last 45–60 seconds. My wife, however, had from 6 to 12 hours of fairly long, fairly regular (3–5 minutes apart) contractions almost every day for a week before our second daughter was born. Your partner may have "bloody show" (a blood-tinged vaginal discharge), backaches, and diarrhea.

PHASE 2 (ACTIVE LABOR) is generally shorter, but far more intense, than the first phase. In the early part of this phase, contractions are about 5 minutes apart and last about 45–60 seconds. If she's been in labor for a while, your partner may be hungry and is still probably able to talk through the contractions. Later in this stage, however, the contractions will get closer together (2–3 minutes apart) and longer (more than 60 seconds). By this time she will have lost her appetite and won't be able to talk through the contractions (she probably won't want to anyway). If you aren't already there, it's time to head off to the hospital.

PHASE 3 (TRANSITION) usually lasts a few hours. You can stop wondering why they call it "labor." Your partner's contractions may be almost relentless—often two or three in a row without a break. She's tired, sweating, her muscles may be so exhausted they're trembling, and she may be vomiting.

STAGE 2 (PUSHING AND BIRTH)
The second stage generally lasts 2–4 hours. This is the shortest and usually the most intense part of the process. Your partner's contractions are still long (more than 60 seconds) but are further apart. The difference is that during the contractions, she'll be overcome with a desire to push—similar to the feeling of having to make a bowel movement.

STAGE 3 (AFTER THE BIRTH)
The baby is born and the placenta needs to be delivered.

What You're Going Through

Starting labor is no picnic, for her or for you. She, of course, is experiencing—or soon will be—a lot of physical pain. You, in the meantime, are very likely to feel a heavy dose of *psychological* pain.

I couldn't possibly count the number of times—only in my dreams, thankfully—I've heroically defended my home and family from armies of murderers and thieves. But even when I'm awake, I know I wouldn't hesitate before diving in front of a speeding car if it meant being able to save my wife or my children. And I know I would submit to the most painful ordeal to keep any one of them from suffering. Somehow just knowing those things, and feeling so sure of what I'd do in a moment of crisis, gives me a strong sense of confidence and control. But helping your partner through labor is not the same as deciding to rescue a child from a burning building.

The most important thing to remember about this final stage of pregnancy is that the pain—yours and hers—is finite. After a while it ends, and you get to hold your new baby. Ironically, however, her pain will probably end sooner than yours. She'll be sore for a few weeks or so, but by the time the baby is six months old, your partner will hardly remember the pain. If women *could* remember the pain, I can't imagine that any of them would have more than one child. But for six months, a year, even two years after our first daughter was born, my wife's pain remained fresh in my mind. And when we began planning our second pregnancy, the thought of her having to go through a remotely similar experience frightened me.

Staying Involved

Being There—Mentally and Physically

Despite your fears and worries, this is one time when your partner's needs—and they aren't all physical—come first. But before we get into how you can best help her through labor and delivery, it's helpful to get a firm idea of how to tell *when* she's actually gone into labor, and what stage she's in once she's there.

STAGE 1: PHASE 1 (EARLY LABOR)

Although the contractions are fairly mild at this point, you should do everything you can to make your partner as comfortable as possible (back rubs, massages, and so forth). Some women may tell you exactly what they want you to do, others may feel a little shy about making any demands—especially things that might seem trivial. Either way, ask her regularly what you can do to help. And when she tells you, do it. If taking a walk makes her feel better, go with her. If doing headstands in the living room is what she wants to do (fairly unlikely at this point), give her a hand. You also need to trust her instincts about what's going on with her body. At some point during every day of my wife's week-long first-stage labor marathon, I became convinced that *this* time it was real and that *this* time she should let me call the doctor. Wisely and firmly, she refused.

Make sure you *both* get something to eat *before* you go to the hospital. In fact, you should bring some food with you. Once you get to the hospital, the nurses won't let your partner eat until after the baby is born, and you're not going to want to try to make a dash to the snack bar between contractions. Finally, try to get some rest. Don't be fooled by the adrenaline rush that will hit you when your partner finally goes into labor. You'll be so excited that you'll feel you can last forever, but you can't. She's got some hormones (and pain) to keep her going; you don't.

STAGE 1: PHASE 2 (ACTIVE LABOR)

One of the symptoms of second-phase labor is that your partner may seem to be losing interest in just about everything—including arguing with you about when to call the doctor. After my wife's contractions had been 2–3 minutes

The Three Stages of Labor and Delivery

STAGE	WHAT'S HAPPENING
Stage 1/Phase 1 (early labor)	♦ Her cervix is effacing (thinning out) and dilating (opening up) up to about 3 centimeters ♦ Her water may break
Stage 1/Phase 2 (active labor)	♦ She's increasingly uncomfortable ♦ Her cervix continues to efface and will dilate to about 7 centimeters ♦ Water may break (if it hasn't already) or may have to be broken
Stage 1/Phase 3 (transition)	♦ Her cervix is now fully dilated ♦ She may feel the urge to push
Stage 2 (pushing and birth)	♦ Increase in bloody discharge ♦ The baby is moving through the birth canal ♦ Doctor may have to do an episiotomy
Stage 3 (after the birth)	♦ The placenta is separating from the wall of the uterus ♦ Episiotomy or tearing (if any) will be repaired

WHAT SHE'S FEELING	WHAT YOU CAN DO
♦ She may be excited but not totally sure that "this is really it" ♦ She may be anxious and restless ♦ She may not feel like doing much of anything	♦ Reassure her ♦ Tell jokes, take a walk, or rent a movie—anything to distract her
♦ She's getting serious and impatient about the pain ♦ She's beginning to concentrate fully on the contractions	♦ Call the doctor and get her to the hospital ♦ Reassure and encourage her ♦ Help her take one contraction at a time ♦ Feed her ice chips ♦ Praise her for her progress ♦ Massage, massage, massage
♦ She may be confused, frustrated, and scared ♦ She may announce that she can't take it anymore and is going home	♦ Do whatever she wants you to do ♦ Try to help her resist pushing until the doctor tells her she should ♦ Mop her brow with a wet cloth ♦ Feed her ice chips ♦ Massage her (if she wants it)
♦ She's feeling confident that she can finish the job ♦ She may have gotten a second wind	♦ Continue to reassure and comfort her ♦ Encourage her to push when she's supposed to and tell her how great she's doing ♦ Encourage her to watch the baby come out (if she wants to and if there's a mirror around) ♦ Let the professionals do their job
♦ RELIEF ♦ Euphoria ♦ Talkative ♦ Strong, heroic ♦ Hungry, thirsty ♦ Empty (of the baby) ♦ Desire to cuddle with her baby (and her partner)	♦ Praise her ♦ Put the baby on her stomach ♦ Encourage her to relax ♦ Encourage her to start nursing the baby, if she feels ready ♦ Bond with her and the baby

apart for a few hours (and so strong that she couldn't talk through them), I was encouraging her to call. She refused. Many women, it seems, "just know" when it's time to go. So, chances are if she tells you "it's time," grab your car keys. If you're still not sure whether the second phase has started, here's a pretty typical scenario that may help you decide:

YOU: Honey, these contractions have been going on like this for three hours. I think we should head off to the hospital.
SHE: Okay.
YOU: Great. Let's get dressed, okay?
SHE: I don't want to get dressed.
YOU: But you're only wearing a nightgown. How about at least putting on some shoes and socks?
SHE: I don't want any shoes and socks.
YOU: But it's cold out there. How about a jacket?
SHE: I don't want a jacket.

Get the point?

Another typical symptom of second-phase labor is (in most people anyway) an uncharacteristic loss of modesty. Birth-class instructor Kim Kaehler says she can always tell what stage of labor a woman is in just by looking at the sheet on her bed (when she's in it and naked). If she's in first phase, she'll be covered up to her neck; in second phase, the sheet is halfway down; by the third phase (see below), the sheet's all the way off.

STAGE 1: PHASE 3 (TRANSITION)

It seems that when laboring women are shown in TV shows, they're often snapping at their husband or boyfriend, yelling things like "Don't touch me!" or "Leave me alone, you're the one who did this to me." I think I'd internalized those stereotypes and by the time we got to the hospital I was really afraid that my wife would behave the same way when she got to the transition stage, blame me for the pain, and push me away. Fortunately, it never happened. The closest we ever came was when we were in labor with our second daughter. The only place my wife could be comfortable was in the shower, and for a while I was in there with her, trying to talk her through the contractions as I massaged her aching back. Then she asked me to leave the bathroom for a while. Sure, I felt hurt for a minute—I felt I should be there with her—but it was clear that she had no intention of hurting me.

Unfortunately, not every laboring woman manages to be as graceful under pressure. If your partner happens to say something nasty to you or throws you unceremoniously out of the room for a while, you need to imagine that while she's in labor her mind is being taken over by an angry rush-hour mob, all trying to push and shove their way onto an overcrowded subway train. Quite often, the pain she's experiencing is so intense and overwhelming that the only way she can make it through the contractions is to concentrate completely on them. Something as simple and well-meaning as a word or a loving caress can be terribly distracting.

So what *can* you do? Whatever she wants. Fast. If she doesn't want you to touch her, don't insist. Offer to feed her some ice chips instead. If she wants you to get out of the room, go. But tell her that you'll be right outside in case she needs you. If the room is pitch black and she tells you it's too bright, agree with her and find something to turn off. If she wants to listen to the twenty-four-hour Elvis station, turn it on. But whatever you do, don't argue with her, don't reason with her, and above all, don't pout if she swears at you or calls you names. She really doesn't mean to, and the last thing she needs to deal with at this moment of crisis is your wounded pride.

STAGE 2: PUSHING

Up until the pushing stage, I thought I was completely prepared for dealing with my wife's labor and delivery. I was calm, and, despite my feelings of inadequacy, I knew what to expect almost every step of the way. The hospital staff was supportive of my wanting to be with my wife through every contraction. But when the time came to start pushing, they changed. All of a sudden, *they* were in control. The doctor was called, extra nurses magically appeared, and the room began to fill up with equipment—a scale, a bassinet, a tray of sterilized medical instruments, a washbasin, diapers, towels. (We happened to be in a combination labor/birthing room; if, in the middle of pushing, you find yourself chasing after your wife, who's being rushed down the hall to a separate delivery room, don't be alarmed. It may feel like an emergency, but it isn't really.)

The nurses told my wife what to do, how to do it, and when to do it. All I could do was watch—and I must admit that at first I felt a little cheated. After all, *I* was the one who had been with my wife through almost every contraction. *My* baby was about to be born. But when the most important part finally arrived, I wasn't going to be anything more than a spectator. And unless you're a professional birthing coach or a trained labor and delivery nurse, chances are you're going to feel like a spectator, too.

The truth of the matter is that although I was feeling left out and would have liked to have been more involved in this stage, it was probably a lot better for my wife that I wasn't. As I watched the nurses do their stuff, I quickly realized that simply holding your partner's legs and saying, "Push, honey. That's great," just isn't enough. *Recognizing* a good, productive push, and, more important, being able to *explain* how to do one—"raise your butt . . . lower your legs . . . keep your head back . . ."—are skills that come from years of experience.

STAGE 2: BIRTH

Intellectually, I had known my wife was pregnant. I'd been to all the appointments and I'd heard the heartbeat, seen the ultrasound, and felt the baby kicking. Still, there was something intangible about the whole process. And it wasn't until our baby started "crowning" (peeking her hairy little head out of my wife's vagina) that all the pieces finally came together.

At just about the same moment, I also realized that there was one major advantage to my having been displaced during the pushing stage: I had both hands free to "catch" the baby as she came out—and believe me, holding my daughter's hot, slimy, bloody little body and placing her gently at my wife's breast was easily the highlight of the whole occasion.

If you think you might want to do this, make sure you've worked out the choreography with your doctor and the nurses before the baby starts crowning. See "Birth Plans" on pages 115–18 for more information.

Your partner, unfortunately, is in the worst possible position to see the baby being born. Most hospitals, however, have tried to remedy this situation by making mirrors available. Still, many women are concentrating so hard on the pushing that they may not be interested in looking in the mirror.

If you were expecting your newborn to look like the Gerber baby, you may be in for a bit of a shock. Babies are generally born covered with a whitish coating called *vernix.* They're sometimes blue and frequently covered with blood and mucus. Their eyes may be puffy, their genitals swollen, and their backs and shoulders may be covered with fine hair. In addition, the trip through the birth canal has probably left your baby with a cone-shaped head. All in all, it's the most beautiful sight in the world.

After the Birth

THE BABY

Your baby's first few minutes outside the womb are a time of intense physical and emotional release for you and your partner. At long last you get to meet the unique little person you created together. Your partner may want to try nursing the baby (although most newborns aren't hungry for the first twelve

Seeing the Baby

Many hospitals have very rigid rules regarding parent/infant contact—feeding may be highly regulated and the hours you can visit your child may be limited. The nursing staff may also bottle-feed the baby—either with sugar-water or with formula. If this isn't what you want, let them know.

Some hospitals, however, are more flexible. The hospital where both our children were born now no longer has a nursery (except for babies with serious health problems). Healthy babies are expected to stay in the mother's room for their entire hospital stay. There are even hospitals that permit the new father to spend the night with his partner and baby. Check with the staff of your hospital to find out their policy.

hours or so), and you will probably want to stroke his or her brand-new skin and marvel at his or her tiny fingernails. But depending on the hospital, the conditions of the birth, and whether or not you've been perfectly clear about your desires, your baby's first few minutes could be spent being poked and prodded by doctors and nurses instead of being held and cuddled by you.

At some point after the birth, your baby will be weighed, measured, given an ID bracelet, bathed, diapered, footprinted, and wrapped in a blanket. Some hospitals also photograph each newborn. After that, most hospitals (frequently required by law) apply a silver nitrate gel or drops to your baby's eyes as a protection against gonorrhea. The thing to remember about all this is that in most cases it can—and should—wait.

If, however, your baby was delivered by C-section, or if there were any other complications, the baby will be rushed off to have his or her little lungs suctioned before returning for the rest of the cleanup routine (see page 159 for more on this).

THE PLACENTA

Before our first child was born it had simply never occurred to me (or to my wife, for that matter) that labor and delivery wouldn't end when the baby was born. While you and your partner are admiring your new family member, the placenta—which has been your baby's life support system for the past five months or so—still must be delivered. Your partner may continue to have mild contractions for anywhere from five minutes to about an hour until this happens. The strange thing about this stage of the delivery is that neither you nor your partner will probably even know it's happening—you'll be much too involved with your new baby.

Once the placenta is out, however, you need to decide what to do with it. In this country most people never even see it, and those who do just leave it at the hospital (where it will either be destroyed or, more likely, sold to a cosmetics company—honest). But in many other cultures, the placenta is considered to have a permanent, almost magical bond with the child it nourished in the womb, and disposal is handled with a great deal more reverence. In fact, most cultures that have placenta rituals believe that if it is not properly buried, the child—or the parents, or even the entire village—will suffer some terrible consequences.

Researcher J. R. Davidson found that in rural Peru, for example, immediately after the birth of a child, the father is required to go to a far-off location and bury the placenta deep enough so that no animals or people will accidentally discover it. Otherwise, the placenta may become "jealous" of the attention paid to the baby and may take revenge by causing an epidemic.

In some South American Indian cultures, people believe that a child's life can be influenced by objects that are buried with its placenta. According to Davidson, parents in the Qolla tribe "bury miniature implements copied after the ones used in adult life with the placenta, in the hopes of assuring that the infant will be a good worker. Boys' placentas are frequently buried with a shovel or a pick, and girls' are buried with a loom or a hoe."

But placentas are not always buried. In ancient Egypt, pharaohs' placentas were wrapped in special containers to keep them from harm. And a wealthy Inca in Ecuador built a solid-gold statue of his mother—complete with his placenta in "her" womb.

Even today, the people of many cultures believe that placentas have special powers. In other parts of Peru placentas are burned, the ashes are mixed with water, and the mixture is then drunk by the babies as a remedy for a variety of childhood illnesses. Traditional Vietnamese medicine uses placentas to combat sterility and senility, and in India, touching a placenta is supposed to help a childless woman conceive a healthy baby of her own.

Whatever you and your partner decide to do, it's probably best to keep it a secret—at least from the hospital staff. Some states try to regulate what you can do with a placenta and may even prohibit you from taking it home (although if you really want to, you can probably find a sympathetic nurse who will pack it up for you). We deliberately left our first daughter's placenta at the hospital. But the second one's is still stored in the freezer (we're planning to honor her birth by planting a tree and using the placenta as fertilizer).

Dealing with contingencies

Unfortunately, not all labors and deliveries proceed exactly as planned. In fact, most of them don't. The American Association of Obstetricians and Gynecologists estimates that more than 30 percent of babies are born by Cesarean section. And a good number of mothers who deliver vaginally are medicated in some way. As with so many other aspects of your pregnancy experience, having good, clear information about what's really going on and what the options are during labor and delivery will help you make informed, intelligent decisions about how to handle the unexpected or the unplanned. The key to getting the information you need is to ask questions—and to keep on asking until you're completely satisfied with the answers you're getting. Find out about the risks, the benefits, the effects on your partner, the effects on the baby. The only exception to this rule is when there is a clear medical emergency. In such a case, you might want to save your questions for later.

Here are a few of the contingencies that can come up during the birth and how they might affect you—and your partner.

PAIN MEDICATION

If you've taken a childbirth class (and even if you haven't), you and your partner may have planned to have a "natural" (medication-free) childbirth. Unfortunately, natural childbirth often sounds better—and less painful—than it actually turns out to be. Because your partner is the one who is experiencing the physical pain, you should defer to her judgment when considering pain medication. This doesn't mean, however, that you don't have anything to say about the issue. What you may want to do is discuss her attitude toward medication thoroughly before she's in labor, so you know whether she wants you to suggest it when *you* get concerned, or wait until *she* requests it. And remember, if you do end up having a discussion about medication sometime during labor, make sure you do it in the most supportive possible way. It's painful to have to watch the one you love suffer, but starting an argument when she's in labor isn't a smart idea (and you're not going to resolve anything anyway).

Many women feel that taking pain medication is a sign of weakness, or that they've failed—as women and as mothers. In addition, some childbirth preparation methods view medication as the first step along a path that ultimately leads to Cesarean section. This is not, by any stretch of the imagination, the rule.

Your nurses or doctor may offer you pain relief, or you can request it yourself. We're not suggesting that you should use—or that you will need—pain

Some of the Most Common Options for Relieving Pain

EPIDURAL

An epidural is usually administered during the second stage of labor, when the pain is greatest. Your partner will be asked to lean over a table or lie on her left side. After a local anesthetic has numbed the area, a large needle, through which a catheter carrying the medication is threaded, will be inserted into the space between the spinal cord and the membrane that surrounds it.

ADVANTAGES

- The effect is felt almost immediately.
- It is the safest, most effective, labor painkiller available.
- Very little of the medication "crosses the placenta" (affects the baby).
- The medication does not make the mother feel drowsy.
- If properly administered (and it usually is), the epidural will block the *pain* of your partner's contractions, while still leaving her able to feel *when* they are starting and, therefore, when to push.

RISKS

- Possible increase in maternal blood pressure.
- Inability to feel the urge to empty the bladder, which can lead to the need for a urinary catheterization.
- If improperly administered, your partner may not be able to feel when to push. This could lead to a forceps delivery (see below), or increase the chance she'll have to have a Cesarean section.
- Occasionally causes nausea, headaches, ringing in the ears, or leg cramps.

medication. But whatever you do, knowing a little about your options is always a good idea.

EXHAUSTION

Pain isn't the only reason your partner might need some chemical intervention. In some cases, labor may be progressing so slowly (or be stalled for so long) that your practitioner may become concerned that your partner will be too ex-

DEMEROL

Demerol is usually given through an IV or a shot in the buttocks. It is generally administered no later than three hours before delivery and in conjunction with a tranquilizer (see below).

ADVANTAGES

- Takes effect almost immediately.
- Generally has little or no effect on your partner's ability to push.

RISKS

- Can cause nausea and vomiting.
- In larger doses, it can make your partner too drowsy to push effectively.
- The medication easily crosses the placenta, causing the baby to be temporarily drowsy at birth, unable to suck properly for a short while, or, in rare cases, unable to breathe without assistance.

SEDATIVES AND TRANQUILIZERS

These do just what you think they might: they relax and calm your partner. They don't have much effect on pain, however.

ADVANTAGES

- May relieve anxiety.
- If taken in a moderate dose, your partner isn't numbed and can still participate fully in the birth.

RISKS

- Can cause nausea and drowsiness.
- Cross the placenta and may cause temporary breathing problems and drowsiness in the baby.

hausted by the time she needs to push. This was exactly what happened during our second labor. After twenty hours of labor and only four centimeters of dilation, our doctor suggested pitocin (a drug that stimulates contractions) together with an epidural. This chemical cocktail removed the pain of labor while allowing my wife's cervix to dilate fully and quickly. I'm convinced that this approach not only did not increase the risk of a C-section but actually prevented one by allowing my wife a well-deserved breather before she started pushing.

Other Common Birth Contingencies

FORCEPS

Forceps are long tongs that are used to guide a stubborn baby's head through the birth canal. If the birth is progressing normally, there's no reason to use forceps. Nevertheless, some doctors routinely use them, usually just to increase the speed of delivery. Most forceps deliveries will leave the baby with bruises in the temple area for a week or two. In rare instances, permanent scarring or other damage can occur. In addition, your partner may need additional medication and a larger-than-normal episiotomy (see below). Make sure you ask your doctor—*before* the birth—whether (and if so, how often) he or she uses forceps. Forceps may legitimately be called for if:

- The baby is in distress and a vaginal birth needs to be speeded up.
- Your partner is too exhausted (or medicated) to push effectively. In this case, using forceps may save your partner from having a C-section.

EPISIOTOMY

An episiotomy involves making a small cut in the perineum (the area immediately below the vagina) to enlarge the vaginal opening and allow for easier passage of the baby's head. About 90 percent of women delivering for the first time under an obstetrician's care have an episiotomy (whether they need it or not). Many women, however, feel that a small amount of tearing is preferable (and less painful) than a routine episiotomy. But the procedure may be legitimately indicated if:

- The baby is extremely large, and squeezing through the vagina might harm the baby or your partner.
- Forceps are used.
- The baby is breech (see below).

BREECH PRESENTATION

If is a baby is breech it means that the feet will be delivered first (only 3–4 percent of babies are born this way). There's nothing you can do to prevent your baby from coming out any way he or she wants to. And in most cases, the fact that the baby is breech doesn't call for any extraordinary measures. Breech presentation does, however, increase your partner's chance of having a C-section.

EXTERNAL AND INTERNAL FETAL MONITORING

This involves attaching a rather complicated machine—complete with graphs, digital outputs, and high-tech beeping—to your partner's abdomen. Fetal monitors are used to monitor your baby's heartbeat and your partner's contractions.

In some respects, fetal monitors are pretty remarkable. If properly hooked up, they are so accurate that by watching the digital display, you will be able to tell when your partner's contractions are starting—even before *she* feels them—and how intense they will be. The forewarning you have may help you coach your partner through the contraction. But if you were thinking that saying something like "Ready, honey? Here it comes—looks like a big one" might be fun, your partner probably won't appreciate the humor.

In many hospitals, laboring women are routinely hooked up to external fetal monitors. Internal fetal monitors (which are actually electrodes attached to the baby's scalp) are also frequently used. But unless there's some compelling reason why you need one (if your partner has been given an epidural, for example, or if there have been signs of fetal distress), you and your partner will be a lot better off without either kind of monitor. Here's why:

- Once the fetal monitor is on, your partner is virtually confined to her bed. No more showers, no more walks to the nursery, no more creative labor positions.
- It can scare the hell out of you. When my wife was hooked up to a fetal monitor during her first labor, we were comforted by the sound of the baby's steady, 140-beats-per-minute heartbeat. But at one point the heart rate dropped to 120, then 100, then 80, then 60. Nothing was wrong—the doctor was just trying to turn the baby over—but hearing her little heart slow down that much nearly gave my wife and me heart attacks.

A final word of advice about fetal monitors: if you absolutely have to have one, make sure they turn the volume down (better yet, all the way off).

Cesarean Section

All things being equal, most parents would prefer to bring their babies into the world "normally." And most of the time, things go the way they're supposed to. But when they don't, the chances of having a Cesarean section delivery increase greatly. In fact, more than 30 percent of all children born in hospitals are delivered by C-section.

What She's Going Through

Most childbirth preparation classes (see pages 102–6) put a great deal of emphasis on natural, unmedicated deliveries. Many women, therefore, feel a tremendous amount of pressure to deliver vaginally, and may actually consider themselves "failures" if they don't—especially after they've invested many hours in a painful labor (for more on this see pages 159–60).

In addition, recovering from a Cesarean is much different than recovering from a vaginal birth (see page 160 for more details). My wife (and I) spent three nights in the hospital after the C-section delivery of our first daughter. But after our second daughter was born (vaginally), we remained in the hospital for only five hours. (We rushed it a little; most people stay twenty-four to forty-eight hours after a vaginal birth.)

What You're Going Through

Your take on the C-section is undoubtedly going to be quite different from your partner's. Researcher Katharyn May found that only 8 percent of men whose partners delivered by C-section objected to the operation; 92 percent were "greatly relieved." Although I didn't participate in this study, it accurately reflects my own experience. It simply had never occurred to me that we might somehow have "failed" when our first daughter was delivered by C-section. On the contrary, I remember feeling incredibly thankful that my wife's suffering would finally end. And seeing how quickly and painlessly the baby was delivered made me wonder why we hadn't done it sooner.

Despite the relief a father may feel on his wife's behalf, a C-section can be a trying experience for him. As a rule, he is separated from his wife while she is being prepped for surgery, and he is not given any information about what's happening. I remember being left in the hall outside the operating room, trying to keep an eye on my wife through a tiny window. Besides being terribly scared, I felt completely helpless—and useless—as the doctors, nurses, and assistants scurried around, blocking my view, getting dressed, washing, opening packages of scalpels, tubes, and who knows what else. Only one person—the pediatrician who would attend the delivery—took a minute to pat me on the shoulder and tell me that everything would be all right. I've never felt more grateful to another person in my life.

When I was finally permitted into the operating room, I was told—no discussion allowed—to sit by my wife's head. There was a curtain across her chest that prevented me from seeing what the surgeons were doing. Whenever I stood up to get a better view the anesthesiologist shoved me back down into my seat. I was too exhausted to argue, but a friend of mine whose partner had a C-section in the same hospital a few years later *did* argue and was able to go around to the "business end" of the operation.

Staying Involved

My friend and I may be the lucky ones; in many hospitals men aren't allowed into the operating room at all. Others permit them in only if they've taken a special C-section class. Hopefully, even before you check in you and your partner will have already told your OB exactly what your preferences are should there be a C-section, and you'll be familiar with any relevant hospital policies. (See pages 16–17 for other things to discuss with your OB.)

Don't forget that although a C-section is a fairly commonplace operation, it is still major surgery. And after the operation, your partner will need some extra special care.

Common Medical Reasons for a Cesarean Section

- **Fetopelvic disproportion.** The mother's pelvis is too small to allow the baby's head to pass through the vagina.
- **Failure of the labor to progress.** Exhausted by an excessively long labor, the mother is unable to push the baby out.
- **Maternal herpes (active).** If the mother has an outbreak of herpes within about four weeks of the birth, there isn't much choice.
- **Placenta problems.** *Abrupto placenta* (separation of the placenta from the uterine wall before labor begins) causes bleeding and can threaten the lives of both mother and baby. *Placenta previa* (the placenta is fully or partially blocking the opening of the cervix) prevents the baby from leaving the uterus.
- **Position of baby.** Under certain circumstances, if the baby is breech (coming out feet first) or transverse (facing in the same direction as the mother instead of facing backward), a C-section may be more likely.
- **Previous C-section birth(s).** Contrary to popular belief, having had one C-section increases the chances of subsequent C-sections by only about 3 percent. Most women with a prior C-section have V-BACs (vaginal births after Cesarean).

First of all, as strange as it may sound, after having a C-section your partner may feel terribly left out. She will have been fully awake during the operation and will be anxious to meet the new baby. But whereas after a vaginal birth the mother gets to see and touch the baby immediately, after a C-section the baby is usually quickly whisked away to have his or her lungs suctioned out. (Although it may seem like a scary emergency procedure, suctioning a C-section baby's lungs is quite routine. In a vaginal birth, as the baby passes through the birth canal, he or she gets what amounts to a natural Heimlich maneuver that squeezes the amniotic fluid out of the lungs. C-section babies need a little help.)

You'll probably get to make a "ceremonial" umbilical cord cut (the surgeons will have already cut the cord while delivering the baby). If the baby is being cared for right in the delivery room, make sure to tell your partner exactly what's happening—she'll want to know. In some hospitals, C-section babies are removed from the delivery room immediately after the birth and

Some of the Most Common Nonmedical Reasons for a Cesarean Section

- **Scheduling.** Doing a C-section delivery means your doctor won't have to wait around for an unpredictably long labor.
- **It's easier.** Many OBs consider C-sections safer than vaginal deliveries.
- **It's Friday.** More operations are performed on Friday afternoons, when tired doctors are eager to get home for the weekend, than at any other time of the week.
- **Fear of lawsuits.** If something goes wrong with the birth—fetal or maternal distress, or even a birth defect—the obstetrician is likely to be blamed for having let the labor go on too long. In some cases, therefore, OBs perform a C-section to speed things up.

taken straight to the nursery, where they're washed, examined, and put through basically the same procedures covered in the preceding chapter. This whole process can take anywhere from a few minutes to a few hours.

Although you might want to remain with your partner and comfort her immediately after the delivery, stay with your baby instead. It's bad enough for a newborn to be deprived of snuggling with one of his parents right away, but it would be worse if the baby couldn't be with *either* of you. Staying with our daughter also eased my paranoia that she might be switched in the nursery (a highly unlikely occurrence, given the rather elaborate security measures in place in most hospitals).

Your Partner's Emotional Recovery

Having an unplanned C-section can trigger a whole host of conflicting emotions in your partner. She, like you, may feel greatly relieved that the pain is over and the baby is safe. At the same time, it's very natural for her to second-guess herself and the decision she made, to start wondering whether there was anything she could have done to avoid the operation, or to believe she's failed because she didn't deliver vaginally. These feelings are especially common when the C-section was performed because labor "failed to progress" (meaning that the cervix wasn't dilating as quickly as the doctors may have thought it should).

If you sense that your partner is experiencing any of these negative emotions, it's important for you to counter them immediately. She really needs to know that no one could have done more, or been stronger or braver than

Facts to Remember about Recovery from a Cesarean Section

- Your partner's incision will be tender or downright painful for at least several days. Fortunately, she'll undoubtedly be receiving some intravenous pain medication.
- The nursing staff will visit quite frequently to make sure that your partner's uterus is getting firm and returning to its proper place, to see whether she's producing enough urine, and to check her bandages.
- Your partner will have an IV until her bowels start functioning again (usually one to three days after delivery). After the IV is removed, she'll start on a liquid diet, then add a few soft foods, and finally return to her normal diet.
- Your partner will need to get up and move around. Despite the fact that a C-section is major abdominal surgery, less than twenty-four hours after the delivery the nurses will probably encourage—and help—your partner to get out of bed and take a couple of rather painful-looking steps.
- Before your partner leaves the hospital the sutures or staples will be removed. Yes, staples. Until I heard the clink as the doctor dropped them into a jar, I'd just assumed that my wife had been sewn up after her C-section.

she was; that she didn't give in to the pain too soon; that she tried everything she could have to jump start a stalled labor; and that the decision she made (or at least agreed to) was the best one—both for the baby and for herself.

Some of these thoughts might seem obvious to you—so obvious that you might think they don't need to be said at all. But they do—especially by you. You were there with her and you know better than anyone else exactly what she went through. So, being comforted and praised by you will mean a lot more to her than hearing the same words from a well-meaning relative.

An Important Warning

Never, never, never suggest to your pregnant partner that she consider a C-section—let your doctor make the first move.

When my wife was pregnant with our second daughter, the pain she had been through during her first labor and delivery was still fresh in my mind. At one point I told her that I was really upset by the thought that she might have to endure another horrible labor, and I suggested that she should consider a C-section.

I had no idea that someone could get so furious so quickly. Even though I had the very best intentions and was sincerely thinking only of her and how to minimize her pain, she thought I was being completely insensitive. Clearly, I had underestimated how incredibly important giving birth vaginally—especially after already having had one C-section—was to her.

Many of the men I've talked to have had similar thoughts about making the C-section suggestion to their partners. Most of them were wise enough not to act on their impulse. And hopefully, you won't either. Telling your partner how you're feeling and what you're going through is, in most cases, the right thing to do. But when it comes to C-sections, really and truly, it's an issue that's just too hot to handle.

Notes:

Gee Honey, Now What Do We Do?

What She's Going Through

Physically

- Vaginal discharge (called *lochia*) that will gradually change from bloody to pink to brown to yellow over the next six weeks or so
- Major discomfort if there is an episiotomy or C-section incision (the pain will disappear over the next six weeks)
- Constipation
- Breast discomfort—starting on about the third day after the birth (when her breasts become "engorged" with milk), and if she's breastfeeding, her nipples will probably be sore for about two weeks
- Gradual weight loss
- Exhaustion—especially if her labor was long and difficult
- Continued contractions—especially while breastfeeding—but disappearing over the next several days
- Hair loss (most women stop losing hair while they're pregnant, but when it's over, they make up for unlost hair)

Emotionally

- Relief that it's finally over
- Excitement, depression, or both (see page 163)
- Worried about how she'll perform as a mother, and whether she'll be able to breastfeed (but over the next few weeks, her confidence will build and these worries should disappear)
- A deep need to get to know the baby
- Impatience at her lack of mobility
- Decreased sex drive

Postpartum Blues and Depression

About 70 percent of new mothers experience periods of mild sadness, weepiness, mood swings, sleep deprivation, loss of appetite, inability to make decisions, anger, or anxiety after the baby is born. These postpartum blues, which many believe are caused by hormonal shifts in a new mother's body, can last for hours or days, but in most cases they disappear within a few weeks. If you notice that your partner is experiencing any of these symptoms, there's not much you can do except be as supportive as possible. Encourage her to get out of the house for a while and see to it that she's eating healthily.

In a small number of cases, postpartum blues can develop into postpartum depression. According to the American College of Obstetricians and Gynecologists, postpartum depression, if not recognized and treated, may become worse or last longer than it needs to. Here are some symptoms to watch out for:

- Postpartum blues that don't go away after two weeks, or feelings of depression or anger that surface a month or two after the birth.
- Feelings of sadness, doubt, guilt, helplessness, or hopelessness that begin to disrupt your partner's normal functioning.
- Inability to sleep when tired, or sleeping most of the time, even when the baby is awake.
- Marked changes in appetite.
- Extreme concern and worry about the baby—or lack of interest in the baby and/or other members of the family.
- Fear of harming the baby or thoughts of self-harm.

Again, most of what your partner will go through after the birth is completely normal and nothing to worry about. So be patient, and don't expect her to bounce back immediately. If you're really concerned, however, encourage your partner to talk with you about what she's feeling and to see her doctor or a therapist.

What's Going On with the Baby

For thousands of years, most people have believed that at birth, infants were capable only of eating, sleeping, crying, and some rudimentary movements. But in the mid-1960s researchers Peter Wolff and Heinz Prechtl discovered that infant behavior they had previously thought to be random actually fell into six clearly defined states that are apparent within just a few minutes after a baby is born. "By recognizing them and realizing when they occur and what the expected responses are in each," write Marshall and Phyllis Klaus, authors of *The Amazing Newborn,* "parents not only can get to know their infants but also can provide most sensitively for their needs." Here's a summary of the six states, based on the Klauses' book.

Quiet Alert

Babies in the quiet alert state rarely move—all their energy is channeled into seeing and hearing. They can (and do) follow objects with their eyes and will even imitate your facial expressions.

Within the first hour of life, most infants have a period of quiet alertness that lasts an average of forty minutes. During his or her first week, the normal baby spends only about 10 percent of any twenty-four-hour period in this state. It is in this state, however, that your baby is most curious and is absorbing information about his or her new world. And while the baby is in this state you will first become aware that there's a real person inside that tiny body.

Active Alert

In this state, the baby will make small sounds and move his or her arms, head, body, face, and eyes frequently and actively.

The baby's movements usually come in short bursts—a few seconds of activity every minute or two. Some researchers say these movements are designed to give parents subtle clues about what the baby wants and needs. Others say these movements are just interesting to watch, and therefore promote parent/infant interaction.

Crying

Crying is a perfectly natural—and for some, frequent—state (for more on this, see pages 181–85). The infant's eyes may be open or closed, the face red, and the arms and legs moving vigorously.

Often, just picking up the baby and walking around with him or her will stop the crying. Interestingly, researchers used to think that babies were soothed by the upright position. It turns out, though, that what makes them stop crying is the *movement toward* the upright position.

Keep in mind, too, that crying is *not* a bad thing—it not only allows the baby to communicate but also provides valuable exercise. So, if your efforts to calm him or her aren't immediately successful (and the baby isn't hungry or stewing in a dirty diaper), don't worry; chances are the tears will stop by themselves in a few minutes.

Drowsiness

This is a transition state that occurs as the baby is waking up or falling asleep. There may still be some movement, and the eyes will often look dull or unfocused.

Leave the baby alone—let him or her drift off to sleep or move into one of the alert stages.

Quiet Sleep

The baby's face is relaxed and the eyelids are closed and still. There are no body movements and only tiny, almost imperceptible mouth movements.

When your baby is in the quiet sleep state, you may be alarmed at the lack of movement and be afraid the baby has stopped breathing. If so, lean as close as you can and listen for the baby's breath. Otherwise, *gently* put a hand on the baby's back and feel it rise and fall. Try to resist the urge to wake the baby up—most newborns spend up to 90 percent of their first few weeks sleeping.

Active Sleep

Eyes are usually closed, but may occasionally flicker open. The baby may also smile or frown, make sucking or chewing movements, and even whimper or twitch—just as adults do in their active sleep state.

Half of a baby's sleep time is spent in quiet sleep, the other half in active sleep, with the two states alternating in thirty-minute shifts. So, if your sleeping baby starts to stir, whimper, or seems to be waking up unhappy, wait a few seconds before you pick him or her up to feed, change, or soothe. If left alone, the baby may very well slip back into the quiet sleep state.

Newborn babies are capable of a lot more than crying, sleeping, and looking around. Just a few hours out of the womb, they are already trying to communicate with those around them. They can imitate facial expressions, have some control over their bodies, can express preferences (most prefer patterned objects to plain objects and curved lines to straight ones), and have remarkable memories. Marshall Klaus describes playing a game with an eight-hour-old girl in which he asked one colleague (who was a stranger to the baby) to hold her and slowly stick out her tongue. After a few seconds, the baby imitated the woman. Then Dr. Klaus took the baby and passed her around to twelve other doctors and nurses who were participating in the game, all of whom were told not to stick their tongues out. When the baby finally came back to the first doctor, she—without any prompting—immediately stuck out her tongue again. Even at just a few hours old, she had obviously remembered her "friend."

If you want your baby to respond to and play with you, try to establish communication during his or her active alert stage. (During the first few months infants are particularly responsive to high contrast, and so black-and-white toys and patterns are often a big hit.) But be patient. Babies are incredibly bright little creatures, but they also have minds of their own. This means that despite your best efforts, your baby may not be interested in performing like a trained seal whenever you wish.

What You're Going Through

Unconditional Love

Sooner or later, almost every writer takes a crack at trying to describe love. And for the most part, they fall short. But there's a line in Maurice Sendak's classic children's book *Where the Wild Things Are* that captures the feeling of loving one's own child exactly: "Please don't go—we'll eat you up—we love you so." As crazy as it may sound, that's precisely what my love for my daughters feels like to me. Whether we're playing, reading a book, telling each other about our days, or I'm just gazing at their smooth, peaceful faces as they sleep, all of a sudden I'll be overcome with the desire to pick them up, mush them into tiny balls, and pop them in my mouth. I know, it sounds nuts, but just you wait.

One of my biggest fears during my wife's second pregnancy was that I wouldn't be able to love our second child as much as the first—that there wouldn't be enough of the consuming, overpowering love I felt for our first daughter to share with the new baby. But I really had nothing to worry about. Three seconds after our second daughter was born, I already wanted to eat her up, too.

Awe at What the Female Body Can Do

Watching your partner go through labor is truly a humbling experience; chances are, your own physical courage, strength, and resolve have rarely been put to such a test. But there's nothing like seeing a baby come out of a vagina to convince you that women are really different from men.

I know that vaginal birth has been around for millions of years and that that's the way babies are supposed to be born. Yet in a strange way, there's something almost unnatural about the whole process—the baby seems so big and the vagina so small (it kind of reminds me of the ship-in-a-bottle conundrum). Ironically, a C-section somehow seems more "normal": when the fetus is full-grown, cut an appropriately sized exit and let the baby out. You'd think that with all the technological advances we've made in other areas, we'd have invented an quicker, easier, less painful way to have children.

Jealousy

"The single emotion that can be the most destructive and disruptive to your experience of fatherhood is jealousy," writes Dr. Martin Greenberg in *The Birth of a Father.*

There's certainly plenty to be jealous about, but the real question is "Whom are you jealous of?" Your partner for being able to breastfeed and for her close relationship with the baby, or the baby itself for taking up more than his or her "fair share" of your partner's attention, and for having full access to your partner's breasts while you aren't even supposed to touch them? The answer is "both."

Now that that the baby's born, communication with your partner is even more important than before. Jealousy's "potential for destruction," writes Greenberg, "lies not in having the feelings but in burying them." So if you're feeling jealous, tell her about it. But if you can't bring yourself to discuss your feelings on this issue with your partner, take them up with a male friend or relative. You'll be surprised at how common these feelings are.

Feeling Pushed Away or Left Out

Another common feeling experienced by new fathers is that of being pushed away or excluded from the new parenting experience. "The mother plays a critical role," writes Pamela Jordan. "She can bring her mate into the spotlight or keep him in the wings. The most promoting mothers . . . brought their mates into the experience by frequently and openly sharing their physical sensations and emotional responses. They actively encouraged their mates to share the experience of becoming and being a father."

While it's easy to give in to your feelings of jealousy, throw up your hands, and leave the parenting to your partner, don't do it. Encourage her to talk about what she's feeling and thinking, and ask her specifically to involve you as much as possible.

A good way to cut down on your potential feelings of jealousy or of being pushed away is to start getting to know your baby right away—even before you leave the hospital. Change as many diapers as you can (if you've never changed one before, get one of the nurses to show you how), give the baby a sponge bath, or take him or her out for a walk while your partner gets some rest.

Amazement at How Being a Parent Changes Your Life

It's virtually impossible to try to explain the myriad ways becoming a parent will change your life. You already know you'll be responsible for the safety and well-being of a completely helpless person. You've heard that you'll lose a little sleep (all right, a lot) and even more privacy. And you've prepared yourself for not being able to read as many books or see as many movies as you did before. These are some of the big, obvious changes, but it's the tiny details that will make you realize just how different your new life is from your old one.

The best way I can describe it is this: Sometimes one of my daughters will put some food into her mouth and after a few chews change her mind, take it out, and hand it to me. Most of the time I take the offering and pop it into my mouth without a second thought. You probably will too. Even more bizarre, since I became a father I have actually had serious discussions with my friends about the color and consistency of the contents of my children's diapers. So will you.

Bonding with the Baby

No one knows exactly where or when it started, but one of the most widespread—and most enduring—myths about child rearing is that women are somehow more nurturing than men and are therefore better suited to parenting.

In one of the earliest studies of father-infant interaction, researcher Ross Parke made a discovery that might shock the traditionalists: the fathers were just as caring, interested, and involved with their infants as the mothers were, and they held, touched, kissed, rocked, and cooed at their new babies with at least the same frequency as the mothers did. Several years later, Dr. Martin Greenberg coined a term, *engrossment,* to describe "a father's sense of absorption, preoccupation, and interest in his baby."

Parke and a number of other researchers have repeatedly confirmed these findings about father-infant interaction, and have concluded that what triggers engrossment in men is the same thing that prompts similar nurturing feelings in women: early infant contact. "In sum," writes Parke, "the amount of stimulatory and affectional behavior depends on the opportunity to hold the infant."

But What If I Don't Bond Right Away?

Although we've spent a lot of time talking about the joys of loving your child and how important it is to bond with the infant as soon as possible, many new fathers (and mothers, for that matter) *don't* feel particularly close to the new baby immediately after the birth.

In a way, this really makes more sense than the love-at-first-sight kind of bonding you hear so much about. After all, you don't even know this new little person. He or she may look a lot different than you expected. And, if your partner's labor and delivery were long and arduous, you may unconsciously be blaming the baby for the difficulties or may simply be too exhausted to fully appreciate the new arrival.

So, if you haven't established an instant attachment with your baby, there's absolutely nothing wrong with you. And, more important, there's no evidence whatsoever that your relationship with or feelings for your child will be any less loving than if you'd fallen head over heels in love in the first second. Just take your time and don't pressure yourself.

Staying Involved

The First Few Days

In the first few days you're going to have to learn to juggle a lot of roles. You're still a lover and friend to your partner, and, of course, you're a father. But for now, your most important role is that of support person to your partner. Besides her physical recovery (which we'll talk more about below), she's going to need time to get to know the baby and to learn (if she chooses to) how to breastfeed.

When our first daughter was born (by C-section), the three of us spent four days in the hospital (which meant three uncomfortable nights on a crooked cot for me). But when our second daughter was born (vaginally), we all checked out less than five hours after the birth. In both cases, though, my first few days at home were mighty busy—cooking, shopping, doing laundry, fixing up the baby's room, getting the word out, screening phone calls and visitors, and making sure everyone got plenty of rest.

Coming Home . . . and Beyond

Within a few minutes after we'd brought our first daughter home from the hospital, my wife and I looked at each other and almost simultaneously asked, "Well, now what are we supposed to do?" An important question, no doubt, and one that seems to come up time and time again.

A NOTE ON RECOVERY

As far as the baby is concerned, there's not much to do in the beginning besides feeding, changing, and admiring him or her. But your partner is a different story. Despite everything you've heard about women giving birth in the fields and returning to work a few minutes later, that's not the way things usually happen. Having a baby is a major shock to a woman's system. And, contrary to popular belief, the recovery period after a vaginal birth is not necessarily any shorter or easier than the recovery period after a C-section. In fact, my wife—who has delivered both ways—says recovering from the C-section was a lot easier.

Whatever kind of delivery your partner has, she'll need some time—probably more than either of you think—to recover fully. According to a recent study, more than 40 percent of new mothers experience fatigue and breast soreness in the first month after giving birth. In addition, vaginal discomfort, hemorrhoids, poor appetite, constipation, increased perspiration, acne, hand numbness or tingling, dizziness, and hot flashes are common for a month after delivery. And between 10 and 40 percent of women feel pain during sexual intercourse, have respiratory infections, and lose hair for three to six months.

Helping the Other Kids Adjust to Their New Sibling

Handling your older children's reactions to their new baby brother or sister requires an extra touch of gentleness and sensitivity. Although kids are usually wildly excited (initially, at least) at their new status as big brother or big sister, most of them will have some adjustment problems later on—as soon as they realize that the new kid is more than just a temporary visitor. My older daughter, for example, who was completely potty trained before her sister was born, regressed and began wetting her bed again a few weeks after we brought our younger daughter home. She also began making increased demands for our attention—demands we weren't always able to satisfy.

One way to help your older children adjust to their new sibling is to make them feel involved from the start. Our older daughter stayed at my parents' house while my wife was in labor with our younger daughter. But as soon as the baby was born, we called our older daughter and told her first. She then got to be the one to make the announcement to the other members of the family that she was a big sister. We also had her come to the hospital right away (even though it was past her bedtime), where she got to hold her new sister "by herself." Later, allowing her to "help" diaper, bathe, feed, and clothe her little sister really made her feel like the baby was "hers."

"Is There Anything We Can Do?"

One of the most common questions you'll hear from people is whether they can help out in any way. Some people are serious, others are just being polite. You can tell one group from the other by keeping a list of chores that need to be done and asking them to take their pick.

One of the nicest, and most helpful, things that was done for us both times we brought a baby home was a group effort by some of our friends. They'd gotten together and, taking turns, brought us meals every day for more than a week. Not having to cook or shop gave us a lot more time to spend together and let us get some rest. And of course, when our friends had their children, we were there with our spinach lasagna and a bottle of wine.

Do You *Really* Want Your Mother-in-law to Move in with You Right after the Birth?

Be careful about having people stay over to help with the newborn—especially parents (yours or hers). The new grandparents may have more traditional attitudes toward parenting and may not be supportive of your involvement with your child. They may also have very different ideas about how babies should be fed, dressed, carried, played with, and so on. If you do have someone stay with you to help out after the birth, make sure they understand that you and your wife are the parents and that what you say ultimately goes.

"Not so fast. I want to be called 'Nana.'"

Here are some things you can do to make the recovery process as easy as possible and to start parenting off on the right foot.

- Help your partner resist the urge to do too much too soon.
- Take over the household chores or ask someone else to help. And if the house is a mess, don't blame each other.
- Be flexible. Expecting to maintain your normal, prefatherhood schedule is unrealistic—especially for the first six weeks after the birth.
- Don't allow your relationship with your partner to be based solely on your child. If she's up to it, go on a date with your partner and leave the baby with a relative or friend.
- Be patient with yourself, your partner, and the baby. You're all new at this.
- Be sensitive to your partner's emotions. Recovery has an emotional component as well as a physical one.
- Make sure to get some time alone with the baby. You can do this while your partner is sleeping or, if you have to, send her out for a walk.
- Control the visiting hours and the number of people who can come at any given time. Dealing with visitors takes a lot more energy than you might think. And being poked, prodded, and passed around won't make the baby very happy. Also, for the first month or so, ask anyone who wants to touch the baby to wash his or her hands first.
- Keep your sense of humor.

Immediate Concerns . . . with Long-term Impact

FEEDING THE BABY: BREAST VS. BOTTLE

In the fifties and sixties—when most people reading this book were born—breastfeeding was out of style and most women our mothers' age were given a wide variety of reasons (by their doctors, of course) not to breastfeed. But in the nineties you'd be hard-pressed to find anyone who doesn't advocate breastfeeding. Even in the medical community, there's general agreement that breastfeeding is just about the best thing you can do for your child.

If you and your partner haven't already decided to breastfeed, here are the reasons why you should:

FOR THE BABY

- Breast milk provides exactly the right balance of nutrients needed by your newborn. In addition, breast milk contains several essential fatty acids that are not found in baby formula.

- Breast milk adapts, as if by magic, to your baby's changing nutritional needs. Neither of our children had a single sip of anything but breast milk for the first seven or eight months of life, and they're both incredibly healthy kids.
- Breastfeeding greatly reduces the chance that your baby will develop food allergies. If your family (or your partner's) has a history of food allergies, you should withhold solid foods for at least six months.
- Breastfed babies are less prone to obesity in adulthood than formula-fed babies. This may be because with the breast, it's the baby—not the parent—who decides when to quit eating.
- Breastfed babies have a greatly reduced risk of developing respiratory and gastrointestinal illness.
- Breastfeeding is thought to transmit to the infant the mother's immunity to certain diseases.

FOR YOU AND YOUR PARTNER

- It's convenient—no preparation, no heating, no bottles or dishes to wash . . .
- It's free. Formula can cost a lot of money.
- It gives your partner a wonderful opportunity to bond with the baby. In addition, breastfeeding will help get your partner's uterus back into shape and may reduce her risk of ovarian and breast cancer.
- In most cases there's always as much as you need, and never any waste.
- Your baby's diapers won't stink. It's true. Breastfed babies produce stool that—at least compared to "real food" stools—doesn't smell half bad.

A Note on Juice

If you and your partner decide not to breastfeed, or decide to supplement breastfeeding with a bottle, don't fill it with juice. A recent study found that children who drink large quantities of fruit juice—especially apple juice—suffer from frequent diarrhea and, in the worst cases, may fail to grow and develop normally. The problem is that babies love juice so much that, if you give them all they want, they'll fill up their tiny stomachs with it, leaving no room for the more nutritious foods they need. The American Dietetic Association recommends that parents refrain from giving their babies juice until they're at least six months old, and then restrict juice intake until age two.

A Special Note on Breastfeeding

As natural as breastfeeding is, your partner and the baby may need anywhere from a few days to a few weeks to get the hang of it. The baby won't immediately know how to latch on to the breast properly, and your partner—never having done this before—won't know exactly what to do either. This initial period, in which cracked and even bloody nipples are not uncommon, may be quite painful for your partner. And with the baby feeding six or seven times a day, it may take as long as two weeks for your partner's nipples to get sufficiently toughened up.

Surprisingly, your partner won't begin producing any real milk until two to five days after the baby is born. But there's no need to worry that the baby isn't getting enough food. Babies don't eat much the first 24–48 hours, and any sucking they do is almost purely for practice. Whatever nutritional needs your baby has will be fully satisfied by the tiny amounts of *colostrum* your partner produces. (Colostrum is a kind of premilk that helps the baby's immature digestive system get warmed up for the task of digesting real milk later.)

Overall, the first few weeks of breastfeeding can be very stressful for your partner. If this is the case, *do not* be tempted to suggest switching to bottles. Instead, be supportive, praise her for the great job she's doing, bring her something to eat or drink while she's feeding, and encourage her to keep trying. You also might want to ask your pediatrician for the name of a local lactation consultant (yes, there really is such a thing).

SLEEPING ARRANGEMENTS

Your pediatrician will probably tell you that your baby should get used to sleeping by him- or herself as soon after birth as possible. The reasoning is that in American culture we emphasize early independence, so babies should adapt quickly to being away from their parents—especially if both parents work and the children are in day care.

But there is another school of thought that maintains that babies should sleep in the same bed as their parents (an idea shared by about 80 percent of the world's population). The rationale is that human evolution simply can't keep pace with the new demands our culture is placing on its children. "Proximity to parental sounds, smells, heat, and movement during the night is precisely what the human infant's immature system expects—and needs," says James McKenna, an anthropologist and sleep researcher.

If You Decide to Share Your Bed with Your Child

Do it because you and your partner *want* to, not because you feel you have to. You're not negligent or overindulgent parents for doing it, so don't be embarrassed by your choice. But remember: no waterbeds—a baby could roll between you and the mattress. Also, overly soft mattresses and pillows may pose a risk of suffocation.

If Family Sleeping *Isn't* for You

Don't feel guilty. You're not a bad or selfish parent for not doing it. Teaching your children to be independent does not mean that you don't have a close bond with them. But don't feel like a failure if you allow an occasional exception, such as when a child is ill or has had a frightening experience.

So which approach is right? Well, given the wide divergence of expert opinions out there, it's a tough call—one you'll ultimately have to make on your own. Our older daughter slept in a bassinet in our room for a month or so until we moved her into her own room. Our younger daughter, however, slept in bed with us for six months before moving to her own room. Neither of them had any trouble making the transition, or any sleep problems thereafter.

Here are a few of the most common questions you're likely to have if you haven't already decided where your child will be sleeping.

- **How will it affect the baby's independence?** There's absolutely no agreement on this. Richard Ferber, author of *Solve Your Child's Sleep Problems,* maintains that "sleeping alone is an important part of a child's learning to be able to separate from his parents without anxiety and to see himself as an independent individual." In contrast, Thomas F. Anders, M.D., a professor of psychiatry, contends that "every child is born with a strong need for lots of close physical contact with a caregiver, and children in whom this need isn't met early in their lives may end up trying to fill it as adults."
- **What about safety?** Most adults—even while asleep—have a highly developed sense of where they are. After all, when was the last time you fell out of bed? So, the risk of accidentally suffocating your baby is pretty slim.
- **How will the baby sleep?** Despite what you might think, co-sleeping children tend to sleep more *lightly* than children who sleep alone

(blankets rustling and parents turning over in bed wake them up). But light sleeping isn't necessarily a bad thing. In fact, there seems to be a correlation between lighter sleep and a lower incidence of SIDS (Sudden Infant Death Syndrome).

Sharing a bed with your infant not only affects your child, but it can also have a serious impact on you. You'll lose a lot of sexual spontaneity, and you may also lose some sleep. Even the soundest-sleeping kids generally wake up every three or four hours; 70 percent of them just look around for a few minutes and soothe themselves back to sleep. But if your baby is in the other 30 percent, he or she may wake up, see you, and want to play.

A Note on Middle-of-the-Night Wake-ups

If your baby wakes up in the middle of the night hungry, and your partner is breastfeeding, you might as well stay in bed and let your partner take care of things. I know that doesn't sound terribly gallant, but, really and truly, there's not much you can do to help. And your sleeping through the 2 A.M. feeding may actually benefit your partner. Whenever I was able to get a full night's sleep, I was fairly fresh for the 7 A.M. child-care shift, allowing my wife a few more precious hours in bed.

If, however, your baby is being bottle-fed (either with formula or expressed breast milk), you should do your fair share of the feedings. You might want to work out a system in which the one who does the 2 A.M. feeding gets to sleep in (or gets breakfast in bed, or whatever).

Sometimes, though, your baby might wake up at two or three in the morning for no other reason than to stay awake for a few hours and check things out. In this kind of situation, you and your partner can either split the child-entertainment duty or stay up together and see what's on late-night TV; if there were any sitcoms or detective shows you missed when you were growing up, you can probably catch the reruns at three in the morning. Thanks to my older daughter's middle-of-the-night awakenings, my wife and I once had the rare opportunity to see what may have been (hopefully) the only episode of "David Cassidy, Teen Detective."

SEX AFTER THE BABY

Most doctors advise women to refrain from intercourse for at least six weeks after giving birth. But before you mark that date on your calendar, remember that the "six-week rule" is only a guideline. Resuming intercourse ultimately depends on the condition of your partner's cervix and vagina, and, more important, on how you're both feeling. It's not uncommon for couples to take as long as six months to fully reestablish their prepregnancy sex life.

Many factors influence when and how a couple decides to resume their sex life. Here are a few:

- When you had sex with your partner before, she was the woman you loved. Now, she's also a mother—a thought that reminds many men of their own mothers and can be a big turn-off. Several studies have shown that many women, too, have a tough time reconciling their roles as lover and mother, and may see themselves as unsexual.
- According to Dr. Jerrold Shapiro, some men have "emotional difficulty being sexual with the part of their wives that produced their children." While I can't say that seeing my daughter coming out of my wife's vagina was particularly erotic, I always found the sight of her feeding our babies rather arousing.
- In the first few weeks after the birth, your partner may focus more on the baby than on you.
- You might be jealous of the baby and his or her intimate relationship with your partner.
- You may feel especially aroused at having concrete proof (the baby) of your virility.

Chances are, you were fairly abstinent during the last few weeks of the pregnancy and you can hardly wait to get your sex life back on track. But you should expect the first few times you have sex after the baby is born to be a period of tentative rediscovery for both of you. Her body has changed, and she may respond differently than she used to. She may still be worried that having sex will hurt, and you may be afraid of the same thing. Go slowly, take your cues from her, and give yourselves plenty of time to get used to each other again.

You may also find that your partner's vagina is much drier than before, making intercourse painful. This doesn't mean she isn't aroused by you; it's simply a common postbirth occurrence—especially if she's breastfeeding. If this happens, invest in a little K-Y jelly, Astroglide, or other similar lubricant.

CHILD CARE

With more and more women entering the work force, it's getting harder to find a traditional dad-goes-to-work-while-mom-stays-at-home kind of family anymore, and it's nearly impossible to find the mom-goes-to-work-while-dad-stays-at-home variety. And even if you or your partner wanted to be a full-time caregiver, you probably couldn't afford it anyway. So, sooner or later, most couples find themselves considering some form of child care.

IN-HOME CHILD CARE

More than 1.4 million children are cared for in their homes during the day by nonrelatives, and another 500,000 are cared for by live-in help.

In-home care is convenient; you don't have to worry about day-care schedules, and your baby can stay in the environment to which he or she has become accustomed. In addition, your baby will receive individual attention, and, if you stay on top of the situation, the caregiver will keep you up to date on your child's development. Finally, by remaining at home your child will be less exposed to germs and illness.

Every time my wife and I have tried to find in-home child care, it has been a traumatic experience. But the first time was the hardest. Besides being afraid that the person we chose would turn out to be an ax murderer, we were worried that no one else could love our daughter as much or care for her as well as we did. While nothing can replace a parent's love, there are many wonderful caregivers out there who can give your baby the next best thing. You just need to know how to find them.

The most common ways to find in-home care are:

- Agencies
- Word of mouth
- Bulletin boards (either caregivers respond to your ad, or you respond to theirs)

The first thing to do is to conduct thorough interviews over the phone—this will enable you to screen out the obviously unacceptable candidates (for example, the ones who are only looking for a month-long job, or those who don't drive if you need a driver). Then invite the "finalists" over to meet with you, your partner, and the baby in person. Make sure the baby and the prospective caregiver spend a few minutes together, and pay close attention to how they interact. My wife and I ruled out a couple of people because they showed absolutely no interest in holding, cuddling, or playing with the baby. And we hired one woman largely because the moment she walked in the door she picked up our daughter and started playing with her. Be sure to get—and check—references (it's awkward, but absolutely essential). Ask each of the references why the baby-sitter left his or her previous jobs, and what the best and worst things about him or her were. Also, make sure to ask the prospective caregiver the questions listed on the following page.

Questions to Ask Prospective Caregivers

- What previous child-care experience have you had (including caring for younger relatives)?
- What age children have you cared for?
- Tell us a little about your own childhood.
- What would you do if . . . (give several examples of things a child might do that would require different degrees of discipline).
- How would you handle . . . (name a couple of emergency situations).
- Do you know baby CPR? (If not, you might want to consider paying for the caregiver to take a class.)
- What are your favorite things to do with kids?
- Do you have a driver's license?
- What days/hours are you available/not available? How flexible can you be if an emergency arises while we're at work?
- Are you a native speaker of any foreign language?

Other Important Topics to Cover

- Compensation (check with other people who have caregivers for the going rate) and vacation.
- Telephone privileges.
- Complete responsibilities of the job: feeding, bathing, diapering, changing clothes, reading to the baby, and so on, as well as what light housekeeping chores, if any, will be expected while the baby is sleeping.
- English-language skills—particularly important in case of emergency (you want someone who can accurately describe to a doctor or 911 operator what's going on).
- Immigration/green card status

You might want to draw up an informal contract, listing all of the caregiver's responsibilities—just so there won't be any misunderstandings.

When you make your final choice, have the person start a few days before you return to work so you can all get to know each other, and so you can spy.

A NOTE ABOUT LIVE-IN HELP

Hiring a live-in caregiver is like adding a new member to the family. The process for selecting one is similar to that for finding a non-live-in caregiver, and you can use most of the questions listed on this page when conducting

What to Look for in a Day-care Center

- The level of training of the staff. Some have degrees in early childhood education; some aren't much more than warm bodies.
- Safety: windows, fences around yards, access to kitchen appliances and utensils (knives, ovens, stoves, household chemicals, and so forth).
- Is it licensed by the National Association of Education and Child Care?
- Overall cleanliness.
- Caregiver/child ratio. (In California, one licensed caregiver can take care of as many as four infants. I personally think that any more than two is too many.)
- Quality, condition, and number of toys.
- Security: what precautions are taken to ensure that kids can be picked up only by the person you select? Do strangers have access to the center?

Before you make your final choice, be sure to take a tour. Spend half an hour or so—when all the kids are there—observing. Are the children happy? Are they doing the kinds of activities you expected?

Finally, in the weeks after you pick the perfect day-care center, make a few unannounced visits—just to see what goes on when there aren't any parents around.

interviews. After you've made your choice, you might want to try out your new relationship on a non-live-in basis for a few weeks, just to make sure everything's going to work out to your satisfaction.

OUT-OF-HOME CHILD CARE

Many people—even those who can afford in-home child care—feel that out-of-home centers are preferable. For one, a good day-care center is, as a rule, much better equipped than your home and offers your child a wide range of stimulating activities. In addition, out-of-home day care gives your child the opportunity to play with other children; this, in the opinion of many experts, helps children become better socialized and more independent. The downside, of course, is that interacting with other kids usually means interacting with their germs—children in out-of-home day care get sick a lot more often than those cared for at home.

Taxes and Child Care

- Be sure to get your caregiver or baby-sitter's social security number; you'll need it to take advantage of the tax deduction/credit for child-care expenses.
- If you pay a baby-sitter or other household worker more than $1,250 a year, you are required to deduct social security taxes. The amount you need to deduct changes every year, so check with the Social Security Administration or your accountant to be sure.

CRYING

Let's face it, babies cry; it's their job. The fact is that 80 to 90 percent of all babies have periods of crying that can last from twenty minutes to an hour *every day*. Still, there's nothing like holding an inconsolably crying child to make even the most seasoned parent feel inadequate.

I think fathers tend to feel this sense of inadequacy more acutely than mothers, perhaps because most men have been socialized to view themselves as less than fully equipped to care for children and therefore have less than complete confidence in their parenting abilities.

When (not if) your child starts to cry, resist the urge to hand him or her to your partner. She knows nothing more about crying babies than you do (or will soon enough). To start with, however, here are a few things you can do to reduce the amount of time your child will spend crying:

- **Take note of what your partner eats while breastfeeding.** After one horrible, agonizing evening of inexplicable crying from our usually happy baby and a frantic call to the doctor, we discovered that the broccoli my wife had eaten for dinner was the culprit.
- **Know your baby.** Within just a few days after birth, your baby will develop distinct cries: "I'm tired," "Feed me now," "Change my diaper," "I'm uncomfortable as can be," "I'm bored in this car seat," and "I'm crying because I'm mad and I'm not going to stop no matter what you do." Once you learn to recognize these cries, you'll be able to respond appropriately and keep your baby happy. It's also important to know your child's routine—some babies like to thrash around and cry a little (or a lot) before going to sleep, others don't.
- **Carry your baby more.** Some studies show that the more babies are held (even when they're not crying), the less they cry.

After you've tried soothing, feeding, changing the diaper, checking for loose diaper pins or uncomfortable clothing, and rocking, the baby may still continue to howl. Sometimes there's really nothing you can do about it (see the section on coping, pages 183–85), but sometimes all it takes is a new approach. Here are a few alternatives you might want to try:

- **Hold the baby differently.** Not all babies like to be held facing you; some want to face out so they can see the world. One of the most successful ways I've learned to soothe a crying baby—and I've tried this on many kids besides my own—is to use Dave's Magic Baby Hold. (Dave, the father of a close friend, supposedly used the Hold to calm his own three children.) Quite simply, have the baby "sit" in the palm of your hand—thumb in front, the other fingers on the baby's bottom. Then have the baby lie face down on the inside of your forearm, with his or her head resting on the inside of your elbow. Use your other hand to stroke or pat the baby's back.
- **Distraction.** Offer a toy, a story, a song. If the baby is diverted by a story or song, you'd better be prepared to repeat it over and over and over . . .
- **Give the baby something to suck on.** Just take a guess why they call them "pacifiers." If you don't approve of pacifiers, you can either help the baby suck on his or her own fingers, or loan out one of yours.
- **Give the baby a bath.** Some babies find warm water soothing. Others freak out when they get wet. If you do decide to try bathing a crying infant, don't do it alone. Holding onto a calm soapy baby is no easy chore. But keeping a grip on a squirming, screaming, soapy baby takes a team of highly trained specialists.
- **Invest in a frontpack.** A lot of crying babies just want to be held all the time, and no matter how strong you think you are, your arms—and back—won't last forever. You'll be able to use your frontpack for other purposes as well—both my daughters traveled hundreds of miles strapped to my chest, while I did my cross-country ski-machine workout. In addition, carrying the baby around in the pack might give you an inkling of what it was like for your partner to be pregnant.
- **Take the baby for a walk or a drive.** A word of caution: this doesn't work for all babies. When she was an infant, my elder daughter would fall asleep in the stroller or the car in a heartbeat. But my younger daughter hates riding in the car, especially when she's tired, and cries even more when she's put in her car seat. If you don't feel like going out, try putting the baby on top of a running washing machine or dryer. There's also a special device called SleepTight that, when attached to

the baby's crib, simulates the feel (and sounds) of a car going fifty-five miles an hour. Call 1-800-NO-COLIC for more information.

COPING WITH CRYING

If you've tried everything you can think of to stop the baby from crying, but to no avail, here are some things that may help you cope:

- **Tag-team crying duty.** There's no reason why both you and your partner have to suffer together through what Martin Greenberg calls "the tyranny of crying." Spelling each other in twenty-minute or half-hour shifts will do you both a world of good. Getting a little exercise during your "time off" will also calm your nerves before your next shift starts.
- **Let the baby "cry it out."** If the crying goes on for more than twenty minutes or so, try putting the baby down in the crib and letting him or her cry. If the screaming doesn't stop after ten or fifteen minutes, pick the baby up and try a different approach for another fifteen minutes or so. Repeat as necessary.

"I'm worried about him. He's not picking at his food."

A Note on Crying in Public

Dealing with a crying child in public was particularly stressful for me. It wasn't that I didn't think I could handle things; rather, I was embarrassed by and afraid of how other people would react. Would they think I was hurting the baby? Would they call the police? If they did, how could I possibly prove that the baby was mine? Fortunately, no one ever called the police, but there was no shortage of comments, which ranged from the seemingly helpful ("Sounds like that baby is hungry") to the blatantly sexist and demeaning ("Better get that baby home to her mother").

Although my fears about my children crying in public may sound a little paranoid (okay, a lot), I know I'm not alone. Just about every father I've spoken to has had similar thoughts in similar situations. I have to admit, however, that most of the women I've mentioned this to (including my dear wife) think I'm completely nuts on this point.

Colic

Starting at about two weeks of age, some 20 percent of babies develop colic—crying spells that, unlike "ordinary" crying, can last for hours at a time, sometimes even all day or all night. The duration and intensity of crying spells peaks at around six weeks and usually disappears entirely within three months.

Since there's no real agreement on what causes colic or on what to do about it, your pediatrician probably won't be able to offer a quick cure. Some parents, however, have been able to relieve (partially or completely) their colicky infants with an over-the-counter gas remedy for adults. Talk to your doctor about whether he or she thinks taking this medication would benefit your child.

- **Get some help.** Dealing with a crying child for even a few minutes can provoke incredible rage and frustration. And if the screams go on for hours, it can become truly difficult to maintain your sanity, let alone control your temper. If you find yourself concerned that you might lash out (other than verbally) at your child, call someone: your partner, pediatrician, parents, baby-sitter, friends, neighbors, clergy person, or even a parental-stress hotline. If your baby is a real crier, keep these numbers handy.

- **Don't take it personally.** Your baby isn't deliberately trying to antagonize you. It's all too easy to let your frustration at this temporary situation permanently interfere with the way you treat your child. "Even if your powerful feelings don't lead to child abuse," write the authors of *What to Expect the First Year,* "they can start eroding your relationship with your baby and your confidence in yourself as a parent unless you get counseling quickly."

PLAYING WITH YOUR BABY

Playing with your child is one of the most important things you can do with him or her. Kids learn just about everything they need to know from playing. Besides, it's fun for you. Some studies indicate that babies who are played with a lot tend to be more attentive and interactive as they grow up, and retain these qualities later in life as well.

As a rule, men and women have different play styles: men tend to stress the physical, high-energy type of playing; women, the social and emotional. Neither kind of parent-child interaction is better—each is different *and* indispensable, and there's no point in trying to compare or rate them.

Several researchers have done extensive studies on the impact of physical play on children and have come up with some interesting conclusions. Ross Parke, for example, found that girls who are exposed to higher than traditional levels of physical play become more assertive in their peer interactions later in life—this is a particularly important finding to those of us who are concerned by all the recent studies showing that our daughters may be shortchanged in their education because they don't speak up in class as often as boys.

In general, babies love physical play, and by the time they're just a few days old, they've already learned which of their parents will play with them which way—and they'll react accordingly. Here are some important things to keep in mind about playing:

- **Use moderation.** It's perfectly fine to play with a baby as young as a few days old, but restrict each session to five minutes or so. Too much playing can make your child fussy or irritable.
- **Take your cues from the baby.** If he or she cries or seems bored, stop what you're doing.
- **Schedule your fun.** The best time for physical play is when the baby is in the active alert state; playing with toys or books is fine during the quiet alert state (see page 164). Also, choose a time when your full attention can be devoted to the baby—no phone calls or other distractions.

Finally, don't play too vigorously with the baby immediately after feeding. Believe me—I learned the hard way.

- **Get comfortable.** Find a place where you can get down to the baby's level—preferably on your back or stomach on the floor or bed.
- **Be patient.** As mentioned above, your baby is not a trained seal—don't expect too much too soon.
- **Be encouraging.** Use lots of facial and verbal encouragement—smiles, laughter. Although the baby can't understand the words, he or she definitely understands the feelings. Even at only a few days old, your baby will want to please you, and lots of encouragement will build his or her self-confidence.
- **Be gentle—especially with the baby's head.** Because babies' heads are relatively large (one-quarter of their body size at birth vs. one-seventh by the time they're adults) and their neck muscles are not yet well devel-

A Note on Dressing Children

Getting a baby dressed is not an easy task; their heads always seem too big to go through the appropriate openings in their shirts, and their hands regularly refuse to come out of the sleeves. There are a few things you can do to make dressing a little easier:

- Reach through the sleeve and pull your baby's hands through—it's a lot easier than trying to shove from the other side.
- Buy pants or overalls whose legs snap open. Some manufacturers make baby clothes that are absolutely beautiful but impossible to put on or take off. The snap-open legs also make diaper changing much easier—you don't have to remove the whole outfit to access the diaper.

Also, don't overdress your baby. For some strange reason, people tend to bundle their children up in all sorts of blankets, sweaters, hats, and gloves—even in the summer. But unless you're Eskimos, there's no reason to dress your children like one. A basic rule of thumb is to have the baby wear the same kind of clothes you do, plus a hat. Layering clothing is sometimes a good way to go—if the baby gets too hot, you can remove a layer.

Finally, remember this simple rule: "If they can't walk, they don't need shoes." It's not only a waste of money, but confining a baby's feet in a hard pair of shoes all day long can actually damage the bones.

oped, their heads tend to be pretty floppy for the first few months. Be sure to support the head—from behind—at all times, and avoid sudden or jerky motions.

A COUPLE OF WARNINGS

- *Never* shake your child. This can make their little brains rattle around inside their skulls, causing bruises or permanent injuries.
- *Never* throw the baby up in the air. Yes, your father may have done it to you, but he shouldn't have. It looks like fun but can be extremely dangerous.

Notes:

Fathering Today

For the first weeks and months after the birth of your child, you'll be spending much of your time in the role of support person for your partner. But after a while, you'll settle into a more "normal" life—one and/or both of you will go back to work, and you might feel like taking in a movie or visiting some friends. And gradually, you'll be figuring out exactly what it means to be a father and how involved you intend to be in your child's life. Do you want to be someone he or she runs to when hurt or sad? Will you know his shoe size or whether she likes pants that zip up or slip on? Will you schedule any medical appointments or play dates, or will you leave those things to your partner?

Whatever you decide, you'll soon come face-to-face with the fact that being a father in America—especially an *involved* one—is going to be tough. Sure, the responsibilities of the job itself are difficult and at times frustrating, but the biggest obstacles you'll face—ones you've probably never even thought about before—are societal.

Only recently have men and women felt able to speak out against the traditional role fathers have played in the family. And only recently has society finally recognized that the distant father is not the ideal father. But in the midst of this newfound freedom to lash out against yesterday's absent, neglectful fathers, today's fathers are falling victim to old stereotypes.

According to one stereotype, men haven't taken an active role in family life because they haven't wanted to. But is this true of today's fathers? Hardly. Many of us realize that the traditional measures of success are not all they're cracked up to be, and we are committed to being a major presence in our children's lives, physically and emotionally. The hitch is that society (and by this I mean all of us) not only won't support us but actively discourages us. Quite simply, Americans don't value fatherhood nearly as much as motherhood. (Even the words have different associations: motherhood is equated

with caring, nurturing, and love, whereas *fatherhood* connotes merely a biological relationship.) As a result, men are rarely accepted if they assume a different role than the one they are "supposed" to assume.

The emphasis on traditional roles starts long before you might imagine. Even before they can walk, children of both sexes are bombarded with the message that fathers are basically superfluous. Just think of the books your parents read to you, and that you'll probably read to your own children. Have you ever noticed that there aren't any fathers in *The Cat in the Hat; Where the Wild Things Are; Are You My Mother?; Goodnight Moon; The Runaway Bunny;* and *Peter Rabbit*?

In the vast majority of children's books, a woman is the only parent, while the man—if he appears at all—comes home late after work and bounces baby around for five minutes before putting her to bed. My local library has a special catalog of children's books with positive female characters—heroines and mothers. As a father who shares the child-care responsibilities equally, I find it extremely frustrating that the library doesn't have a catalog (or even many books) with positive male role models.

In recent years there's been a push to portray more accurately the roles that women and minorities play in shaping our country's history and culture. *Little Black Sambo,* for example, has all but disappeared from library and bookstore shelves, and most new children's books make a conscious effort to take female characters out of the kitchen and the nursery and give them professional jobs and responsibilities. But one group—fathers—continues to be portrayed in the same stereotypical mold as always.

One of my older daughter's favorite books, for example, is *Mother Goose and the Sly Fox,* "retold" by Chris Conover. It's the story of a single mother (Mother Goose) with seven tiny goslings who is pitted against (and naturally outwits) the Sly Fox. Fox, a neglectful, and presumably unemployed, single father, lives with his filthy, hungry pups in a grimy hovel littered with the bones of their previous meals. Mother Goose, a successful entrepreneur with a thriving lace business, still finds time to serve her goslings homemade soup in pretty porcelain cups. The story is funny and the illustrations marvelous, but the unwritten message is that women take better care of their kids than men, who have nothing else to do but hunt down and kill innocent, law-abiding geese.

You'll find the same negative portrayals of fathers in the majority of children's classics. Once in a great while someone will complain about *Babar*'s colonialist slant (you know, little jungle dweller finds happiness in the big city and brings civilization—and fine clothes—to his backward village). But you'll never hear anyone ask why Babar is automatically an "orphan" after his mother is killed by the evil hunter. Why can he find comfort only in the arms of another female? Why do Arthur and Celeste's mothers come alone to the city to fetch their children? Don't the fathers care? Do they even have fathers?

If books were the only place children got messages about the way the world is supposed to be, it might be possible to edit out the negative messages. But sooner or later most kids find themselves in front of some kind of a screen—movie or television—and the most common images of fathers they're likely to see are nearly identical to those perpetuated in print: if fathers are there at all, they're usually fairly useless.

One of the best examples of the negative father image—and the effect it has on our children—is *Bambi,* which, although about fifty years old, is still one of the most popular children's movies of all time. In the early part of the film, Bambi enjoys a warm, nurturing relationship with his mother. And it's not until about halfway through the movie that we learn he has a father—a stern, authoritative, and, at best, fleeting presence in the young deer's life.

At the end of the movie, Bambi himself becomes a father, and, like the only male role model he's ever known, does his fathering from a distant hill.

As significant as movie images are to children, by far the most powerful delivery system for negative portrayals of fathers is the small screen. The average American child spends eight hours a day watching television—a lot more time than he or she spends reading. Clearly, then, the images of fathers that children—and adults—get from television have the potential to do much more damage than the images they get from books.

Overall, men get a pretty raw deal when it comes to the way they're portrayed on television. Frederic Hayward, the director of Men's Rights Inc., in Sacramento, California, conducted a survey of a thousand random TV advertisements and found that "100 percent of the jerks singled out in male-female relationships were male. There were no exceptions. . . . 100 percent of the ignorant ones were male. 100 percent of the incompetent ones were male." And for fathers, the negative portrayals run a little deeper. Besides being depicted as dumber than their wives and children, fathers—if they're part of the commercial family unit at all—are shown as oblivious to the needs of their children. Mothers, it seems, are the only ones who care. Here are a few examples:

- In a spot for Post Raisin Bran, a father and his daughter are oohing and aahing about their cereal. "Somebody must really love us," says Dad. "Who do you think it is?" "Mommy!!!" yelps the child.
- Another breakfast cereal, Kix, is billed as being "Kid tested, Mother approved."
- When it comes time to make lunch, advertisers insist that "Choosy mothers choose Jif."
- In a nationally run magazine ad, Fisher-Price gleefully informs us that "it took Fisher-Price and 2,043 mothers to design a highchair like this."
- In a commercial for Aquafresh toothpaste, a father and child are arguing about whether fluoride or mouthwash is the toothpaste's most important ingredient. They probably would have argued all day, if Mom hadn't stepped in to tell them, "You need both."
- A certain cough medicine is "recommended by Dr. Mom."

And when it comes to what's shown between the commercials, fathers don't fare a lot better. While there are a few exceptions, most fathers in sitcoms are portrayed as buffoonish, easily outwitted men whose main contribution to their families is money (just think of "The Simpsons" and "Married—With Children").

While it's possible to argue that mothers still do most of the shopping and

feeding, the subtle yet critical message contained in these ads is that fathers simply don't care. They don't feed their kids, don't clothe them, and won't be there to take care of them when they're sick. Mothers are the better parents and fathers play, at best, a secondary role in the home.

It seems that we've confused men's lack of training in child care with a lack of interest in or concern about their children. A lot of today's fathers—who, like Bambi, were raised in "traditional" families—simply had no role models, no one to teach them the skills they lack today.

This brings up an interesting contradiction. Many supposedly open-minded people are quick to put the blame on "socio-economic pressures" when discussing hot issues such as crime and drugs. But when discussing fathers' purported indifference toward their children, no one thinks to hold society responsible. Instead, we're told by someone as highly respected as Barbara Jordan, a former congresswoman and advisor to the governor of Texas, "Women have a capacity for understanding and a compassion which a man structurally does not have. . . . He's just incapable of it." When various fathers' rights groups protested her remarks, Jordan defended them, saying they were "based on observable fact." Imagine what would happen if a man had made a similarly inflammatory statement about women. Or African Americans. Or anyone except a man.

Perhaps the most active way we have of discouraging men's involvement with children is by continually portraying men as dangerous. In an article I wrote for the *New York Times Magazine,* I described an incident that took place not along ago. I was pushing my older daughter on the swing at our favorite park, when I heard a little girl start to scream. She was just a few feet away, teetering on the small platform at the top of a long, steep slide. As I watched, she lost her grip on the handrail and began to fall. Without thinking, I leapt over to the slide, caught the girl, and set her down on the sand. I knelt down and was about to ask her if she was all right, when a woman picked the girl up, gave me a withering look, and hustled the child away. "Didn't I tell you not to talk to strange men in the park?" the woman asked her daughter, glaring over her shoulder at me. "Did he hurt you?"

I remember standing there for a few seconds, stunned, as the woman bundled her child into the car and drove off. I wondered what she had been thinking. Hadn't she seen me playing with a happy girl who called me Daddy? It was a cloudless, summer day and as I looked around the park, I realized I was the only man there. That was when it hit me: I—the father—was invisible. What had come to that woman's mind was what was most ingrained and automatic—the stereotyped images of a man in the park, menacing and solitary.

In some twisted way, I can understand these "instinctive" fears. If I'd turned around and seen a strange man kneeling near my daughter, I might have jumped to the worst possible conclusions, too. And when my wife and I interview baby-sitters for our daughters, *I* am the one who has the most serious qualms about hiring a man for the job.

But my "understanding" of these fears is based less on the truth about how men actually *are* with children than on how we've been trained to *view* men with children. I still remember the "safety movies" I saw in about the third or fourth grade—scary images of the sinister, mustachioed men (and they were always men) lurking behind trees in the park or trying to entice us into their cars.

I'm not saying that there aren't some sick men out there, men who do horrible things to children. Men are the perpetrators in most sexual abuse cases (which constitute 11 percent of all cases of abuse and neglect). Yet there are plenty of sick women out there too; women murder more children than men do and are the perpetrators in the majority of physical and psychological abuse cases.

None of this, of course, is meant to imply that men are just hapless victims, or that all the obstacles fathers face are "someone else's" fault. In fact, some of the most significant barriers have been erected by men themselves. In the workplace, for example, where men still occupy the majority of positions of power, men who try to take time off work to be with their families—either as paternity leave or by reducing their work schedules—find that their employers abuse them, treat them like wimps, and question how serious they are about their jobs (see pages 88–92 for more on this).

Despite the many obstacles, some of us have risked our careers and jeopardized our finances to try to break through the "glass ceiling" that keeps us at work—and away from our families. But in many cases, when we finally get home we run into another barrier—this one imposed by none other than our partners.

Here's an all-too-common scenario: When I was visiting some friends not long ago, their six-month-old son started fussing. Colin, who was holding the baby, began rocking him. Suddenly his wife, Marina, appeared and whisked the baby away. "Let me take him, honey," she said. "I think I know what he needs."

I've seen scenes of this kind played out many times before (and not only at Colin and Marina's house), but this time I began to wonder. Did Marina really know what the baby needed? And if so, did she know better than Colin did?

According to a significant amount of research, the answers to my questions are "probably" and "no," respectively. In a variety of studies, researcher Ross Parke found that fathers—despite stereotypes to the contrary—are just as sensitive and responsive to their infants' needs as mothers. They know when something is wrong, and they take appropriate action. So why then, had Colin—a man I knew wanted an active role in raising his children—simply handed his crying son over to his wife? When you factor out sheer laziness from the equation, the answer to that question is a little tougher. What it seems to boil down to is that most of us—men as well as women—simply assume that women know more about kids than men.

In some ways, that may be true. On average, women do spend more time taking care of children than men do, and their skills may be a little sharper than men's. But parenting skills are not innate—they are learned through experience and training. No first-time parents, mothers or fathers, know instinctively how to soothe a colicky baby or prevent diaper rash. In fact, when our older daughter was born, my wife was taught how to breastfeed by a *male* nurse.

Still, the stereotypes persist, and to a great extent women control the amount—and quality—of time men spend with their children. Although most mothers feel that fathers should play an important role in the kids' lives, that role should be "not quite as important as mom's," according to a nationwide survey of mothers, published as *The Motherhood Report: How Women Feel about Being Mothers.* In fact, researchers found that two out of three women seem threatened by equal participation and may themselves be "subtly putting a damper on men's involvement with their children because they are so possessive of their role as primary nurturer."

It may sound as though all these obstacles are almost too numerous to overcome. Well, there may be a lot of them, and they may be quite ingrained, but if you're willing to put in the time and effort, you'll be able to have—and maintain—an active, involved relationship with your children.

Here are some things you can do:

- **Get some practice.** Don't assume that your partner magically knows more than you do. Whatever she knows about raising kids, she's learned by doing—just like anything else. And the way you're going to get better is by doing things, too. Research has shown, for example, that the lack of opportunity may be one of the biggest obstacles to fathers' being more affectionate with their children. As mentioned in the preceding chapter, once they get to hold them, fathers are at least as affectionate with their children—cooing, looking at, holding, rocking, soothing—as their partners are. (So much for the stereotype about men being emotionally distant by nature.)
- **Take charge.** Ultimately, if you don't start taking the initiative, you'll never be able to assume the child-rearing responsibilities you want—and deserve. In all the times I've seen women pluck crying or smelly babies from their husbands' arms, I've never heard a man say, "No, honey, I can take care of this." So, if you find yourself in a situation like that, try a few lines such as: "I think I can handle things" or "That's okay; I really need the practice." And there's also nothing wrong with asking her for advice—you both have insights that the other could benefit from. But have her tell you instead of doing it for you.
- **Don't devalue the things you like doing with the kids.** As discussed in the preceding chapter, men and women generally have different ways

of interacting with their children; both are extremely important to your child's development. So don't let anyone tell you that wrestling, playing "monster," or other so-called guy things are somehow not as important as the "girl things" your partner may do (or want you to do).

- **Get involved in the day-to-day decisions that affect your kids' lives.** This means making a special effort to share with your partner such responsibilities as meal planning, food and clothes shopping, cooking, taking the kiddies to the library or bookstore, getting to know their friends' parents, and planning play dates. Not doing these things can give the impression that you don't think they're important or that you're not interested in being an active parent. And by doing them, you make it more likely that your partner will feel comfortable and confident in sharing the nurturing role with you. But try to log some private, "quality" time with the kids, too. Sure, somebody has to schlepp the kids all over town—to doctor appointments, ballet lessons, or soccer practice—but that shouldn't be the only contact you have with them.
- **Keep communicating.** If you don't like the status quo, let your partner know. But be gentle. If at first she seems reluctant to share the role of child nurturer with you, don't take it too personally. Men are not the only

ones whom society has done a bad job of socializing. Many women have been raised to believe that if they aren't the primary caregivers (even if they work outside the home as well), they've somehow failed as mothers. If your partner does work outside the home, you might want to remind her of what Karen DeCrow, a former president of the National Organization for Women (NOW), says: "Until men are valued as parents, the burden of childrearing will fall primarily to women and frustrate their efforts to gain equality in the workplace."

- **If you're in a position to do something for other men, do it.** All things being equal, try hiring a male baby-sitter once in a while. Or consider asking a male friend instead of the usual women friends to do some baby-sitting when you and your wife want a night out. If you need to ease yourself into it, try the teenage son of some friends. Continuing not to trust men and boys will continue to make men and boys think of themselves as untrustworthy and will make it difficult for them to be comfortable enough in their role as parent to take on as much responsibility as they—and their partners—would like.
- **Get your partner to be your publicist.** Pamela Jordan writes that "men tend not to be perceived as parents in their own right by their mates, co-workers, friends or family. They are viewed as helpmates or breadwinners." The cure? "The mother can mitigate the exclusion of the father by others by including the father in the pregnancy and parenting experiences and actively demonstrating her recognition of him as a key player," Jordan says.
- **Get some support.** Even before your baby is born, you're likely to become aware of the vast number of support groups for new mothers. It won't take you long to realize, however, that there are few, if any, groups for new fathers. And if you find one, it will probably be geared toward men whose contact with their kids is limited to five minutes before bedtime.

After having read this book, you know that men have just as many pregnancy, birth, and child-rearing questions as their partners. So, if you can't find a new fathers' support group in your own neighborhood, why not be a trailblazer and start one of your own?

Here are a few ways you might get going:

- Start meeting regularly with male friends who already have kids. Talk on the phone, go for walks with the kids, meet in a park for lunch.
- Encourage other expecting male friends or new fathers to join you,

and ask them to contact their male friends who have or are about to have children.
- Put up signs in local children's clothing and/or toy stores.
- Check with your partner's doctor, your pediatrician, and your childbirth class instructor about helping you advertise your group.
- Contact the Y or some of the local family-planning agencies to see if they'll help with publicity.
- Check with the people who organize some of the new mothers' groups—maybe they'd be interested in a fathers' auxiliary.

Who knows—if you do a good enough job publicizing your new fathers' group, you might even be able to turn it into a real business. Don't laugh: plenty of people are making money on mothers' groups.

A Final Word

Throughout this book we've talked about the benefits—both to you and to your children—of your being an active, involved father, and about how fatherhood actually begins long before your first child is born. What we haven't touched upon, though, is the positive effect your fatherhood role can have on your relationship with your partner.

Sociologist Pepper Schwartz has found that couples who worked *together* to raise their children "seemed to create a more intimate and stable relationship. They did more together. They talked on the phone together much more and spent more child-related time together. Wives in the study said they believed that raising children together created a more intimate adult relationship." Other research confirms Schwartz's findings. For example, a 1993 study showed that fathers who were actively involved with their children had a much lower divorce rate than those who weren't.

So it's in everyone's best interest for you to do everything you possibly can to become an involved father. It's not easy, but the rewards—for you, your children, and your partner—are incalculable.

Selected Bibliography

Books

American College of Obstetricians and Gynecologists. *The ACOG Guide to Planning for Pregnancy, Birth, and Beyond.* Washington, D.C.: ACOG, 1990.

Beail, N., and J. McGruire, eds. *Fathers: Psychological Perspectives.* London: Junction Books, 1982.

Bitman, S., and S. Zalk. *Expectant Fathers.* New York: Hawthorn Books, 1978.

Bradley, Robert A. *Husband Coached Childbirth.* New York: Harper and Row, 1974.

Cath, H. C., A. Gurwitt, and L. Gunsberg, eds. *Fathers and Their Families.* Hilldale, N.J.: Analytic Press, 1989.

Colman, L. L., and A. D. Colman. *Pregnancy: The Psychological Experience.* New York: Noonday Press, 1991.

Cowan, C. P., and P. A. Cowan. *When Partners Become Parents.* New York: Basic Books, 1992.

Eisenberg, A., H. Murkoff, and S. Hathaway. *What to Expect When You're Expecting.* New York: Workman, 1988.

Grad, R., D. Bash et al. *The Father Book.* Washington, D.C.: Acropolis Books, 1981.

Greenberg, Martin. *The Birth of a Father.* New York: Continuum, 1985.

Klaus, M., and P. Klaus. *The Amazing Newborn.* Reading, Mass.: Addison-Wesley, 1985.

Klaus, M., J. Kennel, and P. Klaus. *Mothering the Mother.* Reading, Mass.: Addison-Wesley, 1993.

Lamb, Michael, ed. *The Role of the Father in Child Development.* New York: John Wiley and Sons, 1981.

Minnick, M. A., K. J. Delp, and M. C. Ciotti. *A Time to Decide, a Time to Heal.* Mullett Lake, Mich.: Pineapple Press, 1990.

Osherson, S. *Finding Our Fathers: The Unfinished Business of Fatherhood.* New York: Free Press, 1986.

Paulaha, Dennis. *An American Child's Portfolio.* Edina, Minn.: Patron, 1991.

Pederson, A., and P. O'Mara, eds. *Being a Father.* Santa Fe: John Muir, 1990.

Shapiro, Jerrold L. *The Measure of a Man.* New York: Delacorte, 1992.

———. *When Men are Pregnant.* New York: Delta, 1993.

Thevenin, Tine. *The Family Bed.* New York: Avery, 1987.

Van de Carr, F. R., and M. Lehrer. *Prenatal Classroom.* Atlanta: Humanics Learning, 1992.

Verny, T., and J. Kelly. *The Secret Life of the Unborn Child.* New York: Delta, 1991.

Verny, T., and P. Weintraub. *Nurturing the Unborn Child.* New York: Delacorte Press, 1991.

Journal articles

Broude, Gwen J. "Rethinking the Couvade: Cross-Cultural Evidence." *American Anthropologist* 90 (1988): 903–11.

Cummings, David. "The Effects of Miscarriage on a Man." *Emotional First Aid* 1, no. 4 (1984): 47–50.

Davidson, J. R. "The Shadow of Life: Psychosocial Explanations for Placenta Rituals." *Culture, Medicine and Psychiatry* 9 (1985): 75–92.

Goldbach, R. C. et al. "The Effects of Gestational Age and Gender on Grief After Pregnancy Loss." *American Journal of Orthopsychiatry* 61 (July 1991): 461–67.

Jordan, Pamela. "Laboring for Relevance: Expectant and New Fatherhood." *Nursing Research* 39 (January–February 1990): 11–16.

Klein, Hillary. "Couvade Syndrome: Male Counterpart to Pregnancy." *International Journal of Psychiatry in Medicine* 21, no. 1 (1991): 57–69.

May, K. A. "Factors Contributing to First-Time Fathers' Readiness for Fatherhood: An Exploratory Study." *Family Relations* 31 (July 1982): 352–61.

———. "First-Time Fathers' Responses to Unanticipated Caesarean Birth: An Exploratory Study." Unpublished report to U.C.S.F., 1982.

———. "Three Phases of Father Involvement in Pregnancy." *Nursing Research* 31 (November–December 1982): 337–42.

———. "A Typology of Detachment/Involvement Styles Adopted During

Pregnancy by First-Time Expectant Fathers." *Western Journal of Nursing Research* 2, no. 2 (1980): 445–61.

Miller, W. E. and S. Friedman. "Male and Female Sexuality During Pregnancy: Behavior and Attitudes." *Journal of Psychology and Human Sexuality* 1, no. 2 (1988): 17–37.

Stainton, M. C. "The Fetus: A Growing Member of the Family." *Family Relations* 34 (July 1985): 321–26.

Teichman, Y., and Y. Lahav. "Expectant Fathers: Emotional Reactions, Physical Symptoms and Coping Styles." *British Journal of Medical Psychology* 60 (1987): 225–32.

Zayas, L. H. "Psychodynamic and Developmental Aspects of Expectant and New Fatherhood: Clinical Derivatives from the Literature." *Clinical Social Work Journal* 15 (Spring 1987): 8–21.

———. "Thematic Features in the Manifest Dreams of Expectant Fathers." *Clinical Social Work Journal* 16 (Fall 1988): 283–95.

Resources

Periodicals

American Baby
249 West 17th Street
New York, NY 10011

Child
110 5th Avenue
New York, NY 10011

Family Life
1290 Avenue of the Americas
New York, NY 10104

Full-Time Dads: The Journal for Caregiving Fathers
P.O. Box 577
Cumberland Center, ME 04021

Men's Health
33 East Minor Street
Emmaus, PA 18098

Parenting Magazine
301 Howard Street, 17th Floor
San Francisco, CA 94105

Parents Magazine
685 Third Avenue
New York, NY 10017

Organizations

Men's Health Network
P.O. Box 770
Washington, DC 20044
(202) 543-6461

Men's Issues Think Tank
4839 305th Avenue, N.E.
Cambridge, MN 55008
(612) 689-5885

National Center for Family Centered Care
7910 Woodmont Avenue, Suite 300
Bethesda, MD 20814
(301) 654-6549
They publish the *National Fathers Network Newsletter*

National Fathers' Rights Organization
(414) 798-9000 or (800) 221-2372

Parents, Inc.
270 Commerce Drive
Fort Washington, PA 19034
(215) 628-2402 or (800) 628-2535

Computer networking

America On-Line (800) 522-6364
Has several forums on Parents Information and Children's Issues. Look for the keyword "parents" or "children."

CompuServe (800) 848-8119
Go issues, select "parent connection."

Delphi (800) 544-4005
Type "groups," select "mensnet."

GEnie (800) 638-9636
Type the word "family" (gets you to the family roundtable); select "1" for the bulletin board. Choose from a variety of topics including Parenting, Parenting for school-age kids, Working parents, For men only.

Internet (USENET) (800) 488-6383
Has several parent- and family-related news groups, including clari.news.children, misc.kids, and clari.news.issues.family.

Prodigy (800) 776-3449
Jump: health, select "health and life-styles," select "bulletin board," select "parenting issues" or "men's issues"

General information

The Birth and Life Bookstore
141 Commercial Street, NE
Salem, OR 97301
(503) 371-4445
Has an incredible catalog of childbirth- and parenting-related books, as well as other resources

Index

F

G

H

T

Cartoon Credits

About the Authors

Armin A. Brott has written on fatherhood for the *New York Times Magazine, Newsweek,* the *Washington Post, American Baby* magazine, and *Parenting* magazine. He lives with his wife and two daughters in Berkeley, California.

Jennifer Ash is the author of *Private Palm Beach* and a contributing editor to *Town and Country.* She, her husband, and their son make their home in New York City.